Macs®

ALL-IN-ONE

A Wiley Brand

Macs®

ALL-IN-ONE

6th Edition

by Paul McFedries

A Wiley Brand

Macs® All-in-One For Dummies®, 6th Edition

Published by: **John Wiley & Sons, Inc.**, 111 River Street, Hoboken, NJ 07030-5774, www.wiley.com

Copyright © 2023 by John Wiley & Sons, Inc., Hoboken, New Jersey

Media and software compilation copyright © 2023 by John Wiley & Sons, Inc. All rights reserved.

Published simultaneously in Canada

No part of this publication may be reproduced, stored in a retrieval system or transmitted in any form or by any means, electronic, mechanical, photocopying, recording, scanning or otherwise, except as permitted under Sections 107 or 108 of the 1976 United States Copyright Act, without the prior written permission of the Publisher. Requests to the Publisher for permission should be addressed to the Permissions Department, John Wiley & Sons, Inc., 111 River Street, Hoboken, NJ 07030, (201) 748-6011, fax (201) 748-6008, or online at http://www.wiley.com/go/permissions.

Trademarks: Wiley, For Dummies, the Dummies Man logo, Dummies.com, Making Everything Easier, and related trade dress are trademarks or registered trademarks of John Wiley & Sons, Inc. and may not be used without written permission. Mac is a registered trademark of Apple, Inc. All other trademarks are the property of their respective owners. John Wiley & Sons, Inc. is not associated with any product or vendor mentioned in this book. *Macs All-in-One For Dummies®*, 6th Edition is an independent publication and has not been authorized, sponsored, or otherwise approved by Apple Inc.

For general information on our other products and services, please contact our Customer Care Department within the U.S. at 877-762-2974, outside the U.S. at 317-572-3993, or fax 317-572-4002. For technical support, please visit https://hub.wiley.com/community/support/dummies.

Wiley publishes in a variety of print and electronic formats and by print-on-demand. Some material included with standard print versions of this book may not be included in e-books or in print-on-demand. If this book refers to media such as a CD or DVD that is not included in the version you purchased, you may download this material at http://booksupport.wiley.com. For more information about Wiley products, visit www.wiley.com.

Library of Congress Control Number: 2022949504

ISBN 978-1-119-93276-5 (pbk); ISBN 978-1-119-93278-9 (ebk); ISBN 978-1-119-93277-2 (ebk)

SKY10039469_120522

Contents at a Glance

Table of Contents

Introduction

When Macs — or *Macintoshes,* as they were known in the early years — first began to roam the earth in January 1984, they caused quite a fuss. A built-in screen! A graphical user interface! Fonts! A *mouse,* for crying out loud! Since then, the Mac, despite never being a huge success commercially, has become a cultural touchstone, the computer that even your mom's mom has heard of. The Mac has always been the computer that the cool kids use.

And the Mac has long had a reputation for being easy to use and friendly to even the greenest of novice computer users. But is that reputation deserved? Are Macs *really* that easy to learn? I wish I could answer a resounding "Yes!" to both questions, but I'd be lying if I did. Sure, Macs are easier to use than their chief rivals: PCs that run Microsoft Windows. And, sure, most folks can learn the basics of using a Mac without much fuss and even less bother.

But here's the thing: Your Mac wasn't cheap, so did you really want to pay all that money just to learn a few basics? Don't you owe it to yourself (or to the person who bought your Mac, if you've been so lucky) to go beyond the basics and really learn what your Mac can do? I'm not saying that you need to turn into a total Mac nerd and master every intricacy and memorize every setting. Forget all that. No, I'm simply suggesting that it's possible to get way more out of your Mac investment without spending a ton of time or effort.

About This Book

Welcome, then to *Macs All-in-One For Dummies,* Sixth Edition. This book is your complete guide to everything Mac-related that's worth knowing. If you're new to Macs, in Book 1, Chapter 1, I begin at the beginning by giving you a tour of your new computer and taking you gently through a few necessary tasks such as using the mouse (or trackpad) and keyboard and shutting down your Mac when you're done for the day. You then take a look around the screen (Book 1, Chapter 2), get your Mac connected to your network and to the internet (Book 1, Chapter 3), learn a few file and folder basics (Book 1, Chapter 4), learn about using apps (Book 1, Chapter 5), and learn a few useful customizations (Book 1, Chapter 6).

Once you've mastered those basics — or, if you have some Mac experience and perhaps you skimmed the chapters in Book 1; no problem! — from there the book slowly and carefully builds your Mac knowledge in topics such as browsing the web, emailing, and doing other internet-related tasks (Book 2); protecting and networking your Mac (Book 3); enjoying music, podcasts, books, photos, and other media (Book 4); and performing day-to-day tasks such as connecting with people, setting up appointments, and creating documents (Book 5).

This book is a reference, which means you don't need to read the chapters in order from front cover to back, and you're not expected to commit anything to memory — there won't be a snap quiz on Friday. You can dip into the book wherever you want to learn what you need to learn or to find answers to your most pressing questions (those that relate to using your Mac, that is). If you're short on time, you can safely skip sidebars (the text in gray boxes) and anything marked with the Technical Stuff icon without missing anything essential to the topic at hand.

To help you navigate this book efficiently, I use the following conventions:

>> *Control-click* means to hold down the Control key and click the mouse. If you're using a mouse that has a left and right button, you can right-click rather than Control-click. If you have an Apple trackpad, tap with two fingers. You find complete explanations of the multitouch gestures in Book 1, Chapter 2.

>> When I refer to the Apple menu — the menu that appears when you click the Apple icon in the upper-left corner of your Mac's screen — I use the symbol. When I talk about menu commands, I use a command arrow, like this: Choose ➪ Recent Items ➪ Calendar. That means to click the Apple icon to open the Apple menu, then click Recent Items in that menu to open a submenu, and then click Calendar in that submenu.

Finally, in this book, you may note that some web addresses break across two lines of text. If you're reading this book in print and want to visit one of these web pages, key in the web address exactly as it's noted in the text, pretending the line break doesn't exist. If you're reading this as an e-book, you've got it easy — just click the web address to be taken directly to the web page.

Foolish Assumptions

In writing this book, I made very few assumptions about you, dear reader. However, to make sure that we're on the same page, I assume that

>> You have a Mac, so you can follow along with my explanations and procedures.

>> If you want to connect with other computers in your home or office, you have the necessary equipment to set up a wired or wireless network.

>> If you want to do internet-related tasks such as surfing the web or sending email, you have an account with an internet service provider.

>> You don't believe that learning how to use a Mac should be all work and no play. Oh, there will be some work for you in these pages, but I also try to inject a little fun as we go along.

Icons Used in This Book

To help emphasize certain information, this book displays different icons in the page margins.

TIP

The tip icon marks shortcuts and points out useful nuggets of information that can help you get things done more efficiently or direct you to something helpful that you might not know. Sometimes tips give you a second, or even third, way of doing a task pointed out in a step.

REMEMBER

Remember icons mark information that's been mentioned previously but is useful for the task at hand. This icon often points out useful information that isn't quite as important as a tip but not as threatening as a warning. If you ignore this information, you can't hurt your files or your Mac, but it may make the task at hand a bit harder or more time consuming.

TECHNICAL STUFF

This icon highlights interesting information that isn't necessary to know but can help explain why certain things work the way they do on a Mac. Feel free to skip this information if you're in a hurry, but try to browse through this information when you have time. You might find out something interesting that can help you use your Mac.

WARNING

Watch out! This icon highlights something that can go terribly wrong if you're not careful, such as wiping out important files or messing up your Mac. Make sure that you read any warning information before following any instructions.

Beyond the Book

In addition to the material in the print or e-book you're reading right now, this product comes with some access-anywhere goodies on the web. Although the Mac uses menus for just about everything, the menu commands have key combination counterparts. I put together a table of the most common key commands, which you can print and keep near your Mac. You also find a table that shows you how to type foreign letters and common symbols and one that summarizes multi-touch gestures. To help you stay up to date with the latest Mac news, I provide a list of Mac websites with hot links, which you can simply click to go to each site. To find the cheat sheet for this book, just go to www.dummies.com and type **Macs All-in-One For Dummies Cheat Sheet** in the Search box.

Where to Go from Here

Dummies books aren't meant to be read cover to cover. However, this book flows from task to task, chapter to chapter, in an order that would be logical if you're learning the Mac for the first time. In that case, feel free to start at Book 1 and go through its chapters to familiarize yourself with how the Mac is organized and how you can make it do what you want it to do. Then mix it up, moving on to fun tasks, such as making FaceTime video calls (Book 2, Chapter 5) or designing a flyer with Pages (Book 5, Chapter 3), and then bounce back to a crucial task, such as backing up (Book 3, Chapter 1).

If you're computer intuitive, you could start with Book 1, Chapter 3 to get your Apple ID and internet connection set up, and then move in the direction you want, whether it's learning about more advanced system functions in Book 3 or organizing and editing your images by using Photos.

If you're familiar with the Mac but want to brush up on the latest, read about Control Center in Book 1, Chapter 2; Maps in Book 2, Chapter 6; Books in Book 4, Chapter 3; and the completely updated Pages, Numbers, and Keynote apps in Book 5, Chapters 3–6.

1

Getting Started with Your Mac

Contents at a Glance

Chapter **1**

From Go to Whoa: Getting to Know Your Mac

The world is divided into two types of people: Those who look before they leap and those who take the plunge without a second thought (or often even a first, for that matter). In the computer world, people who prefer not to look before leaping will fire up their new machine and start banging away: clicking this, pressing that, turning this dial, and twiddling that knob. It's all liberating, I suppose, but for those of us who prefer to give things a good look before leaping, it seems like madness and a recipe for trouble.

This chapter (and the rest of the chapters here in Book 1) is dedicated to members of the look-before-you-leap camp. Sure, it takes a bit more time than just diving in and seeing what happens, but the payoff is a solid grounding in Mac basics that will serve you well throughout your long and illustrious Mac career.

In this chapter, you explore your Mac to get fully acquainted with your new computer. You tour your Mac's hardware doodads, and then you see how to start the machine. From there, you take a close look at controlling your Mac with a mouse or trackpad, and learn the ins and outs of your Mac keyboard. The chapter closes with the details of putting your Mac to sleep, shutting down your Mac, and restarting your Mac.

The Parts Department: Touring Your Mac's Hardware

When you check in to a high-class hotel, the person who carries up your luggage usually gives you a brief tour of your room's amenities. Now, I'm not saying this book is the equivalent of a fancy-schmancy hotel, but I'd like to offer you the same service: a tour of your Mac's amenities.

One problem, though: There are so many different types of Macs that I have no way of knowing what model you have, nor do I have the space to go through every model that's out there. That's not a deal-breaker, however, because I can give you a general tour that will be enough to get you acquainted with your Mac's hardware features. (You can think of the rest of the book as a tour of your Mac's software features.)

The ports report

In computing lingo, a *port* is a connection point on a computer, meaning that you use it to connect something to the machine. So, when I talk about the features of your Mac, what I'm mostly talking about are the various ports you use to attach other devices to your Mac.

The good news about ports is that things are much simpler now than they were even just a few years ago, particularly in the Mac universe. In the old days, something could be connected to your computer in a dizzyingly large number of ways. Now, connections to current and recent Mac models come in just two main flavors: Thunderbolt and HDMI.

Thunderbolt connections

Most Macs come with two or four Thunderbolt ports, which are usually marked with a lightning bolt icon, as shown in Figure 1-1.

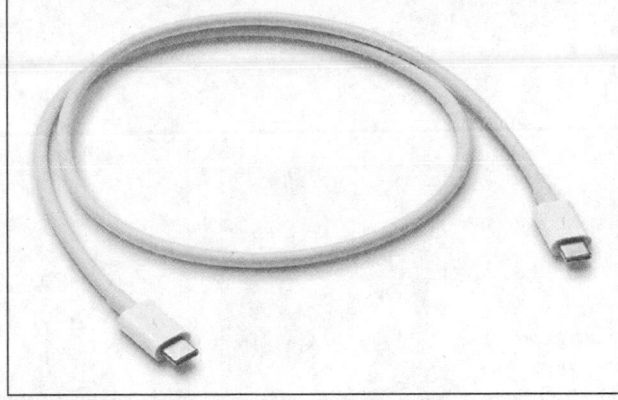

FIGURE 1-1:
Thunderbolt ports and cable.

Thunderbolt ports are the main reason why connecting devices to your Mac is much simpler than it used to be. Why? Because Thunderbolt ports are compatible with several different device types:

>> **Thunderbolt devices:** External monitors, TVs, or external hard drives that also have Thunderbolt ports. These devices can connect to your Mac directly by using a Thunderbolt cable such as the one shown in Figure 1-1, right.

TIP

Thunderbolt devices support *daisy-chaining*, which means you connect Thunderbolt device A to your Mac, Thunderbolt device B to device A, Thunderbolt device C to device B, and so on. You can daisy-chain up to six devices in this way. Sweet!

>> **USB 4 and USB 3.1 Gen 2 devices:** Hard drives, cameras, smartphones, tablets, and printers that have a USB 4 or USB 3.1 Gen 2 port. (USB is short for Universal Serial Bus.) These devices can connect to your Mac's Thunderbolt port by using a USB cable — specifically, a cable that has USB-C connectors, as shown in Figure 1-2, right. Note that each USB-C connector in Figure 1-1, left, has the same shape as each Thunderbolt connector in Figure 1-2, left, which means this cable will connect to your Mac's Thunderbolt port, no questions asked.

>> **DisplayPort devices:** Displays that have a DisplayPort or Mini DisplayPort port. These devices can connect to your Mac's Thunderbolt port using a USB-C-to-DisplayPort (or USB-C-to-Mini-DisplayPort) adaptor or cable.

HDMI connections

Available on the Mac Studio, Mac Pro, Mac mini, and MacBook Pro, the HDMI (High-Definition Multimedia Interface) port (see Figure 1-3, left) is used to connect devices such as external monitors, TVs, and cameras that also have an HDMI port. To make the connection, you use an HDMI cable such as the one shown in Figure 1-3, right.

FIGURE 1-2:
USB-C connectors
and a USB cable.

FIGURE 1-3:
An HDMI port
and a typical
HDMI cable.

TIP

What if you have an iMac, MacBook Air, or other Mac that doesn't come with an HDMI port? You can still connect HDMI devices to your Mac, but you'll need a Thunderbolt-to-HDMI adaptor (a device that has a Thunderbolt connector on one end and an HDMI port on the other). A USB-C-to-HDMI adaptor will also get the job done.

Locating your Mac's ports

Before you can connect anything to your Mac, you need to know where to find your Mac's ports:

> » **Desktop Mac:** If you have an iMac, Mac mini, Mac Pro, or Mac Studio, you'll find the ports on the back of the computer. Some Mac models have a few extra ports you can access:

- *Mac Studio:* Offers a few extra ports on the front of the device.

- *Mac Pro:* Provides some extra ports on top of the computer.

>> **Notebook Mac:** If you have a MacBook Pro or a MacBook Air, the ports are on the sides of the computer.

Figure 1-4 points out the relevant ports and buttons on the back of a Mac Studio. Most Macs come with some combination of these features.

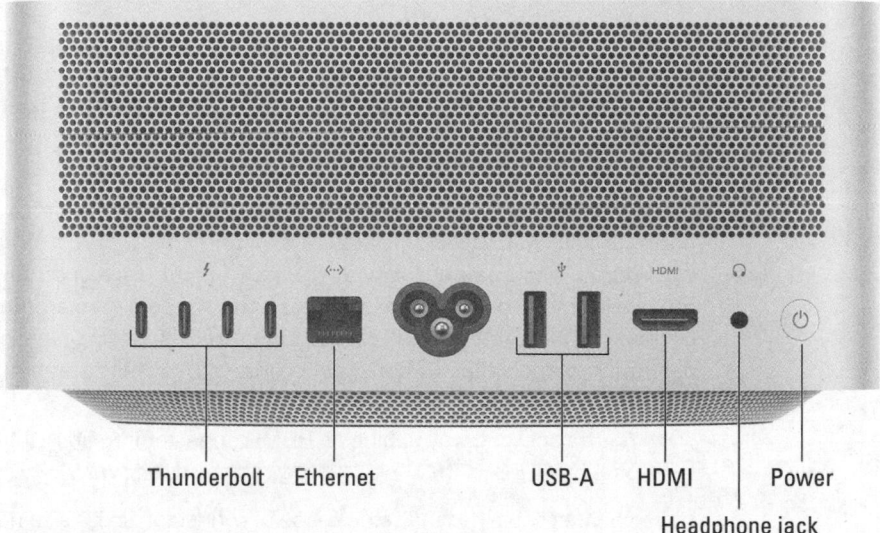

FIGURE 1-4: The ports and buttons that festoon the back of a Mac Studio.

Thunderbolt   Ethernet   USB-A   HDMI   Power

Headphone jack

Note in Figure 1-4 that the Mac Studio, like most Macs, comes with a few other features besides the Thunderbolt and HDMI ports:

>> **Ethernet:** This port (available on the Mac Studio, Mac mini, and Mac Pro) enables you to use an Ethernet cable to connect to a network device, such as a router or broadband modem.

>> **USB-A:** These ports enable you to connect devices such as a hard drive, camera, smartphone, tablet, and printer that have USB-A ports. (USB-A is an older version of USB.)

>> **Headphone jack:** This port enables you to connect a pair of headphones or a set of speakers to your Mac. The headphones or speakers must also have a 3.5mm output jack, and you need a 3.5mm audio cable to connect the device to your Mac.

>> **Power:** You use this button to turn on your Mac, as I describe a bit later in this chapter (see "Cranking Up Your Mac").

Connecting stuff to your Mac

First off, let me note that you actually have two ways to connect a device to your Mac:

>> **With cables:** You connect the device by running a compatible cable from the device to your Mac.

>> **Without cables:** You connect the device wirelessly by using a technology called Bluetooth. See Book 3, Chapter 4 to learn all about Bluetooth devices and connections.

When it comes to making a connection with a cable, it's worth noting that all the ports on your Mac have a particular size and shape that's unique to each type of connection. Fortunately for you, the jack on the corresponding cable that plugs into each type of port has the same size and shape. For example, look at the HDMI port and HDMI cable, shown earlier in Figure 1-3. As you can see, the shape of the port mirrors the shape of both cable connectors. This means two things for you:

>> There's only one way to plug an HDMI connector into an HDMI port, so it's not possible to insert the cable into the port the wrong way.

>> No other cable has the same shape of connector, so it's also not possible to insert the wrong cable into the port.

With these two pieces of good news in mind, connecting anything to your Mac involves the following general steps:

1. **If you're using an adaptor, insert one end of the adaptor into the compatible port on your Mac.**

2. **Connect one end of the cable to your Mac:**

   - *If you're using an adaptor:* Plug one end of the cable into the compatible port on the adaptor.

   - *If you're not using an adaptor:* Plug one end of the cable into the compatible port on your Mac.

3. **Connect the other end of the cable to the compatible port on the device.**

When your Mac recognizes that a new device is attempting to connect, you see the Allow Accessory to Connect? dialog shown in Figure 1-5.

4. **Say "Yeah, that's cool," and click Allow.**

FIGURE 1-5:
When you connect a new device, your Mac asks if it's okay.

Cranking Up Your Mac

Starting your Mac is the most straightforward task you'll learn in this book. Why? Because I can tell you everything you need to know in a mere four words:

Press the power button.

Yep, that's it. Or, I should say, that's it as long as you know where to find the power button on your Mac. Here's where to look, depending on which Mac model you're using:

>> **iMac, Mac Studio, or Mac mini:** The power button is on the back of the device (as shown for the Mac Studio in Figure 1-1).

>> **Mac Pro:** The power button is on top. (On older Mac Pro models, the power button is on the front.)

>> **MacBook Pro or MacBook Air:** The power button is the one in the top-right corner of the keyboard.

A few seconds after you press the power button, your Mac chimes to let you know that it's starting.

When you unpack your Mac and turn it on for the very first time, it asks you to type your name and make up a password to create an account for using your Mac. You use this name and password in the following situations:

>> When you wake or restart your Mac, if you activate those types of privacy settings (see Book 3, Chapter 2)

>> When you install new apps or update the system software

>> When you change some settings in System Settings

>> When you switch from one user to another, if you set up your Mac to work with multiple users (see Book 3, Chapter 3)

REMEMBER

This username and password are different than your Apple ID, which you use for iCloud and making Music Store, App Store, and Apple Books purchases. You can learn about creating an Apple ID in Book 1, Chapter 3.

To guide you through the process of setting up a Mac for the first time, a special application called Setup Assistant runs, asking for your time zone, the date, and whether you want to transfer files and applications from another Mac to your newer one. If you've just upgraded to a new Mac, you don't have to reinvent the wheel and set up everything again. You can migrate settings from your old Mac to your new Mac.

The most important part of this initial procedure is remembering the password you chose because you'll need it to log in to your account, change some of the settings in System Settings, or install new software.

An *operating system* is the program that controls your computer and is almost always stored on your computer's built-in hard drive (rather than on an external drive). On the Mac, the operating system is named macOS (pronounced "mac oh ess") and is followed by a version number, such as 13, followed by a subversion number that's incremented with each new update (so, for example, if the original version is 13.0, the first update is 13.1, the second is 13.2, and so on).

TECHNICAL STUFF

Apple gives a codename to each version of macOS. Early versions of macOS were named after big cats, such as Mountain Lion, Snow Leopard, and Jaguar. Now they're named after places in California, such as Catalina, Big Sur, and Monterey. The current codename is Ventura and its version number is 13.

After the operating system loads and you log in, you can start using your computer to run other applications to do things such as design a poster, send an email, browse the web, calculate your yearly budget, or play a game — you know, all the cool things you bought your Mac for in the first place.

Making Your Mac Do Your Bidding: Mouse, Trackpad, and Keyboard Basics

After you start your Mac, it just sits there doing apparently not much of anything, at least on the surface. Sure, if you stare at the screen long enough, the time in the upper-right corner of the screen will change. But is that all there is? Nope, not even close. However, your Mac won't do anything even remotely useful until you tell it what you want it to do. How do you do that? There are various methods, but the following two are the ones you'll use almost all the time:

>> Use your Mac's mouse or trackpad to select a command, run an app, or perform a task.

>> Use your Mac's keyboard to run a command or type some text.

REMEMBER

What's the difference between a mouse and a trackpad? A *mouse* is an external device that's more or less the size and shape of a bar of soap. When you move the mouse, an arrow onscreen — called, unsurprisingly, the *mouse pointer* — moves in the same direction. A *trackpad* is a flat, rectangular surface that can be either an external device or built into a notebook Mac (just below the keyboard). When you move your finger across the trackpad's surface, the onscreen mouse pointer moves in the same direction.

Maneuvering the mouse

The main purpose of the mouse is to perform the following generic two-step procedure to make something happen on your Mac:

1. **Move the mouse so that you position the mouse pointer over a particular location on the screen.**

2. **Perform the mouse action that makes your Mac do what you want it to do.**

I know that procedure is vague, so let's try to firm things up a bit by running through a quick example:

1. **Move the mouse so that the mouse pointer ends up over the Apple symbol () in the upper-left corner of the screen.**

2. **Press and then immediately release the left mouse button.**

   If you have a mouse that doesn't seem to have any buttons (such as the Apple Magic Mouse), press and then immediately release the left side of the mouse.

Pressing and immediately releasing the left mouse button (or the left side of a Magic Mouse) is known in the mouse trade as *clicking* the mouse. You should now see the Apple menu, as shown in Figure 1-6.

3. **Move the mouse so that the mouse pointer is outside the Apple menu, and then click.**

The Apple menu disappears, just like that.

Move the mouse pointer over the Apple icon and click

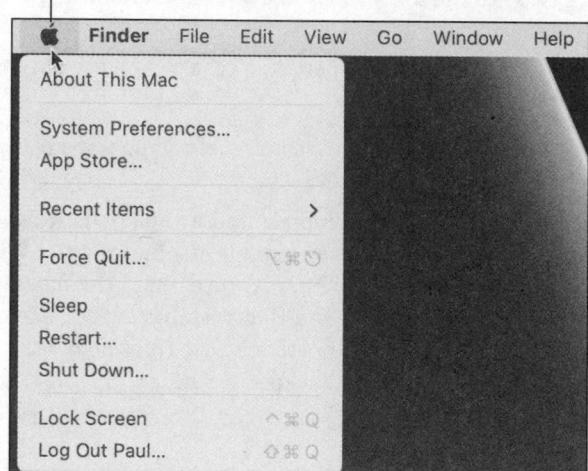

FIGURE 1-6: Clicking displays the Apple menu.

Here are the basic moves you can make with your mouse:

» **Point:** Move the mouse so that the mouse pointer is over some specified location.

» **Click:** Quickly press and release the left mouse button or the left side of a Magic Mouse. You almost always point at something and then click it. Depending on the something, clicking it usually selects it or executes its command or action.

» **Double-click:** Quickly press and release the left mouse button (or, again, the left side of a Magic Mouse) twice in succession, with as little delay as possible between the two clicks. You almost always point at something and then double-click it, which usually opens the thing you double-clicked.

» **Drag:** Point at an item on the screen, hold down the left mouse button (or press and hold the left side of a Magic Mouse), and then move the mouse. As you move the mouse, the item moves along with the pointer — this is the *dragging* part. When the item is in the position you want, release the button and the item stays in its new position.

>> **Right-click:** Quickly press and release the right mouse button or the right side of a Magic Mouse. You almost always point at an item and then right-click it. Depending on the item, right-clicking it usually displays a *shortcut menu* (sometimes called a *context menu*) that contains a collection of commands related to the item. For example, Figure 1-7 shows the shortcut menu that appears when you right-click the desktop.

TIP

If a context menu doesn't appear when you click the right side of your Magic Mouse, you need to set up the Magic Mouse to function like a two-button mouse. Choose ➪ System Settings. Click Mouse in the left sidebar, click the Point & Click tab, and then use the Secondary Click pop-up menu to select Click Right Side. If you're left-handed, you can instead choose Click Left Side, which reverses the clicking sides (that is, regular clicks are now on the right and secondary clicks are now on the left, which might feel more natural).

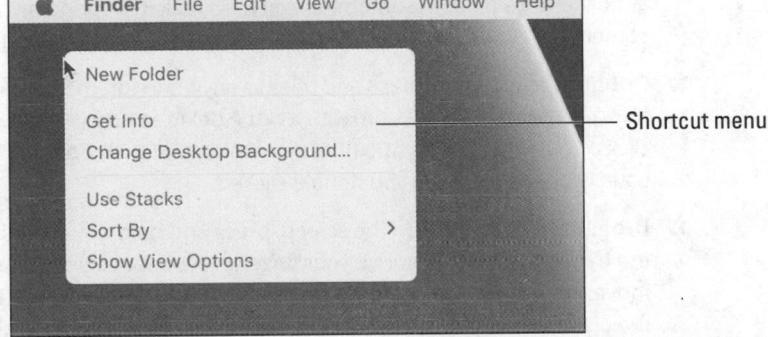

FIGURE 1-7:
Right-clicking typically displays a shortcut menu of commands.

>> **Control-click:** Hold down the Control key while you click. This action has the same effect as right-clicking, so it's used when you have a mouse that has only a single button.

>> **Scroll:** With a Magic Mouse, move a finger up, down, left, or right on the surface of the mouse to slide the content under the mouse pointer in the same direction as you move your finger. Some older mice have a scroll wheel that, when turned, moves the current window content up or down.

>> **Swipe:** With a Magic Mouse, quickly drag two fingers left or right on the surface of the mouse to move back and forth through web pages or to browse photos in Photos.

Getting a feel for the trackpad

All current MacBook Pro and MacBook Air models sport trackpads that take the place of a mouse. The trackpad is the flat, rectangular area below the keyboard. If you have a desktop Mac, you can get in on the trackpad fun by shelling out for the external Magic Trackpad, which operates in the same way as the built-in trackpad on a notebook Mac.

You control your Mac via the trackpad by using *gestures*, which are special movements you make with one or more fingers on the surface of the trackpad. Here's a summary of the gestures you can use with the trackpad:

>> **Point:** Slide a finger across the surface of the trackpad so that the mouse pointer is over some specified location. If you reach the edge of the trackpad but still need to move the mouse pointer in the same direction, just pick up your finger and place it on or near the opposite side of the trackpad, and then continue.

>> **Click:** Quickly press and release anywhere on the surface of the trackpad. You almost always point at something and then click it. Depending on the something, clicking it usually selects it or executes its command or action.

>> **Double-click:** Quickly press and release anywhere on the surface of the trackpad twice in succession, with as little delay as possible between the two clicks. You almost always point at something and then double-click it, which usually opens the thing you double-clicked.

>> **Drag:** Point at an item on the screen, press and hold down on the surface of the trackpad, and then move your finger. As you move your finger, the item moves along with the pointer — this is the *dragging* part. When the item is in the position you want, lift your finger off the trackpad and the item stays in its new position.

>> **Right-click:** Quickly press and release anywhere on the surface of the trackpad using two fingers. You almost always point at an item and then right-click it. Depending on the item, right-clicking it usually displays a shortcut menu that offers a collection of commands related to the item.

TIP

If right-clicking using a two-finger press doesn't work for you, you need to activate this feature. Choose ➪ System Settings. Click Trackpad in the left sidebar, click the Point & Click tab, and then use the Secondary Click pop-up menu to select Click with Two Fingers.

>> **Scroll:** Swipe two fingers up and down or left and right across the trackpad. The window content follows the movement of your fingers.

>> **Rotate:** Place two fingers on the trackpad and turn them clockwise or counterclockwise to move the window contents in a circular motion.

>> **Swipe:** Quickly and briefly slide the tips of two fingers left or right on the surface of the trackpad to move back and forth through web pages or to browse photos in Photos. You can also quickly slide three fingers across the trackpad to perform these tasks:

- Swipe up with three fingers to open Mission Control (see Book 1, Chapter 5), and then tap to close it or tap a different window to switch to it. You can also swipe down with three fingers to return to the previous window.

- Swipe left and right with three fingers to switch between full-screen applications or Desktops (see Book 1, Chapter 5).

REMEMBER

To change these two tasks from three fingers to four fingers, choose ⇨ System Settings ⇨ Trackpad, and then select the More Gestures tab. In the Swipe between Full-Screen Apps pop-up menu, choose Swipe Left or Right with Four Fingers.

>> **Pinch:** Place two fingers slightly apart on the trackpad and then bring them together as if picking up a small item; doing so zooms in on the current window content.

>> **Spread:** Place two fingers together on the trackpad and then move them apart; doing so zooms out on the current window content.

TIP

Choose ⇨ System Settings and then click Trackpad to specify how you want to use the trackpad and to see examples of how the multitouch gestures work, as shown in Figure 1-8.

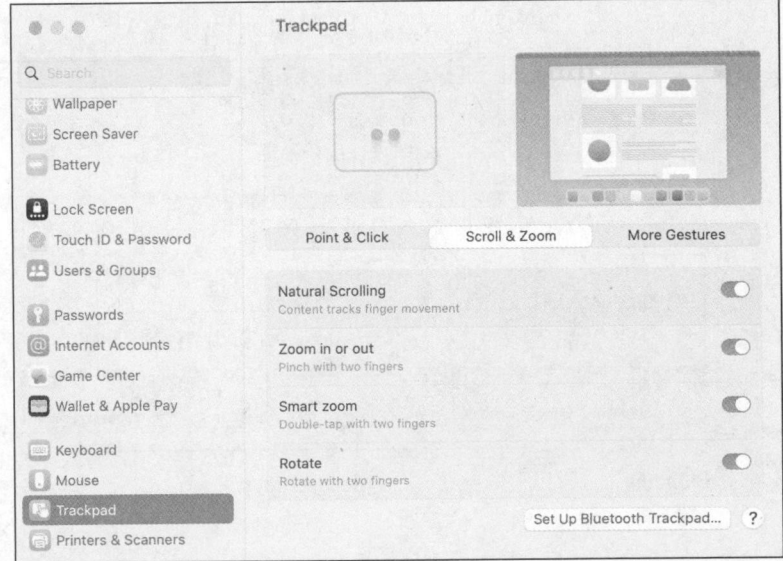

FIGURE 1-8:
See multitouch gestures in action in System Settings.

Comprehending the keyboard

The primary use of the keyboard is to type information. However, you can use the keyboard also to select items and menu commands — sometimes more quickly than by using the mouse. Figure 1-9 shows how the keyboard groups related keys. The next few sections cover each group of keys in detail.

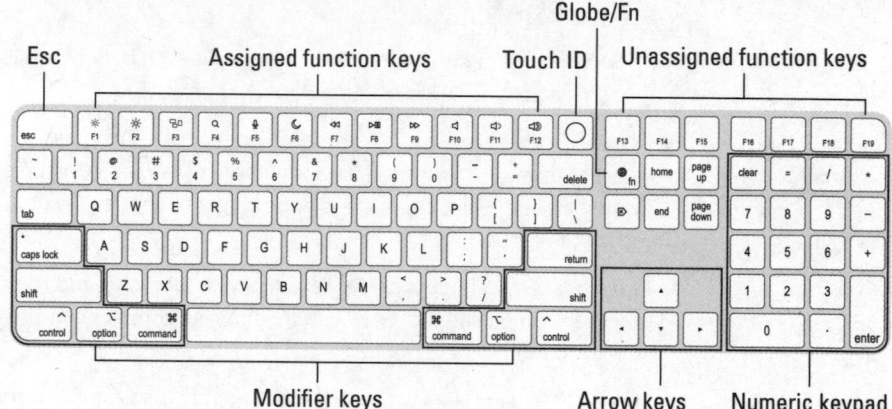

FIGURE 1-9: The parts of a typical full-size Mac keyboard.

REMEMBER

Figure 1-9 shows a diagram of the full-size keyboard that ships with some desktop Mac models. If your desktop Mac came with a smaller keyboard or if you have a notebook Mac, your keyboard has a different arrangement, as shown in Figure 1-10, but most of the keys work the way I describe here.

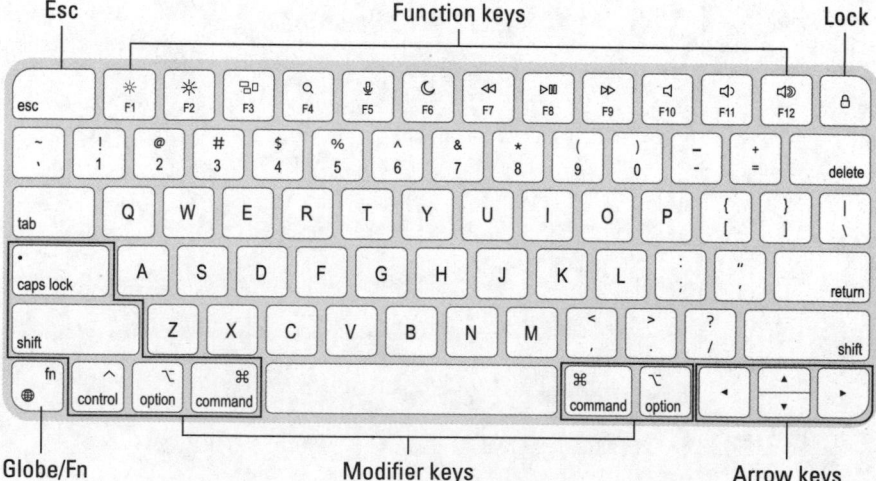

FIGURE 1-10: The parts of a typical regular-size Mac keyboard.

Function and special feature keys

Depending on your keyboard, you may see 12 to 20 function and special feature keys along the top of the keyboard. These keys are labeled F1 through F12/F19, along with an Esc key — short for Escape — and either a Lock key or a Touch ID key.

The function number (F1, F2, and so on) appears on the bottom or in the lower-right corner of the key and a larger icon represents what happens when you press the key, such as dim the screen brightness (F1) or play and pause music you're listening to in Music (F8). The icons on each of these special feature keys are far from self-evident, so check out Table 1-1 to find out what all your Mac's special feature keys do when you press them. (Note that the key assignments vary slightly depending on whether you're using a regular keyboard, a backlit keyboard, or a Magic Keyboard.)

TABLE 1-1   ## Special Features Assigned to Function Keys

Function Key	What It Does
F1	Decreases the display brightness
F2	Increases the display brightness
F3	Displays Mission Control
F4	Regular keyboard: Displays Launchpad
	Magic Keyboard: Opens Spotlight
F5	Regular keyboard: Not assigned
	Backlit keyboard: Decreases backlight brightness
	Magic Keyboard: Enables dictation (press and hold down to activate Siri)
F6	Regular keyboard: Not assigned
	Backlit keyboard: Increases the backlight brightness
	Magic Keyboard: Toggles do not disturb feature
F7	Rewinds the currently playing video or audio
F8	Pauses/plays the currently playing video or audio
F9	Fast-forwards the currently playing video or audio
F10	Mutes whatever sound is currently playing
F11	Decreases the sound volume
F12	Increases the sound volume

So, I hear you asking, why have both the icon and the function number on each key? That's because these special keys can do double-duty:

>> For macOS, the keys perform the tasks outlined in Table 1-1.

>> For your applications, the keys perform special tasks defined by the application. For example, Microsoft Word defines F7 as the keyboard shortcut for running the spell checker and F5 as the shortcut for opening the Find and Replace dialog.

However, if you press the F7 key when you're working in Microsoft Word, your Mac will rewind whatever video or audio you have playing — it won't run Word's spell checker. You run application-specific function keys by pressing and holding down the Fn key and *then* pressing the required function key on the upper row of the keyboard. In Microsoft Word, for instance, pressing Fn+F7 tells Word to run the spell checker, while pressing Fn+F5 opens the Find and Replace dialog. The Fn key is either below the F13 key on full-size keyboards (refer to Figure 1-9) or in the lower-left corner on smaller external keyboards and MacBook keyboards. On the notebook Magic Keyboard, the Fn key doubles as the globe key (which sports a globe icon); if you have a touch bar, it replaces the Fn key.

In other words, holding down the Fn key tells your Mac, "Ignore the special feature controls assigned to that function key listed in Table 1-1 and just behave like an old-fashioned function key."

To reverse the way the Mac's function keys work when you press them, choose ⇨ System Settings, click Keyboard in the left sidebar, and then click Keyboard Shortcuts. In the dialog that appears, click Function Keys, click the Use F1, F2, Etc. Keys as Standard Function Keys switch on, and then click Done. When you activate this option, you *must* hold down the Fn key to perform the commands shown in Table 1-1, but you don't have to hold down the Fn key to use app-specific function keys.

Here's a quick look at the other some keys you might see along the top of your Mac keyboard:

>> **Esc:** This key (it's on the far left) often works as a "You may be excused" command. For example, if a drop-down menu appears on the screen and you want it to go away, press the Esc key.

>> **Lock:** This key (which has a lock icon and appears to the right of the F12 key; refer to Figure 1-10) takes you immediately to the login screen, meaning you can't return to the desktop until you enter the credentials of your Mac user account. See Book 3, Chapter 2 for more info on locking your Mac.

>> **Touch ID:** This key (it has a circular depression — that's the fingerprint reader — Instead of an icon and appears to the right of the F12 key; refer to Figure 1-9) enables you to lock and unlock your Mac by using a fingerprint. See Book 3, Chapter 2 to learn all about Touch ID.

>> **Eject:** This key (which is seen on only older Mac keyboards) ejects a CD or DVD from an external disc drive connected to your Mac.

Alphanumeric keys

When you press an alphanumeric key (that is, a letter, number, or symbol), you're telling the Mac to display that character at the cursor position. (The cursor usually appears as a blinking vertical line on the screen.)

TIP

You can move the cursor by pointing to and clicking a new location with the mouse or by pressing the arrow keys, as explained in the upcoming "Arrow and cursor control keys" section.

TIP

Just because you don't find a character labeled on your keyboard doesn't mean you can't type that character. Holding down Shift, Option, or Shift+Option while pressing another key on the keyboard results in a different symbol or letter, such as an uppercase letter or the symbol for a trademark or square root.

To see all the key combinations, follow these steps:

1. **Choose ⌘ ⇨ System Settings and then click Keyboard.**

2. **Click the Edit button to the right of Input Sources.**

3. **Click the Show Input Menu in Menu Bar switch on.**

4. **Click Done and then close System Settings.**

   An icon for the Input menu (pointed out in Figure 1-11) appears in the menu bar near the top-right corner of your screen.

TIP

   If you don't see the Input menu icon, restart your Mac (see "A fresh beginning: Restarting your Mac," later in this chapter).

5. **Click the Input menu icon and then click Show Keyboard Viewer.**

   A graphic representation of the keyboard appears on your screen.

6. **Hold down the Shift, Option, or Shift+Option keys.**

   The keyboard changes to show the letter or symbol that will be typed when you hold down Shift, Option, or Shift+Option and type a letter or number.

   Refer to the book's cheat sheet for more information about typing special characters. (Turn to the Introduction for instructions on accessing the cheat sheet.)

Input menu icon

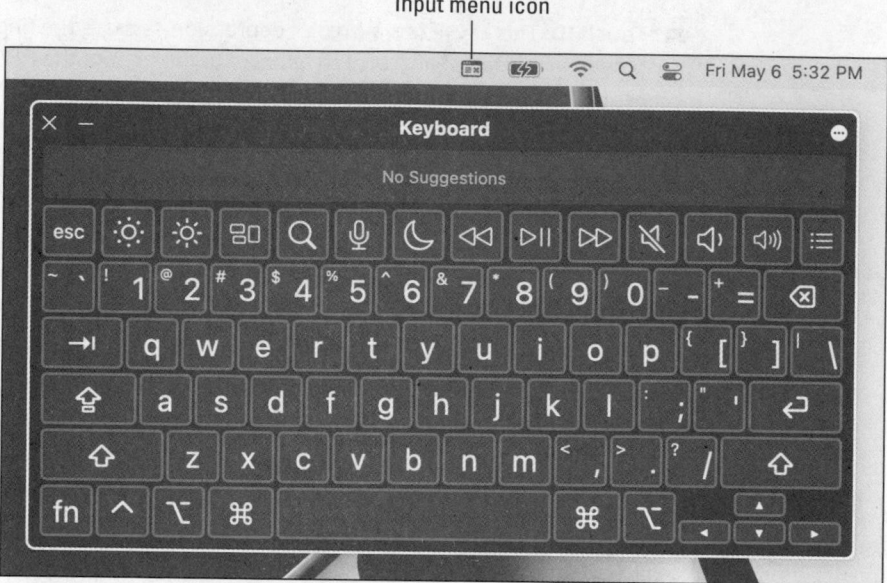

FIGURE 1-11:
The keyboard
viewer.

Besides keys that type letters and characters, you'll find keys that don't type anything but nevertheless play an important role:

» **Delete:** Removes the character to the left of the cursor. If you hold down Delete, your Mac keeps deleting characters to the left of the cursor until you lift your finger.

» **Tab:** Indents text in a word processor and moves from cell to cell in a spreadsheet app, but it can also move from text box to text box in a form, like when you type a shipping address for an online merchant.

» **Return:** Moves the cursor to the next line in a word processor but can also choose a default button (which appears in blue) on the screen. For example, the Print button is the default button in the Print dialog, so pressing Return in the Print dialog sends your document to the printer.

TIP

If you've recently moved to a Mac from the PC world, all this talk of a Return key might have you scratching your head. Scratch no more: The Return key is just the Mac equivalent of the Enter key.

Modifier keys

Modifier keys are almost never used individually. Instead, modifier keys are usually held down while pressing another key. Included in the modifier keys category are the function keys mentioned in a few of the previous sections (which you use in combination with the Fn key), along with the Shift, Control, Option, and ⌘ keys.

Here's an example of how modifier keys work. If you press the S key in a word-processing document, your Mac types the letter *s* on the screen. If you hold down a modifier key, such as the ⌘ key, and then press the S key, the S key is modified to behave differently. In this case, holding down the ⌘ key followed by the S key (⌘+S) tells your word-processing application to issue the Save command.

Most modifier keystrokes involve pressing two keys, such as ⌘+Q (the Quit command), but some modifier keystrokes can involve pressing three or four keys, such as Shift+⌘+3, which saves a snapshot of what you see on your screen as an image file, which is commonly referred to as a *screenshot*.

The main use for modifier keys is to help you choose commands quickly without fumbling with the mouse or trackpad. Every application includes dozens of such keystroke shortcuts, but Table 1-2 lists the common keystroke shortcuts that work the same in most apps.

TABLE 1-2　**Common Keystroke Shortcuts**

Command	Keystroke Shortcut
Copy	⌘+C
Cut	⌘+X
Paste	⌘+V
Open	⌘+O
New	⌘+N
Print	⌘+P
Quit	⌘+Q
Save	⌘+S
Select All	⌘+A
Undo the previous command	⌘+Z
Redo the previous command	⌘+Y

Most Mac apps display their keystroke shortcuts for commands directly on their drop-down menus, as shown in Figure 1-12.

The Caps Lock key, when active (as indicated by the green light on the key), lets you type in all capital letters but doesn't affect the function of modifier keys combined with letters.

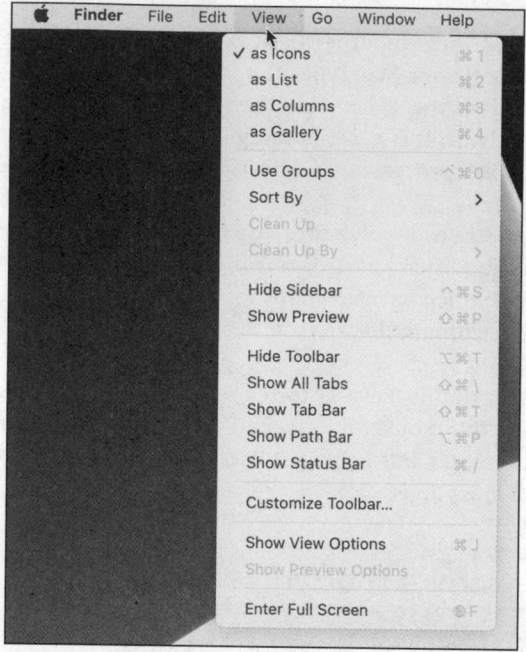

FIGURE 1-12:
Most drop-down menus list shortcut keystrokes for commonly used commands.

REMEMBER

Instead of describing the modifier keys to press by name (such as Shift), most keystroke shortcuts displayed on menus use cryptic graphics. Figure 1-13 displays the different symbols that represent shortcut commands.

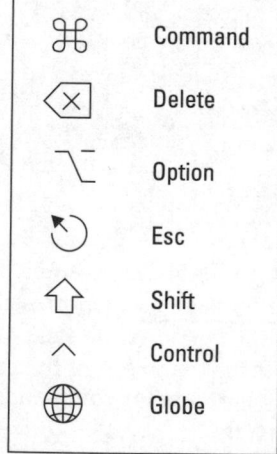

⌘	Command
⌫	Delete
⌥	Option
↻	Esc
⇧	Shift
∧	Control
🌐	Globe

FIGURE 1-13:
A guide to symbols for keystroke commands.

Numeric keypad

Full-size keyboards (refer to Figure 1-9) have a numeric keypad on the right side, which arranges the numbers 0–9 in rows and columns like a typical calculator keypad. The numeric keypad also features other keys that are useful for mathematical calculations. The main use for the numeric keys is to make typing numbers faster and easier than using the numeric keys on the top row of the typewriter keys.

Arrow and cursor control keys

The pointer becomes a cursor when you use the keyboard to enter data in any type of app or even when naming a file. The cursor often appears as a vertical blinking line and acts like a placeholder. Wherever the cursor appears, that's where your next character will appear if you press a keyboard key. You can move the cursor with the mouse or trackpad, or you can move it with the arrow keys.

The up arrow moves the cursor up, the down arrow moves the cursor down, the right arrow moves the cursor right, and the left arrow moves the cursor left. (Could it be any more logical?) Depending on the application you're using, pressing an arrow key may move the cursor in different ways. For example, pressing the right arrow key in a word processor moves the cursor right one character, but pressing that same right arrow key in a spreadsheet may move the cursor to the adjacent cell on the right.

On some Mac keyboards, you may see four additional cursor control keys: Home, End, Page Up, and Page Down. Typically, pressing the Page Up key scrolls up one screen, and pressing the Page Down key scrolls down one screen. Many applications ignore the Home and End keys, but some applications let you move the cursor with them. For example, Microsoft Word uses the Home key to move the cursor to the beginning of a line or row and the End key to move the cursor to the end of a line or row, and ⌘+Home/End moves the cursor to the beginning or end, respectively, of a document.

TIP

Just because you may not see the Home, End, Page Up, and Page Down keys on your Mac keyboard doesn't mean those command keys aren't there. For example, on the MacBook, holding down the Fn key and then pressing the left arrow key acts as the Home key, which moves the cursor to the start of the line that the cursor is in. Pressing Fn+→ jumps the cursor to the end of the current line, Fn+← moves the cursor to the beginning of the current line, Fn+↑ scrolls the text up one page, and Fn+↓ scrolls the text down one page. Also, ⌘+Fn+←/→ moves the cursor to the beginning or end, respectively, of the document. Because seeing is believing, try it on your own Mac keyboard — even if you don't see keys bearing those actual labels.

To the left of the End key on a full keyboard, you may find a smaller Delete key. Like the bigger Delete key, this smaller Delete key also deletes characters one at a time. The difference is that the big Delete key erases characters to the *left* of the cursor, but the small Delete key, sometimes labeled Del, erases characters to the *right* of the cursor. If your keyboard lacks this second Delete key, you can hold down the Fn key while pressing the Delete key to erase characters to the right of the cursor.

Turning Off Your Mac

You can turn off your Mac (or let it rest a bit) in one of three ways — sleep, shut down, or restart. In this section, I explain when and why you'd want to use each option and, of course, how.

Nighty-night: Putting your Mac to sleep

If you're taking a short break from working on your Mac, you don't have to always turn it off and then turn it back on again when you want to use it. To conserve energy, put your Mac to sleep instead of leaving it running while you're away. When you put your Mac to sleep, it turns off the display and shuts down almost every other power-draining component of your Mac and draws only a teensy trickle of power. The great part, though, is that you can instantly wake it up by touching the keyboard, clicking the mouse, swiping the trackpad, or opening the lid (if you use a MacBook Air or MacBook Pro). Presto change-o! Your Mac immediately returns to the same state you left it in, without making you wait to power on as if it were completely shut down.

WARNING

If your Mac is doing a task, such as sending an email or downloading a file, let it finish the task before putting it to sleep.

To put your Mac to sleep, choose one of the following actions:

>> **Choose ⇨ Sleep.** The menu is in the upper-left corner of the screen.

>> **Press and hold down the power button.** Then, when the dialog in Figure 1-14 appears, click the Sleep button (or press the S key on your Mac's keyboard). *Note:* This method does not work on models with Touch ID.

>> **Press Option+⌘+power button.** This puts your Mac to sleep instantly without a dialog appearing. This option is useful if you're shopping online for an anniversary present and your spouse walks into the room. Again, this method doesn't work on models with Touch ID.

>> **If you have a MacBook Pro or MacBook Air, just close its lid.** Your notebook Mac goes to sleep right away.

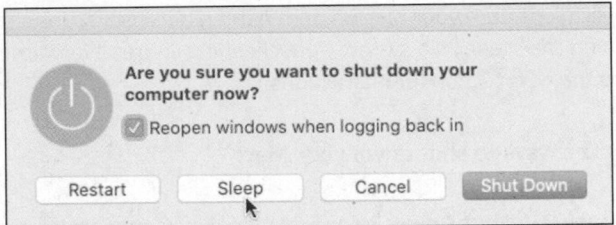

FIGURE 1-14:
Press and hold
down the power
button to display
this dialog.

TECHNICAL STUFF

Depending on which Mac model you own, you may notice a built-in combination power/sleep indicator light that softly pulses like a firefly when your Mac is sleeping. On the MacBook Pro, the power/sleep indicator light is on the front edge below the right wrist rest. On the Mac mini, the indicator light is in the lower-right corner. No such light is anywhere on the iMac or the latest MacBook Air, which appear to be totally in the dark when they're asleep.

Quittin' time: Shutting down your Mac

When you shut down your Mac, open applications are automatically closed, internet and network connections are disconnected, and logged-in users are logged out. It may take a few minutes for your Mac to shut down. You know your Mac is shut down completely when the screen is black, the hard drive and fan are silent, and there are no blinking lights. Here are a few circumstances when you'd want to shut down your Mac:

>> **When you won't be using your Mac for an extended length of time,** turning it completely off can extend its useful life, waste less energy, and save you a few bucks on your yearly energy expense.

>> **When you're traveling,** turn off your MacBook Air, MacBook Pro, or Mac mini before putting it in your wheeled carry-on bag.

TIP

Putting your Mac to sleep is fine if you're carrying your MacBook in a laptop bag or backpack. If you're going through a security line in an airport or other location, sleep is actually exactly what you want so that when the inspector checks your computer, one touch will bring it to life. Security guards may ask you to turn on a computer that is turned off.

>> **If you own a Mac that is user serviceable and want to open the computer** to install a new battery, additional memory, or a video graphics card, be sure to turn it off first.

>> **To resolve weird situations,** such as unresponsive or slow-running applications, turn your Mac off and then on because it runs a number of behind-the-scenes file-system housekeeping chores every time you start it. (See the next section for instructions.)

Here are the ways to shut down your Mac:

>> **Choose ⇨ Shut Down.** A confirmation dialog appears (as shown in Figure 1-15) asking whether you're sure you want to shut down.

Select the Reopen Windows when Logging Back In check box if you want everything you're working on to open the next time you turn on your Mac.

Click the Shut Down button (or Cancel if you change your mind). If you don't click either option, your Mac will shut down automatically after 1 minute.

>> **Press and hold down the power button.** When a dialog appears (refer to Figure 1-14), click the Shut Down button or press the Return key. This method doesn't work on Mac models that support Touch ID.

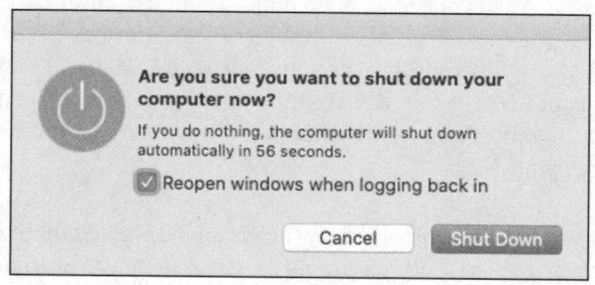

Are you sure you want to shut down your computer now?

If you do nothing, the computer will shut down automatically in 56 seconds.

☑ Reopen windows when logging back in

Cancel   Shut Down

FIGURE 1-15: Click Shut Down to turn off your Mac.

Make sure that your MacBook Air or MacBook Pro is completely shut down before closing the lid, or it may not shut down properly. Even more problematic, it may not start up properly when you next try to turn it on.

To shut down without seeing those bothersome dialogs, do this: Hold the Option key and then choose ⇨ Shut Down. This bypasses the confirmation prompt asking whether you're sure that you want to shut down.

WARNING

You have one more option for shutting down your Mac but proceed with caution. Press and hold ⌘+Control and then press the power button to perform a *force shutdown*, which forces all running applications to shut down immediately. However, this route should never be your first choice when shutting down. Use a force shutdown as your last resort only if your Mac — your *Mac*, not just a stubborn application — is unresponsive and appears to have frozen. If a single application is freezing or acting flaky, force-quit (close) that single application instead of shutting down your entire computer. (See Book 3, Chapter 6 for information on force-quitting a single application.) Performing a force shutdown can cause you to lose any changes you've made since the last time you saved them, so use force shutdown only as a last resort.

A fresh beginning: Restarting your Mac

Sometimes your Mac can act sluggish or applications may fail to run. If that happens, you can shut down and immediately restart your Mac, which essentially clears your computer's memory and starts it fresh.

To restart your computer, you have three choices:

» **Choose ⇨ Restart.**

» **Press the power button.** Then, when a dialog appears, click the Restart button (refer to Figure 1-14) or press the R key. Note that you can't use this method if your Mac supports Touch ID.

» **Press Control+⌘+Eject.**

When you restart your computer, your Mac closes all running applications; you have the chance, though, to save any files you're working on. After you choose to save any files, those applications are closed, and then your Mac will shut down and boot up again.

Chapter **2**

Touring the Screen

The tall-forehead types who specialize in computer science have a genius for coming up with words and phrases that seem designed to not only confuse the rest of us but also to wring the joy out of using a computer. A good example is *user interface,* which sounds like it came straight from a dystopian robot novel. Well, I'm happy to report that I have two pieces of good news for you. First, you won't catch me using the phrase *user interface* anywhere in the rest of this book. Second, what that phrase represents isn't some abstruse computer science concept that requires PhD-level knowledge. Instead, it simply refers to what you see on your screen after you start the Mac and how you use what you see to make your Mac do useful things. Yep, that's it.

In this chapter, I elaborate on that definition by giving you a 50-cent tour of everything you see on your Mac screen and by telling you how to manipulate what you see to make your Mac do the things you want it to do.

Before you get started, if you're new to computers, I hope you didn't skip Chapter 1 because it takes you through the fundamentals of using your Mac's keyboard and its mouse or trackpad. You get a ton of practice using those devices in this chapter, so you need to know the basics before diving in to this material.

Getting to Know the Desktop

When you start your Mac, you end up at a screen that looks more or less like the one shown in Figure 2-1. Welcome to the Mac desktop. Wait, what? *Desktop?* Is this another one of those highfalutin computer science nerd words? Yes. It's a metaphor because the geeks want you to think of the Mac screen as something akin to the top of an actual desk. That is, in the real world, when you want to work with something, you take it out of storage, place it on your desktop, do what you need to do, and then put it back in storage. I hear you: Who works like this anymore? No one!

Desktop   Menu bar   Mouse pointer

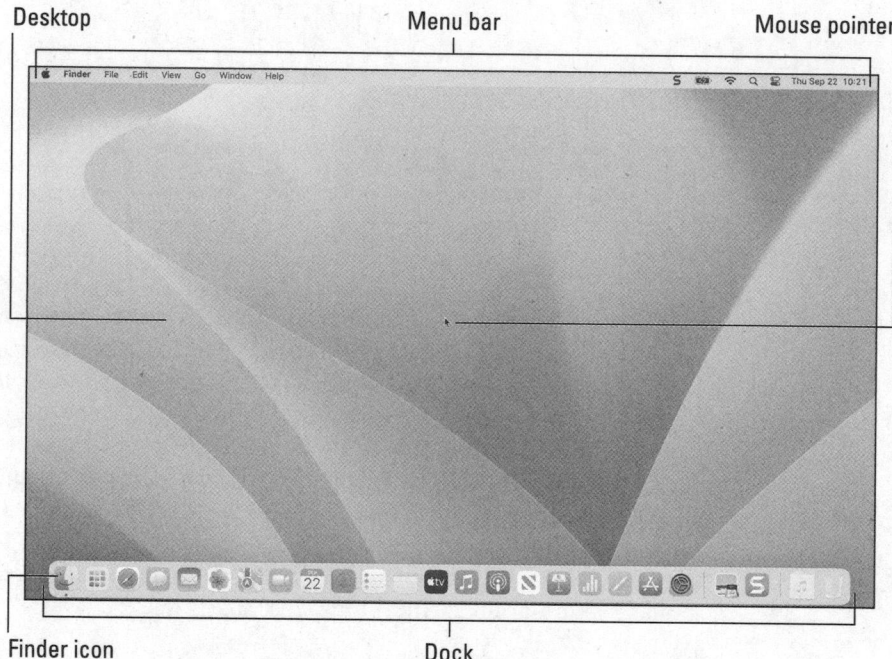

FIGURE 2-1:
The desktop: your
Mac home away
from home.

Finder icon   Dock

The upshot here is that you don't have to think of the Mac desktop as being anything remotely like the top of a physical desk. Instead, just bear in mind that when you do pretty much anything on your Mac, what you work with (that is, any of the menus, dialogs, and windows that I discuss shortly) appears on the desktop. Enough said about all that.

As pointed out in Figure 2-1, although the desktop is mostly empty, it does contain three important items: the menu bar, the dock, and a special app called Finder. The next few sections give you the details on these Mac knickknacks.

Exploring the menu bar

The menu bar runs across the top of your Mac's screen. The menu bar is always accessible and almost always visible, and it provides a single location where you can find nearly every possible command you may need for your computer or the app you're using. The menu bar consists of three parts: the Apple icon, the active app's menus, and the system icons.

The left side of the menu bar contains two crucial Mac features:

>> **Apple icon (🍎):** Click this icon to unfurl the Apple menu, which contains commands for controlling or modifying your Mac. I talk about most of the Apple menu commands elsewhere in the book. (For example, check out Chapter 1 to learn about the Sleep, Restart, and Shut Down commands.)

>> **Active app's menus:** This part of the menu bar changes depending on which app you're using, and it consists of the name of the active app along with several words that represent menus containing commands for controlling that app and its data. The default app that's always active in macOS is Finder (which you find out more about in this chapter), so in Figure 2-1 you see the name Finder in the menu bar along with the Finder's menus: File, Edit, View, Go, Window, and Help. Open System Settings (🍎 ⇨ System Settings), and it becomes the active app; the menu bar now shows the name System Settings along with that app's menus (Edit, View, Window, and Help), as shown in Figure 2-2.

REMEMBER

An *app* (short for *application*) is a software program that you run on your Mac to accomplish some task, such as modifying your Mac's settings (that's what you do with System Settings; see Book 1, Chapter 6) or scheduling an appointment (using the Calendar app; see Book 5, Chapter 2). For general info on working with apps, see Book 1, Chapter 5.

REMEMBER

The app name in the menu bar — that is, Finder in Figure 2-1 and System Settings in Figure 2-2 — also represents a menu. For most apps, this menu contains the command for quitting the app as well as a command for accessing the app's settings.

On the right side of the menu bar, you see the system icons, shown in Figure 2-3, which also points out the name of the default icons. (Note that your Mac might show more or fewer icons.)

System Settings menus

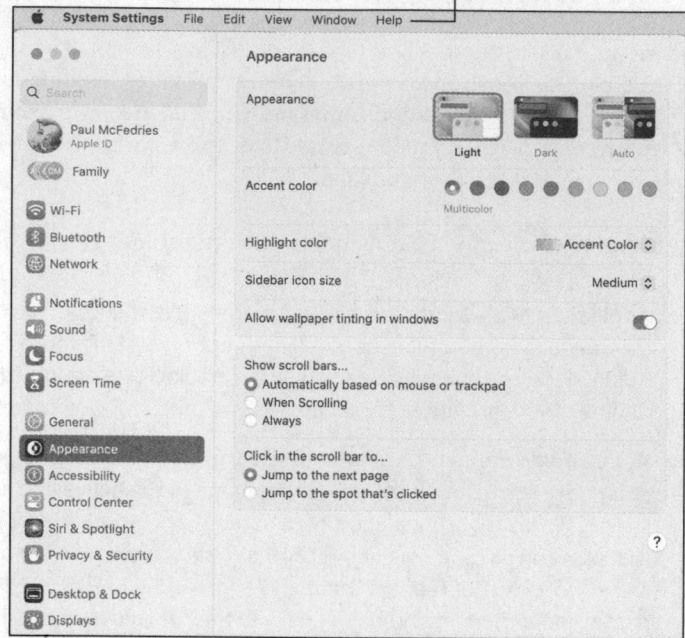

FIGURE 2-2:
With System Settings now the active app, you see its name and menus on the left side of the menu bar.

Third party   Wi-Fi   Control Center

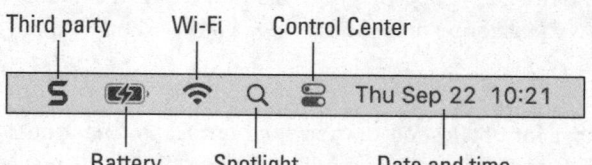

FIGURE 2-3:
The system icons.

Battery   Spotlight   Date and time

These icons generally fall into one of the following three categories:

>> **Status icon:** An icon that tells you the current status of some aspect of your Mac. For example, the battery status icon shows you either that your notebook Mac is running on the power adapter (as shown in Figure 2-2), or the amount of battery power left if your notebook is running on its battery (see Book 3, Chapter 6). Similarly, the Wi-Fi icon shows the strength of the current Wi-Fi network signal (see Book 3, Chapter 4). You can also click a status icon to see more detailed status and related commands.

>> **macOS icon:** An icon that launches a macOS feature. For example, you can click the Spotlight icon to search your Mac (see Book 1, Chapter 4). Similarly, you can click the date or time to open Notification Center (see Book 1, Chapter 6). Of particular interest here is the Control Center icon, which displays Control Center, as shown in Figure 2-4. Control Center gives you

quick access to several system features, such as Wi-Fi, Bluetooth, focus, and volume. I describe each Control Center item as I discuss the related feature in this book.

>> **Third-party icon:** An icon installed by a third-party app. When you click the icon, it runs a command or displays a menu related to the app.

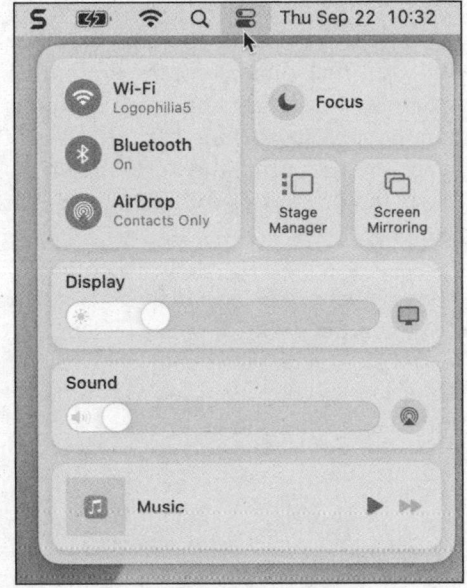

TIP

One big problem with allowing third-party icons on the right side of the menu bar is that they have a rabbitlike tendency to multiply, so your menu bar can get overcrowded in a hurry. If you don't want an icon (whether it's a third-party icon or a macOS icon) cluttering up the menu bar, you can typically remove it by following these steps:

1. **Hold down the ⌘ key.**

2. **Move the mouse pointer over the icon you want to remove.**

3. **Drag the mouse pointer off the menu bar.**

   If nothing happens when you try to drag the icon off the menu bar, it means the icon can't be removed from the menu bar. For example, you can't remove the Control Center icon or the date and time.

4. **Release the ⌘ key and the mouse button.**

If you've removed a menu bar icon and decide you want it back on the menu bar, you can display it again by using the Control Center section of System Settings. For example, you can display or hide the Bluetooth icon choosing ⇨ System Settings, clicking Control Center in the left sidebar, and then using the Bluetooth pop-up menu to select Show in Menu Bar. There are some exceptions, so see Book 1, Chapter 6 for detailed instructions.

The dock

The *dock* is the horizontal strip that runs along the bottom of the desktop. The default dock consists of 20 or so icons, most of which represent an app installed on your Mac. (The dock is home also to icons that represent files and folders.) When you use your Mac for the first time, the dock already has icons for many preinstalled apps, as well as the Downloads folder and the Trash folder (the two icons on the far right of the dock).

When you install a new app on your Mac, it usually adds its own app icon to the dock. You can also add icons to the dock for apps, folders, or files you use frequently (see Book 1, Chapter 5). To help keep your dock icons organized, macOS automatically arranges things so that app icons appear on the left side of a divider and file icons on the right side, as shown in Figure 2-5.

FIGURE 2-5:
The dock displays app icons to the left of the divider and file and folder icons to the right.

App icons

File and folder icons

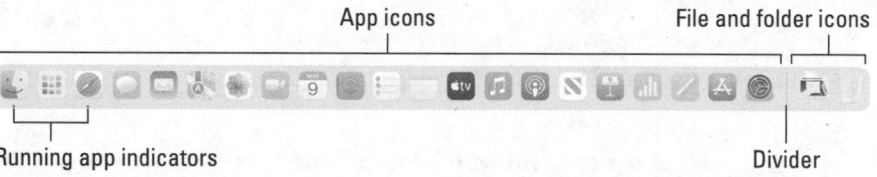

Running app indicators

Divider

You click a dock icon to open the app (or file or folder). If you open an app that isn't on the dock, a temporary icon appears there; when you quit that app, the icon disappears from the dock. Whenever you see a little dot just below the app's icon, it's a visual indicator that the app is running. When you quit an app, its little dot disappears.

For more info about working with apps on the dock, head to Book 1, Chapter 5. To learn how to change the dock's appearance, go to Book 1, Chapter 6.

Finder

Finder is an app that lets you find, copy, move, rename, delete, and open files and folders on your Mac. You can run apps directly from Finder, but using the dock to find and run apps you use frequently is much more convenient.

Finder runs all the time. To switch to Finder, do one of the following:

>> Click an area of the desktop outside any open windows.

>> Click the Finder icon on the dock (pointed out earlier in Figure 2-1).

You know you're in Finder when the app menu just to the right of the icon in the upper left of the screen says Finder (as opposed to Pages, System Settings, or some other app name), as shown previously in Figure 2-1.

Go to Book 1, Chapter 4 to find out how to use and customize Finder, as well as create tabs, tags, and folders in Finder.

Looking at Menus, Dialogs, and Windows

The Mac screen and all its features act like a kind of communication pathway between you and macOS, serving three purposes:

>> To show you all available commands and settings

>> To display information to you

>> To accept input from you

This section tells you how menus, dialogs, and windows serve those three purposes.

Getting the hang of menu commands

Earlier I mentioned that the words you see on the left side of the menu bar, after the icon, represent the active app's menus. Each of these menus contains a group of related commands. For example, the File menu contains commands related to files, such as Open, Save, and Print; the Edit menu contains commands related to making changes to items or data, such as Copy, Paste, and Undo; and the View menu offers commands related to what you see on the screen, such as Hide Toolbar and Enter Full Screen. The number and names of the menus depend on the app.

To run a menu command, follow these general steps:

1. **Move the mouse pointer over the name of the menu that contains the command you want to run.**

2. **Click the menu name.**

macOS drops down a menu of commands you can choose.

3. **Move the mouse pointer over the command you want to run.**

4. **Click the command.**

If the command has a right-pointing arrow (for example, see the Recent Folders command in Figure 2-6), clicking the command will display another menu, which is called a *continuation menu.* Note, however, that you don't have to click such commands; instead, you can just hover the mouse pointer over the command and the menu will appear all by itself.

5. **If macOS displays a continuation menu (as shown in Figure 2-6), click the command you want in that menu.**

macOS runs the command.

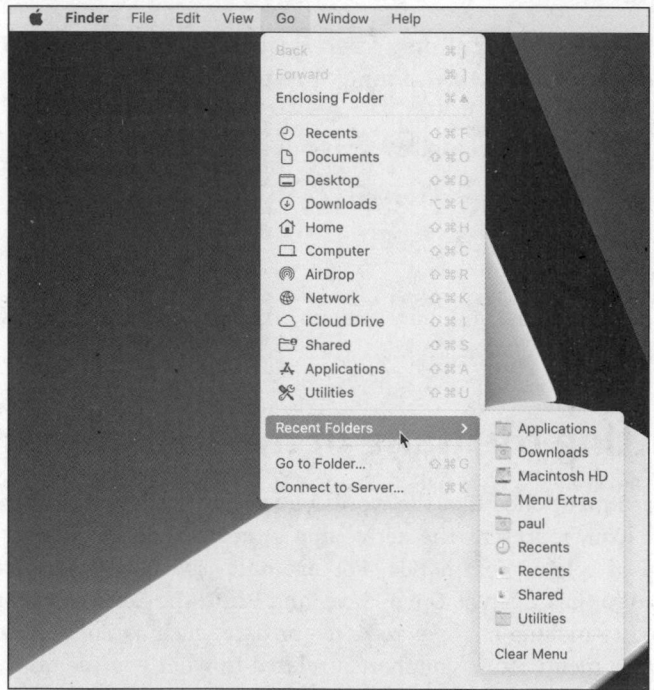

FIGURE 2-6:
Some menu
commands
display
continuation
menus.

TIP

If you see a right-pointing arrow to the right of a command, it means that command displays a continuation menu.

Dealing with dialogs

When your Mac needs information from you or wants to present a choice you can make, it typically displays a *dialog* — essentially an onscreen box that offers a variety of choices. For example, when you run the Save command on a new file, the Save As dialog enables you to specify a name for the file and a location where you want it saved. Similarly, when you run the Print command, the Print dialog box enables you to specify print settings such as the printer and the number of copies.

When a dialog appears, you tell macOS what options you want by manipulating one or more controls. For example, Figure 2-7 shows a typical dialog that offers the following common dialog controls (among others):

>> **Pop-up list:** Click this control to display a list of choices, and then click the item you want.

>> **Slider:** Drag the circle left or right to set a value.

>> **Text box:** Type the value you want.

>> **Spin box:** Click the up or down arrow to set the value you want.

>> **Check box:** Select this control to toggle a setting on (a check mark appears in the box) or off (no check mark appears in the box).

>> **Radio buttons:** In a group of radio buttons, select the one you want (the circle gets filled). In a radio button group, only one button can be selected at a time (that is, displayed with a filled-in circle).

>> **Command button:** Click the button to execute the command written on the button.

Every dialog displays buttons that let you cancel the dialog or complete it. To cancel a dialog, you usually have three choices:

>> Click the Cancel button.

>> Press Esc.

>> Press ⌘ +. (period).

To complete a dialog, you usually have two choices:

>> Click the button that represents the command you want to complete, such as Save or Print. If the dialog is used only to specify settings, the button that completes the dialog and puts the new settings into effect will be labeled OK or Done.

>> Press Return to choose the default button, which usually appears in blue.

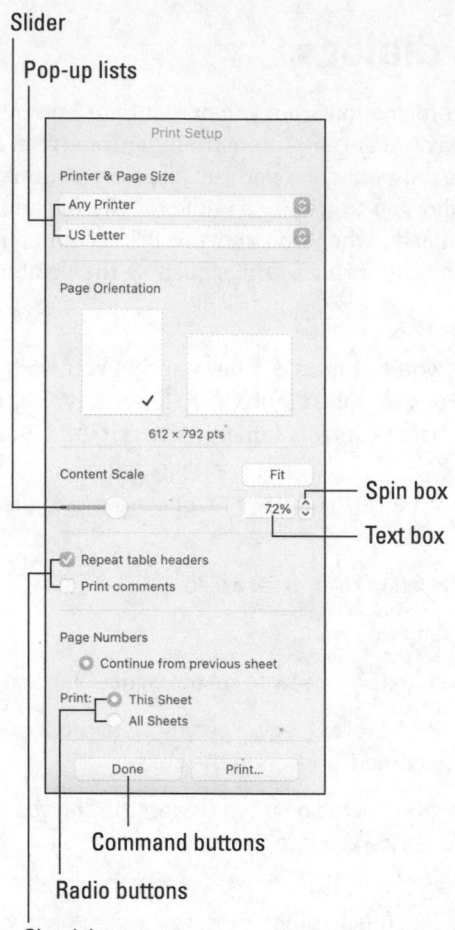

Slider

Pop-up lists

Spin box

Text box

Command buttons

Radio buttons

FIGURE 2-7:
Some common
dialog controls.

Check boxes

Messing with windows

Every app needs to accept, manipulate, or display data. A word processor lets you type and edit text, a spreadsheet app lets you type and calculate numbers, and a presentation app lets you display text and pictures. To help you work with different types of data (such as text, pictures, audio files, and video files), every app displays data inside a rectangular area called a *window*.

For example, choose ⇨ System Settings. Why, look: A box shows up on the desktop, as shown in Figure 2-8. That box is the System Settings window.

Now click the Finder icon on the dock. Lo and behold, a second window appears on the desktop, probably over top of the System Settings window, as shown in Figure 2-9.

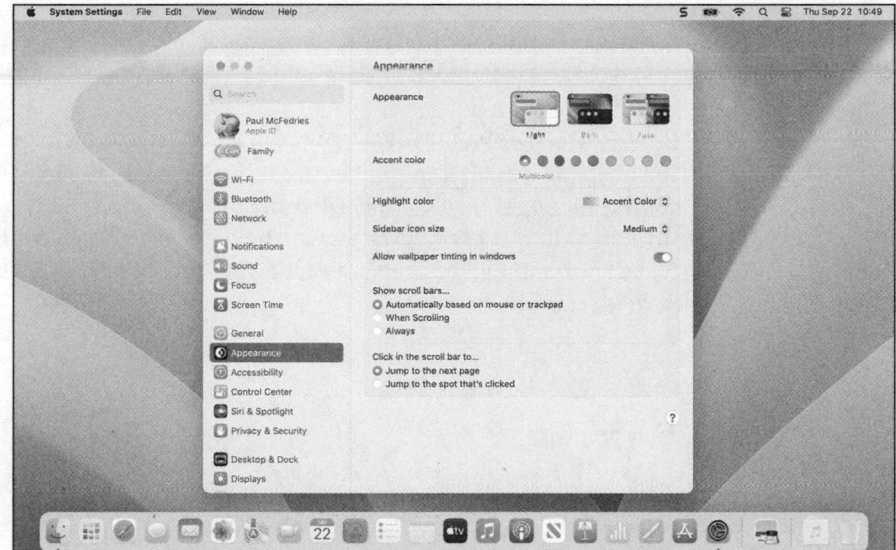

FIGURE 2-8:
Run the System
Settings
command and
the System
Settings window
appears for duty
on the desktop.

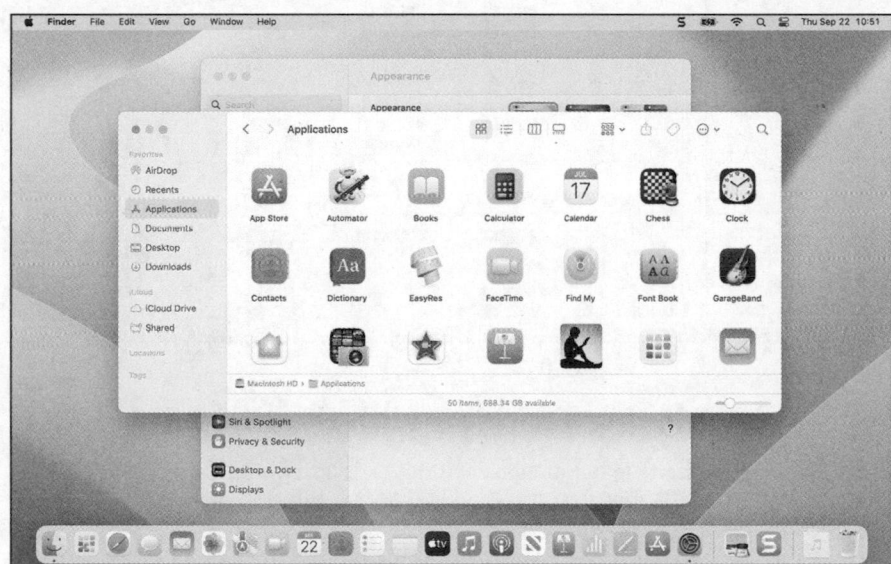

FIGURE 2-9:
Multiple apps
can appear in
windows
onscreen at the
same time.

Dividing a screen into multiple windows offers several advantages:

>> Two or more apps can display data on the screen simultaneously.

>> A single app can open and display data stored in two or more files or display two or more views of the same file.

>> You can copy (or move) data from one window to another. If each window belongs to a different app, this action transfers data from one app to another.

Of course, windows aren't perfect. When a window appears on the screen, it might be too big or too small, it might be hard to find because it's hidden behind another window, or it might display the beginning of a file when you want to see the middle or end of it. Most windows provide built-in controls to control their appearance, as shown in Figure 2-10. The following sections show you what you can do with these controls.

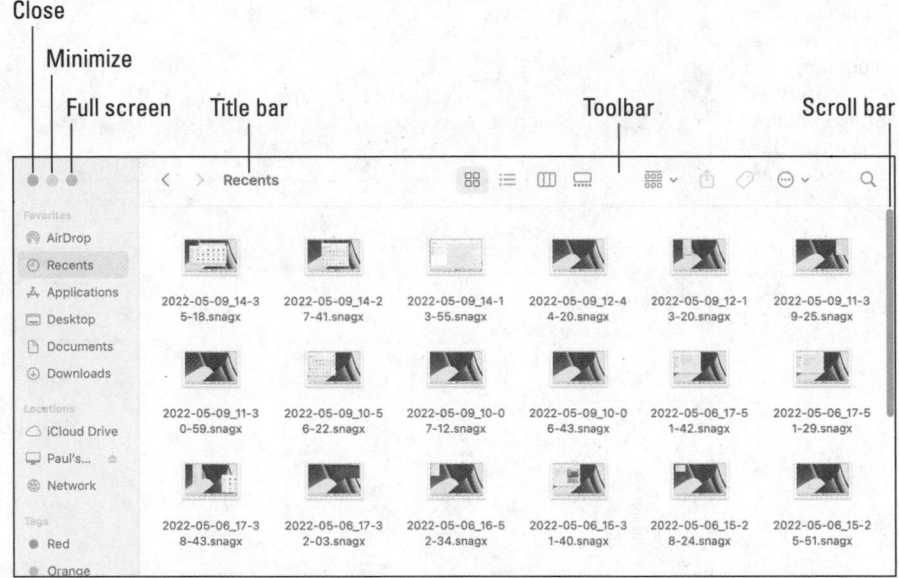

FIGURE 2-10:
Every window provides controls so you can manipulate it.

Moving a window with the title bar

The title bar of every window serves two purposes:

>> It identifies the window by displaying its name.

>> It provides a place to grab when you want to drag (move) the window to a new location on the screen.

To move a window, follow these steps:

1. **Move the mouse pointer into the title bar.**

2. **Drag the title bar until the window is in the position you want.**

3. **Release the mouse button.**

Resizing a window

Sometimes a window may be in the perfect location, but it's too small or too large for what you want to do at that moment. To change the size of a window, follow these steps:

1. **Move the pointer over any corner or edge of the window.**

The regular mouse pointer changes to a resizing pointer that looks like a dash with arrows on both ends. (The resizing pointer has just one arrow if the window has reached its size limit and can only be made smaller or larger.)

2. **Drag the resizing pointer.**

- *To resize the width,* drag the left or right side of the window.
- *To resize the height,* drag the top or bottom side of the window.
- *To resize the width and height at the same time,* drag a corner of the window.
- *To make the window smaller,* drag the edge or corner towards the inside of the window.
- *To make the window larger,* drag the edge or corner away from the window.

The window grows or shrinks while you drag the resizing pointer.

3. **Release the mouse button when you're happy with the new size of the window.**

Closing a window

When you finish viewing or editing data displayed in a window, you can close the window to keep it from cluttering the screen. To close a window, follow these steps:

1. **Move the pointer to the upper-left corner of the window and then click the close icon (the little red button) of the window you want to close.**

If the window doesn't have any data that needs to be saved, you're done. However, many windows contain data that you worked on, so the app might ask if you want to save your data. In that case, the app displays a dialog that asks whether you want to save it.

2. **If a dialog appears, click one of the following choices:**

- *Don't Save (or Delete):* Closes the window and discards any changes you made to the data inside the window. In some apps, this button is named Delete instead of Don't Save.
- *Cancel:* Keeps the window open.

- *Save:* Closes the window but saves the data in a file. If this is the first time you've saved this data, another dialog appears, giving you a chance to name the file and to store the saved data in a specific location on your hard drive.

REMEMBER

Computers typically offer two or more ways to accomplish the same task, so you can choose the way you like best. As an alternative to clicking the close icon, you can click inside the window you want to close and then choose File ➪ Close or press ⌘+W.

Minimizing a window

Sometimes you may not want to close a window, but you still want to get it out of the way so it doesn't clutter your screen. In that case, you can minimize or hide the window, which tucks it onto the dock.

To minimize a window, choose one of the following methods:

» Click the minimize button — the yellow button in the upper-left corner — of the window you want to tuck out of the way.

» Click the window you want to minimize and choose Window➪ Minimize Window.

» Press ⌘+M.

To open a minimized window, choose ➪ Recent Items and then click the minimized app or document in the list, or click the minimized window on the dock.

Employing full-screen view

Most Apple apps and many third-party apps offer full-screen view. When available, the full-screen button (the green dot pointed out earlier in Figure 2-10) appears in the upper-left corner of the app window. When you click the full-screen button, the application fills the screen, and the menu bar is hidden from view. Hover the pointer at the very top of the screen to reveal the menu bar so you can point and click to use the menus. Move the pointer back to the window, and the menu bar disappears again. Press the Esc key or Control+⌘+F to return to normal view or click the full-screen button again, which you find by hovering the pointer over the upper-right corner.

TIP

If you use several applications in full-screen view, swipe left or right with four fingers across the trackpad or press Control+→ or Control+← to move from one application to another.

Zooming a window

If a window is too small to display data, you can instantly make it bigger by using the zoom button, which is what the full-screen button (the green button in the upper-left corner of most windows) turns into when you hold down the Option key. (When you hold down the Option key and move the mouse over the zoom button, a plus sign appears inside.) Option+clicking the zoom button expands the window to its maximum size; Option-clicking the zoom button a second time shrinks the window to its prior size.

REMEMBER

Zooming a window makes the window — not the contents — grow larger. Many apps have sliders or menus that increase or decrease the size of the contents: 100 percent is the actual size; a lower percentage (such as 75 percent) shows more data at a smaller size; and a higher percentage (such as 200 percent) shows less data but may be easier on your eyes. Most word-processing applications have an option for page width.

Scrolling through a window

No matter how large you make a window, it may still be too small to display all the data contained inside. If a window isn't large enough to display all the data inside it, the window lets you know by displaying a vertical scroll bar, a horizontal scroll bar, or both.

You can scroll what's displayed in a window two ways:

>> **Mouse or trackpad scrolling:** Place two fingers on the top of a Magic Mouse or the surface of a trackpad. Then move your fingers up and down to scroll the window contents vertically, or left and right to scroll the window contents horizontally.

>> **Scroll bars:** You can move the contents by

- *Dragging the scroll box:* Click and drag the gray oval scroll box in the scroll bar to move up and down or right and left in the window. This option scrolls through a window faster than mouse or trackpad scrolling.

- *Clicking in the scroll bar:* Scroll up and down or right and left in large increments or directly to the spot where you click.

  Although the scroll bar is the size of the window, it represents the length, or width, of the document; if you want to jump to page 25 of a 100-page document, click and hold in the upper quarter of the vertical scroll bar; to go to page 90, click and hold near the bottom of the scroll bar.

TIP

You can adjust the scroll bar's appearance — or eliminate the scroll bar altogether — which I explain in Book 1, Chapter 6.

TIP

Depending on your Mac model, your Mac's keyboard may have dedicated Page Up and Page Down keys, which you can press to scroll up and down. Not seeing Page Up and Page Down keys on your Mac or MacBook keyboard doesn't mean they aren't there. To use your Mac's invisible Page Up and Page Down keys, see Book 1, Chapter 1.

Getting Acquainted with Siri

If you have an iPhone or iPad, you're probably already familiar with Siri, the virtual assistant built into many Apple devices, including the Mac. A *virtual assistant* is software that can respond to verbal commands. A basic virtual assistant needs to have the capability to respond to commands such as "What time is it?" A more sophisticated virtual assistant can pull together information from several sources.

REMEMBER

The Mac Studio, Mac mini, and Mac Pro don't have built-in microphones. To use Siri on one of these machines, you need to connect either a USB external microphone (see Book 1, Chapter 1) or a Bluetooth microphone (see Book 3, Chapter 4). Once the microphone is connected, you can set up the microphone sensitivity on the Input tab of your Mac's Sound settings (choose System Settings ⇨ Sound).

In this section, I show you how to configure Siri and get Siri working for you.

Enabling Siri

If you didn't enable Siri during your Mac's setup procedure, you can follow these steps to enable it now:

1. **Choose ⇨ System Settings or click System Settings on the dock.**

   The System Settings window appears.

2. **Click Siri & Spotlight.**

   The Siri settings appear.

3. **Click the Ask Siri switch on.**

   macOS asks you to confirm.

4. **Click Enable.**

   macOS asks you to choose a voice for Siri.

5. **Click each voice (Voice 1 through Voice 5) to check them out, and then click the one you prefer.**

The voice you choose isn't set in the digital equivalent of stone. After you complete these steps, at any time you can open System Settings and select Siri. Then use the Language list to choose a language for Siri to speak, use the Voice Variety list to select your preferred variation on your selected language, and use the Siri Voice list to select your preferred voice.

6. **Click Done.**

macOS asks if you'd be willing to share your Siri interactions with Apple as a way of helping to improve Siri. These recordings aren't connected to you or your Apple ID, but some folks aren't comfortable with the idea of Apple employees listening to what they say to Siri.

7. **If you're okay with sharing your Siri requests, click Share Audio Recordings; otherwise, click Not Now.**

macOS enables Siri and you're ready to dive in.

Getting Siri's attention

By default, Siri lies dormant until you wake it up to speak a request. You can catch Siri's ear in two main ways:

» Click the Siri icon in the menu bar. (If you don't see this icon, open System Settings, click Control Center, and then use the Siri pop-up menu to select Show in Menu Bar.)

» If your keyboard has a dictation key (look for a microphone icon on the F5 key), press and hold down that key until Siri appears. Otherwise, press and hold down the ⌘ key, and then press and hold down the spacebar until Siri appears.

TIP

An even faster way to get Siri's attention is with a voice command. To set this up, open System Settings, click Siri & Spotlight, and then click the Listen for "Hey Siri" switch on. macOS takes you through a brief setup procedure to make sure that Siri can recognize your voice. Once that's done, you can now invoke Siri by saying "Hey Siri."

You'll know that Siri is awake and listening to you when you see the Siri window, as shown in Figure 2-11.

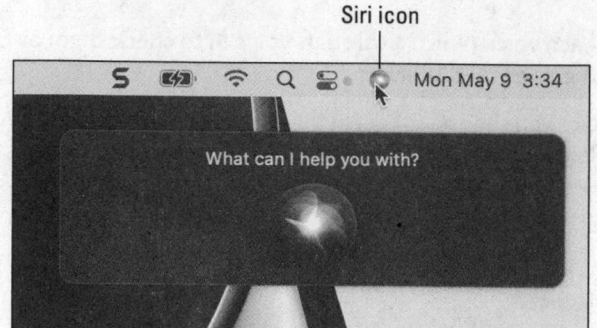

Siri icon

FIGURE 2-11:
This window
appears when
you wake up Siri.

Getting help

Theoretically, the Mac should be so easy and intuitive that you can teach yourself how to use your computer just by looking at the screen. Realistically, the Mac can be confusing and complicated — otherwise, there would be no need for this book! I've done my best to give you steps and tips to handle almost any useful Mac task you come across, but to cover absolutely everything Mac-related would require several books this size! And sometimes it may just help to read the same task explained in a different way. So, any time you are confused when using your Mac and can't find the answers in this book, try turning to your Mac for help with your Mac!

Your Mac offers two types of help:

>> **It can point out specific menu commands to choose for accomplishing a specific task.** For example, if you want to know how to save or print a file, Mac Help will point out the Save or Print command so you know which command to choose.

>> **It can provide brief explanations for how to accomplish a specific task.** By skimming through the brief explanations, you can (I hope) figure out how to do something useful.

Here's how you can access both types of help:

1. **Click the Help menu at the far-right end of the menu bar for any application you're running.**

   Or you can switch to Finder by clicking the Finder icon on the dock, and then click Help.

   A Search text box appears.

2. **Begin typing a word or phrase.**

   If, for instance, you want help with printing a document, type **print**. While you type, a list of possible topics appears.

   Help topics for the application you're running appear first under the Menu Items category, followed by the Help Topics category.

3. **Move your pointer over a Menu Items topic.**

   A floating arrow points to the command on a menu to show you how to access your chosen topic for the application you're running, as shown in Figure 2-12.

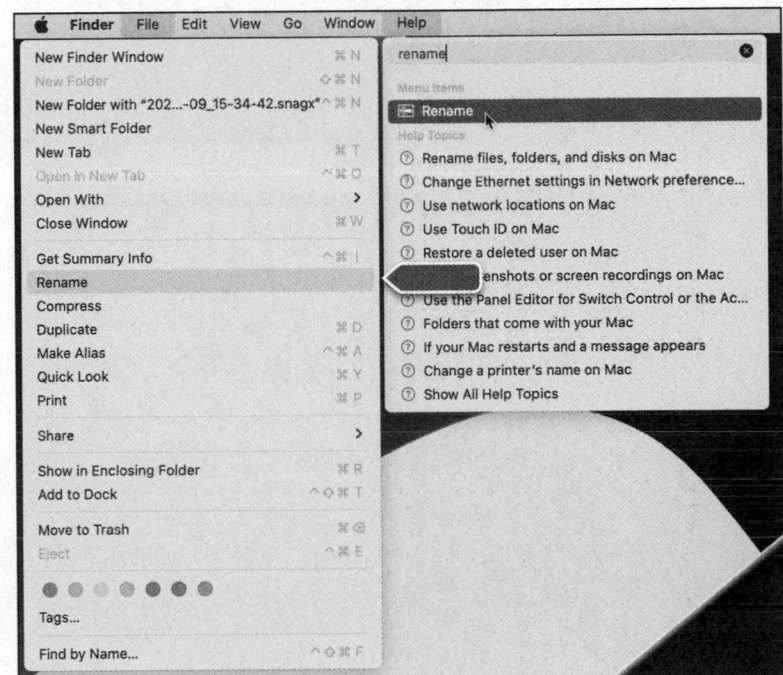

FIGURE 2-12: macOS Help shows you how to access a particular command.

4. **If you want to read a Help article on a specific subject, click one of the topics under Help Topics.**

   If you're accessing Help from Finder, you're taken to a page from the macOS User Guide, as shown in Figure 2-13. You can access the macOS User Guide in Finder also by choosing Help⇨ macOS Help.

   If you're accessing Help from a third-party application, such as Microsoft Word, you're taken to that application's Help documentation.

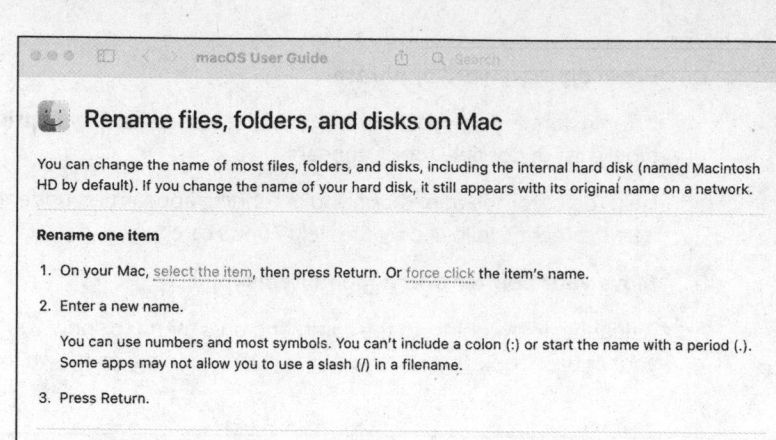

Rename files, folders, and disks on Mac

You can change the name of most files, folders, and disks, including the internal hard disk (named Macintosh HD by default). If you change the name of your hard disk, it still appears with its original name on a network.

Rename one item

1. On your Mac, select the item, then press Return. Or force click the item's name.

2. Enter a new name.

   You can use numbers and most symbols. You can't include a colon (:) or start the name with a period (.). Some apps may not allow you to use a slash (/) in a filename.

3. Press Return.

Rename multiple items

1. On your Mac, select the items, then Control-click one of them.

2. In the shortcut menu, choose Rename.

3. In the pop-up menu below Rename Finder Items, choose to replace text in the names, add text to the names, or change the name format.

   - *Replace text:* Enter the text you want to remove in the Find field, then enter the text you want to add in

FIGURE 2-13:
The macOS
User Guide.

Chapter **3**

Getting Your Mac Online

B elieve it not, there's no law that says a computer has to be connected to the internet. That might sound unthinkable, but the fact is that your Mac is stuffed with useful apps and tools that can be used offline (that is, without jacking in to the internet). So, if you want to use your Mac without connecting to the online world, I say go for it. You'll get no judgment from me.

That said, an offline Mac *does* miss out on a ton of good things. Perhaps the most important is the constant stream of updates that come in over the internet for macOS and your installed apps. Without those updates, your Mac's performance, reliability, and, crucially, its *security* will suffer over the medium to long term. Without an internet connection, you can't surf the web; exchange email or text messages; make FaceTime calls; get directions; play streaming movies, TV shows, or songs; sync your appointments, contacts, and notes across your devices; or share photos, videos, and documents.

If all that sounds like way too much to give up, not to worry: In this chapter, I explain how to connect your Mac to the internet. Then I walk you through creating an Apple ID, which you use for iCloud, FaceTime, and shopping in the iTunes Store, the App Store, and the Apple Book Store. After you have an Apple ID, you discover how to set up iCloud and learn about the various iCloud options. At the end of this chapter, I explain how to add accounts from other providers, such as Microsoft Exchange and Google. Many apps that came with your Mac access information from these accounts, so setting them up at the beginning makes your Mac experience easier down the road.

Introducing Your Mac to the Internet

To get the internet show on the road, in this section I explain how to set up a broadband internet connection, which is a high-speed connection provided by your local cable company, a phone company (which usually calls the connection a digital subscriber line), or satellite. I assume a few things:

>> You already have an internet account with a broadband provider.

>> The broadband provider has given you a device called a broadband modem, which handles the connection.

>> If you're doing the Wi-Fi (wireless networking) thing, you have a wireless router that's already hosting a wireless network.

In this section, you learn about two ways to set up an internet connection:

>> **Direct:** If you're the only person who will be using the internet and don't need to access the connection from different places in your home, you can connect your Mac directly to the modem.

>> **Wireless:** If you share the connection with other people in your home or want to be able to access the connection from anywhere in your home, you can connect your wireless router to the broadband modem and then connect your Mac to your wireless network.

Getting online by connecting your Mac directly to your broadband modem

A broadband modem is a high-speed modem used for digital subscriber line (DSL), cable, or satellite internet access. In almost all cases, the internet service provider (ISP) provides you with a broadband modem compatible with its service. Getting the broadband modem connected is the first step in putting your network together.

Of the two connection types I mention in the introduction to this chapter, by far the most common is the wireless connection. I show you how that works a bit later, but note that such a setup is not required for many situations. For example, if you have only one Mac, you don't have a smartphone or tablet, and don't need to access the connection from different places in your home, there's no need to set up wireless access to the internet, so you should connect the broadband modem directly to your PC. Similarly, even if you have multiple computers, for safety reasons you might prefer that only one of them access the internet. (For example, you might not want small children having direct access to the internet.)

Connecting the Mac and modem

Begin by connecting and plugging in the modem's power adapter. Make sure the modem is turned off. If the modem doesn't come with a power switch, unplug the power adapter for now.

The next step is to attach the cable that provides the ISP's internet connection. How you do this depends on what type of modem you have:

>> **DSL broadband modem:** Run a phone line from the nearest wall jack to the appropriate port on the back of the modem, which is usually labeled *DSL,* as shown in Figure 3-1, left.

>> **Cable broadband modem:** Run a TV cable line from the nearest wall jack to the cable connector on the back of the modem, which is usually labeled *Cable,* as shown in Figure 3-1, center.

FIGURE 3-1:
The DSL port, cable connector, and Ethernet port on the back of the modem.

Now you need to connect your Mac to the broadband modem. All broadband modems have one or more network ports on the back labeled *Ethernet* or *LAN,* as shown in Figure 3-1, right. Run a network cable from the Ethernet port on your Mac to an Ethernet port on the back of the broadband modem

TIP

If you have a MacBook Air, MacBook Pro, or other Mac that doesn't offer an Ethernet port, you need to spring for a USB-C-to-Ethernet adapter. Plug the adapter into a USB-C or Thunderbolt port, and then plug the Ethernet cable into the other end of the adapter.

TIP

Some broadband modems also come with a USB port on the back. If you're working with a Mac that doesn't have an Ethernet port, you might be able to use a USB connection instead by running a USB cable from a USB port on your Mac to the USB port on your broadband modem.

Happily, when you connect your Mac to a broadband modem via an Ethernet port, your Mac recognizes the modem's internet connection right away. Your Mac automatically figures out the proper settings to connect to the internet without making you type a bunch of cryptic numbers and fiddle with confusing technical standards. Yes!

Checking the connection

To make sure your Ethernet connection is up and running, follow these steps:

1. **Choose ⇨ System Settings.**

2. **Choose Network.**

3. **Choose your Ethernet device.**

   In Figure 3-2, the Ethernet connection is made via a device called Belkin USB-C LAN (which is a USB-C to Ethernet adapter).

4. **Read the status line, which appears below the device name.**

   If the status is *Connected*, as shown in Figure 3-2, you're online and good to go. You can click the connection, if you want, but all you'll see is for-geeks-only stuff such as the IP address and the subnet mask. Be sure to give thanks to your favorite deity that you don't have to worry about any of that!

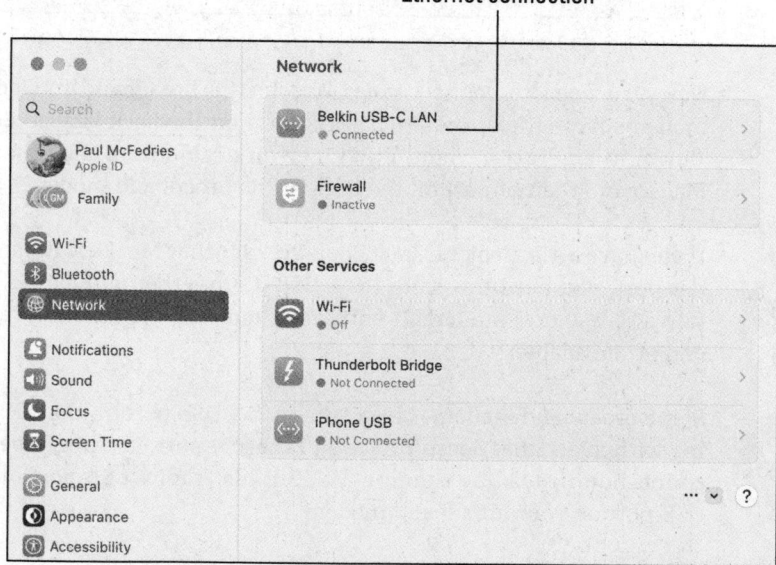

FIGURE 3-2: The current status (fingers crossed) should be *Connected*.

Getting online by using a wireless network to access a broadband connection

Connecting a broadband modem directly to a Mac is the simplest way to get online, but it's not always the most convenient. For example, if other people in your house want to use the internet, they must do so through the same Mac connected to the modem. Similarly, if you have a notebook Mac, you may be able to take it to different places in your house, but you can't take the internet connection with you.

The solution to both problems is to create a wireless network and give it access to your broadband internet connection. The wireless network enables other computers and devices (such as iPhones and iPads) to share the same connection and enables you to access the connection from different parts of your house.

Connecting the modem and router

The first step is to set up your broadband modem so that its internet connection can be shared with each device on your wireless network. You do this by connecting the broadband modem to your wireless router. First, however, make sure that you turn off the modem and disconnect the network or USB cable connecting the router and your Mac.

Examine the back of your wireless router and locate the port it uses for the internet connection. Some access points label this port *WAN* (see Figure 3-3), whereas others use *Internet.* Some routers don't label the internet port at all, but instead place the port off to the side so that it's clearly separate from the router's network ports.

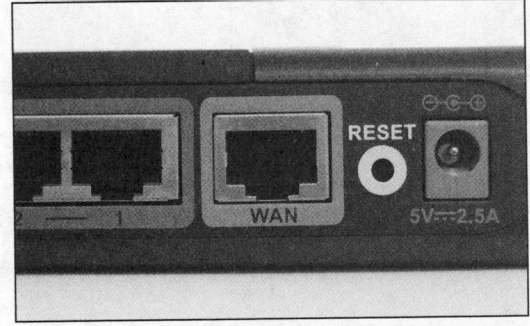

FIGURE 3-3:
The port used for the internet connection.

With the broadband modem and router turned off, run a network cable from one of the broadband modem's network ports to the WAN port on the router.

TIP

On my network, I keep the broadband modem and the wireless router side by side on a desk so that I can easily see the LEDs on the front of both devices (particularly the LED on the broadband modem that indicates a good internet connection). If you do this, purchase a 1-foot Ethernet cable to connect the two devices.

You're now ready to turn on your devices. Begin by turning on the broadband modem and waiting until it has a solid connection with the internet. Then turn on your router.

Connecting to a Wi-Fi network

You connect your Mac to your wireless network by following these steps:

1. **Display a list of nearby wireless networks in one of the following ways:**

    - Click the Wi-Fi icon (see Figure 3-4) on the right side of the menu bar.

    - Click the Control Center icon (also in Figure 3-4) and then click Wi-Fi.

    If you don't see a list of Wi-Fi networks when you click the Wi-Fi icon on the menu bar, click the Wi-Fi switch on. If you still don't see the list, click the Other Networks disclosure arrow.

Wi-Fi icon   Control Center icon

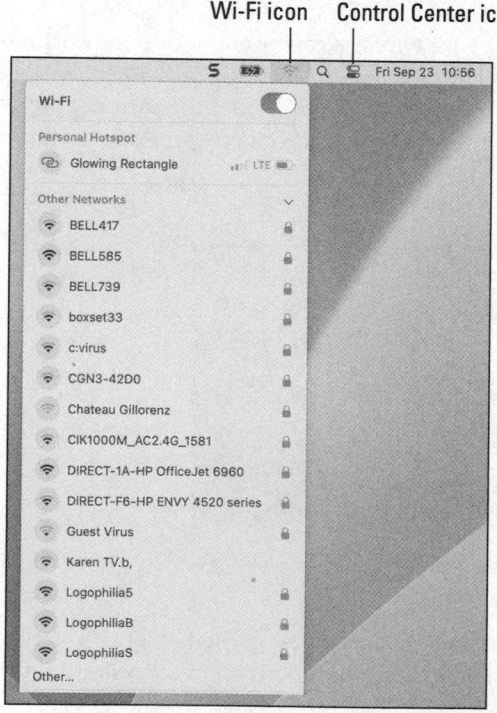

FIGURE 3-4:
Click the Wi-Fi icon to see a list of nearby wireless networks.

REMEMBER

If you don't see the Wi-Fi icon on the menu bar, choose ➪ System Settings, click Control Center in the sidebar, and then use the Wi-Fi pop-up menu to select Show in Menu Bar.

2. **Select the name of your wireless network.**

A lock icon to the left of the network's signal strength indicates a *secured* (also known as *encrypted*) wireless network protected by a password. For a secured network, macOS prompts you for the password, as shown in Figure 3-5.

On the odd chance that you don't see the network you want, you can click Other at the bottom of the list to open the Find and Join a Wi-Fi Network dialog. Enter the name of a network you want to join, select the Security type (if you know it), and then continue with Step 3 (assuming the network requires a password, that is).

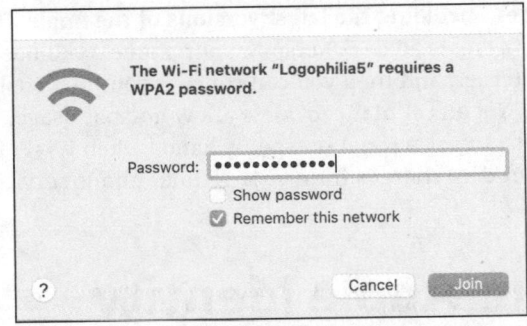

FIGURE 3-5:
To access a secured network, you need to enter the password.

3. **Type the network password.**

4. **(Optional) Select the following options in the password prompt dialog:**

   - *Show Password:* Displays the characters you type instead of dots that hide your password. With long, mixed-character, case-sensitive passwords, it can be helpful to see what you type — just make sure that no one is looking over your shoulder.

   - *Remember This Network:* Remembers that you've connected to the selected network before and then connects to it automatically whenever you're within range of its signal. This option is handy if the network is at a place you visit frequently, such as a friend or relative's house or your workplace. (If you chose to remember more than one wireless network in the same location, your Mac always connects to the one with the strongest signal first.)

5. **Click Join.**

   macOS connects you to the wireless router and, hence, to the internet.

The Wi-Fi icon on the menu bar shows black bars to indicate the strength of the Wi-Fi network signal your Mac is connected to. Like mobile phone reception (and chocolate), more bars are better.

When you connect to a wireless network that doesn't require you to enter a password, your Mac essentially broadcasts any information you type (such as credit card numbers or passwords) through the airwaves. Although the likelihood of anyone monitoring what you're typing may be small, tech-savvy engineers or hackers can "sniff" wireless signals to monitor or collect information flowing through the airwaves. Whenever you connect to a public Wi-Fi network, assume that a stranger is peeking at your data and type only such data that you're comfortable giving away to others. Connecting to a secured network that requires you to type a password to connect to it means all the traffic over that connection is encrypted, so no snoop can monitor or collect what you send or receive.

Many smartphones, including the latest versions of the Apple iPhone, enable you to use the device to create a Wi-Fi hotspot. Your phone's cellular service is used to connect to the internet, and then you can connect your MacBook to your phone's hotspot network. Not all cellular providers allow hotspot usage, and most that do allow it require you to pay a fee. A hotspot is handy when Wi-Fi is unavailable but you may also incur data charges from your cellular phone service provider.

Establishing Your Apple Identity

You become a somebody in the Mac world by setting up your own *Apple ID*, which is an email address and password that uniquely identifies you in the Mac universe. Why is that something you should care about? Because an Apple ID is a way of verifying who you are when it comes time to register new products, purchase goodies from the iTunes Store, App Store, and Book Store, play media using apps such as Apple Music and Apple TV, and access certain Apple services, such as the iCloud online storage service (see "Storing Your Data in iCloud," later in this chapter).

When you turned on your Mac for the first time, a series of questions and prompts appear, including a prompt to sign in to your Apple ID account or create a new Apple ID. If you went ahead and created an Apple ID during setup, no worries: You can safely skip this section and move on with your life. But if, instead, you clicked the Set Up Later link, no problem: Now's your chance to fill that gap.

Signing in with an existing Apple ID

If you already have an Apple ID but haven't yet signed in with it on your Mac, here are the steps to follow:

1. **Choose ⟹ System Settings or click the System Settings icon on the dock.**

2. **Click Sign In near the top of the System Settings sidebar.**

   The Sign In settings appear.

3. **Use the Apple ID text box to enter your Apple ID email address, and then click Next.**

4. **Type your Apple ID password, which appears as dots for security (see Figure 3-6), and then click Next.**

   Your Mac prompts you to enter your Mac's administrator account password.

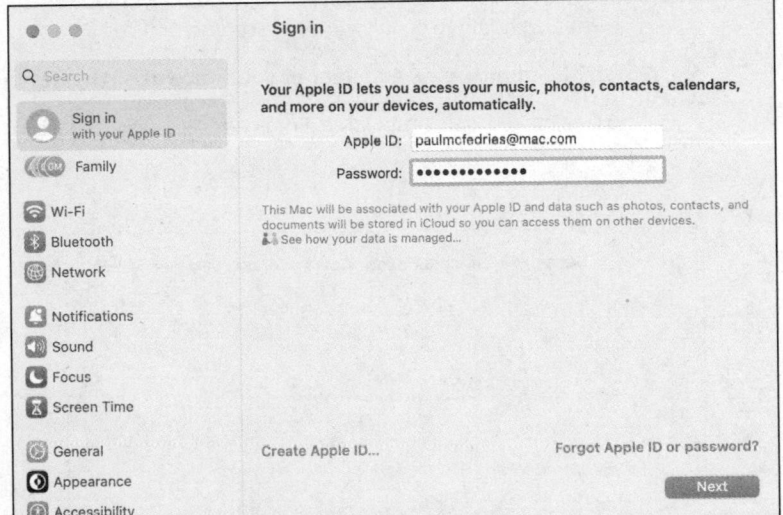

FIGURE 3-6:
The dots prevent
snoops from
reading your
password.

5. **Type your password and click OK.**

   Remember: Enter your Mac account password, not the password for the Apple ID you're signing in to.

   Your Mac asks if you want to turn on Find My Mac, which is a good idea if you travel with your Mac. I cover this feature in Book 3, Chapter 2, so feel free to skip it for now.

6. **Either click Allow, to enable Find My Mac, or click Not Now, to disable it.**

   System Settings signs you in to your Apple ID and displays the Apple ID settings.

Forging a new Apple ID

Here are the steps to follow to create your very own Apple ID:

1. **Choose ⊕ ⇨ System Settings or click the System Settings icon on the dock.**

2. **Click Sign In near the top of the System Settings sidebar.**

    The Sign In settings appear.

3. **Click Create Apple ID.**

    System Settings prompts you to enter your birthday. Why? Mostly because some Apple ID settings and features work differently for young children (in most countries, that means children under the age of 13). Also, Apple might use your birthdate to confirm your identity.

4. **Enter the month, day, and year of your date of birth, and then click Next.**

    The Get Started with Your Name, Email Address, and Password dialog appears, as shown in Figure 3-7.

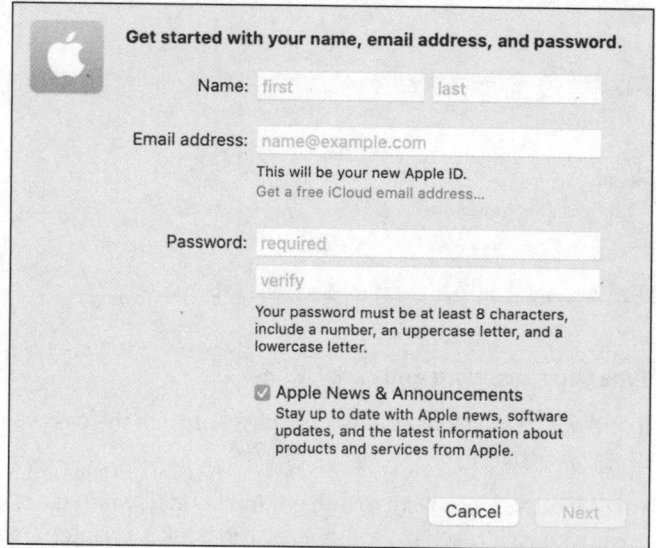

FIGURE 3-7:
Creating an Apple ID requires your name, an email address, and a password.

5. **Type your first name and last name.**

6. **Select the Get a Free iCloud Email Address link.**

    Your Apple ID email address will be *user*@icloud.com, where the *user* part could be your name, nickname, favorite beat poet, or whatever.

Nope, you don't have to create a new iCloud email address if you don't want to. It's perfectly fine to use an existing email address. I recommend going the iCloud address route because it's a bit more convenient to have all your Apple emails and logins under a single, Apple-protected address, but it's not essential.

7. **Fill in the Email Address text box to complete your icloud.com address.**

Use only letters, numbers, and periods. Also, don't choose an address that has already been assigned to someone else. How on earth are you supposed to know that? Unfortunately, you can't, at least not until you click Next in Step 10. Then, if you see a warning that the address you've typed is "no longer available," you need to try again.

Alternatively, if you opted not to create a new iCloud email address, enter an existing email address in the Email Address text box.

8. **Type the password you want to use and then type it again in the second Password text box.**

Your password must be at least eight characters and contain at least one number, one uppercase letter, and one lowercase letter.

9. **(Optional) If you don't want Apple pestering you with company-related messages, deselect the check box for Apple News & Announcements information.**

10. **Click Next.**

If the email address you chose in Step 7 is taken (curses!), System Settings will let you know and you'll need to repeat Steps 7 through 10. Otherwise, System Settings prompts you for a phone number to verify your identity with a text or voice call.

11. **Select your location, type your phone number (including the area code), select whether you want to receive the verification via Text Message or Phone Call, and then click Next.**

System Settings displays a dialog for you to enter the verification code you received via text or call.

12. **Once you get the verification code, type it in the boxes provided.**

Although the dialog comes with a Next button, you won't have to click it because as soon as you enter the last digit of the verification code, your Mac checks the code and automatically shuffles you over to the Terms and Conditions dialog.

13. **Select the I Have Read and Agree To check box and then click Agree.**

Your Mac prompts you to enter your Mac account password.

14. **Type your password and click OK.**

Remember: Enter your Mac account password, not the password for the Apple ID you just set up.

Your Mac asks if you want to turn on Find My Mac, which is a good idea if you travel with your Mac. I cover this feature in Book 3, Chapter 2, so feel free to skip it for now.

15. **Either click Allow, to enable Find My Mac, or click Not Now, to disable it.**

System Settings finishes setting up your Apple ID.

Maintaining your Apple ID

After your existing or new Apple ID is confirmed, you end up at the Apple ID settings window. You can also get there at any time by opening System Settings (choose ⇨ System Settings or click the System Settings icon on the dock) and then clicking Apple ID.

The Apple ID settings window is divided into two sections: The top section lists the different aspects of your Apple ID that you can work with, and the bottom Devices section lists all the devices associated with your Apple ID.

Here's a quick look at each item in the Apple ID settings:

>> **Name, Phone, Email:** Displays your Apple ID name and birthday (see Figure 3-8), each of which you can change by clicking its Edit button. You also get a Reachable At section, which lists the various ways Apple can contact you (such as your Apple ID email address and your phone numbers). You can click + to add more email addresses and phone numbers. Finally, this screen also includes several switches that enable you to opt in to various Apple newsletters.

>> **Password & Security:** Enables you to change your Apple ID password, set up two-factor authentication, and more. I talk about all this later in the book; see Book 3, Chapter 2.

>> **Payment & Shipping:** Displays your current Apple ID payment method and shipping address, if any (see Figure 3-9). If you just created your Apple ID, click Add a Shipping Address to set up the address to which you want items shipped (for example, if you purchase stuff at the Apple Store). Unfortunately (and inexplicably), you can't set up or change your payment info here. Instead, follow these steps:

1. *Click the dock's App Store icon (pointed out in Figure 3-9).*

2. *Choose Store ⇨ Account.*

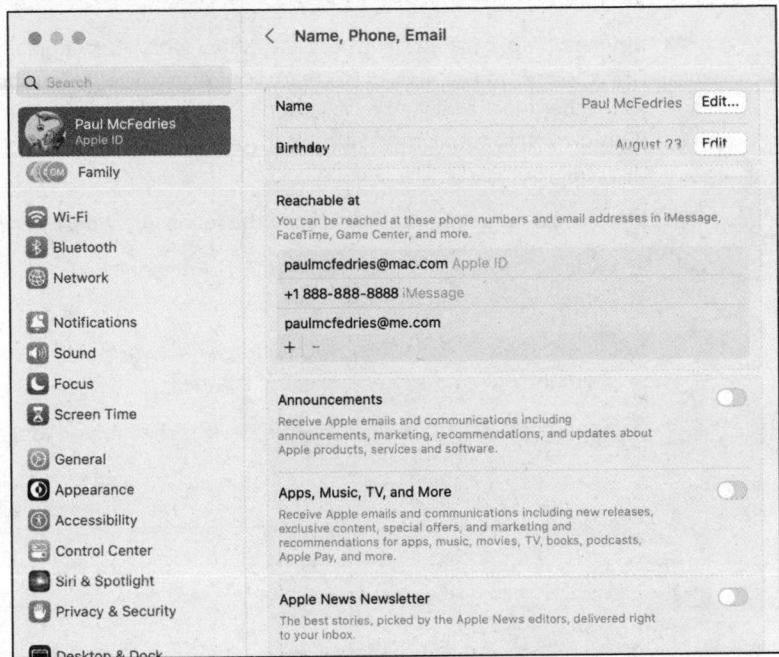

FIGURE 3-8:
The Name,
Phone, Email
screen of the
Apple ID settings.

Getting Your Mac
Online

3. *Click Account Settings.*

4. *Sign in with your Apple ID.*

5. *If this is your first time signing in, click Review, select the Terms & Conditions check box, and click Continue.*

6. *Click Manage Payments.*

7. *Select Edit next to your payment method and then provide the details (such as your credit card number, expiration date, and security code).*

8. *Fill in any missing data (such as your phone number) and then click Done.*

>> **iCloud:** Displays a list of apps and features that work with iCloud. I discuss these apps and features in the next section.

>> **Media & Purchases:** Displays settings for making purchases, including using Touch ID to authorize purchases, specifying when a password is required, and managing your subscriptions.

>> **Family Sharing:** Displays the family members who are part of Family Sharing (see Book 3, Chapter 3), enables you to add new members, and offers access to your family subscriptions, purchase sharing, and location sharing.

WARNING

REMEMBER

» **Devices:** Displays a list of devices associated with your Apple ID. At first you see whatever Mac you used to create your Apple ID. After a while, though, your other Macs and your mobile Apple devices also appear here. Why? Because you can look for devices that you don't recognize, which would be a sign that your Apple ID has been hacked.

If you see an unrecognized device, do the following two things *immediately*:

● Click the device, click Remove from Account, and then click Remove when your Mac asks you to confirm.

● Click Passwords & Security, click Change Password, and then follow the prompts to create a new Apple ID password.

It's also a good idea to remove any old devices that you no longer use.

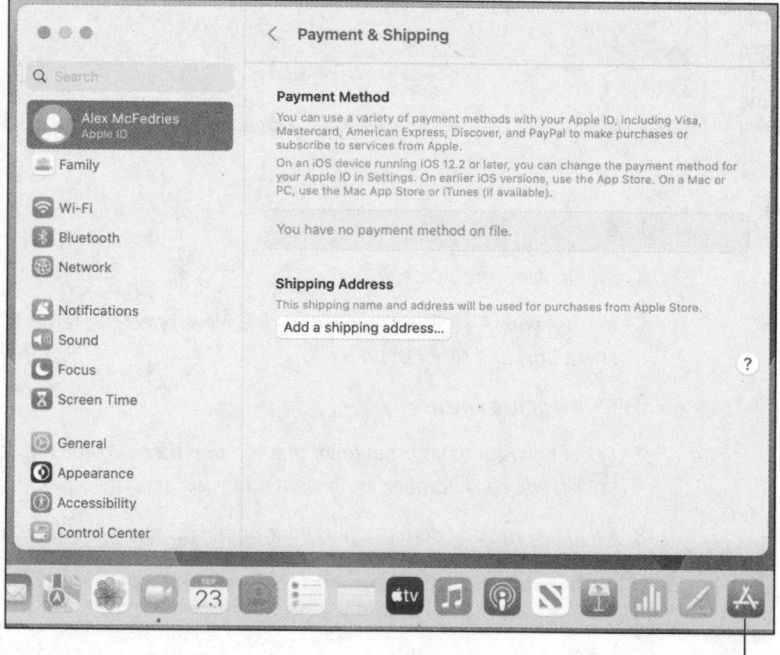

FIGURE 3-9:
The Payment & Shipping screen of Apple ID settings.

App Store icon

Storing Your Data in iCloud

If you have just your Mac and no other computers or mobile devices, life is pretty simple because all your data resides on your Mac and is always there when you need it. However, it's my guess that you likely have multiple devices in your life, such as another Mac, a Windows PC, an iPhone, an iPad, or some combination. Ah, now your life is a little more complicated. For example, what if you have, say, a file or photo on one device and want to use that item on another device?

This kind of problem can be solved in a number of ways, such as using AirDrop (see Book 3, Chapter 5). However, perhaps the simplest and most universal method is to store anything you might want to share across multiple devices in Apple's iCloud service. iCloud remotely stores and syncs data that you access from various devices — your Mac and other Apple devices, such as iPhones and iPads, and PCs running Windows. Sign in to the same iCloud account on different devices, and the data for activated apps *syncs*; that is, you find the same data on all your devices, and when you make a change on one device, that change shows up on the others. Sweet? You know it.

iCloud works with tons of Apple apps and the data within them, including the following:

>> Books

>> Calendar

>> Contacts

>> GarageBand

>> iMovie

>> Keychain

>> Keynote

>> Mail

>> Notes

>> Numbers

>> Pages

>> Photos

>> Preview

>> Reminders

>> Safari

>> Siri

>> TextEdit

WHAT'S ALL THIS ABOUT A CLOUD?

You might be wondering what the *Cloud* part of the name *iCloud* is referring to, so let me take a few minutes of your precious time to explain. In many network diagrams (a diagram that shows how the components of a network are connected), the designer is most interested in the devices that connect to the network, not the network itself. After all, the details of what happens inside the network to shunt signals from source to destination are often extremely complex and convoluted, so all those minutiae would serve only to detract from the network diagram's larger message of showing which devices can connect to the network, how they connect, and their network entry and exit points.

When the designers of network flowcharts want to show the network but not any of its details, they almost always abstract the network by displaying it as a cloud symbol. (It is, if you will, the "yadda yadda yadda" of network diagrams.) At first the cloud symbol represented the workings of a single network, but in recent years it has come to represent the internet (the network of networks).

So far, so good. Earlier in this millennium, some folks had the bright idea that instead of storing files on local computers, you could store them on a server connected to the internet, which meant anyone with the right credentials could access the files from anywhere in the world. Eventually, folks started storing programs on internet servers, too, and started telling anyone who'd listen that these files and applications resided "in the cloud" (meaning on a server — or, more typically, a large collection of servers that reside in a special building called a *data center* — accessible via the internet).

An example of a cloud service is Apple's iCloud, which not only let you store and share data that you can access from all your devices but also comes with a collection of applications — Mail, Photos, Calendar, Pages, and more — that enable you to work online when you sign in with your Apple ID at www.icloud.com/. That's why, as I mention earlier in this chapter, you need an internet connection to use iCloud.

iCloud also works with third-party iCloud-enabled apps, such as Adobe Acrobat and iA Writer.

Here are some situations where iCloud can make your life easier:

>> You want to back up the songs you add to the Music app and TV show collections.

>> You use both a Mac and an iPhone or iPad.

>> You want to access Contacts, Calendar, and Mail from more than one computer — Mac or Windows — say, one at work and one at home.

>> You keep a calendar that other people need to see and maybe even edit.

>> You want to activate Find My Mac to keep tabs on your Mac's location and track it down should it be lost or stolen.

The initial setup on your Mac or the creation of an iCloud Apple ID (as explained previously) activates your iCloud account and places in the cloud a copy of the data in Mail, Contacts, Calendar, Notes, Reminders, and Safari on your Mac. Here, I show you how to work with the iCloud settings, sync devices, and sign in to and use the iCloud website.

TIP

If you use a Windows 10 or 11 PC in addition to your Mac, you can download the iCloud app from the Windows Store, which enables iCloud storage and syncing in Windows. You then access the iCloud apps through iCloud.com and Microsoft Outlook.

Configuring iCloud settings

You can choose which apps you want to use with iCloud and how they can be used. For example, you may want to keep Contacts and Calendars synced across all your devices but prefer that Notes stay separate because you use Notes on your iPhone for shopping lists that you don't need on your Mac. Here's how to customize how you work with iCloud:

1. **Choose \# ⇨ System Settings or click the System Settings icon on the dock.**

2. **Click Apple ID and then click iCloud.**

   The iCloud settings appear, as shown in Figure 3-10. Note that each app on the right side of the window has a switch. When an app's switch is on, your Mac stores that app's data and settings in iCloud, which enables you to sync that same data with your other devices that support iCloud.

3. **For each app for which you don't want to use iCloud, click its switch off.**

4. **Click the Options button to the right of the iCloud Drive icon.**

   The iCloud Drive options window appears (see Figure 3-11). This window enables you to choose which documents are stored in iCloud.

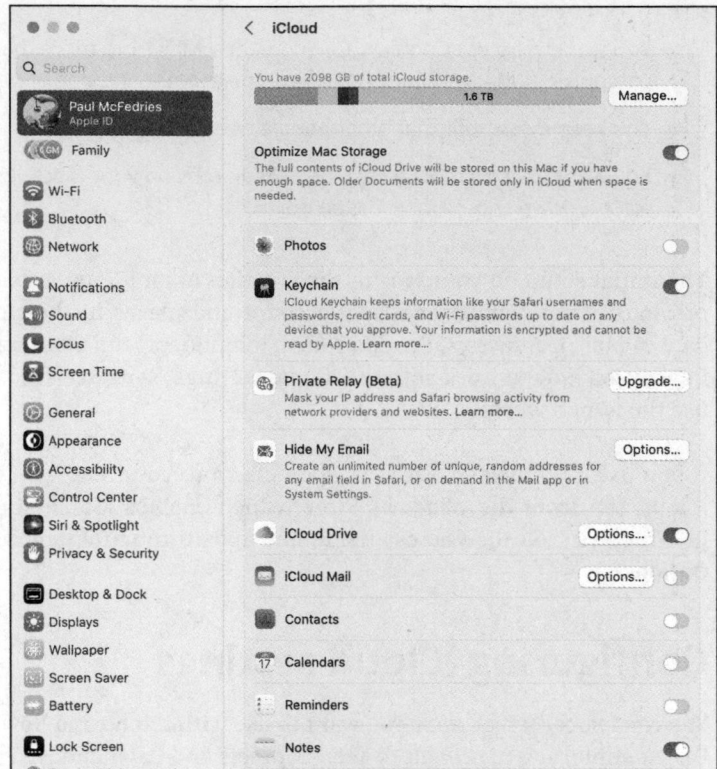

FIGURE 3-10:
Use the iCloud settings to customize how you use iCloud.

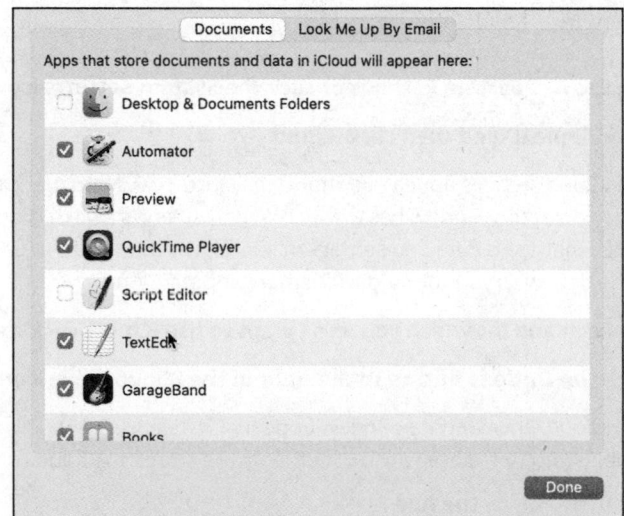

FIGURE 3-11:
Select the documents to store in iCloud.

5. **Specify which documents you want to store in your iCloud drive.**

   Select the check mark that corresponds to each app that contains documents that you want to store in your iCloud drive.

REMEMBER

   The big one in this list is Desktop & Documents Folders. If you select this check box, everything you save to the desktop or to the Documents folder (the default storage folder for most apps) is automatically stored in the same folders in iCloud. That is, your desktop and Documents files are no longer stored locally on your Mac's hard drive but are stored remotely in iCloud. This enables you to share these files with any device that can access your iCloud account. However, it also means that you need an internet connection to access these files.

6. **When you're finished, click Done to return to iCloud settings.**

7. **(Optional) Click the Manage button in the upper right to see the data that occupies your allotted iCloud storage, as shown in Figure 3-12.**

   Each item in the list on the left shows you how much storage that type of data is currently using in iCloud. In most cases, clicking an item displays a button that enables you to delete all files of that type from iCloud. An exception is Backups, which displays a list of the backups of your iOS devices — *not your Mac.* iCloud keeps documents and data for iCloud-enabled apps but *does not back up your entire Mac.* See Book 3, Chapter 1 to learn about backing up your Mac.

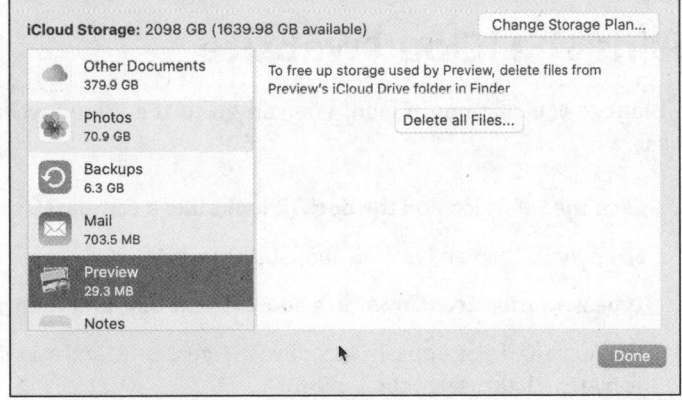

FIGURE 3-12:
Manage storage
for the apps you
use with iCloud.

8. **(Optional) Click the Add Storage button or, if you already pay for an iCloud storage plan, click the Change Storage Plan button.**

   A free iCloud account gives you 5 gigabytes (GB) of storage. You can purchase additional storage — up to 2 terabytes (TB) or 2,000 GB — for a monthly subscription fee, the cost of which depends on where you live.

If you decide to purchase additional storage, click the desired storage amount and then click Next. Follow the onscreen instructions to add your personal and payment information.

9. **Click Done.**

10. **Click the red close icon in the upper left to quit System Settings.**

Syncing with your other devices

Syncing with other devices couldn't be simpler. To sync iCloud-app-specific documents, such as Pages documents, and data from apps such as Calendar and Contacts with your iOS devices, do the following:

1. **Tap Settings on the Home screen of the device you want to sync with iCloud.**

2. **Tap iCloud.**

3. **Sign in to your iCloud account.**

4. **Tap the on position for any apps you want to use.**

   The data in each app is automatically synced between your Mac and your iOS device.

REMEMBER

You must have an internet connection to use iCloud.

Using the iCloud website

To manage your data on iCloud, you can go to the iCloud website. Follow these steps:

1. **Click the Safari icon on the dock (it looks like a compass).**

   See Book 2, Chapter 1 to read about using Safari.

2. **Type *www.icloud.com* in Safari's address text box, and then press Return.**

   The Apple ID dialog appears, as shown in Figure 3-13, and asks if you want to sign in to iCloud using your Apple ID.

3. **Say "But of course!" and click Continue with Password.**

4. **Type your Mac account password (*not* your Apple ID password) and then click Continue.**

   The iCloud website appears. Your name appears in the upper-right corner, and icons that take you to your activated services appear in the window, as shown in Figure 3-14.

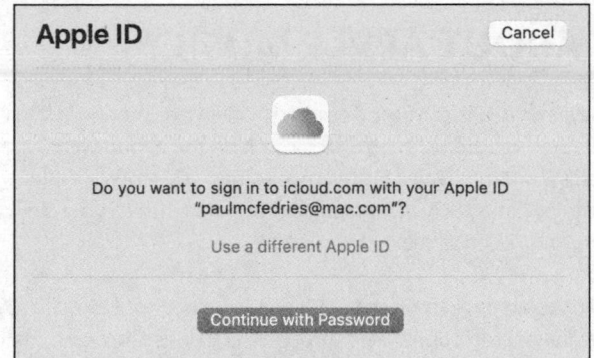

FIGURE 3-13:
Click an icon
to go to the
data you want.

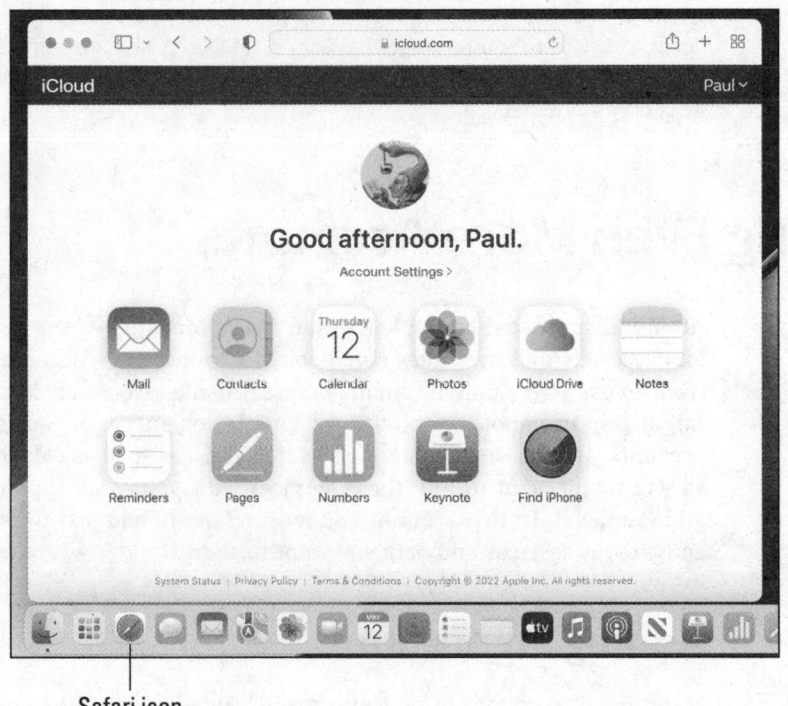

FIGURE 3-14:
Click an icon to
load the iCloud
app you want
to use.

Safari icon

Getting Your Mac
Online

5. **Click an icon to load the app you want.**

6. **To switch to another app, click the iCloud button in the upper-left corner to display the app list, and then click the app you want.**

7. **When you're done with iCloud, click your name in the upper-right corner and then click Sign Out.**

Adding Even More Accounts

After you've created an Apple ID, your Mac's Mail app — the app you use to send and receive email messages (see Book 2, Chapter 3) — automatically configures itself to use your Apple ID email address. Thanks! However, it's possible that you might also use another account for email. Not only that, but many third-party accounts, such as Google, offer associated services such as calendars and contacts, so you might want to link those services with your Mac apps (such as Calendar and Contacts). In this section, I show you how to add accounts to your Mac and activate the services and data you want to share.

Adding an account

Many email accounts offer contact and calendar management and even note-taking services. Your email address and password identify you and give you access to your account. The three types of email accounts you can set up are

>> POP (Post Office Protocol)

>> IMAP (Internet Message Access Protocol)

>> Exchange

A POP email account usually transfers email from the POP server computer to your computer. An IMAP or Exchange email account stores email on its server, which allows access to email from multiple devices. Most individuals have POP accounts, whereas many corporations have IMAP or Exchange accounts. If your organization has other types of accounts, you can talk to them about setting them up.

REMEMBER

You can access your email from Mail (or a different email app) on your Mac, from a web browser on your Mac, or on another computer, such as at your friend's house or in an internet cafe. When you use a web browser, you go to the email provider's website.

Gathering your account information

To make Mail work with your email account, you need to gather the following information:

>> **Your username (also called an *account name*):** Typically, your name in one form or another (such as paul.mcfedries, pmcfedries, or paulmcf) or something similar. Your username plus the name of your email provider or ISP defines your complete email address, such as pmcfedries@gmail.com or *yournamehere*@comcast.net.

>> **Your password:** The password is any phrase you choose to access your account. If someone sets up an email account for you, that person might have already assigned a password, but you can change it.

>> **Your email account's incoming server name:** The mail server name of the computer that contains your email message is usually a combination of POP or IMAP and your email account company, such as pop.comcast.net or imap.gmail.com.

>> **Your email account's outgoing server name:** This is the name of the outgoing mail server that sends your messages to other people. The outgoing server name is usually a combination of SMTP (Simple Mail Transfer Protocol) and the name of the company that provides your email account, such as smtp.gmail.com or smtp.comcast.net.

REMEMBER

If you don't know your account name, password, incoming server name, or outgoing server name, ask the company that runs your email account or search on the provider's website. If you're unable to find the information, chances are you might still be able to set up your email account on your Mac, thanks to the Mail app's capability to detect the most popular email account settings, such as those for Yahoo! and Gmail.

Configuring your account

After you collect the technical information needed to access your account, you need to add it to Internet Accounts on your Mac by following these steps:

1. Choose ⇨ System Settings or click the System Settings icon on the dock or from Launchpad.

2. Click the Internet Accounts button.

The Internet Accounts settings appears and displays a list of your current accounts.

3. Click Add Account.

A dialog appears and displays a list of the account types you can add, as shown in Figure 3-15.

FIGURE 3-15:
Internet Accounts displays a list of the account types you can add to your Mac.

4. Click the name of the account you want to add: iCloud, Microsoft Exchange, Google, Yahoo!, or AOL.

If the type of email account you want to add is not listed (for example, if you have an email account from your company's domain or your personal domain such as StoogeCurly@mydomain.com), click Add Other Account and then choose Mail. You end up face-to-face with the Add a Mail Account dialog.

5. **Type your name, email address, and password, and any other requested information (each type of account is slightly different).**

   As you work through the setup, when you come to the step where you're asked to let macOS work with the email service to perform actions such as sending and receiving email (see Figure 3-16), be sure to click Allow (or whatever the equivalent button is for the service your adding).

   When the setup is complete, your account is verified and a list of services appears, such as Contacts and Calendar, as shown in Figure 3-17.

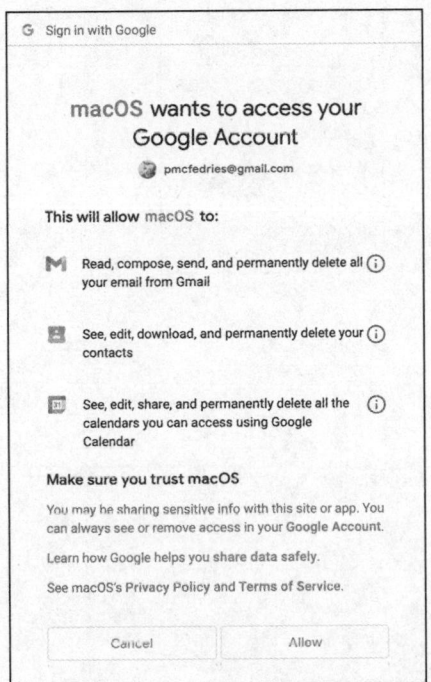

FIGURE 3-16: Give macOS permission to perform the listed email activities on the email service.

6. **Deselect the check box next to each macOS app that you don't want to use with the new account.**

   You should leave the Mail check box selected. If the service offers calendar management, leave the Calendar app selected so you can use the service's calendars with your Mac's Calendars app. However, if the service offers features that you don't want to use with your Mac, deselect the corresponding app check boxes.

7. **Click Done.**

macOS finalizes your new account and adds it to the list in the Internet Accounts pane.

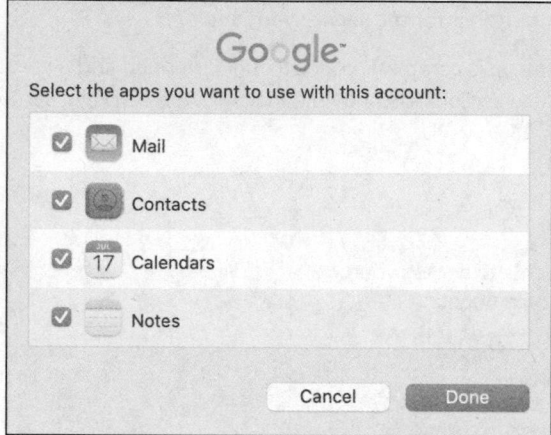

FIGURE 3-17:
The account
displays a list of
its services that
you can use.

IN THIS CHAPTER

» **Becoming fast friends with Finder**

» **Organizing your stuff with folders**

» **Categorizing your stuff with tags**

» **Searching your stuff with Spotlight**

» **Sending your stuff to the trash**

Chapter **4**

Fiddling with Files and Folders

t's possible to use your Mac without creating anything with it. For example, if you use your Mac only to explore the web, exchange email and text messages, and listen to podcasts, you're not creating anything. Nothing wrong with that, of course, but it's more likely that you'll want to use your Mac to make things, such as documents with the Pages app or spreadsheets with the Numbers app. Similarly, it's also likely that you'll use your Mac to work with things you've created elsewhere, such as photos or videos taken with your iPhone or iPad.

An item such as a document, spreadsheet, photo, or video is an example of a *file*, which is the fundamental storage unit on your Mac. Your personal files are stored either on your Mac's internal hard drive or in iCloud (see Book 1, Chapter 3). Ideally, each file is stored with similar files in a location called a *folder*. (Think of an old-fashioned filing cabinet, where paper documents are organized into separate file folders. No idea what I'm talking about? Ask your parents.)

So, when it comes to organizing your personal stuff on your Mac, files and folders are the key. This chapter familiarizes you with the way your Mac organizes your files and folders. I begin by explaining Finder, which is the tool you use to organize your Mac's files and folders. Next, I show you how to create and manage folders. I also tell you about *tags,* which help you quickly identify and find folders and files. Later in the chapter, I shine a light on your Mac's search tool, Spotlight Search. And at the end of the chapter, I spell out the procedure for deleting a file or folder.

Getting to Know Finder

You view, manage, and organize your Mac's files and folders using an app called *Finder*. (And if you add storage to your Mac — such as one or more external hard drives or USB flash drives — Finder is the place to go to manage those drives.)

To access Finder, click the Finder icon (the smiley face icon on the far left of the dock). Finder is divided into three parts, as shown in Figure 4-1:

» A *toolbar* runs across the top of the window and contains buttons you use to control and manage the files and folders in Finder.

» A left pane displays the sidebar, which by default shows the following sections:

- *Favorites:* Provides one-click access to a few commonly used folders.

- *iCloud:* Provides access to iCloud Drive as well as to any files you've shared with others via iCloud.

- *Locations:* Provides access to any connected storage devices, such as external hard drives, Flash drives, and memory cards (for example, the SDXC cards supported by the MacBook Pro). You use this section also to access your network.

- *Tags:* Enables you to view files and folders that have been tagged. (See "Playing Tag: Classifying Files and Folders for Quick Access," later in this chapter.)

» A right pane showing the contents of the selected drive or folder (or search results if you performed a search). If you switch to list, column, or gallery view, the right pane also shows a hierarchy of files — and even other folders — stored inside folders.

The right pane may be further divided into *tabs*, which are essentially windows within the main Finder window that display different folders open simultaneously, although only the one in view is active. (See "Keeping tabs on multiple folders," later in this chapter.)

TIP

You can choose to hide or show either or both the toolbar and sidebar by choosing the appropriate command from Finder's View menu.

Handling devices

The Locations category of the sidebar lists any devices, remote or cabled, connected to your Mac, as well as any mounted disk images, which can appear when you download software updates or large files.

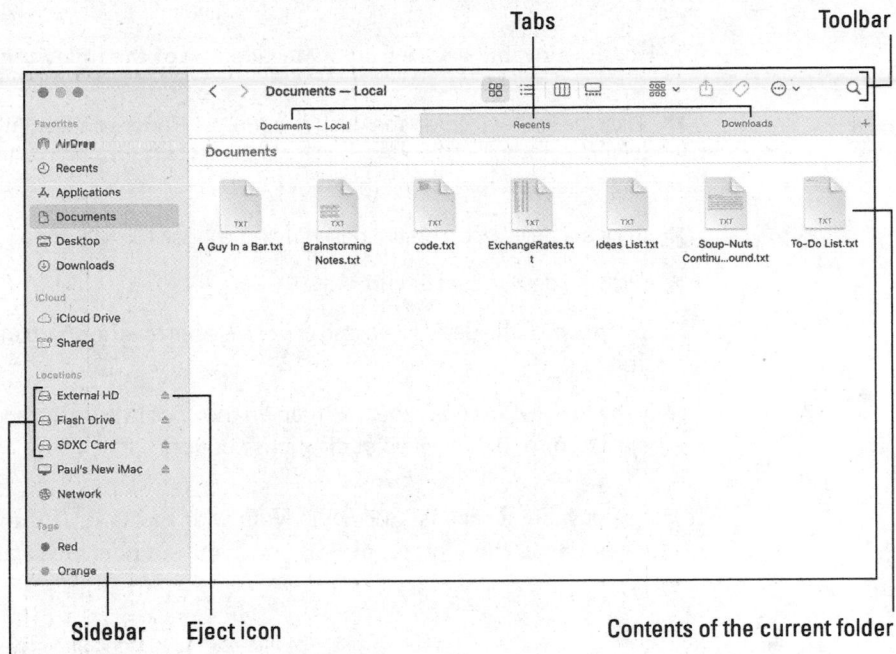

Tabs   Toolbar

Sidebar   Eject icon   Contents of the current folder

Connected devices

FIGURE 4-1:
Finder displays the files, folders, and devices connected to your Mac.

TIP

Strangely, the one device you don't see here is your Mac! To correct that, choose Finder ➪ Settings, click the Sidebar tab, and then select the check box beside the name of your Mac. When you click your Mac in the Locations category of the sidebar, you see the internal hard disk drive (HDD) or solid-state drive (SSD), which is named Macintosh HD by default. This is the drive that your Mac boots from. If your desktop Mac has a second hard drive installed, it appears in the Locations list.

The other devices listed here are those that you plug into your Mac, such as an external hard drive, a USB flash drive, or a memory card, each of which is shown as connected in Figure 4-1. These removable devices can be connected and disconnected at any time.

To connect a removable device to your Mac, just plug it in with the appropriate Thunderbolt or USB cable. The icon for the device appears in the Locations list and on the desktop.

You can eject a removable drive when you no longer need to access it or want to take it with you. Ejecting a removable hard drive or USB flash drive removes its icon from Finder and the desktop and allows you to then safely disconnect it from your Mac.

WARNING

If you physically try to disconnect a removable drive before you eject it, your Mac might mess up the data on that drive. Always eject removable drives before physically disconnecting them.

To eject a removable device from a Mac, do one of the following:

>> Click the Finder icon on the dock to open the Finder window. In the Finder window's sidebar, click the eject icon (labeled in Figure 4-1) next to the connected drive you want to remove.

>> Click the device icon on the desktop and choose File ⇨ Eject.

>> Click the device icon and press ⌘+E.

>> Control-click the device icon and choose Eject from the shortcut menu that appears.

>> Drag the device icon to the trash can on the dock (the trash can turns into an eject icon); and then let go of the mouse button.

If the removable device is a CD/DVD, your Mac ejects it. If the removable device is plugged into a Thunderbolt or USB port, you can now physically disconnect the device.

Understanding folders

All the data you create and save by using an application (such as a word-processing document or a photograph you copy from your smartphone to your Mac's hard drive) is stored as a *file*. Although you can store files on any storage device, the more files you store on a device, the harder it is to find the one file you want at any given time. (But using Spotlight, described later in this chapter, is a great way to find things.) Much like you would place related paper documents in a manila folder rather than stack them willy-nilly on your desk, folders on your Mac help you organize and manage electronic files on a storage device in a logical way. You can even store folders inside other folders.

Initially, every Mac hard drive contains the following folders:

>> **Applications:** Contains all the apps installed on your Mac. When you open Launchpad, you see all the apps stored in the Applications folder.

>> **Library:** Contains data and settings files used by applications installed on your Mac, fonts, and plug-ins used by applications such as internet web browsers.

>> **System:** Contains files used by the macOS operating system. You shouldn't change this folder.

WARNING

Never delete, rename, or move any files or folders stored in the Library or System folder, or else you might cause your Mac (or at least some apps on your Mac) to stop working. Files in the Library and System folders are used by your Mac to make your computer work. If you delete or rename files in either folder, your Mac might not operate the way it's supposed to — or (worse) grind to a halt.

>> **Users:** Contains any files that you — and anyone else who uses your Mac — create and save, including documents, pictures, music, and movies.

The Users folder contains Home folders; each account on your Mac is assigned a Home folder when the account is set up. (See Book 3, Chapter 3 for more information about creating accounts.) The Home folder has the same name as the account and shouldn't be renamed. The Home folder of the user who is logged in looks like a little house.

Each Home folder automatically contains the following folders when an account is set up. Note that these folders have icons on them.

- **Desktop:** Contains any application and document icons that appear on your Mac's desktop.

- **Documents:** Contains any files you create and save using different applications. (You'll probably want to organize this folder by creating multiple folders inside it to keep all your files organized in a logical, easy-to-manage way.)

- **Downloads:** Contains any files you download from the internet. After you download the files, you'll want to move them to an appropriate folder or, if you download apps, install them.

- **Library:** Contains folders and files used by any applications installed on your Mac. (**Note:** There are three Library folders: one stored on the top level of your hard drive, another inside the System folder, and one hidden inside your Home folder, which you can see by holding down the Option key and choosing Go ⇨ Library.)

- **Movies:** Contains video files created by iMovie and certain other applications for playing or editing video, such as Final Cut Pro X or QuickTime Player.

- **Music:** Contains audio files, such as music tracks stored in Music or created by GarageBand or another audio application, such as Audacity or Logic Pro X.

- **Pictures:** Contains digital photographs, such as those you import to Photos.

- **Public:** Provides a folder that you can use to share files with other user accounts on the same Mac, or with other users on a local area network (LAN).

Every drive (such as your hard drive) can contain multiple folders, and each folder can contain multiple folders. A collection of folders stored inside folders stored inside other folders is a *hierarchy*. It's important to know how to view and navigate through a folder hierarchy to find specific files, and I tell you how to do that in the "Navigating Your Mac's Devices and Folders" section, later in this chapter.

Customizing Finder settings

As you look at the figures in this book, you might say to yourself, "My Finder doesn't look like that." You probably have different Finder settings than I do. You can choose the items you see in Finder's sidebar and also how Finder behaves in certain situations by setting Finder settings to your liking. Follow these steps, and remember that you can always go back and change them later if you think of a better setup:

1. **Click the Finder icon on the dock.**

   A Finder window opens.

2. **Choose Finder ⇨ Settings.**

   The Finder Settings window opens.

3. **Click the General tab at the top, if it isn't selected.**

4. **Select the check boxes next to the items you want to see on your desktop.**

   You can select any or all of the following: Hard Disks; External Disks, CDs, DVDs, and iPods; and Connected Servers.

5. **In the New Finder Windows Show drop-down list, choose which folder you want to open each time you open Finder.**

6. **(Optional) Select the Open Folders in Tabs Instead of New Windows check box if you want this option in the Action menu, which is in Finder's toolbar.**

   You can have more than one folder open simultaneously. They can be opened in separate windows, which tend to clutter the desktop, or in separate tabs within one Finder window. See the section "Keeping tabs on multiple folders," later in the chapter, to learn about tabs.

7. **Click the Sidebar tab.**

   The Sidebar settings pane opens, as shown in Figure 4-2.

8. **Select the check boxes next to the items you want to see in Finder's sidebar.**

   When Finder is open, you can show and hide the items in each category by clicking the disclosure arrow, which appears to the right of a category title (such as Locations) when you hover your mouse pointer over the category title in the sidebar.

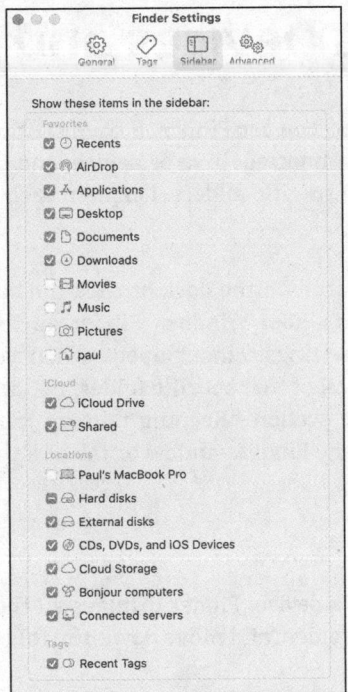

FIGURE 4-2:
You can choose
the items listed in
Finder's sidebar.

9. **Click the Advanced tab to work with the following options:**

   - *Show All Filename Extensions:* Displays the file extension of every filename on your Mac. File extensions are the two or more letters after a filename, such as .docx or .txt.

   - *Show Warning before Changing an Extension:* Opens a dialog if you save a file as a different type, such as saving a .docx file as .txt.

   - *Show Warning before Removing from iCloud Drive:* Displays a warning dialog when you delete a file from your iCloud drive.

   - *Show Warning before Emptying the Trash:* Gives you a chance to bail before you empty the trash.

   - *Remove Items from the Trash after 30 Days:* Automatically empties any file in the trash older than 30 days.

   - *Keep Folders on Top:* If you select In Windows When Sorting by Name, Finder organizes all the current folder's subfolders at the top of the list. If you select On Desktop, Finder organizes all the desktop's folders at the top.

   You can also set the search level for Spotlight search, which I discuss in the "Spotlight settings" section, later in this chapter.

10. **To close the Finder Settings window, click the red close icon in the upper-left corner.**

Navigating Your Mac's Devices and Folders

To access files stored on your Mac, you use Finder to navigate the different folders and devices. First you choose a connected drive or device, and then you can open and exit folders or jump between specific folders. I explain each method throughout these sections.

REMEMBER

To open Finder, click the Finder icon on the dock or click the background of your desktop and choose File ⇨ New Finder Window. Finder opens to the folder or device you specified in Finder settings. Finder opens when you double-click a folder, too, but it opens at the level of that specific folder, not at the highest point of the Finder hierarchy. See the section "Keeping tabs on multiple folders" to learn about opening more than one Finder window or tab at a time.

Opening a folder

When you open Finder and click a device, Finder displays all the files and folders stored on that device. To open a folder (and move down the folder hierarchy), you have several choices:

>> Double-click the folder.

>> Click the folder and choose File ⇨ Open.

>> Click the folder and press ⌘+O.

>> Click the folder and press ⌘+↓.

>> Right-click (or Control-click) the folder and choose Open in New Tab from the shortcut menu that appears.

REMEMBER

Each time you open a folder within a folder, you're essentially moving down the hierarchy of folders stored on that device.

Keeping tabs on multiple folders

Tabs are a way of having several folders open in one pane at the same time so you don't have to close and open folders to switch between them or use the Back and Forward arrows. To open a folder in a new tab, you have two choices:

>> Right-click (or Control-click) the folder and choose Open in New Tab from the shortcut menu that appears.

>> Click the folder, click the action icon (the three-dots-in-a-circle icon; see Figure 4-3), and then click Open in New Tab.

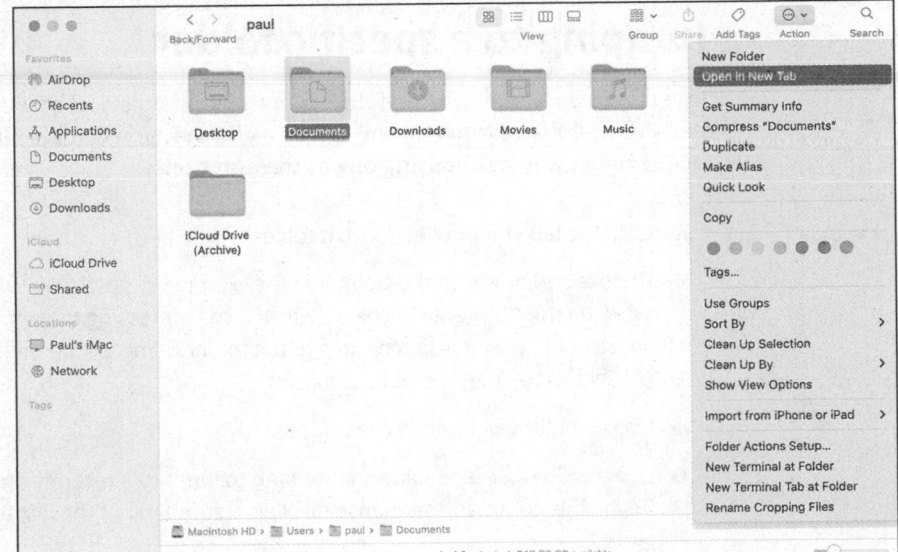

FIGURE 4-3:
Opening the
Documents folder
in a new tab.

TIP

Want to know how I convinced Finder to show the toolbar icon labels in Figure 4-3? Choose View ➪ Customize Toolbar to open a window of toolbar customization options. Use the Show pop-up menu to select Icon and Text. While you're here, you can customize the toolbar's icons: Drag the icons you want to see from the window to the toolbar. To delete icons you don't need, drag them off the toolbar and they disappear in a puff of virtual smoke. When you've completed your customizations, click Done.

TIP

Hold down the Option key while clicking the Action button, and Open in New Tab becomes Open in New Window.

Another way to add a new tab to Finder is to first create the tab and then use the new tab to navigate to the device or folder you want to view. Finder gives you three ways to add a new tab:

>> Choose File ➪ New Tab.

>> Press ⌘+T.

>> Click the create a new tab icon, which is the + icon that appears to the right of the last tab when you have two or more tabs already open in Finder.

To close a tab, hover the mouse pointer over the tab and then click the X that appears on the left side of the tab.

Jumping to a specific folder

By moving up and down the folder hierarchy on a device, you can view the contents of every file stored on the device. However, you can also jump to a specific folder right away by choosing one of these options:

» Click the tab you opened for that folder.

» Choose a folder from the Go menu; for example choose Go⇨Utilities. Folders listed on the Go menu can be accessed also by pressing the appropriate shortcut keys, which appear next to the folder name on the menu, such as ⌘+Shift+U to open the Utilities folder.

» Click a folder displayed in the sidebar.

» Use the Go ⇨ Recent Folders command to jump to a recently opened folder. (Using this command sequence displays a submenu of the last ten folders you visited.)

» To open the Library folder, hold down the Option key and choose Go ⇨ Library.

REMEMBER

If you display the contents of a folder in list, column, or gallery view, you can view folder hierarchies directly in Finder. (You find out more about using the list, column, and gallery views later in the "Taking in the View: Working with Finder's Views" section.)

Jumping back and forth

While you navigate from one folder to the next, you might suddenly want to return to a folder for a second look. To view a previously viewed folder, you can choose the Back command in one of three ways:

» Click the back arrow (<).

» Choose Go ⇨ Back.

» Press ⌘+[.

After you use the Back command at least once, you can choose the Forward command, which reverses each Back command you chose. To choose the Forward command, pick one of the following ways:

» Click the forward arrow (>).

» Choose Go ⇨ Forward.

» Press ⌘+].

Moving to a higher folder

After you open a folder, you might want to go back and view the contents of the folder that encloses the current folder. To view the enclosing folder (and move up the folder hierarchy), choose one of the following:

>> Choose Go ⇨ Enclosing Folder. This option changes the tab if you're using tabs.

>> Press ⌘+↑. This option changes the tab if you're using them.

>> Hold down the ⌘ key, click the folder name in the Finder window title bar to display the hierarchy of enclosing folders, and then click an enclosing folder. In Figure 4-4, for example, the Documents folder is open, so when I hold down ⌘ and click Documents in the title bar, the pop-up menu shows the current folder at the top, followed by each enclosing folder (Documents is enclosed by paul, which is enclosed by Users, which is enclosed by Macintosh HD, which is enclose by Paul's MacBook Pro).

>> Hold down ⌘ and click the document title in an open app window to see the document's folder hierarchy, then click an enclosing folder. Note that this trick doesn't work for new, unsaved documents.

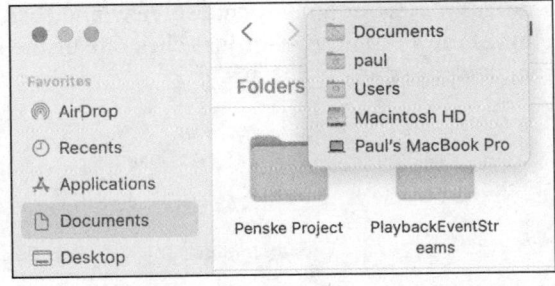

FIGURE 4-4:
Hold down ⌘ and click the current folder name to see the enclosing folders.

Following the folder path

When you move up, down, and sideways among multiple layers of a folder hierarchy, it's easy to lose track of where you are. Fortunately, Finder always knows exactly where you're located and has some tools that can help you get your bearings.

In Finder, choose View ⇨ Show Path Bar. Displayed at the bottom of the Finder window is the series of folders that lead to the folder you're currently viewing. Double-click any of the folders in the series to switch to that folder's view. If you misplace or can't find a file, click in the Search field of the Finder window, and then type the name of the file or a word or phrase it contains. Click the file you seek from the list of matches that appears, and then use the path bar to see where the file is hiding.

REMEMBER

The Back command is not the same thing as the Enclosing Folder command. If you open an external drive and then switch to the Utilities folder on your hard drive, the Back command returns Finder to the external drive, but the Go ⇨ Enclosing Folder command opens the Applications folder where Utilities resides.

Taking in the View: Working with Finder's Views

Finder shows the contents stored on a device, such as a hard drive, which acts like a giant folder. If your Mac's hard drive contains a large number of files and folders, trying to find a particular file or folder can be frustrating. To organize a folder's contents, Finder can display the contents of a folder in four views, which I discuss throughout this section. You can also preview files, and I tell you how to do that here as well.

To switch to a different view in Finder, choose View and then choose As Icons, As Lists, As Columns, or As Gallery — or just click one of the view icons on the toolbar, as shown in Figure 4-5.

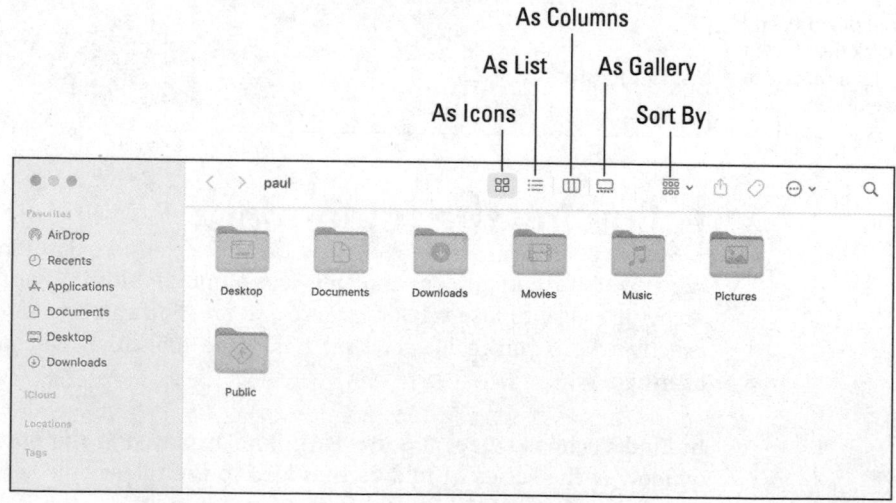

FIGURE 4-5:
Use the View menu or the toolbar icons to change Finder's view.

Using icon view

Icon view (choose View ➪ As Icons, click As Icons, or press ⌘+1) displays all files and folders as icons (refer to Figure 4-5). To organize files in icon view, you can manually drag icons where you want or have your Mac automatically arrange icons based on certain criteria, such as name or date modified.

To arrange icons within icon view manually, follow these steps:

REMEMBER

1. **Move the pointer over an icon you want to move.**

   To select two or more icons, holding down the ⌘ or Shift key and clicking the icons.

2. **Click and drag the mouse.**

   Your selected icon(s) moves when you move the mouse.

3. **Release the mouse button when you're happy with the new location of your icon(s).**

TIP

When you arrange icons manually, they might not align. To fix this problem, make sure that no items are selected and then choose View ➪ Clean Up to straighten them.

Manually arranging icons can be cumbersome if you have dozens of icons you want to arrange. As a faster alternative, you can arrange icons automatically in icon view by following these steps:

1. **Click the sort order arrow (labeled in Figure 4-5) to open the pop-up menu, or choose View ➪ Clean Up By.**

2. **Choose an option.**

   Note that all options except the first (Name) create sections to group similar files and folders:

   - *Name:* Arranges icons alphabetically.

   - *Kind:* Arranges items alphabetically by file extension, clustering documents, images, and music tracks, for instance.

   - *Application:* Groups items by application type.

   - *Date Last Opened:* Puts files and folders you opened today in the Today section, those you opened yesterday in the Yesterday section, and so on for the Previous 7 Days, Previous 30 Days, and Earlier.

   - *Date Added:* Organizes files and folders by the date you added them, dividing them in the same time intervals as Date Last Opened. Added files and folders may be ones that were copied or downloaded from another source as well as ones you created.

- *Date Modified:* Arranges the most recently modified items at the top of the window and divides the others in the same time intervals as Date Last Opened.

- *Date Created:* Arranges the most recently created items at the top of the window and divides the others in the time intervals as with Date Last Opened.

- *Size:* Arranges the largest sized files and folders at the top of the window. Files are grouped by size divisions, such as From 100MB to 10GB, From1MB to 100MB, and From 10KB to 1MB.

- *Tags:* Arranges icons alphabetically by the tag name assigned to a file. Icons with no tags appear near the top of the window, followed by tagged icons with the applied tags in alphabetical order (for example, Blue, Gray, Green, Home, and so on). You can add or delete tags by choosing Finder ⇨ Settings and clicking the tags icon, and then choosing which icons are displayed in the Finder sidebar.

Using list view

By default, list view (choose View ⇨ As List, click As List, or press ⌘+2) displays each item by name, size, the date it was last modified, and the kind of item it is, such as a folder or a PDF (Portable Document Format) file. The biggest advantages of list view are that it always displays more items than icon view in the same amount of space, it displays hierarchies of folders as indented items (shown in Figure 4-6), and you can select items from multiple folders at the same time.

TIP

Another advantage you get with list view is that you can customize the columns that Finder displays. Right-click any column header and then use the pop-up menu that appears to display or hide columns, as needed.

You can change the width of a column by hovering the mouse pointer over the right edge of the column header until the pointer becomes a vertical line crossed by a two-headed arrow (labeled in Figure 4-6). Click and drag left or right to make the column narrower or wider. You can also move a column by clicking and dragging its header to the left or right. Only the Name column must remain as the first column. Additionally, if you click a column heading in list view (such as Name or Date Modified), Finder sorts your items by that column in ascending order; click the header again to change to descending order. The order in which the files are displayed is indicated by an up arrow (ascending order, as shown in Figure 4-6) or a down arrow (descending order).

Drag the right edge of a column header to change the width

Disclosure arrow   Sort order arrow   Column headers

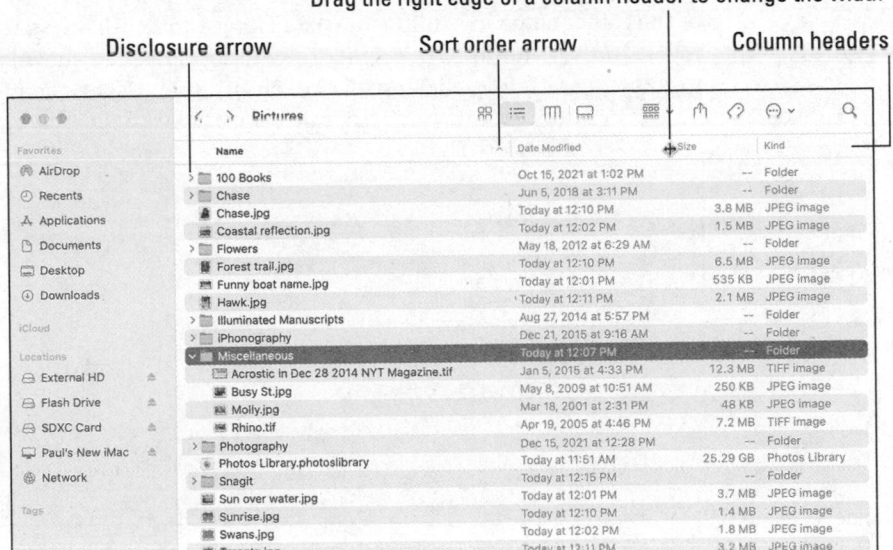

FIGURE 4-6:
List view displays items in rows and folders as hierarchies.

TIP

In any view, click the Sort By icon to change the sorting criteria.

When you view a folder in list view, subfolders are identified by a folder icon and a right-pointing arrow icon, which is called a *disclosure arrow*. Clicking a disclosure arrow expands that folder to display its contents — files, more folders, whatever — and the disclosure arrow now points down instead of to the right. Clicking the downward-pointing arrow collapses that folder to hide its contents. If you Option+click a folder that has a disclosure arrow, Finder displays the contents of not only the top-level folder but also of any subfolders contained within it. Option+click the top-level folder to collapse and close all the folders.

When you expand more than one folder, list view makes it easy to move files and folders from one folder to another. Select multiple folders or files or both at one time by holding down the ⌘ key and clicking each item you want to select. Then click and hold down on *one* of the selected items and drag them all to wherever you want to move them — to another folder in that view, to the desktop, or to trash on the dock. If you have another folder, device, or drive open in a separate tab, you can drag the items to the tab. Then when the tab is highlighted, release the mouse or trackpad button, and the items will be moved to that folder, device, or drive.

Using column view

Column view (choose View ➪ As Columns, click As Columns, or press ⌘+3) initially displays files and folders in a single column. As with List view, all folders display a disclosure arrow next to the folder name (but the arrow is to the right of the folder name in column view). Clicking a folder displays the contents of that folder in the column to the right. To get to the display shown in Figure 4-7, for example, I started by clicking Macintosh HD, then Users, then Paul.

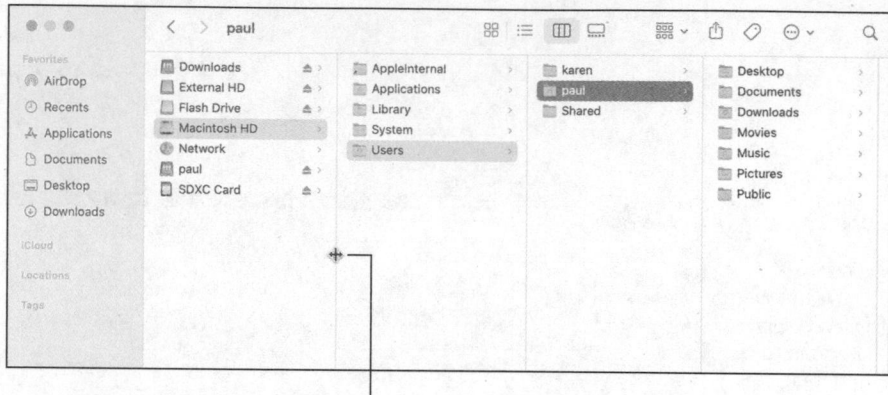

FIGURE 4-7:
Column view displays the folder contents in adjacent columns.

Drag the right border of a column to change the column's width

When you click an application, a document, or an image, the rightmost column shows a preview of the item.

You can adjust the width of a column by hovering the mouse pointer over the right border of the column until the pointer becomes a vertical line crossed by a two-header arrow (labeled in Figure 4-7). Drag the border left or right to make the column narrower or wider.

Using gallery view

Gallery view (choose View ⇨ As Gallery, click As Gallery, or press ⌘+4) combines list view with the graphic elements of icon view, as shown in Figure 4-8. In Finder, gallery view lets you choose files or folders by flipping through enlarged icons of those files or folders. The enlarged icons provide a view of the contents of a file, as shown in Figure 4-8, which can make finding a particular file or folder easier.

Changing your view options

In any Finder view — icon, list, column, or gallery — you can change the view options. You can also choose to make one style view the default for every folder you open in a Finder window, or you can set different views for different folders. From any of the four views, choose View ⇨ Show View Options or press ⌘+J.

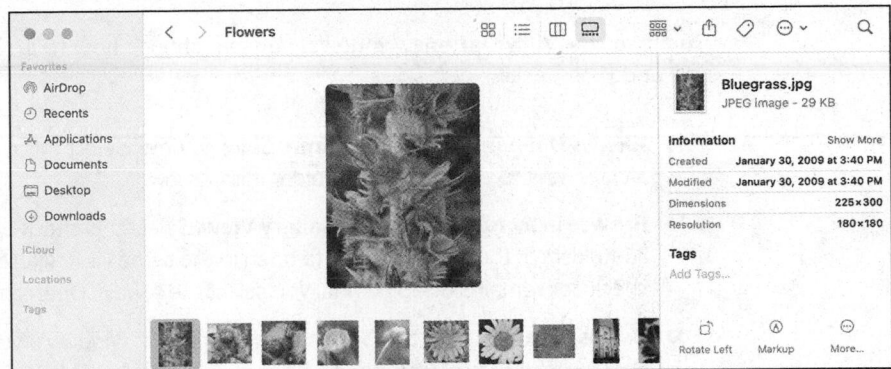

FIGURE 4-8:
Gallery view displays both icons and item names.

The View Options window opens; the options you see depend on the current view. In Figure 4-9, the View Options windows for the following views are shown from left to right:

>> **Icon view:** Scale the size of the icons and the grid spacing, adjust the text size and position, and add color to the background.

>> **List view:** Set the same options. Choose small or large icons, the text size, and the columns you want to see displayed.

>> **Column view:** Choose the text size and whether you want to see icons and the preview column.

>> **Gallery view:** Choose the size of the thumbnails you want to see.

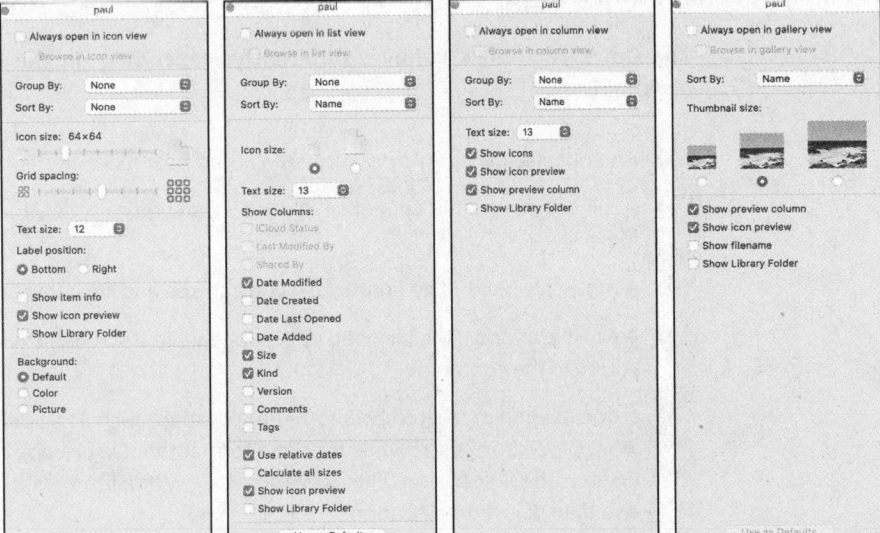

FIGURE 4-9:
Use View Options to customize how you view Finder and folders.

Fiddling with Files and Folders

In any of the View Options windows, you can choose how to arrange or sort folders and files:

>> **Always Open in Icon/List/Column/Gallery View:** Select this check box if you always want to see the current folder in that view.

>> **Browse in Icon/List/Column/Gallery View:** Select this check box if you want subfolders of the current folder to open in the same view. (Note that this check box remains disabled until you select the Always Open check box.)

>> **Use as Defaults:** Click this button at the bottom of window if you want Finder and any folders to always open with this view (not available in Column view).

Using Quick Look to sneakily peek at the contents of a file

Quick Look enables you to see the contents of a file for many file types without having to run the application you would normally use to create, view, and save the file. To run Quick Look on a file, select the file in Finder and then do one of the following:

>> Click the action icon (three-dots-in-a-circle; refer to Figure 4-3) and then select Quick Look.

>> Press the spacebar.

Finder displays an enlarged preview of the selected file, as shown in Figure 4-10.

The Quick Look view behaves differently, depending on the type of file you're peeking into:

>> An audio file plays in its entirety, so you can hear its contents.

>> A full-size picture file appears in a window, so you can see what the picture looks like.

>> A movie file plays in its entirety, so you can see and hear its contents.

>> A PDF file or an HTML file (web page) appears in a scrollable window that lets you read the contents.

>> A document file (created by another application, such as a spreadsheet or word processor) is scrollable if it's in a format that Quick Look recognizes or displays the first screen of its contents along with a listing of its name, size, and date of last modification.

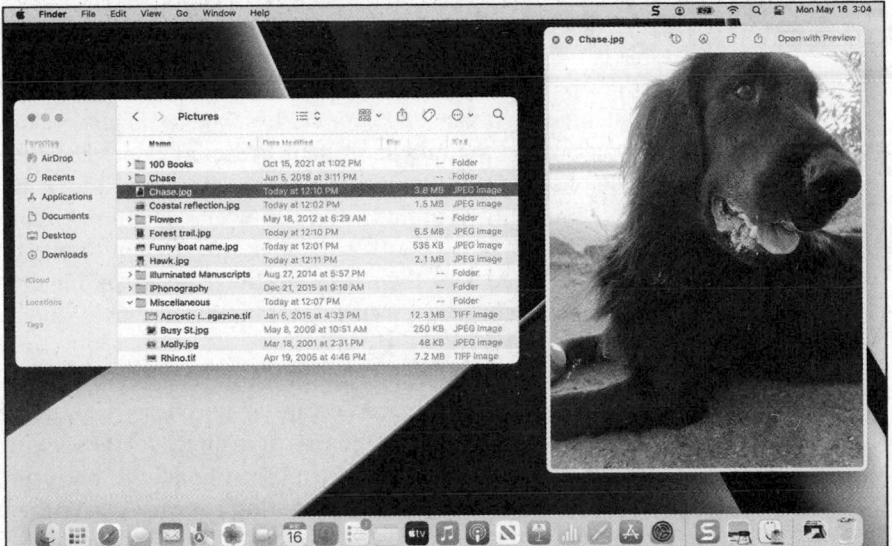

FIGURE 4-10:
Click a file icon
and press the
spacebar to
preview the file's
contents with
Quick Look.

>> A folder appears as an icon listing its name, size, and last modified date.

>> An application icon is displayed along with a name, size, and last modified date.

TIP

If you don't have the app that a file was created in, chances are that you can view it as an image by using the Preview app. From Preview, you can search, copy, and print — but not edit — image and PDF documents. Click the Preview icon in Launchpad (see Book 1, Chapter 5 to learn about Launchpad). Choose File ⇨ Open, and then click the file you want to view in Chooser, which looks and functions like Finder.

You have four options to close the Quick Look display:

>> Click the red close icon in the upper-left corner.

>> Press the spacebar.

>> Press the Escape key.

>> Click the app icon to open the file. The associated app is listed on the button at the top of the Quick Look window. (In Figure 4-10, the button is Open with Preview.)

Organizing 101: Forging Folders

When it comes to organizing your clothes, you *could* just make a big pile of everything you own in the middle of your bedroom floor. That would, at least, have the value of simplicity! But the cost of that simple system is that, after a while, it would be a nightmare to find what you want (not to mention the wrinkles). No, I think we can all agree that it's much more efficient to organize your clothes so that similar things have their own locations: socks in one drawer, underwear in another drawer, shirts and jackets hanging in the closet, and so on.

Organizing your Mac's stuff is similar. Yep, you could store all of your personal files — that is, everything you create or purchase (say, using the iTunes Store or the Book Store) with your Mac — in a single folder for simplicity's sake. But believe me when I tell you that, even if you're a light Mac user, you're eventually going to have *thousands* of files, so making a messy pile of them in a single folder is going to lead to Mac misery.

Fortunately, besides letting you navigate your way through different folders, Finder also lets you create folders. The main purpose for creating a folder is to group related files and folders. You create a folder in Finder or in the Save As dialog. The next sections walk you through each method.

Creating a folder from the Finder menu

To create a folder from the Finder menu, follow these steps:

1. **Click the Finder icon on the dock.**

   Finder appears.

2. **Navigate to and open the folder where you want to store your new folder.**

3. **Choose File ⇨ New Folder (or press Shift+⌘+N).**

   An untitled folder icon appears with its name selected.

4. **Type a descriptive name (which must also be unique in the enclosing folder) for your folder and then press Return.**

   Your new folder is christened and ready for use.

Creating a folder using Save or Save As

Finder isn't the only way to create a new folder. When you save a file for the first time or save an existing file under a new name, you can also create a new folder to store your file at the same time. You use the Save As command, which is the

Duplicate command in apps that support versions, such as Pages or Numbers. (To find out more about Mac's version control feature, see the nearby sidebar, "Saving multiple versions of documents.") To create a folder from the Save or Save As dialog, follow these steps:

1. **Create a new document in any application, such as Microsoft Word or Apple Pages.**

2. **Do one of the following:**

   - *If this is the first time you're saving the document:* Choose File ⇨ Save.

   - *If you've already saved the document:* Choose File ⇨ Save As or File ⇨ Duplicate. Choosing File ⇨ Save at this point saves only changes to the current document without opening a dialog.

   A Save As dialog appears, as shown in Figure 4-11.

Where pop-up menu

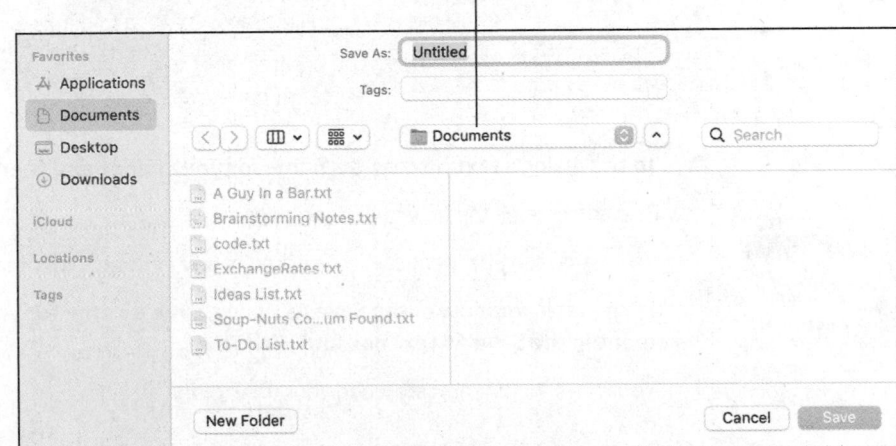

FIGURE 4-11: Create a folder while you're saving a file.

3. **If you don't see the New Folder button, click the downward-pointing arrow to the right of the Where pop-up menu.**

   The Save As dialog expands to display your Mac's storage devices and common folders in a Finder-like presentation.

4. **In the sidebar of the dialog, click the location where you want to create a folder and open the folder where you want to create a new folder.**

5. **Click the New Folder button (or press Shift+⌘+N).**

   A New Folder dialog appears.

6. **In the dialog's text box, type a name for your folder and then click Create.**

   The app creates the new folder and opens it.

   This name can't be identical to the name of any existing folder in that location.

REMEMBER

7. **In the main window of the Save As dialog, type a name for your document in the Save As text box and click Save.**

   Your new document is stored in your new folder.

Playing Tag: Classifying Files and Folders for Quick Access

Tags provide a way to categorize similar files. Although every file should have a unique name (you can have duplicates if they're stored in different folders but I don't recommend this), you can apply the same tag to many files or folders and then search for or view files by tag. For example, suppose you have lots of photos of dogs scattered throughout various folders. If you apply a tag named, say, *Dogs*, to each of those images, you can quickly and easily search for all your pooch pics just by searching for the tag Dogs. Finder will find them no matter where they're located.

You can add tags to new files when you save them for the first time or add tags to existing files and folders — and then with a click, access everything attached to a single tag.

You can tag a file or folder by a color, but then you have to remember what each color means. Tags become more effective when you name the colors and add other named tags. You can also assign a color to the named tags, but your choices are limited to the seven predetermined colors.

Setting tag preferences

To give more meaningful names to the colored tags, click the desktop outside a window and then choose Finder ⇨ Settings ⇨ Tags. Click the color name of one of the tags to select it, and then type a new name. For example, Green could become Garden Ideas. You can do several other tasks in the Tags pane of the Finder Settings window:

REMEMBER

>> **Display tags in the sidebar.** Deselect the check box beside each tag you don't want to see in the Finder sidebar and select the check box next to each tag you do want to see. When you click a tag in the sidebar, all files with that tag will appear in the right pane of the Finder window.

The Tags section of Finder's sidebar has an All Tags button that, when clicked, will open a list that shows all your tags, including those you chose not to display in the sidebar.

>> **Access tags from the Finder menu.** Drag tags from the list to the box at the bottom of the window to designate favorite tags that you want to see in Finder's File menu.

>> **Change tag colors.** Click the colored circle next to a tag name and choose a different color or no color from the list.

If you don't see Tags in the sidebar, choose Finder ⇨ Settings to open the Finder Settings window, click the Sidebar button in the toolbar, and make sure the check box next to Recent Tags is selected.

Tagging existing files and folders

If you have thousands of files on your Mac, you probably won't go through and tag them all, but you may want to tag the files that you access frequently or are related to a project. To tag an existing file or folder:

1. **Click the Finder icon on the dock to open a Finder window.**

2. **Navigate to and then click the folder or file you want to tag.**

3. **Click the File menu and then do one of the following:**

- *Click a color from the tags at the bottom of the menu.* The tag is added to your folder or file.

- *Click Tags to see more tag options or create a tag name. In the Tags window that appears, as shown in Figure 4-12, type a new tag name or click Show All (at the bottom of the Tags list) to see all your tags and then click one from that selection.* When you type a new tag name, it appears in the Tags list.

  Or click the edit/add tags icon (labeled in Figure 4-12) in the Finder toolbar and click the tag you want to add to the file or folder (click Show All if you don't see all your existing tags) or type a name to create a tag.

4. **Click or create other tags you want to add to the file or folder.**

You can add as many text tags as you want. You're limited to the seven preset colors, although you can use the same color for more than one tab. Go to Finder ➪ Settings ➪ Tags and click the colored circle next to a tag to change its color.

Edit/add tags

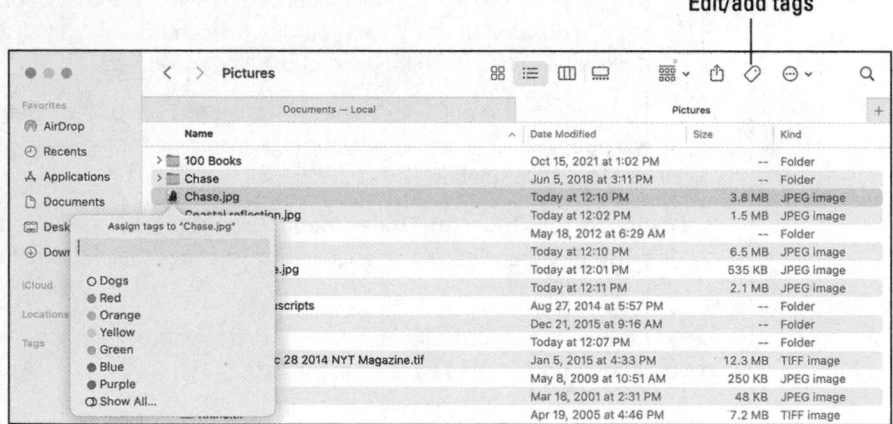

FIGURE 4-12:
Descriptive tags
help you find files
and folders fast.

To delete tags from a file or folder, click the file or folder once, and then click the Edit Tags button in the Finder window toolbar. Click to place the pointer to the right of the tag you want to delete and then press the Delete key.

Tagging new files

When you create a file of any kind, you save it at some point with a name and location. The Save As dialog has a Tag field where you can tag the new file with an existing tag or tags, or create a tag that you can then use for other files as well.

From the app, choose File ⇨ Save or Save As and then click the Tags field. The list of colored tags appears, with the Show All option at the bottom. Click the tag you want to use from the list or type a new tag to add it to the Show All list.

Finding your tagged files

To find files with the same tag, click Finder on the dock and then click the tag in the sidebar (or click All Tags and then click the tag you want). All files and folders with that tag appear in the contents pane on the right side of the Finder window.

Fiddling with Files and Folders

After you create a file (by using an application such as a word processor) or a folder (by using Finder or a Save As dialog from an application), you might need to change or edit the name of that file or folder to correct a misspelling or to change the name. Additionally, you might need to move or copy that file or folder to a new location or delete it. To move, copy, or delete items within a folder or any of its subfolders, you first have to select the item(s), and I tell you how to do that in just a sec.

REMEMBER

To make sure that you're copying, moving, or changing the correct file, you may want to open it first. However, this can take time. A faster way to view the contents of a file is to click that file in the Finder window and then click the Quick Look command (or press the spacebar) to take a peek into the file's contents (refer to Figure 4-10).

Selecting stuff in Finder

No matter how you view the contents of a folder, selecting items remains the same. You always have to select an item before you can do anything with it, such as copy or delete it. You can select items in three ways:

>> Select a single item (file or folder) by clicking it.

>> Select multiple items by selecting the first item and then holding down the ⌘ key and clicking each of the other items.

>> Select a range of contiguous items by clicking alongside the first item you want to select and then dragging the mouse up or down to the last item you want to select. Or in list, column, or gallery view, click the first item, hold down the Shift key, and then click the last item; all items between the first and last are selected.

Renaming files and folders

Keep these rules in mind when naming and renaming files and folder:

>> **Number of characters:** File and folder names can't be longer than 255 characters.

>> **Character restrictions:** You can't use certain characters when naming files or folders, such as the colon (:). Additionally, some applications might not let you use the period (.) or slash (/) characters in a filename.

>> **Duplicate folder names:** One folder can't have the same name as another folder in the same location. For example, you can't store two folders named Tax Info in one folder (such as the Documents folder). You can, however, store two folders with the same name in two different locations — and if you try to move one of them to the same place as the other, your Mac asks whether you want to merge the two folders into one folder with the same name or replace one with the other.

>> **Duplicate filenames:** You can store two identically named files in different folders. If you try to move a file into a folder that already contains a file with the same name, a confirmation dialog asks whether you want to replace the older file with the new one or keep both (in which case the new file has the word *copy* appended to the name).

>> **File extensions:** You can also store identically named files in the same location if (and only if) the files have different file extensions. That means you can have a word processor document named My Resume and a spreadsheet file also named My Resume stored in the same folder.

TECHNICAL STUFF

A file's complete name consists of two parts: the name and the file extension. The name is any descriptive name you choose, but the file extension identifies the type of file. An application file has the . app file extension, a Microsoft Word file has the . doc or . docx file extension, a Pages file has the . pages file extension, and a Keynote file has the . key file extension.

So, for example, you could have in the same folder two files that appear to be named My Resume, with one file a Microsoft Word file with the full name My Resume.docx and the other a Pages file with the full name My Resume.pages.

TIP

To view a file's extension, click that file and choose File ⇨ Get Info (or press ⌘+I). An Info window appears and displays the file extension in the Name & Extension section, as shown in Figure 4-13. To always view the file extensions for this file, deselect the Hide Extension check box. To view extensions for all files in Finder, follow the instructions in the earlier section, "Customizing Finder settings."

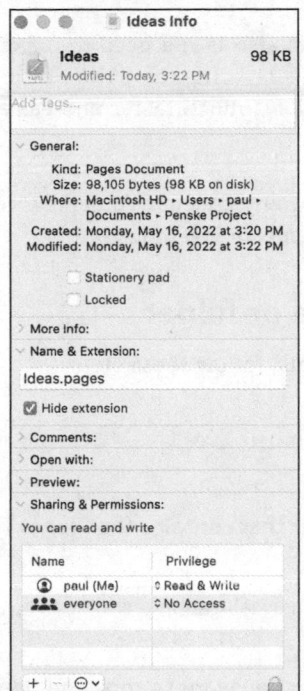

REMEMBER

Folders don't need file extensions because file extensions identify the type of file, and folders can hold a variety of different types of files.

For a fast way to rename a file or folder, follow these steps:

1. **Click a file or folder that you want to rename and then press Return.**

   The file or folder's name appears highlighted.

WARNING

   When editing or typing a new name for a file, changing the file extension can confuse your Mac and prevent it from properly opening the file because it can no longer identify which application can open the file. Don't modify or remove the file extension.

2. **Type a new name (or use the left- and right-arrow keys and the Delete key to edit the existing name) and then press Return.**

   Your selected file or folder appears with its new name.

Copying a file or folder

You can copy a file or folder and place that copy in another location. Why would you want to do that? Copying a file is a quick way of making a backup. Many people store copies of crucial files on an external storage device, such as a hard drive

Fiddling with Files and Folders

or flash drive. Copying a file is useful also if you need to make a new file that's similar to the original. Rather than re-creating the parts of the original that you don't need to change, it's almost always much faster and easier to make a copy and then modify the copy as needed.

When you copy a folder, you also copy any files and folders stored inside. To copy a file or folder, you can use either menus or the mouse.

Using menus to copy a file or folder

To copy a file or folder by using menus, follow these steps:

1. **Click the Finder icon on the dock.**

    Finder appears.

2. **Navigate to (and open) the folder that contains the files or folders you want to copy.**

    Use the sidebar and the various other navigation techniques I outline earlier in this chapter to find what you want.

3. **Select one or more files or folders you want to copy and then choose Edit ⇨ Copy (or press ⌘+C).**

4. **Navigate to and open the folder where you want to store a copy of the file or folder.**

5. **Choose Edit ⇨ Paste (or press ⌘+V).**

    You have your own cloned file or folder right where you want it.

REMEMBER

You can also create an alias of a file or folder, as I explain in Book 1, Chapter 5. An *alias* — a shortcut — points to the actual file or folder, acting like a remote control for opening the file. Because it points to the actual file (and not a copy), the alias does *not* constitute a backup of the original or a duplicate that you can modify.

Using the mouse or trackpad to copy a file or folder

Using the menus to copy a file or folder is simple, but some people find clicking and dragging items with the mouse more intuitive. You can drag between two separate devices (such as from a flash drive to a hard drive) or between different folders on the same device. Just follow these steps:

1. **Click the Finder icon on the dock.**

    Finder shows its face.

2. **Navigate to the folder that contains the file you want to copy and double-click the folder to open it.**

3. **Click the folder and choose File ⇨ New Tab.**

   A new tab appears showing Recents. Alternatively, you can choose File New Window, and a window containing Recents appears. (If you specified a different default folder for new windows as I described earlier in the "Customizing Finder settings" section, you'll see that folder instead of Recents.)

4. **Click the new tab or window and navigate to the folder where you want to move the file.**

5. **Using your mouse, click to select one file or folder or ⌘-click to select multiple files or folders.**

6. **Hold down the Option key and drag your selected file(s) or folder(s) to the second tab.**

   A green plus sign appears near the pointer while you drag the mouse.

7. **Release the mouse button when the second tab is highlighted.**

   When you hear the basso sound effect, the selected files and folders have been successfully copied to the folder you selected.

REMEMBER

Dragging a file or folder to a new location on the *same* device (such as from one folder to another on the same hard drive) always moves that file or folder (unless you hold down the Option key, which ensures that the original stays where it is and a copy is created in the new location). On the other hand, dragging a file or folder from one device to a *different* device (such as from a USB flash drive to a hard drive) always copies the file or folder — unless you use the ⌘ key, which moved the file or folder by creating a copy on the destination drive and deleting the original.

Moving a file or folder

You can move files and folders in Finder by following similar steps as for copying — just don't hold down the Option key.

However, thanks to your Mac's *spring-loaded folders* feature, you can also move files and folders without opening a second tab. Drag the file or folder you want to move over the icon of the destination device or folder and wait a moment or two until the folder springs open. (You can keep springing subfolders open this way until you reach the one you want.) Let go of the mouse button to move the file or folder. To adjust how long it takes for folders to spring open, choose ⇨ System Settings, click Accessibility in the sidebar, and then click Pointer Control. Drag the Spring-Loading Speed slider to adjust how quickly or slowly folders spring open when you hover over them with a selected file or folder.

REMEMBER

Don't release the mouse button until you're sure you're moving the file to the desired folder. If in doubt, press Esc to abandon the move operation and leave things the way they were.

Copying or moving multiple files

You can select several files from different locations and copy or move them into a folder. To select the files, use any of the techniques I outline earlier in the "Selecting stuff in Finder" section. Drag any one of the selected files to the folder where you want to place them (remember to hold down Option if you're copying the files). Finder drags the files as a group, and the number of files appears in a red circle on top of the group. Drag the group over the folder where you want to place them until the folder is highlighted, and then release them.

If you want to create a folder for a group of files, select the files as I describe in the preceding paragraph. Choose File ⇨ New Folder with Selection. A new folder is created called New Folder with Items, which you can rename as I explain earlier in the "Renaming files and folders" section. If the grouped files are from the desktop, invoke the command from the desktop and the new folder appears there.

Zip, Zip: Archiving Files and Folders

Files and folders take up space. If you have a bunch of files or folders that you don't use but want or need to save (such as old tax information), you can archive those files. *Archiving* grabs a file or folder (or a bunch of files or folders) and compresses them into a single file that takes up less space on your hard drive than the original file(s), unless you're archiving files that don't compress, such as certain types of images, videos, and audio files.

After you archive a group of files, you can delete the original files. If necessary, you can later unpack the archive file to retrieve all its files.

The easiest way to archive files on a Mac is to compress them into a single Zip file. Zip files represent the standard archiving file format used on Windows computers, but they work like a charm on Macs, too. (By the way, Zip isn't an acronym. It just sounds speedy.) Here are the steps to follow to compress some files and folders into a Zip archive:

1. **Click the Finder icon on the dock.**

   Finder comes to the fore.

2. **Navigate to and open the folder that contains the file or folder you want to archive.**

3. **Select one or more items you want to archive.**

4. **Choose File ⇨ Compress.**

   If, for instance, you select three items in Step 3, the Compress command displays Compress 3 items.

   After invoking this command, an archive file named Archive.zip appears in the folder that contains the items you selected to compress. (Yep, you're right: the name Archive.zip is both boring and unhelpful. You'll want to give your new Zip archive a more descriptive name right away.) If you compress a folder, the Zip file has the same name as the folder but with the .zip extension.

REMEMBER

To open a Zip file, double-click it. Doing so creates a folder inside the same folder where the Zip file is stored. Now you can double-click this newly created folder to view the contents that were stored in the Zip file.

Searching for Lost Files

No matter how organized you try to be, there's a good chance you might forget where you stored a file. To find your wayward files quickly, you can use the Spotlight feature.

With Spotlight, you type a word or phrase to identify the name of the file you want or the content you want inside that file. Spotlight displays a list of files that match what you typed. Say you want to find all the files related to your burning interest in kumquats. If you typed **kumquat**, Spotlight would find all files that contain *kumquat* in the filename — or in the file itself, if it's one your Mac can peer into (such as a Pages document or an Excel spreadsheet).

Running a Spotlight search

Spotlight searches for text that matches all or part of a filename and data stored inside a file. *Hint:* When using Spotlight, search for distinct words. For example, searching for *A* will be relatively useless because so many files use *A* as part of the filename and in the content. However, searching for *ebola* will narrow your search to the files you most likely want.

Spotlight searches your entire computer. To restrict a search to a specific folder, be sure to check out the next section.

To use Spotlight, follow these steps:

1. **Click the Spotlight icon — the magnifying glass — near the upper-right corner of the menu bar.**

   Alternatively, press ⌘+Spacebar. The Spotlight pop-up window appears.

2. **In the text box at the top of the pop-up window, type a word or phrase.**

   While you type, Spotlight displays the files that match your text, organized by file type. If you click one of the matching files, a quick view window opens, as shown in Figure 4-14.

3. **Click a file to open it or click Search in Finder at the bottom of the results to see the entire list of matches in a Finder window.**

   Narrow your search by setting more limited criteria in the Finder window, as described next.

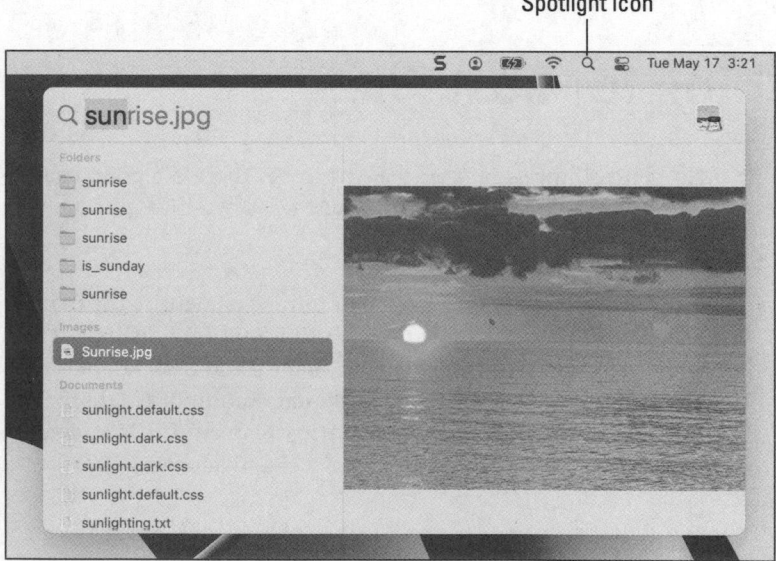

Spotlight icon

FIGURE 4-14:
Click a matching file in the Spotlight search results to see a preview.

Running a Finder search

The preceding steps enable you to search your entire computer for files. However, you can narrow your search to a specific folder or device attached to your Mac. To search a folder or attached device, follow these steps:

1. **In Finder, open the folder or click the device you want to search.**

2. **Click the magnifying glass icon in the upper-right corner of the Finder window.**

   Finder displays the Search text box.

   You can open a new Finder search window for the current folder by pressing Option+⌘+Space.

3. **In the Search text box, enter the word or phrase you want to use as the search text.**

   Finder searches your entire Mac and displays a list of files and folders that match your search text.

4. **In the Search bar that appears just below the Finder toolbar, select the name of the folder or device.**

   This tells Finder to narrow its search to just that folder or device.

5. **Click the plus button (+) next to Save on the right side of the Search bar.**

   Finder displays a new search criterion (see Figure 4-15). All search criteria take the following general form:

   attribute operator value

   where *attribute* is the file or folder property that you want to search, such as Kind (the file type, such as Image or Folder), Name (the file or folder name), or Contents (what's in the file or folder); *value* is the example of *attribute* that you're searching for; and *operator* is how you want Finder to match the *attribute* and *value*.

   For example, the default operator is the keyword Is, which means Finder matches files and folder where *attribute* equals *value*.

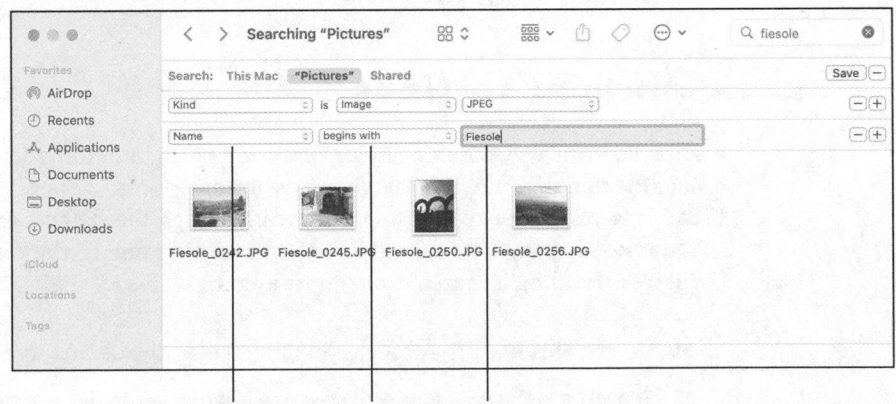

FIGURE 4-15:
Add one or more criteria to narrow your search.

Attribute field   Operator field   Value field

6. **In the attribute field (the first field), choose a file or folder attribute: Kind, Name, Contents, Last Opened Date, or Last Modified Date. Click Other to open a window that lets you choose more specific attributes to search by.**

7. **In the operator field (the second field), choose the operator you want to use.**

   For certain attributes — particularly Kind and Contents — the operator is a fixed value (Is and Contains, respectively), so you can't change it.

8. **In the value field (the third field), choose or enter the attribute value you want to search for.**

   For example, if you want to narrow your search results to see only images, choose Kind in the attribute field and then choose Image in the value field. In some cases, Finder adds an extra field to narrow your search even more. If you choose Image, for example, Finder adds a second value field in which you can choose a specific image type, such as JPEG.

   Similarly, if you want to narrow your search to see only files with a name that begins with the word *Sasquatch*, choose Name in the attribute field, Begins With in the operator field, and then enter **Sasquatch** in the value field.

9. **(Optional) Repeat Steps 5 through 8 to add another rule for the search criteria.**

   Figure 4-15 shows a search with two criteria rules added.

10. **(Optional) If you want to use this search criteria again in the future, click Save, type a name for the search, and then click Save.**

    A button named after the search word appears next to the other searchable device names.

11. **When you find the file you're looking for, click the item to open it or drag and drop it to a new location.**

Spotlight settings

When you run a search in a Finder window, Spotlight automatically searches This Mac, meaning it runs the search over your entire Mac. Where Spotlight runs its search is called the search *scope*. You can change the default scope by choosing Finder ➪ Settings ➪ Advanced and then selecting one of the following from the When Performing a Search drop-down menu:

>> **Search This Mac:** The scope is your entire Mac (the default scope).

>> **Search the Current Folder:** The scope is whatever folder you have open in Finder.

>> **Previous Search Scope:** The scope of any new search is the same as whatever you used as the scope of your most recent search. If you searched This Mac last time, the scope will be Search This Mac this time. Similarly, if you searched only the current folder last time, your scope this time will be whatever folder you're in.

You can also set preferences for the types of results Spotlight gives you. Choose ➪ System Settings and click Siri & Spotlight. Select the check boxes next to the categories you want Spotlight to include when searching, as shown in Figure 4-16. Deselect check boxes next to types of categories you want Spotlight to ignore. For example, you may not want applications to be included in your search results, in which case you would deselect the Applications check box.

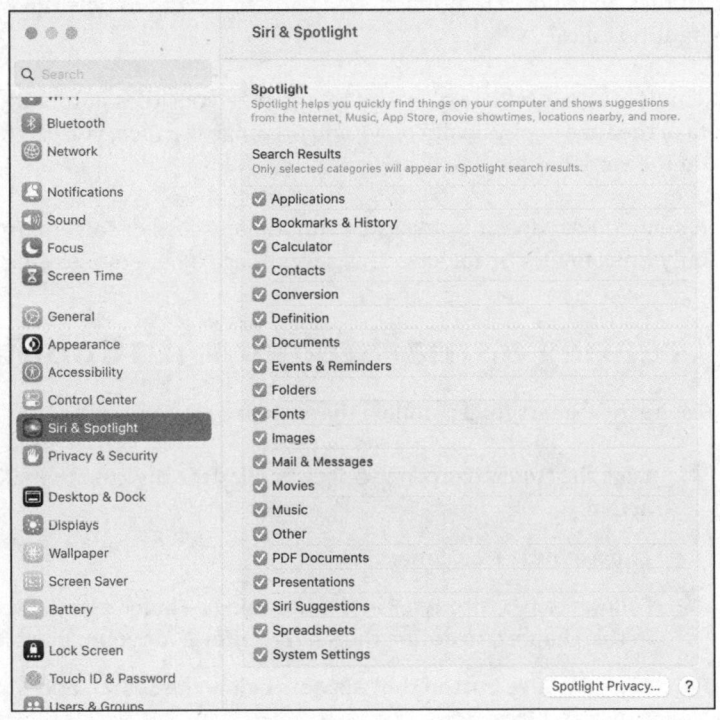

FIGURE 4-16:
Use Spotlight settings to specify which categories you want to see in your search results.

You can also prevent Spotlight from searching specific locations. To do this, click the Spotlight Privacy button, and then use one of the following techniques to specify a location where you don't want Spotlight to search:

>> Click Add (+), select the folder you want Spotlight to skip, and then click Choose.

Fiddling with Files and Folders

>> In Finder, display the folder you want Spotlight to skip, drag the folder to the Spotlight window, then drop it inside the Prevent Spotlight from Searching These Locations box in the Privacy dialog.

Using smart folders

Spotlight can make finding files and folders fast and easy. However, if you find yourself searching for the same types of files repeatedly, you can create a *smart folder*, which essentially works behind the scenes with Spotlight to keep track of a bunch of files that share one or more common characteristics. For example, you can tell a smart folder to store info about only those files that contain *rose* in the filename or the file; and from now on, you can look in that smart folder to access all files and folders that match *rose* without having to type the words in the Spotlight text box.

Think of smart folders as a way to organize your files automatically. Rather than take the time to physically move and organize the files, you can have smart folders do the work for you.

TECHNICAL STUFF

A smart folder doesn't physically contain any files or folders. Instead, it contains only links to files or folders. This saves space by not duplicating files.

Creating a smart folder with Spotlight

To create a smart folder, follow these steps:

1. **Click the Finder icon on the dock or click the desktop to make Finder active.**

2. **Choose File ⇨ New Smart Folder.**

3. **Follow Steps 3 through 9 in the "Running a Finder search" section, earlier in this chapter, to define the search criteria for your smart folder.**

4. **Click the Save button that appears below the Search text box.**

   A Save As dialog appears.

5. **Click in the Save As text box and type a descriptive name for your smart folder.**

6. **Choose a location to store your smart folder from the Where pop-up menu (or click the down arrow and navigate to the location where you want to save your smart folder).**

7. **(Optional) Select or deselect the Add to Sidebar check box.**

Select the check box if you want the smart folder to appear in the sidebar in the Favorites section. Deselect the check box if you don't want to see your smart folder in the sidebar.

8. **Click Save.**

Your smart folder appears in your chosen location. Instead of displaying an ordinary folder icon, smart folder icons have a gear inside a folder.

REMEMBER

After you create a smart folder, it automatically keeps your list of files and folders up to date at all times. If you create new files or folders that match the criteria used to define a smart folder, that new file or folder name will appear in the smart folder automatically. Delete a file, and the smart folder deletes its link to that file as well.

Deleting a File or Folder

To delete a file or folder, you first have to place that item in the trash. But putting an item in the trash doesn't immediately delete it. In fact, you can retrieve any number of files or folders you've thrown away. Nothing is really gone — that is, permanently deleted — until you empty the trash.

WARNING

Deleting a folder deletes any files or folders stored inside it. Therefore, if you delete a single folder, you might really be deleting 200 other folders containing files you might not have meant to get rid of, so always check the contents of a folder before you delete it, just to make sure it doesn't contain anything important.

To delete a file or folder, follow these steps:

1. **Click the Finder icon on the dock, and then navigate to and open the folder that contains the file or folder you want to delete.**

2. **Select the files and folders that you want to delete.**

3. **Choose one of the following:**

   ● Choose File ➪ Move to Trash.

   ● Drag the selected items onto the trash icon on the dock.

   ● Press ⌘+Delete.

   ● Control-click a selected item and choose Move to Trash from the shortcut menu that appears.

Retrieving a file or folder from the trash

When you move items to the trash, you can retrieve them again as long as you haven't emptied the trash since you threw them out. If the trash icon on the dock appears filled with crumbled up paper, you can still retrieve items from the trash. If the trash icon appears empty, it doesn't contain any files or folders that you can retrieve.

To retrieve a file or folder from the trash, follow these steps:

1. **Click the trash icon on the dock.**

   A Finder window appears, showing all the files and folders you deleted since the last time you emptied the trash.

2. **Select the item (or items) you want to retrieve, drag them onto a device or folder in which you want to store your retrieved items, and then release the mouse button.**

TIP

You can put the deleted file back in the same location from which it was deleted. In the Finder window that appears after you click the trash icon, select the file, and then click the actions icon (gear) and choose Put Back from the drop-down menu.

Emptying the trash

Every deleted file or folder gets stored in the trash, where it eats up space on your hard drive until you empty the trash. When you're sure that you won't need items you trashed any more, you can empty the trash to permanently delete the files and free up additional space on your hard drive.

To empty the trash, do one of the following:

>> Click the Finder icon on the dock (or click the desktop) and choose Finder ⇨ Empty Trash.

>> Control-click the trash icon on the dock and choose Empty Trash from the shortcut menu that appears.

>> If you want to examine the files in the trash before deleting them, Control-click the trash icon and choose Open from the pop-up menu. This opens a Finder window and shows all the files in the trash.

>> Click the Finder icon (or the desktop) and press ⌘+Shift+Delete.

A dialog appears, asking whether you're sure that you want to remove the items in the trash permanently. Click OK (or Cancel).

Chapter **5**

Managing Apps

You've probably noticed that after you start your Mac and the desktop shows up, your Mac just kind of sits there doing nothing. Sure, the time in the upper-right corner changes regularly, and you might see the odd notification, especially if your Mac is online and receiving email or other incoming, notification-worthy data. But that's about it. Congratulations: Your Mac is now a very expensive paperweight!

But, of course, it doesn't have to be this way. You paid good money for your Mac, and you want to it to do something useful (or fun or interesting or whatever floats your boat). The secret here is that you have to tell your Mac what you want it to do. And the way you do that is by launching and using one or more apps. An *app* (short for *application*) is a software program designed to perform a specific function. The Calendar app, for example, knows all about maintaining your schedule, so any time you need to schedule an appointment, you use Calendar to get it done. Similarly, if you need to create a spreadsheet for work, the Numbers app is the place to be.

In this chapter, you explore the world of apps on your Mac. You learn how to start and stop apps, install and uninstall apps, work with apps on the dock and desktop, and perform a fistful of techniques for taming the apps on your Mac.

Firing Up an App

Other than Finder (which is always running), you can't do anything with an app until you run it. Running an app is also referred to as *launching* or *starting* an app. Your Mac offers a little less than a million ways to start an app. I won't go through them all, but I will explain a few of the most popular methods. Here are quick descriptions of these methods, each of which I explain in more detail in the sections that follow:

>> Click an app or a document icon on the dock.

>> In Finder, either double-click an app in the Applications folder or double-click a document associated with the app you want to run. (For example, double-clicking a word-processing document opens the default word-processing app, which is usually Pages.)

TIP

To open the Applications folder from a Finder window, choose Go ⇨ Applications or press Shift+⌘+A.

>> Click an alias of the document. (See "Alter Egos: Creating Aliases for Documents," later in this chapter, for more on aliases.)

>> Find the app with the Spotlight Search feature and then select the app in the search results.

>> Click Launchpad on the dock and then click the icon for the app you want to open. If you have a trackpad, pinch your thumb and three fingers to open Launchpad, and then click the desired app icon.

>> Choose an app from the Apple (⌘) menu's Recent Items menu or the dock's recent apps section.

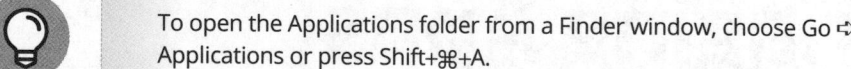

TIP

When you attach a device, such as a digital camera or a mobile phone, an app such as Photos or Music may launch automatically, depending on the settings you choose.

Running an app from the dock

The dock contains icons that represent some (but by no means all) of the apps installed on your Mac. By default, the dock comes pre-stuffed with a variety of apps that Apple thinks you might want to use right away. However, you can always add your favorite apps to the dock and remove the dock icons that you never use.

To run an app from the dock, move the pointer over the app icon that you want to run and click. (What? Were you expecting something difficult?)

"That's all well and good," you grumble, "but how am I supposed to know which icon represents which app?" That's a first-rate question, and I have what I hope is a first-rate answer: Hover the mouse pointer over any dock icon and macOS helpfully displays a little label that tells you the name of the app. For example, when you hover the mouse pointer over the icon that looks like a compass, you see a label that says Safari, as shown in Figure 5-1. Safari is your Mac's web browser (which you become fast friends with in Book 2, Chapter 1).

FIGURE 5-1:
Hover the mouse pointer over a dock icon to see a label that identifies the icon.

The dock doesn't just give you one-click access to apps. It's chock-full of features that enable you to get much more out of your apps. Let's take a look at what else you can do with the dock:

>> **See at-a-glance which apps are running:** If you see a dot under an app icon (see Figure 5-2), it means the app is currently running (as long as you didn't turn off this feature, as I describe in Book 1, Chapter 2).

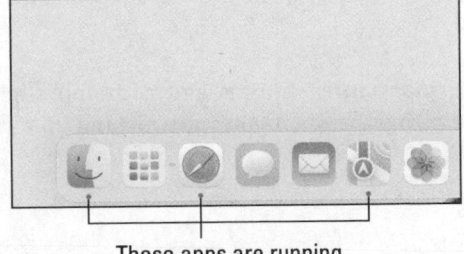

FIGURE 5-2:
The dock identifies running apps with a dot.

These apps are running

>> **Switch between running apps:** Click a running app's dock icon to switch to that app. For example, if you want to switch to the Photos app from the Mail app, click the Photos app icon on the dock. Doing so immediately displays the Photos window and displays the Photos name in the application menu portion of the menu bar at the top of the screen. Clicking the Photos app icon brings Photos to the forefront, but the Mail app doesn't close or quit on you; it just moseys to the background, waiting for its turn to step into the limelight again.

>> **Switch to a specific window of a running app:** Click the window if it's visible. If it isn't visible, right-click the app's dock icon and then click the window name in the menu that appears.

>> **Add a running app's icon to the dock:** Right-click the running app's temporary dock icon and then choose Options ⇨ Keep in Dock. (For another method to add icons to the dock and to learn how to remove icons from the dock, see the section "Messing with Dock Icons," later in this chapter.)

>> **See which windows you've minimized:** *Minimized* windows are tucked out of sight but still open. (You minimize a window by clicking the yellow minimize button in the top-left corner of the window.) By default, you see a thumbnail version of the minimized window on the right end of the dock. Click the thumbnail to bring the window back to full size.

>> **Hide all windows that belong to a specific app:** Right-click the app's dock icon and then click Hide. To reveal the windows, click the app on the dock or in Launchpad.

TIP

You can hide the dock by choosing ⇨ System Settings ⇨ Dock & Dock. Set the Automatically Hide and Show the Dock switch on, and the dock will be hidden until you move the mouse pointer to the bottom of the screen. Hiding the dock is a handy way to gain screen real estate if you're working with a small screen.

Running an app from Launchpad

If the app you want to open isn't stored on the dock, you can hunt down that app by opening the Applications folder in a Finder window or by using a Spotlight search. Nothing's wrong with those methods, but let me introduce you to one that's almost always faster: Click the dock's Launchpad icon (labeled in Figure 5-3).

TIP

If you use a trackpad, place three fingers and a thumb slightly apart on the trackpad and bring them together as if you were picking up a small object. *Voilà!* Launchpad launches.

FIGURE 5-3:
Click Launchpad
to see icons for
all your installed
apps.

Launchpad

TIP

If you use Launchpad a lot, consider creating a keyboard shortcut for it. Choose ⇨ System Settings (or click the System Settings icon on the dock), click Keyboard in the sidebar, and then click Keyboard Shortcuts. Click Launchpad & Dock, select the Show Launchpad check box, and then press the key or key combination you want to use to open Launchpad.

Launchpad shows all the apps in the Applications folder, using multiple screens depending on how many apps are installed on your Mac. All the apps that came with your Mac and all the apps you installed have an icon in Launchpad.

You can have multiple Launchpad screens. To move from one Launchpad screen to another, hold down the mouse button and move the mouse left or right, swipe left and right with two fingers on the trackpad, or press ⌘+→ or ⌘+←.

To open an app, just click the app icon in Launchpad.

TIP

If you have quite a few Launchpad screens, don't bother hunting for the app you want to launch. Instead, start typing the name of the app. Launchpad switches to showing only the apps with names where at least one of the words begins with what you've typed. When you see the app you want, click it to launch it.

To leave Launchpad without opening an app, click anywhere on the background or press Esc.

You can do the following to manage the appearance of Launchpad:

» Drag an icon to change its location in Launchpad; drag it to the very right or left edge to move the icon to another screen. You can move only one icon at a time.

» Drag one icon and drop it on another to create a folder that holds both icons, and then drag other icons into the folder. Click the folder once to open it, and then double-click the name to highlight it and type in a new name. To remove an icon from a folder, just drag it from its folder into Launchpad.

TIP

You can drag an icon from Launchpad to the dock to add the icon to the dock.

Running an app from Finder

Because an app's icon might not appear on the dock, you have to be able to access icons another way. Finder can help you launch any app from the Applications folder.

To run an app from Finder, follow these steps:

1. **Click the Finder icon on the dock.**

2. **Choose Go ⇨ Applications.**

You can also press Shift+⌘+A.

Finder displays the apps installed on your Mac.

3. **Scroll through the Applications folder until you see the app icon you want and then double-click the icon to run the app.**

You might have to double-click a folder that contains an app icon and then double-click the app icon.

Your chosen app appears, typically with a blank window, ready for you to do something application-y, such as typing text. Other apps, such as Music, may be filled with brightly colored icons.

A file on the Mac appears as a graphically descriptive icon with a name. An icon can represent an app, a document, or a link, known as an *alias*, to either of those:

» **App files** do something, such as let you play a game of chess, or send, receive, and organize your email. App icons are often distinct enough to help you identify the type of app they represent. For example, the Safari app icon appears as a compass, the Photo app icon appears as a sort of color wheel, and the Mail app icon (for sending and receiving email) appears as a sealed envelope.

>> **Document files** hold data created by apps, such as a report created in a word-processing app, a budget created in a spreadsheet app, or a movie created in a video-editing app. Document icons often appear as a dog-eared page showing a thumbnail image of the content and the suffix of the file type stamped on the bottom, such as *web*, *docx*, or *html*. Folders look like folders, and image files such as JPG, PNG, or TIFF may appear as thumbnails of the image.

>> **Aliases** represent links to documents. You find out more about aliases in the "Alter Egos: Creating Aliases for Documents" section, later in this chapter.

As an alternative to starting an app and then having to find and open the file you want to work with, the Mac gives you the option of double-clicking the document icon you want to open. This opens the app with your double-clicked document ready for action.

You have several ways to find and open a document:

>> Click the Finder icon on the dock and then click the Documents folder in the sidebar (or choose Go ⇨ Documents or press Shift+⌘+O) to open the Documents folder.

>> Click the desktop and press Shift+⌘+D to open Finder and display the Desktop folder.

>> Click the Finder icon on the dock and then navigate to the location of the folder that contains your document. Double-click the folder to see the documents within.

>> Type the document name or a word or phrase it contains in the Spotlight Search field in the Finder window or desktop menu bar.

If the document you want is one you worked on recently, open a Finder window and then either click Recents in the sidebar or choose Go ⇨ Recents (or press Shift+⌘+F) to see a list of files you've used recently. You also have the option to select a folder you opened recently by choosing Go ⇨ Recent Folders and then clicking the folder name in the continuation menu that appears.

Double-click your document file when you find it to open it. Your Mac loads the default app that's associated with that file type (if the app isn't already running) and displays your chosen document in a window. Most of the time, the default app will be the app that you used to create the document.

TIP

To see which app is the default for a document, right-click the document and click Get Info. In the info window that appears, click the Open With disclosure arrow to see the default app. If you want, you can use the Open With pop-up menu to choose a different default app for this document. If you want all documents of this file type to use the new app, click Change All and then click Continue when macOS asks you to confirm.

If your Mac can't find the app that created the document, it might load another app or ask you to choose an existing app on your Mac that can open the document.

Sometimes if you double-click a document icon, an entirely different app loads and displays your file. This can occur if you save your file in a different file format. For example, if you save a Keynote presentation as a PDF document, it will open with Preview (or whatever app you've selected to open PDF documents with).

Running an app with Spotlight

As an alternative to clicking an app's dock or Launchpad icon (see the next section) or locating an app or document by clicking through folders, you can use your Mac's handy Spotlight feature to quickly open apps or documents for you. I explain Spotlight in detail in Book 1, Chapter 4. You can use Spotlight to run apps and open documents in two ways:

>> **Via Finder:** Click the Finder icon on the dock, click in the Search text box, type all or part of the app name, and then double-click the app in the search results.

>> **From the desktop menu bar:** Click the Spotlight icon (the magnifying glass) on the right side of your Mac's menu bar (or press ⌘+spacebar) and begin typing the first few letters of the app name. Double-click the app when it appears in the search results window.

Running an app you used recently

The thing about apps is that when you use one once, you'll often use it again pretty soon. That's probably why macOS maintains not one but *two* areas where it keeps track of apps you've used recently:

>> **The Recent Items menu:** Choose ⬤ ⇨ Recent Items and then choose the app you want to run from the Applications list, which shows your ten most recently used apps. You can also choose a recently created or viewed document or other file to automatically launch the associated app and load the document or file.

TIP

By default, macOS shows the ten most recent apps you've used. To change that number, choose ● ⇨ System Settings (or click System Settings on the dock), click Desktop & Dock in the sidebar, and then modify the number in the Recent Documents, Apps, and Servers spin box.

» **The recent apps dock area:** This area, which is just to the right of the dock divider (see Figure 5-4), displays icons for the last three apps you launched, provided those apps don't already have an icon on the dock. If you find that you don't use this area, you can score some extra dock real estate by turning off this feature: Choose ● ⇨ System Settings (or click System Settings on the dock), click Desktop & Dock in the sidebar, and then click the Show Recent Applications in Dock switch off.

Recent apps

FIGURE 5-4:
The dock's recent apps area displays the three most recently used apps.

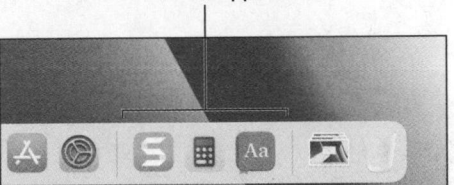

Flitting from One App to Another

Your Mac doesn't care how many apps you have running at the same time: Whether it's 2 or 22, your Mac is cool with whatever's going on.

Why run multiple apps at the same time? Usually because you need those apps for some common purpose. For example, if you're working on a project, you might have Pages open to write a project report, Numbers open to crunch some project data, Safari open to research some aspect of the project, and Mail open to correspond with your project colleagues.

Similarly, you might do most of your work in an app such as Pages but leave productivity apps such Mail, Messages, Calendar, and Contacts open so that you can access them quickly when you need them.

Ah, but there's the rub: When you have multiple apps running, how do you switch from one app to another? At this point in your Mac education, you won't be the least bit surprised to hear that your Mac offers quite a few ways to switch among different apps. Here are the techniques you'll use most often:

>> **Using the dock:** Click a running app's dock icon to switch to that app.

>> **Using Application Switcher:** Hold down ⌘ and press tab to open Application Switcher, which displays icons of all running apps. With the ⌘ key held down to keep Application Switcher open, press the tab key to cycle the highlight left-to-right through the icons of the running apps; note that the highlighted app icon also displays the app name (see the Pages icon in Figure 5-5). When you've highlighted the app you want to work with, release the ⌘ key and macOS switches you to that app.

Holding down both Shift and ⌘ while pressing tab cycles the highlight through the icons from right to left. You can also hold down ⌘, press tab once, and then use the arrow keys to navigate left and right.

If an app has several files open in different windows, Application Switcher just switches you to that app, but you still have to find the specific window to view.

FIGURE 5-5:
The Application Switcher displays icons of running apps.

>> **Clicking a window:** A fast but somewhat clumsier way to switch between apps is to rearrange your windows so you can see two or more windows at one time. To switch to another window, click anywhere inside that window.

>> **Using Mission Control:** To see thumbnail versions of all the open windows on your desktop and other desktops spaces (which I get to in just a bit; see "Organizing Multiple Desktops with Spaces"), press F3 to launch Mission Control. (You can also swipe up on the trackpad with three or four fingers or

click the Mission Control icon in Launchpad to open Mission Control, as shown in Figure 5-6.) Then click the window you want to work in.

TIP

To choose how many fingers you need to open Mission Control, click System Settings on the dock and select Trackpad from the list. (You have this choice only if you use a trackpad.) Click the More Gestures tab, and then open the Mission Control pop-up menu and choose Swipe Up with Three Fingers or Swipe Up with Four Fingers.

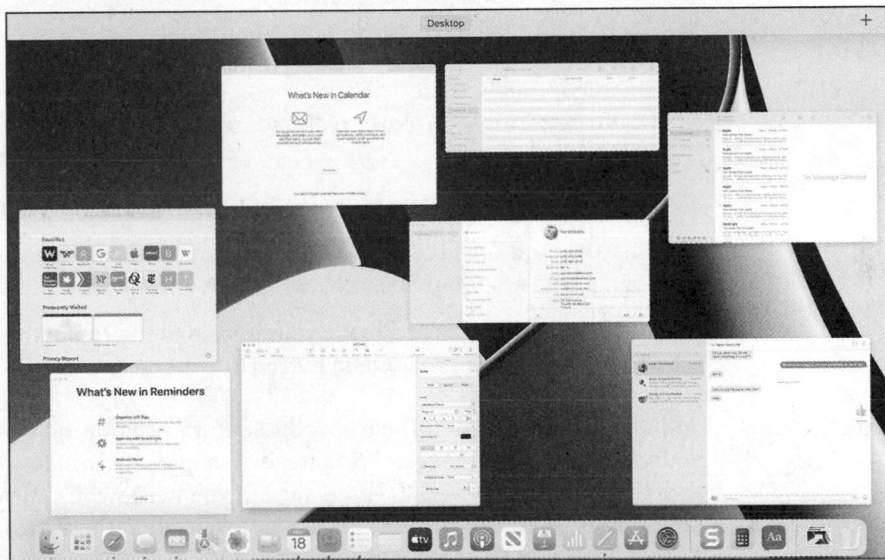

FIGURE 5-6: Mission Control shows everything that's open on your desktop.

TIP

If you want to cycle through two or more open windows from the same app, press ⌘+` (that's the backtick character, which lives on the key to the left of numeral 1 on most keyboards).

Another way to switch between apps is to set up entire desktops, which I explain in the section "Organizing Multiple Desktops with Spaces," later in this chapter.

Working in Split-View Mode

Sometimes you need to work in two windows at the same time. For example, you might have Pages open while you write a report and also have Safari running with some research for that report. Wouldn't it be nice if there was an easy way to have the windows arranged so that you could see both windows and you could switch from one to another without having to call up Application Switcher?

Yep, sure, you could move and size the windows just so, but why go to all that trouble when macOS is happy to do it for you using a handy feature called split-view mode? To work in split-view mode, do the following:

1. **Launch the two apps you want to use, such as any two of Pages, Numbers, Keynote, or Safari.**

2. **In one of the app windows, hover the mouse pointer over the full-screen button, the green button in the upper-left side of the window.**

   A pop-up menu appears.

3. **Choose Tile Window to Left of Screen.**

   macOS moves and sizes the app window so that it takes up the entire left side of the screen. macOS also displays reduced versions of your other open windows on the right.

4. **Click the other application you want to use in split-view mode.**

   macOS moves and sizes the app window so that it takes up the entire right side of the screen, so you're now officially in split-view mode.

5. **To exit split-view mode, move your mouse to the top of the screen and then click the exit full-screen button in either app window.**

TIP

Split-view mode is useful, but macOS Ventura offers a new tool for organizing your screen: Stage Manager. With Stage Manager, the window you're working in gets the bulk of the screen (center stage, if you will), while all your other running apps appear as thumbnails off to the side (waiting in the wings, if you will). Click a thumbnail and that app comes to the fore. To use Stage Manager, choose ⇨ System Settings (or click the System Settings icon on the dock), click Desktop & Dock in the sidebar, and then click the Stage Manager switch on. In the window that appears, click Turn on Stage Manager.

Quittin' Time: Shutting Down an App

When you're finished with an app for the day (or for a while), you should shut it down. Why? Because shutting down an app you no longer need offers two important benefits:

» Running apps uses system resources (such as memory), so shutting down an unneeded app frees up its resources for other apps to use.

» Running apps usually have one or more windows open on the desktop, so quitting an app removes those windows and makes your desktop less cluttered and easier to navigate.

Note that you can get the same benefits by closing one or more of an app's open documents rather than shutting down the entire app.

REMEMBER

You don't have to be paranoid about your Mac's resources and constantly shut down apps. macOS is pretty good about managing those resources, even if you're running lots of apps. If you notice that your Mac is a bit sluggish, by all means shut down any apps you don't need right now.

Closing a document

If you want to stop working with or viewing a specific document but want to keep the app running, you can close just that particular document. You have three ways to close a document window:

>> Choose File ⇨ Close.

>> Press ⌘+W.

>> Click the red close icon in the top-left corner of the document window.

TIP

If you just want to create some space on the desktop, you don't have to close the document. Instead, you can click the document's yellow minimize button (in the top-left corner of the document window) to minimize the window to the dock. Click the document or app icon on the dock to quickly reopen the document.

WARNING

If you close an app's only remaining document, the app itself usually remains running. Therefore, be careful not to think that you can quit an app just by closing all its open documents (as you can in the Windows world).

If you try to close a document that has unsaved changes, a confirmation dialog appears, asking whether you want to save your file.

Quitting an app

To shut down an app, you have three choices:

>> Click the application menu and choose Quit (such as Photos ⇨ Quit Photos to shut down the Photos app).

>> Press ⌘+Q.

>> Right-click the app icon on the dock and choose Quit from the contextual menu that appears.

REMEMBER

If you try to shut down an app that displays a window containing a document that you haven't saved yet, a confirmation dialog appears asking whether you want to save your file.

Force-quitting an app

Despite the Mac's reputation for reliability, there's a chance that an app will crash, freeze, or hang, which are less-than-technical-terms for an app screwing up and not reacting when you click the mouse or press a key. When an app no longer responds to any attempts to work or shut down, you might have to resort to a last-resort procedure known as a *force-quit*.

WARNING

If you force-quit an app, you will lose any data you changed between the time of your last save and right before the app suddenly froze or crashed. For instance, say you're typing a sentence and then perform a force-quit before pressing ⌘+S to save it — that sentence would be missing the next time you reopen that document.

As the name implies, force-quitting makes an app shut down whether it wants to or not. Here are the two easiest ways to force-quit an app:

>> **Choose ⇨ Force Quit (or press ⌘+Option+Esc).** The Force Quit Applications dialog appears, as shown in Figure 5-7. Frozen or crashed apps might appear in the Force Quit Applications dialog with the phrase *Not Responding* next to its name. Click the app you want to force-quit and then click the Force Quit button. If you select Finder, the Force Quit button reads Relaunch.

FIGURE 5-7:
If an app has crashed, the Force Quit Applications dialog shows *Not Responding* beside the app name.

>> **Right-click an app icon on the dock and choose Force Quit from the shortcut menu that appears.** If the app hasn't really crashed or if your Mac thinks the app hasn't crashed, you won't see a Force Quit option in this pop-up menu. In that case, you may want to wait a minute or so to give the app some time to come to its senses (it might just be busy completing a long or intensive operation). If you wait awhile, and the app still appears stuck but you don't see the Force Quit option, hold down the Option key, right-click the app icon on the dock, and then choose Force Quit.

TIP

Most apps present you with the original and a recovered version of the document you were working on before a force-quit. Look at both to determine which is the most recent or most correct version, and then proceed as follows, depending on which file is the better one:

>> **Original file:** Save the file by choosing File ⇨ Save. If you're not happy with the original document, click the close icon (the red button in the upper-left corner) of the recovered file. When asked whether you want to save it, click Don't Save.

>> **Recovered file:** Close the original file, and then click the window of the recovered file to make it active. Choose File ⇨ Save and give the recovered file the same name as the original file. Click Replace when asked in the confirmation dialog.

TIP

If the documents you're comparing are lengthy and were created in an app that lets you compare versions, save the original and recovered versions using different names, compare both version in the app, and continue with the one you like best.

Alter Egos: Creating Aliases for Documents

An alias in the real world is a new name that refers to an existing person. An *alias* in the Mac world is a new file that points to an existing document. The only thing the alias contains is the location of the original document. This means that when you double-click the alias, macOS grabs that location info and uses it to open the original document.

This might strike you as odd behavior. Why bother creating an alias at all? Why not just work with the original document directly? Great questions! Here's are two scenarios where aliases come in handy:

>> Some documents are buried deep inside a folder hierarchy where you might need to navigate a half dozen or more folders and subfolders to finally get at

the document. Too much effort! By creating an alias for the document and storing that alias in an easy-to-reach place (such as the desktop or Documents folder), you drastically reduce the time and effort needed to open the document.

>> Some documents are useful in multiple contexts. For example, you might require the same document in several projects. You could store copies of the document in each project folder, but if the document requires an edit, you're stuck with editing all the copies. Too much work! Instead, keep one copy of the document in whatever folder makes sense, and then create aliases for the document in the other folders where you use the document.

REMEMBER

I talk about creating aliases for documents in this section, but you can also create aliases for folders and apps.

Here are the steps to follow to create an alias for a document:

1. **Click the Finder icon on the dock.**

2. **Open the folder that contains the document you want to work with.**

3. **Select the document.**

4. **Choose File ⇨ Make Alias.**

   You can also right-click the document and then click Make Alias, or press Control+⌘+A.

   Finder creates a new file with two characteristics that identify the file as an alias (see Figure 5-8):

   • The icon of the file has an arrow in the bottom-left corner.

   • The suggested name of the file is the same as the original document but with the word *alias* appended.

5. **Type the name you want to use for the alias and then press Return.**

   You don't have to keep the *alias* part of the suggested name, if you don't want to. Most folks find that having the arrow in the bottom-left corner is enough to remember that the file is an alias.

An alias is just another file, so you can perform all standard file-related tasks. In particular, you can move the alias to a new location — because it's pointless to store the original document and the alias in the same location.

TIP

You can store an alias on the desktop for fast access or in specific folders to organize apps and documents without moving them to a new location.

FIGURE 5-8:
An arrow and the
word *alias* in the
filename identify
a file as an alias.

Messing with Dock Icons

The dock includes several apps already installed on your Mac, but if you install more apps (see "Welcoming New Apps to Your Mac," later in this chapter), you might want to add their icons to the dock as well. One way to add an app icon to the dock is to click and drag the icon to the dock.

When you drag an app icon to the dock, you aren't physically moving the app from the Applications folder to the dock; you're just creating a link, or *alias*, from the dock icon to the actual app (which is still safely stashed in its folder). Here's how to create a new dock icon by dragging an app to the dock:

1. **Click the Finder icon on the dock.**

2. **Choose Go⇨Applications.**

   You can also press Shift+⌘+A.

   Finder displays the contents of the Applications folder.

3. **Drag the icon of the desired app to the dock.**

   Make sure that you drag the app icon to the left of the dock divider, which is labeled out in Figure 5-9. To the left of the divider, you see app icons. To the right of the divider, you can store file or folder icons.

4. **Drag the app icon left or right along the dock until the icon is in the position you prefer, and then release it.**

   Your chosen app icon now has its own place on the dock.

Be careful not to drag the app icon to the trash icon unless you really want to delete it from your hard drive.

WARNING

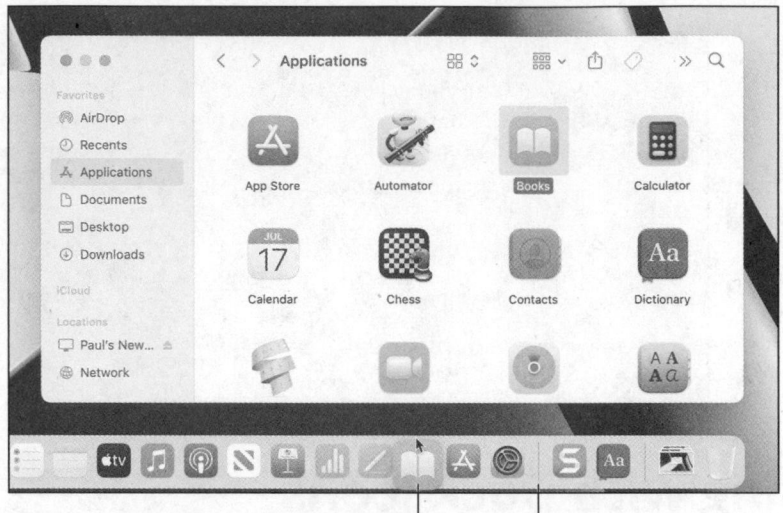

FIGURE 5-9:
Drag the app icon
to the left of the
dock divider.

The Books app icon in the process   Divider
of being dragged to the dock

TIP

You can also add an app icon to the dock when the app is open. Remember that the dock displays the icons of all running apps at all times, but when you exit an app, that app's icon — if it's not a dock resident — will disappear from the dock. To give a running app dock residency, right-click the running app's icon on the dock (or click and hold down on the app icon) and choose Options ⇨ Keep in Dock from the shortcut menu, as shown in Figure 5-10. Now when you exit from this app, the app icon remains visible on the dock.

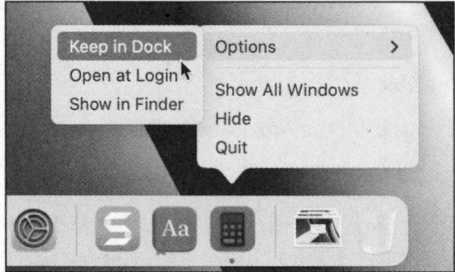

FIGURE 5-10:
You can give
temporary app
icons permanent
dock residency.

Adding file and folder aliases to the dock

You can always find the files and folders you want by using Finder. However, you might find that switching to Finder constantly just to access the contents of a particular folder can be tedious. As a faster alternative, you can store aliases to files and folders directly on the dock.

Accessing files from the dock

If you have a file that you access regularly, consider placing an icon for that file directly on the dock. That way, the file icon remains visible at all times (whenever the dock is visible), giving you one-click access to your frequently used files. To place a file icon on the dock, follow these steps:

1. **Click the Finder icon on the dock.**

2. **Navigate to the folder containing the file you use frequently.**

3. **Drag the file to the dock into any space to the left of the trash icon.**

   The icons on the dock slide apart to make room for the icon. To open this file, just click its file icon.

You can add more than one icon, but too many will clutter up the dock. If you've got lots of files you'd like to access from the dock, consider making stacks, as I describe in the next section.

REMEMBER

A file icon on the dock is just an alias or link to your actual file. If you drag the file icon off the dock to delete it from the dock, your original file remains untouched.

Creating stacks on the dock

Rather than clutter the dock with multiple app or file icons, consider storing a folder on the dock. A folder icon, when stored on the dock, is a *stack*. After you create a stack on the dock, you can view its contents by clicking the stack. By default, the dock comes with a prefab stack: the Downloads folder, which is the icon you see just to the left of the trash icon.

TIP

To load the app or open the file, you can click the stack on the dock and then click the app or file icon. The downsides include losing the shortcut menus for the items in the stack and not being able to open a document in an app other than the one in which it was created.

To store a stack on the dock, follow these steps:

1. **Click the Finder icon on the dock to open a new Finder window.**

2. **Navigate to a folder you use frequently.**

3. **Drag the folder to the dock into any space to the right of the rightmost divider but before the trash.**

   The dock icons slide apart to make room for your stack to give your folder a place all its own.

Alternatively, you can create a folder anywhere. In the folder, create aliases for the apps or documents you use frequently, and then drag that folder to the dock as outlined in the previous steps.

Opening files stored in a stack

After you place a stack on the dock, you can view its contents — and open a file in that stack — by following these steps:

1. **Click a stack folder on the dock.**

The files and folders in the stack appear as a stack of single icons neatly arranged in an arc above the icon. At the top of the stack is an Open in Finder link. Click the link to view all the files in a Finder window. If a file contained in the folder represented by the stack is open, the icon shows a piece of paper emerging from the folder.

2. **Click the file you want to open and your chosen file opens.**

Or click Open in Finder link to see the files in a Finder window.

TIP

Right-click (two-finger tap on a trackpad) a stack icon to display a shortcut menu of options for customizing the way a stack folder appears on the dock (as a stack or folder) and how its contents are displayed when you click it, as shown in Figure 5-11.

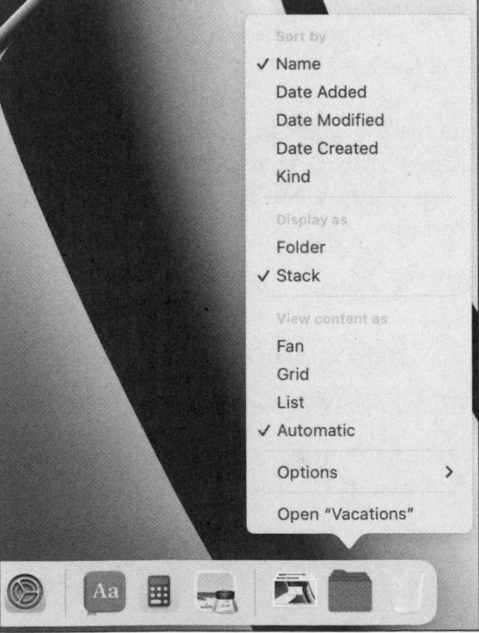

FIGURE 5-11:
Control-click a stack to display a shortcut menu.

Rearranging icons on the dock

After you place app, file, and folder icons on the dock, you may want to rearrange their order. How you rearrange the dock is up to you! To rearrange icons on the dock, drag the icon that you want to move sideways until the icon is in its new position, and then release.

While you move an icon, its neighbors move to the side to show you where the icon will appear when you let go of the mouse button.

TIP

You can rearrange icons on the dock how you want, but two icons you can't move or remove are the Finder and trash icons, which won't budge no matter how hard you try to drag them.

Removing icons from the dock

Right from the get-go, you might see icons on the dock for apps that you rarely use. Or you might think having the Launchpad icon on the dock is redundant because opening the Launchpad is a quick operation. Rather than let those icons take up precious dock real estate, get rid of them and make room for the icons of apps and files you use frequently. It's like keeping salt and pepper on the counter and the mustard seed in the cupboard. You have two ways of removing an icon from the dock:

>> Drag the icon up and off the dock until you see a Remove screentip over the icon, then release the mouse button. Your unwanted app icon disappears.

>> Right-click the app or file icon and choose Options ⇨ Remove from Dock from the shortcut menu.

Note: Removing an icon from the dock doesn't remove or delete the actual file. To remove apps, see the "Uninstalling Apps" section, later in this chapter.

REMEMBER

Here are two things you can't do with icons on the dock:

>> You can never remove the Finder and trash icons from the dock.

>> You can't remove an app icon from the dock if the app is still running.

Organizing Multiple Desktops with Spaces

Spaces multiplies your Mac's single display into as many as 16 separate virtual screens, or desktops. The main purpose of Spaces is to help organize multiple apps running at the same time. Rather than cram multiple app windows on a single desktop, Spaces lets you store multiple apps in separate desktops. One desktop might contain only internet apps, such as Safari and Mail, whereas a second desktop might contain only Microsoft Word and the Mac's built-in Dictionary app. Each desktop can have its own desktop picture and a customized dock.

If one app has multiple windows open, you can store each app window on a separate desktop. For example, if you have a word processor and open a personal letter and a business letter, you could store the personal letter's window on one desktop and the business letter's window on a second desktop.

You manage each space individually, but you can see all of them and move windows from one space to another in Mission Control, or by swiping left or right with three fingers.

Your Mac starts you off with one desktop, which you can see both by opening Mission Control, which is where you create additional desktops. Apps in full-screen view, which you activate by clicking the green full-screen button in the upper right corner, act as a space, too.

Creating desktops

When you're ready to add another desktop, you can do so by following these two steps:

1. **Open Mission Control by using one of these methods:**

    - Press F3.

    - Swipe up on the trackpad with three or four fingers (the number of fingers that opens Mission Control is determined in the Trackpad section of System Settings).

2. **Click the plus sign in the upper-right corner of the screen.**

    A new desktop space appears with the name Desktop 2. Subsequent desktops will be named Desktop 3, Desktop 4, and so on up to Desktop 16, as shown in Figure 5-12.

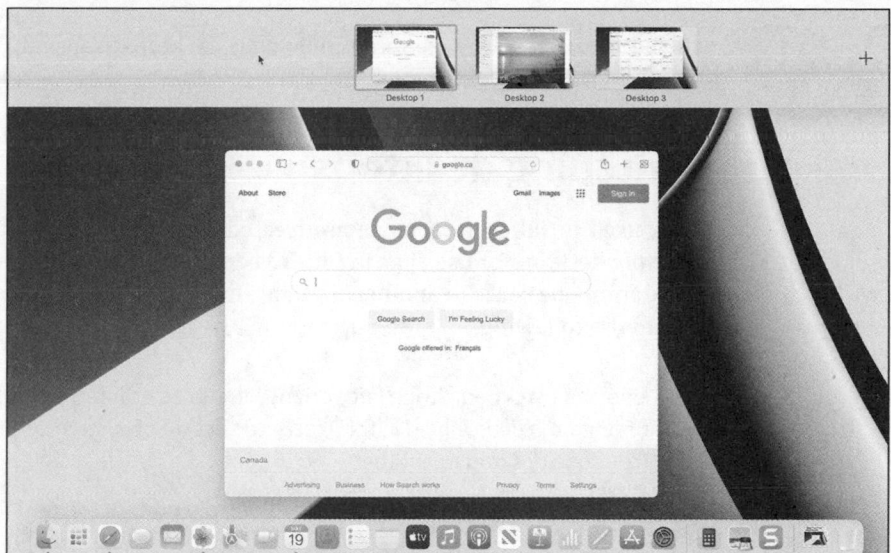

FIGURE 5-12:
Create additional desktops from Mission Control.

You can give each desktop space a personal desktop image and dock. Open Mission Control and click the desktop you want to work in. Then do the following:

» **Set the picture for that desktop:** Navigate to the desktop for which you want to set the picture and go to ⇨ System Settings and click Wallpaper, as I explain in Book 1, Chapter 6.

» **Choose which apps you want to open on that desktop:** Right-click an icon on the dock, click Options, and then click This Desktop (to open the app only on this desktop), All Desktops (to open the app on every desktop), or None (to open the app on the current desktop), as shown in Figure 5-13.

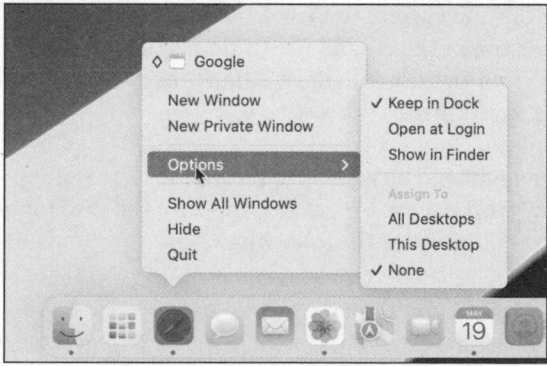

FIGURE 5-13:
Use the Options for each app icon on the dock to customize each desktop.

WARNING

All the changes you make to an individual desktop disappear when you remove that desktop from spaces.

Switching desktops

Apps used in full-screen mode are treated as desktop spaces. When you create multiple desktops or use apps in full-screen mode or both, you want to be able to move from one space to another. To move from one desktop space to another, you can do the following:

>> **Use the trackpad:** Swipe left or right with three or four fingers (the number of fingers is determined in the Trackpad section of System Settings) to move from one desktop to another.

>> **Use Mission Control:** Enter Mission Control and click the desktop you want.

>> **Switch between desktops:** Hold down the Control key and press the left- or right-arrow keys.

Moving app windows to different desktops

Earlier I mention that when you right-click a dock icon and then choose Options ➪ None (the default assignment), when you run the app, it appears on the desktop you're currently working in. For example, if you're on Desktop 1 and you run the Safari web browser, Safari appears on Desktop 1. If you leave Safari running, switch to Desktop 2, and then try to open Safari there, macOS will just switch you back to Desktop 1.

If, instead, you switch to a desktop, right-click a dock icon, and then choose Options ➪ This Desktop, when you run the app, macOS switches back to that desktop (if it's not the current one) and then opens the app on that desktop. For example, if you're on Desktop 1 and run Options ➪ This Desktop on the Safari dock icon, and then from Desktop 2 launch Safari, macOS first switches to Desktop 1 and then opens Safari there.

Either way, you might end up with an app running on a desktop other than the one you're currently working on. To get the app into the desktop you want, you can move it there by doing one of the following:

>> **Move the window via Mission Control:** Go to Mission Control and click the desktop that has the window you want to move. That desktop is now active. Go to Mission Control again and drag the window from the active desktop, which appears in the main part of the screen, to the thumbnail (at the top of the screen) of the desktop where you want to move the window.

>> **Move the window via the dock:** Go to Mission Control and click the desktop where you want the window to be. On the dock, right-click the app you want to move, and then choose Options ⇨ This Desktop.

>> **Move the window via dragging it:** From the desktop, click the title bar of the window you want to move and drag to the far left or right edge of the screen until it shifts to the neighboring desktop. Release the mouse or trackpad button or keep going until you reach the desktop you want to move the window to.

Customizing Mission Control settings

Mission Control lets you choose some of the ways you view and interact with it. Choose ⇨ System Settings, click Desktop & Dock in the sidebar, then scroll down to the Mission Control section (see Figure 5-14).

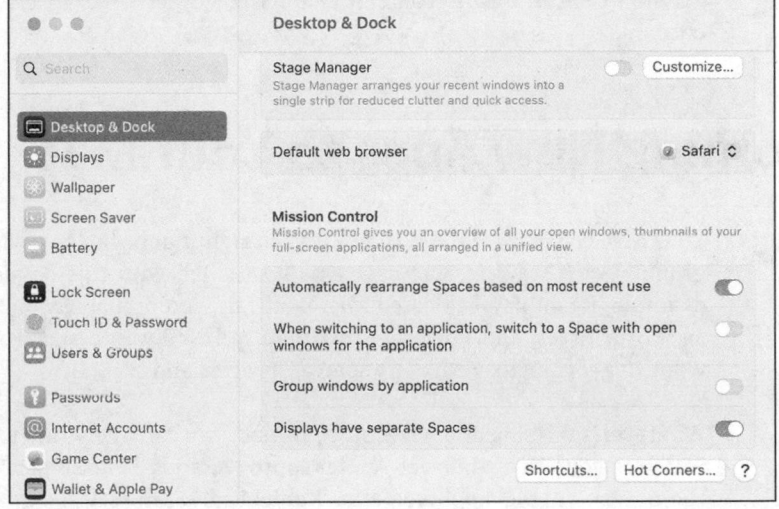

FIGURE 5-14:
Set Mission
Control settings.

Select the switches next to the features you want to activate:

>> **Automatically Rearrange Spaces Based on Most Recent Use:** Moves your desktop spaces around so the most frequently used are first. If you're a creature of habit and like to find things where you put them, turn this switch off.

>> **When Switching to an Application, Switch to a Space with Open Windows for the Application:** When you open an app, your desktop scrolls automatically to the desktop that has a window open and uses that app. If this option is

off, when you click an app on a desktop, it opens on that desktop even if the app is already open on another desktop. And just clicking the app icon on the dock moves you from one window on a desktop to another window of the same app on another desktop.

>> **Group Windows by Application:** When you have multiple windows of multiple apps open and go to Mission Control, the windows are grouped by app.

>> **Displays Have Separate Spaces:** If you use multiple displays, this option lets you have different spaces for each display.

Click Shortcuts and then, in the Keyboard and Mouse Shortcuts dialog that appears, you can use the pop-up menus to set keyboard or mouse shortcuts to access Mission Control, to see Application Windows, and to Show Desktop.

Click the Hot Corners button to assign one of the screen's four corners to Mission Control. Open the pop-up menu next to the corner you want to assign to Mission Control, and choose it from the menu. When you move the pointer to that corner, Mission Control opens. You can also assign other tasks to the remaining three corners.

Welcoming New Apps to Your Mac

Your Mac comes with more than 40 apps right out of the box. That's a lot of programs, but it's a rare Mac user who's satisfied with this default collection. For example, if you're a dedicated Microsoft fan, you probably want to use apps such as Word, Excel, and PowerPoint. If you're heavily into social media, you likely want to get your fix with apps such as Twitter and WeChat.

Whatever's missing app-wise on your Mac, you can likely find it in the App Store, which is your Mac's hub for Apple-approved apps. (Please take a moment to say the phrase "Apple-approved apps" quickly five times. I'll wait.) You can search for the app you want, or you can browse through categories such as Games, Graphics & Design, Photo & Video, and Productivity.

Even better, if you have a newish Mac that runs on Apple silicon, you also get to run iPhone and iPad apps right on your Mac. Nice!

TECHNICAL STUFF

What's all this about *Apple silicon?* Well, for many years, the heart of every Mac computer was a central processing unit (CPU) made by the giant chip manufacturer Intel. However, a few years ago (late 2020, to be semi-precise), Apple started building Macs that use CPUs designed and manufactured by Apple. These original chips were named M1, with subsequent processors named M1 Pro, M1 Max, and M1

Ultra. (As I was writing this in mid-2022, Apple announced the next-generation M2 chip.) To see whether your Mac uses Intel chips or Apple silicon, choose ➪ About This Mac. In the window that appears, read the Chip value. If it says "Apple *something*," as shown in Figure 5-15, you've got Apple silicon and can run iPhone and iPad apps on your Mac.

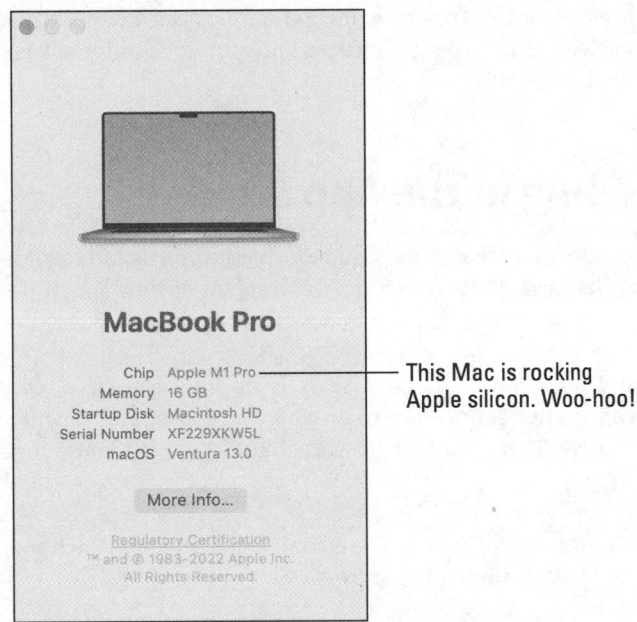

MacBook Pro

Chip	Apple M1 Pro
Memory	16 GB
Startup Disk	Macintosh HD
Serial Number	XF229XKW5L
macOS	Ventura 13.0

More Info...

Regulatory Certification
™ and © 1983–2022 Apple Inc.
All Rights Reserved.

This Mac is rocking Apple silicon. Woo-hoo!

FIGURE 5-15: The Chip value tells you what kind of processor runs your Mac.

These apps cost a fortune, right? Well, yep, a few of them do, but most don't. In fact, quite a few pricing options are available in the App Store:

>> **Free:** That's right: Lots of apps are gratis and most of them are fully functional programs. However, be careful because some free apps are lite versions of full-featured apps that cost money. These scaled-down versions either have limited features or display advertising. Many free apps have options or upgrades you can purchase in the app.

>> **Paid:** Many apps have a price you pay up front to use the app. Prices range from a dollar or two for simple apps up to a few tens of dollars for more sophisticated software.

>> **Subscription:** You pay a monthly or yearly fee and in return you not only get to use the app but also get regular updates. When you purchase a subscription, your Apple ID credit card is charged for each period; you can stop a subscription at any time.

Some subscriptions are updates to an app's data (just like a magazine subscription). Other subscriptions enable certain options in an app (for example, editing tools) for a repeating period of time.

>> **Freemium:** This model starts with a free version of an app. Then you can add premium levels with new functionality or options. This is also referred to as "try before you buy." Many apps offer so-called *in-app purchases*, where the app is free but you pay for extra app knickknacks. Examples of in-app purchases are additional functions or features, chips for online poker games, or music for instrument apps.

Shopping in the App Store

The App Store is a great place to look for new apps to add to your Mac. In this section and the next, I give you a quick rundown of how the App Store is organized and how to use it to purchase and download apps.

REMEMBER

Like the iTunes Store, the App Store is an online service, so you need to have an active internet connection to browse, purchase, and download apps. You also need an Apple ID, so head for Book 1, Chapter 3 to get yours if you don't have one already.

When you first click the App Store from the dock or Launchpad, a window opens similar to the one shown in Figure 5-16.

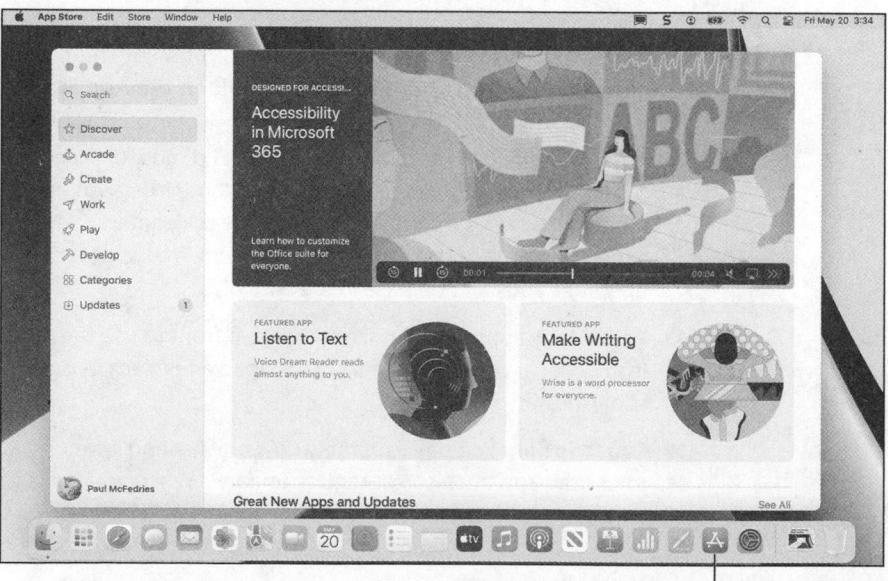

FIGURE 5-16:
The App Store window.

App Store icon

The App Store window is divided into two panes. The left pane contains different areas of the app such as Discover, Arcade, Create, Work, and Play. The right pane of the window displays the contents of whatever area you select in the left pane.

The App Store opens with the Discover area displayed, which shows some featured apps and a long list of sections designed to help you discover great new apps. These sections change constantly, but you usually find the following:

» **Great New Apps and Updates:** This section contains a list of newly released and updated apps and games. These are probably the equivalent of paid ads. Click a link to learn more about the featured software and purchase it if it floats your boat.

» **Optimized for Mac with M1:** This section features apps that have been updated to take advantage of the features of Apple's M1 processor. (You see this section only if your Mac runs Apple silicon.)

» **Great iPhone and iPad Apps for Mac with M1:** This section features iOS (iPhone) and iPadOS (iPad) apps that you can run on your Mac without modification. (You see this section only if your Mac runs Apple silicon.)

» **Top Free Apps and Top Free Games:** These sections feature the most popular free apps and games. Click the See All link to expand either list to see the complete list of free app or games. Click a link to learn more about the app and possibly add it to your treasure trove of apps.

» **Top Paid Apps and Top Paid Games:** These sections feature the most popular paid apps and games. Click the See All link to expand either list to see the complete list of free app or games. Click a link to learn more about the app or purchase it.

» **Editor's Choice:** This section features apps that the Apple staff currently like.

» **Quick Links:** This section has links that, when clicked, give you more information about in-app purchases and other App Store information.

When you find an app that interests you, click the app name or icon to open the app information screen. You'll see the name and description for the current version of the app (see Figure 5-17), and also these items:

» **Price/Get button:** If you're looking at a paid app, this button tells you the price, If you're looking at a free app, the button is named Get, instead.

» **Sample images:** In the center of the window, you see several sample images that you can click through to see what the app looks like and get an idea of how it works.

>> **Ratings and Reviews:** Users can give a simple star rating, from zero to five, or write a review. Reviews help you decide if the item is worth downloading or purchasing.

>> **Information box:** Check here for the category, release date, version number, language used, age-appropriate rating, and system requirements.

>> **More By:** Lists other apps by the same developer.

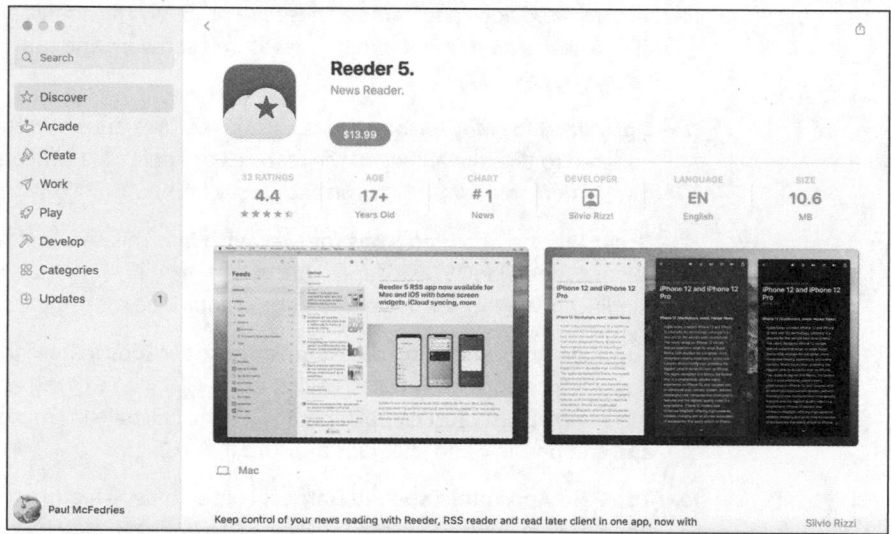

FIGURE 5-17:
The information screen helps you decide whether to purchase or download an app.

The information on the app you're reviewing for purchase may be slightly different. For example, if this is an upgrade or revision from a previous version of the app, you'll see a section called What's New. And, of course, the whole thing may change when Apple decides to try something different.

Setting up a payment method from the App Store

If you plan on downloading one or more paid apps (or free apps that offer in-app purchases), you need a way to pay from your Apple ID account. In most countries, payment can happen in one of two ways:

>> **By using a payment method such as a credit card, a debit card, Apple Pay, or a PayPal account:** If you didn't enter a payment method when you created an Apple ID, you can do so from the App Store by choosing Store ⇨

Account. This displays recent purchases. Click Account Settings and then click the Manage Payments link that appears to the right of Payment Information. In the window that opens, click Add Payment and enter the payment information for the method you want to use.

>> **From your Apple ID balance:** You can add funds to your Apple ID in two ways:

- *Transferring funds from your default Apple ID payment method:* Choose Store ⇨ Account and then click Account Settings to open the Account Information window. In the Apple Account section, click Add Money and then click an amount. The App Store transfers the funds from your Apple ID's default payment method and your new balance appears in the Apple Account section of the Account Information window.

- *Redeem an Apple Gift Card:* Choose Store ⇨ Account, click Redeem Gift Card to open the Redeem Code window, type the gift card code, and then click Redeem. The amount of the card or certificate is added to your account.

REMEMBER

However you choose to pay for your app purchases, a prompt asks for your password to confirm your intent before making the final purchase. (This prompt may not be shown for some free apps.)

Downloading apps from the App Store

When you find something you like in the App Store, do one of the following to download it:

>> **Free app:** Click Get, and then click Install.

>> **Paid app:** Click the price button, click Buy App, and then click Buy when App Store asks you to confirm.

Either way, if you're prompted to sign in with your Apple ID, enter your Apple ID email address, click Get, enter your Apple ID password, and then click Get one last time.

In short order, your new app is downloaded to the Applications folder and you find the icon on Launchpad on your Mac.

If you ever have a problem with a purchase, follow these steps:

1. Go to https://reportaproblem.apple.com/.

2. Enter the Apple ID and password that you used to buy the item, and then click Sign In.

3. **Choose your problem from the menu.**

4. **Follow the onscreen steps.**

TIP

If you want to limit the types of downloads that others who use your Mac can make, you can set up separate user accounts and apply Parental Controls. If you apply Parental Controls to your account, those controls apply to you as well. See Book 3, Chapter 3.

Updating Apps and System Software

Developers are constantly working to improve and enhance their apps or fix bugs that have been pointed out by disgruntled customers. Likewise, when Apple offers an operating system upgrade, developers must update their apps to make them compatible with the new version of macOS. You want to keep your apps up to date to take advantage of these improvements.

Updating your apps

A badge on the App Store's Updates heading lets you know when any apps you downloaded from the App Store have updates that need to be installed.

Click Updates to see what's available, as shown in Figure 5-18. You now have two choices:

» To update a single app, click the app's Update button.

» To update every app that has an available update, click the Update All link.

FIGURE 5-18:
Open the Updates area of the App Store to see what apps need updating.

This badge tells you how many apps need updating

Updating macOS

When macOS has an available update, you see a badge on the dock's System Settings icon (as shown in Figure 5-19). macOS updates almost always contain crucial security fixes, so you should always install an available update as soon as possible.

WARNING

macOS updates can take a half an hour or more to download and install, so run an update only at a time when you won't need your Mac for a while.

To install an update:

1. **Save all your work and close your open apps.**

2. **Click the dock's System Settings icon (or choose ⇨ System Settings).**

3. **Click General in the sidebar and then click Software Update.**

   The Software Update settings appear and tell you which version of macOS is available (refer to Figure 5-19).

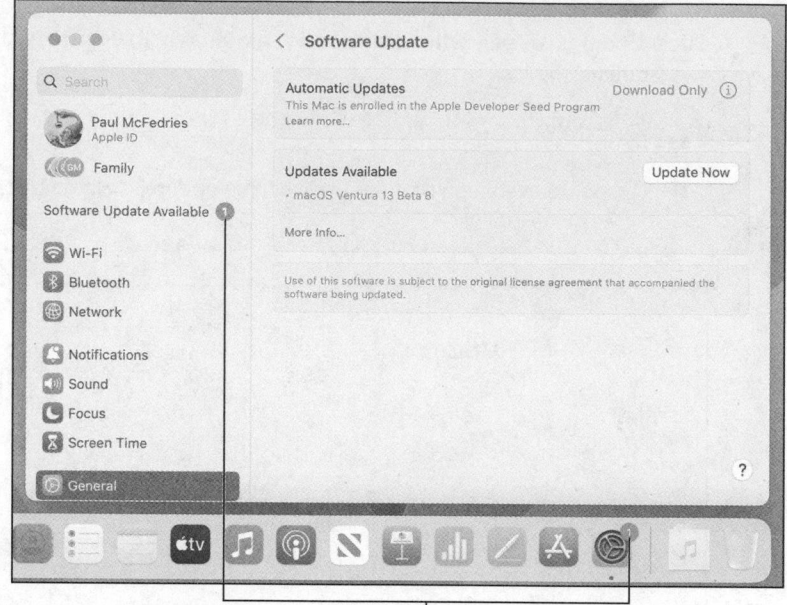

FIGURE 5-19:
Open the
Software Update
settings to
install a pending
macOS update.

These badges usually mean a macOS update is available.

4. **Click Update Now.**

   The legalese of the macOS software license agreement shows up.

5. **Click Agree.**

   macOS asks for your Mac account password.

6. **Type your Mac account password and then click OK.**

   The macOS update downloads (which usually takes a while since these updates tend to be multi-gigabyte behemoths) and then installs. Your Mac will almost always restart during this process (which is why I asked you to save your work in Step 1).

Automating the update process

You can set up your Mac to automatically check for updates to macOS and apps downloaded from the App Store by following these steps:

1. **Choose ⇨ System Settings (or click the System Settings icon on the dock).**

2. **Click General in the sidebar and then click Software Update.**

3. **Click the *i*-in-a-circle (info) to the right of Automatic Updates.**

The Automatically dialog appears with switches for each software update setting.

4. **To automate macOS updates, click the following three switches to On:**

   - Check for Updates

   - Download New Updates when Available

   - Install macOS Updates

5. **To automate app updates, click the Install App Updates from the App Store switch on.**

6. **Click Done.**

   When prompted, enter your Mac admin account password to allow these changes.

Your Mac now automatically checks for and installs any updates that come down the pipe for macOS and your installed apps.

WARNING

The automatic update process is safe and you shouldn't lose any data. Note my use of the word *shouldn't*. Not very reassuring, is it? Sorry, but there *is* a small possibility that you could lose unsaved changes during the update process. Therefore, I highly recommend that at the end of each workday you save all your work and shut down all your apps.

Uninstalling Apps

If you no longer use or need an app or if it's an old version that is no longer compatible with your macOS version, you can always remove the app from your hard drive. Since the process of adding an app to your Mac is called *installing*, you won't be a bit surprised to learn that the process of removing an app from your Mac is called *uninstalling*. By uninstalling an app, you free up space on your hard drive and make your Applications folder a bit less cluttered.

REMEMBER

An app downloaded from the App Store remains available in your purchase records even if you remove the app from your hard drive. You can download the app again in the future, as long it's still available.

Uninstalling a Mac app is typically as simple as dragging and dropping its app icon into the trash. If you've purchased an app in the App Store, you can remove it via Launchpad, and I explain how later in this section. Apps that are preinstalled on your Mac are extremely difficult to remove; I suggest that you don't try to remove them.

To uninstall an app, follow these steps:

1. **Make sure that the app you want to uninstall isn't running. If it is running, shut it down by choosing the Quit command (⌘+Q).**

2. **Click the Finder icon on the dock.**

   Finder appears.

3. **Click the Applications folder in the Finder sidebar to display the apps installed on your Mac, and then click the app icon you want to uninstall.**

   You can display installed apps also by choosing Go⇨Applications or by pressing Shift+⌘+A.

   If the app is in a folder, open the folder before deleting it. Many companies that sell apps store them all in a folder. (Microsoft 365 is a good example of this.) If the folder contains multiple apps, select the desired app and go to Step 4. If the folder contains an uninstaller for the program you want to remove, run it and say, "Adios" to the program.

4. **Choose File ⇨ Move to Trash.**

   Alternatively, you can drag the app icon or folder to the trash icon on the dock, or press ⌘+Delete to move the app icon or folder to the trash.

   TIP

   In some cases, you might be prompted for your administrator password when you move an app file to the trash. If so, type your password and then click OK or press Return.

   WARNING

   Before emptying the trash, make sure that you want to permanently delete any other apps or documents you might have dragged into the trash. After you empty the trash, any files contained therein are deleted from your hard drive forever.

5. **Choose Finder ⇨ Empty Trash.**

   Alternatively, you can right-click the trash icon and choose Empty Trash or press ⌘+Shift+Delete to empty the trash. The keyboard shortcut works only when you're applying it from the desktop.

TIP

From Launchpad, you can delete apps purchased in the App Store. Hold down the Option key, and all the icons begin to wiggle and jiggle. Those you can delete from the Launchpad have an X in the upper left. Click the X. A confirmation dialog asks whether you really want to delete the app. Click Delete if you do; click Cancel if you don't.

Paying Attention to App Security

Apple makes it easy to keep your Mac free from the worst malware hazards by implementing a technology called Gatekeeper. To see how Gatekeeper works, choose ⟹ System Settings and then click Privacy & Security. In the Security section (see Figure 5-20), you see the Allow Apps Downloaded From setting, which offers two options:

>> **App Store:** Select this option to allow your Mac to install only apps that you get via the App Store.

>> **App Store and Identified Developers:** Select this option to allow your Mac to install only apps that you get via the App Store and from identified developers. An *identified developer* is one that is known to Apple and offers apps checked by Apple before they're released. The checks are designed for two critical security concerns:

- Does the app run and does it run as described in the documentation?

- Does the app contain code that could cause damage to the device or to other apps?

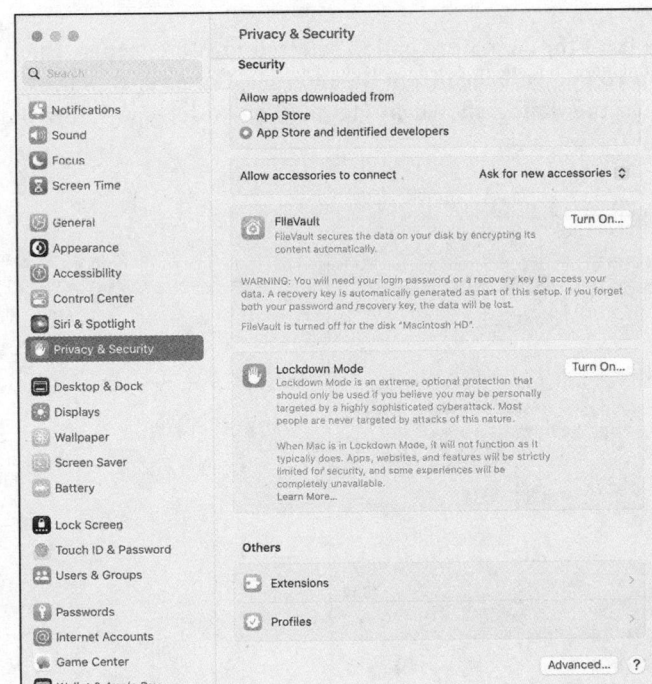

FIGURE 5-20:
The Gatekeeper options ensure that only software checked by Apple can be installed on your Mac.

If you have the App Store and Identified Developers option selected for Gate-keeper, when you download an app from a website (rather than getting it from the App Store) and try to install the app, Gatekeeper displays the dialog shown in Figure 5-21 to confirm that you want to proceed. Click Open if you're sure or click Cancel if you have second (or third) thoughts.

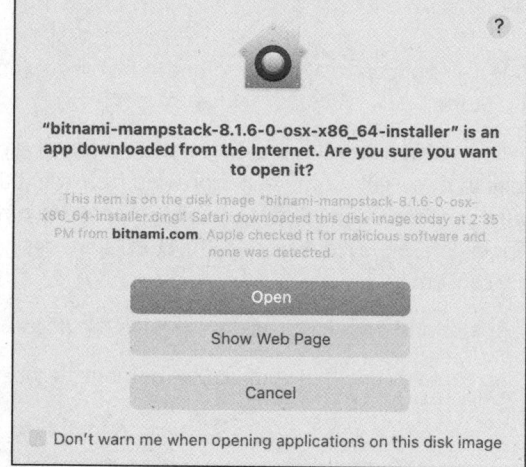

FIGURE 5-21:
With Gatekeeper on the job, you Mac asks you to confirm whenever you try to install an app downloaded from the internet.

If you have the App Store option selected for Gatekeeper, when you try to install an app you downloaded from the internet, Gatekeeper wags its finger at you and displays the dialog shown in Figure 5-22 to let you know that it's refusing to launch the installer.

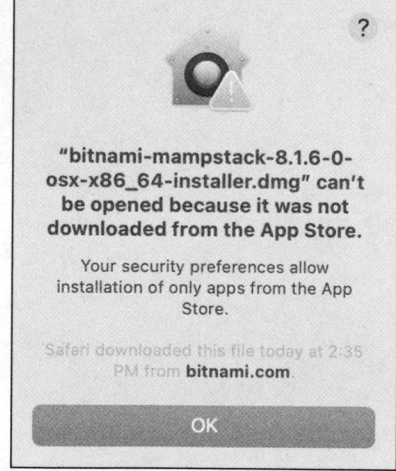

FIGURE 5-22:
With Gatekeeper set to allow only apps from the App Store, it will refuse to install anything you download from the internet.

Too bad for you, right? Not necessarily. If you're absolutely certain — I'm talking 1,000% certain — the app is from a legit developer, you can launch the app installation anyway by following these steps:

1. **Attempt to install the app and, when you see the dialog presented earlier in Figure 5-21, click OK.**

2. **Choose ⇨ System Settings (or click System Settings on the dock).**

3. **Click Privacy & Security.**

In the Security section, you now see a message that says the app you just tried to install was blocked, as shown in Figure 5-23.

4. **Click Open Anyway.**

Gatekeeper asks if you're sure about this.

5. **Click Open.**

Gatekeeper allows the installation to proceed.

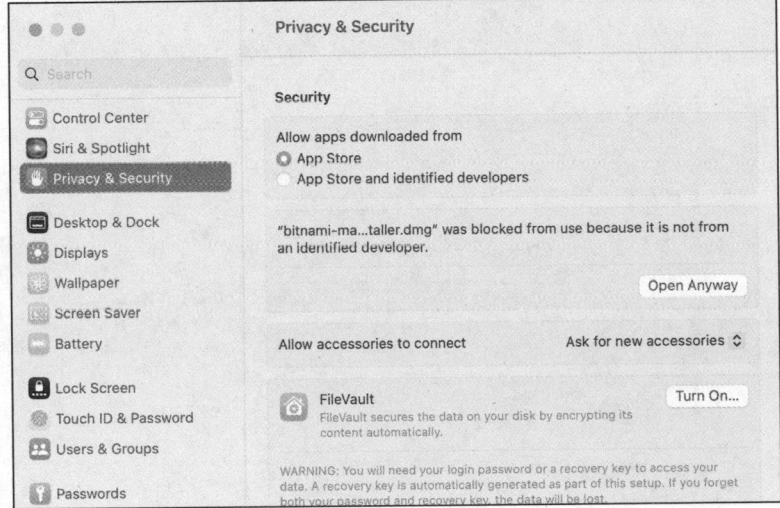

FIGURE 5-23: When Gatekeeper blocks an app installation, you see a message to that effect under the Gatekeeper options.

IN THIS CHAPTER

» Changing the desktop, display, and dock

» Setting the date and time

» Adjusting alert sounds

» Taking control of notifications

» Working in split-screen mode

Chapter **6**

Changing How Your Mac Looks, Sounds, and Feels

O ne of the hallmarks of being a human being is the uncontrollable urge to put a personal stamp on things. We show the world our personal style through the clothes we wear and the haircuts we get; we decorate our homes inside and out; we pierce this and tattoo that. A cookie-cutter life? Not for us, thanks.

That sense of (optionally rugged) individuality extends to your Mac, too. At the factory, your Mac is configured with the appearance, sounds, and overall feel that Apple thinks are a good fit for most people. But Apple certainly doesn't know you or have the slightest inkling of your personal style or how you like to work and play. A cookie-cutter Mac? Not for us, thanks.

In this chapter, I show you how to customize your Mac so that you can thumb your nose at Apple's herd-based settings and put the "personal" in personal computer. Here you explore many of the settings found in System Settings. I show you how to customize your desktop image, set up screen savers, and adjust the screen resolution. I explain how to use Notification Center and how to set the date and time.

Navigating System and App Settings

Before getting down to the nitty-gritty of specific Mac customizations, let's take a step back and get to know how they work in macOS. Configuration options and preferences are known in the Mac universe as *settings*. That's a good name for them because it speaks to the heart of the matter: You customize and configure your Mac and its applications because you prefer to set up your system in that way. It really is as simple as that, and you'll soon see that locating and working with Mac settings is usually a quick and painless process.

WARNING

If you're coming to the Mac from Windows, you should know right off the bat that when you change Mac settings there's more potential for making a mistake than when you set Windows options. In Windows, configuration options and settings appear in a dialog box, and you generally click OK to apply your changes, or you click Cancel if you change your mind or make a mistake. Not so in the Mac scheme of things. In most cases, as soon as you modify a setting, the new setting goes into effect immediately, and the only way to cancel the change is to revert the setting to its previous setting. Bear that in mind as you work with settings on your Mac.

Messing with the system settings

The macOS *system settings* help you configure and customize various aspects of your Mac, including colors, desktop background, security, power settings, user accounts, and software updates. A default Mac setup comes with nearly three dozen system setting categories, and third-party programs sometimes add new categories to the settings.

To view the system settings, your Mac gives you two choices:

>> Click the System Settings icon on the dock.

>> Choose ⇨ System Settings.

Either way, the System Settings window appears, as shown in Figure 6-1.

For the most part, you set system settings by using the following general procedure:

1. **In the sidebar that runs along the left side of the System Settings window, click the item that represents the settings you want to work with.**

Your Mac displays the settings.

2. **If the displayed settings offer categories, click the category you want to work with.**

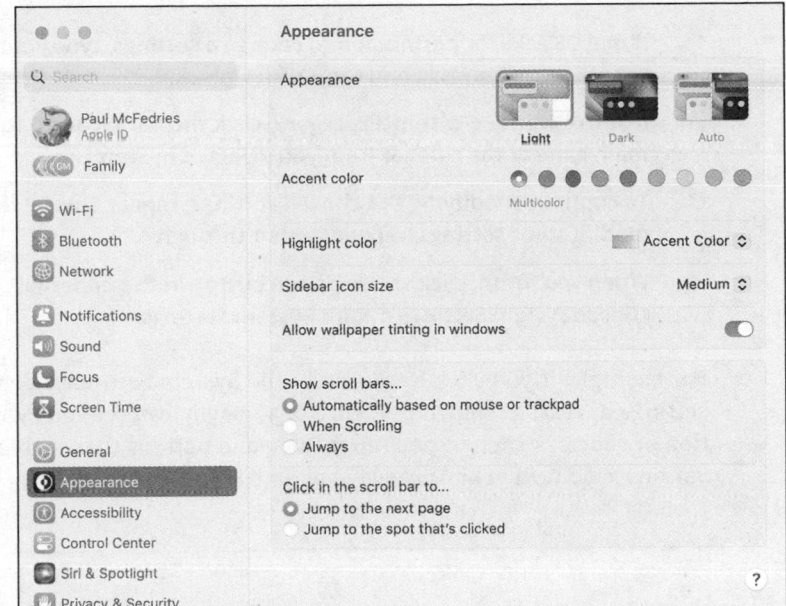

FIGURE 6-1:
Use the System
Settings app
to customize
and configure
your Mac.

3. Make your changes to the settings.

The Mac settings appear as controls such as text boxes, on/off switches, check boxes, option buttons, pop-up menus, and lists.

If you change a setting that deals with security or privacy, macOS prompts you for your Mac's administrator account password, as shown in Figure 6-2.

If you're the only person who uses your Mac, you're the administrator, so your Mac username should already be filled in. To learn more about the different Mac user account types, see Book 3, Chapter 3.

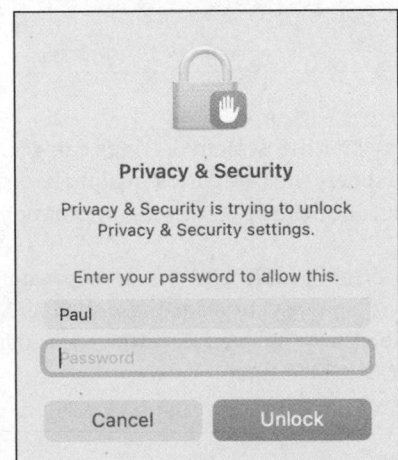

FIGURE 6-2:
Your Mac
requires a
password to
unlock important
settings to avoid
unauthorized
changes.

4. **If macOS asks for permission to change a settings, type your administrator account password and then click Unlock.**

5. **If you're working within a category, click the back icon (<) to return to the main pane of the sidebar item you selected in Step 1.**

6. **To continue modifying the chosen settings, repeat Steps 2 through 4; to modify other settings, repeat Steps 1 through 4.**

7. **When you finish, click the red close button in the upper-left corner or choose System Settings ⇨ Quit System Settings.**

For example, if you click Keyboard in the System Settings sidebar, the Keyboard settings appear, as shown in Figure 6-3. As you can see, this window is a collection of sliders, switches, pop-up menus, and buttons that enable you to configure various aspects of your Mac's keyboard.

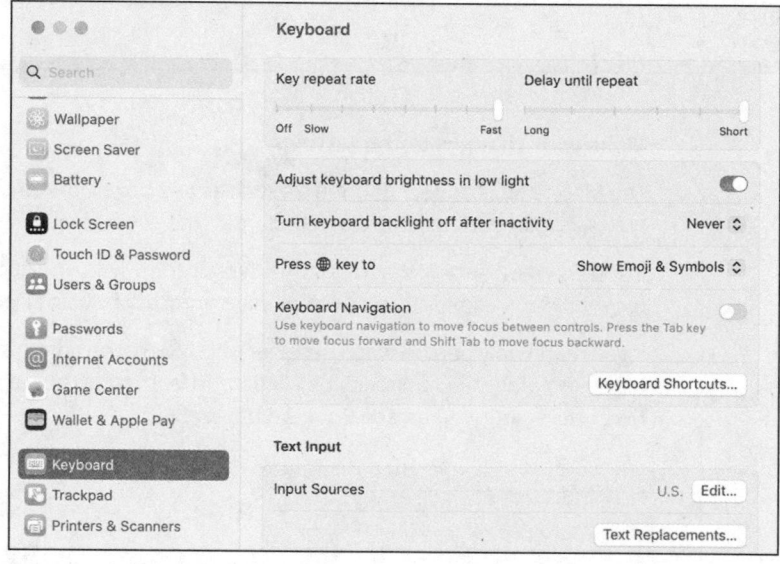

FIGURE 6-3:
In System Settings, click Keyboard to customize your Mac's keyboard.

TIP

You can directly jump to many specific System Settings categories by clicking the View menu (which handily displays the categories in alphabetical order) and then clicking the category you want in the drop-down menu that appears.

REMEMBER

If you share your Mac with other people and set up separate user accounts as explained in Book 3, Chapter 3, some system settings, such as Network or Date & Time apply to all users, while others, such as Desktop & Dock as well as app settings, are specific to the user who sets them.

Tweaking app settings

The system settings let you configure your Mac as a whole, but almost all Mac apps are customizable as well, and they come with their own collection of settings. If you're used to the Windows way of things, you know that locating the settings for Windows programs is often a frustrating guessing game. Happily, there's no guessing when it comes to finding the settings for Mac apps. That's because on the menu bar for every Mac app, you see the name of the app next to the Apple menu. To view the app's settings, click the app name in the menu bar and then click Settings.

For example, click any empty section of the desktop to display the Finder menu bar, click Finder, and then click Settings.

Figure 6-4 shows the Finder Settings window that appears. This is a typical app settings window in that it displays several icons across the top: General, Tags, Sidebar, and Advanced. These icons represent the different categories of settings that the app provides. Click an icon to see the settings associated with that category. These icons are usually called tabs (the term I use in this book) or panels.

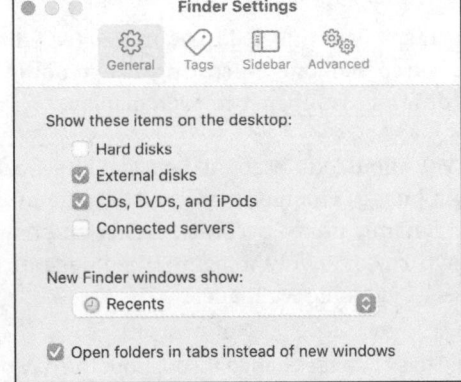

FIGURE 6-4:
The Finder Settings window is divided into four tabs: General, Tags, Sidebar, and Advanced.

TIP

In all Mac apps that have settings (and that's the vast majority of Mac apps) you can open the app settings also by pressing ⌘+, (comma).

Here's the general procedure to follow when you work with app settings:

1. **In the macOS menu bar, click the menu named after the app and then click Settings.**

   The application displays its settings. For example, click an empty section of the desktop and then choose Finder ➪ Settings to open the Finder Settings window shown in Figure 6-4.

2. **Click the tab that contains the settings you want to modify.**

3. **Make your changes to the settings.**

   As with the system settings, app settings appear as controls such as text boxes, check boxes, switches, option buttons, pop-up menus, and lists.

4. **Repeat Steps 2 and 3 to set other app settings.**

5. **When you finish, click the close button or press Esc.**

Trying Out a New Desktop Wallpaper

By default, the desktop displays a decorative background image, which is for some reason called a *wallpaper*. (Do *you* know of anyone who has wallpapered their desk?) Perhaps surprisingly, that image isn't set in stone because you're free to wallpaper your desktop with a different image. Your Mac comes with several ready-to-use desktop wallpapers, but you can display any image you want, such as a photo shot with your mobile device. (Head over to Book 4, Chapter 4 to learn more about working with photos on your Mac.)

TIP

If you have two or more displays connected to your Mac (as I discuss a bit later in the "Two monitors are better than one: Mirroring or extending the display" section), you can assign a different wallpaper to each display.

Before getting started, you should know about a special effect called *dynamic wall-paper*, in which dynamic images change to match the time of day. For example, as night comes on, the dynamic image becomes darker and may even show stars and the moon; when daytime come around again, the image turns lighter. macOS Ventura offers two types of dynamic wallpaper:

>> **Dynamic Desktop:** These images change throughout the day by increasing (when it's light) or decreasing (when it's dark) the overall brightness of the image.

>> **Light & Dark Desktop:** These images change throughout the day by inverting the image colors (lighter colors change to darker colors and vice versa).

If you don't like having your desktop wallpaper change in this way, you can select a static (or *still*) wallpaper that's always light or always dark.

To select a new desktop wallpaper, follow these steps:

1. **Right-click anywhere on the desktop and choose Change Wallpaper.**

   Or you can choose System Settings (or click the System Settings icon on the dock) and then click Wallpaper in the sidebar.

   The Wallpaper settings appear, as shown in Figure 6-5.

   The monitor preview at the top shows you what your desktop looks like with the current wallpaper; this preview changes as you select different wallpapers.

   Below the preview, you see the name of the current wallpaper (in Figure 6-5, the name is Ventura Graphic); to the right of the name, you see a control that enables you to customize the wallpaper. The control you see depends on the type of wallpaper you select.

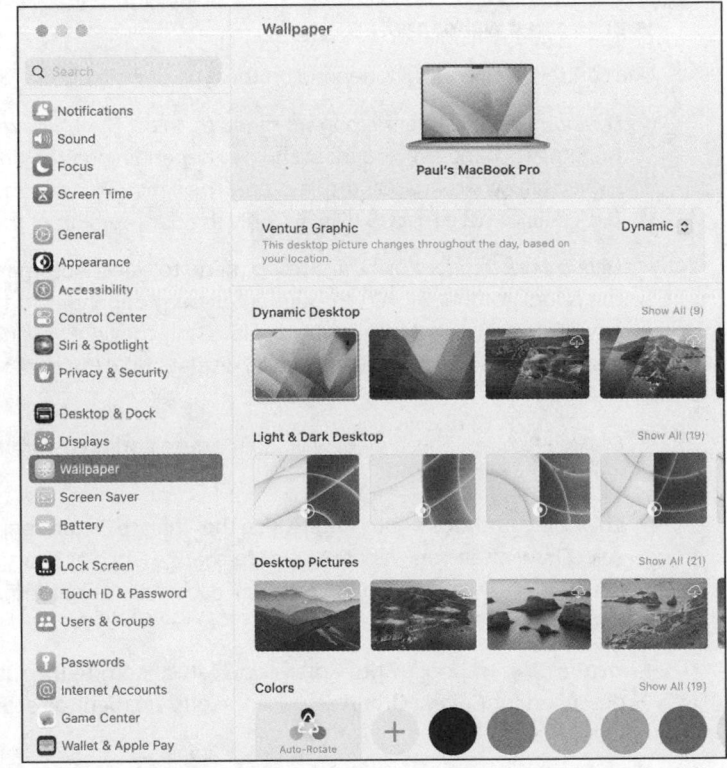

FIGURE 6-5:
Wallpaper settings let you choose a different desktop image or color.

2. **In each of the sections — Dynamic Desktop, Light & Dark Desktop, Desktop Pictures, Colors, and Pictures — you can see all available wallpapers either by scrolling the strip of thumbnails to the left, or by clicking Show All to expand the section.**

3. **Click the wallpaper you want to use.**

Some sections offer extra controls to help you make a selection:

- *Colors:* Instead of clicking an existing color swatch, you can click + (add) and then use the controls in the Colors dialog (such as the color wheel) to specify the color you want to use as a desktop background. Another possibility is to click Auto-Rotate, which tells macOS to cycle through different wallpaper colors throughout the day.

- *Pictures:* Click Auto-Rotate to tell macOS to cycle periodically through the images in your user account's Pictures folder. To add another folder to the Wallpaper pane, click Add Folder, use the chooser dialog to navigate to and select the folder that contains the images you want to use, and then click Choose. If you have a photo album that contains the images you want, use the Add Photo Album pop-up menu to select the album.

4. **Use the control (or controls) below the desktop preview to customize your selected wallpaper.**

The controls you work with depend on the type of wallpaper:

- *Dynamic Desktop:* Use the pop-up menu to select Dynamic, where the brightness changes throughout the day depending on the time of day; Light (Still), where macOS displays only the light version of the image; or Dark (Still), where macOS displays only the dark version of the image.

- *Light & Dark Desktop:* Use the pop-up menu to select Automatic, in which the colors gradually invert throughout the day depending on the time of day; Light (Still), in which macOS displays only the light version of the image; or Dark (Still), in which macOS displays only the dark version of the image.

- *Desktop Pictures:* This type of wallpaper doesn't offer customization controls.

- *Colors:* If you choose Auto-Rotate, use the Change Picture pop-up menu to select how often you want the color to change (such as Every 30 Minutes or Every Hour). If you want macOS to pick each color at random, select the Randomly check box.

- *Pictures:* If you choose Auto-Rotate, you can customize the rotation as described for Colors. Otherwise, use the pop-up menu to select one of the following:

  Fill Screen: Expands the image in all four directions until it fills the entire desktop. The image may be cropped if the image aspect ratio is different from that of the screen.

Fit to Screen: Expands the image in all four directions until the image is the same height as the desktop (or, in some cases, the same width as the desktop). If the aspect ratio does not match that of the screen, there will be blank space on the left and right side of the image (or in some cases, above and below the image). In that case, you can click the color swatch to the right of the pop-up menu and then select the color you want to use for the blank spaces.

Stretch to Fill Screen: Expands the image in all four directions until it fills the entire desktop, but it might increase the width or height nonproportionately if the image aspect ratio does not match that of the screen.

Center: Centers the image on the screen without resizing the image. If you choose an image that's smaller than the desktop, white space will appear around the image. Again, you can click the color swatch to the right of the pop-up menu and then select a color to fill the blank spaces

5. **To close the System Settings window, click the red close icon in the upper-left corner of the window.**

   Or choose System Settings ⇨ Quit or press ⌘+Q.

Setting Up a Screen Saver

A *screen saver* is an animated image that appears onscreen after a fixed time interval when your Mac doesn't detect any keyboard, trackpad, or mouse activity. When selecting a screen saver, you can choose an image to display and the amount of time to wait before the screen saver starts.

TIP

For an eco-friendlier alternative to using the screen saver, you can configure your Mac to turn off its display after a specified amount of idle time; see Book 3, Chapter 2.

To choose and configure a screen saver, follow these steps:

1. **Choose ⇨ System Settings or click the System Settings icon on the dock.**

2. **In the System Settings sidebar, click Screen Saver.**

   The Screen Saver settings appear, as shown in Figure 6-6.

3. **Click the screen saver you want to use.**

4. **If your chosen screen saver can be customized, click Options to see a dialog that contains the settings you can modify.**

FIGURE 6-6:
You can choose
your screen saver
on the Screen
Saver pane.

For screen savers that require an image source, use the Source pop-up menu to choose where you want the screen saver to get its images:

- *Colors:* Click this command to have the screen saver style use random colors.

- *Choose Folders:* Click this command to select the folder from which the screen saver style get its images.

- *Photo Library:* Click this command to select which Photos app library you want the screen saver style to use for its images.

For source-based screen savers, you can also select the Shuffle Slide Order check box to have the screen saver style display the source images in random order.

5. **When you're finished working with the screen saver options, click Done.**

6. **(Optional) Click the Show with Clock switch on to display the time with your screen saver.**

TIP

To learn how to set the idle time interval after which your screen saver kicks in, see Book 3, Chapter 2. You can also use a hot corner to invoke the screen saver whenever you feel like it; see "Enabling hot corners," later in this chapter.

7. **To close the System Settings window, click the red close icon in the upper-left corner of the window.**

   Alternatively, choose System Settings ➪ Quit or press ⌘+Q.

Remodeling the Display

Because you'll be staring at your Mac's screen a lot, you might want to modify how the screen looks and how it shows information. Some changes you can make include altering the brightness, changing the desktop size (resolution), and selecting another color scheme for the onscreen menus, windows, and dialogs. The next few sections take you through all these and more.

Adjusting the screen brightness

The screen *brightness* is a measure of the underlying luminosity of the screen. If you find that your Mac's display is either so bright that everything appears washed out or so dark that you can't read anything, you should adjust the brightness to solve the problem. Your Mac gives you four ways to adjust the brightness:

» **Control Center:** Click the menu bar's Control Center icon near the upper-right corner of the screen, then drag the Display slider left (darker) or right (brighter) as needed.

» **System Settings:** Choose ➪ System Settings, click Displays in the sidebar, and then drag the Brightness slider left (darker) or right (brighter) as needed.

» **Automatic:** Choose ➪ System Settings, click Displays in the sidebar, and then click the Automatically Adjust Brightness switch on to have your Mac automatically set the optimum screen brightness based on the ambient light.

» **Keyboard:** Press F1 to decrease the display brightness; press F2 to increase the display brightness.

Setting the screen resolution

Your Mac's screen is composed of teensy dots called *pixels*, each of which can display multiple colors. Amazingly, everything you see on the screen consists of these pixels. So why don't the items you see on your screen look all jagged and pointillist? It's because the pixels are so small and packed together so tightly that everything looks smooth from the normal viewing distance.

The pixels are arranged in a grid that consists of a certain number of columns and a certain number of rows. The number of columns and rows determines the *resolution* of the screen, and the current resolution affects how your screen looks as follows:

>> **The higher the resolution,** the more pixels there are to display what's onscreen, so the sharper the image but the smaller everything appears.

>> **The lower the resolution,** the fewer pixels there are to display what's onscreen, so the less sharp the image but the larger everything appears.

TECHNICAL
STUFF

When dealing with resolution, you often need to know the difference between physical pixels and display pixels. *Physical pixels* are the actual pixels that are part of the display itself; the number of physical pixels is fixed and can't be changed. *Display pixels* are the pixels that your Mac sends to the display; display pixels depend on the resolution you set, which means the number of display pixels varies depending on the current resolution.

In other words, if you have good eyesight (or strong glasses) and you want your screen to look its best, go with a higher resolution. If your eyesight isn't what it used to be and you don't mind giving up a bit of image quality, go with a lower resolution.

WARNING

Confusingly, selecting your Mac display's highest possible resolution isn't always the best strategy. Every display comes with a *native* or *default* resolution. When you use this default resolution, it means that the pixels macOS sends to the display precisely line up with the physical pixels of the display itself. This puts your Mac's best face forward, so to speak, because it makes everything look sharp and correct on your screen. You usually can choose a higher resolution than this default, but screen performance will suffer if you do.

To change the screen resolution, follow these steps:

1. **Choose ⇨ System Settings or click the System Settings icon on the dock.**

2. **In the System Settings sidebar, click Displays.**

   The Displays pane appears, as shown in Figure 6-7.

3. **Select one of the following:**

   - *Default:* Sets the resolution to the native resolution of the display.

   - *Scaled:* Choose one of the thumbnail images on either side of Default to set a lower or higher resolution. From left to right, the resolutions run from lower to higher, with the lowest resolution marked as Larger Text on the far left and the highest resolution marked as More Space on the far right.

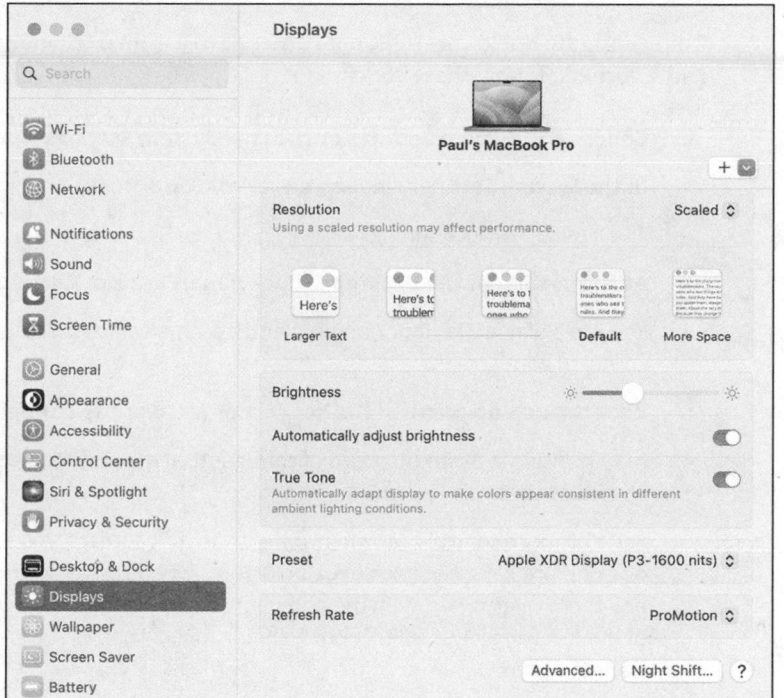

FIGURE 6-7:
Use the Displays
pane to change
the display
resolution.

TIP

Hover the mouse pointer over a thumbnail to see a tooltip that shows you the exact resolution (such as 2560 x 1440, which means 2,560 pixel columns by 1,440 pixel rows).

Your Mac immediately changes the resolution so you can see how it looks. If you don't like the resolution, try again until you find one that's easy on your eyes.

4. **When you're happy with the screen resolution, click the close button in the System Settings window.**

Enabling hot corners

A *hot corner* is a corner of your display that acts as a trigger for some action when you move the mouse pointer to that corner. By default, macOS uses the lower-right corner to trigger the Quick Note feature, which enables you to quickly crank out a note using the Notes app.

To reconfigure the lower-right hot corner or to assign a trigger to any of the other three corners, follow these steps:

1. **Choose ⇨ System Settings or click the System Settings icon on the dock.**

2. **In the System Settings sidebar, click Desktop & Dock.**

   The Desktop & Dock settings appear.

3. **At the bottom of the Desktop & Dock pane, click Hot Corners.**

   You see a dialog with four pop-up menus, each of which corresponds to a corner of your screen.

4. **Click the pop-up menu of the hot corner you want to configure.**

   macOS displays a pop-up menu of commands that you can assign to the hot corner, as shown in Figure 6-8.

   TIP

   For a bit more control over when you activate hot corners, you can also specify one or more keys that need to be held down when you move the mouse pointer to that corner. With the pop-up menu displayed, hold down or more of the following keys: Shift, Control, Option, or ⌘. Then click the command you want to assign.

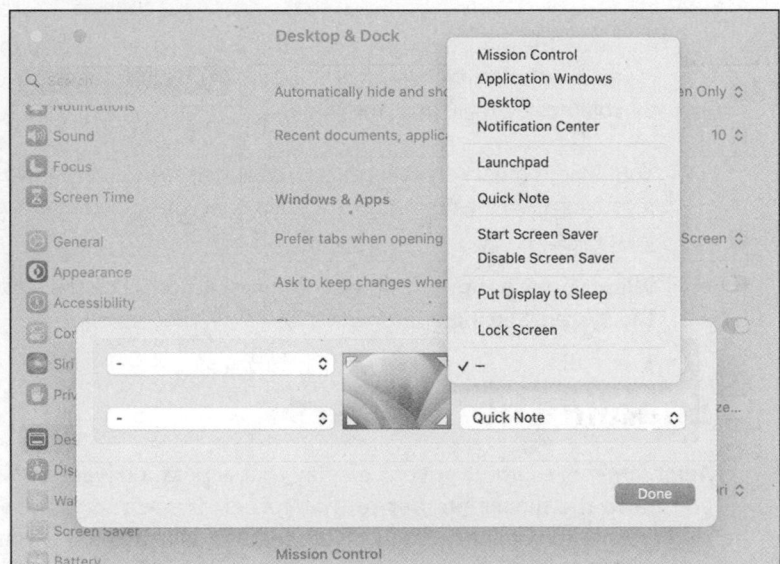

FIGURE 6-8:
Each pop-up menu defines a function for its corresponding hot corner.

5. **Click the command that you want macOS to carry out when you move the mouse pointer to that corner.**

6. **Repeat Steps 4 and 5 to define other hot corners you want to use.**

TIP

You can define multiple hot corners to do the same task, such as defining the two top corners to start the screen saver and the two bottom corners to put the display to sleep.

7. **Click Done.**

8. **To close the System Settings window, click the red close icon in the upper-left corner of the window.**

Alternatively, choose System Settings ➪ Quit or press ⌘+Q.

Using night shift

Clicking the Night Shift button in the Displays pane (choose ➪ System Settings ➪ Displays) lets you schedule a shift in the general colors of the screen. Research has shown that the normal bluish screen display (a cool color) can interfere with sleep, so you may get a better night's sleep by using a display biased toward the yellow end of the palette (warm) rather than blue.

Choose Custom from the Schedule pop-up menu and, as you see in Figure 6-9, you can set night shift to be active at specific times of day depending on the clock or on sunrise and sunset.

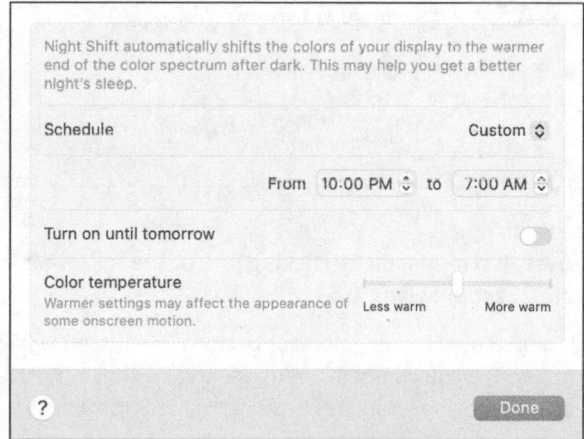

FIGURE 6-9:
Get a better night's sleep with night shift.

Repainting the screen colors

Another way to change the appearance of the screen is to modify the colors used in screen components such as windows, menus, and dialogs. To change the color of these screen items, follow these steps:

1. Choose ⌥ ➪ **System Settings or click the System Settings icon on the dock.**

2. **In the System Settings sidebar, click Appearance (if it isn't selected already).**

The Appearance settings show up, as shown in Figure 6-10.

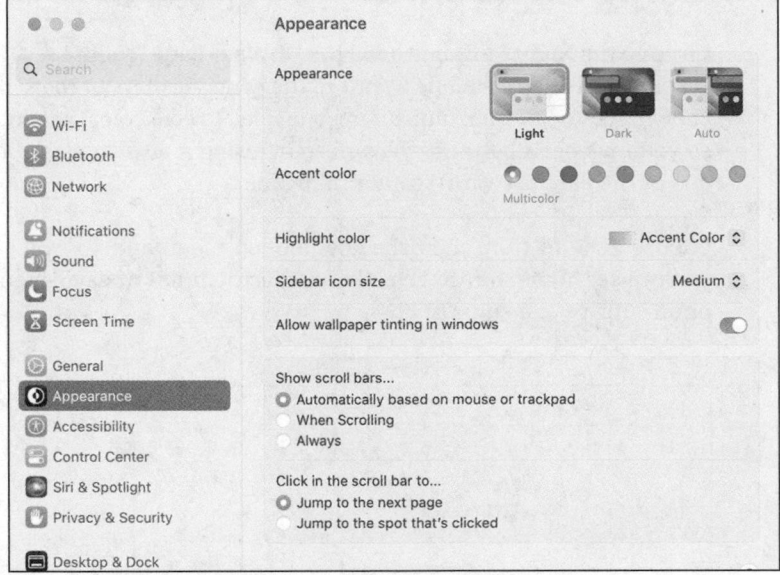

FIGURE 6-10: The Appearance pane offers a few settings to modify colors.

3. **Set the overall screen look by clicking one of the following in the Appearance section: Light, Dark, or Auto.**

The Light option uses lighter colors for buttons, menus, and windows, while the Dark option — you guessed it — uses darker colors. With the Auto option, macOS adjusts the appearance of buttons, menus, and windows throughout the day based on ambient lighting.

4. **Click the Accent Color you feel like seeing.**

macOS uses the accent color for things like pop-up menu arrows, the background of selected check boxes and option buttons, and the background of the highlighted or selected menu command.

5. **From the Highlight Color pop-up menu, choose the background color of items you select.**

6. **When you're done, click the close button in the System Settings window.**

Two monitors are better than one: Mirroring or extending the display

If you find your Mac desktop is getting a tad overcrowded, it might be time to invest in some extra real estate. I'm talking here about *screen* real estate, which you add to your Mac by connecting an external device such as a monitor or even a nearby Mac or iPad. Once the connection has been made, you can configure the external device to operate in either of the following ways:

» **Mirror the display:** The external device displays exactly what's shown on your Mac's display. Mirroring doesn't give you more room for app windows, but it's handy if you want to show a presentation or if your Mac has a relatively small screen and you want to work with a larger display.

» **Extend the display:** The external device acts as an extension of your Mac's desktop, meaning you can move app windows from your Mac's display to the external display.

Connecting an external monitor

If you have an external monitor you want to use, connect that monitor to your Mac using a cable to make an HDMI, Thunderbolt, or USB–C connection between the monitor and your Mac. Your Mac recognizes the extra monitor right away and sets it up as an extension to your Mac's desktop. To configure the extra monitor, follow these steps:

1. **Choose ⇨ System Settings or click the System Settings icon on the dock.**

2. **In the System Settings sidebar, click Displays.**

   The Displays settings appear, and you now see two display thumbnails, as shown in Figure 6-11.

3. **Click Arrange and change the display positions as needed.**

   The Arrange Displays dialog appears. Drag the desktop thumbnails to tell macOS how the displays are positioned relative to each other. For example, if the external monitor sits to the left of your Mac, drag the external monitor's thumbnail to the left of your Mac's thumbnail. This way, when you move your mouse pointer to the left edge of your Mac's display, the pointer continues naturally onto the desktop of the external monitor.

FIGURE 6-11:
With another
display connected
to your Mac, the
Displays pane
shows a display
thumbnail for
each display.

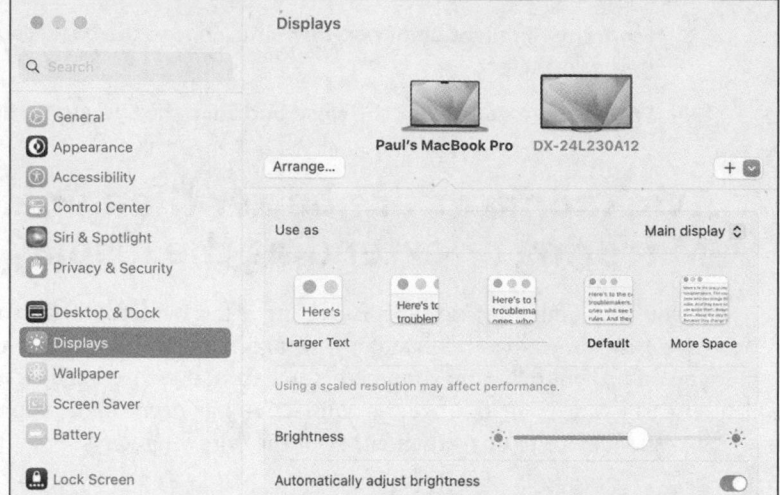

You can also drag the menu bar (the faint white strip across the top of the thumbnail of your Mac display) to a different display.

4. **Click Done when you're ready to return to the Displays pane.**

5. **Click your external monitor.**

6. **Click the Use As pop-up menu and then select how you want macOS to use the external monitor.**

   Your choices are Main Display, Extended Display, or Mirror for *Display*, where *Display* is the name of your Mac's display.

7. **(Optional) Configure settings such as the resolution and brightness.**

8. **To close the System Settings window, click the close icon in the upper-left corner of the window.**

   Alternatively, choose System Settings ➪ Quit or press ⌘+Q.

When you no longer need to use the connected display, disconnect the display's cable from your Mac.

Connecting a Mac or iPad using Sidecar

An alternative to using a cable to connect an external monitor to your Mac is to take advantage of a feature called Sidecar, which enables a Mac or an iPad on the same network and signed in with the same Apple ID to connect wirelessly as a second display. Follow these steps to add a Mac or an iPad as a display to your Mac:

1. **Make sure the Mac or iPad is on the same network as your Mac and is signed in with the same Apple ID.**

2. **Choose ⮕ System Settings or click the System Settings icon on the dock.**

3. **In the System Settings sidebar, click Displays.**

   The Displays pane appears.

4. **Click the + (add display) drop-down menu that appears below and to the right of the display thumbnail.**

   macOS displays a menu of nearby Macs and iPads that are eligible to connect.

5. **In the Mirror or Extend To section of the menu, click the Mac or iPad you want to connect.**

   Once the connection is complete, you'll see two display thumbnails (similar to what's shown earlier in Figure 6-11).

TIP

   Another way to connect a Mac or an iPad is to click the menu bar's Control Center button, click Screen Mirroring, and then click the Mac or iPad you want to use. You can then click Display Settings to continue with these steps.

6. **Configure the connected Mac or iPad as I describe in Steps 3 through 8 of the "Connecting an external monitor" section.**

When you no longer need to use the connected Mac or iPad, return to the Displays pane, click the thumbnail for the connected device, and then click Disconnect.

Renovating the Dock, Menu Bar, and Control Center

By default, the dock appears at the bottom of the screen, and the icons have a standard size. Like most things on your Mac, however, the dock is customizable. For example, you can move the dock to the left or right side of the screen, which gives you a bit more vertical space for your app windows.

The dock occupies a fixed amount of horizontal real estate at the bottom of your screen, which means the dock icons shrink a little each time you add another icon. (I explain how to add icons to the dock in Book 1, Chapter 5.) The bad news here is that if you add lots of items to the dock, the icons could become so small that you would barely be able to make out which is which. The good news here is that you can always see the name of each icon by hovering the mouse pointer over it. The even better news is that you can turn on magnification in the Desktop & Dock section of System Settings, which increases the size of the dock icons when you move the pointer over them, as shown in Figure 6-12.

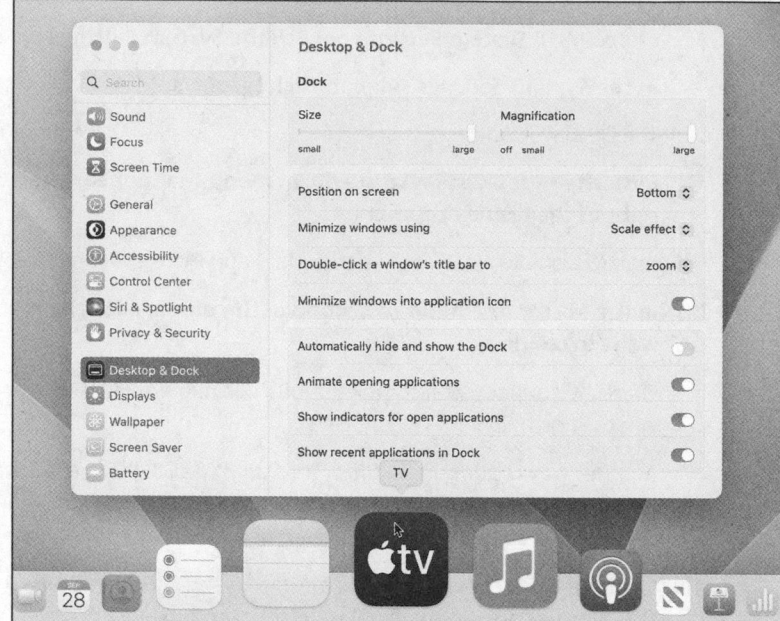

FIGURE 6-12:
With dock magnification turned on, hovering the mouse pointer over an icon increases its size for easier readability.

To make these and other changes to the dock's appearance, follow these steps:

1. Choose ➪ **System Settings or click the System Settings icon on the dock.**

2. **In the System Settings sidebar, click Desktop & Dock.**

The Desktop & Dock settings appear (refer to Figure 6-12).

3. **Drag the Size slider to adjust the size of the dock.**

When you drag the Size slider to the left to decrease the size of the dock, the icons shrink as well. Note, too, that dragging the Size slider to the right might not increase the size of the dock if it's already at its maximum width.

4. **If you want to see a larger version of any dock icon when you hover the mouse pointer over it (as demonstrated in Figure 6-12), drag the Magnification slider to adjust the magnification level that macOS applies.**

The Magnification feature is especially helpful if you have a small dock with a lot of items on it.

REMEMBER

5. **Use the Position on Screen pop-up menu to select your preferred location for the dock: Bottom, Left, or Right.**

6. **Use the Minimize Windows Using pop-up menu to select which special effect you want macOS to apply to windows that you minimize to (and restore from) the dock:**

- *Genie Effect:* The window is minimized to the dock with an effect that's reminiscent of a genie flowing into a magic lamp. When you restore the window, it returns to the desktop with an effect that's like a genie flowing out of a magic lamp.

- *Scale Effect:* The window is minimized to the dock by moving down and to the right and shrinking as it moves. When you restore the window, it moves up and to the left to its previous position and expands as it moves.

7. **Use the Double-Click a Window's Title Bar To pop-up menu to decide what happens when you double-click a window's title bar.**

   The default action is Zoom, which expands the window to take up the maximum available vertical space on your desktop. The alternative actions are Minimize or Do Nothing.

8. **For the rest of the dock settings, use the switches to turn them on or off, as you prefer:**

   - *Minimize Windows into Application Icon:* When this switch is on, macOS minimizes each window into its dock icon. This gives you more dock room, but it means you have to click and hold down (or right-click) the app's dock icon to restore a minimized window from the menu that appears. If you turn this switch off, macOS minimizes windows to the right side of the dock (to the left of the trash icon).

   - *Automatically Hide and Show the Dock:* Click this switch on to hide the dock and give your apps some extra vertical space. To bring the dock back onscreen temporarily, move the mouse pointer to the bottom of the screen.

   - *Animate Opening Applications:* When this switch is on, it means that when you click an app's dock icon, macOS bounces the icon to indicate that the app is opening. Click this switch off to skip this effect.

   - *Show Indicators for Open Applications:* Click this switch off to prevent macOS from showing the little black dot under the icon for each running app.

   - *Show Recent Applications in Dock:* Click this switch off to remove the Recent Applications area from the dock.

9. **In the Menu Bar section of the Desktop & Dock settings, use the following pop-up menus to customize the following menu bar settings:**

   - *Automatically Hide and Show the Menu Bar:* Choose Always to hide the menu bar and give your apps a bit more vertical headspace. To bring the menu bar back onscreen temporarily, move the mouse pointer to the top of the screen; choose In Full Screen Only to hide the menu bar only when you run any app in full screen mode; choose In Desktop Only to hide the menu bar except when you run an app in full-screen mode; choose Never to always keep the menu bar onscreen.

- *Recent Documents, Applications, and Servers:* Set the number of recent files, apps, and servers you see when you choose ⇨ Recent Items.

10. **In the System Settings sidebar, click Control Center.**

11. **Use each module pop-up menu listed in the Control Center Modules section to decide whether you want that module to appear also as a menu bar icon.**

Some modules can be either on the menu bar full-time, or never on the menu bar. The pop-up menu for these modules offers the following two options:

- *Show in Menu Bar:* Always display the module in the menu bar.

- *Don't Show in Menu Bar:* Never display the module in the menu bar.

Other modules represent features that aren't always active (such as Screen Mirroring and Now Playing), so it usually makes sense to see these modules in the menu bar only when you're using them. The pop-up menu for these modules offers the following three options:

- *Always Show in Menu Bar:* Display the module in the menu bar even when it's not active.

- *Show When Active:* Display the module icon in the menu bar only when you're using the module.

- *Don't Show in Menu Bar:* Never display the module in the menu bar, even when it's active.

12. **Scroll down to the Other Modules section and, for each module listed, decide whether you want that module displayed in Control Center or the menu bar or both by using the following controls:**

- *Show in Menu Bar:* Click this switch on to show the module in the menu bar.

- *Show in Control Center:* Click this switch on to show the module in Control Center.

13. **Scroll down to the Menu Bar Only section and then customize the following items to your heart's content:**

- *Clock:* Click Clock Options and then use the dialog controls to customize the appearance of the menu bar date and time. If you don't want to display the date and time, use the Show Date pop-up menu to select Never.

- *Spotlight:* Configure whether Spotlight appears in the menu bar by using this pop-up menu to choose Show in Menu Bar or Don't Show in Menu Bar.

- *Siri:* Configure whether Siri appears in the menu bar by using this pop-up menu to choose Show in Menu Bar or Don't Show in Menu Bar.

- *Time Machine:* Configure whether Time Machine appears in the menu bar by using this pop-up menu to choose Show in Menu Bar or Don't Show in Menu Bar.

14. **To close the System Settings window, click the close icon in the upper-left corner of the window.**

Alternatively, choose System Settings ➪ Quit or press ⌘+Q.

Setting the Date and Time

Keeping track of time might seem trivial, but knowing the right time is important. That way, your Mac can determine when you created or modified a particular file and keep track of appointments you've made through apps such as Reminders and Calendar.

Of course, keeping track of time is useless if you don't set the right time to begin with. To set the proper date and time, follow these steps:

1. **Choose ➪ System Settings or click the System Settings icon on the dock.**

2. **In the System Settings sidebar, click General and then click Date & Time.**

The Date & Time settings appear.

Several settings in the Date & Time pane are locked. You can change them only by entering your Mac's administrator account credentials.

REMEMBER

3. **Leave the Set Date & Time Automatically switch on to have your Mac automatically determine the current date and time.**

Your Mac gets the current date and time from an online time server. The default time server is time.apple.com, but you can click Set if you want to choose a different one.

This feature works only if you're connected to the internet. If you aren't connected to the internet, click the Set button next to Date and Time to pick a date and set the time.

4. **(Optional) Click the Set Time Zone Automatically Using Your Current Location switch on if you want the clock to change automatically when you travel to a different time zone.**

This feature works when you have an internet connection and have turned on Location Services (see Book 2, Chapter 6).

5. **To close the System Settings window, click the close icon in the upper-left corner of the window.**

   Alternatively, choose System Settings ⇨ Quit or press ⌘+Q.

Fine-Tuning Sounds

Your Mac can play a wide variety of sounds, from simple alert boops to full-fledged symphonies. With a few tweaks here and there, you can make your Mac as easy on your ears as your Mac's screen is easy on your eyes.

Customizing your Mac's sound effects

Your Mac communicates with you not only by displaying dialogs and notifications but also via sound effects that accompany certain operations. Of particular note is your Mac's alert sound, which plays every time your Mac wants you to pay attention to what's happening on the screen. For example, you hear the alert sound when you try to close an app without saving an open document.

To customize your Mac's sound effects, follow these steps:

1. **Choose ⇨ System Settings or click the System Settings icon on the dock.**

2. **In the System Settings sidebar, click Sound.**

   The Sound settings appear.

3. **Use the Alert Sound pop-up menu to choose the alert sound you want your Mac to use.**

4. **Use the Play Sound Effects Through pop-up menu to choose the output device you want your Mac to use to display its sound effects.**

   The default value is Selected Sound Output Device, which refers to whatever device you've selected in the Output tab (described in the section that follows). Alternatively, you can select a specific sound output device that's connected to your Mac.

5. **Set the alert loudness by dragging the Alert Volume slider to the left (quieter) or right (louder).**

6. **(Optional) Click the following switches on or off as desired:**

   - *Play sound on startup:* When on, tells macOS to play its iconic startup sound.

- *Play User Interface Sound Effects:* When on, lets you hear such sounds as the crinkling of paper when you empty the trash or a whooshing sound if you remove an icon from the dock.

- *Play Feedback When Volume Is Changed:* When on, beeps to match the sound level while you increase or decrease the volume.

7. **Either click the close button to close System Settings or leave the Sound pane onscreen and continue with the next section.**

Configuring sound output and input

Every Mac can play sound through speakers (built-in or external) or headphones, from making the simplest beeping noise to playing streaming music like a stereo. Three primary ways to modify the sound on your Mac involve volume, balance, and input/output devices:

» **Volume:** Defines how loud your Mac plays sound by default. Many applications, such as Music, also let you adjust the volume, so you can set the default system volume and then adjust the volume within each application, relative to the system volume, as well.

» **Balance:** Defines how sound plays through the right and left stereo speakers. By adjusting the balance, you can make sound louder coming from one speaker and quieter coming from the other.

» **Input/output:** Depending on your equipment, you might have multiple input and output devices — speakers and headphones as two distinct output devices, for example. By defining which input and output device to use, you can define which one to use by default.

To customize your Mac's sound input and output settings, follow these steps:

1. **Choose ⇨ System Settings or click the System Settings icon on the dock.**

2. **In the System Settings sidebar, click Sound.**

    The Sound settings appear.

3. **Click the Output tab to display the Output settings, as shown in Figure 6-13.**

4. **Click the output device you want to use if you have another output option connected to your Mac, such as headphones, external speakers, or Apple TV.**

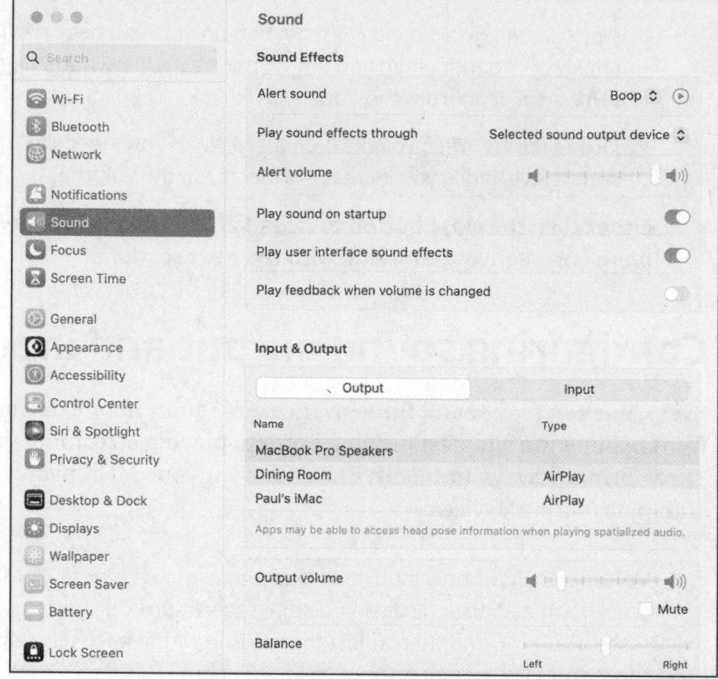

FIGURE 6-13:
Adjust volume and balance of sound output from apps like Music.

5. **Drag the Output Volume slider to the left (to decrease the output volume) or to the right (to increase the output volume).**

   To mute all sound output, select the Mute check box.

   Output volume defines the maximum volume that sound-playing apps can emit. For example, if you set the output volume at 75 percent and then play a song in the Music app with the Music volume at 100 percent, the song plays at just 75 percent of the Mac's maximum output capacity.

TIP

   You can also adjust the output volume by clicking the Control Center icon in the menu bar and then dragging the Sound slider left (to decrease the volume) or right (to increase the volume). Your Mac keyboard also has dedicated volume keys: F10 (mute), F11 (decrease volume), and F12 (increase volume).

6. **(Optional) Drag the Balance slider to adjust the balance between the left and right speakers.**

7. **Click the Input tab to open the Input settings, as shown in Figure 6-14.**

8. **Click the input device you want your Mac to use to receive sound.**

9. **Drag the Input Volume slider to adjust the default input volume.**

   To make sure the input volume is at the right level, speak a few test words into your sound input device. While you're speaking, keep an eye on the Input Level indicator. If the input level bars stop more or less in the middle, the input volume is just right; if the bars stop far to the left, increase the input volume; if the bars stop far to the right, decrease the input volume.

10. **To close the System Settings window, click the close icon in the upper-left corner of the window.**

   Alternatively, choose System Settings ➪ Quit or press ⌘+Q.

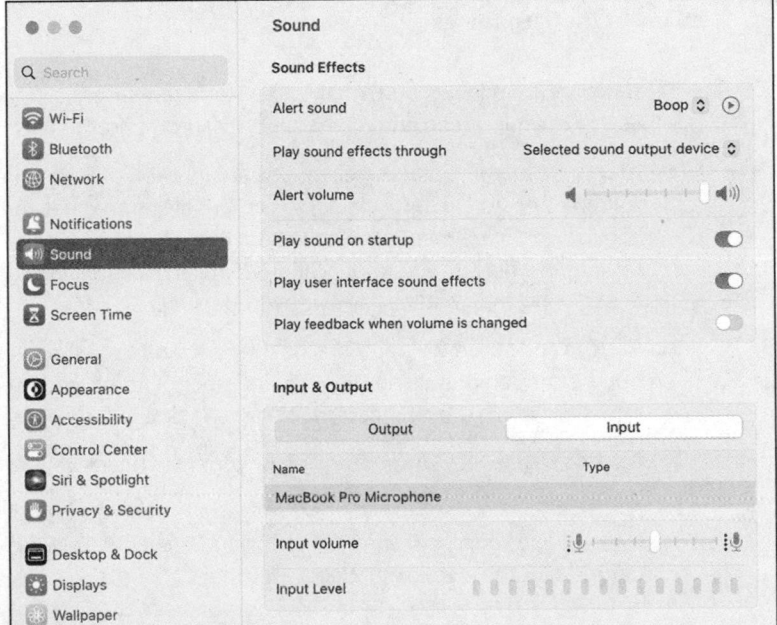

FIGURE 6-14:
Input settings let you define how to record sound.

Putting the "No" in Notifications

When your Mac wants to pester you, er, I mean, tell you or remind you of something, it alerts you. It used to be those alerts were few and far between, but today with bells ringing for birthdays, beeps telling you that you've got mail, and banners flying across the screen with the latest tweet, your Mac can sound like a noisy traffic jam.

macOS gives you two ways to reduce the noise generated by notifications:

» **Notification Center settings:** Enable you to customize notifications app by app. For each app on your Mac, you can configure everything from specifying the notification types you want to see to shutting off notifications altogether.

>> **Focus:** Enables you to shut off some or all notifications so that you can concentrate on what you're doing.

The next two sections provide the details on these methods for nixing notifications.

Configuring notification settings

One of the things that makes notifications such a bother is that there are just so many of the darn things:

>> **Banners** are mini-windows that appear for a few seconds in the upper-right corner of your screen and then disappear automatically.

>> **Alerts** are banners that remain onscreen until you click an action button, such as Reply or Later. In particular, *time-sensitive* alerts are ones that can't wait, so you can configure macOS to show them even if you're using a Focus to temporarily hide all other notifications. Similarly, *critical* alerts are those that are so important that they always override a focus.

>> **Badges** appear on the app icons on the dock and Launchpad as white numbers in red circles, indicating the number of items that need your attention, which can be messages to be read or apps to update.

>> **Sounds** play to let you know an app or your Mac needs your attention.

>> **Notification Center** holds items from various apps, such as a Facebook post by someone you follow or upcoming calendar events. To view Notification Center, click the menu bar's clock.

To personalize how you receive notifications, follow these steps:

1. **Choose ⇨ System Settings or click the System Settings icon on the dock.**

2. **In the System Settings sidebar, click Notifications.**

   The Notifications settings appear, as shown in Figure 6-15. Your settings may look slightly different based on the apps you have installed on your Mac.

   The Applications Notifications section lists the apps that use notifications, listed in alphabetical order. Below each app is a summary of the notification types currently turned on for the app. For example, in Figure 6-15 you can see that the current notification types for the Calendar app are Badges, Sounds, Alerts, and Time Sensitive. The word *Off* is displayed below each app for which you have turned off notifications, such as the Books app in Figure 6-15.

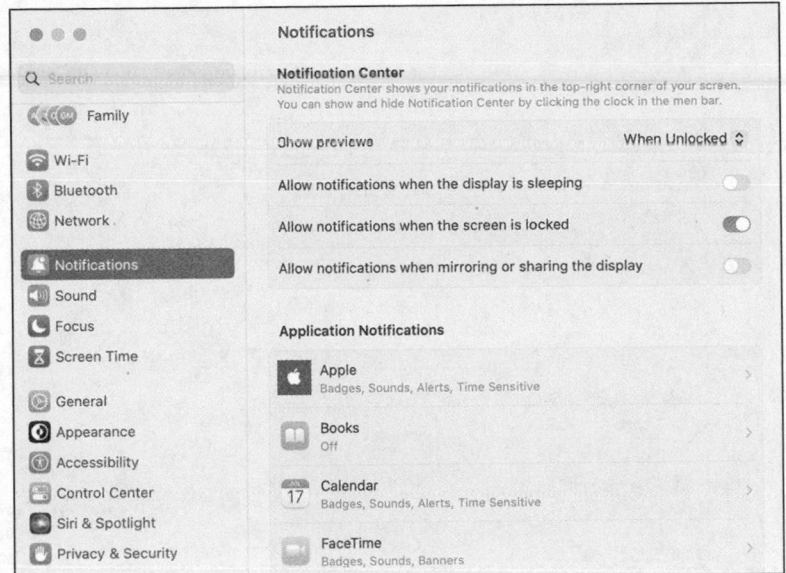

FIGURE 6-15:
Use the
controls in the
Notifications
pane to manage
notifications for
your Mac apps.

3. **(Optional) Configure the following global notification settings:**

   - *Show Previews:* Same as the Show Previews settings for an individual app (see Step 7), but this setting applies to all your apps.

   - *Allow Notifications When the Display Is Sleeping:* Click this switch on to see notifications even when your Mac's display is asleep.

   - *Allow Notifications When the Screen Is Locked:* Click this switch on to see notifications when your Mac's screen is locked.

   - *Allow Notifications When Mirroring or Sharing the Display:* Click this switch on to see notifications when you've mirrored or shared your Mac display onto another device.

4. **Click the app you want to work with.**

   System Settings displays the notification settings for the app. Figure 6-16 shows the pane that appears for the Calendar app.

5. **If you don't want to see any notifications for this app, click the Allow Notifications switch off, and then skip to Step 8.**

6. **Click the alert style you prefer: None, Banners, or Alerts.**

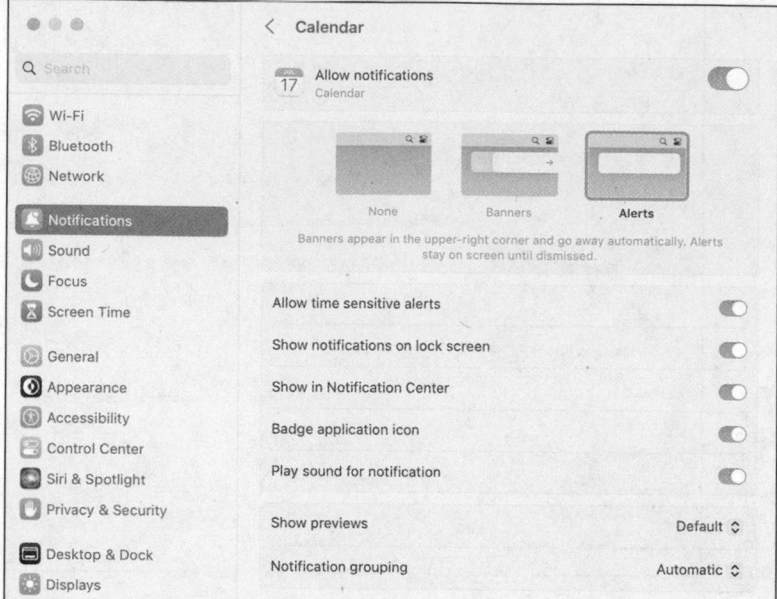

FIGURE 6-16:
Use the controls in an app's notifications pane to manage how that app alerts you.

7. **Configure the settings to customize the type of notifications you want for the app.**

The available settings vary from app to app, but the following are the most common ones:

- *Allow Critical Alerts:* When on, allows the app to send critical alerts.

- *Allow Time Sensitive Alerts:* When on, allows the app to send time-sensitive alerts.

- *Show Notifications on Lock Screen:* When on, macOS displays any notifications issued while your Mac was asleep. These notifications appear in the login window when you wake up your Mac.

- *Show in Notification Center:* When on, displays the app's recent (within the past week) notifications in Notification Center.

- *Badge App Icon:* When on, displays badge notifications on the app's icon on the dock and in Launchpad.

- *Play Sound for Notifications:* When on, macOS plays a sound along with each app notification.

- *Show Previews:* Displays a preview of the content of the notification (such as the first few lines of an incoming email message). The default is When Unlocked, which means you see the preview only when you're logged in to your Mac account. The other two options are Always (you see previews also in the login screen, which could present privacy issues) and Never (disables all previews).

- *Notification grouping:* Determines how Notification Center groups the app's notifications. Automatic (the default) lets macOS determine the groupings; By App groups the notifications by app; and Off displays the notifications individually instead of in groups.

8. **Repeat Steps 4 through 7 to customize notifications for any other app you want to work with.**

9. **To close the System Settings window, click the close icon in the upper-left corner of the window.**

   Alternatively, choose System Settings ⇨ Quit or press ⌘+Q.

Getting your attention back with Focus

Tweaking notification settings app by app, as I describe in the preceding section, works well, particularly for apps that send a lot of notifications your way. Sometimes, however, you really want to bear down and get some work done, whether you're completing an important project, studying for a test, or finally getting started writing the Great [Insert Nationality Here] Novel. In those situations, you want to work distraction-free, so even a single notification can throw you off.

You *could* turn off the Allow Notifications switch (refer to Figure 6-16) for every app, and then turn each switch back on again when you've finished your work, but I assume you have a long list of more important things to do. Fortunately, macOS offers a much faster and easier way to silence notifications: Focus. With the Focus feature activated, your Mac temporarily stops all notifications, so you get to work (or play or meditate or whatever) in blissful silence. And, just in case there are some notifications you don't want to miss, Focus enables you to set up exceptions for specific people, apps, and alerts (such as time-sensitive alerts).

Smartly, macOS understands that different distraction-free scenarios require different types of notification exceptions. For example, if you're meditating, you probably want no notification exceptions, while if you're concentrating on a work task, you might still want to allow notifications from certain team members and some work-related apps.

For each kind of situation, you can use Focus to set up a *focus.* (Wait, what? The feature itself is called Focus, but each scenario you create within it is called a focus? Alas, yes.) You can customize each focus in two ways:

>> You can set up exceptions to allow notifications from specific people or apps when the focus is turned on.

>> You can configure the focus to turn on automatically at a specific time, when you arrive at a specific location, or when you start using a specific app.

The main focus you'll use is called Do Not Disturb, which silences all notifications (even time-sensitive ones).

Turning on a focus

You turn on a focus via Control Center:

1. **Click the menu bar's Control Center button.**

2. **Click Focus.**

   The Focus window appears, as shown in Figure 6-17.

3. **Click the focus you want to use.**

   macOS turns on the focus.

4. **(Optional) If the focus also offers temporary activations — such as For 1 Hour and Until This Evening — you can click one of those to have your Mac turn off the focus automatically after the specified period.**

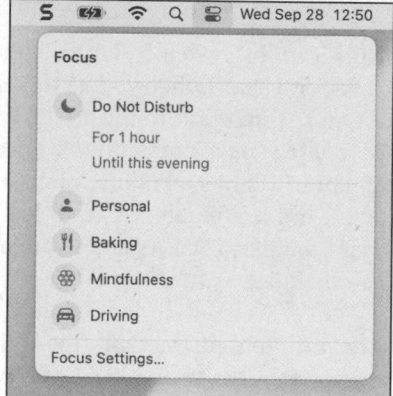

FIGURE 6-17: You turn on a focus via Control Center.

REMEMBER

If you didn't set up your focus to turn off automatically, repeat Steps 1 through 3 when you're ready to turn off the focus (clicking the focus in Step 3 is a toggle that turns the focus on and off).

Customizing a focus

To make Focus work for you, it's usually necessary to tweak a particular focus in some way, such as allowing people or apps exceptions and configuring the focus to turn on automatically. Here are the steps to following customize a focus:

1. **Choose ⌘ System Settings or click the System Settings icon on the dock.**

2. **In the System Settings sidebar, click Focus.**

   The Focus settings appear. By default, you see two predefined focuses: Do Not Disturb and Personal. If you have an iPhone, you also see a focus named Driving.

3. **Click the focus you want to modify.**

   If you see a Driving focus, note that you can tweak that focus only on your iPhone.

4. **To create an exception for a person, click Allowed People, click + (add people) to see a list of your contacts, click the person, and then click Add.**

   Repeat as needed for each person you want to add as an exception.

   Instead of allowing one or more people, you might prefer to block one or more people. In that case, use the Notifications pop-up menu to select Silence Some People, and then follow Step 4 as needed to specify who you want silenced during the focus.

   To allow some FaceTime calls, use the Allow Calls From pop-up menu to choose who you want to hear from when the focus is on, such as Favorites, All Contacts, or Everybody. Leave the Allow Repeated Calls switch on if you want insistent callers to get through.

5. **Click Done to return to the focus settings.**

6. **To create an exception for an app, click Allowed Apps, click + (add) to see a list of your installed apps, click the app, and then click Add.**

   Repeat as needed for each app you want to add as an exception.

   Instead of allowing one or more apps, you can instead block one or more apps. To do this, use the Notifications pop-up menu to select Silence Some Apps, and then follow Step 6 as needed to specify all the apps you want silenced during the focus.

7. **Click Done to return to the focus settings.**

8. **To have the Focus turn on automatically, click Add Schedule to open the Set a Schedule dialog, and then select how you want the focus to turn on:**

   - *Time:* Turn the focus on (and off) at a specified time. In the dialog that appears, choose a From time to turn on the focus and a To time to turn off the focus. You can also deselect the button for each day of the week that you don't want to turn on the focus. Click Done.

- *Location:* Turn on the focus when you arrive at a specified location, and turn off the focus when you leave that location. In the dialog that appears, select the location and then click Done.

- *App:* Turn on the focus when you start using a specified app, and turn off the focus when you quit the app. In the dialog that appears, click the app and then click Done.

9. **Click < (back) to return to the Focus pane.**

10. **To allow people to bypass the focus if they have important news, click Focus Status and make sure the Share Focus Status switch is set on.**

   Otherwise, turn this switch off to tell macOS not to share your Focus status with your apps. Alternatively, leave that switch on and then turn off the switch for each focus for which you don't want to share your status.

11. **To close the System Settings window, click the close icon in the upper-left corner of the window.**

   Alternatively, choose System Settings ➪ Quit or press ⌘+Q.

Creating a focus

If the default Do Not Disturb and Personal focuses aren't suitable for a particular situation, you can create your own focus. Here's how it's done:

1. **Choose ➪ System Settings or click the System Settings icon on the dock.**

2. **In the System Settings sidebar, click Focus.**

   The Focus settings appear.

3. **Click Add Focus.**

4. **Do one of the following:**

   - *Click a predefined focus — Gaming, Mindfulness, Reading, or Work.* Customize the focus as I describe in the preceding section.

   - *Click Custom.* Then type a name for your custom focus, click a color, click an icon, and then click OK.

   The settings for your custom focus appear.

5. **To close the System Settings window, click the close icon in the upper-left corner of the window.**

   Alternatively, choose System Settings ➪ Quit or press ⌘+Q.

Chapter **7**

Making Your Mac More Accessible

Not everyone has perfect eyesight, hearing, or eye-hand coordination. If you have trouble with your vision, hearing, or ability to use the keyboard, trackpad, or mouse (or all three), using a computer can be difficult. That's why every Mac comes with special Accessibility features that you can turn on and modify for your needs. These features fall under three categories — seeing, hearing, and interacting — all of which I introduce you to in the following pages.

If you're interested in getting the most out of the Accessibility features, especially VoiceOver, I recommend that you read Apple's extensive instructions for all the Accessibility features on both the Help menu and online at www.apple.com/support/accessibility.

Mitigating Vision Limitations

Those of you who are no longer spring chickens (or even summer chickens, for that matter) know one thing for certain: The older you get, the worse your eyesight becomes. Sure, you can ramp up your eyeglass prescription or invest in extra-strength reading glasses, but even that may not be enough when it comes to reading text and deciphering icons on your Mac screen. And, of course, if your eyesight problems go beyond simple afflictions such as farsightedness or astigmatism, a change of eyewear isn't going to help you make sense of what's happening on your monitor.

Whatever the source of your visual challenges, you can't work with your Mac if you can't see what your Mac is trying to show you onscreen. Fortunately, macOS offers a number of tools to make things easier to see, reduce visual distractions, and even hear audio translations of what's on the screen. Your Mac includes three settings categories to help you overcome visual challenges:

>> **VoiceOver:** Allows your Mac to read text, email, and even descriptions of the screen in a computer-generated voice. VoiceOver can speak more than 30 languages and analyzes text paragraph by paragraph, so the reading is more natural and, well, humanlike. You can set up settings for specific activities: for example, reading headlines at a faster speaking rate than the article itself. And special commands make browsing web pages easier.

>> **Zoom:** Sets up keyboard shortcuts so you can enlarge (zoom) the screen.

>> **Display:** Enables you to customize your Mac's display to compensate for your vision limitations, such as inverting the screen colors so you see white or light-colored text on a dark background.

To modify the vision assistance features of your Mac, follow these steps:

1. **Choose ⇨ System Settings and click Accessibility in the sidebar.**

    Or right-click the System Settings icon on the dock and choose Accessibility from the menu that opens.

    The Accessibility settings appear.

    TIP

    If you find yourself frequently messing with the Accessibility settings, do yourself a favor and click Control Center in the System Settings sidebar. Then, in the Accessibility Shortcuts section, click the Show in Menu Bar switch on. (To get Control Center access to your Mac's accessibility features, click the Show in Control Center switch on.) This enables you to access many of the accessibility features I talk about in this chapter — such as VoiceOver, Zoom, and Sticky Keys — from your Mac's menu bar.

2. **Click VoiceOver.**

    The VoiceOver settings, shown in Figure 7-1, appear.

3. **Make your selections from the following three options:**

    • *VoiceOver:* Click this switch on to enable VoiceOver, which provides spoken or Braille descriptions of items on the screen. This option also provides control of the computer via the keyboard.

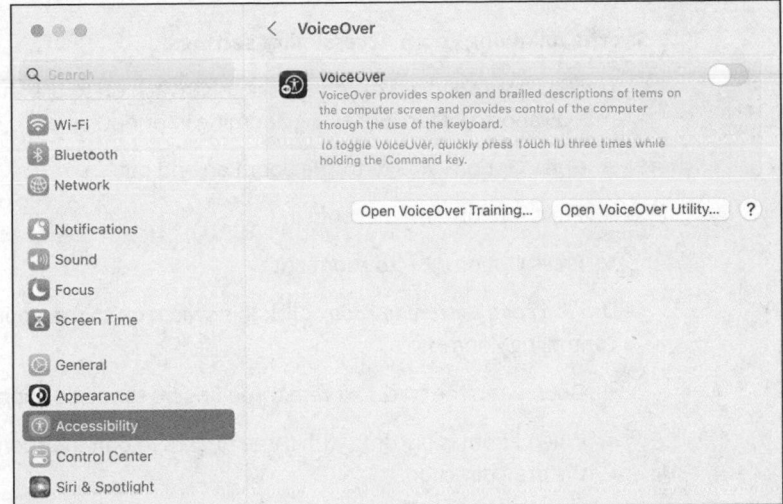

FIGURE 7-1:
Get spoken descriptions of items onscreen by enabling VoiceOver.

- *Open VoiceOver Training:* Click this button to listen to the Mac's digital computer voice show you how to use the VoiceOver option.

- *Open VoiceOver Utility:* Click this button to open a dialog with options for the VoiceOver Utility. This dialog is divided into a series of sections such as Verbosity, Speech, Navigation, and Web. For example, in Speech, you choose a computer voice you like and the rate at which the voice speaks to you.

When you're done with VoiceOver, click < (back) to return to the Accessibility settings.

4. **Click Zoom.**

The Zoom section of the Accessibility settings appears, as shown in Figure 7-2.

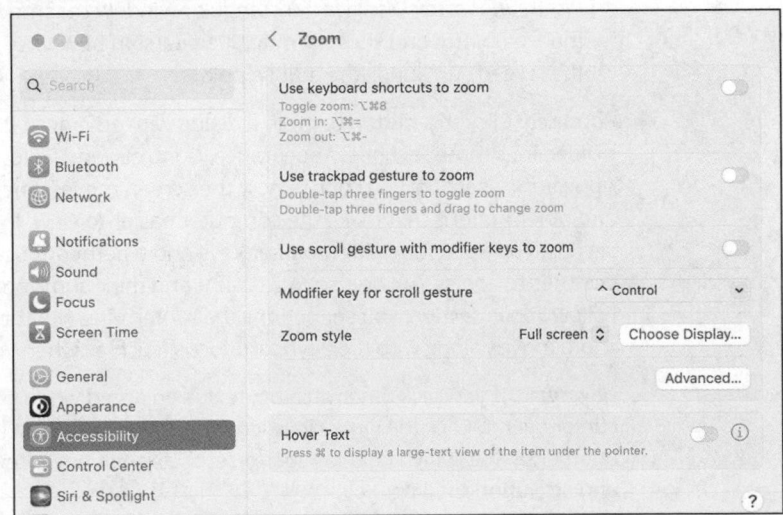

FIGURE 7-2:
The Zoom settings enable you to control zooming in on screen stuff.

5. **Set the following Zoom Accessibility settings:**

- *Use Keyboard Shortcuts to Zoom:* Click this switch on to use the default macOS shortcuts for controlling Zooming in or out.

  - Press Option+⌘+8 to toggle Zoom on and off.

  - Press Option+⌘+= to zoom in.

  - Press Option+⌘+- to zoom out.

- *Use Trackpad Gesture to Zoom:* Click this switch on to use your trackpad for controlling Zoom:

  - Double-tap the trackpad with three fingers to toggle Zoom on and off.

  - When Zoom is on, drag with three fingers to pan the zoomed screen in the drag direction.

- *Use Scroll Gesture with Modifier Keys to Zoom:* Click this switch on to use the scroll wheel on a mouse to zoom. In the drop-down list, choose one of the following modifier keys: Control, Option, or ⌘.

- *Zoom Style:* Use the pop-up menu to choose what portion of the screen you want to zoom:

  - *Full Screen:* Zooms the entire screen. If you have a secondary display connected to your Mac, click Choose Display to select which display you want to zoom.

  - *Split Window:* Splits the screen horizontally into two panes. The bottom pane shows the regular (unmagnified) screen, and the top pane shows the zoomed version of the portion of the screen that includes the mouse pointer.

  - *Picture-in-Picture:* Displays a rectangular window that moves with the mouse pointer and shows a magnified version of whatever portion of the screen surrounds the mouse pointer.

- *Advanced:* Click this button to open a dialog with advanced Zoom settings, divided into three sections: Appearance, Controls, and Follow Focus. In the Appearance section, you choose how the screen moves when zoomed in, and other options that make the computer easier to view. In the Controls section, you set options for modifier keys and whether to use trackpad gestures to zoom. You also set maximum and minimum zoom. In the Follow Focus section, you set options that determine whether and how the zoom moves along with the keyboard focus (such as when you press Tab).

- *Hover Text:* If you click this switch on, text is enlarged when you hover your cursor over it. Click the i-in-a-circle icon (hover text settings) to open another dialog, which enables you to set the size of hover text, the font, and activation modifier key.

TIP

The zooming options can be particularly helpful when working with photo-editing apps or when aligning several objects in a drawing or page layout app.

6. **When you're done with Zoom, click < (back) to return to the Accessibility settings.**

7. **Click Display to open the Display accessibility options.**

    The dialog is divided into three sections: Display, Cursor, and Color Filters (in Figure 7-3, you see the Display and Pointer sections).

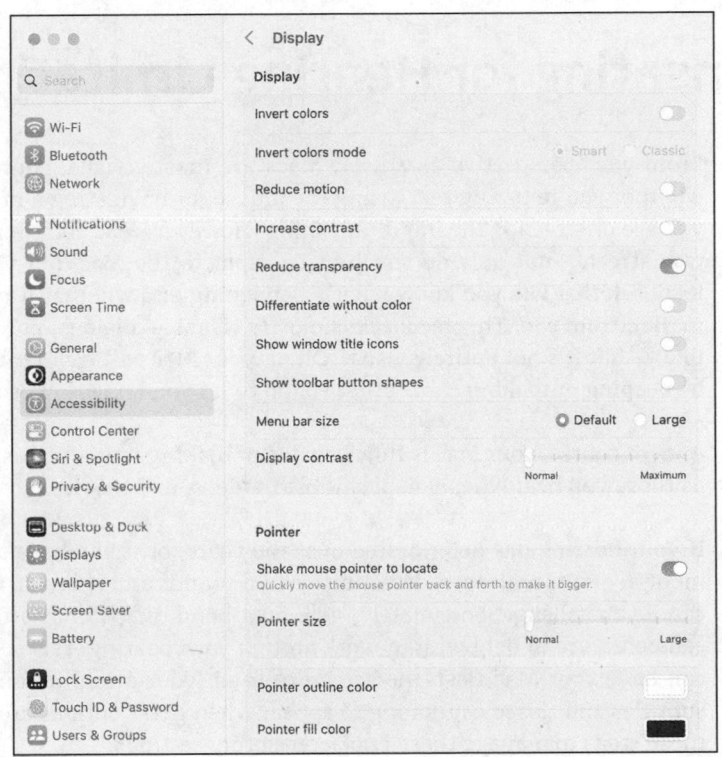

FIGURE 7-3:
Configure the Display settings for easier screen viewing.

8. **Click the following tabs and select the options you want to activate:**

    - *Display:* Turn on the Invert Colors switch to change the display to white text on a black screen. If you choose Invert Colors, don't enable Night Shift. You can also increase contrast, reduce motion when you open applications or switch desktops, or reduce the transparency apparent with some backgrounds. The last option makes it easier to read text.

    - *Pointer:* In this section, you can change the cursor size, outline color, and fill color. Shaking the mouse pointer to locate it is enabled by default. This option enlarges the cursor when you shake the mouse from side to side or move a finger quickly on the trackpad.

- *Color Filters:* In this section, if you enable color filters, you can convert the display to grayscale, or choose one of four color filters. Again, my advice is to experiment with the different options to see which one you prefer.

9. **To quit System Settings, click the close icon or press ⌘+Q. Or click < (back) and go on to the next section to set up other Accessibility functions.**

Compensating for Hearing Limitations

From your perspective as a user, Macs are mostly visual contraptions. That is, whether you're typing text, using the mouse, or navigating a menu system, what you see onscreen is the important thing. However, Mac communication is a two-way street —not only do you provide input to the Mac, but your Mac provides feedback that lets you know what's happening and whether it needs more information from you. This feedback is mostly visual — dialogs, notifications, and the like — but it's not entirely visual. Often, your Mac will try to catch your attention by beeping or making some other sound to let you know something's happening.

And, of course, your Mac is fully capable of making more interesting sounds, such as those you hear when you play music, videos, and movies.

If your hearing has deteriorated over the years, or if you have a hearing impairment in one or both ears, detecting system sounds and enjoying music and movies can be a challenge. Fortunately, help is at hand. macOS has a few tools that you can configure to help with or work around your hearing issues. For example, you can have your Mac flash the screen to catch your attention and you can set up subtitles and closed captioning to appear when these options are available. Follow these steps to manage these two accessibility settings:

1. **Choose ⇨ System Settings and click the Accessibility icon.**

Or right-click the System Settings icon on the dock and choose Accessibility from the menu that opens.

The Accessibility settings appear.

2. **Click Audio.**

The Audio section of the Accessibility settings appears, as shown in Figure 7-4.

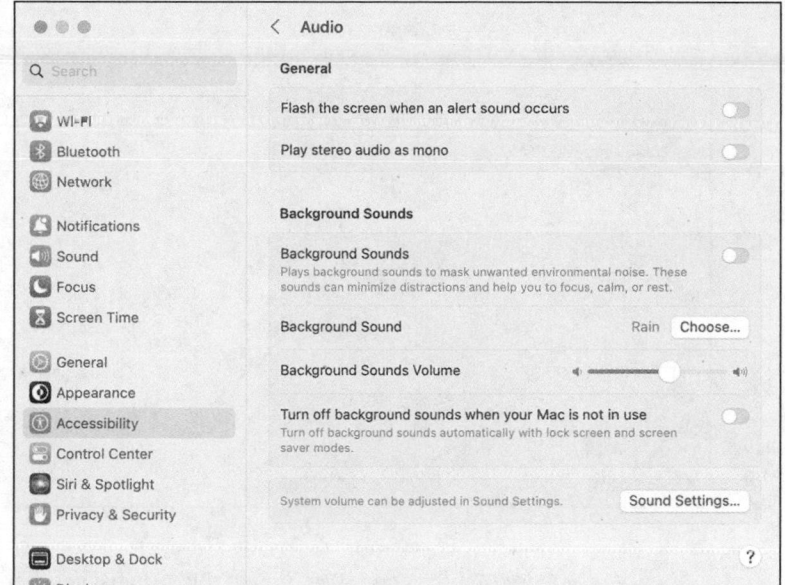

FIGURE 7-4:
Your Mac's Audio
accessibility
settings.

3. **Click the Flash the Screen When an Alert Sound Occurs switch on.**

   When this option is on, your Mac flashes the screen when an alert sound is played.

4. **(Optional) Click the Play Stereo Audio as Mono switch on to remove the stereo effect from music or other stereo-enabled sounds your Mac plays.**

REMEMBER

   Use the Sound Settings to adjust the volume of alerts and other audible output, as I explain in the section on fine-tuning sounds in Chapter 6 of this minibook.

   When you're done with Audio, click < (back) to return to the Accessibility settings.

5. **Click Captions.**

   The Captions settings appear, as shown in Figure 7-5. You use these settings to select how you want to see subtitles or closed captioning, when these services are available.

6. **Make your selections from the following options:**

   - *Style for Subtitles and Captions:* Click one of the choices in the list to see a preview and decide whether you want to select it. Or click the plus button to create a custom subtitle style. In the window that opens, type a name for your new subtitle; choose the typeface, size, and color from the pop-up menus; and then click Done. The new subtitle style is added to the list.

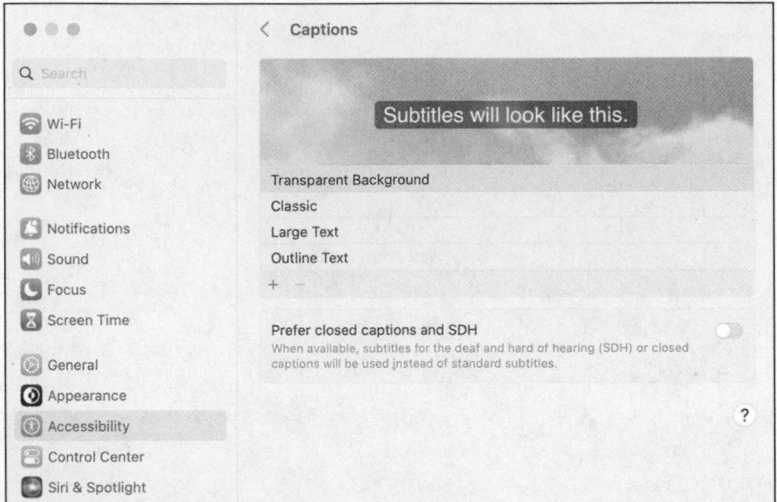

FIGURE 7-5:
Use the Captions
accessibility
settings to set up
closed captioning.

- *Prefer Closed Captions and SDH:* Turn on this switch if you want to see these types of captions rather than subtitles. SDH, which is short for subtitles for the deaf and hard of hearing, offers more information (such as descriptions of sound effects and the name of whoever is currently speaking) than simple subtitles.

7. **Click the close icon or press ⌘+Q to quit System Settings. Or click < (back) and then go on to the next section to set up other Accessibility functions.**

REMEMBER

If you're watching movies, TV shows, or other video in one of your Mac's media player applications (such as Apple TV or QuickTime Player), you may have closed caption options available, depending on the source of the video. Some apps have controls for subtitles and closed captioning in their menus.

Overcoming Physical Challenges

Using a Mac might seem at first blush to be more of a mental exercise. After all, it appears as though you spend lots of time in front of the screen reading things, looking at things, and thinking about things.

However, if you mapped out your Mac time, you'd almost certainly find that you spend great chunks of time on physical tasks: using your keyboard to press keys and type longer passages and using your mouse or trackpad to point at, click, double-click, and drag things — not to mention whatever gesticulations and hands-on techniques you use to cajole your computer into behaving sensibly for a change.

This surprisingly physical side of using a Mac means that if you have physical challenges, you may find it hard to perform certain tasks (and a few may be mission impossible). Fortunately, it doesn't have to be that way. If you have physical limitations or find eye–hand coordination challenging, you can use several Mac options to improve your control of the user interface. You find each of the following in the Motor section of the Accessibility settings.

Easing keyboard limitations

If you have physical limitations using the keyboard, the Mac offers two solutions: sticky keys and slow keys. Sticky keys can help you use keystroke shortcuts, such as ⌘+P (Print), which usually require pressing two or more keys at the same time. By turning on sticky keys, you can use keystroke shortcuts by pressing one key at a time in sequence. Press the modifier key first, such as the ⌘ key, and it "sticks" in place and waits until you press a second key to complete the keystroke shortcut.

The slow keys feature slows the reaction time of the Mac every time you press a key. Normally when you press a key, the Mac accepts it right away, but slow keys can force a Mac to wait a long time before accepting the typed key. That way, your Mac will ignore any accidental taps on the keyboard and patiently wait until you hold down a key for a designated period before it accepts it as valid.

To turn on sticky keys or slow keys and other keyboard accessibility features, follow these steps:

1. **Choose ⇨ System Settings and click the Accessibility icon.**

   Or right-click the System Settings icon on the dock and choose Accessibility from the menu that opens.

   The Accessibility settings appear.

2. **In the Motor section of the window, click Keyboard.**

   The Keyboard settings appear, as shown in Figure 7-6.

3. **Click the Enable Full Keyboard Access switch on to enable you to use your Mac entirely from the keyboard.**

4. **Turn on the following switches, as desired:**

   - *Sticky Keys:* Click this switch on to enable the Sticky Keys option. Then click the *i*-in-a-circle (options) to open another window with the following check boxes: Press the Shift Key Five Times to Toggle Sticky Keys, which lets you turn the feature on and off from the keyboard; Beep When a Modifier Key Is Set, which causes a beep to sound after you set a modifier key such as Option or ⌘, after which you can press the next key of the keyboard shortcut; or Display Pressed Keys on Screen, which displays a modifier key such as ⌘ or Alt onscreen. By default, the key is displayed in the upper right of the screen, but you can choose another option from the drop-down menu to the right of the Display Pressed Keys on Screen check box.

- *Slow Keys:* Click this switch on to create a slight delay between when you press a key and when it's activated. Click the *i*-in-a-circle (options) and you can select the Use Click Key Sounds check box to hear a sound like a typewriter when you press a key. You can also vary the delay between when you press a key and when it's recognized by macOS by dragging the Acceptance Delay slider.

- *Accessibility Keyboard:* Click this switch on and a virtual keyboard appears on your screen. When you press a key, it's highlighted on the Accessibility keyboard. You can also click a key from the Accessibility keyboard to add it to a document or email you're creating. As you type, word suggestions appear above the keyboard.

TIP

Click the Panel Editor button to open the Accessibility Keyboard Active Panel Collection and create a custom panel. In this panel, you can add buttons to the Accessibility keyboard that perform certain actions. After saving your changes, your customizations appear on the accessibility keyboard.

TIP

You can click the *i*-in-a-circle (options) to the right of the Accessibility Keyboard switch to open a new dialog with even more ways to customize the Accessibility Keyboard.

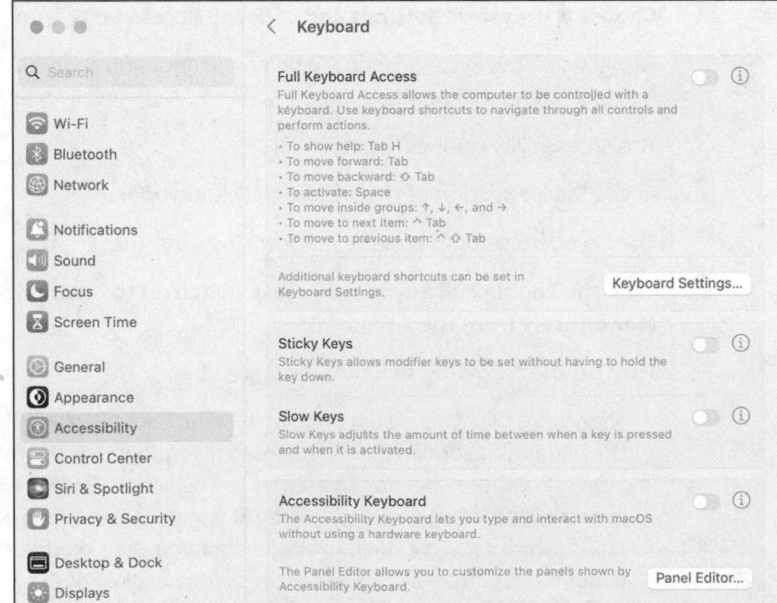

FIGURE 7-6:
Sticky keys and slow keys can make your keyboard easier to use.

Making the mouse and trackpad easier to use

If you have physical limitations using the mouse or trackpad, your Mac offers several Pointer Control settings that can help. For example, you can turn on the Mouse Keys feature, which lets you control the mouse through the numeric keys. To set up Pointer Control, follow these steps:

1. **Choose ⇨ System Settings and click the Accessibility icon.**

Or right-click the System Settings icon on the dock and choose Accessibility from the menu that opens.

The Accessibility settings appear.

2. **In the Motor section, click Pointer Control.**

The Pointer Control settings appear, as shown in Figure 7-7.

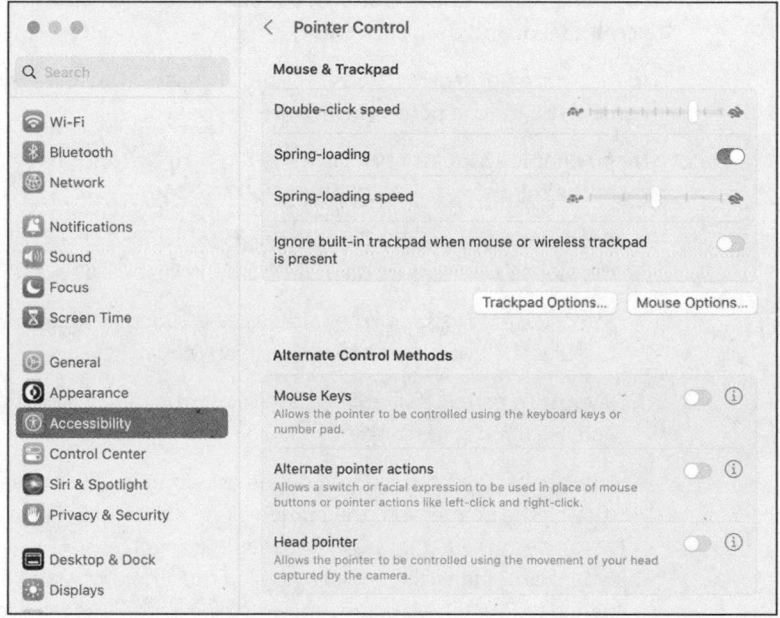

FIGURE 7-7:
Use the Pointer Control settings to make your mouse or trackpad easier to use.

3. **In the Mouse & Trackpad section, drag the sliders to specify Double-Click Speed and Spring-Loading Speed.**

What on earth is a *spring-loading speed*? It's a drag-and-drop thing. As you might know, when you drag a file or folder and hover it over another folder, after a time that folder opens, and you can then drop your item in the open folder. The time you must hover over the folder before it opens is the spring-loading speed. If you don't want to use spring loading, click the Spring-Loading switch off.

4. **(Optional) If you have a MacBook, click the Ignore Built-In Trackpad When Mouse or Wireless Trackpad Is Present switch on.**

Don't turn on this switch if you don't have a mouse or wireless trackpad present. If you do, you won't be able to use your computer and will have to hold down the Start button to force-restart your Mac.

5. **Click the Trackpad Options button if you use a trackpad.**

This opens a dialog that enables you to turn off using the trackpad or inertia or both for scrolling. (If you click the Use Inertia When Scrolling switch off, it means scrolling stops immediately when you lift your finger from the trackpad; otherwise, scrolling comes to a gradual stop when you lift your finger.) Click the Use Trackpad for Dragging switch on and then choose one of the following options from the Dragging Style pop-up menu: Without Drag Lock, With Drag Lock, or Three-Finger Drag.

6. **(Optional) Click Mouse Options, use the dialog that shows up to set the scroll speed, and then click OK.**

7. **In Alternate Control Methods section, click the Mouse Keys switch on to control the mouse pointer using the keyboard.**

8. **If you enabled Mouse Keys, click the *i*-in-a-circle (options) and choose from the following (click OK when you're done):**

   - *Press the Option Key Five Times to Toggle Mouse Keys On or Off:* Lets you turn the Mouse Keys feature on or off from the keyboard.

   - *Ignore Built-In Trackpad When Mouse Keys Is On* (only Macs with trackpads): Disables the trackpad when you turn on Mouse Keys.

     If you turn on this switch, you have to use the mouse keys to deselect it and use the trackpad again.

   - *Initial Delay:* Drag the slider to define how long the Mac waits before moving the pointer with the numeric key. A short value means that the Mac may immediately move the pointer as soon as you press a number or letter key. A long value means that you must hold down a key for a longer period before the Mac starts moving the pointer. Choose a long value if you use a compact keyboard so you can type normally without moving the mouse and move the mouse without typing a series of the same letter.

   - *Maximum Speed:* Drag the slider to adjust how fast the Mouse Keys feature moves the pointer with the keyboard.

9. **Click the Alternate Pointer Actions switch on to use switches or facial expressions instead the usual mouse actions (such as pressing F11 instead of left-clicking).**

10. Click the Head Pointer switch on to control the mouse pointer by moving your head (which your Mac follows by using the camera).

11. Click the close icon or press ⌘+Q to quit System Settings.

Getting on Speaking Terms with Your Mac

The Speakable Items feature lets you control your Mac by using spoken commands.

Chapter 2.

TIP

If you prefer, you can type commands to Siri. To do so, in the Accessibility section of System Settings, click Siri and click the Type to Siri switch on. Then click the Siri Settings button to choose Siri settings.

Setting up the microphone

You can use your Mac's built-in microphone; there is also often a microphone built into monitors and displays. If you're going to be dictating or talking to your Mac, make sure the microphone is turned on and you know where it is. If you speak directly to the microphone, your voice will be picked up much better than if you're looking out the window on a busy street. Look at the mic.

DICTATING AND SPEAKING TO YOUR MAC AND TALKING TO SIRI

You may think that speaking to your Mac and talking to Siri are the same, but they're quite different. You can use your voice and the Mac's built-in microphone to ask your Mac to carry out tasks. For example, when you're dictating some text to Pages or to a text field in Keynote, you can issue editing commands such as "Delete last sentence." Dictating text and speaking commands let you use your voice instead of a keyboard or trackpad.

On the other hand, when you're talking to Siri, you often aren't asking Siri to do something that you could do with the keyboard ("Delete last sentence" for example). Instead, you're asking Siri to do a higher-level task than typing or erasing. For example, you might say, "Siri, what time is my next appointment?"

And make sure it's turned on. Open System Settings by choosing ➪ System Settings, and then click Sound. For the purpose of setting up your microphone, click the Input tab (see Book 1, Chapter 6). You can adjust the input volume as you want. Note that you may have several input devices, but in this window you select only one of them to be used.

You now should have your Mac set up so that you can speak to it or to a connected display.

Setting up Speakable Items

To use the Mac's built-in voice recognition software, you have to define its settings and then assign specific types of commands to your voice. You define the Speakable Items settings to choose how to turn on voice recognition and how your Mac will acknowledge that it received your voice commands correctly. For example, your Mac may wait until you press the Esc key or speak a certain word before it starts listening to voice commands. When it understands your command, it can beep.

To define the Speakable Items settings, follow these steps:

1. **Choose ➪ System Settings and click Accessibility in the sidebar.**

   Or right-click the System Settings icon on the dock and choose Accessibility from the menu that opens.

   The Accessibility settings appear.

2. **Click Voice Control in the Motor section of the Accessibility pane.**

3. **Click the Voice Control switch on.**

4. **Use the Language and Microphone menus to select which language and microphone you want to use with Voice Control.**

5. **Click the Play Sound When Command Is Recognized switch on.**

   When this option is enabled, your computer will play a sound when Voice Control recognizes a command.

6. **Click the Commands button.**

   A list of commands you can enable with Voice Control is displayed. The first command is Open Siri. I suggest you copy the commands you'll use frequently, paste them in a Pages document, print a copy, and keep this list by your computer.

TIP

When you open an application and hover your cursor over a menu, a numbered list is displayed when Voice Control Is enabled. Speak the number to perform the command.

7. **To add a custom command:**

   a. *Click + (add).*

   b. *Use the When I Say text box to type the word or phrase you want to say to invoke the command.*

   c. *Use the While Using pop-up menu to select the app in which you want the command to run.*

   d. *Use the Perform pop-up menu to select the command you want to run.*

   e. *Click Done.*

8. **Click the close icon to exit System Settings.**

Making Your Mac More
Accessible

Using the Internet

2

Contents at a Glance

Chapter 1

Wandering the Web

There are many solid and sensible reasons to own a Mac. However, I'd bet good money that if every Mac user was asked to write down their top five reasons for getting a Mac, some variation of "To surf the web" would appear on almost every list. Whether you're 18 or 80, a world traveler or a homebody, a bon vivant or a penny-pincher, your life probably includes browsing the seemingly endless trove of wit, wisdom, and weirdness that is the World Wide Web.

Happily, your Mac is an excellent web-wandering machine thanks to its sharp screen and its inclusion of Safari, which is the web browser of choice in the Mac world. In this chapter, you get to know Safari and explore its many features for browsing. You delve into Safari's long list of techniques for navigating sites, including searching the web and finding sites you visited previously. You also learn how to work with tabs, which are an essential feature for efficient web browsing.

Bear in mind that this chapter is only the beginning of your Safari schooling. See Book 2, Chapter 2 for much more Safari goodness.

Surf's Up: Browsing Websites

After you connect to the internet (as explained in Book 1, Chapter 3), you can run a web browser app to browse online. The most popular browser for the Mac is the one that comes with it: Safari. So, without further ado (not that there's been much ado so far, mind you), crank up Safari by clicking the dock's Safari icon, which is labeled in Figure 1-1. The figure shows the Safari window that appears and points out a few important landmarks.

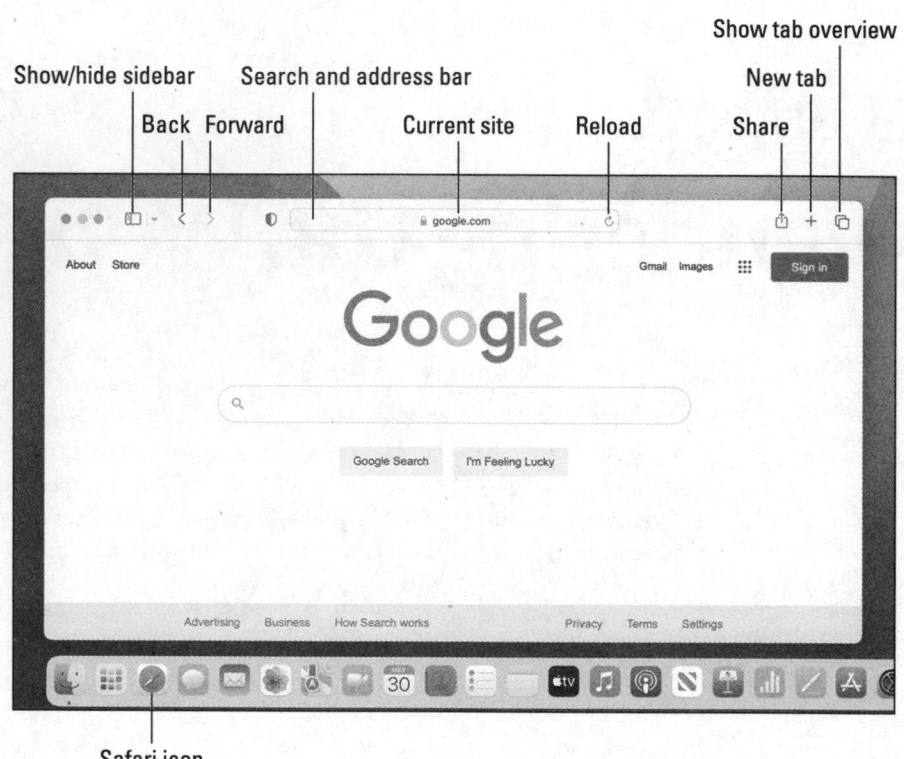

FIGURE 1-1:
The Safari app is your Mac's default web browser.

The top strip of the Safari window is called the *toolbar*. Here are a few toolbar tools that you need to know about right off the bat (I discuss each tool in more detail elsewhere in this chapter and the next):

» **Show/hide sidebar:** Toggle on and off Safari's sidebar, which gives you access to your bookmarks and your reading list (see Book 2, Chapter 2).

» **Search and address bar:** Type the address of a web page (see "Typing a web page address") as well as search for information on the web (see Book 2, Chapter 2).

» **Current site:** Display the name of the current website you're visiting.

>> **Back and forward:** Retrace your web-surfing steps (see "Going back in time").

>> **Reload:** Refresh the current web page.

>> **Share:** Share a web page address via email, text, and more. See Book 2, Chapter 2.

>> **New tab:** Create a new browser tab (see "One-Window Surfing: Browsing with Tabs").

>> **Show tab overview:** View thumbnail versions of your open tabs (again, see "One-Window Surfing: Browsing with Tabs").

TIP

Surprisingly, the Safari toolbar isn't fixed, which means you can add or remove tools at will. To put your personal stamp on the toolbar, choose View ⇨ Customize Toolbar. In the pane that opens, you add a tool to the toolbar by dragging the tool icon from the pane to the toolbar. To get rid of a tool, drag it off the toolbar. Click Done when you're, well, done.

Surfing Techniques

Surfing or *browsing* the web means using a web browser such as Safari to flit merrily from one web page to another. (Actually, the "merrily" part is optional; the techniques for surfing grumpily are the same.) You can use four basic methods to navigate to a web page:

>> Type the web page address if you know it.

>> Click a link that points to the web page.

>> Search the web for the web page you want.

>> Navigate back to the web page if it's one you visited recently.

The next few sections describe each technique in just the right amount of detail.

Typing a web page address

The most direct way to surf to a web page is to type the page's *address* (also known, at least among the web's nerdiest denizens, as *URL*, or Uniform Resource Locator). Most website addresses, such as `https://www.apple.com/mac`, consist of these parts:

>> **https://www:** Identifies the address as part of the World Wide Web (WWW) and that this website exchanges information securely by using a method called Hypertext Transfer Protocol Secure (HTTPS). Some sites omit the www

portion of the name. Just keep in mind that www is common but not always necessary for many web page addresses.

>> **The domain name of the website (such as** apple**):** Identifies the server computer that hosts the web page. Most domain names are abbreviations or smushed-together names of the company, organization, or person, such as whitehouse for the White House website and paulmcfedries for my domain.

>> **An identifying extension (such as** .com**):** Identifies the type of website, as shown in Table 1-1. Many websites use a two-letter extension that identifies the site's home country, such as .uk for the United Kingdom or .ca for Canada.

>> **The web page location on the server (such as** /mac**):** Identifies the directory or similar location of the web page within the server. On Apple's site, for example, www.apple.com/mac is the page for Mac-related stuff, while www.apple.com/iphone is the page for iPhone info.

TABLE 1-1

Common Web Address Extensions

Three-Letter Extension	Type of Website	Examples
.com	Often a commercial website, but can be another type of website	www.apple.com
.gov	Government website	www.nasa.gov
.edu	School website	www.mit.edu
.net	Network, sometimes used as an alternative to the .com extension	www.earthlink.net
.org	A nonprofit organization website	www.redcross.org
.mil	Military website	www.army.mil

When you know the address of the page you want to visit, you type the address directly into Safari as follows:

1. **In Safari, click in the search and address field (refer to Figure 1-1).**

If the search and address text box already contains an address, Safari selects it.

2. **Type the address of the web page you want to visit.**

TIP

Almost all web page these days use HTTPS, so you can skip the opening `https://` part of the address and Safari will add it for you automatically.

As you type the address, Safari autocompletes it with a likely match, usually based on your viewing history, and then highlights the part it added. In Figure 1-2, I typed **app**, and Safari autocompleted that to `apple.com`. You can see, too, other potential matches listed below; as you type more letters, the choices narrow. You have several ways to proceed here:

- If the autocompleted address is the one you want, move on to Step 3.

- If you want to use the autocompleted address but add more to it, press the right arrow key and type the rest of the address.

- If you don't want to use the autocompleted address, continue typing.

- If you want to use a page from the pop-up list that appears, press the down arrow key until you highlight the page you want.

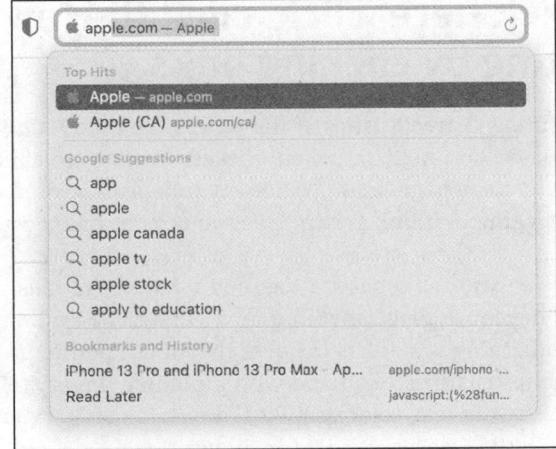

FIGURE 1-2:
Begin typing an address, and Safari auto-completes a potential match.

3. **Press Return.**

Safari displays the web page corresponding to the address you typed or selected. For example, I typed `apple.com/mac` and I ended up at the page shown in Figure 1-3.

REMEMBER

Safari's address and search text box only shows the domain name of the web page. For example, even though I typed `apple.com/mac` and correctly ended up at the address `https://www.apple.com/mac`, you can see in Figure 1-3 that Safari just shows `apple.com` in the address and search bar.

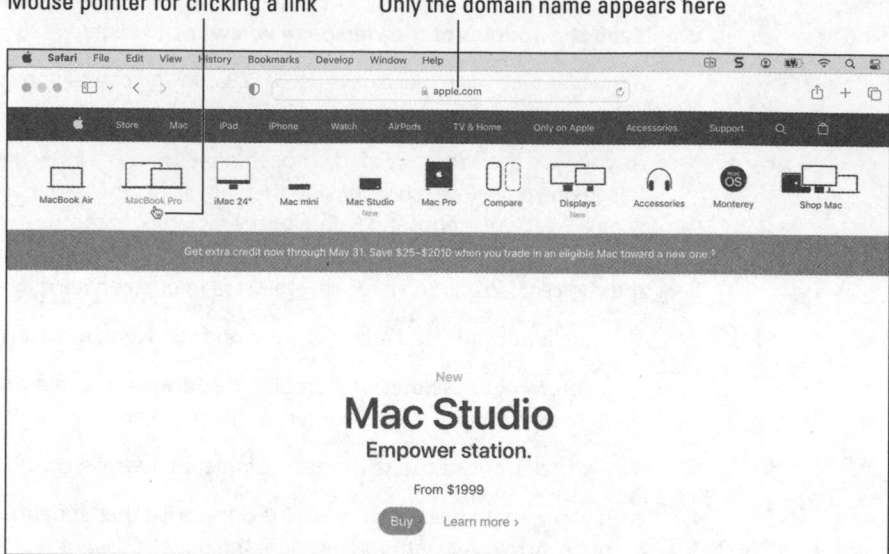

Mouse pointer for clicking a link   Only the domain name appears here

FIGURE 1-3:
Whatever the address of the page you surfed to, Safari displays only the domain name in the address and search field.

Click, click here, click, click there: Navigating by clicking links

One of the defining characteristics of the web is the link. A *link* is a special word, phrase, image, or button that, when clicked, whisks you directly to another web page. Not just any page, mind you. Every link is associated with one and only one page, so clicking that link always takes you to the link's associated page.

Okay, so how can you tell what's a link and what isn't? Alas, it's not that easy because these days just about anything on a page can be a link. The only way to be sure that something is a link is to hover the mouse pointer over it. If it's a link, the mouse pointer changes to a hand with a pointer finger (refer to Figure 1-3). If the link is text, the text color usually changes, as well. (You might be able to discern this with the *MacBook Pro* text in Figure 1-3.)

Putting the web to work: Searching for sites

You don't need to be an experienced web surfer to know that the web is incomprehensibly big. We're talking here a total number of pages measured in the *billions*. Nope, that's not a typo. *Billions.*

How in the name of Tim Berners-Lee (the fellow who invented the web) are you supposed to find anything in such an intimidatingly vast collection? If you don't have the address of the page you want, and you don't know of any site that has a link to the page you want, all is not lost. You can, instead, search for what you're looking for. Special websites called *search engines* specialize in finding stuff on the web. Whether you want to find the website for a specific company or person or more general information about a topic, a search engine can help you locate whatever you're looking for.

Google is probably the most well-known search engine (and is Safari's default search engine), but others include DuckDuckGo and Bing, which you can designate as the default search engine. Here's how to use Safari to access search engines and then start your (search) engine:

1. **In Safari, type your search text in the search and address field.**

See the upcoming "Searching tips" sidebar for some pointers on constructing useful search queries.

As you type the search text, Safari displays a pop-up menu that includes a section titled Google Suggestions (refer to Figure 1-2), which includes some sample Google searches related to what you've typed so far. You have several ways to proceed:

- Keep typing until your search text is complete.

- If your completed search text has generated an autocomplete address, press the spacebar.

- If you want to use one of the items in the Google Suggestions list, instead, press the down arrow key until you highlight the item you want.

2. **Press Return.**

Safari forwards your search text to Google, which displays its results, as shown in Figure 1-4. Generally speaking, the first few results (that is, the first few results after the inevitable ads and other sponsored content!) are the most relevant to your search text. Google usually displays many pages of results, but there's never much point going beyond a page or two.

Each result is a link. These links generally take you to web pages, but you can also click one of the buttons at the top of the results web page — Images, Shopping, Videos, and so on — to see results in other types of media.

3. **Click a result that looks promising.**

Safari takes you to the page (or whatever).

4. **If that page wasn't what you wanted, click the back icon (labeled in Figure 1-1) to return to the search results, and then try again.**

5. **Repeat Steps 3 and 4 as needed.**

SEARCHING TIPS

Given the billions of web pages on the web, your search can turn up more exact results if you better define your search terms. Here are a few ways you can specify your search terms:

- Use quotation marks around a phrase to find the words exactly as you typed them. For example, if you type **John Quincy Adams** in the Search field, your result contains references for **John** Smith and Jane **Adams** in **Quincy**, Massachusetts, as well as references to the former president. If you type **"John Quincy Adams"** your search results contain only websites that contain the name as you typed it.

- To match pages that contain all your search terms, separate each term with the word AND (all-uppercase); for example, type **rutabaga AND recipe AND delicious**.

- To match pages that contain one or more of your search terms, separate each term with the word OR (all-uppercase); for example, type **rutabaga OR neep OR swede**.

- Confine your search to a specific website by adding site: *domain*. For example, if you want references to John Quincy Adams from the White House website, type **"John Quincy Adams" site:whitehouse.gov**.

- To exclude pages that contain a particular word, place a hyphen before that word. For example, type **rutabaga -turnip**.

- Don't worry about using small articles and prepositions like *a, the, of, about;* or using capital letters (except with the AND and OR operators which, as I mentioned, must be all uppercase).

- Check your spelling. If you mistype a word or phrase, the search engine might look for pages that contain that misspelled word or phrase, which probably won't be the page you really want to see.

If you want to switch the default search engine from Google to DuckDuckGo, Bing, or some other service, do the following:

1. **Choose Safari ⇨ Settings.**

2. **Click the Search tab.**

3. **Use the Search Engine pop-up menu to choose the search engine you prefer: Yahoo!, Bing, DuckDuckGo, or Ecosia.**

4. **Click the close icon in the upper-left corner of the settings window.**

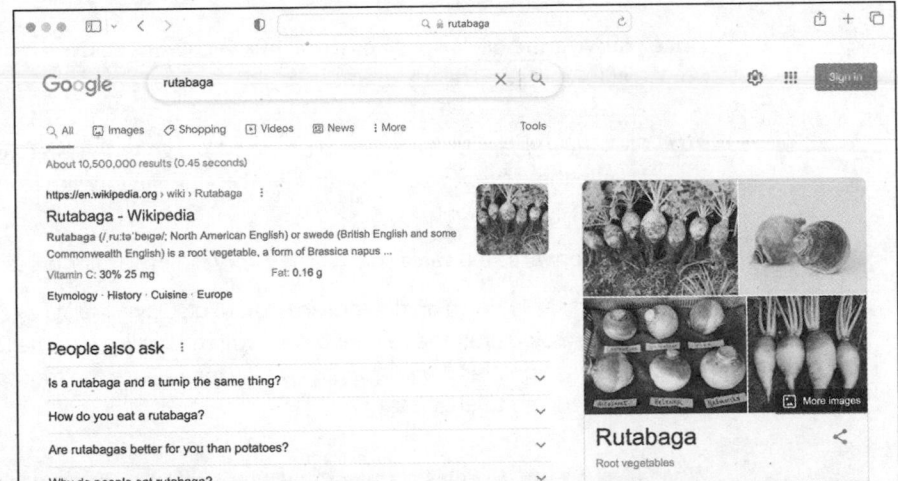

FIGURE 1-4:
Words or phrases
you search for
appear as links
in the search
results.

TIP

If you search for websites and find yourself wandering down a number of blind alleys because the web pages you navigate to aren't what you're looking for, return to your search results and start afresh. Choose History ⇨ Search Results SnapBack (or press Option+⌘+S), and the results instantly replace whatever page you were viewing.

Going back in time

If you visit a web page and want to visit it again, Safari gives you a couple of options. If the page was one you visited in your current surfing session (that is, between the time you started Safari and then quit the app), you can go back to that page by using any of the following techniques:

>> Click the back icon (labeled in Figure 1-1) to return to the page you visited just prior to the current page. You can keep clicking the back icon until you return to the page you want.

TIP

To go back, you can also choose History ⇨ Back or press ⌘+[.

>> Click and hold down on the back icon to display a list of pages you've previously visited in this session. Drag the mouse into the list and, when the mouse pointer is over the page you want, release the mouse button to select (and go to) that page.

Once you've gone back a page or three in the current session, you can also reverse your tracks and go forward again:

TIP

» Click the forward icon (labeled in Figure 1-1) to go to the page you visited just after to the current page. You can keep clicking the forward icon until you get to the page you want.

To go forward, you can also choose History ⇨ Forward or press ⌘+].

» Click and hold down on the forward icon to display a list of pages you visited in this session after the current page. Drag the mouse into the list and, when the mouse pointer is over the page you want, release the mouse button to select (and go to) that page.

What if you want to revisit a page that you surfed to in an earlier session, say a day, a week, or even a month ago? No problem! Safari stores a list of your visited web pages in its History menu. To use the History menu to revisit a web page, click History on Safari's menu bar. Using the History menu that appears (see Figure 1-5), you have three choices:

» If the page you want appears in the list of recent pages, click the page in that list.

» If you visited the page on one of the displayed dates, click the date you visited and then click the page on the continuation menu that appears.

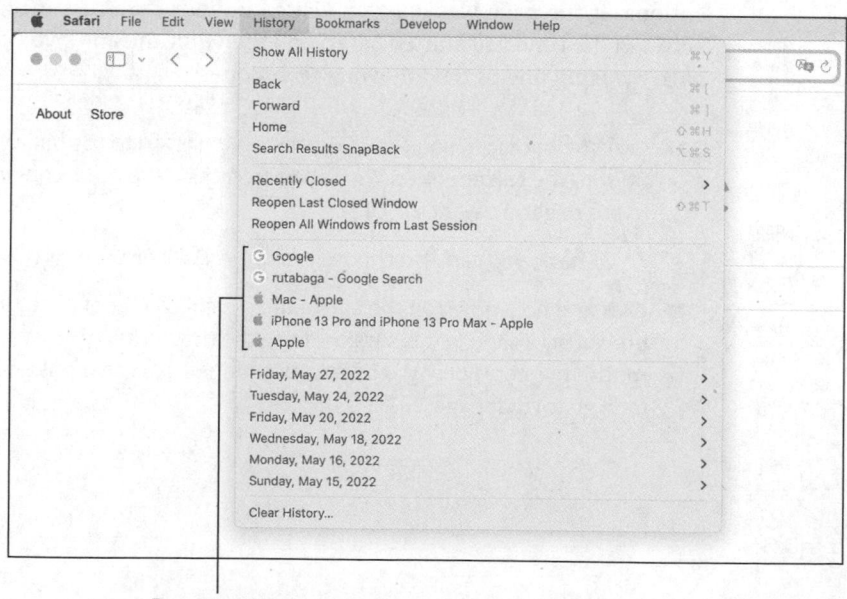

FIGURE 1-5:
The History menu lets you revisit previously viewed websites.

Recent pages

>> If you visited the page on some other date, click Show All History (or press ⌘+Y) to open the History page, click the date you visited, and then click the page. If you're not sure when you visited the page, use the Search box to find the page you want.

TIP

By default, Safari keeps a log of the sites you visit for a year. To change the length of time you want to keep your browsing history, choose Safari ⇨ Settings and click the General button on the toolbar. Use the Remove History Items pop-up menu to choose a period after which a site visit is deleted by Safari.

You can erase some or all of your web browsing history at any time by choosing History ⇨ Clear History, selecting a time frame (such as The Last Hour or Today), and then clicking Clear History.

Distraction-Free Reading with Reader View

You only have to visit a few web pages to learn a painful truth of the web: It's usually hard to find the content amongst all the ads, site promotions, navigation buttons, pop-ups, and other bothersome bric-a-brac that infest modern websites. It's a plague upon the Earth, but Safari can help inject a little sanity into your surfing with *reading view*. This view removes all that non-essential (at least to us surfers) stuff and offers up a simple, unadorned, ready-to-read version of the page.

To give you an example of what a difference reading view can make, check out the page versions shown in Figure 1-6. The page on the left is what you see when you first surf to it, while the page on the right is the same page in reading view.

Show reader view

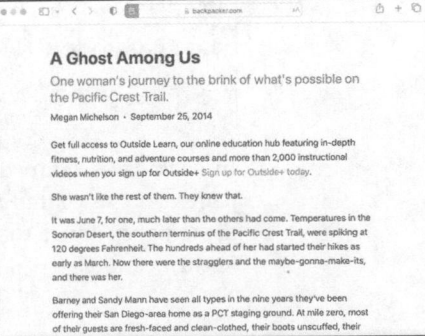

FIGURE 1-6:
The original page (left) and its reading view equivalent (right).

To invoke reading view, Safari offers these methods:

» Click the show reader view icon, labeled in Figure 1-6 (left).

» Choose View ⇨ Show Reader (or press Shift+⌘+R).

One-Window Surfing: Browsing with Tabs

When you want to keep track of more than one web page while browsing a second (or third or fourth) page, you could open two (or three or four) separate browser windows (by choosing File ⇨ New Window or pressing ⌘+N). You *could* do that, but the problem is that you would quickly end up with an absurd number of windows cluttering your desktop.

Fortunately, there's a handier way to keep multiple web pages open in Safari: using tabs. In a Safari window, a tab is a separate section that contains a web page. (Yep, this is similar to the Finder tabs I explain in Book 1, Chapter 4.) You're free have as many tabs open as your Mac's memory will allow (although in practice you don't want to go much beyond 20 tabs). The advantage of using multiple tabs versus multiple windows is that everything fits within a single Safari window (no desktop clutter!) and each tab — and therefore each page — is just a click away (one-click access!).

Manufacturing a new tab

By default, Safari always shows just a single web page in its window; there's nary a tab in sight. Not to worry, though, because Safari gives you all kinds of ways to add a new tab to the window:

» In Safari's toolbar, click the + (new tab) icon (labeled in Figure 1-7).

» Choose File ⇨ New Tab.

» Press ⌘+T.

In each case, Safari displays the Start Page, which contains your favorite pages, pages you've visited frequently, your reading list, and more. Either click one of these pages or use the address and search field to type the page address and press Return.

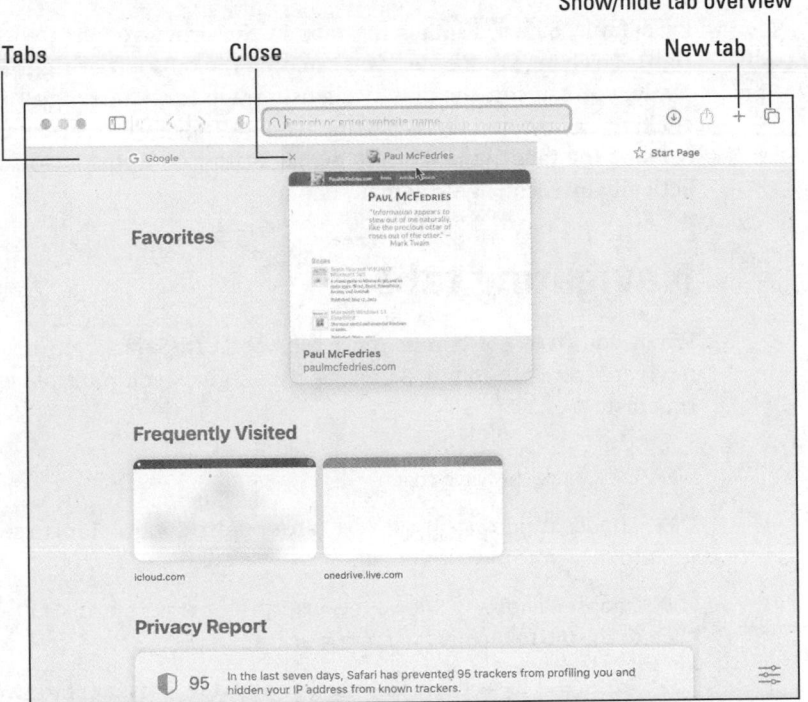

Tabs · Close · Show/hide tab overview · New tab

FIGURE 1-7:
Safari surfing
with a few tabs.

An alternative way to rustle up a new tab is to load a link or address into its own tab. You have two ways to go here:

>> **To load the page into a new tab but stay on the current page:** Either hold down ⌘ and click the link or type the page address in the address and search field, and then press ⌘+Return.

>> **To load the page into a new tab and switch to that tab:** Either hold down Shift+⌘ and click the link or type the page address in the address and search field, and then press Shift+⌘+Return.

Figure 1-7 shows Safari with three tabs on the go. Note that when you hover the mouse pointer over a tab, Safari displays a thumbnail image of the page that loaded in that tab.

TIP

To see thumbnail images of all your open tabs, choose View ⇨ Show Tab Overview (or press Shift+⌘+\ or click Show Tab Overview, labeled in Figure 1-7). To return to your regularly scheduled tabs, choose View ⇨ Hide Tab Overview (or press Shift+⌘+\ or click Hide Tab Overview).

TIP

By default, Safari displays the tabs in the order you created them, from left to right. To change that order, you can drag the tabs left or right as needed. Alternatively, you can sort the tabs by choosing Window ⇨ Arrange Tabs By (or by right-clicking any tab and then clicking Arrange Tabs By), and then clicking either Title (to sort the tabs alphabetically by page title) or Website (to sort the tabs alphabetically by each page's domain name).

Navigating tabs

When you have got two or more tabs open in Safari, you need to know how to navigate from tab to tab. Safari, as usual, gives you multiple ways to accomplish this task:

>> Click a tab to switch to it.

>> Choose Window ⇨ Show Next Tab (or press Control+Tab) to switch to the tab to the left of the current tab.

>> Choose Window ⇨ Show Previous Tab (or press Control+Shift+Tab) to switch to the tab to the right of the current tab.

>> Press ⌘+1 to switch to the first (leftmost) tab, press ⌘+2 to switch to the second tab, and so on up to pressing ⌘+9 to switch to the ninth tab.

Working with tab groups

When you're researching a project for work or school, chances are you'll end up opening a few Safari tabs with pages related to that project. If another task comes along, you might end up opening a few more tabs with pages related to that task. Now you have an event to plan, and a few more Safari tabs get opened.

Having different collections of tabs related to different projects is all in a day's web work, but navigating and organizing all those tabs quickly becomes a real chore. Some folks create separate Safari windows for each project, but then you're back to the problem of window overpopulation on your desktop. Is there a better way?

I'm glad you asked because, yes, there is a better way: tab groups. A *tab group* is a collection of Safari tabs that appear in the Safari window only when you select that group. You can create a tab group for each project, task, and event that you're working on and quickly switch from one to the other as needed, all in a single Safari window.

To create a tab group, you have two options:

>> **Create a tab group from the open tabs:** Open just the tabs you want in your tab group and then choose File ⇨ New Tab Group with *X* Tabs (where *X* is the number of tabs you have open). Safari displays the sidebar and adds the new tab group. Type a name for the tab group and then press Return.

>> **Create and then populate an empty tab group:** Choose File ⇨ New Empty Tab Group (or press Control+⌘+N). Safari displays the sidebar and adds the new tab group. Type a name for the tab group and then press Return. For each tab you want to include in the tab group, right-click the tab, click Move to Tab Group, and then click the name of the tab group.

Once you have a tab group or two set up, how you open a tab group depends on whether you have the sidebar displayed. The sidebar is a pane that appears on the left side of the Safari window and that contains not only your tab groups but also your bookmarks, reading list, and shared links (see Book 2, Chapter 2).

First, here are the techniques you use to show and hide the sidebar:

>> **Show the sidebar:** Choose View ⇨ Show Sidebar. You can also press Shift+⌘+L or click the Show Sidebar button (which then turns into the Hide Sidebar button).

>> **Hide the sidebar:** Choose View ⇨ Hide Sidebar. You can also press Shift+⌘+L or click the Hide Sidebar button (which then turns back into the Show Sidebar button).

TIP

To make the sidebar pane wider or narrower, move the pointer to the right edge of the sidebar until it becomes a vertical line with an arrow on both sides, and then drag the edge right or left.

With that out of the way, you can now use either of the following techniques to open a tab group:

>> **Sidebar displayed:** Your groups appear in the Tab Groups section, as shown in Figure 1-8, top. Click a tab group to open it.

>> **Sidebar hidden:** Your groups appear in a drop-down list called the tab group picker, to the right of the Show Sidebar button, as shown in Figure 1-8, bottom. Click the Tab Group Picker and then click the tab group you want to open.

In the sidebar, you can also right-click any tab group to perform maintenance tasks such as renaming the group, showing the tab overview (thumbnails of the tabs in the group), and deleting the group.

Show/Hide Sidebar

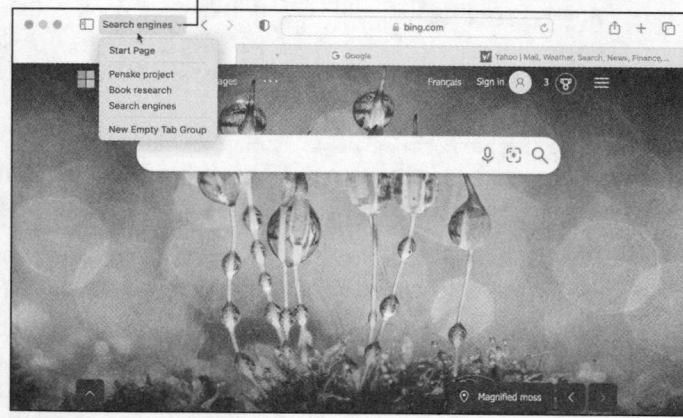

Tab Group Picker

FIGURE 1-8:
Your tab groups
appear in the
sidebar's Tab
Groups section
(top) or in the
tab group picker
(bottom).

Closing tabs

When you no longer need a tab, you should close it to reduce clutter in the Safari window. Here are the techniques you can use:

» To close a single tab, hover the mouse pointer over the tab and then click X, which is the close icon (labeled in Figure 1-7). For the current tab, you can also choose File ⇨ Close Tab or press ⌘+W.

» To close all the tabs to the left of a particular tab, right-click that tab and then click Close Tabs to the Left.

» To close all the tabs except a particular tab, either right-click that tab and then click Close Other Tabs or Option-click that tab's close icon.

TIP

I can't tell you how many times I've accidentally closed a tab that I wanted to keep open. And, just to prove that Murphy's Law (anything that can go wrong will go wrong) is still in effect, the tab that you close by accident will be the tab that has the most important information. If you close a tab inadvertently, Safari has two remedies you can try: If you haven't closed any other tabs in the meantime, choose History ➪ Reopen Last Closed Tab, or press Shift+⌘+T. Otherwise, choose History ➪ Recently Closed and then select the tab from the continuation menu that appears. You're welcome!

Managing tab settings

Safari offers a few useful settings related to tabs. Here's how to work with these settings:

1. **Choose Safari ➪ Settings.**

2. **Click the Tabs button on the toolbar.**

Safari's Tabs settings appear, as shown in Figure 1-9.

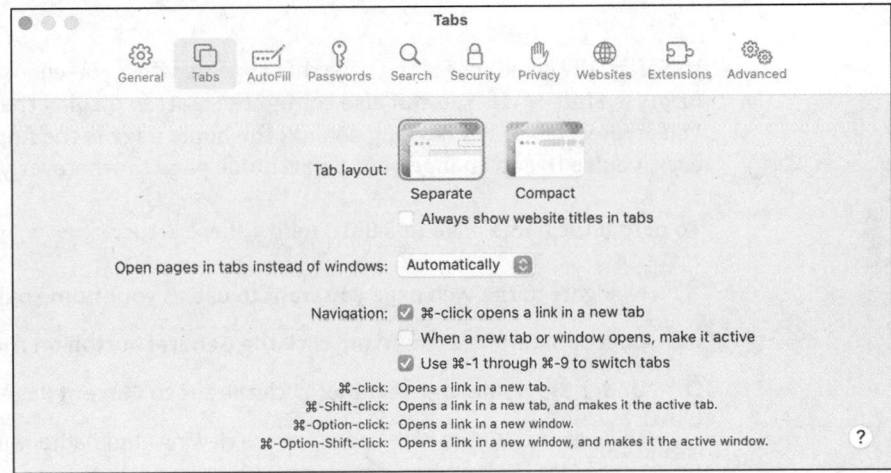

FIGURE 1-9:
Choose your tab settings.

3. **Click the tab layout you prefer.**

The Separate layout shows the tabs below the address and search field. To gain a little extra vertical space, click the Compact layout, which incorporates the tab buttons into the Safari toolbar.

4. **From the Open Pages in Tabs Instead of Windows pop-up menu, choose when you want pages to open in tabs instead of windows.**

5. **Select the check boxes to activate one or all of the following choices:**

- *Always Show Website Titles in Tabs:* By default, when you have lots of tabs open (or the Safari window is narrow), Safari displays each website's icon in the tab instead of the page title. If you prefer to always see the titles, select this check box.

- *⌘-Click Opens a Link in a New Tab:* When this check box is selected, pressing ⌘-click on a link opens the linked page in a new tab and leaves the current web page open.

- *When a New Tab or Window Opens, Make It Active:* When this check box is selected, opening a link or address in a new tab automatically switches you to that tab.

- *Use ⌘+1 through ⌘+9 to switch tabs:* When this check box is selected, you can press the ⌘ key and a number to surf through your open tabs.

6. **Click the close icon.**

Setting Your Safari Home Page

In Safari, the *home page* is the page that appears when you choose History ➪ Home or press Shift+⌘+H. You can also configure Safari to display the home page when you create a tab or window. By default, the home page is the Apple website. However, you're free to change your Safari home page to whatever you prefer.

To define the home page in Safari, follow these steps:

1. **Navigate to the web page you want to use as your home page.**

2. **Choose Safari ➪ Settings and click the General button on the toolbar.**

3. **Under the Homepage text box, click the Set to Current Page button.**

   The website address of the page you are viewing automatically fills the Homepage field, as shown in Figure 1-10.

   If the current web page isn't the one you want to use as the home page, you can instead type the correct address in the Homepage text field.

4. **(Optional) If you want Safari to open to your home page when you restart or reopen Safari or when you create a new Safari window, choose Homepage in the New Windows Open With pop-up menu.**

5. **(Optional) If you want Safari to display your home page when you create a new tab, choose Homepage in the New Tabs Open With pop-up menu.**

6. **Close the Safari settings pane.**

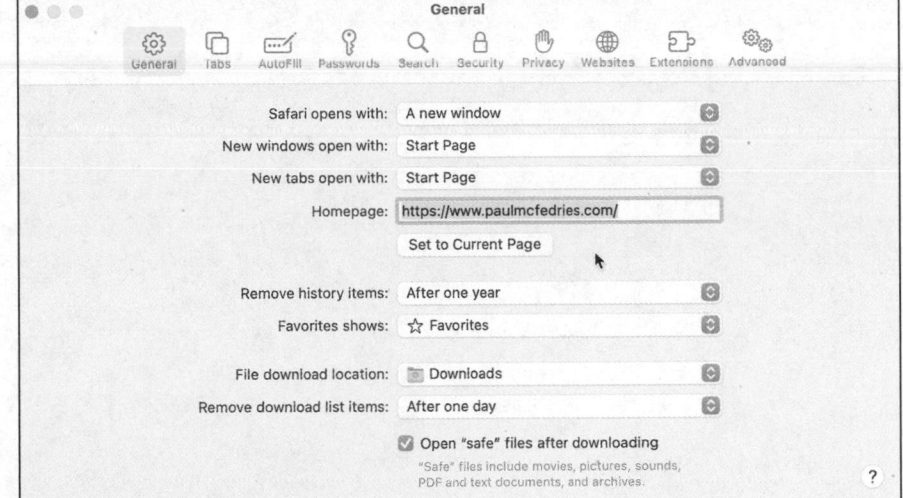

FIGURE 1-10:
Set your Safari
home page here.

Scouring Web Page Text

You can search for a word or phrase in the text on a web page, and Safari will find and highlight each occurrence of the word or phrase. Here's how:

1. **Navigate to the web page you want to search.**

2. **Choose Edit ⇨ Find ⇨ Find or press ⌘+F.**

Under the toolbar, the Find text field appears.

3. **Type the word or phrase you want to find.**

Safari highlights each occurrence of the search phrase, and a left arrow and a right arrow appear to the right of the Search field. Safari also shows how many instances of the search word or phrase have been found. The first occurrence of your query is shown with a yellow highlight.

4. **Use the navigation arrows to go to the next (right arrow) or previous (left arrow) occurrence of the search term.**

5. **Click Done to close the Find banner or choose Edit ⇨ Find ⇨ Hide Find Banner (or press Shift+⌘+F).**

Chapter **2**

Order Out of Chaos: Organizing Web Pages

Assuming you still read things in hard copy, imagine if you just placed whatever reading material you wanted to save in a random location in your home. That is, everything you read that's worth keeping — every worthwhile book, magazine, newspaper, letter, postcard, pamphlet, and ransom note — gets deposited willy-nilly somewhere in your abode. Can you imagine how much time you'd waste trying to find anything?

Now imagine that instead of scouring just your home for the item you want, you have to scour the entire world! That's essentially the problem in a nutshell when you don't organize the web pages that come your way. Sure, most of the pages you read won't be worth a second look, but you'll be surprised at just how many pages you'll come across that are worth not just a second look but also a third or even a hundredth.

In this chapter, I tell you how to use the Safari features that organize favorite websites you want to revisit, manage the articles you want to read later, and list the links to articles your friends have sent you via text messages. These are, respectively, your bookmarks, reading list, and shared with you links. You also delve into useful browsing topics, such as accessing text message links, managing passwords and credit cards, protecting your privacy on the web, sharing web pages, and downloading files. Along the way, you find tips and tricks to make your surfing experience more fun and productive.

REMEMBER

As you read the chapter, remember that you can access your bookmarks, reading list, and shared links from Safari's sidebar, which you open by choosing View ⇨ Show Sidebar or by clicking the show sidebar icon.

Saving Sites for Subsequent Surfs: Managing Bookmarks

A *bookmark* is way of saving any web page that you think you'll visit again. You might, for example, bookmark a favorite news site or an oft-used reference page. Click a bookmark and Safari opens the saved web page, just like that.

Safari gives you three locations to save bookmarks: the favorites bar, the Bookmarks menu, and the Bookmarks sidebar.

The *favorites bar,* shown in Figure 2-1, gives you one-click access to web pages you visit most frequently. Choose View ⇨ Show Favorites Bar (or press Shift+⌘+B) and the favorites bar shows up below the address and search text field. Each item you see on the favorites bar is a bookmark to a web page. Safari ships with a few default favorites to get you going.

FIGURE 2-1:
The favorites bar offers lickety-split access to your favorite pages.

You can place as many bookmarks as you like on the favorites bar, but you'll see only as many as can fit in the width of the Safari window. If Safari isn't wide enough to display all your bookmarks, the show more bookmarks icon appears at the right end of the favorites bar, as pointed out in Figure 2-1. Click the icon to open a menu that displays the bookmarks that don't fit. You can get around that problem by making the Safari window wider (if possible) or by grouping bookmarks into folders on the favorites bar (which I get to in just a bit).

The Bookmarks menu, shown in Figure 2-2, is where you'll perform many of your bookmark management chores. The bottom part of the menu is where all your bookmarks appear, organized as follows:

>> Your bookmark folders (such as the Social Media folder shown in Figure 2-2) appear at the very bottom.

>> Your favorites — that is, the bookmarks that appear on the favorites bar — appear in the Favorites submenu.

>> Individual bookmarks that you saved to the Bookmarks menu (such as the Paul McFedries and Wikipedia bookmarks shown in Figure 2-2) appear above the Favorites submenu.

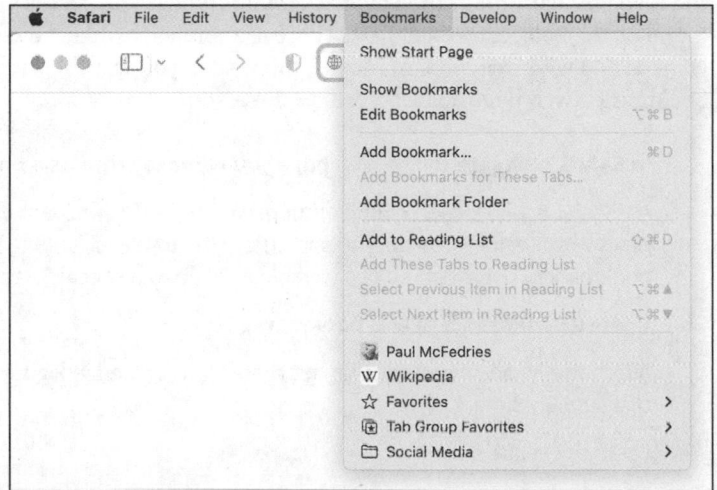

FIGURE 2-2:
The Bookmarks
menu is where
you manage and
save bookmarks.

Finally, Safari also offers the Bookmarks sidebar, which you display by showing the sidebar and then clicking Bookmarks (or by choosing View ⇨ Show Bookmarks Sidebar or by pressing Control+⌘+1). As you can see in Figure 2-3, the Bookmarks sidebar contains the same bookmarks and folders as the bottom part of the Bookmarks menu. (Well, not *exactly* the same: The individual bookmarks on the Bookmarks menu — Paul McFedries and Wikipedia in Figure 2-2 — now appear in the sidebar's Bookmarks Menu folder.) Clicking the disclosure arrow to the left of a folder displays the bookmarks within or collapses them if it's already open. Click a bookmark to open that web page.

REMEMBER

Bookmarks behave the same whether they appear on the favorites bar, on the Bookmarks menu, or in the Bookmarks sidebar: Click a bookmark and Safari opens the linked web page, no questions asked.

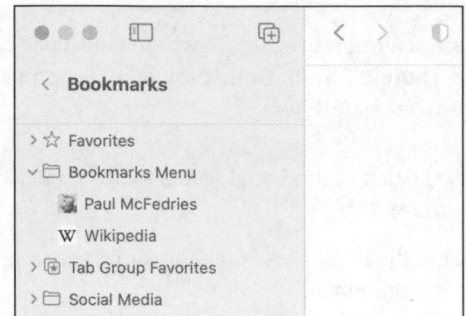

FIGURE 2-3:
The Bookmarks
sidebar shows
your bookmarks
and folders.

Adding a bookmark

By default, Safari comes stocked with several prefab bookmarks already placed on the favorites bar and in the Favorites folder (which you access via the Bookmarks menu or the Bookmarks sidebar). There are some sensible choices here, but you'll want to add your own bookmarks for those sites you want to save for posterity. To bookmark a web page address, follow these steps:

1. **In Safari, navigate to the web page you want to store as a bookmark.**

   REMEMBER

   A website is a collection of one or more web pages. If you want to bookmark a news website, for instance, you should use the top-level landing page as the bookmarked page instead of a web page linked to a specific article.

2. **Choose Bookmarks ⇨ Add Bookmark.**

   Alternatively, press ⌘+D or click the share icon (labeled in Figure 2-1) and then click Add Bookmark.

   Safari opens the dialog shown in Figure 2-4.

   TIP

   You can add a bookmark also by clicking the address to select it, dragging the address, and then dropping it on the favorites bar or inside a folder in the Bookmarks sidebar.

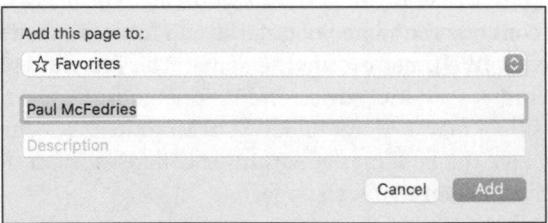

FIGURE 2-4:
Choose a
location for your
bookmark and
optionally edit
its name.

3. **Click the Add This Page To pop-up menu and choose a location for storing your bookmark.**

   You can choose Bookmarks (which places the bookmark at the bottom of the Bookmarks menu and the bottom of the Bookmarks sidebar), Favorites, the Bookmarks menu, or a specific folder. (You discover how to create a bookmark folder in the next section, "Storing bookmarks in folders.")

4. **(Optional) Type a new name for the bookmark if you don't want to keep the default name.**

5. **Click Add.**

   Your new bookmark appears where you placed it.

TIP

To sync your bookmarks across all devices, turn on Safari in iCloud on your Mac and your iOS devices, or Safari on a Windows computer with iCloud. See Book 1, Chapter 3 to learn about using iCloud.

Storing bookmarks in folders

After you save a bunch of bookmarks, they can start to clutter the Bookmarks menu or the favorites bar. To organize your bookmarks, you can store related bookmarks in the same folder. There are two ways to create a bookmarks folder. There are two ways to create a bookmarks folder: in the Bookmarks sidebar and using the Bookmarks editor. You use both methods in this section.

Follow these steps to use the Bookmarks sidebar to create and populate a bookmarks folder:

1. **Choose View ⇨ Show Bookmarks Sidebar to open the Bookmarks sidebar.**

2. **Choose Bookmarks ⇨ Add Bookmark Folder.**

   An Untitled Folder is added to the bottom of the Bookmarks sidebar.

3. **Type a name for the folder and press Return.**

4. **In the Bookmarks sidebar, open the folder (such as Favorites or Bookmarks Menu) that contains the bookmark you want to store in your new folder.**

5. **Drag the bookmark and then drop it in the new folder.**

   Safari moves the bookmark to the new folder.

6. **Repeat Steps 4 and 5 to move additional bookmarks to the folder.**

   After you create a folder, you can add bookmarks at any time.

TIP

Another way to create and populate a bookmarks folder is to open a tab for each page you want to include in the new folder, and then choose Bookmarks ➪ Add Bookmarks for These *X* Tabs (where *X* is the number of tabs you have open). Select a location for the new folder, type a folder name, and then click Add.

TIP

If you have tons of bookmarks, it will be difficult to drag them onto the folder. To solve this dilemma, choose File ➪ New Window. Resize the new window and position it alongside another browser window. Open the Bookmarks sidebar in both windows and drag bookmarks from one window to the folder you want to populate in the other window.

Follow these steps to use the Bookmarks editor to create and populate a bookmark folder:

1. **Choose Bookmarks ➪ Edit Bookmarks to display the Bookmarks editor.**

   If you want the new folder to be placed inside an existing folder, click Favorites Bar, Bookmarks Menu, or another folder in the left column.

2. **Click the New Folder button.**

   An untitled folder is added to the bottom of the list or to the folder you selected in Step 1.

3. **Type a name for the folder and press Return.**

4. **(Optional) Click the disclosure triangle to the left of a folder name to display the bookmarks and folders within that folder.**

   This step is useful if you have bookmarks in another folder that you want to move to the new folder.

5. **Drag each bookmark you want to move into the new folder.**

6. **Choose Bookmarks ➪ Hide Bookmarks Editor.**

Rearranging or deleting bookmarks

Safari saves your bookmarks and bookmark folders in the order you create them, adding them to the bottom of an ever-growing list. If you continue to add bookmarks to the Bookmarks menu without placing them in folders, you may find that you have a gazillion bookmarks listed willy-nilly and can't remember what half of them link to (guilty as charged). As time passes, you probably have bookmarks you no longer use or that no longer work.

The solution is to rearrange the bookmarks you want to keep in a more sensible order and to delete the bookmarks that no longer spark joy. The procedures for moving and deleting bookmarks are the same whether you work in the Bookmarks sidebar or the Bookmarks editor. Follow these steps to put your bookmarks in a more logical order and delete any you no longer want:

1. **In Safari, choose Bookmarks ➪ Edit Bookmarks.**

   Or choose View ➪ Show Bookmarks Sidebar.

2. **Do one of the following:**

   - *Bookmarks editor:* Click the disclosure triangle next to the folder name that contains the bookmark.

   - *Bookmarks sidebar:* Click the folder you want to move or delete.

   The contents, which might include bookmarks and additional folders that contain other bookmarks, are listed below.

   Click the additional folders to see the bookmarks contained within. You may need to repeat this step several times to find the bookmark you want.

3. **Drag the bookmark or bookmark folder you want to move up or down the list to a new folder or position.**

   Drag the bookmark or folder beyond the last item in a folder to move it out of the folder. A line shows where the item is being moved to; if you move it into a folder, the folder is highlighted.

   Safari moves your chosen bookmark to its new location.

4. **To change the order in which bookmarks are displayed, drag them up and down within the collection or folder.**

5. **To delete a bookmark:**

   - *Bookmarks editor:* Click the bookmark that you want to delete and press Delete.

   - *Bookmarks sidebar:* Right-click the undesired bookmark and choose Delete from the context menu.

WARNING

   You can also delete a folder this way, but all the bookmarks and folders within the deleted folder will be deleted.

   To restore a bookmark you mistakenly deleted, press ⌘+Z or choose Edit ➪ Undo Remove Bookmark.

TIP

6. **To return to the most recent web page you viewed, choose Bookmarks ➪ Hide Bookmarks Editor.**

7. **To close the sidebar, click the show/hide sidebar icon (labeled in Figure 2-1).**

Renaming bookmarks and folders

You may want to bookmark several web pages from the same website but find that you'll have trouble differentiating them in the Bookmarks menu or Bookmarks sidebar because the displayed name begins with the website and then the slashes and such to specify the web page. You can rename bookmarks and folders to something that's more meaningful, which will help you find your bookmarks more quickly. Here's how to rename in the Bookmarks editor and the Bookmarks sidebar:

>> **Bookmarks editor:** Choose Bookmarks ⇨ Edit Bookmarks. The Bookmarks editor opens. Click the bookmark or folder you want to rename and then press Return. The name of the bookmark or folder opens for editing. Type the new name you want to use or click the text to edit it, and then press Return. After you finish editing your bookmarks, choose Bookmarks ⇨ Hide Bookmarks Editor.

>> **Bookmarks sidebar:** Choose View ⇨ Show Bookmarks Sidebar. Right-click the bookmark or folder you want to rename and choose Rename from the context menu. The name of the bookmark or folder opens for editing. Type the new name you want to use or click the text to edit it, and then press Return.

Importing and exporting bookmarks

After you collect and organize bookmarks, you might become dependent on your bookmarks to help you navigate the web. Fortunately, if you ever want to switch browsers, you can export bookmarks from one browser and import them into another browser.

To export bookmarks from Safari, follow these steps:

1. **Choose File ⇨ Export ⇨ Bookmarks to open the Export Bookmarks dialog.**

2. **(Optional) Type a descriptive name for your bookmarks if you don't want to keep the default name of Safari Bookmarks.**

3. **Click the Where pop-up menu and choose where you want to store your exported bookmarks file.**

   You can click the arrow button to the right of the Where pop-up menu to expand the Export Bookmarks dialog to its full size, enabling you to store the bookmarks in any folder in your Mac's file system.

4. **Click Save.**

After you export bookmarks from one browser, it's usually a snap to import them into a second browser. To import bookmarks into Safari, follow these steps:

1. **In Safari, choose File ⇨ Import From, and then choose an option from the continuation menu.**

The options vary depending on which web browsers you have installed. On my computer, I have a copy of Firefox, and the continuation menu gives me the option of importing Firefox bookmarks or importing a Bookmarks HTML file.

If you choose to import from another web browser on your computer, a dialog opens giving you the option of which type of bookmarks you want to import. For example, if you import from Firefox, you can import Bookmarks, History, and Passwords. After deciding which options you want to import, click the Import button.

If you choose Bookmarks HTML file, a dialog appears and you follow the next steps to complete the import.

2. **Navigate to the folder where the exported bookmarks file is stored.**

3. **Click the bookmarks file you want to use and then click the Import button.**

Your imported bookmarks appear in an Imported folder that includes the date when you imported the folder. At this point, you can move this folder or its contents to the Bookmarks sidebar or Bookmarks menu to organize them. (See the earlier section, "Rearranging or deleting bookmarks.")

Setting up a Web Page Reading List

Here's a surfing scenario you'll come across time and again in your web career: You find a fascinating or useful page that you're dying to read, but you just don't have time right now. What's a busy body to do? You could leave the tab open, but that adds unnecessary clutter to the Safari window. You could bookmark the page, but bookmarks are really for pages you'll visit multiple times.

A better solution is to add the page to your Safari *reading list*, which is a collection of pages that Safari stores for you. You can use the Reading List sidebar to access those pages and read them whenever you have some spare time.

Safari offers two techniques for adding stuff to your reading list:

» **Add a single page:** Navigate to the web page you want to add to the reading list, and then choose Bookmarks ⇨ Add to Reading List. Alternatively, press Shift+⌘+D or click the share icon (labeled in Figure 2-1) and then click Add to Reading List.

>> **Add multiple pages:** Open a tab for each page you want to add to the reading list, and then choose Bookmarks ⇨ Add These *X* Tabs to Reading List (where *X* is the number of tabs you have open).

When you're ready to read one or more of your saved articles, you can display the sidebar and then click Reading List, or choose View ⇨ Show Reading List Sidebar (or press Control+⌘+2). As you can see in Figure 2-5, the Reading List sidebar shows the title of the article, its source website, and the first few words of the article. Click the article you want to read and Safari loads the page for you.

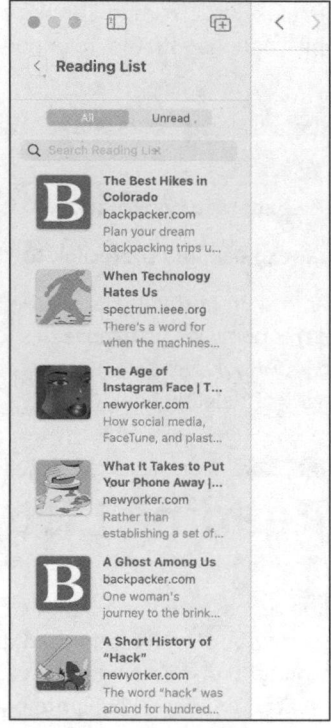

FIGURE 2-5:
The Reading List sidebar stores web pages you want to read later.

REMEMBER

Your reading list is available also on the Start Page that Safari displays when you create a new tab or open a new window. Scroll down to the Reading List section. If you don't see the page you want, click Show All.

Here are a few useful techniques for navigating and managing your reading list:

>> **Navigating reading list items:** To move to the next page in your reading list, either scroll past the bottom of the current reading list page or choose Bookmarks ⇨ Select Next Item in Reading List. To move to the previous page

in your reading list, either scroll past the top of the current reading list page or choose Bookmarks ⇨ Select Previous Item in Reading List.

>> **Controlling the reading list display:** Scroll up to show the All and Unread buttons. Click All to see every reading list page or click Unread to see only those pages you haven't read yet.

>> **Marking a page as unread:** Right-click the page and then click Mark as Unread.

>> **Searching for a page:** If your reading list is very long, use the Search Reading List text box to locate the page you want. (Safari searches the page title, website domain, and summary text, but not the entire page text.)

>> **Saving a page for offline reading:** Right-click the page in the Reading List sidebar and then click Save Offline. You can now read the page text even if your Mac isn't connected to the internet (say, on a long plane ride).

>> **Deleting a page from your reading list:** Right-click the page and then click Remove Item.

>> **Deleting the entire reading list:** Right-click any page, click Clear All Items, and then click Clear when Safari asks you to confirm.

Accessing Links Shared with You via Text

If you have a busy texting life via your Mac's Messages app (see Book 2, Chapter 5) and your connected devices such as your iPhone, part of that life is getting tons of links to cool or fun or useful web pages. That's awesome, but it's never easy to find a link that someone sent you in a text last week or last month. That's okay, though, because Safari has you covered thanks to the Shared with You sidebar, which gathers all those text message links — or, to be more accurate, all the links texted to you by people in your Contacts list — into one handy location.

For all this to work, you need to configure Messages to share links with Safari. This feature is on by default, but you ought to follow these few steps to make sure:

1. **Click the dock's Messages icon.**

   The Messages app appears.

2. **Choose Messages ⇨ Settings.**

   The Messages settings appear.

3. **Click the Shared with You tab.**

4. **Select the Safari check box, if it isn't already selected.**

5. **Click the close icon.**

With that chore out of the way, return to Safari, choose View ➪ Show Sidebar (or click the show sidebar icon, labeled in Figure 2-1) and then click Shared with You. As shown in Figure 2-6, the Shared with You sidebar that appears displays the domain, title, and main image from each shared link, as well as telling you who sent the link. Click a shared link to open the page in Safari.

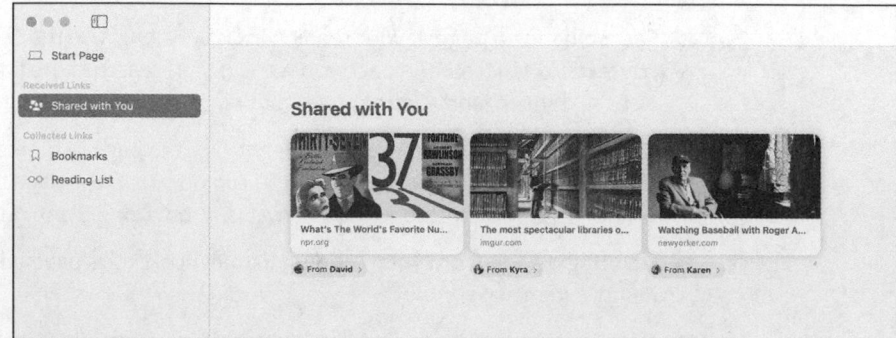

FIGURE 2-6:
The Shared with You sidebar gathers web page links that your contacts have texted.

REMEMBER

You can access your shared links also via the Start Page that Safari displays when you create a new tab or open a new window. Scroll down to the Shared with You section.

You can open and manage your shared links also by using these techniques:

>> **Opening a link in a new window:** Right-click the link and then click Open in New Window.

>> **Opening a link in a tab group:** Right-click the link, click Open in Tab Group, and then click the tab group in the continuation menu that appears.

>> **Replying to the person who sent you the link:** Right-click the link and then click Reply.

>> **Deleting a link:** Right-click the link and then click Remove Link.

Allowing Safari to Store Passwords, Credit Cards, and Other Personal Info

The web is an exciting, dynamic resource, but it has its share of drudgery as well. I'm talking here about the personal info that you have to type over and over again as you go from site to site: usernames, passwords, your email address, your physical address, your phone number, your credit card number and that expiration date you can never remember. It's endless and it can quickly turn surfing the web into a joyless experience.

To regain some of that joy, why not farm out some or all of that drudge work to Safari? Using a feature called AutoFill, Safari can remember all the personal data I just mentioned and can fill it in for you automatically when you come across a web form that requires it. How this works depends on the type of data:

>> **Your information from Contacts:** Safari displays an AutoFill icon on the right side of a web form text field. Click that icon and then click your name, as shown in Figure 2-7, to have Safari fill in the form field (or fields) from your Contacts card. In some fields, clicking the AutoFill icon displays a list of possible entries; click the item you want to use to fill in the field.

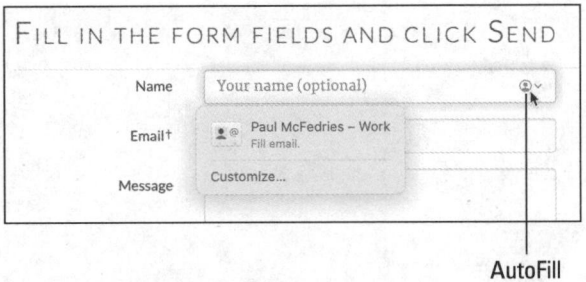

FIGURE 2-7:
Click the AutoFill icon and then click your name to fill in form fields using your Contacts card.

AutoFill

>> **Usernames and passwords:** The first time you visit a website that requires a username and password, you can take one of the following two routes:

- *Use the Safari-generated password:* Safari automatically creates a strong password for the site, as shown in Figure 2-8. If you click Use Strong Password, Safari not only uses its generated password but also saves your login data to AutoFill.

- *Use your own password:* If you use the Other Options drop-down menu to click Choose My Own Password, you can enter your own password. After you submit the form, Safari displays the dialog shown in Figure 2-9 to ask if you want to save the password. Click Save Password to save the password and the username to AutoFill. If you want to skip the save just this time, click Not Now. If you never want to save the site's login data, click Never for This Website.

It's a good idea to click Never for This Website for sensitive sites such as financial institutions and corporate portals.

TIP

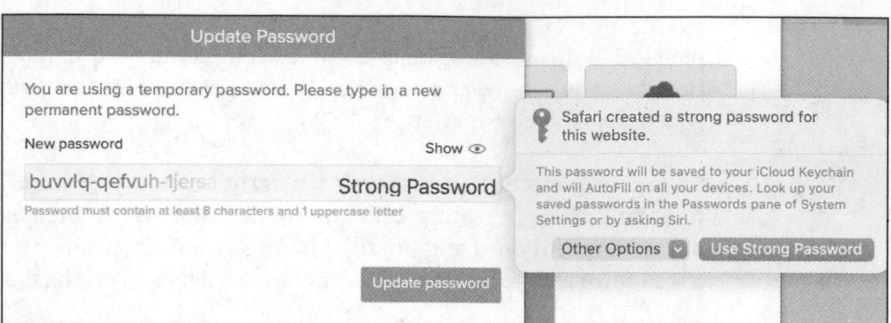

If Safari saved your site login data, the next time you visit the website's login page, Safari displays a drop-down menu for the saved login, as shown in Figure 2-10. Click the login in the pop-up and Safari automatically fills in your username and password.

>> *Credit cards:* If you've added one or more credit cards to Safari (see "Adding credit cards," a bit later), Safari displays a drop-down menu with a list of your saved credit cards when you click inside a credit card data field, as shown in Figure 2-11. Click the card you want to use, and Safari automatically fills in the credit card data.

>> *Other form fields:* Safari remembers what you enter the first time you fill in a form and use that data if the same website later asks you for the same information again.

FIGURE 2-10:
If you allow Safari
to save a
website's login
data, Safari
prompts you to
fill in that data
automatically the
next time you
visit the site's
login page.

FIGURE 2-11:
If you've added
one or more
credit cards to
Safari, navigating
to a credit card
form field
displays a list of
your saved cards.

Choosing the types of personal info Safari can store

Passwords? Credit card numbers? These are sensitive hunks of precious data, so is AutoFill — or, rather, is the data stored by AutoFill — safe? The short answer is "Yes." The longer answer is "Yes, but you need to take some steps to ensure the safety of your AutoFill data":

>> **Don't share your Mac user account with anyone:** Safari stores your AutoFill data in encrypted form, so it's protected from snoops. However, if someone else logs in to your Mac using your account, that person has full access to your

AutoFill data, meaning the person can log in to your websites and use your saved credit card info.

» **Don't leave your Mac unattended with your account logged in:** If you leave your Mac and stay logged in, any miscreant who happens along can use your Mac without your authorization, which also means using your AutoFill data without permission. If you'll be leaving your Mac unattended, be sure to lock your Mac or log out of your account.

Another step you can take is to decide what types of data you're willing to let Safari store using AutoFill. Here's how:

1. Choose Safari ⇨ Settings.

The Safari settings appear.

2. Click the AutoFill icon on the toolbar (labeled in Figure 2-7).

The AutoFill settings appear, as shown in Figure 2-12.

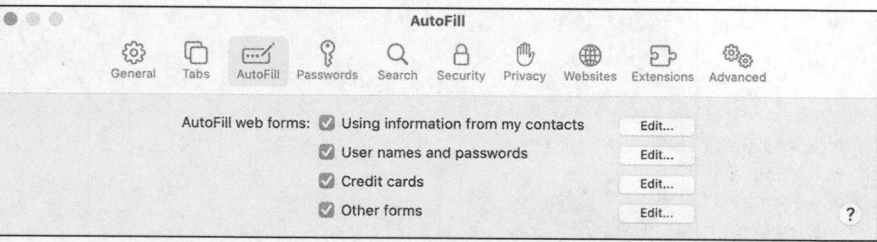

FIGURE 2-12:
Use the AutoFill settings to decide which types of personal data you want Safari to save.

3. For each of the settings, deselect the check box for each type of data that you don't want Safari to store using AutoFill.

4. (Optional) For each AutoFill data type, you can click the associated Edit button to edit, add, and delete saved items.

Safari will prompt you for your Mac admin account password when you click the Edit button associated with the User Names and Passwords setting and the Credit Cards setting.

5. Click the close icon.

Adding credit cards

If you want to have Safari automatically fill in your credit card number, expiration date, and the name on your card when visiting a site that requires payment info, you first need to add your credit card info to Safari.

REMEMBER

The one piece of credit card info that Safari doesn't save is the card's security code. As a security precaution, you have to enter this code yourself whenever you use the card online.

Here are the steps to follow to add one or more credit cards to Safari:

1. **Choose Safari ➪ Settings.**

   The Safari settings appear.

2. **Click the AutoFill icon on the toolbar.**

   The AutoFill settings appear.

3. **Make sure the Credit Cards check box is selected and then click the Edit button to the right of Credit Cards.**

   The Credit Cards Are Locked dialog appears.

4. **Enter your Mac user account password and then click Unlock.**

   The dialog refreshes showing information for any credit cards you've saved.

5. **Click Add.**

6. **Type the card description, card number, expiration date, and cardholder name.**

7. **Click Add.**

8. **Repeat Steps 6 and 7 to add all the credit cards you want Safari to AutoFill for you.**

9. **Click Done.**

10. **Click the close icon.**

Enhancing Online Security and Privacy

It's a cold, cruel online world, but Safari is built with your privacy and security in mind. For example, Safari encrypts your web browsing to help avoid internet eavesdropping and potential digital theft. And, instead of letting websites access your information automatically when you fill out forms, Safari detects forms and presents your information in drop-down fields so you can choose which information to insert. Safari also offers three more tools to help you stay safe and secure during your online jaunts: private browsing, security and privacy settings, and security recommendations. The next three sections provide the not-even-close-to-gory details.

Browsing privately

Safari keeps track of your browsing history, but that's not always a good thing. For example, if you use Safari on a public Mac, perhaps in a library, you may not want to leave a trace of where you've been. More likely, if other people have access to your Mac user account, they also have access to your browsing history.

You can clear your browsing history from a specified time frame (as I explain in Book 2, Chapter 1), such as from the last hour or from today and yesterday. That's great if you remember to do it, but it's also a blunt instrument because it deletes everything in the chosen time frame, which might mean you lose some valuable sites.

A better solution most of the time is Safari's *private browsing* feature, which keeps your web browsing history private by

>> Not saving which websites you visit, which means they don't show up in History

>> Removing any files that you downloaded from the Downloads window (Window ⇨ Downloads)

>> Not saving names or passwords that you enter on websites

>> Not saving search words or terms that you enter in the search and address field

To get private browsing on the job, choose File ⇨ New Private Window (or press Shift+⌘+N). You know private browsing is active when you see the word *Private* next to the show sidebar icon and the address and search field has a dark gray background, as shown in Figure 2-13. You can use the navigation buttons during the session, but when you close Safari, or close the private window, your viewing history is erased. In short, opening a private window is an excellent solution when you're surfing for your spouse's anniversary present!

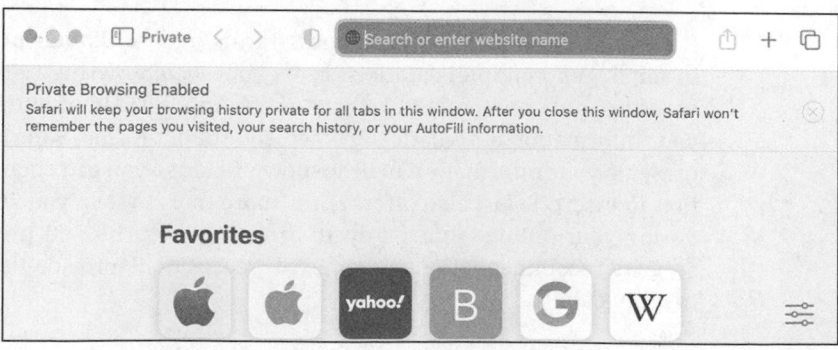

FIGURE 2-13: A private browsing window shows *Private* in the toolbar and displays the address and search field with a gray background.

Setting security and privacy settings

Safari sensibly sets a few security- and privacy-related settings, but you might want to customize these settings to suit your own level of paranoia. (As some wag once said, "When everyone is out to get you, being paranoid is just good thinking.") Let's take a spin around these settings:

1. **Choose Safari ➪ Settings.**

   The Safari settings appear.

2. **Click the Security button on the toolbar.**

   The Security settings appear.

3. **You'll want to leave these check boxes selected, but here's what they mean so you can decide for yourself:**

   - *Warn When Visiting a Fraudulent Website:* When you open a website that Safari finds suspicious, you receive a warning that requires you to confirm or cancel opening the page. Safari uses Google Safe Browsing to determine if a site is fraudulent.

   - *Enable JavaScript:* JavaScript is a language used for displaying page content, processing forms, and requesting data from the server. Some nefarious websites also use JavaScript for dark purposes, so it might be tempting to deselect this check box. However, doing so would almost certainly mean that every web page you visit would act wonkily or not display at all.

4. **Click the Privacy button on the toolbar.**

   The Privacy settings appear.

5. **Again, the default settings here probably work best for most people, but let's see what everything means so that you can choose your own path:**

   - *Prevent Cross-Site Tracking:* Makes it harder for companies to track your browsing across multiple websites. I strongly suggest that you *not* deselect this option.

   - *Hide IP Address from Trackers:* Tells Safari not to provide your Internet Protocol (IP) address to sites that are known to track you across the web. Since your IP address can uniquely identify your internet connection, trackers can use that address to identify you as you surf from page to page. That sucks, so you'll want to leave this check box selected.

   - *Block All Cookies:* Almost all websites require cookies to function properly, which is why this check box is deselected by default. (And it's why, if you select this check box, Safari warns you that websites may not work and asks you to confirm your choice.) Best to leave this setting deselected.

TECHNICAL STUFF

Cookies are generally benign pieces of information that websites you visit use to save data about you. For example, an online store might use a cookie to save your shopping cart. Cookies may also be used for user authentication or to store specific information such as your site preferences. When you surf to a website, that site gives you a cookie so that the next time you go to that website, it recognizes you because it sees you have one of its cookies.

- *Manage Website Data:* Safari keeps a list of websites that have stored data that can be used to track your browsing. This data includes not only cookies but also website files and a more modern alternative to cookies called local storage. You can click the Manage Website Data button and see who's tracking what, and then select specific sites you would like to remove.

TIP

To enable quick surfing without interruptions, do not block all cookies, but visit the Privacy settings frequently, click Manage Website Data, and remove suspect sites.

- *Allow Websites to Check for Apple Pay and Apple Card:* Enables websites that support Apple Pay and Apple Card to check whether these are enabled on your Mac.

- *Allow Privacy-Preserving Measurement of Ad Effectiveness:* Enables advertisers to measure the effectiveness of their ads without associating any ad activity or metrics with you.

6. **Click the close icon.**

Checking out Safari's password security recommendations

The passwords you use on websites protect your site account and data, but not all passwords are created equal. In fact, many passwords suffer from some (or, shudder, even all) of the following problems:

» **You reuse the password:** I know, we all do it. We take our favorite or go-to password and use it on multiple sites. It's easier than trying to memorize a unique password for every site, am I right? True, but here's the problem: If that password gets into the wrong hands, every site in which you reused that password is immediately vulnerable.

» **The password is weak:** A weak password is one that can be guessed easily by a malicious user. 123456 is an obviously weak password, but so is an ostensibly clever password such as p4ssw0rd. See the sidebar "Forging a strong password" to learn how to up your password game.

» **The password has been leaked:** Most websites that require credentials store user passwords on their servers. However, servers can (and do) get hacked and those saved passwords stolen. If the site was sloppy about how those passwords were stored, the passwords end up sold to a cybercriminal or exposed for all to see. If your password is one of them, it's said to have been *leaked*.

FORGING A STRONG PASSWORD

When you're setting up a website account, it's not enough to use any old password that pops into your head. To ensure the strongest security for your account, you need to make the password robust enough that it's impossible to guess and impervious to software programs designed to try different password combinations. Such a password is called a *strong password*. Ideally, you should build a password that provides maximum protection while still being easy to remember.

The easiest way to do this is to use the strong password that Safari generates automatically when you create the website account. However, if you prefer to create your own passwords, you need a few tips to reduce the chances of your account being compromised. Lots of books will suggest ridiculously abstruse password schemes (I've written some of these books myself), but you really need to know only three things to create strong-like-a-bull passwords:

- **Use passwords that are at least 12 characters long.** Shorter passwords are susceptible to programs that just try every letter combination. You can combine the 26 letters of the alphabet into about 12 million five-letter word combinations, which is no big deal for a fast program. If you use 12-letter passwords — as many experts recommend — the number of combinations goes beyond mind-boggling: 90 quadrillion, or 90,000 trillion!

- **Mix up your character types.** The secret to a strong password is to include characters from the following categories: lowercase letters, uppercase letters, punctuation marks, numbers, and symbols. If you include at least one character from three (or, even better, all five) of these categories, you're well on your way to a strong password.

- **Don't be obvious.** Because forgetting a password is inconvenient, many people use meaningful words or numbers so that their passwords will be easier to remember. Unfortunately, this means they often use obvious things such as their name, the name of a family member or colleague, their birth date, or their Social Security number. Being this obvious is just asking for trouble. Adding 123 or ! to the end of the password doesn't help much either. Password-cracking programs try those.

One of the benefits of having Safari save your website passwords (see "Allowing Safari to Store Passwords, Credit Cards, and Other Personal Info") is that it can examine your passwords to see if they have been reused, are weak, or have been leaked. If one or more of these problems apply to one your saved passwords, Safari displays a recommendation designed to set things right. You should peruse these recommendations regularly by following these steps:

1. **Choose Safari ⇨ Settings.**

   The Safari settings appear.

2. **Click the Passwords button on the toolbar.**

   Safari asks you for your Mac account password.

3. **Type your password and then press Return.**

   The Passwords settings appear. The list on the right includes a Security Recommendations section that shows you which of your passwords have problems.

4. **Click a recommendation.**

   Safari displays the details of the problem. Figure 2-14 displays a typical example.

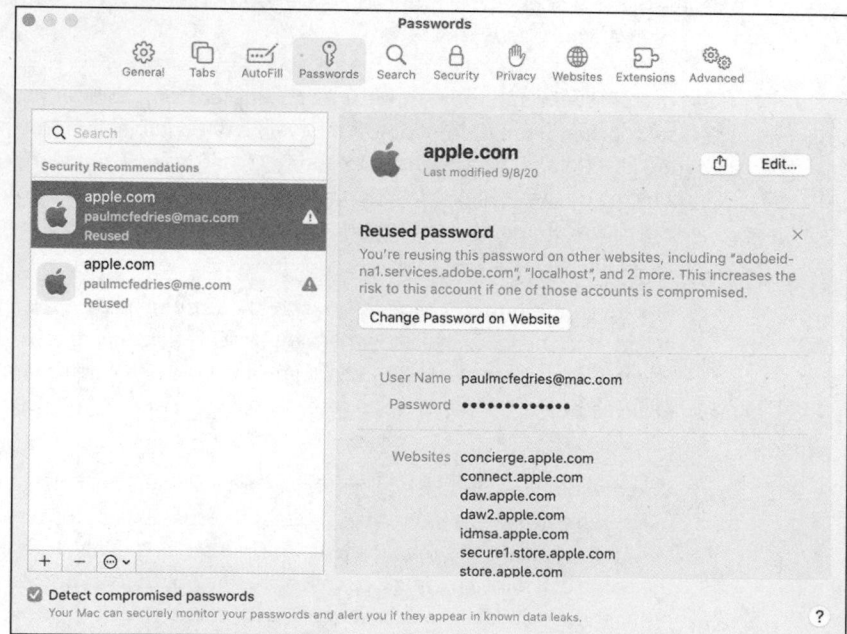

FIGURE 2-14: The Passwords settings display security recommendations for problematic passwords.

5. **Follow the recommended action, such as clicking Change Password on Website for a password that you've reused elsewhere.**

   If the password is one you no longer use (say, because you deleted your account on the website), you can click – (delete) at the bottom of the list, and then click Delete Password when Safari asks you to confirm.

6. **Repeat Steps 4 and 5 until you've gone through all the recommendations.**

7. **Click the close icon.**

"Check This Out": Sharing a Web Page

Useful, fun, or just plain weird web finds are treasures that cry out to be shared with friends, family, colleagues, the members of your disc golf team, or anyone else who you think might be interested. (Just be careful not to overdo do it: No one likes an over-sharer.)

To share a link to web page, first use Safari to navigate to the page. Then click the share icon on the toolbar (labeled way, way back in Figure 2-1) or choose File ⇨ Share. The menu that appears includes the following sharing options:

- » **Email This Page:** Sends a link to the web page in an email message. The Mail application loads and opens a new email message containing your web page link. Fill in the address and subject fields, write an accompanying message, and click Send. (See Book 2, Chapter 3 to learn about Mail.)

- » **Messages:** Sends a link to the web page that the recipient can click to open the web page with their web browser. A message bubble opens. Fill in the address field and click Send. (See Book 2, Chapter 5 to learn about Messages.)

- » **AirDrop:** Sends the link to other Macs on the same network with AirDrop opened.

- » **Notes:** Adds the URL to Notes and opens the application. Add any text to remind you why you shared the web page to Notes.

- » **Open in News:** Opens the News app and displays the web page, where you can save the story, use the page to suggest similar stories, and more. (See Book 4, Chapter 2 to get the scoop on News.)

- » **Reminders:** Adds the URL to Reminders and opens a Reminders window. Add any text to clarify why you shared the URL to reminders, and then set a date and a time.

From out There to in Here: Downloading Files

Part of the web's appeal is that you can find interesting content — such as music tracks or free demos of apps you can try before you buy— that you can download and install on your Mac. (When you copy a file from the web and store it on your computer, that's *downloading*. When you copy a file from your computer to a website — such as your electronic tax forms that you file electronically on the IRS's website — that's *uploading*.)

WARNING

Download a file only if you trust the source. If you visit an unknown website, that website might be trying to trick you into downloading a file that could do harmful things to your Mac, such as delete files, spy on your activities, or even bombard you with unwanted ads, so be careful. Safari has built-in protections that scan websites and downloads to warn you of potential dangers. To discover ways you can protect your Mac (and yourself) from potentially dangerous internet threats, take a look at the earlier section on protecting your web-browsing privacy and consult Book 3, Chapter 2.

When you find a file you want to download, follow these steps:

1. Click the Download link or download icon to begin downloading the file you want to save on your Mac's hard drive.

If you've never downloaded from the website before, a dialog appears asking you if you want to allow downloads from the website.

2. Click Allow.

If you allow downloads, an animated circle swoops to the downloads icon on the dock. A download icon appears to the left of the share icon on the Safari toolbar. If you're downloading a large file, a blue progress bar appears below the icon indicating the progress of the download. When the bar disappears, your download is complete.

3. When the file has completely downloaded, click the downloads icon on the Safari toolbar.

A pop-up menu appears listing the files that have been downloaded.

If the file is still downloading, you see a circular icon with an arrow, which indicates the progress of the download.

4. Double-click the file to open it. Or if you downloaded an application, install it.

Alternatively, you can go to the Downloads stack on the dock and open the file from there.

If you click the magnifying glass icon to the right of a file displayed in the Downloads window, Safari opens a Finder window and displays the contents of the Downloads folder. The file you downloaded is highlighted.

5. **After opening a downloaded file, click the downloads icon and then click the Clear button.**

The Downloads list is cleared, but the downloaded file still remains in the Downloads folder, or another location if you changed the default location in Safari Settings.

TIP

By default, downloaded files are saved to the Downloads folder. To change the destination folder, choose Safari ➪ Settings and click the General button. From the File Download Location pop-up menu, choose Other, and then click the destination folder in Chooser. Alternatively, you can choose Ask for Each Download, and Safari will prompt you for the location where you want to save the file.

While the Safari Settings are open, choose to open safe files, such as PDFs, photos, and movies, as soon as the download is finished by selecting the Open "Safe" Files after Downloading check box.

Chapter **3**

Exchanging Messages with Mail

When you think about it, there's a mind-bogglingly large number of ways to talk to someone these days: You can text someone; you can use social media to send that person a direct message; you can use a communications platform such as Zoom or Teams to exchange posts or chat messages; you can connect with a voice or video call.

And, of course, you can email that person. Email has been around seemingly forever and is starting to get a noticeably fusty odor about it, as though it's past its "best before" date. Email does have a slightly old-fashioned feel, but that doesn't mean its day is done. Far from it. After all, more than 4 billion people use email around the world and chances are most of the folks you know have at least one email account. Even millennials still use email, for crying out loud!

The staying power of email means you'll be sending and receiving email messages for a very long time, so it pays to get comfy with your Mac's email app: Mail. In this chapter, you take a tour of the Mail app, and then you get right down to business by learning how send a message. You also learn how to reply to a message, forward a message, send files as attachments, and even undo a sent message. You also explore Mail's features for receiving and reading incoming missives. It's a veritable email feast, so let's get the banquet started.

REMEMBER

To learn how to add accounts to your Mac, head back to Book 1, Chapter 3 for all the details.

Inspecting the Mail Window

To start your Mail journey, click the dock's Mail icon (labeled in Figure 3-1). If you see a message asking whether you want to use mail privacy protection, select the Protect Mail Activity radio button and click Continue. You end up looking at a window that looks suspiciously like the one shown in Figure 3-1.

Sidebar Message list New message Message preview Toolbar

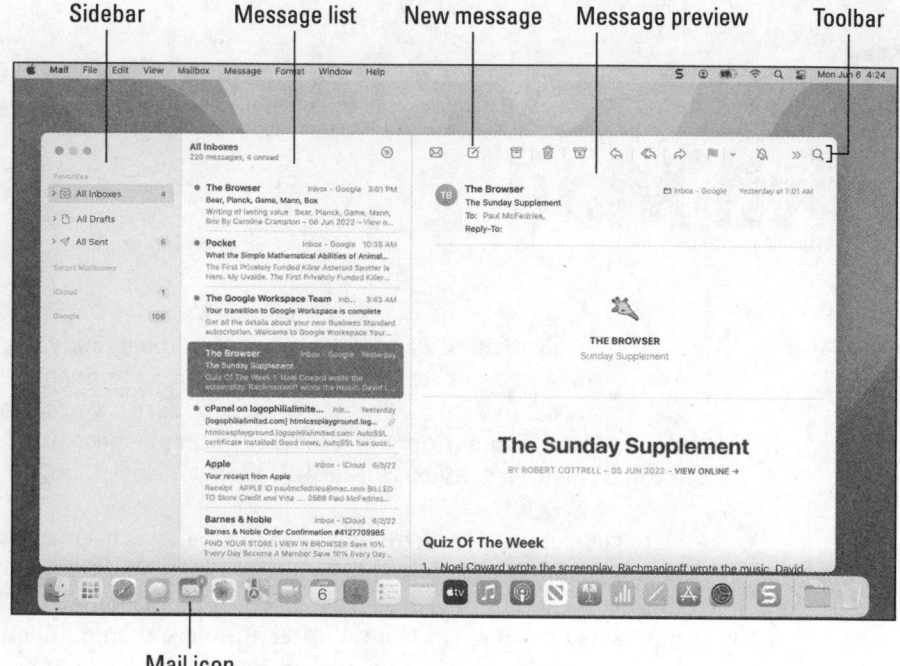

Mail icon

FIGURE 3-1:
Clicking the dock's Mail icon brings you face-to-face with the Mail app.

The default Mail window is divided into three vertical strips. Here's a quick look at each of these columns:

>> **Sidebar:** Shows a list of your mailboxes, which are the locations that Mail uses to store your messages. *Hint:* Choosing View ⇨ Hide Sidebar and View ⇨ Show Sidebar (or pressing Control+⌘+S) hides and displays the sidebar, which by default has three sections:

- *Favorites:* Shows your Inbox mailbox (which stores messages as you receive them), your Drafts mailbox (which stores copies of emails you've created but not yet sent), and your Sent mailbox (which stores a copy of each message you send). If you have more than one account, all your Inbox mailboxes are consolidated as All Inboxes, all your Drafts mailboxes are consolidated as All Drafts, and all your Sent mailboxes are consolidated as All Sent. In each case, you can click the disclosure arrow to see the individual Inbox or Sent mailboxes for each account. If you click an account, such as your Gmail account under All Inboxes, you see only the messages you've received through that email account.

TIP

Wherever you are in Mail, you can immediately jump to Inbox (or All Inboxes) by pressing ⌘+1, Drafts (or All Drafts) by pressing ⌘+2, and Sent (or All Sent) by pressing ⌘+3.

- *Smart Mailboxes:* Shows your smart mailboxes, which you set up to organize your messages (see Book 2, Chapter 4).

- *Accounts:* Shows an item for each account (iCloud and Google in Figure 3-1). You might also see an On My Mac item for local mailboxes. Click an account's disclosure arrow to see all the account's mailboxes. Besides Inbox and Sent, you usually also see the following: Drafts (messages you're composing but haven't yet sent), Junk (spam messages), Trash (deleted messages), and Archive (messages you've saved just in case you need to reference them down the road).

➤➤ **Message list:** Shows the messages in whatever mailbox you selected in the sidebar. By default, the messages are sorted with the most recent message at the top. You can change the sort order by choosing View ⇨ Sort By and then clicking a sort option from the continuation menu.

TIP

To make it easier to view and read your messages, you can change the width of Mail's main columns to taste. Hover the pointer over the right border of the column you want to resize, and then drag the border right (to make the column wider) or left (to make the column narrower).

- *Message preview:* Displays the content of whatever message you've clicked in the message list. Note the toolbar at the top of the message preview. You learn what these buttons do as you go through this chapter. The top part of the preview, just under the toolbar, displays the message *header,* which offers some basic info about the selected message, including the sender, subject, and date and time you received it. The rest of this column shows the content of the selected message.

Shipping Out Emails

After you configure your Mail account(s) and are familiar with the buttons and panes, you can start writing and sending email to anyone with an email address. In this section, I describe how to write and send an email, attach files and photos, and customize the appearance of your messages.

To be clear, when I talk about sending an email, I'm really talking about doing three similar but different things:

>> **Sending an original message:** You're initiating an email conversation with one or more other people.

>> **Replying to a message you've received:** Someone sent you a message, and now you're holding up your end of the conversation by sending a response to that message.

>> **Forwarding a message you've received:** Someone sent you a message, and now you're sending a copy of that message to one or more other people.

The next three sections take you through each technique.

Creating and sending an original message

When you want to initiate an email conversation with one or more people, you have to create and send an original message. Follow these steps:

1. **In Mail, choose File ⇨ New Message.**

Alternatively, press ⌘+N or click the New Message button (labeled in Figure 3-1).

A New Message window appears, as shown in Figure 3-2.

Although the steps here instruct you to click in each field, you can also press the tab key to move from field to field.

TIP

2. **Click the To text box and type an email address or do one of the following:**

- *Click + (add) at the right end of the field to open Contacts and select recipients from there.*

- *Begin typing a name you have stored in Contacts, and Mail will automatically fill in that person's email address (as long as it's part of the person's Contacts card). If a person has more than one email address, click the one you want from the list that appears.*

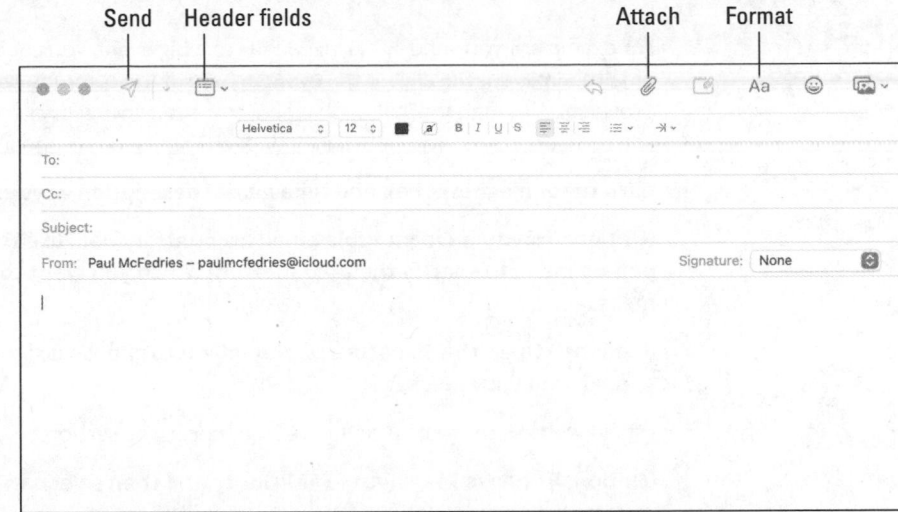

Send Header fields   Attach   Format

FIGURE 3-2:
Use this window
to compose an
original message.

3. **(Optional) Click the Cc text box and add an email address or addresses using one of the methods in Step 2.**

The Cc (courtesy copy) field is where you type email addresses of people whom you want to receive a copy of the message. That is, these are the people you want to keep informed but who don't necessarily need to write a reply. The email address you add to the Cc field will be visible to all recipients.

4. **(Optional) Choose View ⇨ Bcc Address Field and then use the Bcc text box to add an email address or addresses using one of the methods in Step 2.**

You can also show the Bcc field by pressing Option+⌘+B or by clicking the header fields icon (pointed out in Figure 3-2) and then selecting the Bcc Address Field command.

The Bcc (blind courtesy copy) field sends a copy of your message to email addresses that you type here, but those email addresses will not be visible to other recipients.

TIP

When sending a particularly important message, many people type the recipient's email address in the To field and their own email address in the Cc or Bcc fields. This way, they can verify that their message was sent correctly.

5. **(Optional) Choose View ⇨ Reply-To Address Field and then use the Reply To text box to type an email address that replies will be sent to that's different than the address the message is being sent from.**

You can also show the Reply To field by pressing Option+⌘+R or by clicking header fields icon (pointed out in Figure 3-2) and then selecting the Reply-To Address Field command.

For example, if you send 1,000 invitations to a big event, you could create an email address specifically for the event on one of the common service providers. Although the invitation is sent from you, invitees respond to the special address, and your inbox isn't clogged with 1,000 responses.

6. **Click the Subject text box and type a brief description of your message.**

7. **(Optional) If you have multiple email accounts in Mail, use the From pop-up menu to specify the account from which you want to send the message.**

8. **(Optional) Open the Signature pop-up menu to choose a signature to appear with your message.**

   I show you how to create a signature in an upcoming section.

9. **(Optional) Choose Message ⇨ Set Priority and then select an option that reflects the urgency (or lack thereof) of your message.**

   The priority options are High, Normal (the default), and Low. Use High priority only if your message is truly urgent or earth-shatteringly important.

10. **Click in the Message field (the blank expanse at the bottom of the window) and type your message.**

11. **(Optional) If you want to gussy up your message with different typefaces, colors, and other font effects, click the toolbar's Format button (labeled in Figure 3-2) to display the formatting options (refer to Figure 3-2).**

    Use the font, size, and color pop-up menus to change the look of your message, and click effects such as bold and italics. You can also format lists with bullets or numbers.

12. **Click the send icon, which I point out in Figure 3-2.**

Replying to a message

You'll often find yourself responding to messages others send to you. Your reply can contain the text that you originally received so the recipient can better understand the context of your reply.

To reply to a message, follow these steps:

1. **In Mail's sidebar, click the Inbox mailbox.**

   The middle column lists all the messages stored in your Inbox mailbox. If you have more than one email account, either click All Inboxes or click the Inbox mailbox of the account in which the message you want to reply to appears.

2. **Select a message in the Inbox that you want to reply to.**

3. **Select one of the following commands.**

   Or you can click buttons on the heads-up display, which is revealed when you hover the pointer over the center of the line between the message header and the message preview (as demonstrated in Figure 3-3). The heads-up display contains the delete, reply, reply all, and forward icons; if the message includes one or more attachments, the heads-up display also includes the Attachment drop-down list.

   - *Message ⇨ Reply:* Opens a response message addressed to the sender only. You can also click the toolbar's reply icon (labeled in Figure 3-3) or press ⌘+R.

   - *Message ⇨ Reply All:* If the message was sent to you and several other people, this option sends your response to everyone (except Bcc recipients, whom you don't know about) who received the original message. You can also click the toolbar's reply all icon (labeled in Figure 3-3) or press Shift+⌘+R.

4. **Write your reply in the space above the original message.**

5. **Click the send icon.**

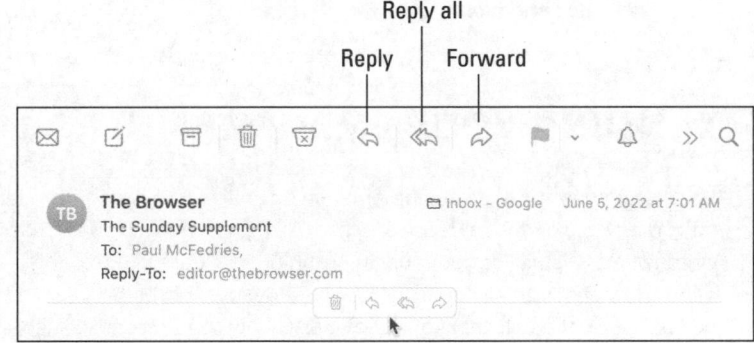

FIGURE 3-3:
For each message you receive, you can click reply, reply all, or forward.

Forwarding a message

Often, you'll receive a message that you think will be of interest to someone else who wasn't one of the original recipients. In that case, you can forward a copy of the email to that person, along with a bit of text explaining why you're forwarding the message.

To forward a message, follow these steps:

1. In Mail's sidebar, click the Inbox mailbox.

The middle column lists all the messages stored in your Inbox mailbox. If you have more than one email account, either click All Inboxes or click the Inbox mailbox of the account in which the message you want to reply to or forward appears.

2. In the Inbox, select a message that you want to forward.

3. Choose Message ⇨ Forward.

Alternatively, click the forward icon on the toolbar (refer to Figure 3-3) or press Shift+⌘+F.

If you want to send an exact copy of the original message as an attachment, choose Message ⇨ Forward as Attachment.

TIP

To both reply and forward the message, click the reply or reply all icon. Then click in the Cc, or Bcc field and type the email address of the person you want to forward the message to.

4. Write your message to the recipient in the space above the original message.

5. Click the send icon.

MINDING YOUR EMAIL MANNERS

Because composing and sending either an original message or a reply takes very little time, many people take a decidedly informal approach to all email. That's fine, but whether you're emailing your aunt in Austin or your boss in Boston, you should bear in mind a few etiquette guidelines. Nothing overly fussy or restrictive, mind you — there's no Emily Post of email, thankfully — but just a few commonsense suggestions based on mutual respect between you and your recipient(s):

- If you're sending a message to a large number of people — particularly if all or most of these people don't know each other — place all the addresses in the Bcc field. This keeps everyone's address private. In the To field, you can put your own address.

- Try to respond to all messages in a timely manner. No, fortunately, this doesn't mean you have to dash off a response within seconds of receiving an email. Personally, I try to respond to all my messages within a couple of hours, or by the end of the day, at least. However, replying within 24 hours of receipt is fine for almost all messages.

- Conversely, don't expect your recipients to respond to your messages immediately. Also, remember that everyone — yep: *everyone* — is super-busy these days, so don't conclude your message with a plea for a quick response. That's just not cool.

- When you reply to or forward a message, Mail includes — or *quotes* — the entire original message. However, if your reply or forward deals with only part of the original message, you should delete everything that's not relevant from the quoted text. One quick way to do this is to select the part of the original you want to include, and then click the reply icon or forward icon. In the new message that appears, Mail includes only the part of the original message that you selected.

- Unless the sender specifically says something like "No response necessary," you should acknowledge all non-junk email messages you receive. Even a quick "thanks" lets the sender know you received the message.

- Give your subject lines a bit of thought. Vague subjects such as "Question" or "Please help" are just annoying. A short sentence that captures the essence of your message is always helpful and almost always gets your message answered sooner.

- Be sure to always practice the three "Bs" of email: be good, be brief, and be gone. Being good means writing in clear, understandable prose that isn't marred by sloppy spelling or flagrant grammar violations. Being brief means getting right to the point without indulging in a rambling preamble. Always assume that your addressee is plowing through a stack of email and has no time or patience for verbosity. State your business and then practice the third "B": Be gone!

Customizing some useful sending settings

Like other Mac apps, Mail offers settings that let you customize and personalize your messages. The next two sections take you through a few useful settings that apply to sending email messages.

Keeping up appearances

In this section, I talk about how your outgoing messages appear. Whether you write a new message, reply to a message, or forward a message to another person, you have several choices about how that message looks. Choose Mail ⇨ Settings and then traipse through the following steps:

1. **Click the Fonts & Colors button on the toolbar to choose the font for outgoing messages.**

2. **Click the Select button next to the Message Font field and use the Fonts dialog to choose a Collection, Family, Typeface, and Size, as shown in Figure 3-4.**

Here you're setting the default font that Mail uses when you start any new message. Remember that you can also change the message font on individual messages using the format bar (refer to Figure 3-2).

TIP

While you're here, you might also want to fiddle with the font that Mail uses to display the message list. Click the Select button that appears to the right of the Message List Font field and use the Fonts dialog to make your selections.

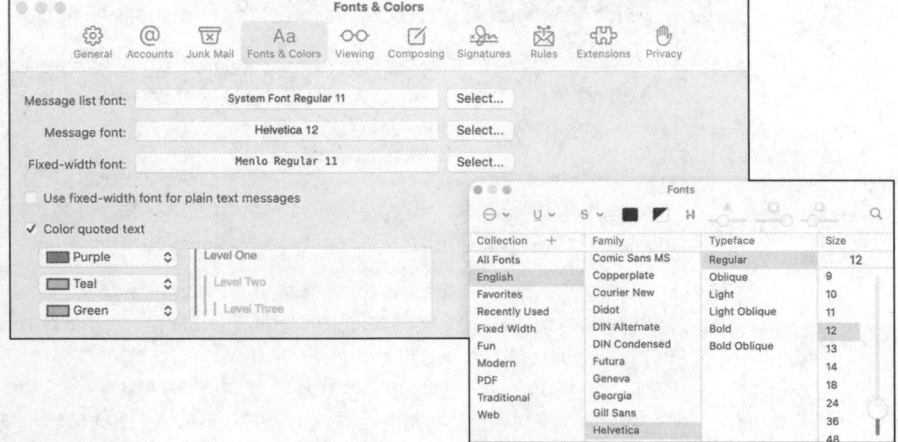

FIGURE 3-4:
Use the Fonts dialog to customize your message font.

3. **Click the Select button next to the Fixed-Width Font field and use the Fonts dialog to change this font.**

REMEMBER

A *fixed-width font* is one where every character has the same width, whether it's a *w* or an *i*. These fonts tend to look like they were produced by a typewriter (assuming you know what that ancient piece of technology is and what its text looks like!).

TIP

In the Fonts dialog, click the Fixed Width collection to see all the available fixed-width type families.

Plain text messages don't use any font formatting, which makes your messages smaller and readable by people using even very old email technology (which is admittedly very rare these days). If you want Mail to use your fixed-width font when you create a plain text message (by choosing Format ⇨ Make Plain Text when composing a message), select the Use Fixed-Width Font for Plain Text Messages check box.

4. **Leave the Color Quoted Text check box selected to change the color of text as it's quoted in an ongoing message conversation.**

The levels here refer to how often text has been quoted. For example, when you reply to an original message, that message's text is quoted at level one; if your recipient sends back a reply that includes the original text, then that text is now quoted at level two.

For each level of quoted text, click the color swatch pop-up menu and then select the color you want to use for text at that level. Click Other to open a color selector and choose a custom color.

5. **Click the Composing button on the toolbar to make choices about the appearance of outgoing messages, as shown in Figure 3-5.**

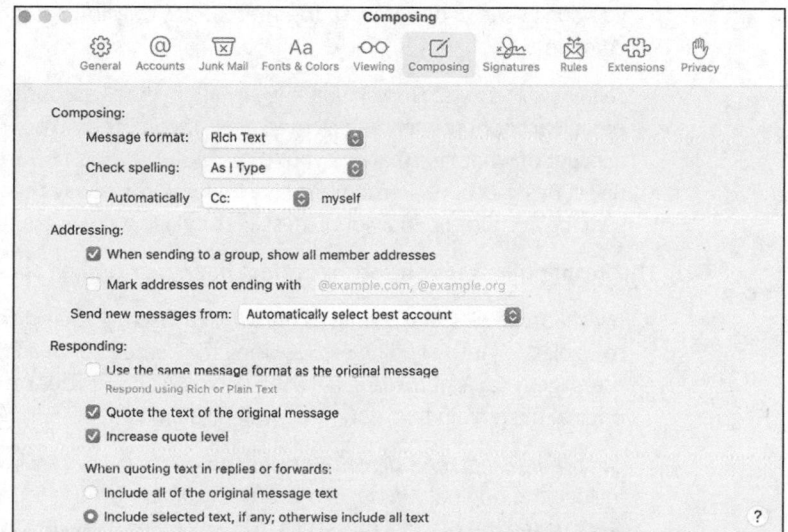

FIGURE 3-5:
Customize how outgoing messages look.

6. **The Composing section offers the following settings:**

- *Message Format:* Choose from Plain Text or Rich Text, which takes advantage of stylized text functions such as bold, italic, and underlining.

- *Check Spelling:* Activate one of the spell-checking options: As I Type, When I Click Send, or Never.

- *Automatically x Myself:* Select the check box and then use the pop-up menu to select either Cc: or Bcc: to receive courtesy copies (visible or blind, respectively) for every message you send. The courtesy copy will show up in your Inbox in addition to the copy that Mail stores in your Sent messages mailbox.

7. **The Addressing section presents these settings:**

- *When Sending to a Group, Show All Member Addresses:* When selected, this setting tells Mail to display each group member's email address when you choose a Contacts group as the message recipient. If you deselect this check box, Mail only displays the group name, not the addresses of individual members.

- *Mark Addresses Not Ending With:* Select the check box and type one or more domain names, separated by commas, in the text box. Now any recipient address you specify that doesn't use these domain names gets marked in red by Mail. What's the point? To alert you when you're sending a message to someone outside a trusted domain. For example, if you type the domain used by your company email addresses, all recipients outside the company appear in red, but company recipients will not. This can help ensure that you don't send proprietary or for-internal-use only information outside the company.

- *Send New Messages From:* If you have multiple email accounts, choose the default account for sending all messages. If you prefer that Mail choose the account of whatever mailbox you're currently viewing, choose Automatically Select Best Account. Remember, too, that you can always change the sending account on individual messages by using the From field.

8. **The Responding section settings affect how your replies appear:**

- *Use the Same Message Format as the Original Message:* Select this check box to cajole Mail into sending replies using the same format as the original message. That is, if the original used rich text, so will your reply; if the original used plain text, your reply will be plain text, as well.

- *Quote the Text of the Original Message:* Leave this check box selected to include the original message in your reply. If for some reason you don't want to see the original messages in your replies (I don't recommend this), deselect this check box.

- *Increase Quote Level:* Leave this check box select to have Mail indent the original text one level. If you have an ongoing conversation, the original text indents one more level with each response.

- *When Quoting Text in Replies or Forwards:* By default, Mail includes either all the original text or whatever text you select in advance of choosing the Reply, Reply All, or Forward command. This is the Include Selected Text, If Any; Otherwise Include All Text option. If you'd prefer that Mail always include the entire original text when quoting, select the Include All of the Original Message Text option.

Signing your message

A *signature* is a chunk of text that appears at the bottom of an outgoing message or reply. The signature gives you an opportunity to provide a little extra info about yourself to the recipient, such as your phone number and website, or express your personality and wit with an amusing image or a snappy quotation. If you have multiple email accounts, you can assign a different signature to each account. You can also create multiple signatures and then choose which you want to use depending on the tone and occasion of your message. Here's how to create message signatures:

1. **Choose Mail ⇨ Settings and then click the Signatures button on the toolbar.**

2. **Click the account name in the first column and then click + (plus sign) at the bottom of the second column.**

   Mail makes a signature suggestion, such as your first name or your first and last name with your email address.

3. **To change the default signature that Mail created, click the text to select it and then edit as needed.**

   You can also copy and paste an image from another app.

   To insert a website link, leave the cursor in the Signature block but choose Edit ⇨ Add Link. Type the URL (or copy and paste or click and drag from Safari) and then click OK. Recipients can click the link, and the website opens in the recipient's default browser. You can also select typed text or an image and then choose Edit ⇨ Add Link; the link is applied to the selected item.

4. **Repeat Steps 2 and 3 to create other signatures, such as a professional signature you use for work and another you use for messages sent to friends.**

   Hint: Double-click the signature name (Signature #1, Signature #2, and so on) to give the signature a more meaningful name.

5. **(Optional) Click All Signatures, and then click and drag signatures from the second column to a different account name to use the same signature for different accounts.**

   The number of signatures associated with each account is shown under the account name.

   When you show the signature field in outgoing messages, you see only the signatures associated with the account you're using to send the message.

6. **Click the close icon.**

You can edit your signature within a message if the signature text isn't quite appropriate in that instance.

Including a file along for the ride

When you send an email, you're sending text that you compose on the spot. However, sometimes the message you want to convey already exists in a separate file, which could be a PDF document or a document you created using Pages or Numbers. In that case, you can include the file along with your email message, a process known in the email trade as *attaching* the file. The file you attach is called — no surprises here — an *attachment*.

Anyone receiving your message and file attachment can then either open the file right from your message or save the file to their computer and open the file later. Many people need to share files or digital images, and file attachments are one way to share files with others.

REMEMBER

Your email provider may limit the maximum file size you can send. For example, some providers set a maximum size of 10MB or 20MB. Your recipients, too, may have limits on the file size they can receive.

If you have a file larger than 60 to 70 percent of the maximum limit, you might have to send your files through a free remote storage and file-sharing service, such as Hightail (`www.hightail.com`), SendThisFile (`www.sendthisfile.com`), or Dropbox (`www.dropbox.com`). As of this writing, each of these services have an option for a free account, but if you need to send humongous files, you'll have to upgrade your account. Refer to each site for current pricing.

Alternatively, if you have an Apple ID, you can take advantage of a service called Mail Drop. If Mail detects that the file or files you're sending exceed your email provider's maximum size, Mail will upload the attachments to iCloud and your recipient has 30 days to download them. Mail Drop is enabled automatically on your iCloud account but not in your other accounts. To control whether Mail uses Mail Drop for an account, choose Mail ⇨ Settings, click Accounts in the toolbar, click the account you want to modify, then either select or deselect the Send Large Attachments with Mail Drop check box.

To attach a file to a message, follow these steps:

1. **In Mail, open a new message window as described in one of the previous sections.**

   You can open a new message window to create a new message, reply to an existing message, or forward an existing message.

2. **Choose File ⇨ Attach Files.**

   Alternatively, click the attach icon, which looks like a paper clip (refer to Figure 3-2), or press Shift+⌘+A.

A browse dialog appears.

3. **Navigate through the folders to get to the file you want to send and then click it.**

TIP

To select multiple files, click the first file, hold down the ⌘ key, and then click each of the other files you want to send. To select a range of files, click the first file, hold down the Shift key, and then click the last file you want to send.

4. **Click Choose File.**

If you have just one file, it's pasted into your message. If you paste multiple files, the file is particularly large, or the file is in a format that Mail can't display, such as FileMaker or ePub, you see an icon for the attached file in the message window.

TIP

By default, an image attachment is sent full size. To change the size of the attached image, choose Small, Medium, Large, or Actual Size from the Image Size pop-up menu to the right of Message Size.

TIP

To send a single file as a file or to facilitate sending multiple files, select the file(s) in Finder, and then choose File ➪ Compress. Finder creates a Zip file that comprises the selected files. If the Zip file is small enough, attach it to your message.

5. **Address your message, add a subject line, and type your message.**

6. **Click the send icon.**

If you're using the macOS Ventura (or later) version of Mail, the app is often smart enough to recognize when you forget to include an attachment. For example, if you include in your message some text along the lines of "See the attached file," but you don't actually attach anything to your message, Mail displays a dialog like the one shown in Figure 3-6 asking if you meant to add an attachment. If Mail got it wrong, just click Send Anyway; otherwise, click Cancel, attach your file, and then click the send icon once again.

FIGURE 3-6:
Mail can often recognize when you forget to attach a file.

You can set rules for all email attachments by choosing Edit ⇨ Attachments and selecting one or both of the following:

» **Always Send Windows-Friendly Attachments:** Makes sure that Windows users can read your attachments. This option is best selected because you can never be 100 percent sure which operating system your recipient will use to read your attachment.

» **Always Insert Attachments at End of Message:** Inserts the attachment at the bottom, so the recipient may have to scroll down to get to the attachment. Whether you select this option is a personal preference. If you want the attachment in the middle of the message — a photo, for example — don't select this check box.

You can also choose Edit ⇨ Include Attachments with Replies and choose whether Mail attaches the original message's attachments to your reply. Selecting Never here is usually the best option because it avoids creating bigger messages that take longer to send, and the person who sent you the attachment should have it anyway. Alternatively, select Ask to have Mail prompt you to include the attachments; select When Adding Recipients to have Mail include the original attachments only if you're sending your reply to more people than the original sender; or select Always to always include the attachments.

Attaching a photo to your message

You could use the steps in the preceding section to attach a photo to your message, but a better method in most cases is to go directly to Photo Browser, which shows photo previews instead of a list of names that don't mean anything to you until you open them, like DSC174.

Photo Browser also enables you to take a photo using your iPhone or iPad camera. For this to work, your Mac and your iPhone or iPad must be signed in to the same Apple ID (and have two-factor authentication turned on), be on the same Wi-Fi network, and have Bluetooth turned on. Your Mac needs to be running macOS Mojave or later, your iPhone iOS 12 or later, and your iPad iPadOS 13 or later.

To use Photo Browser, do the following:

1. **In Mail, open a new Message window, as described in one of the previous sections.**

    You can open a new Message window to create a message, reply to an existing message, or forward an existing message.

2. **Click the Photo Browser icon, pointed out in Figure 3-7.**

Photo Browser

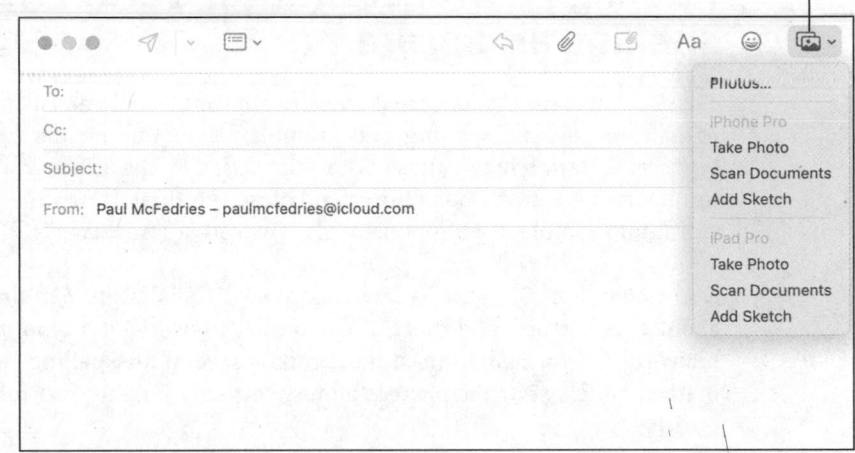

FIGURE 3-7:
Click the Photo
Browser icon
to access your
photos on your
iPhone or iPad
camera.

3. **Choose one of the following commands:**

- *Photos:* Mail opens Photo Browser. Scroll through thumbnails from your Photos and Photo Booth photos, events, and albums until you find the photo you want. Double-click an event or album to see the photos in the event or album; double-click a photo to see an enlarged preview in the bottom half of the browser window. Drag the selected photo or photos into your message.

TIP

To select multiple photos, click the first file, hold down the ⌘ key, and then click each of the other photos you want to send. To select a range of photos, click the first photo, hold down the Shift key, and then click the last photo you want to send.

- *Take Photo:* Opens the camera app on the iPhone or iPad. Take your photo, tap Use Photo (or Retake to try again), and your photo gets inserted into the message.

4. **(Optional) Use the Image Size pop-up menu to adjust the image size by selecting Small, Medium, Large, or Actual Size.**

The larger the photo, the larger the message file will be, making it potentially slower to send and receive, although the better resolution is useful if the photo is destined to be printed.

5. **Address your message, add a subject line, and type a message.**

6. **Click the send icon.**

TIP

In Book 4, Chapter 4, I explain how to send photos directly from Photos.

Putting your best foot forward: Checking spelling and grammar

These days, there's a concerted effort to appear all cool and casual when it comes to matters such as spelling and grammar. Everyone claims to not care about typos and to not judge those who fall victim to the greengrocers' apostrophe (an apostrophe erroneously inserted before the final "s" in the plural form of a word; for example, typing "mistake's" instead of "mistakes").

Don't believe it. Oh, sure, a few enlightened souls might genuinely be sanguine about email errors, and most of us do tend to overlook a typo or two. However, know this: If your email message contains several misspellings and a few grammatical gaffes, your recipient is almost certainly judging you for it, and not in a positive way.

Fortunately, Mail has your back because not only does it come with a spelling and grammar checker, but those tools are turned on by default and are checking for errors as you type. The spell checker will underline suspected misspelled words in red to help you find potential problems easily as you create the message. Even better, the spell checker will also correct some misspellings automatically. To make sure these options are working for you, do the following:

>> Choose Edit ⇨ Spelling and Grammar ⇨ Check Spelling ⇨ While Typing.

>> Choose Edit ⇨ Spelling and Grammar ⇨ Correct Spelling Automatically.

The spell checker can fix most errors, but not all of them. To nip any other spelling and grammar errors in the bud, follow these steps:

1. **Start a new message, a reply to an existing message, or a forwarded message.**

2. **Type your message.**

3. **Choose Edit ⇨ Spelling and Grammar ⇨ Show Spelling and Grammar.**

   The spelling and grammar checker does its thing, with a Spelling and Grammar dialog showing the first problem word. Note that, by default, Mail checks for only spelling errors. To include grammar mistakes in the process, select the Check Grammar check box.

4. **Click one of the following buttons:**

   - *Change:* Changes the misspelled word with the spelling that you choose from the list box on the left

   - *Find Next:* Finds the next misspelled word

- *Ignore:* Tells Mail that the word is correct

- *Learn:* Adds the word to the dictionary

- *Define:* Launches Mac's Dictionary application and looks up and displays the word's definition in the Dictionary's main window

- *Guess:* Offers best-guess word choices

5. **Click the send icon.**

REMEMBER

The spelling and grammar checker can't catch all possible errors (words like *fiend* and *friend* can slip past because the words are spelled correctly), so make sure that you proofread your message after you finish spell-checking and grammar-checking your message.

Later, dude: Scheduling a send

If you're using macOS Ventura or later, Mail enables you to send a message later rather than right away. For example, you might want to email a special announcement at a certain time. If you're not going to be near your Mac at that time, you can tell Mail when you want the message sent.

To schedule a send, click the drop-down arrow that appears to the right of the send icon. In the drop-down menu that appears, Mail offers one or more default times, examples of which you can eyeball in Figure 3-8. To specify a custom time, click Send Later to open the Send Later dialog, choose a date and time, and then click Schedule.

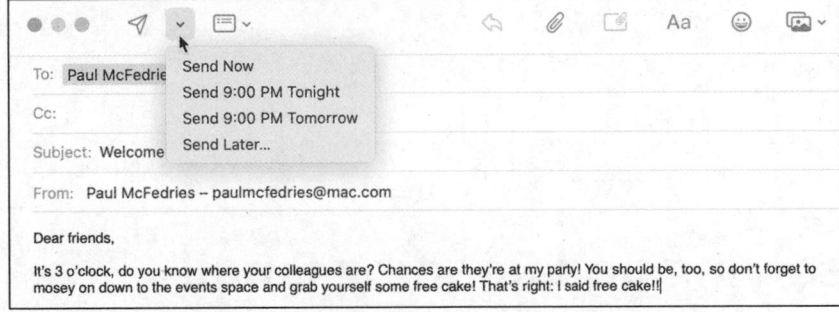

FIGURE 3-8:
Mail enables you to send a message at a later time.

Back from the brink: Undoing a send

Have you ever clicked the send icon, immediately realized that you forget to add something crucial to your message or made a major, perhaps career-destroying blunder, and then yelled at the computer "Undo! Undo!"? Hey, we've all been there.

Happily, if you're using the macOS Ventura (or later) version of Mail, you really *can* retrieve a sent message before anyone else sees it. No, yelling "Undo!" at your Mac still doesn't work, but you can click the Undo Send link that appears at the bottom of the sidebar, as shown in Figure 3-9. Undo Send sticks around for only 10 seconds (by default; see the Tip, below), though, so if you want to prevent an unsound message from being delivered, you have to think fast.

TIP

If 10 seconds is too short an interval, you can ask Mail to give you a bit more time to undo your sends. Choose Mail ➪ Settings, click Composing in the toolbar, and then use the Undo Send Delay pop-up menu to select a time that works for you: 10 Seconds, 20 Seconds, or 30 Seconds. If you never make mistakes (*raises eyebrow*), you can choose off to deactivate the Undo Send feature.

FIGURE 3-9:
By default, Mail gives you up to 10 seconds to claw back a sent message.

Receiving and Reading Email

Email uses the proverbial two-way street, meaning that not only do you send messages to friends, family, colleagues, and perhaps even a few complete strangers, but you also receive messages from anyone who has something to say to you. The emails you receive could be replies to your messages, forwarded messages, or original messages. Your address might be on the To line, the Cc line, or the Bcc line, but however each new message is sent, it winds up in the Inbox mailbox of your email account.

Retrieving email

This is the point in the book where you might expect me to insert a long-winded, multistep procedure for receiving email in the Mail app. True enough, but I'm not going to do that. Why not? Because to retrieve incoming missives in Mail, you don't have to do anything! Mail automatically knows whenever a new message arrives on your mail provider's incoming mail server and grabs that message right away. You don't need to lift even so much as a finger.

That said, it *is* possible to check for and retrieve email manually in Mail. To do so, choose Mailbox ➪ Get New Mail. (You can also press Shift+—+N or click the get mail icon, labeled in Figure 3-10.)

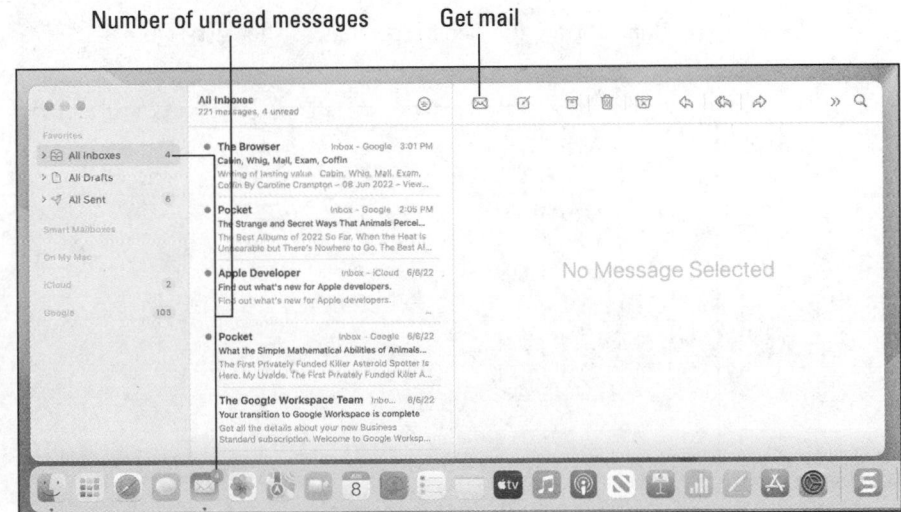

Number of unread messages   Get mail

FIGURE 3-10:
Mail tells you
the number of
unread messages
in the app and in
the dock icon.

TIP

If you don't want Mail to check for new messages on a particular account for a while, you can temporarily disable that account. Choose Mail ➪ Settings, click Accounts in the toolbar, click the account you want to turn off, then deselect the Enable This Account check box.

The number of unread messages appears in the sidebar next to the Inbox (or All Inboxes, if you have multiple accounts) label and in a badge on the Mail icon on the dock, as shown in Figure 3-10, as well as in Launchpad. Unread messages also appear in the message list with a blue dot to the left of the sender's name.

The figure doesn't show the number of unread messages in Launchpad.

Customizing a few handy receiving settings

Mail offers a few useful settings for controlling how it checks for and receives incoming messages. For example, you can configure Mail to check for new mail automatically at fixed intervals of time, such as every 5 or 15 minutes, or you can always check for new messages manually. To configure these and other receiving settings, follow these steps:

1. **In Mail, choose Mail ⇨ Settings.**

2. **Click the General button in the toolbar.**

   Mail displays the General settings, as shown in Figure 3-11.

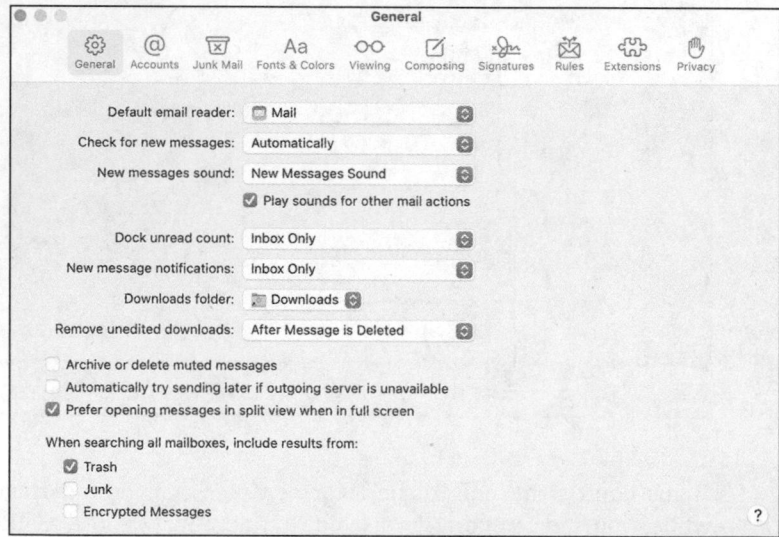

FIGURE 3-11: The General settings offer a few options related to receiving messages.

3. **From the Check for New Messages pop-up menu, choose an option to determine how often to check for new messages.**

   Automatically will get your new mail whenever you open Mail and continuously as long as Mail remains open. Choose Every Minute, Every 5 Minutes, Every 15 Minutes, Every 30 Minutes, or Every Hour to check at the chosen interval. If you prefer to receive messages on your own terms, choose Manually.

4. **(Optional) Choose a sound to play when you receive new messages from the New Messages Sound pop-up menu.**

   By default, the New Messages Sound plays when a new message is received. You can choose a different sound from the plethora of sounds on this menu. You can also choose None in case any sound bothers you.

5. **Use the pop-up menus to select your preferences for the following options:**

   - *Dock Unread Count:* Choose whether the number in the badge on the Mail icon on the dock reflects unread messages in just your inbox (Inbox Only), in all your mailboxes (All Mailboxes), or just messages you received today (Today).

   - *New Message Notifications:* Indicate which types of communications you want Notification Center to manage: Inbox Only, VIPs, Contacts, or All Mailboxes, or new messages received today. (See Book 1, Chapter 6 to learn about Notifications.)

   - *Downloads folder:* Specify the default location that Mail uses when you save a file attachment.

   - *Remove Unedited Downloads:* Indicate whether to remove unedited downloads after the message is deleted, when Mail quits, or never.

6. **Click the close icon.**

Mail can check for new messages only if you leave Mail running. If you quit Mail, it can't check for new messages periodically.

Reading email

You'll be happy to hear that reading email is almost as easy as receiving it. In fact, I can tell you the entire process in just two quick steps:

1. **In the sidebar, click the mailbox that contains the message you want to read.**

2. **In the message list, either click the message to display its contents in the message preview pane or double-click the message to open it in a separate window.**

The advantage of the message preview pane is that you can scan your messages quickly by clicking each one without having to open a separate window. The advantage of reading a message in a separate window is that you can resize that window and see more of the message without having to scroll as often as you would if you were reading that same message in the preview pane.

I should mention, too, that Mail organizes your messages by *conversation*, which is the thread of messages with the same subject. This way, you don't have to scroll through to find responses from different people on different days but can follow the conversation exchanges as they occurred. To view your messages separately instead, choose View ➪ Organize by Conversation and turn off that feature.

The number to the right of the subject line in the message list shows how many exchanges make up the conversation. You can also see the "speakers" in the conversation by clicking the arrow next to the number. To expand all the messages in message list, choose View ➪ Expand All Conversations. Choose View ➪ Collapse All Conversations to collapse them again.

Viewing and saving file attachments

When you receive a message that has a file attachment, you see a paper clip next to the sender's name in the message list and also on the message. To save a file attachment, follow these steps:

1. **Click a message with an attachment icon (paper clip) in the message list.**

   If the attachment is an image, it appears in the body of the email. If the attachment is a document, an icon for the document type is displayed with the name of the document.

2. **If the attachment is a document, double-click the attachment icon within the message to view the attachment in the application it was created in.**

3. **Choose File ➪ Save Attachments.**

   If the email message contains more than one attachment, all will be saved in the folder you specify in the next step.

4. **In the dialog that opens, choose the folder where you want to save the attachments.**

   By default, Mail saves your attachments into the Downloads folder, unless you designate another folder in the General pane of Mail settings.

5. **Click Save.**

TIP

You can also just click and drag attachments from the message body to the desktop or a Finder window or folder. To do so, hold down the ⌘ key to select more than one attachment, and then click and drag any one of the selected attachments to the desktop or a Finder window.

TIP

Right-click an attachment to display a context menu of options. The options differ depending on the file type of the attachment, but in most cases, you'll be able to preview the attachment, view it in its default application, save the document, and so on.

WARNING

Before you download an attachment, make sure that you can trust it. That's easier said than done because if your computer has been compromised, the attachment may appear to come from one of the addresses in your contact list. A good way to check an email address is to hover your cursor over the name. Don't click it, but wait to see if the email address refers to the address you expect. Unfortunately, sometimes you discover that the true sender is not who you think it is. Fortunately, the Mac is less vulnerable to malware than other devices, but in today's world, you have to be extra careful.

Adding an email address to Contacts

Typing an email address every time you want to send a message — if you can even remember the address — can get tedious. Mail searches your messages as well as Contacts for matches when you begin to type a name in an address field. Nonetheless, you may want to add the people behind those addresses to Contacts on your Mac so your addresses are all in one place.

When you receive an email from someone whose name and address you want to remember, that person's email address in Contacts by following these steps:

1. **In the sidebar, click the mailbox that contains the message from the person whose address you want to save.**

2. **In the message list, select the message.**

3. **Choose Message ⇨ Add Sender to Contacts.**

Although nothing appears to happen, your chosen email address is now stored in Contacts.

Adding an email contact to your VIPs list

If you have a business associate or a friend with whom you converse frequently, you can add this person to your VIPs list. When you add people to this list, their names appear below VIPs in the sidebar of the Mail app. After adding someone to this list, any message from them that you don't delete is easily retrieved by clicking their name. To add a person to your VIPs list, follow these steps:

1. **In the sidebar, click the mailbox that contains the message from the person you'd like to add to your VIPs list.**

2. **In the message list, select the message.**

3. **Right-click the person's name in the From field, and choose Add to VIPs from the context menu that appears.**

   The person is added to your VIPs list. Click the person's name in your VIPs list, and every email the person has sent will appear in the message list.

IN THIS CHAPTER

» **Searching for messages**

» **Creating mailboxes to store related messages**

» **Using smart mailboxes and rules to ease organization**

» **Cleaning up junk email**

» **Deleting and archiving messages**

Chapter **4**

Getting More Out of Mail

P eople used to complain about serious problems such as pollution, overpopulation, and poverty. Now all anybody talks about is how many emails they have in their inbox. That's unsurprising, I suppose, because almost everybody gets *way* too much email.

There's not much that Mail can do to reduce the avalanche of email you receive in a day, but Mail does offer quite a few tools that can help you not get buried under all those messages. For example, Mail has a search feature that enables you to locate specific text stored in a message. You can also get Mail to remind you to deal with a particular message. When you find the messages you want, you may want to group them into their own mailbox. Even better, you can set up smart mailboxes, where Mail automatically puts related messages in the same mailbox, or you can create rules for what mail goes to which mailbox. You learn the specifics of these features and more in this action-packed chapter.

"Where's Waldo's Message?" Searching Your Email

One method that many people use today to organize their email is to eschew any organization. That is, they just let the messages come in and accumulate in their inbox. Then, when they need to deal with a particular message, they use Mail's powerful search feature to miraculously pluck the message out of the mailbox maelstrom.

This seems like sheer madness to me, but even if you go the opposite route and take full advantage of Mail's organization tools such as mailboxes, smart mailboxes, and message rules, it can still take time to find what you want. Fortunately, Mail's search feature can help even the hyperorganized.

You can use search to scour your email for all or part of the name of the person who sent the message, the subject line of the message, or text in the message. To give search a whirl, follow these steps:

1. **In Mail, open the mailbox you want to search.**

   TIP

   To include trash, junk, or encrypted messages in your search, choose Mail ⇨ Settings ⇨ General and select the Trash, Junk, or Encrypted Messages check boxes, or any combination of those three.

2. **Click the search icon (the magnifying glass icon in the upper-right corner of the window).**

3. **Type a word, phrase, or partial phrase that you want to find.**

   As you type, Mail uses the message list to display the messages that match your text.

4. **(Optional) To create a smart mailbox search:**

   a. *Click + (save) at the top of the message list to open a smart mailbox window.*

   b. *Type a name for your new smart mailbox search.*

   c. *Choose any options you want to customize your search.*

   d. *Click OK to save your smart mailbox search.*

   I explain smart mailboxes in depth in the "Organizing on Autopilot: Creating Smart Mailboxes" section, later in this chapter.

5. **Click a message to read it.**

Getting Mail to Remind You to Deal with a Message

One of the most common reasons that we forget to respond to, forward, or in some other way deal with a received message is that it simply gets buried under all the messages we receive after it. With each new message that gets stuffed into our already overburdened inbox, that message moves farther and farther down Mail's message list. Out of sight, as they say, is out of mind.

Fortunately, if you're using the macOS Ventura (or later) version of Mail, you can bring a message back into sight and therefore back into mind. The feature is called Remind Me and it works like this:

1. **In the sidebar, click the mailbox that contains the message you want to be reminded to deal with later.**

2. **In the message list, select the message.**

3. **Choose Message ⇨ Remind Me, and then select a time when you want to be reminded.**

   Your choices are Remind Me in 1 Hour, Remind Me Tonight (this one appears only if it's not yet evening), or Remind Me Tomorrow. To set a custom date and time, click Remind Me Later, use the Remind Me dialog to choose a date and a time, then click Schedule.

When the reminder time arrives, Mail automatically moves the message to the top of the message list and marks the message with a Remind Me label, as shown in Figure 4-1. Note, as well, that a Remind Me mailbox also appears in the Favorites section with a badge that tells you how many messages Mail is currently reminding you to handle.

FIGURE 4-1:
Mail can remind you to deal with a message by resurfacing that message to the top of the message list.

Creating a Mailbox to Store Related Messages

When you receive an email message, no matter who sent it, what the subject line is, or what the message contains, Mail unceremoniously dumps the message into the Inbox of the account to which the missive was sent. You can search for messages and use Remind Me to resurface messages, but neither is a viable long-term solution for managing an Inbox groaning under the weight of hundreds or thousands of messages.

Leaving everything in an overstuffed Inbox can lead to three big problems:

>> Individual messages get pushed down the message list as new messages come in, to the point where you either forget about the message or have trouble finding it.

>> If your Inbox contains multiple conversations about the same topic, it can be hard to find and navigate all those related messages.

>> When you've dealt with a message, just leaving it in your Inbox can make it close to impossible to find later.

To fix these problems, you can create your own mailboxes for organizing related emails. For example, creating a mailbox named Penske Project enables you to use that mailbox to store every email conversation about the Penske project. When you need to locate a Penske-related message from a last week, last month, or even last year, you know exactly where to find it.

Creating a shiny mailbox

To create a mailbox, follow these steps:

1. **In Mail, choose Mailbox ⇨ New Mailbox.**

   A New Mailbox dialog appears, as shown in Figure 4-2.

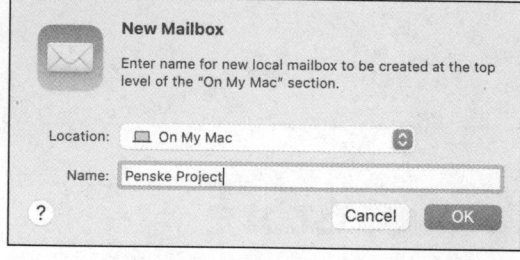

FIGURE 4-2:
Choose a location and type a name for your new mailbox.

2. **Use the Location pop-up menu to choose a destination for your new mailbox.**

3. **In the Name text box, type a name for your mailbox.**

4. **Click OK.**

   Your mailbox appears in the sidebar under the location you chose in Step 2. (You might need to click the location's disclosure arrow to see your mailbox.)

TIP

If you don't like the name of your mailbox, feel free to change it. Either click the mailbox in the sidebar and then choose Mailbox ⇨ Rename Mailbox, or right-click the mailbox and then click Rename Mailbox. Type the new name and then press Return.

Moving a message to a mailbox

When you create a mailbox, it's empty. To store a message in that mailbox, you must manually move the message to the mailbox. Here's how it's done:

1. **In Mail, display the mailbox that contains the message you want to move.**

2. **Click to select the message.**

TIP

To select multiple, nonconsecutive messages, click the first one, and then hold down the ⌘ key while clicking each of the other messages. To select multiple consecutive messages, click the first message, hold down the Shift key, and then click the last message.

3. **Choose Message ⇨ Move To and then click the mailbox in the continuation menu that appears.**

Alternatively, make sure the destination mailbox is visible in the sidebar, and then drag the message and drop it on the mailbox in the sidebar.

Your selected message now appears in the mailbox.

Deleting a mailbox

You can delete a mailbox by following these steps:

1. **In Mail, click the mailbox you want to delete.**

2. **Choose Mailbox ⇨ Delete Mailbox.**

Alternatively, right-click the mailbox and then click Delete Mailbox.

A confirmation dialog appears, asking whether you're sure that you want to delete your mailbox.

WARNING

When you delete a mailbox, you delete all the messages stored inside.

3. **Click Delete.**

Organizing on Autopilot: Creating Smart Mailboxes

Creating your own mailboxes and moving related messages into them is a great way to bring a bit of tidiness to that mess you call an Inbox. However, the biggest problem with creating and using mailboxes is *remembering* to move your messages to them. It's okay, I get it: You start off with the best intentions, but then you get busy, a tsunami of messages floods in, and your Inbox quickly gets out of your control once again. Wouldn't it be nice to have an assistant to manage your mailboxes for you?

Well, duh, but that's never going to happen. But how about the next best thing? I'm talking about a Mail feature called the *smart mailbox*, which automates the process of organizing related messages. A smart mailbox differs from an ordinary mailbox in three ways:

>> A smart mailbox lets you define the type of messages you want to store automatically; that way, Mail organizes your messages without any additional work from you.

>> A smart mailbox doesn't contain any messages; instead, it links to the messages, which are still stored in the Inbox mailbox (or any mailbox that you move them to).

>> Because smart mailboxes contain only links to the original messages, a single message can have links stored in multiple smart mailboxes.

REMEMBER

Mail comes with one prefab smart mailbox called Today. You might think this smart mailbox is the place to go to see every message you've received today, but that's not quite right. The Today smart mailbox contains only messages that you've *read* today. It doesn't contain new, unread messages.

Creating a smart mailbox

To create a smart mailbox, you need to define a name for your smart mailbox along with the conditions that define the types of messages you want Mail to store automatically in your smart mailbox. Here are the steps to follow:

1. **In Mail, choose Mailbox ⇨ New Smart Mailbox.**

   A dialog for defining your new smart mailbox appears.

2. **In the Smart Mailbox Name text box, type a name for your smart mailbox.**

3. **Open the Contains Messages That Match pop-up menu and choose one of the following:**

- *All:* Mail creates a link for a message in the smart mailbox only if that message matches every condition you specify in the steps that follow.

- *Any:* Mail creates a link for a message in the smart mailbox only if that message matches one or more of the conditions you specify in the steps that follow.

4. **Open the first condition pop-up menu and choose an option, such as From or Date Received.**

5. **Open the second condition pop-up menu (if any) and choose an operator to apply to your first condition (for example, Contains or Ends With).**

6. **In the condition text box (if any), type a word or phrase that you want to use for your condition.**

7. **(Optional) Click + (add condition) and repeat Steps 4 through 6.**

Figure 4-3 shows a smart mailbox with three conditions added. Note that the first condition uses both pop-ups and the text box, the second condition uses just the two pop-ups, while the third condition uses only the first pop-up.

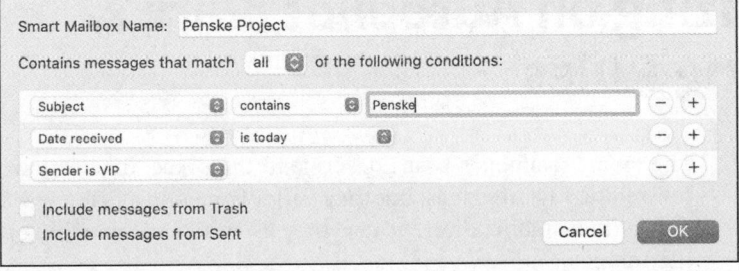

FIGURE 4-3: The conditions you add define how smart your smart mailbox is.

8. **Click OK.**

Your smart mailbox appears in the Smart Mailboxes section of the sidebar. If any messages match your defined criteria, you can click your smart mailbox's icon to see a list of those messages.

TIP

If you decide to change the name of your smart mailbox, either click the smart mailbox in the sidebar and then choose Mailbox ⇨ Rename Mailbox, or right-click the smart mailbox and then click Rename Mailbox. Type the new name and then press Return.

REMEMBER

The messages stored in a smart mailbox are just links to the actual messages stored in your Inbox mailbox. If you delete a message from a smart mailbox, the message remains in the Inbox; if you delete a message from the Inbox, it is deleted also from the smart mailbox.

Deleting a smart mailbox

Deleting a smart mailbox doesn't physically delete any messages because a smart mailbox contains only links to existing messages. To delete a smart mailbox, follow these steps:

1. **In Mail, click the smart mailbox you want to delete.**

2. **Choose Mailbox ⇨ Delete Mailbox.**

   Alternatively, right-click the smart mailbox and then click Delete Mailbox.

   A confirmation dialog appears, asking whether you're sure that you want to delete your smart mailbox.

3. **Click Delete.**

Organizing on Autopilot, Part 2: Creating Rules

The smart mailboxes that I describe in the preceding section are a powerful tool for organizing messages, but they suffer from one glaring weakness: They provide only *virtual* organization because they leave all your matching messages cluttering the Inbox.

If you want *real* organization where your messages are moved out of the Inbox and into a specific mailbox, and you want to avoid the drudgery of moving all your messages manually, may I introduce you to rules? A *rule* is a set of conditions that Mail applies to incoming messages, combined with one or more actions that Mail applies to a message if it matches those conditions.

The condition could be who the message is from, a word or phrase found in the subject line or message body, whether the message has an attachment, and so on. The action could be moving the message to a mailbox, replying to or forwarding the message, or even deleting the message.

To create a rule, follow these steps:

1. Choose Mail ➪ Settings to open the Mail settings window.

2. Click the Rules button on the toolbar.

The Rules window appears.

3. Click Add Rule.

A dialog for defining your new rule appears.

4. In the Description text box, type a brief description of what your rule does.

5. Open the If *X* of the Following Conditions Are Met pop-up menu and select one of the following for *X*:

- *All:* Mail performs the action of Step 10 only if the incoming message matches every condition you specify in the steps that follow.

- *Any:* Mail performs the action of Step 10 only if the incoming message matches one or more of the conditions you specify in the steps that follow.

6. Open the first condition pop-up menu and choose an option, such as From or Subject.

7. Open the second condition pop-up menu (if any) and choose an operator to apply to your first condition (for example, Contains or Begins With).

8. In the condition text box (if any), type a word or phrase that you want to use for your condition.

9. (Optional) Click + (add condition) and repeat Steps 6 through 8.

10. In the Perform the Following Actions section, use the first pop-up menu to specify the type of action you want Mail to apply to any message that matches the conditions you set up in Steps 5 through 8.

11. Use the rest of the action's pop-up menus (the number and content of the pop-up menus depends on which action you selected in Step 10) to complete the action.

12. (Optional) Click + (add action) and repeat Steps 10 and 11 to specify more actions to apply to any matching message.

Figure 4-4 shows an example rule with three conditions and two actions.

13. When you finish defining your rule, click OK.

Mail asks whether you want to apply your new rule to your messages.

14. Click Apply.

Mail applies the rule to your current messages and applies the rule's actions on any messages that match the conditions you specified.

15. Click the close icon of the Rules window.

Mail will now run the rule on any new messages that come in.

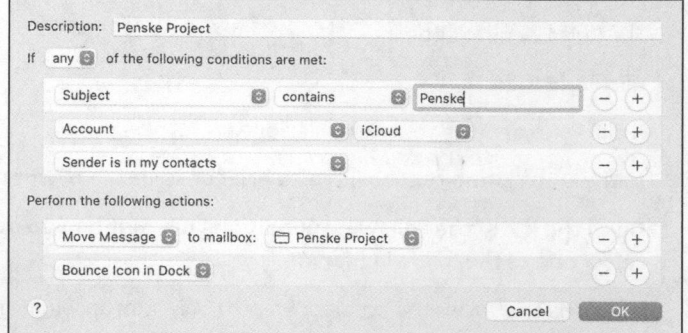

FIGURE 4-4:
Define a rule by
adding one or
more conditions
and actions.

REMEMBER

To modify a rule, choose Mail ⇨ Settings ⇨ Rules, click the rule, and then click Edit.

Dealing with Junk Email

Just like you receive junk mail in your paper mailbox, soon after you get an email address, you're going to start receiving junk email (or *spam*). While you can't entirely stop it, Mail has filters that help limit the inevitable flow of junk email so you can keep your email account from getting overwhelmed, and — perhaps more important — limit the dispersion of your email address and the personal information on your computer that can be accessed through your email.

WARNING

Most junk email messages are advertisements trying to sell you various products, but some junk email messages are scams to trick you into visiting bogus websites that ask for your credit card number or (worse) your bank account info. This form of spam is called *phishing*. Other times, junk email might contain an attachment masquerading as a free application that secretly contains a computer virus. Or a junk email might try to trick you into clicking a web link that downloads and installs a computer virus on your Mac. By filtering out such malicious junk email, you can minimize potential threats that can jeopardize your Mac's integrity or your personal information.

Filtering junk email

Filtering means that Mail examines the content of messages and tries to determine whether the message is junk. Your first task is to enable junk mail filtering and then set the filtering options you prefer:

1. Choose Mail ➪ Settings.

2. Click Junk Mail on the toolbar.

The Junk Mail settings appear.

3. In the Junk Mail Behaviors tab, select Enable Junk Mail Filtering.

Mail enables the rest of the settings in the Junk Mail Behaviors tab, as shown in Figure 4-5.

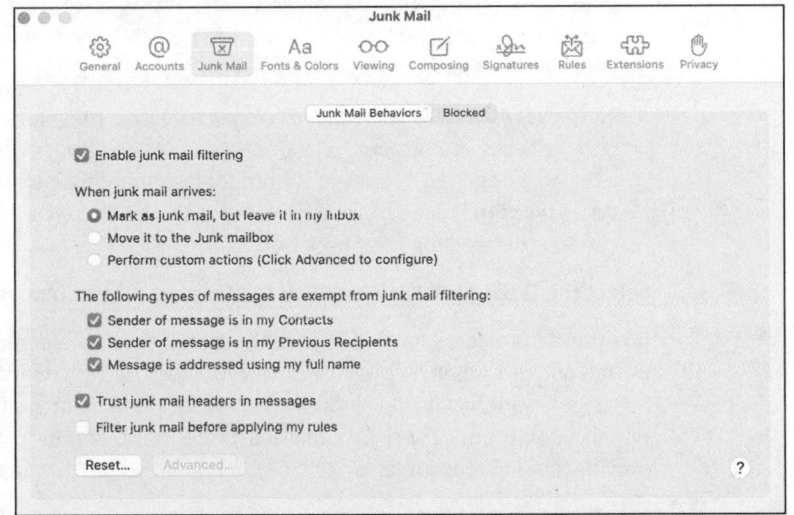

FIGURE 4-5: Use the Junk Mail Behaviors tab to enable and configure Mail's junk mail filtering.

4. Select one of the following options from the When Junk Mail Arrives section:

- *Mark as Junk Mail, But Leave It in My Inbox:* Identifies spam messages as junk mail, but doesn't do anything else with them.

- *Move It to the Junk Mailbox:* Identifies spam messages as junk mail and tosses them into the Junk mailbox. This option nicely separates junk mail from non-junk, but it does mean you need to check your Junk mailbox frequently to make sure Mail hasn't moved any legit messages there by accident.

- *Perform Custom Actions:* Enables you to define one or more custom actions to handle junk mail; see Step 8.

5. **Make sure that each of the following check boxes is selected (as they are by default) to specify the types of messages to exempt from junk mail filtering:**

Keeping these check boxes selected helps keep legitimate messages out of your Junk mailbox.

- *Sender of Message Is in My* Contacts: People in your Contacts aren't likely to spam you (otherwise you're hanging out with the wrong crowd), so leaving this check box selected exempts messages from those people.

- *Sender of Message Is in My Previous Recipients:* Even if the sender isn't in your Contacts, if you sent a message to that person in the past, new messages from that person won't be considered junk.

TIP

This setting assumes you don't have regular email conversations with spammers! To make sure you don't have any dodgy addresses in your list of previous recipients, choose Windows ➪ Previous Recipients. If you see a recipient that you think might be a spammer, click the recipient and then click Remove From List.

- *Message Is Addressed Using My Full Name:* As a rule, most junk messages don't address you by your full name, so leaving this check box selected is usually a good idea. However, it's not foolproof because some spammers do use your full name. If you find you get a lot of that type of spam, consider deselecting this check box.

6. **Select the Trust Junk Mail Headers in Messages check box.**

Many email providers have utilities running on their email servers that try to sniff out junk email before it lands in your inbox. If the provider flags a message as junk, it will add a note to that effect in the message header. When you select this check box, Mail trusts the mail that your email provider identifies as junk.

7. **Select Filter Junk Mail before Applying Rules.**

If you choose this option, mail is filtered through Mail's junk mail filter before applying your custom filter rules.

8. **If you select Perform Custom Actions in Step 4, click the Advanced button.**

A rule dialog opens with several conditions and a single (incomplete) action. You need to set up your own rule for junk mail:

a. *Choose Any or All in the If drop-down menu.* This determines whether any or all of the following conditions must be met before Mail filters suspect messages as Junk.

b. *Use the pop-up menus to set up rules for filtering incoming mail. Use + and − to the right of each rule to add or delete a rule.*

c. *Use the pop-up menus In the Perform the Following Actions section to indicate what you want Mail to do when a message arrives that meets the established rules.*

d. *Click OK.* Advanced Junk Mail settings have been applied.

9. **Click Close.**

Training mail to recognize junk

To improve accuracy, Mail allows you to train it by manually identifying junk email that its filter didn't catch.

After a few weeks of watching you identify junk email, the Mail app's filters begin to recognize common junk email. Even better, if you configured Mail to automatically move junk messages to the Junk mailbox (as I describe in the "Filtering junk email" section), your Inbox will be kept free from most junk email so you can focus on reading the messages that matter to you.

To train Mail to recognize junk email, follow these steps:

1. **In Mail's sidebar, click the Inbox (or All Inboxes) mailbox.**

A list of messages appears in the message list. Any messages Mail thinks are junk have brown text in the preview pane.

2. **Click a message that Mail filters as Junk.**

You have three options:

- *Load Remote Content:* You *could* click this button to download images and other remote content found in the message, but I highly recommend you don't do that. Loading that content only alerts the spammer that your email address is working, meaning you'll just get more junk mail. Click Load Remote Content only if you're certain the message isn't junk.

- *Not Junk:* If you choose this option, the message text in the Mail Preview column becomes black.

- *Move to Junk:* If you choose this option, the message is moved to the Junk mailbox.

After sorting through the message Mail thinks are junk, you can make your own decisions on any remaining messages you think are suspect.

3. **Click a message to review it.**

   If you think the message is junk, proceed to Step 4.

4. **Choose Message ⇨ Move to Junk or click the Junk button on the toolbar.**

   This tells the Mail application's filters what you consider junk email. The message is moved to the Junk mailbox.

5. **Click the Junk mailbox.**

6. **If you have multiple email accounts, click the Inbox disclosure arrow and then choose the account from which you moved the message.**

   Mail displays the messages in the message list, and the text for messages Mail thinks are junk is light brown.

7. **Click the message you marked as Junk.**

   A banner runs across the top of the message. If you accidentally marked the message as Junk, click the Move to Inbox toolbar button, and Mail moves the message to the appropriate Inbox. If the message is well and truly junk, don't do anything, except maybe empty the mailbox if it overfloweth with digital debris.

WARNING

The cleverness and prowess of spammers and phishers increases daily. Keep an eye out for these tipoffs to counterfeit requests:

>> Misspelled words

>> Logo design, colors, or type that is slightly different than that of the legitimate company

>> Sender addresses that don't match the company name

TIP

To verify an email address you think is bogus, click the disclosure arrow to the right of the name in the From field to display the entire email address. If something is decidedly stinky in Helsinki, move the email to Junk.

Blocking bad senders

After you apply Junk Mail behaviors, most senders of junk email are blocked. This is a good thing, but you might find that Mail misses some spam. If you notice that some of that missed junk is coming from a particular address, you can block that address. The word *block* here implies that you never see messages from that address, but that's not true. Instead, Mail allows the message into your Inbox but marks the message with a "This message is from a blocked sender" banner at the top of the message preview. (As you see in the steps that follow, you have the option of automatically sending blocked messages to the Trash mailbox.)

REMEMBER

Alas, spammers rarely use the same address twice, so blocking and address is much more useful if you receive messages from someone who's abusive, annoying, rude, or threatening.

To enable and fine-tune Mail's blocked mail filtering, follow these steps:

1. **Choose Mail ⇨ Settings.**

2. **Click the Junk Mail toolbar button.**

3. **Click the Blocked tab.**

4. **Make sure that the Enable Blocked Mail Filtering check box is selected.**

5. **Choose one of the following in the When Email from Blocked Addresses Arrives section:**

- *Mark as Blocked Mail, But Leave It in My Inbox:* Mail marks blocked messages with light brown text in the message list and displays buttons for dealing with the email.

- *Move It to the Trash:* Mail automatically moves messages from blocked senders to the Trash mailbox.

6. **Click the close icon to exit the dialog.**

If you receive a message from someone you want to block, click the message in the message list, right-click the sender's name, and then click Block Contact.

Deleting or Archiving a Message

After you're done with a message — that is, you've read it, replied to it, or forwarded it — what happens next? You have a few options. You could just let the message languish in your Inbox, but only if you prefer to become a less productive person over time. You could move the message to a mailbox that contains related messages, which is probably the best course of action with any email that contains useful or important content.

However, most of the emails you receive probably don't rise to that "useful or important" benchmark, so what's to become of all those other messages you get throughout the day? For those messages, you have two choices:

>> **Delete them:** This is the way to go for messages that you're certain you won't ever need to look at again.

>> **Archive them:** This is the route to take for messages that you want to save, just in case, but don't merit creating a new mailbox for storing them.

Taking a message out to the trash

By deleting unneeded messages, you can keep your Inbox uncluttered — and if you're using an IMAP or Exchange account, free up space on the mail server where your email messages are stored.

To delete a message, select it in the message list of whatever mailbox the message resides, then use one of the following techniques:

>> Choose Edit ⇨ Delete.

>> Click the trash can icon (delete selected messages).

>> Press ⌘+Delete.

>> Right-click the message and then click Delete in the shortcut menu.

REMEMBER

Deleting a message doesn't immediately erase it; instead, the message is stored in the Trash mailbox. If you don't empty the trash, you still have the chance to retrieve deleted messages, as outlined in the next section.

Retrieving messages from the trash

Each time you delete a message, Mail stores the deleted messages in the account's Trash mailbox. If you deleted a message by mistake, you can retrieve it by following these steps:

1. **In Mail, display the mailboxes of the account to which the message was sent.**

2. **Click the account's Trash mailbox.**

   A list of deleted messages appears.

3. **Click the message you want to retrieve.**

4. **Choose Message ⇨ Move To ⇨ Inbox.**

   If you have multiple inboxes, choose the one to which you want to move the message from the pop-up list.

Emptying the Trash mailbox

Messages stored in the Trash mailbox continue to take up space, so you should periodically empty the Trash mailbox by following these steps:

1. **In Mail, choose Mailbox ⇨ Erase Deleted Items.**

   A submenu appears, listing all the email accounts in Mail.

2. **Take one of the following actions.**

   - Click In All Accounts to erase all deleted messages.

   - Click the name of a specific email account to erase deleted messages only from that particular account.

TIP

You can set up Mail to automatically move deleted messages to the trash and permanently erase those trashed messages after a month, a week, a day, or upon quitting Mail. To configure this option, choose Mail ⇨ Settings, click the Accounts toolbar button, click a mail account in the Accounts column, and then click Mailbox Behaviors. Use the Erase Deleted Messages pop-up menu to select how often you want Mail to empty the Trash mailbox for the selected account: Never, After One Day, After One Week, After One Month, or When Quitting Mail. While you're here, note that you can also use the Erase Junk Messages pop-up menu to select how often you want Mail to clean out the Junk mailbox.

Archiving a message

If you want to reduce the number of messages you see in your mailboxes but not delete the messages — say, at the end of the year or when a project is complete — you can create an archive of those messages. Archived messages are kept in a mailbox in Mail but removed from active mailboxes. To archive messages, do the following:

1. **Click the mailbox that contains message you want to archive.**

2. **Select the message.**

3. **Choose Message ⇨ Archive, or press Control+⌘+A.**

   The selected message is moved to the account's Archive mailbox.

Chapter **5**

Chatting with Messages and FaceTime

When you need to reach out to someone in your family, posse, or team, you can always use email, as I describe in Book 2, Chapters 3 and 4. But what if what you want to share is just a quick update or question? In that case, email seems like overkill. So, what's the alternative? A little thing the internet's tall-forehead types invented quite a few years ago: instant messaging (or, to be cool, IM). As the name implies, *instant messaging* involves sending a message that gets delivered to its recipient right away. The vast majority of instant messages are text messages, which is why most folks refer to IM as *texting*.

The texting tool-of-choice in the Mac world is the Messages app, which also enables you to share photos and videos (assuming your recipient's texting app supports such things; most do these days). In this chapter, you explore all that Messages has to offer.

Another way that your Mac lets you chat with folks near and far is via the FaceTime app. If the other person is using a Mac, an iPhone, or an iPad, you can conduct audio-only or face-to-face conversations over an internet connection. This chapter tells you everything you need to know to set up and use FaceTime.

Getting the Messages Party Started

Messages uses your Apple ID to send messages to other people who have Messages installed on their Mac, iPhone, or iPad. Yep, that's right: You can use Messages to chat only with peeps who have Apple devices. However, a bit later in this section, I show you a trick that enables your Mac to send and receive messages from anyone.

Launching Messages

To use Messages, you have to sign in to Apple's iMessage service using your Apple ID. Messages prompts you do to this the first time you launch the app, so in the following steps, everything after Step 1 is a one-time-only deal:

1. **Click the Messages icon (pointed out in Figure 5-1) on the dock or Launchpad to launch Messages.**

   The first time you fire up Messages, it prompts you to sign in to iMessage with your Apple ID.

New message

FIGURE 5-1:
Messages
enables you to
chat up a storm.

Messages

2. **Type your Apple ID email address, and then click Sign In.**

   A Password field appears just below the email address.

3. **Type your Apple ID password, and then click Sign In.**

   You're now signed in to the iMessage service. If you see an overview of some Messages app features, click OK.

   Messages asks if you want to all the app to share when you have notifications turned off while using a focus (see Book 1, Chapter 6 to learn about the Focus feature).

4. **Click either OK or Don't Allow, as you prefer.**

   Messages opens, ready to start messaging (refer to Figure 5-1).

iMessage versus SMS/MMS: What's the Difference?

One point of confusion that I need to clear up right off the bat is that the modern texting world consists of two types of messages:

>> **iMessages:** These messages can include not only text but also a wide variety of other media, such as photos, videos, maps, voice recordings, stickers, and animated GIFs. You can also see when the other person is typing a reply, use Apple Pay, and more. You can send iMessages only to folks who have an iPad, an iPhone, or another Mac (or even an iPod touch, if you know anyone who still uses one).

>> **SMS/MMS:** SMS (short messaging service) messages are text-only affairs, while MMS (multimedia messaging service) can include photos, videos, and audio.

The problem is that your Mac's Messages app knows how to send and receive only iMessages. If you want to exchange messages with someone who doesn't have an iPad, an iPhone, or a Mac, those messages need to be SMS or MMS messages. Are you stuck? Not at all! In the next section, I show you how to configure a feature called text message forwarding that enables your Mac to send and receive SMS/MMS messages via your iPhone.

REMEMBER

In this chapter, I refer to all the missives you send or receive with the Messages app as *text messages*. Unless I specify otherwise, this umbrella term refers to both iMessages and SMS or MMS messages and includes those missives that contain media, not just text.

Forwarding SMS/MMS messages to and from your Mac via your iPhone

By default, your Mac is an iMessage-only device. However, if you have an iPhone, you can configure it to forward SMS/MMS messages, which means two things happen:

>> When you receive an SMS/MMS message on your iPhone, you see it also in your Mac's Messages app.

>> When you use your Mac's Messages app to send a text message to someone who doesn't use a Mac, an iPhone, or an iPad, that message is sent as an SMS/MMS message via your iPhone.

REMEMBER

Text message forwarding is a Continuity feature, which means to use it your Mac and iPhone must be signed in to the iMessage service using the same Apple ID. Also, your Mac must be running OS X Yosemite or later and your iDevice must be running iOS 8 or later.

Here are the steps to follow to set up text message forwarding for your Mac:

1. **On your Mac, open Messages.**

2. **On your iPhone, open Settings.**

3. **Tap Messages.**

4. **Tap Text Message Forwarding.**

   Settings displays a list of devices that can use text message forwarding.

5. **Click the switch beside your Mac on, as shown in Figure 5-2.**

   On your Mac, Messages displays a dialog telling you that it can now send and receive iPhone text messages, as shown in Figure 5-3.

6. **On your Mac, click Turn On.**

   Messages turns on text message forwarding.

REMEMBER

You can now communicate with people who don't have an Apple device, but messages will be exchanged through SMS text messages or MMS multimedia-type missives. If you're involved in an SMS/MMS schmooze-fest, your message bubbles will be green. If you're exchanging iMessages with others, your bubbles will be blue. The distinction is important because most of the fancy multimedia tricks I tell you about in this chapter won't work unless you're exchanging iMessages.

FIGURE 5-2:
On your iPhone, set your Mac's switch on to enable text message forwarding.

Allow these devices to send and receive text messages from this iPhone.

Paul's MacBook Pro (Mac)

Paul's MacBook Air 4 (Mac)

Paul's New iMac (Mac)

iPad Pro (iPad)

FIGURE 5-3:
On your Mac, confirm that you want to receive and send text messages via your iPhone.

Messages can send and receive your iPhone text messages on this Mac.

You can turn this on now, or set it up later on your iPhone in Messages settings.

Turn On   Not Now

Tweaking Messages to suit your texting style

Before getting down to the details of using Messages to do the texting thing, it's worth taking a few minutes to run through a few settings that affect how Messages works:

1. **Choose Messages ➪ Settings.**

2. **Click the General button on the toolbar.**

3. **Click Set Up Name and Photo Sharing.**

This feature configures Messages to share your name and your photo with the people you specify. It's a good idea to share these things with at least the people in your Contacts so they can identify your messages more readily. Follow these substeps:

a. *Click Continue.*

b. *Click Customize; select (or take) a photo or select an emoji or memoji; and then click Done.*

   c. *Click Continue.*

   d. *If your Mac asks if you want to use this photo everywhere, click Use.*

   e. *Click the Share Automatically pop-up menu and then click Contacts Only.* If you prefer that Messages ask you if you want to share your name and photo, click Always Ask instead.

   f. *Click Done.*

4. **Set the following options, as you prefer:**

   - *Keep Messages:* Choose an option from the pop-up menu to specify how long Messages saves your text conversations: 30 Days, One Year, or Forever.

   - *Application*: In this section, the default options are to notify you when messages from unknown contacts appear; to notify you when your name is mentioned in a conversation; to automatically play full-screen visual effects; and to play message sound effects.

   - *Message Received Sound:* Open the pop-up menu to choose your preferred sound to indicate that a message has been received.

   - *Text Size:* Click this pop-up menu to either choose a preset text size or click Other to select a custom text size.

   To learn about the options in the Shared with You tab, see Book 2, Chapter 2.

5. **Click the close icon.**

Texting and More with Messages

The bulk of your Messages career will be spent exchanging simple text messages with friends and maybe even the odd foe. However, Messages is capable of handling much more than text. As you learn in the sections to come, you can also use Messages to perform the following amazing feats:

>> **Enhance messages with media:** Your messages can include photos, emojis, GIFs, special effects, and more.

>> **Create group chats:** You can conduct conversations with multiple people and even give your group a special name and photo.

>> **Share a screen:** If the person you're texting is using a Mac, you can ask that person to share their screen, which means you see what's on that person's Mac display and you can use your mouse and keyboard to control that person's Mac as though you're sitting in front of their computer. Likewise, you

can invite your chat partner to take screen control of your Mac as though they were sitting in front of your computer.

» **Share a file:** You can use a text message to send any file from your Mac to the person you're texting with.

Initiating a text chat

When you open Messages, the window has two parts. The left pane shows a list of your previous and active chats — or *conversations*, as Messages prefers to call them — and the right pane shows the messages in whatever conversation is currently selected.

If you're just getting started, the right pane will be a blank expanse of white and the left pane will include just a single conversation titled New Message. Not to worry: You'll have both panes brimming with conversations and text before you know it.

To that end, to initiate a chat with someone, follow these steps:

1. **Click the new message icon (refer to Figure 5-1) in the top-right corner of the conversation pane.**

    You can also choose File ⇨ New Message or press ⌘+N.

    If you're just getting started with Messages, a new conversation is started for you automatically, so you can skip to Step 2.

    A new conversation named New Message appears at the top of the conversation list, and a blank screen appears on the right.

2. **In the To text field, begin typing the name of the person you want to text.**

    As you type, you see a list of contacts who match what you've typed. Under each contact, you see either a phone number or an email address, which is the default method for sending a text to that person.

    What if the person you want to text isn't in your Contacts app? No sweat: Just use the To field to type the person's phone number or email address, and then skip to Step 4.

3. **When you see the contact you want to text, you have two choices:**

    - If you're cool with the default texting method, click the contact.

    - If you want to change the texting method, click the right-pointing arrow to the right of the contact, and then click the method you want to use (see Figure 5-4).

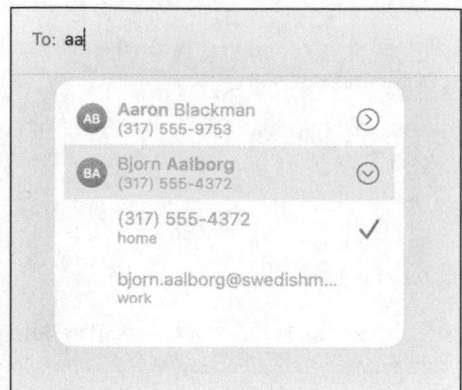

FIGURE 5-4:
You can select a preferred texting method for a contact.

As an alternative to Steps 2 and 3, click + (add) in the upper-right corner to open a list of your contacts (from the Contacts app). You can search for a contact or scroll through the list to find the person you want. Click the contact, and then click the texting method (phone number or email).

The contact appears in the To field and the person's name and avatar appear in the left column.

4. **In the text box at the bottom of the chat window, type a message, and then press Return to send your message.**

   If you're itching to enhance your message with a photo or an emoji, see the next section.

   The person you're texting receives a notification and your message appears in their copy of Messages when they next launch the app.

REMEMBER

Just because someone is connected to the internet doesn't necessarily mean that person is in front of their device and wants to chat. So, if you find your messages falling on deaf ears (deaf fingertips?) and the person isn't bothering to reply to your messages, it likely means the person you're trying to text has gone fishing or is otherwise busy and will get to your message eventually.

Not getting a reply might also mean that the person has blocked you and therefore isn't receiving your messages on purpose. Ouch! If you ever feel like blocking someone yourself, click a conversation with that person, choose Conversation ⇨ Block Person, and then click Block when Messages ask you to confirm.

Getting fancy with photos, emojis, and other message effects

These days, is a text a real message if it doesn't include at least one emoji? Is a photo a real image if it's not texted to at least one person? I don't know the answers to these philosophical conundrums, but I do know that you can enhance your texts with emojis, photos, and much more:

>> **Inserting an emoji:** Click the emojis icon, which is the smiley face that appears to the right of the text message field (and is labeled in Figure 5-5). In the pop-up window that appears, scroll or search for the emoji you want, and then click it to insert it into your message.

>> **Inserting a photo:** Click the apps icon, which appears just to the left of the text message field (and is labeled in Figure 5-5). Then click Photos, search or scroll for the photo you want, and click it to insert the photo into the message.

>> **Inserting a memoji:** Click the apps icon, click Memoji Stickers, and then click the memoji type and style to insert the memoji into the message.

>> **Inserting a GIF image:** Click the apps icon, click #images, search or scroll for the image you want, and then click it to insert the GIF into the message.

>> **Inserting a message effect:** Type your message, click the apps icon, click Message Effects, click the effect you want, and then click the send icon (up arrow beside your text). Message sends the text and displays the effect on the recipient's device.

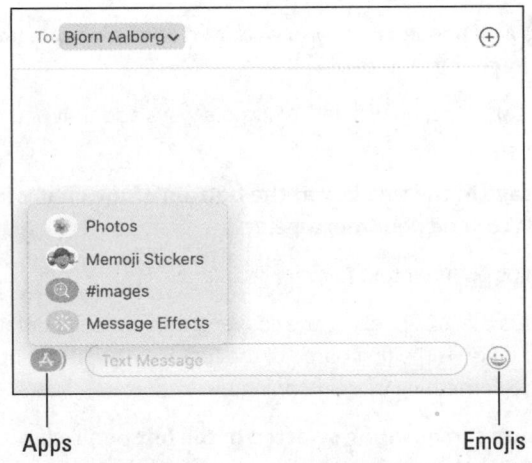

FIGURE 5-5:
Use the emojis and apps icons to add some fun to your message.

Apps   Emojis

The more the merrier: Setting up a group text

As fun and convenient as it is to text with one person, imagine the entertainment or productivity possibilities when you text with two or more people. Yep, that's right: Messages lets you create conversations with multiple people. In fact, you can have up to 32 people (including yourself) in an iMessage text chat and up to 10 people (including yourself) in an SMS/MMS chat.

REMEMBER

Although Messages makes it easy to add more people to an existing group conversation, for some inexplicable reason it doesn't offer a way to turn a single-person conversation into a group text. Boo!

Here are the steps to follow to set up and manage a group text:

1. **Click the new message icon (refer to Figure 5-1) in the top-right corner of the conversation pane.**

    You can also choose File ➪ New Message or press ⌘+N.

2. **Add a person to the group text using any of the following methods:**

    - Use the To text field to start typing the name of the person, and then click the person when they appears in the list of matches from Contacts.

    - Click + (add) in the upper-right corner to display your contacts, search for a contact or scroll through the list to find the person you want, click the contact, and then click the texting method (phone number or email).

    - Use the To text field to type the phone number or email address of the person you want to include in the group text.

3. **Repeat Step 2 as needed until you've added all the people you want to participate in your group text.**

    If you forget someone, no worries: You can always add that person to the group text later.

4. **Type a message in the text box at the bottom of the chat window and press Return to send your message.**

    Messages ships out your text to every recipient.

    Messages adds the group text to the conversation pane. By default, the name of the conversation is the first name of the first few recipients, but you can change that to something more meaningful.

5. **With the group conversation selected in the left pane, click the *i*-in-a-circle (details) in the upper-right corner of the window.**

    Alternatively, right-click the conversation in the left column and then click Details from the context menu.

    Messages opens a pop-up window that shows the details of the group text.

6. **(Optional) To change the group name and avatar, click Change Group Name and Photo, type the group name in the window that**

appears, select an avatar (a photo, an emoji, text, or a memoji), and then click Done.

Messages returns you to the details window.

7. **(Optional) To add another person to the group text, click Add Member; type the name, phone number, or email address of the person you want to add; and then press Return.**

8. **Click outside the details window to close it.**

Messing with messages

Once you have some conversations percolating, Messages gives you quite a few ways to manage your conversations and messages:

>> **Undoing a send:** If you send a message by mistake, you can revoke the message up to 15 minutes after you shipped it. (To recall a sent message, you need the macOS Ventura or later version of Messages.) In the message window, right-click the message you want to cancel, and then click Undo Send. Note that depending on how long it took you to undo the send, your recipient might have seen the message anyway.

>> **Editing a message:** If you send a message that contains a spelling mistake, claims that Dustin Hoffman was in *Star Wars,* or has some other error, you can make changes to the message up to 15 minutes after you sent it. (To edit a message, you need the macOS Ventura or later version of Messages.) In the message window, right-click the message you want to modify, and then click Edit. Make your changes, then press Return or click the check mark button. Note, however, that although your recipient sees your edited message at first, that person still has the option of viewing your original message.

>> **Pinning a conversation:** In the conversations pane, Messages displays the conversations in order according to the time (and date) of the most recent message. If you have a ton of conversations going, you might find that an important conversation keeps slipping down the list, making it hard to find. To prevent that, you can *pin* the conversation, which tells Messages to always display the conversation at the top of the pane. Right-click the conversation and then click Pin.

>> **Marking a conversation as unread:** As a way to remind yourself to follow up on a conversation, you can tell Messages to display the conversation as unread. (You need the macOS Ventura or later version of Messages to mark messages as unread.) Click the conversation and then choose Conversation ➪ Mark as Unread. (You can also press Shift+⌘+U or right-click the conversation and then click Mark as Unread.)

TIP

To view only your unread messages, choose View ⇨ Unread Messages (or press Control+⌘+4).

» **Deleting a conversation:** If you no longer need a conversation, you can reduce clutter in the conversations pane by selecting the conversation and then choosing Conversation ⇨ Delete Conversation. (You can also right-click the conversation and then click Delete.) When Messages asks you to confirm, click Delete.

» **Recovering a deleted conversation:** If you deleted a conversation by accident, you have up to 30 days to recover it before Messages deletes it for good. (You need the macOS Ventura or later version of Messages to recover a deleted conversation.) Choose View ⇨ Recently Deleted (or press Control+⌘+5), click the conversation, and then click Recover. When Messages asks you to confirm, click Recover X Messages (where X is the number of messages in the conversation you're recovering).

Sharing a screen during a text conversation

In Book 3, Chapter 4, I talk about sharing your screen with another Mac user or having another Mac user share their screen with you. It's an amazingly useful technique but what's even more amazing is that you can invoke it right from a text conversation.

Assuming you're already texting with another Mac user and that conversation is selected in Messages, here's what you do to invoke screen sharing:

» **To take control of the other person's Mac:** Choose Conversation ⇨ Ask to Share Screen.

» **To ask the other person to take control of your Mac:** Choose Conversation ⇨ Invite to Share My Screen.

Once the invitation is accepted (again, see Book 3, Chapter 4 for details), the Screen Sharing app shows up and the sharing fun begins.

Sending a file along with a text message

While you're texting with someone, you might want to send that person a file. It might be a Pages document you want the person to review, a PDF file you want them to read, or a video file you want them to view. Whatever the reason, you can use either of the following techniques to ship out a file along with a text message:

>> Choose Conversation ⇨ Send File, use the document chooser to select the file, and then click Open.

>> Open a new Finder window, locate the file you want to share, and then drag the file from Finder and drop it inside the conversation pane. If you want to share a photo, you can also drag it from the Photos app and drop it in the conversation pane.

Either way, Messages adds the file to a new text message and displays a thumbnail version of the file. Type some explanatory text below the file thumbnail (if necessary) and then press Return to send the message.

Making Calls with FaceTime

Instant messaging gives you rapid responses and quick input, but sometimes seeing a friendly familiar face makes an exchange that much better. With *FaceTime*, the video chat app that comes with your Mac, you can communicate with people who use a Mac, an iPhone, or an iPad (or even a iPod touch).

REMEMBER

FaceTime, like Messages, uses the internet to communicate, so make sure you have a connection.

FaceTime uses the information in Contacts to call an iPhone with a phone number and a Mac, an iPad, and an iPod touch with an email address. You also need an internet connection and an Apple ID. If you don't have an Apple ID, you can set one up in FaceTime, or see Book 1, Chapter 3 for detailed instructions.

In this section, I show you how to sign in to FaceTime, call your friends, and accept incoming calls. I also tell you how to add your favorite peeps so you can call them lickety-split.

Signing in to FaceTime

To use FaceTime to make or receive calls on your Mac, you have to turn on FaceTime and sign in to your account. To sign in to FaceTime, follow these instructions:

1. **Click the FaceTime icon (pointed out a bit later in Figure 5-6) on the dock or in Launchpad.**

   The FaceTime window opens, and you see the video from your Mac's camera in the video pane.

If this is the first time you've used FaceTime, go to Step 2. If not, go to the next section.

2. **Enter your Apple ID in the User Name field.**

    If you don't have an Apple ID, click Create New Apple ID and fill in the form that appears to the right of the video window, and then click Next to finish setting up an Apple ID.

3. **Enter your password in the Password field.**

4. **Click Next.**

    Your Mac verifies your credentials and then activates FaceTime.

    The calling pane opens. You can close the FaceTime window, but you remain signed in so you can receive calls.

Making a call with FaceTime

After you enable FaceTime and sign in to your account, you can make and receive calls. To make a call, follow these steps:

1. **If FaceTime isn't already running, click the FaceTime icon (see Figure 5-6) on the dock or in Launchpad.**

    The FaceTime window opens, and you see a live video feed from your Mac's camera in the video pane, as shown in Figure 5-6.

2. **Click New FaceTime.**

    The New FaceTime window appears.

3. **In the To field, start typing the name, email address, or phone number of the person you want to call.**

    As you type, FaceTime offers a list of suggested contacts.

4. **Click the name of the person you want to call.**

    That person's name appears in the text field.

5. **Choose how you want to call the contact:**

    - *Audio and video:* To call the person using both audio and video, click the FaceTime icon.

    - *Audio only:* To call the person using audio only, click the FaceTime icon's drop-down arrow and then click FaceTime Audio (see Figure 5-7). If the contact has an iPhone, you can alternatively click the displayed phone number.

FIGURE 5-6:
The FaceTime
window after
you've signed in.

FaceTime

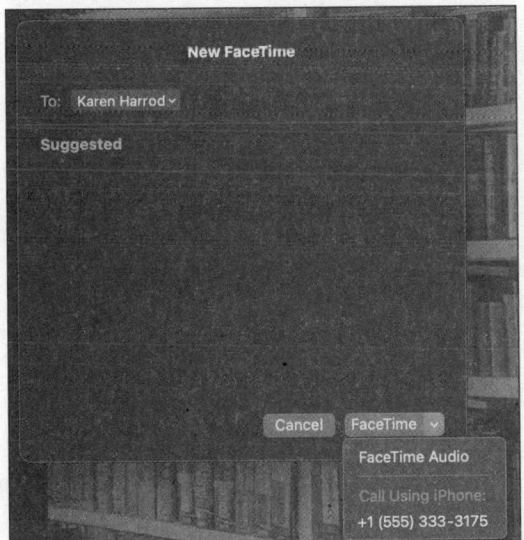

FIGURE 5-7:
Getting ready to
make a call.

Your recipient's device rings, letting them know a FaceTime call is en route. If
the person doesn't answer or declines the call, the person's name appears in
the video window with the message "*Name* is not available for FaceTime"
(where *Name* is the name of the contact).

**Chatting with Messages
and FaceTime**

If the person accepts your video call, you see their face in the main part of your screen. A small window appears where you see yourself, which is what the person you called sees.

6. **Use the icons on the screen (see Figure 5-8) to do the following:**

- *View the sidebar:* Display the name and number of the person you're chatting with. I suggest you use this in full-screen mode (choose Video ⇨ Enter Full Screen). If you don't, part of the video window is hidden.

- *Mute audio:* Mute your microphone so the person you're chatting with can't hear you. Click the icon again to unmute your microphone.

- *Pause video:* Stop your video feed. Click the icon again to resume your video feed.

- *Share screen:* Share a window or your entire screen with your caller.

- *Take a picture:* Take a picture of the other person's video feed.

- *End Call:* Terminate the call.

7. **To terminate your call, click the end icon (red circle with an X) or close the FaceTime window.**

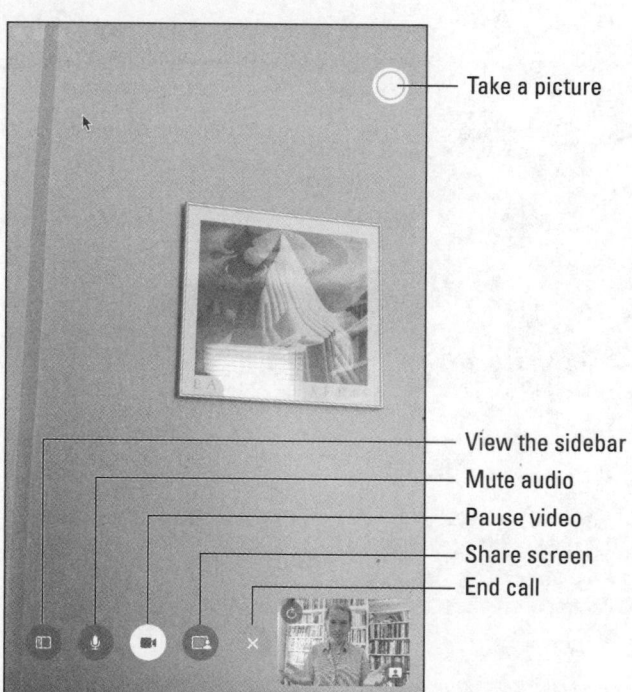

Take a picture

View the sidebar

Mute audio

Pause video

Share screen

End call

FIGURE 5-8:
Use the FaceTime icons to control your call.

Initiating an audio or a video call from Messages

To tie together the two main subjects of this chapter, note that you can initiate a FaceTime call from Messages. Here's how it's done:

1. **Click the conversation with the person you want to call.**

2. **Near the top-right corner of the message pane, click the FaceTime icon (the video camera icon; see Figure 5-9).**

3. **Choose how you want to call the contact:**

   - *FaceTime Audio:* Click this command to call the person using audio only.

   - *FaceTime Video:* Click this command to call the person using audio and video.

   Your Mac launches FaceTime, which then makes the call.

FIGURE 5-9:
Initiate a
FaceTime audio
or video call
from a Messages
conversation.

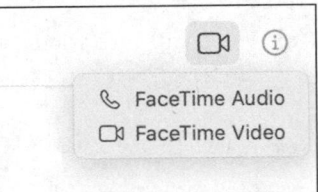

Receiving a FaceTime call

You can receive calls when you launch FaceTime and sign in, as I describe earlier. If someone calls you, FaceTime automatically opens, and you see the following:

>> Your Mac's video feed in the video pane

>> The name or phone number of the person who is calling you

>> The type of call (FaceTime Video or FaceTime Audio)

>> Two buttons that give you the option to accept or decline the phone call, as shown in Figure 5-10

FIGURE 5-10:
You can accept or decline incoming FaceTime calls.

Click Accept to open the video call or click Decline to reject the call.

TIP

If the incoming call is FaceTime video but you're not up for some camera time, click the drop-down arrow beside Accept and then click Accept as Audio.

REMEMBER

If you don't want to receive FaceTime video call invitations, choose FaceTime ⇨ Turn FaceTime Off (or press ⌘+K).

Chapter **6**

Exploring the World with Maps

If you're on a business trip and you get dropped off at the conference center or your hotel, you might ask yourself, "Okay, I know what city I'm in, but where am I *exactly*?" If you have a family driving vacation coming up, you might ask yourself, "Okay, I know where we're going, but what's the best route to get there and how long will it take?" If you find yourself in an unfamiliar part of town, you might ask yourself, "Okay, I know where I am, but where's the nearest café (or restaurant or bookstore)?"

First, wow you ask a lot of questions. Second, did you know that your Mac can answer these and many similar questions? Specifically, the Maps app was made to tackle any question related to location, getting directions (whether you're driving, walking, taking transit, or cycling), and finding nearby businesses and landmarks. Maps has access to a digital representation of just about every mappable object in the world. Maps knows almost every country and county, city and town, street and avenue, business and building, park and playground.

In this chapter, you explore the landscape of the Maps app. You learn how to find your present location and locate an address you know. You investigate how to get directions from one place to another and then make those indications available on your mobile device. You also learn how to share the locations and directions you discover.

Wherever You Go, There You Are

The simplest use of the Maps app is to determine your current location. That might not be useful if you're using a desktop Mac that doesn't go anywhere. But if you have a luggable Mac such as a MacBook Air or MacBook Pro and you always take your Mac on business trips and similar jaunts, seeing your current location on a map can be quite handy. In the following sections, I tell you how to find your location and use the Mac's gestures to navigate.

Enabling location services for Maps

Your Mac has a feature called *location services* that allows apps to determine your current location based on the location of your Mac. Location services performs this trick by gathering information from nearby Wi-Fi networks. Location services is turned off by default, so to enable Maps to determine your current location, you need to not only turn on location services but also need allow Maps to access the data that location services gathers. Follow these steps:

1. **Click the System Settings icon on the dock.**

   Or choose ⌘ ⇨ System Settings.

2. **Click Privacy & Security.**

3. **Click Location Services.**

4. **Click the Location Services switch on.**

   System Settings asks for your Mac admin password to allow this change.

5. **Type your password and then click Unlock.**

   System Settings turns on the Location Services switch, as shown in Figure 6-1. If you happen to also see a switch for Maps, go ahead and click that switch on, which will save you a step the first time you launch Maps.

   Learn more about the Privacy & Security settings in Book 3, Chapter 2.

TIP

6. **Click the close icon of the System Settings window.**

REMEMBER

Apple's emphasis on privacy extends to location services. Why? Because although knowing your location can add great value to some apps (particularly Maps), other apps would use that precious and private information to track you. Creepy! Happily, Apple won't let that happen. When you see a message from an app requesting the use of location services, you can rest assured that the description of why the app needs to access your location is checked carefully by Apple's app review team.

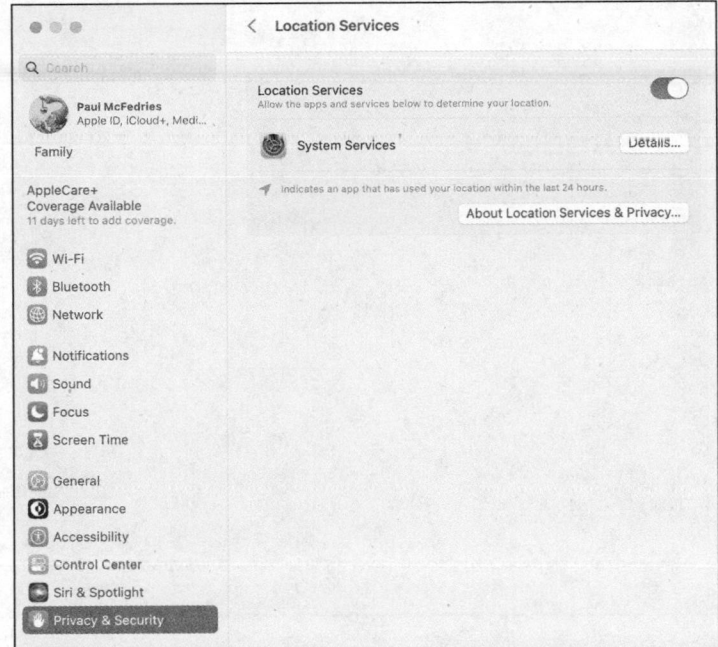

FIGURE 6-1:
Turn on the
switch for Loca-
tion Services.

Launching Maps

When you're ready to unfold Maps, follow these steps:

1. **Click the Maps icon on the dock (see Figure 6-2) or in Launchpad, and click OK to grant Maps permission to use your location.**

   Maps requests permission to use your location. (Don't worry: You see this request only the first time you launch Maps.)

   Note that you won't see this request if you were able to set the Maps switch on in the preceding section.

2. **If you see a What's New in Maps window, click Continue.**

3. **If you see a window asking you to turn on notifications, click either Enable Notifications or Not Now, as you prefer.**

   The Maps window finally appears and displays a map with your current location at the center, indicated by a blue dot.

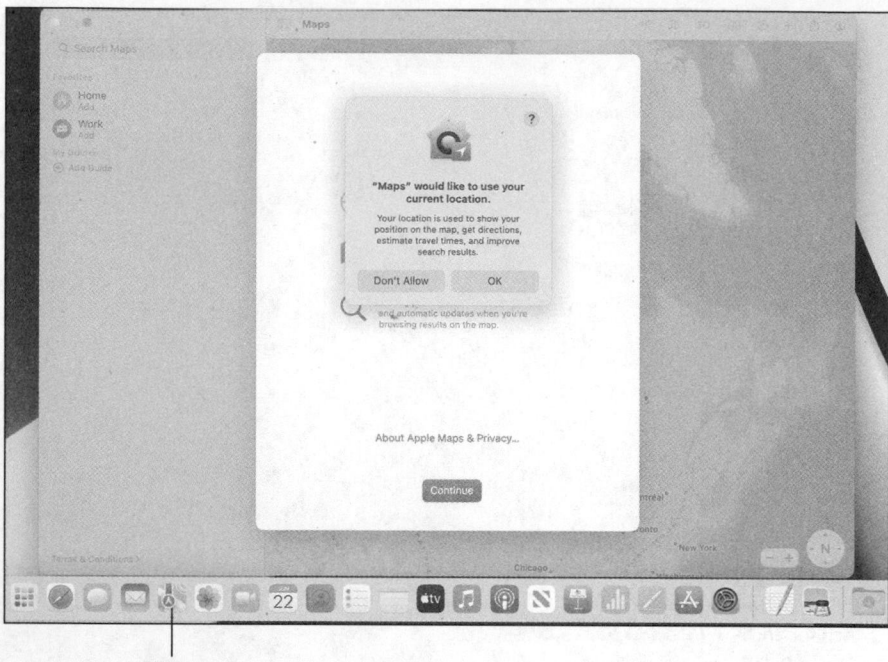

Maps

"You are here": Showing your location on the map

Although Maps shows your current location by default when you launch the app, after you've used Maps to scroll around, search for other locations, or get directions from some Point A to some Point B, your current location will be long lost.

To bring your current location back into view, use any of the following techniques:

>> Choose View ➪ Go to Current Location.

>> Press ⌘+L.

>> Click the show your current location icon on the Maps toolbar, which is labeled in Figure 6-3.

Whichever method you use, Maps brings up a map of your current neighbor-hood. Your exact location is the blue dot on the map, like you see in Figure 6-3. If a pulsing circle appears around the blue dot, your location is approximate; the smaller the circle, the more precise your exact (or nearly exact) location. A compass appears in the lower-right corner of the Maps window and points north.

Current location   Show your current location

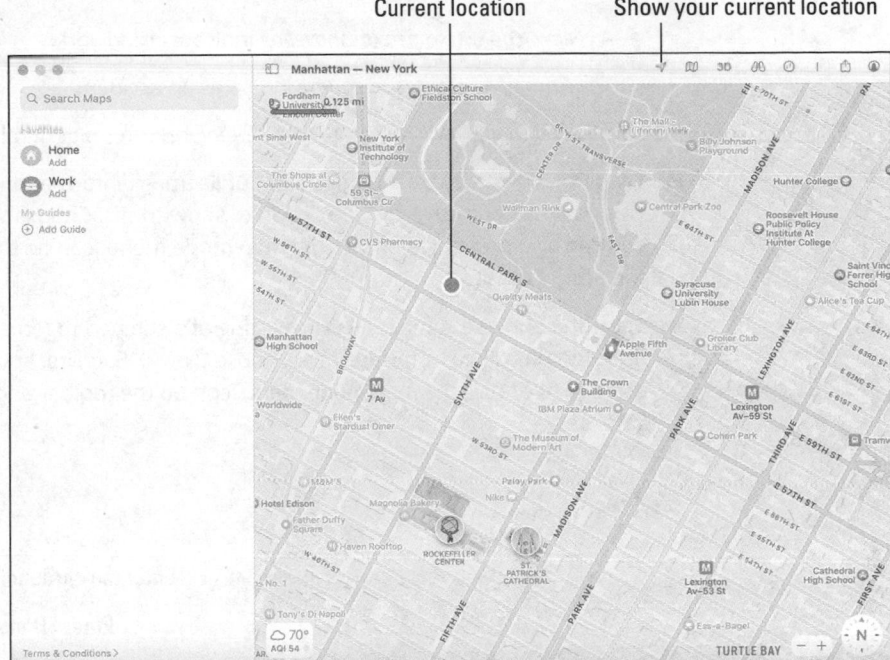

FIGURE 6-3:
The blue dot
indicates your
current location.

Navigating Maps

Maps has icons and menus to change the view and navigate the map, but Maps also takes advantage of the multitouch gestures offered by a trackpad. Figure 6-4 points out the icons you see on the Maps toolbar.

Maps offers four *map modes*, which control the look and features of the map:

» **Explore:** Shows you a map with street names and route numbers. This is the default view. Choose View ➪ Explore. You can also press ⌘+1 or click the map mode menu icon on the toolbar and then click Explore.

» **Driving:** Shows you a map with street names and route numbers and color-coded traffic information. Choose View ➪ Driving. You can also press ⌘+2 or click the map mode menu icon on the toolbar and then click Driving. Here are the colors and symbols that Maps uses to display the current traffic conditions:

- *Red* shows where traffic is heavy and stop-and-go.

- *Orange* means traffic is moving slowly.

- *A white dash in a red circle* icon means the road is closed.

- *A yellow icon with a person shoveling* indicates roadwork.

- *The front of a car in a red square* indicates an accident.

- *A yellow triangle with an exclamation point* indicates a general alert.

>> **Transit:** Shows the street names and public transit information for your area. This map does not give you the option to show traffic. Choose View ⇨ Transit. You can also press ⌘+3 or click the map mode menu icon on the toolbar and then click Transit.

>> **Satellite:** Shows a satellite view consisting of a stitched-together series of photographs taken from satellites. Choose View ⇨ Satellite. You can also press ⌘+4 or click the map mode menu icon on the toolbar and then click Satellite.

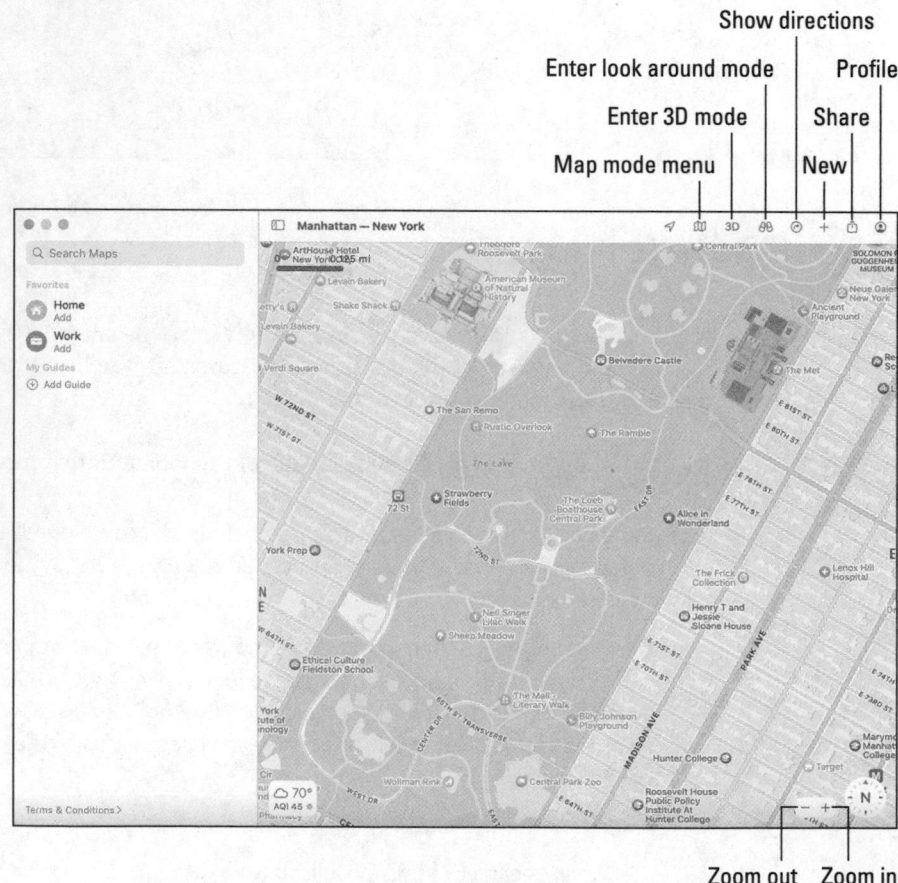

Show directions

Enter look around mode

Profile

Enter 3D mode

Share

Map mode menu

New

FIGURE 6-4: Use Maps' toolbar icons to control the view and perform other map-related tasks.

Zoom out   Zoom in

Change the orientation and size of the map by doing the following:

>> Click the + or − beside the compass to zoom in or out of the map, respectively. (On the View menu, you can also click Zoom In or Zoom Out, or you can press ⌘++ or ⌘+-.) As you zoom in or out, the scale changes. (If you don't see the scale, choose View ⇨ Show Scale.)

>> Double-click the mouse or trackpad to zoom in; hold down the Option key while double-clicking to zoom out.

>> On a trackpad, use the spread and pinch gestures with your thumb and forefinger (or the two fingers that are comfortable for you) to zoom in and out of the map, respectively.

>> Scroll to move the map up, down, or sideways.

>> Choose View ⇨ Show 3D Map (or press ⌘+D or click the enter 3D mode icon on the toolbar) to switch to 3D view, which just tilts the map in explore, driving, and transit mode but becomes 3D in satellite view. Use the slider that appears to the right of the compass to adjust the angle of the tilt.

>> Click and hold down the pointer on the compass and drag left or right to rotate the map.

>> Press Option+← to rotate the map counterclockwise or Option+→ to rotate the map clockwise.

>> Tap the compass icon, which appears in the lower-right corner to return to a north-facing orientation.

Navigating Your World

Even if you don't take your Mac with you or have internet access while traveling, you can still use Maps to calmly plan your trip before grabbing your car keys or backpack. After you come up with a route for your trip, print the directions or send them to your iPhone or iPad and be on your way.

In the sections that follow, I show you how to find addresses or points of interest and store them in Maps, and then I show you how to get from one place to another.

Mapping points of interest

You may know your way around your city or town but not know some of the street names — or perhaps you're headed to a city on business and want to find bookstores near your hotel. In these situations, you don't need directions as much as a location or information. Maps can work with a specific street name and number as well as inexact addresses, such as an intersection, a neighborhood, or a landmark. Use these steps to find either:

1. **(Optional) Click the show your current location toolbar icon if you want to orient the map on your present whereabouts.**

2. **Click the Search Maps text box at the top left of the window.**

3. **Type one of the following in the Search field:**

   - *An address* in the form of a street name and number or an intersection, with the city and state, or just the name of a city or town.

   - *A neighborhood, landmark, or service* such as SOMA (South of Market) San Francisco, Liberty Bell, or bookstores Philadelphia.

   - *The name* of a person or business stored in your Contacts. If you enter a common name, Maps will give you a list of suggestions, as well as a name or names from your Contacts app.

   A list of potential matches from Contacts and the Maps database appears.

4. **If you see the address you seek in the list, click it to show the location on the map.**

   Otherwise, finish typing the complete search terms or address and press Return.

   A pin on the map indicates the address you selected. If your search returned multiple locations, Maps displays a pin for each one (where the name of the location is written on a flag attached to the pin), as shown in Figure 6-5. In this case, I did a search for *ice cream* in SoHo, New York City.

   After you search for addresses, Maps remembers them. In subsequent searches, they show up as suggestions.

   TIP

5. **(Optional) Click the pushpin on the map to see information about the location.**

   An information window opens (see Figure 6-6) that shows some basic information about the location, the contents of which depends on the type of location. For a business, for example, you get useful details such as the phone number and address, the web address, and the business hours.

   If listed, click the web page address to find out more about the location you found, such as the menu of a restaurant or special exhibits at a museum.

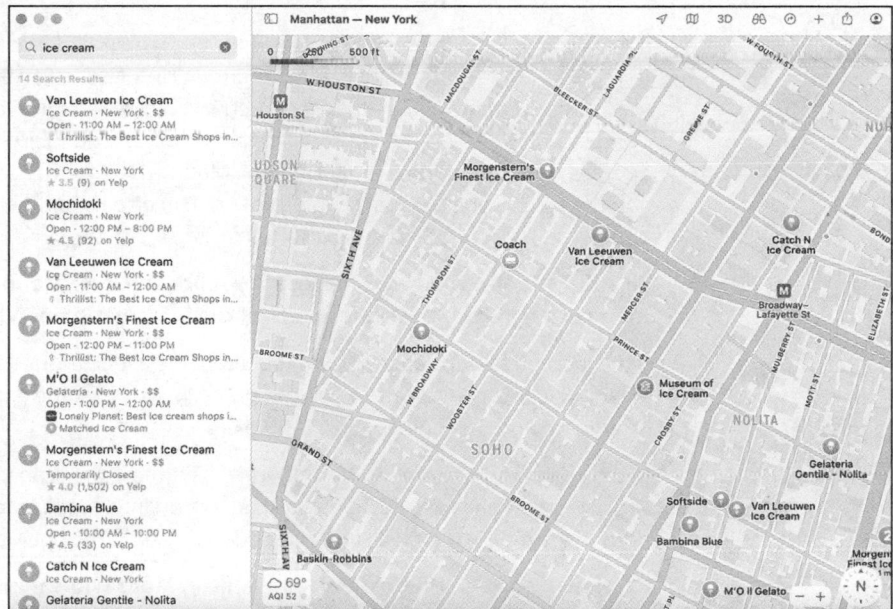

FIGURE 6-5:
Run a search and Maps shows you all the matching locations in the displayed map area.

More

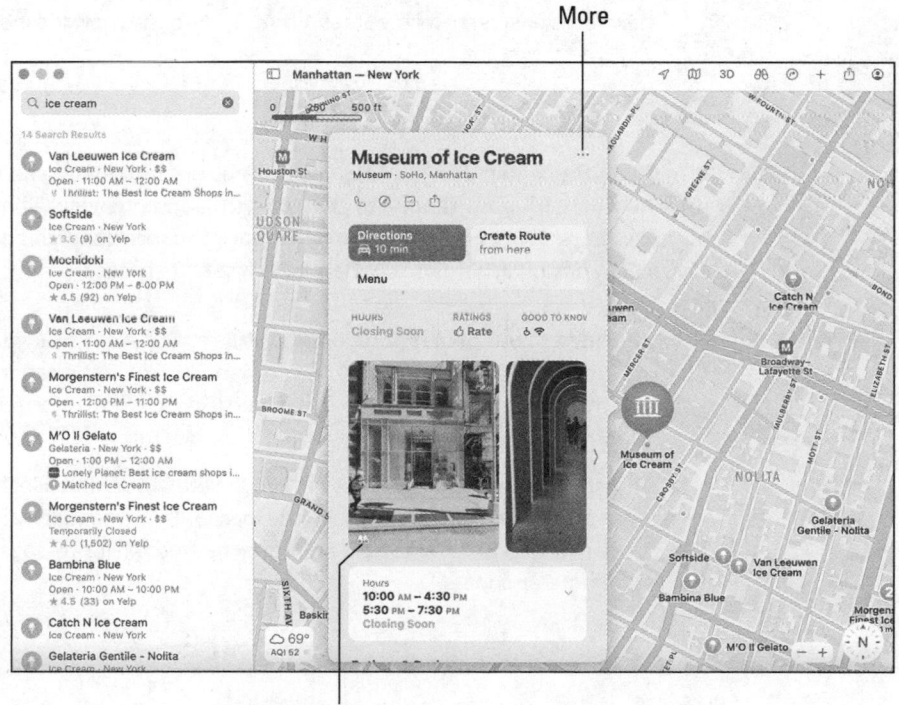

FIGURE 6-6:
The Info window offers up a few details about the location.

Look Around icon

TIP

If you want to keep the location in Maps for future use, click the more icon (three dots in the upper-right corner) and then click Add to Favorites to add the location as a favorite. In the More menu, you can also click Share Add to Contacts, which opens the Contacts app and creates a new card with the address and other pertinent information. Modify the information as needed and then click Done to save the information. You also have other sharing options, as I show you in the next section.

6. **To see a street-eye view of the location, click the look around icon (binoculars) in the lower-left corner of the information window.**

   If the location's information window doesn't have a look around icon, choose View ⇨ Show Look Around (or you can press ⌘+K or click the enter look around icon on the toolbar).

   In the Look Around window, drag let or right to rotate the scene; you can also click the street ahead to move forward or click an intersecting street to turn onto that street. To exit look around mode, click X in the upper-left corner.

7. **(Optional) To keep this location available in Maps while you search for another, create a new tab by choosing File ⇨ New Tab.**

   Alternatively, press ⌘+T or choose New ⇨ New Tab on the toolbar. Once your new tab is onscreen, follow Steps 1 through 6 for the new location.

Sharing what you find

When you find a location in Maps, you might want to share the map and location information with your iPhone or iPad or with someone else. That's not a problem because Maps gives you lots of ways to share the locations you discover. How you share depends on where or to whom you want to share:

» **Sharing to your own iPhone or iPad:** This option is useful if you find a location on your desktop Mac and you want to take that location with you as you travel with your iPhone or iPad. Open the location's information window, click More ⇨ Send to Device, and then click the iPhone or iPad you want to use.

» **Sharing to someone else:** This option is useful if you find a location that you want someone else to have. Open the location's information window, click More ⇨ Share, and then select a sharing method: Mail, Messages, AirDrop, Notes, or Reminders.

Dropping a pin

If there's no pin on the location you want to save or share, right-click the location you want to pin and choose Drop Pin from the context menu. A red pin shows up on the map with a flag that reads Dropped Pin. If the pin isn't exactly where you want it, click and drag it to the correct location. Maps also displays the location's information screen with the standard options.

To remove the pin, choose More ⇨ Remove (or right-click the dropped pin and choose Remove Pin from the context menu). You can add a bookmark for the pin and use it as a starting or ending point when asking for directions, which I explain next.

Can I get there from here? Asking for directions

Maps finds directions from your current location to where you're going or between two addresses that you provide or find. Follow these steps to ask Maps for directions:

1. **In Maps, use one of the following techniques to display the Directions interface:**

   - *Click the show directions icon on the toolbar.* You see the Directions pane with all the fields blank.

   - *Search for a location (or drop a pin), display the location's information window, and then click Directions.* You see the Directions pane with the location in the To field and My Location (that is, your current location) in the From field.

2. **To specify a starting point, delete any existing location in the From field (click the X on the right end of the field), and then type a name or address for the new starting point.**

   To use your current location as the starting point, type **My** and then click My Location in the search results.

   As you type, suggestions appear; click one or type the complete address.

3. **To specify a destination, delete any existing location in the To field (click the X on the right end of the field), and then type a name or address for the new destination.**

   As you type, potential matches appear; click one or type the complete address. To swap the To and From points of the directions, drag the fields up or down.

4. **Use the icons at the top of the Directions pane to specify the mode of transportation you'll be using: driving, walking, transit, or cycling.**

   Maps displays one or more routes under the Options label in the Directions pane, and you see each route on the map, as shown in Figure 6-7. The distance and estimated travel time are displayed for each route. If more than one route is available, Maps displays alternate routes in light blue and the travel time for each. Click the route you want to follow to make it the main route.

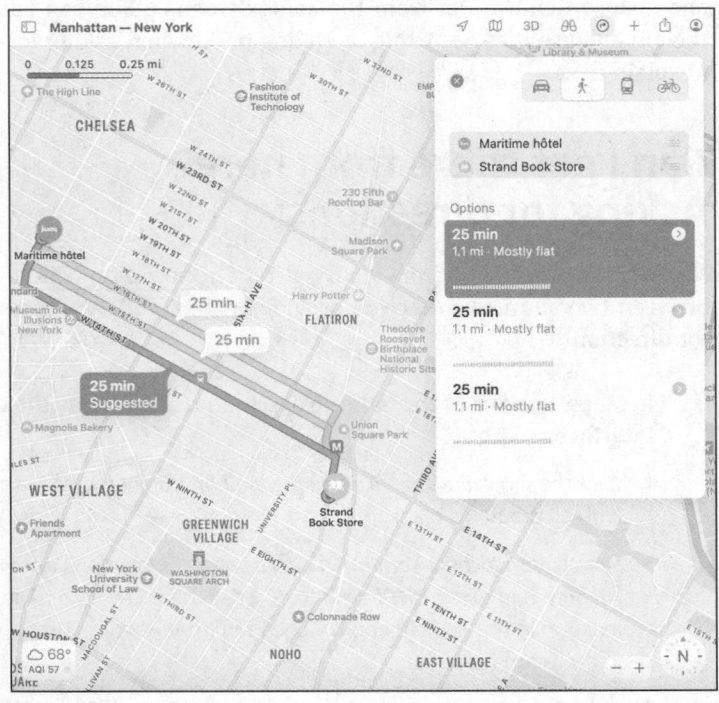

FIGURE 6-7:
Fill in the starting point and destination you want on the Directions pane to see potential routes.

5. **(Optional) If you need to make a stop along the way, click Add Stop and type the name or address of the stop location.**

6. **(Optional) If you want to leave at a particular time instead of right away (which might affect the estimated travel time), click Plan, click either Leave or Arrive, and then enter a date and time.**

7. **Click the disclosure arrow to the right of the route you want to take.**

   Maps displays a list of point-to-point directions.

8. **(Optional) Share the directions as I explain earlier.**

3
Beyond the Basics

Contents at a Glance

Chapter **1**

Backing Up and Restoring Your Data

Technical writing rule #57: Before discussing backups, write a long jeremiad — using your most scolding, schoolmarmish voice — that back-handedly accuses the reader of being too lazy to perform backups, that runs through a litany of potential devilments that can befall data, and that includes at least one it-happened-to-me-so-it-can-happen-to-you story of data-loss misery and woe.

Dear reader, you'll be happy to hear that I'm going to break this old rule. Why? Because if you're reading this chapter, it means you already know your data is at risk, you've already heard the nightmare stories of precious, irreplaceable files lost, and you already *want* to protect your data. Therefore, you don't need a lecture from me. Instead, you just want to know how you can protect your Mac data from harm and how to recover your data should your Mac's hard drive go kaput. I hear you and you've come to the right place.

In this chapter, I start by explaining some of the different backup options. Then I show you how to set up Time Machine to perform regular automatic back-ups. I also talk about recovering an individual file and restoring your Mac with the Time Machine backup in the unfortunate event that you lose all your files (perhaps when your disk dies). I include a brief explanation of AutoSave and

Versions, which you find in Apple apps such as Pages and Keynote, as well as in many third-party apps. And if you purchase a new Mac, you'll want to make a backup of your old Mac and then move all your stuff to the new one — I show you how to do that, too.

Using iCloud to Store Your Data

One way to keep your data safe is to use iCloud to store it. When your data is in iCloud, Apple handles backups of iCloud data automatically. Although this option means you don't have to worry about backups yourself, there are many reasons for not relying solely on iCloud, so I discuss some other backup methods in this chapter.

One of the great features of iCloud is that, after it's set up, it just works — with one very big exception: iCloud relies on a network connection, so it works only if you're connected to the internet.

iCloud offers 5GB of storage space for free, plus space for up to 1,000 photos and any purchased media, apps, and books. (To learn how to get more storage by paying for a monthly subscription, see Book 1, Chapter 3.) iCloud automatically synchronizes the contents of the Contacts, Calendar, Reminders, and Notes apps, as well as Safari bookmarks. This process happens automatically when you turn on iCloud.

You can sync documents created with an iCloud-enabled app, such as Pages or Numbers, and stored on iCloud between multiple Macs or between your Mac and your iPhone, iPad, iPod touch, or Windows PC (which requires iCloud for Windows, a free download from the Microsoft Store.) Even if you don't sync with another device, you can turn on iCloud and store your data remotely.

To turn on iCloud data, follow these steps:

1. **Choose ⇨ System Settings.**

   The System Settings dialog appears.

2. **Click your Apple ID.**

3. **Sign in to your Apple ID, if you aren't signed in already.**

   Your account information appears.

4. **Click iCloud.**

5. **Click iCloud Drive.**

6. **Click Turn On.**

7. **Click the Options button.**

   System Settings displays the dialog shown in Figure 1-1. The Documents tab lists all the apps and locations that can store data on iCloud.

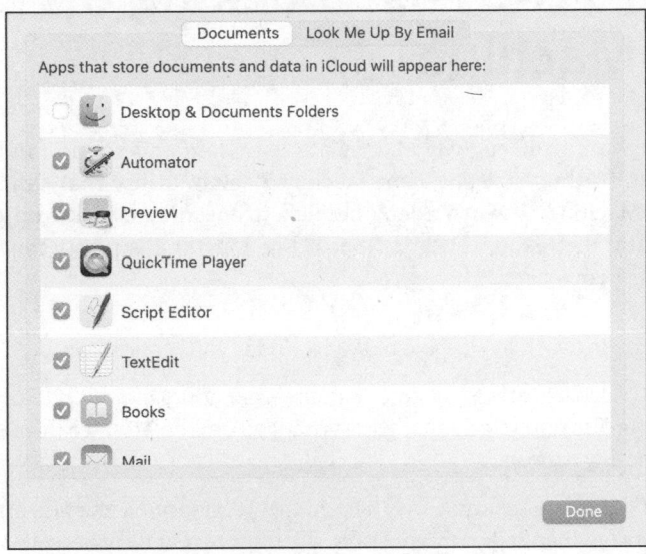

FIGURE 1-1:
You can choose which locations and apps can store data on iCloud Drive.

8. **Select the check box beside each app and location for which you want to store data on iCloud; deselect the check box beside any item for which you don't want to store data in the cloud.**

TIP

You can explore the various options, but start with the defaults before you make too many changes. Many people select most of the options shown in Figure 1-1 so that all the documents for those apps (Automator, Preview, QuickTime Player, and so forth) are backed up and shared to all your devices with the same Apple ID.

The first option, Desktop & Documents folder, is a little tricky. When you turn that option on, the Desktop and Documents folders on your Mac are backed up to your iCloud Drive continually. Each is named with the name of your Mac. Be careful about "cleaning up" apparently duplicate files because they may be copies created on a device other than the one you're running on now. Also, be careful about turning Desktop & Documents Folders on and off because you may accidentally create duplicate copies of the files. In general, turn that option on (or don't) and leave it.

REMEMBER

iCloud Drive doesn't back up apps not purchased in the App Store or Word documents or that 1,001st photo, so you should consider iCloud as a syncing tool for your Mac and a backup tool only for iOS devices.

Blasting into the Past: Backing Up with Time Machine

If you want to keep your Mac's data both safe and sound (and I know you do), look no further than the Time Machine backup utility that ships with every Mac. Time Machine is worth a look because it doesn't just back up your current data once and then stop working. Nope, Time Machine is pretty much always at work to guard your data:

>> The initial Time Machine backup includes your entire Mac.

>> Time Machine runs another backup every hour, and this backup includes just the files and folders that you've changed or created since the most recent hourly backup.

>> Time Machine runs a daily backup that includes only the files and folders you've changed or created since the most recent daily backup.

>> Time Machine runs a weekly backup that includes only the files and folders you've changed or created since the most recent weekly backup.

All these tasks are automated, so Time Machine is a set-it-and-forget-it deal, which is exactly what you want in a backup application. However, Time Machine doesn't stop there. It also keeps old backups:

>> It keeps the last 24 hourly backups.

>> It keeps the last month's worth of daily backups.

>> It keeps all the weekly backups until the backup location gets full, at which point it begins deleting the oldest backups to make room for more.

Keeping these old backups is what gives Time Machine its name. That is, it enables you to go back in time and restore not just a file but also a specific version of a file. For example, say on Monday you created a document and added some text, and then spent Tuesday editing that text. If on Friday you realize that during Tuesday's edits you deleted some of the original text that you'd now give your eyeteeth to get back, there's no problem: Time Machine enables you to restore the version from Monday.

Setting up Time Machine

To use Time Machine, you need to connect an external hard drive to your Mac with a USB or Thunderbolt cable.

TIP

The external hard drive you use to back up your Mac with Time Machine should have oodles of storage space and, ideally, you should use that drive *only* for Time Machine backups. The bigger the hard drive, the further back in time you can go to recover old files and information.

REMEMBER

If you're using a MacBook and you connect an external drive that doesn't have its own power supply, plug your Mac into a power supply. The drive will function when your Mac runs on its battery, but not as long as it will when your computer is plugged into a power source.

To set up Time Machine to back up the data on your Mac's primary hard drive to an external hard drive, follow these steps:

1. **Connect the external hard drive to your Mac.**

   If your Mac asks whether you want to allow the accessory to connect, click Allow.

   You see a notification asking if you want to use the connected drive to back up your Mac using Time Machine.

2. **Move your mouse pointer over the notification, click the Options button that appears, and then click Set Up, as shown in Figure 1-2.**

   Your Mac opens System Settings and displays the Time Machine settings.

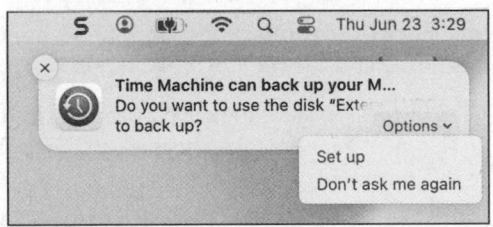

FIGURE 1-2: You see this notification after you connect the external hard drive.

3. **Click Add Backup Disk.**

   System Settings displays a list of available disks.

4. **Click the external drive you just added, and then click Set Up Disk, as shown in Figure 1-3.**

   System Settings displays the options for using the external drive for backups, as shown in Figure 1-4.

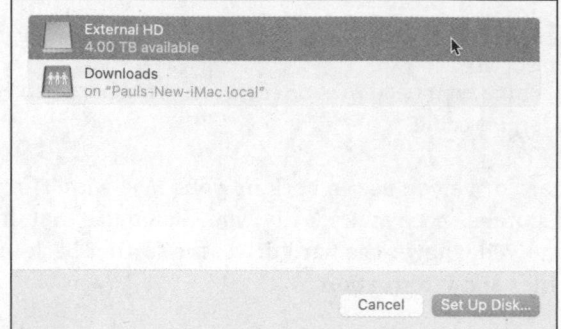

FIGURE 1-3:
Select the drive
you want to use
to store your
Time Machine
backups.

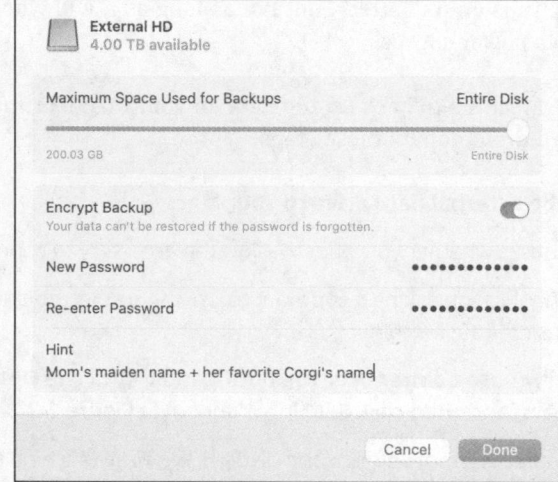

FIGURE 1-4:
Use this dialog
to configure your
Time Machine
hard drive.

5. **Use the Maximum Space Used for Backups slider to set how much hard drive space you want to set aside for storing backups.**

Your best move here, by far, is to leave the slider all the way to right at the Entire Disk setting. This gives Time Machine the most storage space, which means it can store the maximum number of backups.

6. **If you want to encrypt the backup hard drive, leave the Encrypt Backup switch set on and then type a password in the New Password and Re-enter Password text boxes. You can also type a password reminder (nothing too obvious, of course!) in the Hint text box.**

Why encrypt your Time Machine hard drive? Because although it might not be easy to steal your Mac, it's almost certainly trivial to steal your Time Machine external hard drive. Without encryption, the thief can access your backups and, hence, your data. You can avoid that fate by encrypting the hard drive, which means only someone who knows the password can view the backups.

WARNING

If you forget your password, you can't restore your Mac from your backup drive, so choose wisely. Better yet, copy the password and store it in a safe place.

7. **Click Done.**

Time Machine gets the hard disk ready for action, and then dives right into the initial backup.

8. **(Optional) Click Options and then use the dialog that appears (see Figure 1-5 in the next section) to modify the following settings (click Done when you're finished):**

- *Back Up Frequency:* Use this pop-up list to select how often you want Time Machine to run backups. Once Every Hour is the default and works best for most people. If you don't use your Mac much, you might prefer to try a less frequent backup schedule, such as Once Every Day or Once Every Week. You could also go the Manually route if you're sure you won't forget!

- *Back Up on Battery Power:* Click this switch on to have Time Machine run backups when your MacBook is using its battery. Creating backups uses a lot of juice, so most folks leave this switch off.

- *Exclude These Items from Backups:* This list contains the locations that Time Machine skips during each backup. See the next section to learn more about this feature.

9. **Click the close icon to close the Time Machine settings.**

WARNING

Don't interrupt Time Machine during the first backup — for example, by shutting down your Mac or yanking out the cable for the Time Machine hard drive. You can continue working while Time Machine runs in the background.

Skipping files you don't want to back up

Unless you specify otherwise, Time Machine backs up everything on your Mac to which your account has access except temporary files, such as your web browser's cache. Time Machine also sensibly excludes your Downloads folder and the hard drive that Time Machine is using.

To save space, you can identify other files and folders you're not concerned about losing that you want Time Machine to ignore. For example, you may not want to back up your Applications folder if you purchased your apps through the App Store, which lets you download them again if necessary. Or you may choose to skip backing up media you purchased and downloaded from iTunes because if you lose them you can download them again, so there's no need to waste that precious space on your Mac's backup drive.

To tell Time Machine which files or folders to skip, follow these steps:

1. **Choose ⌘ ⇨ System Settings or click the System Settings icon on the dock.**

2. **Click General and then click Time Machine icon to open the Time Machine settings.**

3. **Click Options to open the Time Machine options dialog.**

4. **Under the Exclude These Items from Backups list, click the plus sign (+).**

   A file and folder chooser dialog appears.

5. **Locate and then select the file or folder you want Time Machine to ignore.**

TIP

You can select multiple items by holding down the ⌘ key and then clicking what you want Time Machine to ignore.

6. **Click Exclude.**

   You return to the Time Machine options and your selected item now appears in the Exclude These Items from Backups list. For example, in Figure 1-5, I added the Applications folder to the exclusion list.

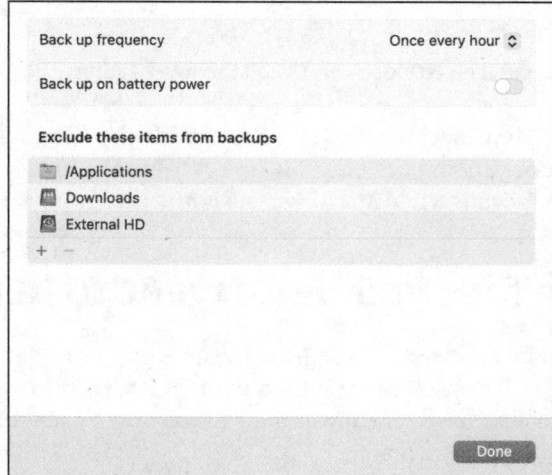

FIGURE 1-5:
Click + to choose items you don't want Time Machine to back up.

7. **To remove an exclusion, click it in the Exclude These Items from Backups list and then click the minus sign (−).**

8. **Repeat Steps 4 through 7 as needed to set up all the items you want excluded from your backups.**

HOW TIME MACHINE DOES ITS BACKUP THING

After its initial backup of your Mac's hard drive, Time Machine automatically performs an incremental backup of any data changed on your Mac's hard drive (providing the backup drive is attached) every hour. Time Machine saves hourly backups for the past 24 hours, daily backups for the past month, and weekly backups for everything older than a month. Time Machine skips backing up files you create and then delete before the next hourly backup.

When your external backup hard drive starts running out of free space for more backups, Time Machine deletes the oldest files it finds to make room for the newer ones.

If you use a portable Mac, when the external drive isn't connected, Time Machine saves a snapshot on your Mac's internal drive; the next time you connect the external drive, the backup resumes.

9. **Click Done.**

You're returned to the Time Machine settings.

10. **Click the close icon to close the Time Machine settings.**

Recovering files and folders

If you delete a file by accident, you can always open the trash to drag it back out. However, recovering a file just isn't possible in plenty of situations:

>> You delete the file and then empty the trash.

>> You overwrite the file with another file of the same name.

>> Your Mac's hard drive develops a problem that corrupts the file.

>> You make and save substantial edits to the file.

The good news is that if you've had Time Machine on the job for a while, you can probably go back in time, locate a version of the file, and then restore it to its original location. Time Machine even lets you keep the existing file if you still need the newer version. Note that I'm talking here about files, but you can also recover folders and even your entire hard drive.

To see how this works, first know that Time Machine consists of two components:

» **The Time Machine settings:** Keep track of in-progress backups (as shown in Figure 1-6) and tweak Time Machine settings. Choose ⇨ System Settings ⇨ General ⇨ Time Machine.

» **The Time Machine app:** Recover files you deleted or changed from earlier backups. You run the Time Machine app from your Applications folder.

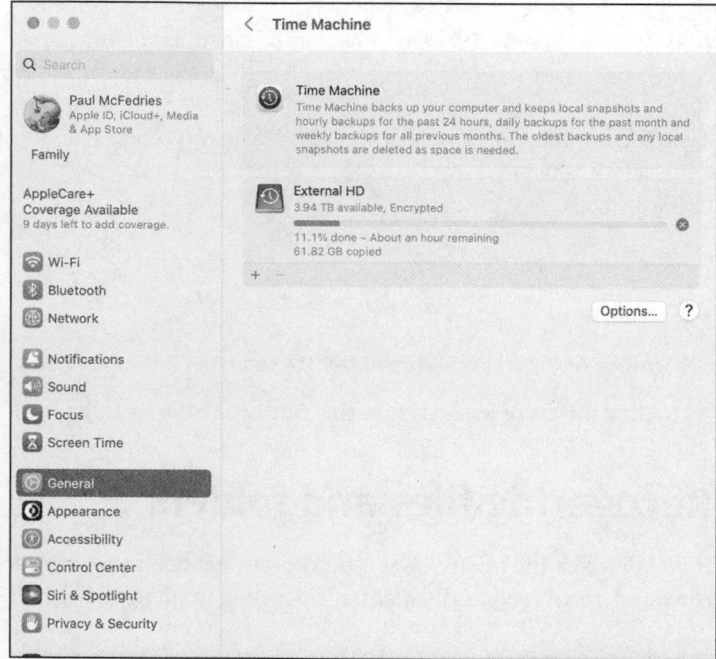

FIGURE 1-6:
The Time Machine settings with a backup in progress.

After you configure Time Machine to back up your Mac, you can use the Time Machine app to retrieve old files or information you deleted or changed after Time Machine backed them up. Here are the two ways to use the Time Machine recovery application to recover files, folders, or other pieces of information, such as address cards, email messages, or events from Calendar:

» By running an application and then opening the Time Machine app

» By opening a new Finder window, navigating to the folder that contains (or used to contain) the file or folder you want to restore, and then running the Time Machine app

The following steps show you how to use both methods:

1. **Open the app for the type of data you want to recover:**

   - *To recover data from an app:* Launch the application.

   - *To recover files or folders or both:* In any Finder window, open the location that contains (or used to contain) the files or folders or both that you want to recover.

2. **Click the magnifying glass (search) in your Mac's menu bar, type Time Machine, and then click Time Machine in the search results.**

   Your Mac opens the Time Machine app, shown in Figure 1-7, using a Finder window.

   The middle of the Time Machine app window consists of a stack of windows for the app you opened. Each window in the stack represents a previous version of the app data that was captured by a Time Machine backup. The idea is that you go back in time to the window version that contains the data you want to recover.

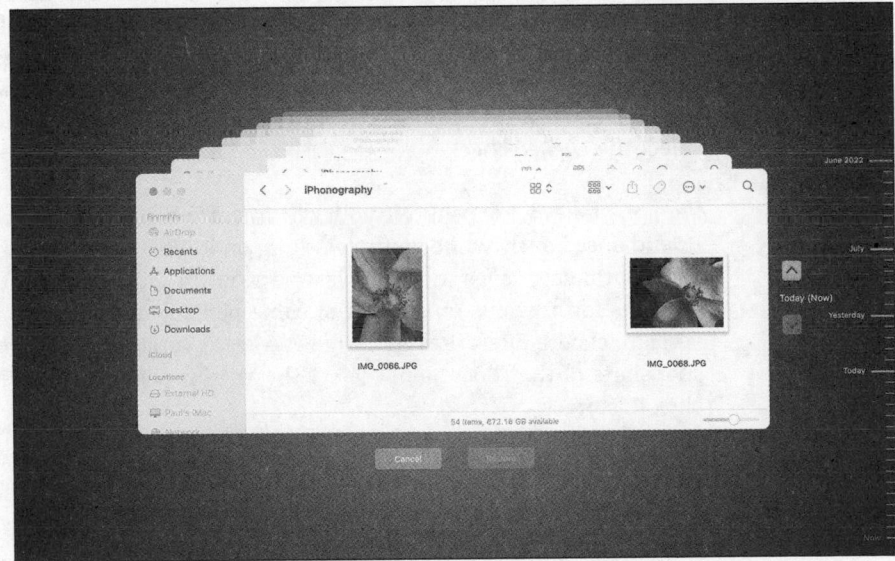

FIGURE 1-7:
You can use the
Time Machine
app to restore
data from an app
or a Finder folder,
as shown here.

3. **Choose one of the following ways to locate the data from the past that you want to recover:**

   - *Click the up arrow (backward) or down arrow (forward) to the right of the stack of app windows.* Click the up arrow to move the app window backward in time to previous Time Machine backups. Click the down arrow to work your way forward to more recent Time Machine backups.

- *Click an app window behind the frontmost window.* Time Machine goes back in time to that window and moves the window to the front of the stack.

- *Click a date (and, for recent backups, a time) in the timeline along the right edge of the screen.* Time Machine goes back in time to that backup date (and time) and moves the corresponding app window to the front of the stack.

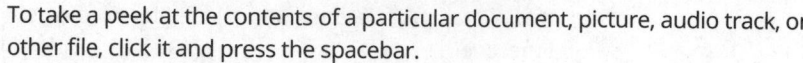

To take a peek at the contents of a particular document, picture, audio track, or other file, click it and press the spacebar.

4. **When you locate the data you want to recover, select it.**

5. **Click the Restore button.**

The Time Machine app closes, returns you to the original app window, and restores the data.

Understanding Versions

Some apps — such as Pages, Numbers, Keynote, TextEdit, and Preview — have AutoSave and Versions functions, which automatically save your files while you work. AutoSave saves your document whenever you make changes. If you make a series of changes that you don't want to lose, you can choose to lock the document at that point. You have to unlock it to make future changes or use it as a template for a new document. To lock a document, hover the pointer near the file name at the top center of the window, click the disclosure triangle that appears, and then select the Locked check box.

Versions takes a snapshot of your document when it's new, each time you open it, and once hourly while you're working on it. Versions keeps those hourly snapshots for a day, saves the day's last version for a month, and then saves weekly versions for previous months. If at some point you want to go back to an earlier version, choose File ⇨ Revert To ⇨ Browse All Versions, and Time Machine shows snapshots of that document. Select the version you want to revert to, and then click Restore.

Restoring your entire backup

If your system or startup disk is damaged, you may have to restore your entire backup to your Mac. If you use Time Machine, you're worry-free. Here's how to restore your Mac with Time Machine:

1. If your Mac is running, choose ⟳ Shut Down and then click Shut Down when macOS asks you to confirm.

2. Press and hold down the power button until you see the text *Loading Startup Options*.

If you have an Intel-based Mac, press the power button to turn on your Mac, immediately press and hold down ⌘+R until you see the macOS Utilities dialog, and then skip to Step 4.

After a few seconds, you see an icon for each of your Mac's startup disks (this will usually be just Macintosh HD) and an Options button.

3. Click Options and then click Continue.

Your Mac boots into the Recovery app.

4. Select Restore from Time Machine and then click Continue.

The Restore from Time Machine dialog appears with instructions and important information.

5. Click Continue.

The Select a Restore Source dialog appears, showing you drives connected to your machine.

6. Click the drive where your backup is stored.

For an external drive, you need to unlock it before you can continue. Click Unlock, type your Mac administrator password, and then click Unlock. Your Mac unlocks the drive.

7. Click Continue.

Your Mac displays a list of Time Machine backups.

8. Select the date and time of the backup you want to use and then click Continue.

The Select a Destination dialog appears. In most cases your system drive is the only drive shown.

9. Click the drive and then click Continue.

Time Machine begins copying your backup from the drive to your Mac.

10. Breathe a sigh of relief that you back up regularly!

Moving Your Backup from an Old Mac to a New Mac

Sooner or later, your Mac will be outdated, and you'll want to move your files to a new Mac. Apple has a handy Migration Assistant application to perform this task. You can transfer your files directly by connecting one Mac to the other with a Thunderbolt cable or over a network. If the old Mac is kaput, however, you can use your Time Machine backup. Follow these steps:

1. **On the new Mac, connect the external drive that contains the Time Machine backups.**

2. **Choose ➪ System Settings or click the System Settings icon on the dock.**

3. **Click General.**

4. **Click Transfer or Reset.**

5. **Click Open Migration Assistant.**

   The Migration Assistant introduction dialog opens.

6. **Click Continue, enter your Mac admin password, and press Return.**

   Migration Assistant automatically quits any open apps, the desktop closes, and a Migration Assistant window opens.

7. **Select the From a Mac, Time Machine Backup, or Startup Disk option and then click Continue.**

   Migration Assistant searches for sources to use.

8. **Select the drive from which you want to transfer your backup and then click Continue.**

9. **Choose the backup you want to use, and then click Continue.**

10. **Select the check box beside each type of information you want to transfer.**

    You can transfer applications, user accounts and data, other files and folders, system settings, printers, and network settings.

11. **Click Continue.**

    Migration Assistant begins transferring the selected data.

12. **When the transfer is complete, click Restart Now, and then click Done when the Migration Completed window appears.**

IN THIS CHAPTER

» Safeguarding your Mac with a password

» Locking your Mac

» Using a fingerprint to log in to your Mac

» Encrypting your documents

» Configuring firewall and privacy settings

Chapter **2**

Protecting Your Mac against Local and Remote Threats

One of the sad facts of modern life is that all computers are vulnerable to attacks of various kinds. Yep, Windows PCs are the target of most malicious hacks, but Mac users shouldn't be complacent: Miscreants would love to break into your Mac and steal or trash your data or use your Mac to attack other computers. Macs, like all computers, can fall prey to two kinds of threat.

The first kind of threat is the type that gets all the publicity these days: *remote* exploits from internet-based rapscallions who try to trick you into installing malicious software (*malware*, for short) or giving away personal data such as your credit card, government ID, or website password by spoofing legit emails and websites (a practice known as *phishing*).

But a second type of threat rarely gets discussed: *local* exploits from scoundrels who gain physical access to your Mac (say, by sitting down in front of a desktop Mac or by stealing a MacBook). These hands-on hoodlums look to steal your private data or install software that gives them control over your Mac or that logs everything you type (such as passwords and banking credentials).

In this chapter, you explore these two types of threat and, more importantly, you delve into the available Mac tools that you can use to thwart all threats — be they physical or virtual, local or remote.

REMEMBER

This chapter isn't the only place in the book where I talk about security. Here are a few more places to check out:

>> To get some info related to app security, see Book 1, Chapter 5.

>> To learn how to surf the web securely and privately, check out Book 2, Chapter 2.

>> To learn how to encrypt your Time Machine backups, see Book 3, Chapter 1.

>> To set limits on a child's user account, see Book 3, Chapter 3.

Battening Down Your Mac's Hatches with a Password

Your Mac's first line of defense is your account password. Note that I'm talking here about your Mac user account, not your Apple ID. Your user account password protects your Mac because you — or some evildoer sitting down at your Mac — must enter the correct password before gaining access to the desktop when you start your Mac and when your Mac has been in sleep mode.

As a rule, your account password should be difficult for someone to guess but easy for you to remember. Unfortunately, in practice, people often use simple — as in, lousy — passwords. To make your password difficult to guess but easy to remember, you should create a password that combines upper- and lowercase letters with numbers or symbols or both, such as OCHSa*co2010alum! (which abbreviates a phrase, in this case, *Ocean City High School all-star class of 2010 Alumnus!*). When you create your user accounts, take advantage of Password Assistant to have your Mac create a password for you. Of course, it may be harder to remember but also harder to guess. When in doubt, record your password and store it in a safe place. For example, you could store all your passwords in a document, and then transfer that file to a USB drive that you keep in a secure location.

TIP

One way to create strong passwords is to combine the first letters of the words in a phrase that you'll never forget with the name of a dearly departed pet, and then for extra security tweak the characters a bit; for example, use a zero in place of the letter o or the number 1 or an exclamation point (!) in place of the letter i. By picking a memorable phrase or lyric, such as "I'm walkin' on sunshine" (reduced to Iw0s, where the third character is a zero instead of the letter o), paired with the name of your long-gone pet hermit crab, Louise (used as Lou!se, where the fourth character is an exclamation point instead of the letter i), you end up with a password (Iw0sLou!se) that you'll remember easily but is very hard for some lowlife to guess.

Changing your password

If you think your Mac user account password might be too simple or too easy to guess, you should upgrade your password to something stronger right away. You might also consider changing your Mac user account password regularly — say, every few months.

To change your Mac user account password, follow these steps:

1. **Choose ⇨ System Settings or click System Settings on the dock.**

The System Settings window appears.

2. **Click the Users & Groups icon to open the Users & Groups settings, shown in Figure 2-1.**

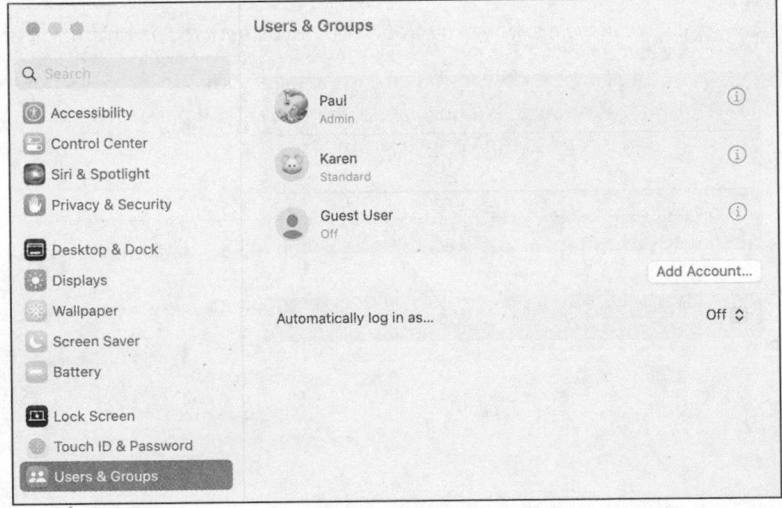

FIGURE 2-1:
Users & Groups settings let you change your user account details.

3. **Click the _i_-in-a-circle (info) to the right of your username.**

   System Settings opens a dialog for configuring your user account.

4. **Click the Change Password button.**

   A dialog appears, displaying text boxes for typing your old password and for typing a new password twice to verify that you typed your new password correctly.

5. **In the Old Password text box, enter your current password.**

6. **In the New Password text box, enter your new password.**

   If you want your Mac to evaluate your password or invent a password for you, click the key icon to the right of the New Password text box. Password Assistant opens, as shown in Figure 2-2. Then do the following:

   a. _In the Type pop-up menu, choose the type of password you want._ Manual lets you type a password that you invent, and Password Assistant rates the security level of your password. The other four types offer various character combinations and security levels: Letters & Numbers; Numbers Only; Random; or FIPS–181-compliant, which creates a password that meets U.S. federal standards.

   b. _Drag the Length slider to set how many characters you want your password to have._ The password appears in the Suggestion field.

   c. _Check the password strength by examining the Quality bar._ Red means your password is not secure, orange indicates so-so security, yellow means your password is fairly secure; and green indicates a strong password that's safe to use. Also, the longer the color bar, the stronger the password.

   d. _Repeat substeps a through c until you have the password you want._

   e. _Click the close icon._ The chosen password is inserted as bullets in the New Password text box. If you didn't select the password manually, it's also added to the Verify text box.

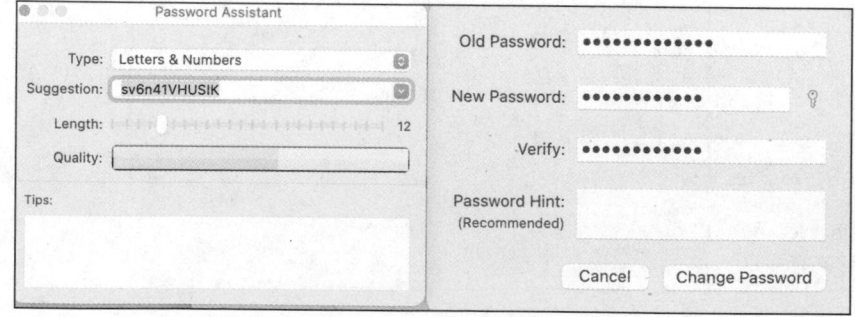

FIGURE 2-2:
Let Password Assistant help you choose a password.

7. **In the Verify text box, enter your new password (if Password Assistant didn't do that for you already).**

8. **Use the Password Hint text box to type a word, phrase, or special code that will help you remember your password just in case you forget it later.**

WARNING

Adding a hint can help you remember your password, but it can also give an intruder a clue about what your password might be, so don't make your hint too on-the-nose. Using my Iw0sLou!se example, you might use the hint "favorite song crab." The intruder would have to know you pretty darn well to figure out that one!

TIP

macOS should be configured to show password hints. After you complete these steps, click Lock Screen and then make sure the Show Password Hints switch is set on.

What happens if you forget your password? At the login screen, click the question mark (?) to the right of the Enter Password field. macOS displays your password hint, which (fingers crossed!) will be enough to jog your memory.

REMEMBER

9. **Click Change Password.**

The password dialog disappears and returns you to the user account options dialog.

10. **Click Done.**

11. **Click the close icon or choose System Settings ⇨ Quit System Settings.**

Safety first: Locking your Mac

Applying a strong password to your Mac user account (as I describe in the preceding section) is Job One when it comes to Mac security. However, your password isn't much good if some malefactor is able to sit down at your Mac keyboard while you're logged in. Sure, your Mac sensibly requires your password to change certain crucial system settings, but there's still a ton of mischief an unauthorized user can get up to.

To prevent this, you should lock your Mac every time you're about the leave it unattended. Here are three ways you can lock your Mac:

» **Display the lock screen:** Choose ⇨ Lock Screen or press Control+⌘+Q.

» **Put your Mac to sleep:** Choose ⇨ Sleep.

» **Log out of your account:** Choose ⇨ Log Out *Name* (where *Name* is your Mac account username) or press Shift+⌘+Q.

WARNING

Full disclosure: Putting your Mac to sleep does *not* actually lock your Mac, at least not right away. By default, your Mac has to be asleep for at least five minutes before it locks. Yikes! Fortunately, in the steps coming up in just a second, I show you how to reduce (or even eliminate) that time interval.

Locking your Mac manually is great — *if* you remember to do it! If you find that you sometimes forget, I understand. It happens to all of us. Fortunately, you can configure your Mac to display the screen saver and turn off the display after a period of inactivity *and* you can set things up so that you need to enter your Mac account password after the screen saver begins or the display is turned off. Here are the steps to follow:

1. **Choose ⌘ ⇨ System Settings or click System Settings on the dock.**

   The System Settings window appears.

2. **Click Lock Screen.**

   The Lock Screen settings appear, as shown in Figure 2-3.

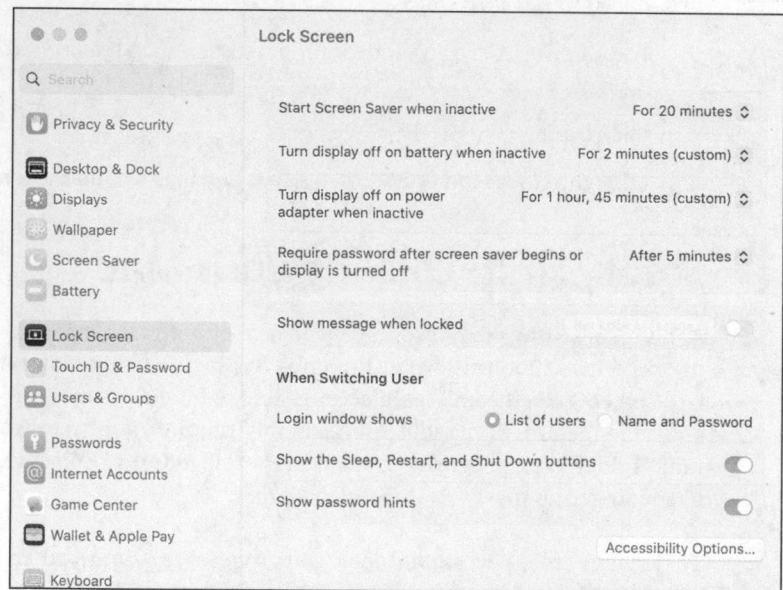

FIGURE 2-3:
Use the Lock Screen settings to automatically lock your Mac.

3. **Use the Start Screen Saver When Inactive pop-up menu to choose the amount of idle time after which your Mac cranks up its screen saver.**

   For this setting (and the next two), you need to make a tradeoff between convenience and security. On the one hand, if you choose the shortest intervals, you might find yourself constantly waking up your Mac (and entering your password, depending on the interval you choose in Step 6); on the other hand, if you choose the longest intervals, your unattended Mac might remain unlocked for too long if you forget to lock it manually. Good luck!

4. **If you have a MacBook, use the Turn Display Off on Battery When Inactive pop-up menu to choose the amount of idle time after which your Mac turns off its display while running on battery power.**

5. **Use the Turn Display Off on Power Adapter When Inactive pop-up menu to choose the amount of idle time after which your Mac turns off its display while running on the power adapter.**

6. **Use the Require Password after Screen Saver Begins or Display Is Turned Off pop-up menu to select an interval after which you must enter your account password to get back to the desktop.**

   The shorter the interval, the greater the security, so consider choosing Immediately, After 5 Seconds, or After 1 Minute.

   When you change this setting, macOS prompts you to enter an admin account password.

7. **Type the password and then click Modify Settings.**

8. **(Optional) Set a screen-lock message:**

   a. *Click the Show Message When Locked switch to On.*

   b. *Enter your Mac admin account password and then click Modify Settings.*

   c. *Click the Set Lock Message button.*

   d. *Type a message that will appear when your screen is locked, such as "Out to Lunch" or "Be Back at 2:30" or "Don't Even Think about Touching My Mac" or "You touch my Mac, I break your face."*

   e. *Click OK.*

9. **(Optional) Configure your Mac to log you out of your account after a specified period of inactivity:**

   a. *Click Privacy & Security.*

   b. *Click Advanced.*

   c. *Click the Log Out Automatically after Inactivity switch on.*

   d. *Enter your Mac admin account password and then click Modify Settings.*

   e. *Use the Log Out After spin box to set the number of minutes of inactivity after which your Mac logs you out of your account.*

   f. *Click Done.*

10. **Click the close icon or choose System Settings ⇨ Quit System Settings.**

Applying password protection

For further protection, you can also password-protect your Mac to disallow an unauthorized person to access to your Mac. By applying password protection to different parts of your Mac, you increase the chances that you'll be the only one to control your computer.

REMEMBER

If you're the only person who has physical access to your Mac, you won't have to worry about password protection, but if your Mac is in an area where others can access it easily, password protection is one extra step in keeping your Mac private.

All the choices here are optional, but I recommend choosing those that best meet your needs. To password-protect different parts of your Mac, follow these steps:

1. **Choose ⇨ System Settings or click System Settings on the dock.**

   The System Settings window appears.

2. **Click Users & Groups.**

3. **Use the Automatically Log In As pop-up menu and choose off.**

   With this setting off (which is the default), you always have to enter a password to log in to your Mac.

4. **Click Privacy & Security.**

5. **At the bottom of the window, click Advanced.**

6. **Click the Require an Administrator Password to Access System-Wide Settings switch on.**

   A *system-wide* setting is one that applies to every user account on your Mac.

   When this switch is on, nobody can modify your Mac's system-wide settings (such as the one you're adjusting right now!) without knowing your Mac's administrator password.

   Appropriately, your Mac asks you to enter your admin password.

7. **Type your admin password and then click Unlock.**

8. **Click Done.**

Another layer of security: Adding two-factor authentication to your Apple ID

Having a strong password protecting your Apple ID is a great start, but what if some delinquent somehow gets hold of that password? No matter how remote that possibility might seem, it pays to set up a second line of defense. For your Mac, that extra safeguard comes in the form of a feature called *two-factor authentication*. When you activate two-factor authentication on your Apple ID, you not only enter your Apple ID password but also confirm your identity using a trusted phone number or a trusted device, such as your iPhone.

Fortunately, Apple now configures two-factor authentication automatically whenever you create a new Apple ID, so you should be good to go. Just to make sure, follow these steps:

1. **Click the System Settings icon on the dock (or choose ➭ System Settings).**

   The System Settings window appears.

2. **Click your Apple ID.**

3. **Click Password & Security.**

   The Password & Security settings appear.

4. **If the Two-Factor Authentication setting is off, click Turn On and then follow the prompts.**

Securing Your Mac with the Touch of a Finger: Using Touch ID

You've got to have a strong-like-bull password protecting your Mac, but passwords suffer from two problems:

» **You have to remember them.** And with each of us having to store dozens of passwords in our tired brains, retrieving any one password is getting more and more difficult.

» **They can fall into the wrong hands.** If some ne'er-do-well learns or discovers your password, your Mac is in big trouble.

So that's why many people are turning to a form of security that can't be forgotten or fall into the hands of a nefarious user: *biometric security*. That's just a highfalutin name for using some part of your body to confirm that you really are you. In the Mac world, biometric security comes in the form of Touch ID, where you use one (or more) of your fingerprints to confirm your identity.

REMEMBER

To use Touch ID, you need either a MacBook Pro or MacBook Air with built-in Touch ID or an Apple Magic Keyboard that supports Touch ID. These devices come with a fingerprint reader. The idea is that you first use the fingerprint reader to scan a fingerprint from at least one of your fingers. Then you can use your fingerprint to unlock your Mac, use Apple Pay, confirm purchases in the App Store, iTunes Store, and Apple Books, and confirm that you want to use password AutoFill.

Setting up your Mac for Touch ID is a fairly quick one-time process:

1. **Click the System Settings icon on the dock (or choose ⇨ System Settings).**

The System Settings window appears.

2. **Click Touch ID & Password.**

The Touch ID & Password settings appear.

3. **Click Add Fingerprint.**

macOS prompts you to enter your Mac user account password.

4. **Type your password and then click Unlock.**

The Place Your Finger dialog appears.

5. **Place the finger you want to use with Touch ID on your Mac or Magic Keyboard's Touch ID key, which is the fingerprint reader.**

The Touch ID key is in the top-right corner of recent Mac keyboards.

6. **Lift and place the finger repeatedly.**

Each time you rest the finger on the Touch ID reader, place it in a slightly different position so that the Touch ID gets a chance to read the entire fingerprint.

When your entire fingerprint has been scanned, you see the Touch ID Is Ready dialog.

7. **Click Done.**

8. **(Optional) Repeat Steps 3 through 7 to scan other fingerprints, as you prefer.**

9. **Use the switches to specify which Mac features you want to use with Touch ID.**

Figure 2-4 shows the default settings. If you want to use Touch ID to confirm purchases you make in the iTunes Store, App Store, and Apple Books, click that switch on.

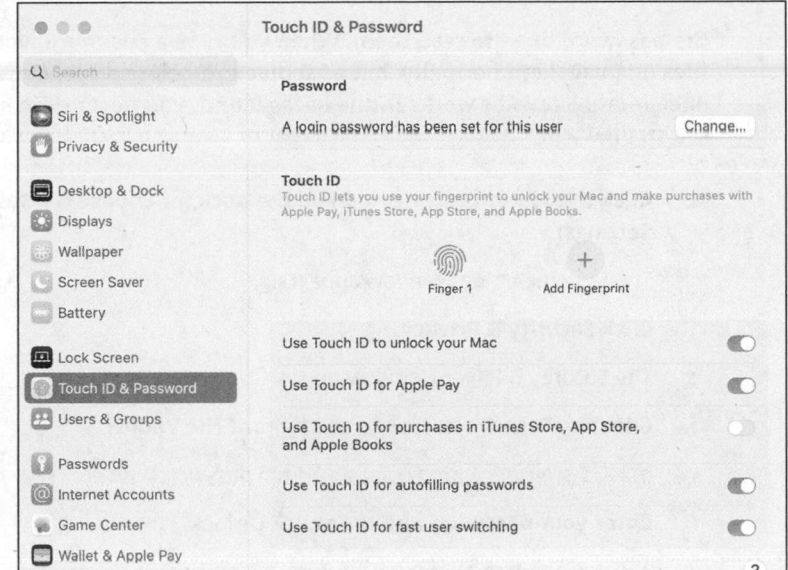

FIGURE 2-4:
Use the Touch
ID & Password
settings to set
up one or more
fingerprints and
to specify which
Mac features you
want to use with
Touch ID.

10. **Click the close icon or choose System Settings ⇨ Quit System Settings.**

11. **Choose ⇨ Log Out *User* (where *User* is your account username), click Log Out, and then use your Mac account password to log back in.**

Touch ID is now enabled.

Encrypting Data with FileVault

Encryption scrambles your files so that even if people can access your files, they can't open or edit them unless they know the correct password. When you use FileVault, your Mac encrypts your entire drive, which means everything on your Mac is secure. If you have multiple users on your Mac, you must enable them so each can sign in with their password.

FileVault uses an encryption algorithm called Advanced Encryption Standard (AES), which is the latest U.S. government standard for scrambling data that even national governments with supercomputers can't crack — at least not in a realistic time frame.

Setting up FileVault

FileVault scrambles your files so that only your password (or the system's master password) can unlock the files to enable you — or someone you trust and give the password to — to read them. When you type a password, you can access your files and use them normally, but as soon as you close a file, FileVault scrambles it once more. FileVault works in the background; you never even see it working. To set up FileVault:

1. **Click the System Settings icon on the dock (or choose ⇨ System Settings).**

   The System Settings window appears.

2. **Click Security & Privacy.**

   The Security & Privacy window opens.

3. **Click the Turn On button to the right of File Vault.**

   macOS prompts you to enter an admin password.

4. **Enter your password and then click Unlock.**

   A dialog appears, as shown in Figure 2-5, giving you options for how to unlock your disk and reset your password if you forget it.

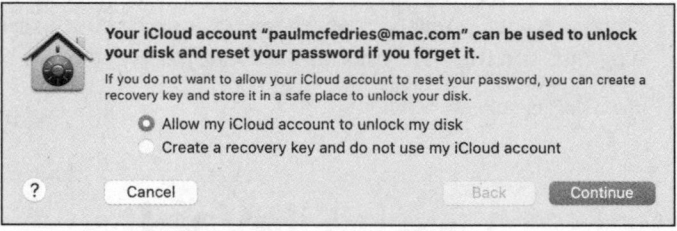

FIGURE 2-5: Choose the type of FileVault security you want to use.

Your iCloud account "paulmcfedries@mac.com" can be used to unlock your disk and reset your password if you forget it.

If you do not want to allow your iCloud account to reset your password, you can create a recovery key and store it in a safe place to unlock your disk.

○ Allow my iCloud account to unlock my disk
○ Create a recovery key and do not use my iCloud account

[?] Cancel   Back   Continue

5. **Select one of the following options:**

   - *Allow My iCloud Account to Unlock My Disk:* With this option, which is the simplest, you use your iCloud password to unlock your disk.

   - *Create a Recovery Key and Do Not Use My iCloud Account:* With this option, a security key that you use to unlock your disk is created. You're prompted to record the key and save it in a safe place.

6. **Click Continue.**

   macOS encrypts your Mac.

TIP

FileVault works also with external hard drives, so your data is safe wherever it's stored.

Turning off FileVault

If you turned on FileVault and later change your mind, you can always turn it off:

1. **Click the System Settings icon on the dock (or choose ⇨System Settings).**

The System Settings window appears.

2. **Click Security & Privacy.**

The Security & Privacy window opens.

3. **Click the Turn Off button to the right of File Vault.**

macOS prompts you to confirm.

4. **Click Turn Off Encryption.**

macOS removes the encryption from your Mac.

Blocking the Bad Guys with a Firewall

The security features I discuss earlier in this chapter — a strong password, locking your computer, setting up Touch ID, and encrypting your data with FileVault — protect your Mac against local threats, but when you connect your Mac to the internet, you essentially open a door to remote threats. A highly technical person (such as a malicious hacker) situated anywhere in the world could access your Mac, copy or modify your files, install malware, or erase all your data. To keep out intruders, you need a special program called a *firewall*.

A firewall does two things:

>> It blocks remote access to your Mac.

>> It makes exceptions for good resources such as website data (so you can still surf the web) and email messages (so you can still receive email).

Every Mac comes with a software firewall that can protect you whenever your Mac connects to the internet.

DEALING WITH NASTY MALWARE AND RATs

Two big threats exploit personal computers that aren't protected by properly configured firewall settings or properly configured router firewall settings. The first of these threats — *malware* — consists of programs that sneak onto your computer and then secretly connect to the internet to do merely annoying (and offensive) things (retrieve pornographic ads that appear all over your screen) or more serious things (infect your computer with a virus that can erase your personal data). Or they can keep track of every keystroke you type on your computer, which in turn is transmitted to a snooping program on a malevolent person's computer so the hacker can find out personal info such as credit card numbers, usernames, and passwords.

A second type of program that requires an outgoing internet connection is a remote access Trojan (RAT). Malicious hackers often trick people into downloading and installing RATs on their computers. When installed, a RAT can connect to the internet and allow the hacker to control the computer remotely over the internet, including deleting and copying files, conducting attacks through this computer, and sending junk email (spam) through this computer.

Although computer malware and RATs written and released by hackers typically target PCs running Windows, security experts agree that it's only a matter of time before the same digital nastiness begins infecting Macs. To guard against potential viruses, spyware, and RATs, your Mac displays a dialog that alerts you when you run a program for the first time. This feature can alert you if a virus, spyware, or a RAT tries to infect a Mac. For further protection, consider purchasing a router with built-in firewall features or installing an antivirus and antimalware program.

TECHNICAL STUFF

Many people use a special device called a router to connect to the internet. A *router* lets multiple computers use a single internet connection, such as a high-speed broadband cable or DSL internet connection. Routers include built-in hardware firewalls and using one with your Mac's software firewall can provide your Mac with twice the protection. To learn how to configure your router's firewall settings, refer to the router's user guide or look for more information in the support section of the router manufacturer's website. If all else fails, contact your ISP support staff.

Although the default settings for your Mac's firewall should be adequate for most people, you may want to configure your firewall to block additional internet features for added security. For example, most people will likely need to access email and web pages, but never need to transfer files by using FTP (short for File Transfer Protocol). If you fall into this category, you can safely block the FTP service.

WARNING

Don't configure your firewall unless you're sure that you know what you're doing. Otherwise, you may weaken the firewall or lock programs from accessing the internet and not know how to repair those problems.

To activate and configure your Mac's firewall, follow these steps:

1. **Click the System Settings icon on the dock (or choose ⇨ System Settings).**

The System Settings window appears.

2. **Click Network.**

The Network settings appears.

3. **Click Firewall.**

The Firewall settings appear.

4. **To turn on your Mac's firewall, click the Firewall switch on.**

5. **Click Options to display the firewall's custom settings, as shown in Figure 2-6.**

The top half of the dialog enables you to block all incoming connections and enable incoming connections from apps or services you specify, such as Dropbox. The bottom half of the dialog offers three on/off switches. Incoming connections options are discussed in the next step.

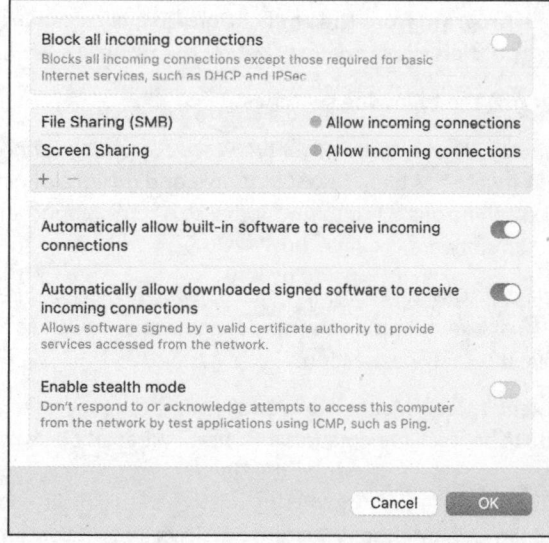

FIGURE 2-6:
Use this dialog to configure your Mac's firewall.

6. (Optional) Click the Block All Incoming Connections switch on.

If you turn on this setting, the firewall allows only essential communications for basic internet and email access; the firewall also blocks sharing services, such as Music sharing or Messages screen sharing. When you select this option, macOS disables all the other options in the dialog.

Steps 7 through 11 are optional and enable you to allow incoming connections for other software applications. If you're satisfied that no other applications will need incoming connections, skip to Step 12.

7. Click + (add) to add applications that you want to allow or block from communicating over the internet.

A chooser dialog appears.

8. Click Applications in the sidebar, and then click a program that you want to allow to be accessed via the internet, such as Dropbox or Skype.

If any other apps require incoming connections, select them. You can select multiple applications by clicking the first application and then ⌘-clicking additional applications.

9. Click Open.

Your chosen program appears in the Applications category.

10. Click the pop-up button to the right of an application in the applications list and choose Allow Incoming Connections or Block Incoming Connections.

11. To remove a program from the applications list, click the program name to select it and then click – (delete) below the program list.

12. Turn on (or off) the following switches:

- *Automatically Allow Built-In Software to Receive Incoming Connections:* The built-in software has been tested by Apple and millions of users. Problems can still creep through, but this option allows normal functioning of your Mac and its software.

- *Automatically Allow Downloaded Signed Software to Receive Incoming Connections:* Allows typical commercial applications such as Microsoft Word to receive incoming connections.

- *Enable Stealth Mode:* Makes the firewall refuse to respond to any outside attempts to contact it and gather information based on its responses.

13. Click OK to close the dialog.

14. Click the close icon or choose System Settings ➪ Quit System Settings.

Cranking Up Your Privacy Settings

Your Mac is a treasure trove of data goodies, such as contacts, calendars, media, photos, and documents. That data is useful to you, of course, but many apps out there believe your data is useful to *them*. That's sometimes true — for example, a social media app might need access to your photos — but it's also true that many apps seek access to data unnecessarily. macOS does a good job of asking your permission when an app seeks to use your data, but you can also control this access yourself.

Your Mac also comes with hardware features that some apps seek to use, such as the camera, microphone, and Bluetooth. Again, macOS gives an app access to these features only if you say so, but you can also control this access manually. For example, if you gave an app access to your camera, you might later decide that wasn't a good idea. That's not a problem because you can revoke that access at any time.

To make changes to your Mac's privacy settings, follow these steps:

1. **Click the System Settings icon on the dock (or choose ⇨ System Settings).**

   The System Settings window appears.

2. **Click Privacy & Security.**

   The Privacy & Security settings appear, as shown in Figure 2-7.

3. **In the Privacy section, click the resource — such as an app or a hardware feature — you want to modify.**

   You see a list of the apps that have requested access to the data in the selected app.

TIP

   To learn more about the privacy settings associated with Location Services, see Book 2, Chapter 6.

4. **To revoke an app's access to the data, click the app's switch to off; to allow access, click the app's switch to on.**

5. **Click < (back) to return to the Privacy & Security settings page.**

6. **Repeat Steps 3 through 5 to adjust the privacy settings for the resources you want to modify.**

7. **Click the close icon or choose System Settings ⇨ Quit System Settings.**

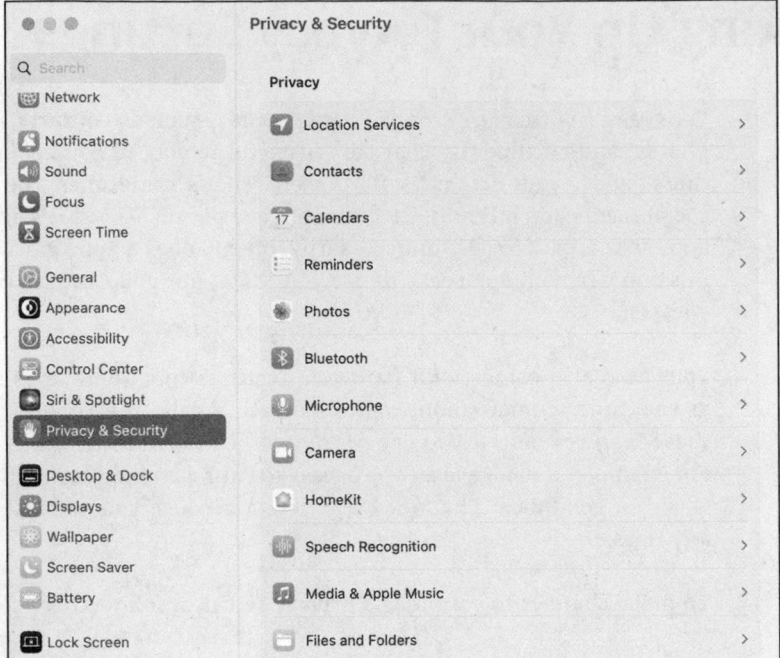

FIGURE 2-7:
Use the Privacy
settings to
choose which
apps access data
from your Mac or
other apps.

IN THIS CHAPTER

» **Adding other users to your Mac**

» **Switching from one user to another**

» **Sharing subscriptions and other data with your family**

» **Monitoring and restricting how others use your Mac**

» **Keeping kids safe with parental controls**

Chapter **3**

Sharing Your Mac

t's possible that you're the only person who ever uses your Mac. If that's the case, what are you doing reading this chapter? May I suggest Book 3, Chapter 4?

However, if you have people around who regularly use your Mac for work or for play, please read on because you'll want to learn how to share you Mac safely and conveniently.

Even if you don't share your Mac with other people, you might still want to share other goodies, such as an Apple Music or Apple TV+ subscription or an app, a book, a movie, or a TV show you've purchased. With Family Sharing, you can share all this and more with up to five people in your family.

In this chapter, you learn not only how to add and manage users on your Mac but also how to set up content and usage restrictions and set time limits for apps and websites. You also explore the convenience of Family Sharing and learn how to share subscriptions and media with other members of your family and how to set up and control children's accounts.

Populating Your Mac with Multiple Users

You probably have family members or colleagues who are clamoring to use your Mac, and who can blame them? Sessions that you supervise are fine, of course, but you probably don't want people messing with your Mac when you're not around because they could accidentally delete important info or modify your settings.

The solution is to let the other person access the Mac using a different user account. You have two ways to go here:

>> **Activate the built-in Guest account:** This is a good way to go if you have to give people only occasional access because it's easy to configure and they can't do any damage with the Guest account, which is a highly secure account.

>> **Create a new user account:** This is the way to go if you want to allow another person to save files, set up email and chat accounts, and configure their own settings.

TIP

If you're looking to configure your Mac for a child, you can certainly create a new user account. However, monitoring and controlling that child's Mac usage is much easier if you do it via Family Sharing. See "All in the Family: Organizing Family Sharing," later in this chapter.

Activating the Guest account

If the built-in Guest account best serves your needs, follow these steps to activate it:

1. **Click the System Settings icon on the dock (or choose ⇨ System Settings).**

The System Settings window appears.

2. **Click Users & Groups.**

The Users & Groups settings appear.

3. **In the list of user accounts on the right, click the *i*-in-a-circle (info) to the right of Guest User.**

4. **Click the Allow Guests to Log in to This Computer switch.**

System Settings prompts you for your Mac administrator password.

5. **Type your Mac admin password and then click Unlock.**

The Allow Guests to Log in to This Computer switch now appears on, as shown in Figure 3-1.

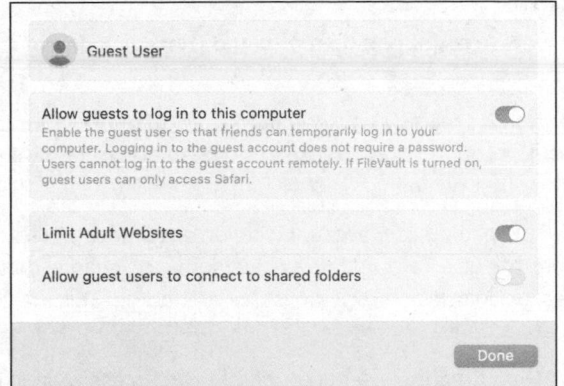

FIGURE 3-1:
Set the Allow
Guests to Log in
to This Computer
switch on to
activate the guest
account.

6. **If you don't want your guests to access certain adults-only websites, leave the Limit Adult Websites switch set on.**

7. **If you want guests to be able to access your shared folders from another computer on the network, click the Allow Guest Users to Connect to Shared Folders switch on.**

To learn about shared folders, see Book 3, Chapter 5.

8. **Click Done.**

In the lists of accounts, the status of Guest User changes from Off to Login, Sharing.

9. **Click the close icon or choose System Settings ➪ Quit System Settings.**

Creating a new user account

If a shiny, new user account is what you need, follow these steps to set it up:

1. **Click the System Settings icon on the dock (or choose ➪ System Settings).**

The System Settings window appears.

2. **Click Users & Groups.**

The Users & Groups settings appear.

3. **Below the list of user accounts, click Add Account.**

System Settings displays a dialog that enables you to specify the new user's settings.

4. **Click the New Account pop-up menu and then click one of the following account types:**

- *Administrator:* Creates a new administrative account. This is just as powerful as your account, so use this type of account only if you explicitly trust the other person.

- *Standard:* Creates a user account with lower security privileges. For example, the user can't update system software, change many system settings, or unlock system settings that are locked. This is a good choice for most accounts.

- *Sharing Only:* Creates a user account that can access your shared folders from another computer on your network but can't log in to your Mac. For this to work, you need to share one or more of your Mac's folders with this account, as I describe in Book 3, Chapter 5.

5. **In the Full Name text box, type the account's display name.**

6. **In the Account Name text box, type the account's username.**

7. **Type the account's password in the Password and Verify text boxes and a hint in the Password Hint text box.**

   If you want your Mac to evaluate your password or invent a password for you, click the key icon to the right of the New Password text box to open Password Assistant (see "Changing your password," in Chapter 2 of this minibook).

8. **Click Create User.**

   Your Mac creates the new account and adds it to the list of accounts in the Users & Groups settings.

9. **Click the close icon or choose System Settings ⇨ Quit System Settings.**

Switching user accounts

If you activated the Guest account or created one or more new user accounts on your Mac, you need to know how to switch back and forth between them. Here are the basic steps:

1. **Choose ⇨ Log Out *User*, where *User* is the name of the currently logged in user.**

   You can also start the logout by pressing Shift+⌘+Q. Your Mac asks you to confirm the logout.

2. **If you want macOS to restore your open windows the next time you log in, select the Reopen Windows When Logging Back In check box.**

3. **Click Log Out.**

   You can also wait until the 60-second timer runs out, at which point your Mac logs you out automatically.

   Your Mac logs out the account and displays the login screen.

4. **Click the user account you want to use.**

   Your Mac prompts you for the account password.

5. **Type the password and then click Log in.**

The only problem with this scenario is that your Mac shuts down all your running apps when you log out. Even if you selected the Reopen Windows When Logging Back In check box, you might not get all your windows back the way you had them, and having to restart everything can take a bit of time.

To avoid these problems, you can use *fast user switching*, which leaves your programs running when you log out and reinstates them just as they were when you log back in. To enable fast user switching, follow these steps:

1. **Click the System Settings icon in the Dock (or choose ⇨ System Settings).**

   The System Settings window appears.

2. **Click Control Center.**

   The Control Center settings appear.

3. **In the Other Modules section, scroll down to the Fast User Switching section.**

4. **Click the Show in Menu Bar pop-up menu and then click how you want fast user switching to appear in the menu bar:**

   - *Full Name:* Shows the current user's full name.

   - *Account Name:* Shows just the current user's account name.

   - *Icon:* Shows just the fast user switching icon.

5. **(Optional) If you want to access fast user switching from Control Center, click the Show in Control Center switch on.**

6. **Click the close icon or choose System Settings ⇨ Quit System Settings.**

With fast user switching activated, you can switch between accounts by clicking the fast user switching icon (or the current user's full name or account name) on the menu bar, as shown in Figure 3-2. The current user is identified by a white check mark in an orange circle, while any other logged-in user is identified by a white check mark in a gray circle (see Figure 3-2).

Logged-in user

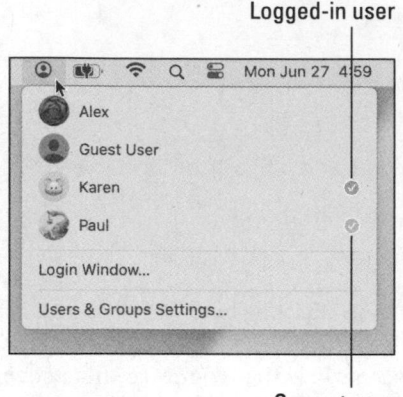

FIGURE 3-2:
With fast user switching on, click the icon (or current account name) on the menu bar to switch user accounts and leave your running programs open.

Current user

TIP

If you set up Touch ID on your Mac (see Book 3, Chapter 2), use your Touch ID finger to press down on the Touch ID key until it clicks, then click Switch User in the screen that appears.

Deleting a user account

After you create one or more accounts, you may want to delete an old or unused account. When you delete an account, your Mac gives you the option of retaining the account's Home folder, which may contain important files. To delete an account, follow these steps:

1. **Make sure that the account you want to delete is logged out and also that you're logged in to your administrator account.**

2. **Choose ⇨ System Settings or click System Settings on the dock.**

   The System Settings window appears.

3. **Click the Users & Groups icon to open the Users & Groups settings.**

4. **Click the *i*-in-a-circle to the right of the account you want to delete.**

5. **Click the Delete Account button.**

   macOS asks you to confirm.

6. **Click OK.**

   Yet another confirmation dialog appears, asking whether you really want to delete this account and presenting options to save the Home folder of the account, as shown in Figure 3-3. Select one of the following radio buttons:

   • *Save the Home Folder in a Disk Image:* Saves the home folder and its contents in a compressed disk image (DMG) file. This keeps the files compressed, so they take up less space on the hard drive than if you choose the next option (which does not compress the files contained in the Home folder). Choosing this option is like stuffing things in an attic to get them out of sight but still keeping them around in case you need them later.

- *Don't Change the Home Folder:* Keeps the Home folder and its contents exactly as they are before you delete the account, so you can browse through the files in the folder at any time.

- *Delete the Home Folder:* Wipes out any files the user may have created in the account.

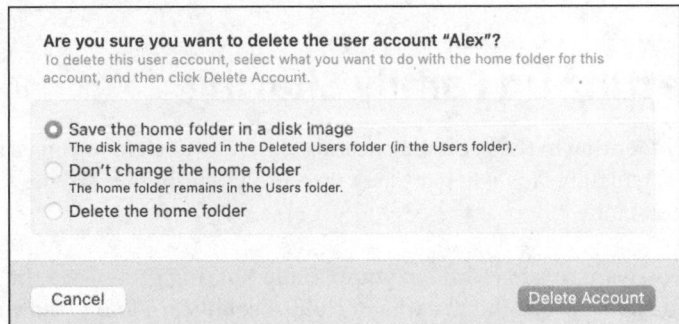

Are you sure you want to delete the user account "Alex"?
To delete this user account, select what you want to do with the home folder for this account, and then click Delete Account.

○ Save the home folder in a disk image
The disk image is saved in the Deleted Users folder (in the Users folder).

○ Don't change the home folder
The home folder remains in the Users folder.

○ Delete the home folder

Cancel   Delete Account

FIGURE 3-3:
Do you really
want to delete?

7. **Click Delete Account.**

   Your Mac deletes the specified account.

8. **Click the close icon or choose System Settings ⇨ Quit System Settings.**

All in the Family: Organizing Family Sharing

If you have a family, one of the biggest problems you face is dealing with the rising costs associated with everyone having their own subscriptions, apps, and media. Surely (you say to yourself) there must be a way to share some of these costs across the entire family.

Another problem you run into is wondering what your kids are up to on their devices. Surely (you say to yourself) there must be a way to monitor and restrict the apps and content that children use and see on their devices.

I'm happy to report that, yep, there *is* a way not only to share subscriptions and purchases among family members but also to monitor and restrict how children interact with a Mac or other Apple device. That way is called *Family Sharing* and it enables you to share Apple subscriptions such as Apple Music and Apple TV+, share Apple purchases such as apps, books, and media, and use Screen Time to monitor and restrict family member usage right from the convenience of your Mac account.

Family Sharing requires one adult to be the family organizer — in the sections that follow, I assume that's you — and the organizer can invite up to five family members to join the group. Everyone invited needs to have their own Apple ID. (If needed, you can create an Apple ID when adding a child to your Family Sharing group.)

Setting up Family Sharing

As I mention in the preceding section, I hereby designate you as the family organizer, which means you get to set up Family Sharing and invite your family members to join.

TIP

If you want to add a child to your Family Sharing group, see the following section "The kids are alright: Creating a child account for Family Sharing."

Here are the steps to follow to set up Family Sharing and invite one or more members of the family to join:

1. **Choose  ⇨ System Settings or click System Settings on the dock.**

   The System Settings window appears.

2. **Click Family, which appears just below your Apple ID.**

   The Family settings appear, which at first just provide an overview of Family Sharing.

3. **Click Set Up Family.**

   Once you've set up Family Sharing (that is, run through these steps at least once), you can click Add Member to invite more people to your family group.

   The Invite People to Your Family dialog appears and displays a list of the items you'll be sharing (such as your Apple subscriptions).

4. **Click Invite People.**

   The Send Invitations dialog appears.

5. **Choose how you want to send the invitation:**

- *Mail:* Sends the invitation via email. Use this method if the person isn't on your network or nearby. Click Mail, and then click Continue. In the new email message that appears, type the person's email address, then click Send. On their device, the family member opens the email messages, selects the invitation, and then selects Join Family.

- *AirDrop:* Sends the invitation via AirDrop. Use this method if the person's device is on the same Wi-Fi network. Click AirDrop, and then click Continue. In the AirDrop window that appears, click the family member's device. On their device, the family member clicks Show Invitation, then Join Family.

- *Invite in Person:* Enables the person to accept the invitation directly on your Mac. Use this method if the person is nearby and can enter their Apple ID credentials to accept the invitation. Click Invite in Person, and then click Continue. The family member then enters their Apple ID email address and password, and clicks Continue.

For Mail or AirDrop, Family Sharing displays a dialog letting you know the invitation was sent.

6. **Click Done.**

macOS turns on Family Sharing.

7. **Click the close icon or choose System Settings ⇨ Quit System Settings.**

Configuring what gets shared

As the family organizer, you get to decide exactly what gets shared with your family members who join your group: subscriptions, purchases, and your location. Here are the steps to follow to configure what gets shared to your Family Sharing group:

1. **Choose ⇨ System Settings or click System Settings on the dock.**

The System Settings window appears.

2. **Click Family, which appears just below your Apple ID.**

The Family settings appear.

3. **Click Subscriptions.**

The Subscriptions pane appears.

By default, Family Sharing automatically shares all your Apple subscriptions, except iCloud+.

4. **To share a subscription, click it in the Available to Share section, and then click Share with Family.**

   You can also use this pane to manage your existing subscriptions (click Manage), view related Apple Subscriptions (click Apple Subscriptions), or view family-friendly subscriptions (click Discover to the right of Subscriptions for family).

   When you've completed your work in the Subscriptions pane, click < (back).

5. **(Optional) If you want to share purchases with your family group, click Purchase Sharing, click Continue, and then click Turn on Purchase Sharing.**

6. **(Optional) If you want to share your location with your family group, click Location Sharing, and then click the switch on next to each family member with whom you want to share your location.**

   If you don't want your location shared automatically with each new family member, click the Automatically Share Location switch off.

7. **Click the close icon or choose System Settings ⇨ Quit System Settings.**

The kids are alright: Creating a child account for Family Sharing

If you have a child who has access to a Mac, it's best to set up a *child account* for that person because that type of account gives you a few extra controls that can help you as the parent or guardian sleep better at night. For example, you can activate the Ask to Buy feature, which means your child requires the permission of a parent or guardian to download or purchase anything from the App Store, iTunes Store, or Apple Books. You can also use the Screen Time feature to set limits on apps, notifications, content, communications, and when the child can use the Mac.

Here are the steps to follow to create a child account:

1. **Choose ⇨ System Settings or click System Settings on the dock.**

   The System Settings window appears.

2. **Click Family, which appears just below your Apple ID.**

   The Family settings appear.

3. **Click Add Member.**

   The Invite People to Your Family dialog appears.

4. **Click Create Child Account.**

The Create a Child Account dialog appears.

5. **Click Verify You're an Adult.**

The Parental Consent dialog appears.

6. **Enter the security code for your Apple ID credit card, and then click Continue.**

The Parental Consent Terms and Conditions dialog appears.

7. **Pretend to read the terms and conditions, select the I Have Read and Agree with These Conditions check box, and then click Agree.**

The Enter the Child's Information dialog appears.

8. **Enter the child's first name, last name, and date of birth, and then click Next.**

macOS creates a new Apple ID based on your child's name.

9. **Type the child's new account password (twice) and then click Next.**

The Two-Factor Authentication dialog appears to let you know that when your child signs in to a new device or website, you'll receive a verification code on the phone associated with your Apple ID.

10. **Click Next.**

Yet another set of terms and conditions appears. Who can say why?

11. **Select the check box and click Agree.**

A dialog appears, letting you know that Ask to Buy is turned on for you child. Ask to Buy is a feature that notifies you when your child attempts to purchase something through Family Sharing's Purchase Sharing feature (assuming you have that turned on) and asks you to approve that purchase (or not).

12. **Click Continue.**

A dialog asks if you want to share the child's location with your family group.

13. **Click Share Location.**

If you don't think your child would be cool with this, you can click Set Up Later, instead.

System Settings returns you to the Family settings, where you now see an account for your child.

14. **Click the close icon or choose System Settings ⇨ Quit System Settings.**

Setting a family member as a parent or guardian

In a family group, a parent or guardian can create child accounts, manage Screen Time parental controls, handle Ask to Buy requests, and more. If you want another person in your family group to share these responsibilities with you, follow these steps to set up that person as a parent or guardian:

1. **Choose ⌘ ⇨ System Settings or click System Settings on the dock.**

   The System Settings window appears.

2. **Click Family, which appears just below your Apple ID.**

   The Family settings appear.

3. **Click the family member you want to configure.**

4. **Click Parent/Guardian.**

5. **Click the Set as Parent/Guardian switch on.**

6. **Click Done.**

7. **Click the close icon or choose System Settings ⇨ Quit System Settings.**

Removing a family member

If one of your family members no longer wants to be part of your group, you can follow these steps to remove that person:

1. **Choose ⌘ ⇨ System Settings or click System Settings on the dock.**

   The System Settings window appears.

2. **Click Family, which appears just below your Apple ID.**

   The Family settings appear.

3. **Click the family member you want to remove.**

4. **Click Remove *Name* from Family (where *Name* is the family member's first name).**

   Family Sharing asks you to confirm.

5. **Click Remove *Name*.**

   Family Sharing removes the family member.

6. **Click the close icon or choose System Settings ⇨ Quit System Settings.**

Using Screen Time to Achieve Mac-Life Balance

The phrase *work-life balance* refers to a kind of equilibrium where the demands of your job and your personal life are roughly equal. However, if you feel like your life is out of balance, although it's possible that too much work is the culprit, may I suggest that too much *technology* might be just as much to blame? Specifically, if in your leisure hours you spend most of your time on your Mac using apps, exchanging messages, and perusing websites, there's a good chance that besides work-life balance, you also need *Mac-life* balance.

Fortunately — and ironically — your Mac can help. Using a feature called Screen Time, you can work towards Mac-life balance in two ways:

>> You can view reports that tell you which apps you use the most and how long you use them.

>> You can set up restrictions that enforce downtime, limit which apps you use and when, and control the content you see.

You can use Screen Time to see reports and set up restrictions not only for yourself but also for a child who either has a user account on your Mac or is a Family Sharing member.

Enabling Screen Time

To begin, follow these steps to activate Screen Time:

1. **Choose ⇨ System Settings or click System Settings on the dock.**

   The System Settings window appears.

2. **Click Screen Time.**

   The Screen Time settings appear.

3. **Click the Enable Screen Time switch on.**

   macOS enables the Screen Time settings, as shown in Figure 3-4. (In Figure 3-4, note that you see the Family Member pop-up menu only if you've activated Family Sharing; see "All in the Family: Organizing Family Sharing," earlier in this chapter.)

4. **Click the Use Screen Time Passcode switch on.**

   macOS prompts you for a four-digit code.

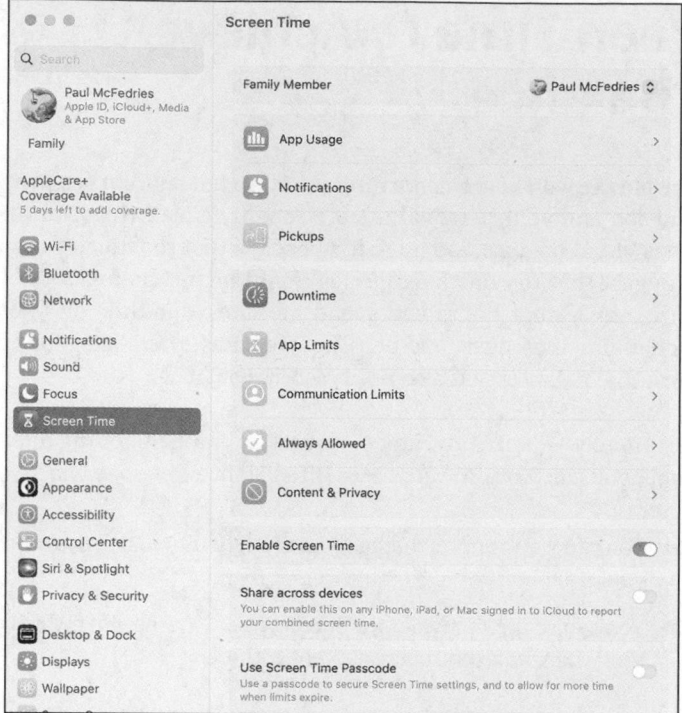

FIGURE 3-4:
Enabling Screen
Time is your first
step towards
Mac-life balance.

5. **Type the code, and then type the same code a second time.**

   macOS prompts you for your Apple ID credentials.

6. **Type your Apple ID email address, click Next, type your Apple ID password, and then click Next.**

   macOS applies the passcode, which is required to change Screen Time settings and perform tasks such as adding on time when certain limits run out.

REMEMBER

If you also want to set up Screen Time for a child who has a user account on your Mac (and if you're not using Family Sharing), log in to the child's account and then repeat the preceding steps.

Displaying Screen Time settings

In the rest of this chapter, I talk about how to modify various Screen Time settings, such as setting up downtime schedule, applying time limits to apps and websites, and setting up content restrictions. In each case, you'll need to first display the Screen Time settings. How you do that depends on whether you want to modify the settings for you or for a child and whether you're using Family Sharing (see "All in the Family: Organizing Family Sharing," earlier in this chapter). Here are the possibilities:

» **To display your Screen Time settings:** Choose ⍟ System Settings (or click System Settings on the dock) and then click Screen Time. If you have Family Sharing turned on, make sure your name appears in the Family Member pop-up.

» **To display the Screen Time settings of a child who is a Family Sharing member:** Choose ⍟ System Settings (or click System Settings on the dock). From here, you have two choices:

  • Click Screen Time, and then use the Family Member pop-up menu to select the child.

  • Click Family, click the child's name in the list of members, and then click Screen Time.

» **To display the Screen Time settings of child who has a user account on your Mac:** Log in to the child's user account, choose ⍟ System Settings (or click System Settings on the dock), and then click Screen Time.

Monitoring Mac usage

To see how you or a child are using apps and the Mac, open the Screen Time settings (see "Displaying Screen Time settings") and click the following:

» **App Usage:** Shows a chart of app usage, a list of the apps used, the total time for each app, and whether an app has reached its time limit.

» **Notifications:** Shows a chart of notifications received by you or the user as well as a list of the apps that generated the notifications (and how many notifications each app displayed).

» **Pickups:** Shows a chart that displays each instance of waking your Mac and the first app you use after waking it (the first post-wake app is known as a *pickup*).

TIP

For each chart, you can use the controls above the chart to choose a time frame (single day or an entire week) and to navigate to the previous (left arrow) or next (right arrow) day or week.

Setting up a downtime schedule

One of the easiest (and, I suppose, one of the most obvious) ways to achieve Mac-life balance is to use your Mac less. However, that's usually easier said than done when faced with the siren songs of the web, that cool game that everyone's playing, an overflowing inbox, and too many text conversations to count.

If you (or one of your children) can't resist the call to sit down in front of the Mac, let the Mac itself force the issue by enforcing downtime. In the Screen Time world, *downtime* means you can't use your Mac. If you try, you get a message telling you that it's your downtime, which is your cue to go do something that doesn't require your Mac.

To use downtime, you can turn it on manually as needed or set up a schedule. Here's how it works:

1. **Display your or your child's Screen Time settings.**

   See "Displaying Screen Time settings," earlier in the chapter for the details. The Screen Time settings appear.

2. **Click Downtime.**

   The Downtime settings appear.

3. **If you want to control downtime manually, click the Downtime switch on and skip to Step 5.**

   The step that follows show you how to set up a downtime schedule.

4. **Use the Schedule pop-up menu to select one of the following:**

   - *Every Day:* Sets up the same downtime schedule each day. Use the From control to set the start of downtime (the default is 10:00 PM) and use the To control to set the end of downtime (the default is 7:00 AM).

   - *Custom:* Sets up a different downtime schedule for each day of the week, as shown in Figure 3-5. For each day you want to schedule downtime, click the day's switch to on, use the left control to set the start of downtime, and use the right control to set the end of downtime. If there's a day you don't want to schedule downtime, click that day's switch off (as shown for Saturday in Figure 3-5).

5. **Click the close icon or choose System Settings ➪ Quit System Settings.**

REMEMBER

If you turned downtime on manually, you turn it off by displaying the Screen Time settings, clicking Downtime, then clicking the Downtime switch off.

Configuring time limits for apps and websites

One of the biggest reasons why people overdo it on their Macs is an app or a website that's way too interesting, way too much fun, or way too addictive. You really *want* to do something else (such as eat or sleep or talk to a human being), but you just can't tear yourself away.

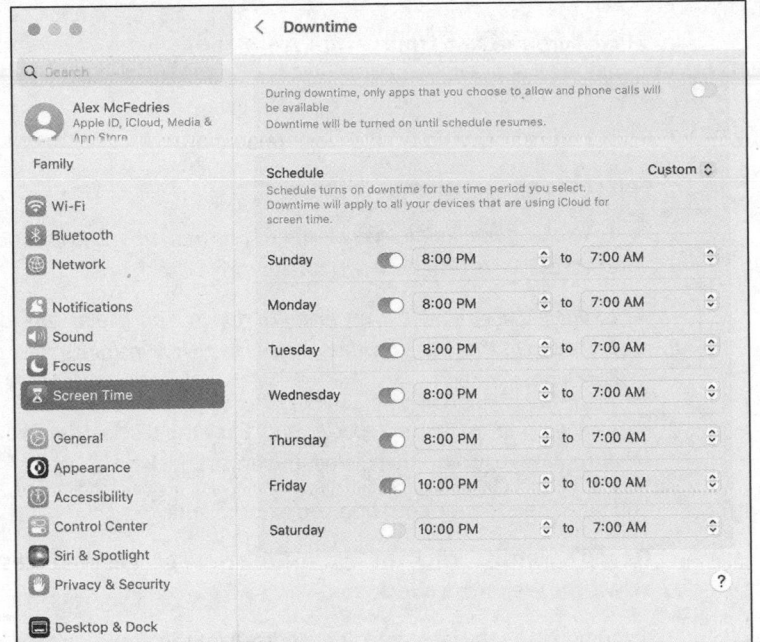

FIGURE 3-5:
You can set up a custom downtime schedule for each day of the week.

No judgement: We've all been there. If you have one or more apps or websites eating up your precious time and feel helpless to stop, the help you need is sitting right in front of you. No, not this book, silly. I'm talking about your Mac, specifically the Screen Time feature called app limits. With *app limits,* you select the apps and websites that are causing you trouble, and then you set a maximum amount of time that you're allowed to spend on those apps and sites. And, of course, you can also set up app limits for your children.

When that maximum time is reached, macOS displays a message telling you that you've reached your limit. You can opt for a little more time if you're in the middle of something. A child can send a request to you (or to another parent or guardian if you're using Family Sharing) for more time.

To set up app limits, you select your problematic apps or enter your hard-to-leave websites, and then set a time limit that applies either every day or on a custom schedule. Here are the full steps to follow:

1. Display your or your child's Screen Time settings.

See "Displaying Screen Time settings," earlier in the chapter for the details. The Screen Time settings appear.

2. Click App Limits.

The App Limits settings appear.

3. **Make sure the App Limits switch to set on.**

4. **Click Add Limit.**

   The Create a New App Limit dialog appears.

5. **Select the apps you want to limit:**

   - *To apply a time limit to every installed app (and to every app subsequently installed):* Select the All Apps & Categories check box.

   - *To apply a time limit to every installed app in a particular category (and to every app in that category that you subsequently install):* Select the category check box.

   - *To apply a time limit to a specific app:* Click the disclosure arrow next to the app's category, and then select the app's check box.

   Repeat as needed for each app you want to limit.

6. **To add a website, click the disclosure arrow beside Websites, and then select the website's check box.**

   If you don't see the website, click + (add), type the domain name, and then press Return. macOS adds the website and selects its check box.

   Repeat as needed for each website you want to limit.

7. **Set the time limit for the selected apps and websites:**

   - *Every Day:* Select this radio button and then set the maximum number of hours and minutes you want to apply. In Figure 3-6, for example, I've set a maximum time of 1 hour and 30 minutes for the Social and Games categories.

   - *Custom:* Select this radio button, click Edit, and then use the Daily Time Limit dialog to set the maximum number of hours and minutes to apply each day. Click Done.

     The time you set is the maximum amount of time you or your child can spend on each of the selected apps.

REMEMBER

8. **If you're setting app limits for a child, select the Block at End of Limit check box (which should be selected by default).**

   This forces the child off the app. The child will then have to request extra time from you.

9. **Click Done.**

   You're returned to the App Limits settings, where you now see a list of the categories, apps, and websites that have time limits.

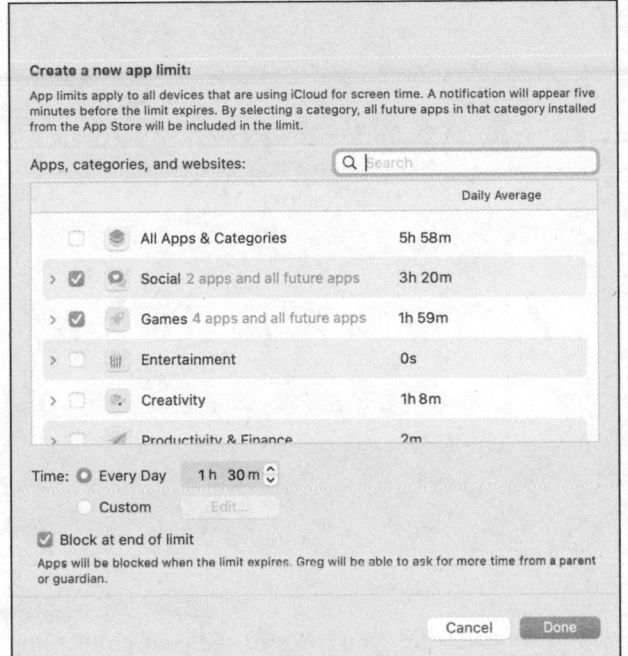

Create a new app limit:

App limits apply to all devices that are using iCloud for screen time. A notification will appear five minutes before the limit expires. By selecting a category, all future apps in that category installed from the App Store will be included in the limit.

Apps, categories, and websites: 🔍 Search

			Daily Average
☐	🗂	All Apps & Categories	5h 58m
☑		Social 2 apps and all future apps	3h 20m
☑		Games 4 apps and all future apps	1h 59m
☐		Entertainment	0s
☐		Creativity	1h 8m
☐		Productivity & Finance	2m

Time: ◉ Every Day 1h 30m ⬍
       ○ Custom Edit...

☑ Block at end of limit

Apps will be blocked when the limit expires. Greg will be able to ask for more time from a parent or guardian.

Cancel   Done

FIGURE 3-6:
You can set up app time limits for all apps, for app categories, or for individual apps and websites.

TIP

To make changes to an item in the App Limits page, hover the mouse pointer over the item and then click the Edit button that appears. In the Edit App Limit dialog that appears, you can change the time limit, click Edit Apps to change the apps included in the item, or click Remove Limit to delete the app limit.

10. **Click the close icon or choose System Settings ⇨ Quit System Settings.**

With app limits in effect, you see (or your child sees) a notification when five minutes of available time are left. When the time limit is reached, the options that appear depend on whether it's you or your child who's affected:

» **You:** When the Time Limit message appears, either close the app (good for you!) or click Ignore Limit. If you went with Ignore Limit (cheater!), you can then click how much extra time you want, as shown in Figure 3-7.

» **Your child:** When the Time Limit message appears, the child's only choices are to close the app window or click Ask for More Time. If the child clicks the latter, they can then click One More Minute (to get a one-time-only extra minute with the app), Enter Screen Time Passcode (to bypass the limit), or Send Request (which sends you a notification to ask for more time). If you receive such a notification, click Options in the notification and then click Approve for 15 minutes; Approve for an Hour; Approve All Day, or Don't Approve.

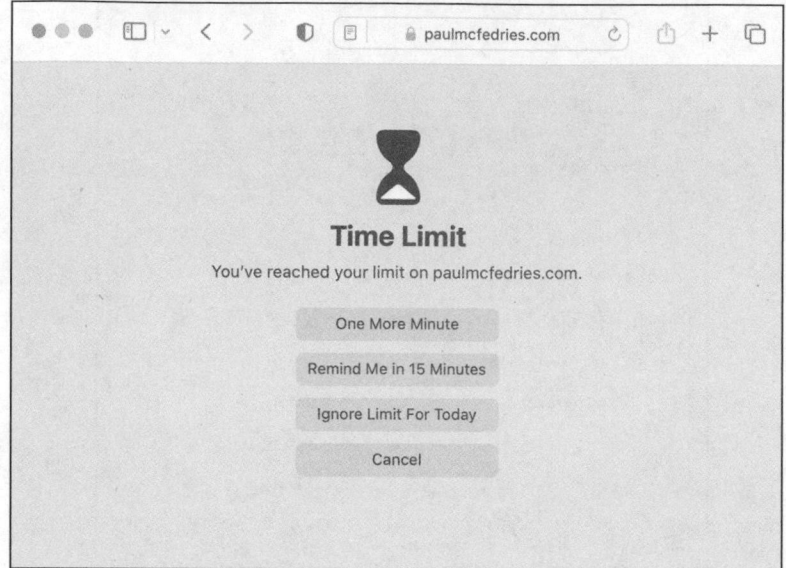

FIGURE 3-7:
You can ignore
your own time
limit, but try
to be strong!

TIP

If you miss the notification, you can still see your child's app limit requests by opening System Settings, clicking Screen Time, selecting the child in the Family Member pop-up, and then clicking Requests.

Setting communication limits

You can use app limits (which I discuss in the preceding section) to restrict the amount of time your child spends using communications apps such as Messages and FaceTime, but you might want to set limits also on *who* your child can communicate with using those apps (as well as the Phone app on your child's iPhone, if they have one).

You can restrict contact communication during screen time and during downtime by following these steps:

1. **Display your child's Screen Time settings.**

   See "Displaying Screen Time settings," earlier in the chapter, for the details. The Screen Time settings appear.

2. **Click Communication Limits.**

   The Communication Limits settings appear, as shown in Figure 3-8.

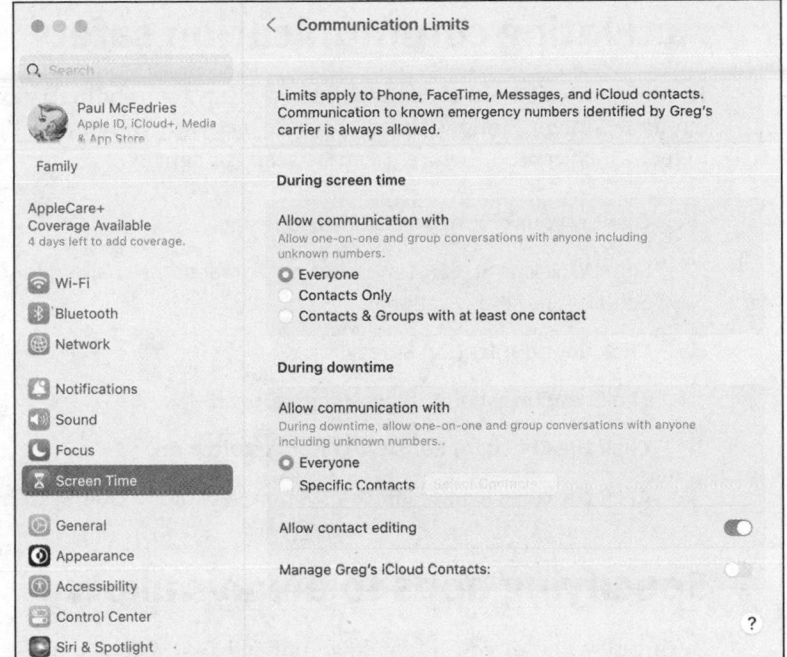

FIGURE 3-8:
Use the Communication Limits settings to restrict who your child can communicate with.

3. **In the During Screen Time section, select an option to determine who your child can communicate with while Screen Time is active.**

   You probably don't want to leave the default Everyone option selected. Select either Contacts Only or Contacts & Groups with at Least One Contact.

4. **In the During Downtime section, select an option to determine who your child can communicate with while downtime is active.**

   Again, you probably don't want to leave the default Everyone option selected. Select Specific Contacts, select the contacts or contacts you want your child to communicate with, and then click Done.

5. **(Optional) If you don't want your child to make changes to their contacts, click the Allow Contact Editing switch off.**

6. **(Optional) If you want to manage your child's iCloud contacts, click the Manage *Name*'s iCloud Contacts switch on (where *Name* is the child's first name).**

   Note that this only sends a request to the child to approve your management of their iCloud contacts. Access the child's Screen Time settings, click Requests, and then click Approve.

7. **Click the close icon or choose System Settings ⇨ Quit System Settings.**

Activating communication safety

If you're worried about your child receiving (or sending!) text messages with explicit content, follow these steps to activate communication safety, which detects such content before it can be seen (or sent):

1. **Display your child's Screen Time settings.**

See "Displaying Screen Time settings," earlier in the chapter, for the details. The Screen Time settings appear.

2. **Click Communication Safety.**

The Communication Safety settings appear.

3. **Click the Check for Sensitive Photos switch on.**

4. **Click the close icon or choose System Settings ⇨ Quit System Settings.**

Specifying apps to always allow

During downtime, you might have noticed that a few apps were still available, such as Maps. What's up with that? Screen Time includes a feature called Always Allowed that enables you to specify which apps you (or your child) can still use during downtime or if you selected All Apps and Categories when you set up app limits. To customize the Always Allowed feature, follow these steps:

1. **Display your or your child's Screen Time settings.**

See "Displaying Screen Time settings," earlier in the chapter, for the details. The Screen Time settings appear.

2. **Click Always Allowed.**

The Always Allowed settings appear.

3. **In the During Downtime section, click the option to specify who you or your child can communicate with: Everyone or Specific Contacts.**

4. **If you go with Specific Contacts, click Edit Contacts and use the dialog that appears to add one or more contacts (click + to add each contact), and then click Done.**

5. **For each app you want to use during downtime or when you use All Apps and Categories for app limits, click the app's switch on.**

If there are any currently allowed apps that you don't want to use, click each app's switch off.

6. **Click the close icon or choose System Settings ⇨ Quit System Settings.**

Applying content and privacy restrictions

One of the main benefits of Screen Time is that it enables you to apply a set of restrictions designed to keep your child safe from harmful content, protect your child's privacy, and prevent your child from doing things that might be harmful to your Mac. Here are some examples from the four types of restrictions you can apply:

» **Content:** You can restrict web content to disallow adult websites or allow just specified websites; you can block explicit language in Siri; you can disallow profiles in the Music app; you can disallow private messaging in Game Center; and you can prevent your child from joining multiplayer games.

» **Store:** You can set allowable ratings for movies, TV shows, and apps; you can disallow explicit books, music, and videos; and you can disallow installing apps, deleting apps, and making in-app purchases on iOS.

» **App:** You can block access to the camera and to specific apps, such as Book Store; you can also disallow specific apps on iOS.

» **Preference:** You can block settings changes on iOS for features such as cellular data, the child's Apple ID account, and the device passcode.

Follow these steps to set these and other content and privacy restrictions:

1. **Display your or your child's Screen Time settings.**

   See "Displaying Screen Time settings," earlier in the chapter, for the details. The Screen Time settings appear.

2. **Click Content & Privacy.**

   The Content & Privacy settings appear.

3. **Click the Content & Privacy switch on.**

4. **Click Content Restrictions and then use the settings that appear (see Figure 3-9) to restrict web content, Siri, Music & TV, Game Center, and Multiplayer Games. Click < (back) when you're done.**

5. **Click Store Restrictions and then use the settings that appear to specify the allowed content on the Mac (in the Allowed Content section) and on iOS (in the Allowed on iOS section). Click < (back) when you're done.**

6. **Click App Restrictions and then use the switches that appear to turn off access to Mac features (in the Allowed section) and iOS features (in the Allowed on iOS section). Click < (back) when you're done.**

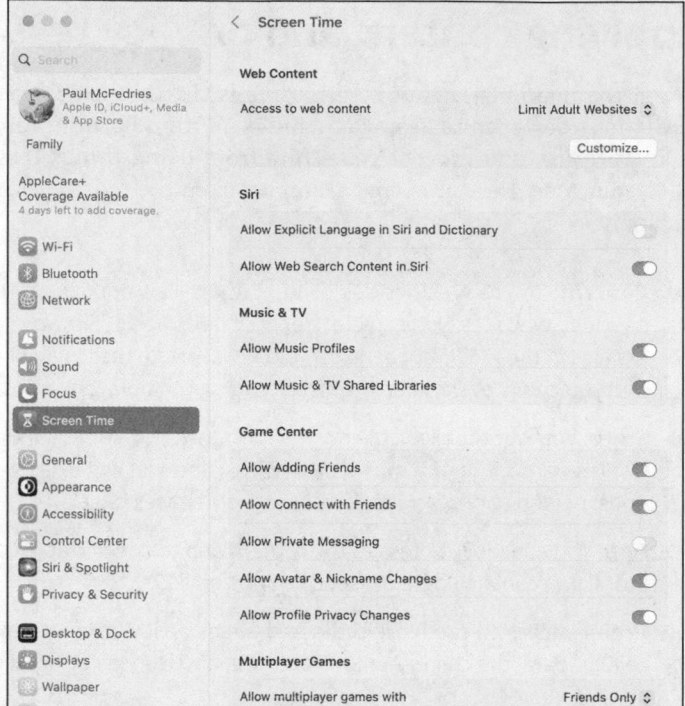

FIGURE 3-9:
The Content
Restrictions
settings.

7. **Click Preference Restrictions and then use the switches that appear to turn off access to iOS preferences. Click < (back) when you're done.**

8. **Click the close icon or choose System Settings ⇨ Quit System Settings.**

Chapter **4**

Networking Your Mac

I f you have just a single Mac in your home or small office, and if you're the only person who uses that computer, your setup is inherently efficient. You can use the machine whenever you like and everything you need — your apps, your printer, your scanner, your internet connection, and so on — are readily available.

Things become noticeably less efficient if you must share the Mac with other people. For instance, you might have to wait for someone else to finish a task before you can get your own work done, you might need to have separate apps for each person's requirements, and you might need to set up separate folders to hold each person's data. User accounts and fast user switching in macOS ease these problems (see Book 3, Chapter 3), but they don't eliminate them. For example, you still have to twiddle a thumb or two while waiting for another person to complete their work.

A better solution is to increase the number of Macs available. At home, for example, the current trend is to buy a nice machine for Mom and Dad to put in their office, while the kids inherit the old Mac for their games and homework assignments.

Now you have several computers kicking around the house or office, but they're all islands unto themselves. If you want to print something using another Mac's printer, you're forced to copy the file to a memory card or other removable media, walk that media over to the other computer, and then print from there. Similarly, if multiple computers require internet access, you face the hassle (and expense) of configuring separate connections.

So now you must take the final step on this road: Connect everything together to create your own small network. This gives you all kinds of benefits:

>> A printer (or just about any peripheral) attached to one computer can be used by any other computer on the network.

>> You can transfer files from one computer to another.

>> Users can access disk drives and folders on network computers as though they were part of their own computer. In particular, you can set up a folder to store common data files, and each user will be able to access these files from the comfort of their machine. (For security, you can restrict access to certain folders and drives.)

>> You can set up a wireless portion of your network, which enables you to access other computers and the internet from just about anywhere in your house or office.

After you understand the concept of networking, networks aren't so difficult to set up. In this chapter, I show you how to set up a simple wired or wireless network — a few computers, a printer, and a modem. I then talk about another connectivity protocol — Bluetooth — which lets you connect devices (such as a keyboard, a mouse, or headphones) wirelessly, as well as share files between devices.

Creating a Wired Network

Setting up networks is easy with Macs because of *Bonjour,* Apple's implementation of zero-configuration networking, which is part of your Mac's operating system. With Bonjour, your Mac seeks and discovers the peripheral devices and computers on your local network and you don't have to do any complicated configuring. You may see the word *Bonjour* in some of the networking settings windows.

The simplest wired network connects two computers, using a USB or Thunderbolt cable or a cable that conforms to a networking cable standard called *Ethernet.* Your Mac has an Ethernet port or a Thunderbolt port or both. If you plug a cable into the ports of two Macs, you have a simple network, as shown in Figure 4-1.

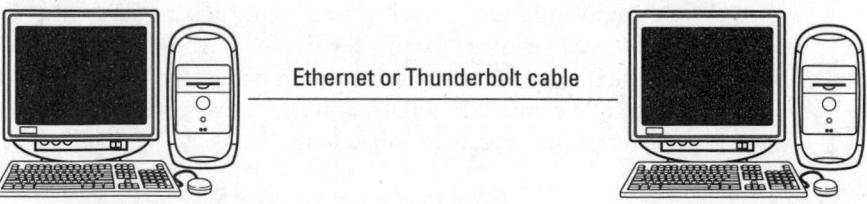

FIGURE 4-1:
A simple network connects two Macs via Ethernet or Thunderbolt cable.

Ethernet or Thunderbolt cable

TIP

All data transfer speeds in this section (and, in fact, in almost every article or book you read) are maximum possible speeds, which are generally achieved only in the most ideal circumstances. Your mileage, as they say, might vary.

All recent Mac models have one or more Thunderbolt/USB 4 ports that support Thunderbolt 4, USB 4, and USB 3.1 connections. Some Macs also come with one or more USB-A ports. Thunderbolt 4 and USB 4 both offer two-way 40 Gbps (gigabits per second) connections, while USB 3.1 has a top speed of 10 Gbps and USB-A maxes out at 5 Gbps.

Ethernet ports are a bit harder to find. The Mac Pro offers two Ethernet ports, and the Mac mini and Mac Studio come with an Ethernet port as standard equipment. An Ethernet port is an optional upgrade on an iMac. In all cases, the top Ethernet speed is 10 Gbps. If you have a MacBook or other Mac that doesn't have a built-in Ethernet port, you can buy a Thunderbolt-to-Gigabit-Ethernet adaptor from Apple.

TECHNICAL
STUFF

Ethernet cables are often identified by the speeds at which they can send data. The earliest Ethernet cables were Category 3 (Cat 3) cables and could transfer data at 10 megabits per second (Mbps). The next generation of Ethernet cables was Category 5 cables, which could transfer data at 100 Mbps. Category 5e and Category 6 (Cat 5e/6) cables transfer data at 1,000 Mbps, or one gigabit per second (Gbit/s). With networking, speed is everything and Category 6a (Cat 6a) and Category 7 (Cat 7) transfer data at 10 Gbit/s. Category 7a supports transfer speeds of 100 Gbit/s.

Because it's physically impossible to connect more than two devices with a single cable, wired networks with three or more devices use a *hub*. Each device connects to the hub, which indirectly connects each device to every other device also connected to the hub, as shown in Figure 4-2.

An improved variation of a hub is a *switch.* Physically, a hub and a switch both connect multiple devices in a single point (refer to Figure 4-2).

With a hub, a network acts like one massive hallway that every computer shares. If many computers transfer data at the same time, the shared network can get crowded with data flowing everywhere, slowing the transfer of data throughout the network.

With a switch, the switch directs data between two devices. As a result, a switch can ensure that data transfers quickly, regardless of how much data the other devices on the network are transferring at the time.

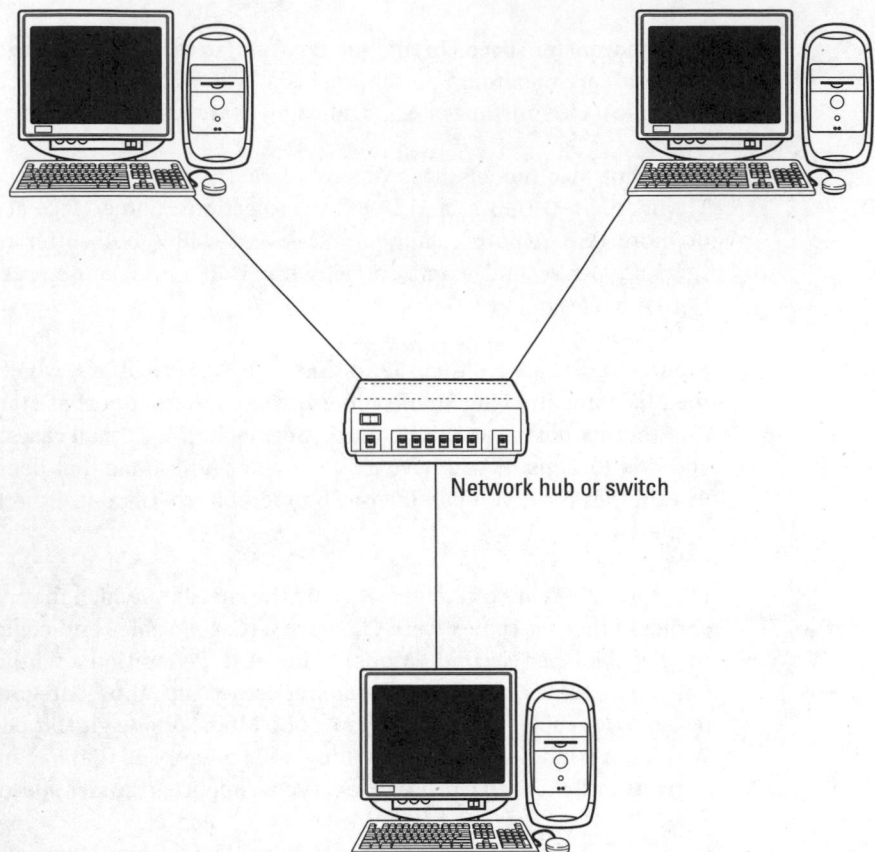

FIGURE 4-2:
A hub or switch
allows multiple
computers to
connect together
in a network.

Network hub or switch

A variation of a switch is a *router*, which often adds a firewall by using Network Address Translation (NAT) and Dynamic Host Configuration Protocol (DHCP). NAT uses one set of Internet Protocol (IP) addresses — which identify the computers and peripherals on the network — for local network traffic and another set for external traffic. This eliminates the risk of your device having the same address as another device. DHCP lets the router assign a different IP address to the same device each time it connects to the network.

Because routers cost nearly the same as ordinary hubs and switches, most wired networks rely on routers. So, if you want to create a wired network of computers, you need

>> Two or more devices — computers, printers, scanners, modems, external drives

>> A network switch or router with a number of ports equal to or greater than the number of devices you want to connect

>> Enough cables (and of sufficient length) to connect each device to the network switch or router

REMEMBER

The speed of a wired network depends entirely on the slowest speed of the components used in your network. So, if you plan to use the fastest cables in your network, make sure your network switch is designed for those cables. If not, you'll have the fastest Ethernet cables connected to a slow network switch, which will run only as fast as the slowest part of your network.

After you connect your computers and peripherals to the hub or switch and turn everything on, follow these steps to make sure that your Mac is connected:

1. **Choose ⇨ System Settings or click System Settings on the dock.**

   The System Settings window opens.

2. **Click Network.**

3. **Beside Ethernet or Thunderbolt, or whichever type of network cable or connection you use, you should see a green light and the word *Connected* below, as shown in Figure 4-3.**

   If you don't see a wired connection such as Ethernet or Thunderbolt, you may see the green light next to Wi-Fi, which is a wireless connection. If you don't see any green dots, you don't have any connection. Don't worry if you have several (or many) connections that are not enabled (they'll have red dots).

I explain how to set up file sharing in Book 3, Chapter 5. After you set up sharing, you see other computers on your network in Finder's Network folder.

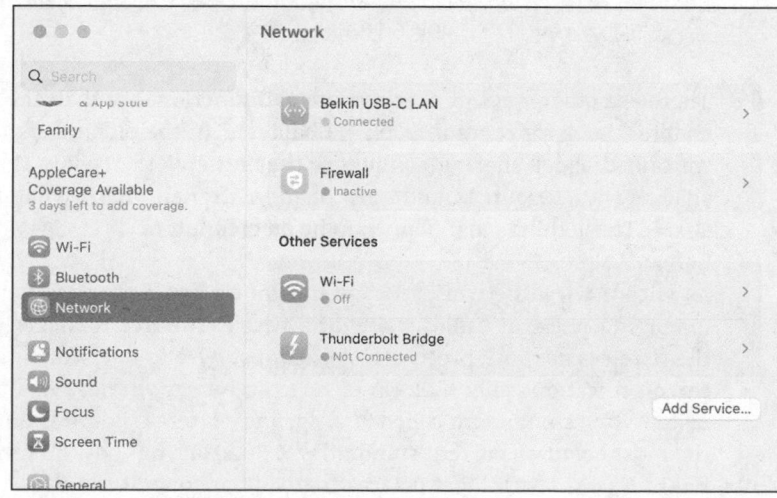

FIGURE 4-3:
The Network settings show you which network connections are active.

When you set up a wired network, the router may have wireless capabilities. If so, you can use an Ethernet cable to connect to the router a computer or printer that stays in one place, and then connect to the wireless network connection on your MacBook to work from your lawn chair in the garden or connect to the network from a desktop Mac in another room in the house. To do so, turn on Wi-Fi and select the network, as I explain in the next section.

"Look, Ma, No Wires!" Setting Up a Wireless Network

Essentially, a wireless network is no different from a wired network, except (of course) that there are no wires. Instead, radio waves take their place. Wireless networks can be a bit slower than wired networks, but unless you transfer big files, going wireless is probably a tidier and more cost-effective alternative because there are no cables to buy and tack along the baseboard. I show you how to create a wireless network that uses a wireless router and eventually a cable modem or DSL modem.

I'd be remiss if I didn't mention two downsides to wireless networks:

>> Potential interference from cordless phones, microwave ovens, and other nearby devices. This type of interference is difficult and frustrating to track down because the source of interference may well be a cellphone that is on only at certain times — and not when you're troubleshooting interference.

>> Less security because of the risk of others intercepting the signal unless you encrypt your communications.

TIP

There are other ways of sharing data and functionality than those you see in this chapter. Look for them in Book 3, Chapter 5. In the olden days (a few years ago), we talked about sharing computers over a network. Today, the emphasis is on sharing files, resources, and functionality. After all, that's what you really want to share. These things just happen to be on computers.

As with a wired network, you need a router for a wireless network. Instead of managing physical cables, though, a wireless router manages signals based on the wireless network protocols. The earliest wireless networks followed a technical specification called 802.11b or 802.11a. Newer wireless equipment followed a faster wireless standard called 802.11g, and a later standard is 802.11n. For a while, the most common current standard was 802.11ac, but now all recent Macs support Wi-Fi 6 (802.11ax). Most devices that support one of the 802.11 family protocols are compatible with one another to a large extent.

THE HAZARDS OF WIRELESS NETWORKING

To access a wired network, someone must physically connect a computer to the network with a cable. However, connecting to a wireless network can be done from another room, outside a building, or even across the street. As a result, wireless networks can be much less secure because a wireless network metaphorically shoves dozens of virtual cables out the window, so anyone can walk by and connect to the network.

When you create a wireless network, you can make your network more secure by taking advantage of a variety of security measures and options. The simplest security measure is to use a strong password that locks out people who don't know the password. Three types of passwords are used for wireless networks:

- **Wired Equivalent Privacy (WEP)** is an older protocol and offers minimal (almost useless) protection. Because it's an older protocol, it may not work on all your devices. Passwords use either 5 or 13 characters. WEP is no longer recommended; I'm listing it here only so that you know what it is if you're working with a device that uses WEP.

- **Wi-Fi Protected Access (WPA)** is better than WEP because it changes the encryption key for each data transmission.

- **Wi-Fi Protected Access 2 (WPA2)** is the best choice because it uses the more secure Advanced Encryption Standard (AES) to encrypt the password when it's transmitted.

For further protection, you can also use encryption. *Encryption* scrambles the data sent to and from the wireless network. Without encryption, anyone can intercept information sent through a wireless network (including passwords). Still another security measure involves configuring your wireless network to let only specific computers connect to the network. Doing this prevents an intruder from gaining access to the wireless network because their computer is not approved to access the network.

Ultimately, wireless networking requires more security measures simply because it offers potential intruders the ability to access the network without physically being in the same room, house, or building. Wireless networks can be as safe as wired networks — as long as you turn on security options that can make your wireless network as secure as possible.

When setting up a wireless network, make sure that your router uses the same wireless standard as the built-in wireless radio or wireless adapter plugged into each of your devices. All new and recent Macs connect to Wi-Fi routers that use one to six types (a, b, g, n, ac, or ax) of the wireless 802.11 network standards.

You can buy any brand of wireless router to create a network or rent one from your internet service provider (ISP). (In fact, most ISP broadband modems now also include a wireless router.) Existing products work well for many people and are still available as new from a number of online vendors. Any router you choose will come with specific software and instructions for setting up your network. The basic steps are as follows:

1. **Connect a Mac to the router directly by using a cable (such as a USB or Ethernet cable).**

2. **Use the connected Mac to log in to the router's configuration pages.**

   See your router manual to learn how to access the configuration pages and what credentials you need to enter.

3. **Display the wireless or Wi-Fi settings.**

   Figure 4-4 shows a typical wireless network configuration page.

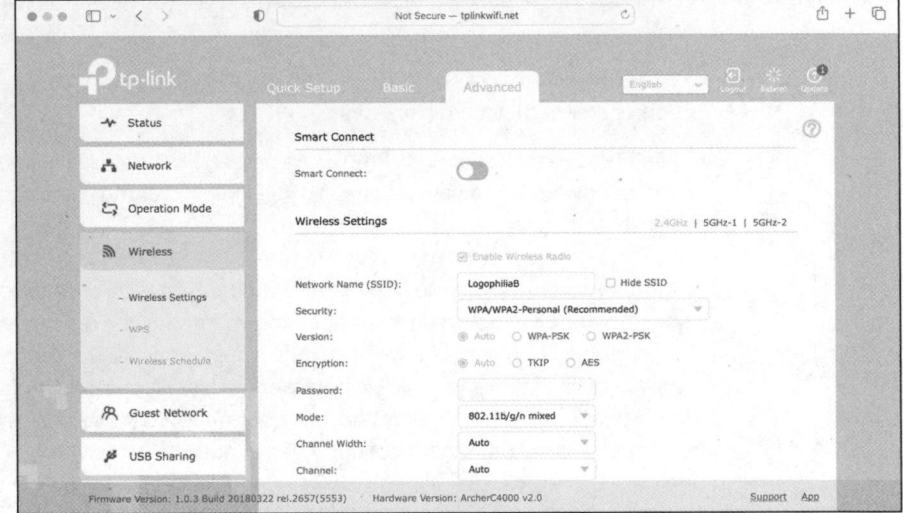

FIGURE 4-4:
A typical configuration page for a wireless network.

4. **Define your wireless network, which usually includes at least the following:**

   - *Give your network a name so devices on the network can then find and connect to your Wi-Fi network.*

   - *Give your network a strong password.*

   - *Choose which security type you want to use.*

WPA2 provides the most security (see the nearby sidebar, "The hazards of wireless networking," for more information).

5. **Click Save or whatever button saves your settings.**

6. **Perform a few of other setup chores:**

   - *Define how you connect to the internet. This is usually dynamic IP, but see the information you received from your internet service provider (ISP).*

   - *Update the router's default login credentials with a unique username and a strong password.*

   - *Make sure the router's hardware firewall is enabled.*

7. **Click Save or whatever button saves your settings.**

8. **Log out of the router's configuration pages.**

TECHNICAL STUFF

Because of physical obstacles, wireless networks don't always reach certain parts of a room or building, resulting in dead spots where you can't connect wirelessly. Walls or furniture can disrupt the wireless signals. You can add a device called an *access point,* also known as a *range extender,* which picks up the signal and rebroadcasts it beyond the reach of the Wi-Fi router, extending your wireless network range. The newest Wi-Fi protocol — 802.11ax — uses a technology that is better at penetrating walls, which will make this problem less troublesome in the future.

The difference between an access point and a router is that the router is at the center of the network, allowing the computers to share printers (see the next chapter), internet connections, and external hard drives. The *access point* is what allows the devices with wireless capabilities to connect to the network from a greater distance.

Connecting Devices Using the Magic of Bluetooth

That mass of wires and cables under your desk doesn't have a name, although some of the more waggish suggestions I've heard are *corducopia, quagwire,* and *nerdnest.* In the end, though, it doesn't much matter because let's face it: Wires are so last century. Wireless is the way to go and your Mac is already configured to use a wireless technology called Bluetooth. In the rest of this chapter, I cover what Bluetooth is; how to set up your Mac with Bluetooth; how to connect your Mac with various Bluetooth devices such as a mouse, keyboard, headset, and cellphone; and how to configure your Mac's Bluetooth capabilities.

A BIT OF BLUETOOTH BACKGROUND

You're probably familiar with Wi-Fi, the standard that enables you to perform networking chores without the usual network cables. Bluetooth is similar in that it enables you to exchange data between two devices without any kind of physical connection between them. Bluetooth uses radio frequencies to set up a communications link between the devices.

Bluetooth is a short-distance networking technology, with a maximum range of about 33 feet (10 meters). You can use your Mac's Bluetooth capabilities to make connections with a wide variety of devices, including

- Another Mac
- iPhone or iPad
- Mouse (such as Apple's Wireless Mighty Mouse)
- Keyboard (such as Apple's Wireless Keyboard)
- Headset
- Speakers
- Printer
- Digital camera

**TECHNICAL
STUFF**

The Bluetooth name comes from Harald Bluetooth, a tenth-century Danish king who united the provinces of Denmark under a single crown, the same way that, theoretically, Bluetooth will unite the world of portable wireless devices under a single standard. Why name a modern technology after an obscure Danish king? Here's a clue: Two of the most important companies backing the Bluetooth standard — Ericsson and Nokia — are Scandinavian.

Working with Bluetooth devices

One of the great advantage of devices that have Bluetooth built-in is that such devices don't require any other equipment to connect with each other. That sounds like magic, but it's true. The connection process generally follows these steps:

>> **Bring the Bluetooth device within 33 feet of your Mac:** Bluetooth works reliably only within this range; the closer the device to your Mac, the better.

» **Make your device discoverable:** Unlike Wi-Fi devices that broadcast their signals constantly, most Bluetooth devices broadcast their availability only when you say so, which is known as making the device *discoverable*. This makes sense in many cases because you usually only want to use a Bluetooth device such as a mouse or keyboard with a single computer. By controlling when the device is discoverable, you ensure that it works only with the computer you want it to.

» **Pair your Mac and the device:** To *pair* two Bluetooth devices is to establish a wireless connection between them so that they can exchange information. So, can any nearby Bluetooth device pair with your Mac? Nope. Before a device can pair with your Mac, that pairing requires your approval. For some Bluetooth devices, your Mac generates a 6-digit passkey that you must then type into the Bluetooth device (assuming, of course, that it has some kind of keypad). In other cases, the device comes with a default passkey that you must type into your Mac to set up the pairing. All other Bluetooth devices set up an automatic pairing (although, again, with your approval) using an empty passkey.

Pairing a Bluetooth device

Using wireless devices is a blissful state because, with no cord to tie you down, it gives you the freedom to interact with your Mac from just about anywhere. Wi-Fi devices are often cumbersome because they require a separate transceiver, and these tend to be large and take up a USB port. Since your Mac already has Bluetooth, however, you don't need anything else to use a Bluetooth-compatible device.

Follow these general steps to pair a Bluetooth device:

1. **Choose ⇨ System Settings or click System Settings on the dock.**

The System Settings window opens.

2. **Click Bluetooth.**

The Bluetooth settings appear.

3. **Make sure the Bluetooth switch is on.**

Click the Bluetooth status icon in the menu bar, and then choose Set up Bluetooth Device. The Bluetooth Setup Assistant appears and starts looking for nearby Bluetooth devices.

4. **Perform whatever steps are required to make your device discoverable.**

For example, if you have an Apple Magic Mouse or wireless keyboard, slide the power switch off and then on again.

After a brief (I hope!) pause, the Bluetooth device shows up in the Nearby Devices list, as shown in Figure 4-5.

5. **In the Nearby Devices list, move the mouse pointer over the device you want to pair, and then click the Connect button that appears (refer to Figure 4-5).**

    Your Mac connects with the device.

    When your Mac connects with a device that requires a passkey for pairing, macOS displays a passkey.

6. **If required, use the Bluetooth device to type the passkey.**

    If the device is (or has) a keyboard, be sure to also press Return.

    You're ready to use your Bluetooth device.

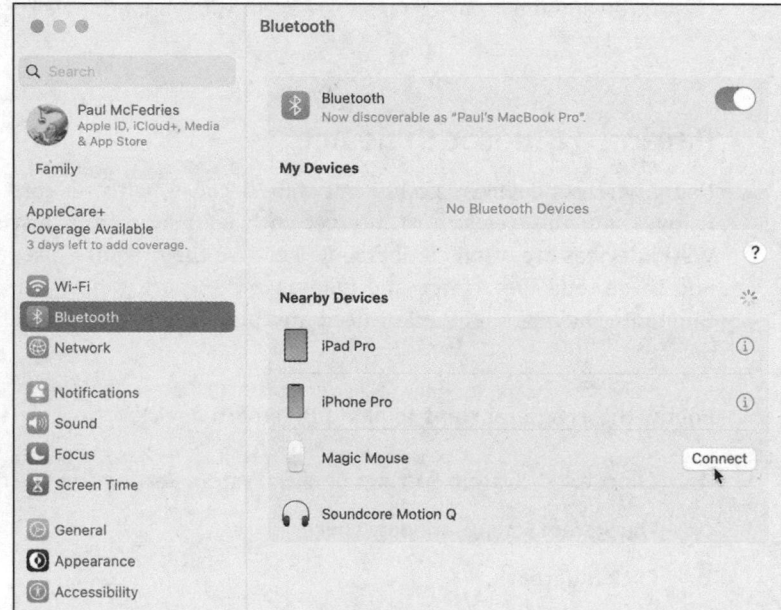

FIGURE 4-5:
When your Mac discovers a Bluetooth device, it displays the device in the Nearby Devices list.

Easier access to Bluetooth devices and settings

If you think you'll be configuring your Bluetooth devices often — or if, more likely, you think you'll be checking their battery levels often — consider adding the Bluetooth icon to your Mac's menu bar:

1. **Choose ➪ System Settings or click System Settings on the dock.**

    The System Settings window opens.

2. **Click Control Center.**

3. **Open the Bluetooth pop-up menu and select Show in Menu Bar.**

4. **Click the close icon or choose System Settings ⇨ Quit System Settings.**

Now you can click the Bluetooth icon in the menu bar to display a list of your connected devices. As you can see in Figure 4-6, the Bluetooth menu that appears also shows the current battery level for each device. (You can use this menu also to toggle your Mac's Bluetooth antenna on and off and to jump directly to the Bluetooth settings.)

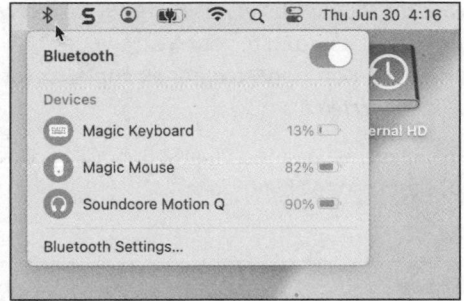

FIGURE 4-6:
Click the Bluetooth menu bar button to see your connected Bluetooth devices and their battery levels.

If your menu bar is getting crowded, another way to access Bluetooth stuff quickly is via Control Center (see Book 1, Chapter 6). Click the Control Center icon on the menu bar and then use either of the following techniques:

>> Click the Bluetooth icon to toggle the Bluetooth antenna off and on.

>> Hover the mouse pointer over the Bluetooth section and click the disclosure arrow that appears. macOS displays a Bluetooth menu just like the one shown in Figure 4-6.

Configuring your Bluetooth device

When you connect a Bluetooth device, in most cases you just go ahead and start using it. However, your Mac gives you a limited set of options for working with your Bluetooth device. For example, you can monitor the battery levels of these devices.

If you use multiple Bluetooth devices of the same type, the list of Bluetooth devices can get confusing because you don't have any direct way to tell one device from another. To avoid this, you can often give your devices unique names (although not all Bluetooth devices support renaming). Here are the steps to follow to rename a Bluetooth device:

1. **Choose ⌘ ⇨ System Settings or click System Settings on the dock.**

   Alternatively, click the Bluetooth icon on the menu bar, click Bluetooth Settings, and then skip to Step 3.

   The System Settings window opens.

2. **Click Bluetooth.**

   The Bluetooth pane appears (see Figure 4-7) and displays two lists:

   - *My Devices:* Displays the Bluetooth devices currently paired with your Mac. If the device is currently connected to your Mac, the device status shows as *Connected;* if the device is not connected (for example, it's turned off), the device status is *Not Connected*.

   - *Nearby Devices:* Displays the unpaired Bluetooth devices currently discoverable and within range of your Mac.

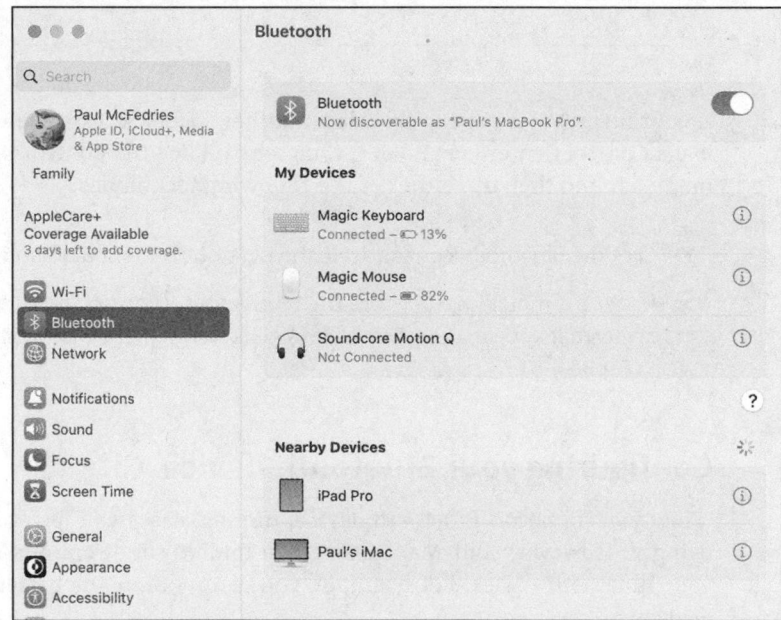

FIGURE 4-7:
The Bluetooth pane display lists of paired and unpaired Bluetooth devices.

3. **Click the *i*-in-a-circle (info) to the right of the device you want to rename.**

4. **Type the new name and then click Done.**

System Settings updates the device's name. This name is stored on the device itself, so you'll see this name even if you pair the device with another computer.

5. **Click the close icon or choose System Settings ⇨ Quit System Settings.**

Disconnecting and reconnecting a Bluetooth device

If you won't be working with a Bluetooth device for a while, you should disconnect it by using either of the following techniques:

» Open System Settings, click Bluetooth, hover the mouse pointer over the device, and then click Disconnect.

» Click the Bluetooth icon on the menu bar and then click the connected device.

Reconnecting the device is just a matter of repeating either technique (although in the Bluetooth settings, you hover the mouse over the device and then click Connect).

Forgetting a Bluetooth device

One common Bluetooth conundrum is what to do when you want to use a paired Bluetooth device with another Mac or with a device such as an iPhone or iPad. Turning the Bluetooth device off and then back on again doesn't help because it just connects to your Mac again. And disconnecting the Bluetooth device doesn't make it available to other computers or devices for pairing.

The secret is that you have to tell you Mac to *forget* the device, which means that your Mac not only disconnects from the device but also will no longer automatically pair with the device.

To forget a Bluetooth device, follow these steps:

1. **Choose ⇨ System Settings or click System Settings on the dock.**

   Alternatively, click the Bluetooth icon in the menu bar, click Bluetooth Settings, and then skip to Step 3.

   The System Settings window opens.

2. **Click Bluetooth.**

   The Bluetooth settings appear.

3. **Click the *i*-in-a-circle (info) to the right of the device you want to forget.**

4. **Click Forget this Device.**

   System Settings asks you to confirm.

5. **Click Forget Device.**

   System Settings disconnects from the device and removes the device from the My Devices list.

6. **Click the close icon or choose System Settings ⇨ Quit System Settings.**

Exchanging files with Bluetooth

If you have a Bluetooth device that can work with files such as documents, music, and images, or data such as appointments and addresses, you can exchange files between your Mac and the Bluetooth device. Bear in mind, however, that this feature is useful only for small files. Bluetooth isn't the fastest technology out there, so these transfers can be glacially slow. Small items such as addresses and appointments transfer reasonably fast, but it can take a few minutes to transfer a single MP3 file. Still, if you have no other way to transfer data, Bluetooth will do in a pinch.

You can transfer files from your Mac to a Bluetooth device by using your Mac's Bluetooth File Exchange utility or from a Bluetooth device to your Mac by activating and configuring your Mac's Bluetooth Sharing feature.

Browsing a Bluetooth device

When you browse a Bluetooth device, you examine the contents of the device and, optionally, get one or more files from the device. You do this using the Bluetooth File Exchange utility, as I demonstrate in the following steps:

1. **In Finder, choose Go ⇨ Utilities.**

   You can also press Shift+⌘+U. Finder opens the Utilities folder.

2. **Double-click Bluetooth File Exchange.**

3. **If you see a file chooser, click Cancel.**

4. **Choose File ⇨ Browse Device.**

   You can also press Shift+⌘+O. The Select Bluetooth Device dialog appears and displays a list of available Bluetooth devices, as shown in Figure 4-8.

5. **If your Mac is not already paired with the device you want to browse, click the device's Connect button and wait until the pairing is complete.**

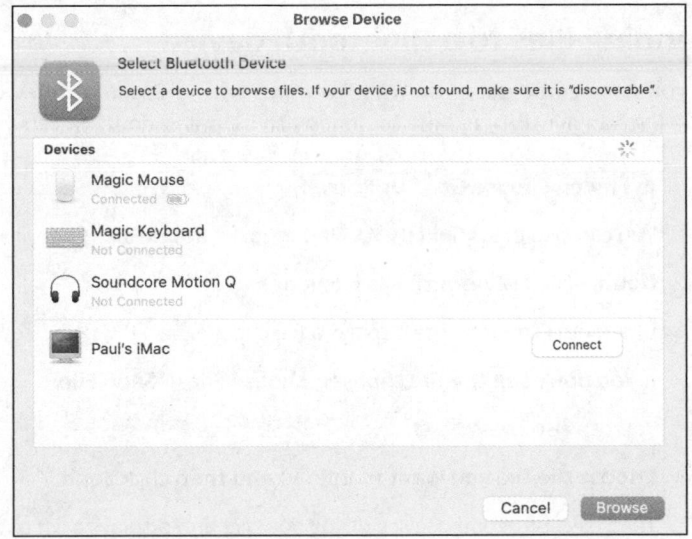

FIGURE 4-8:
The Select
Bluetooth Device
dialog displays
a list of nearby
Bluetooth
devices.

REMEMBER

Want to browse your iPhone or iPad? That would be awesome but, alas, it's not possible. If you try, Bluetooth File Exchange displays the message *The device does not have the necessary services.*

For some devices (such as another Mac), your Mac displays the dialog shown on the left in Figure 4-9, and the other device shows the dialog shown on the right. If the codes match, click Connect on the other device to accept the pairing request.

FIGURE 4-9:
Make sure the
code displayed
by your Mac (left)
matches the code
displayed on
the other device
(right).

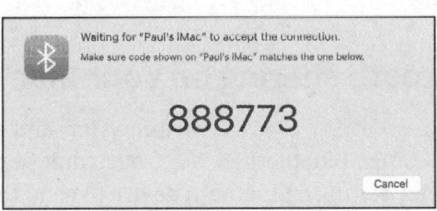
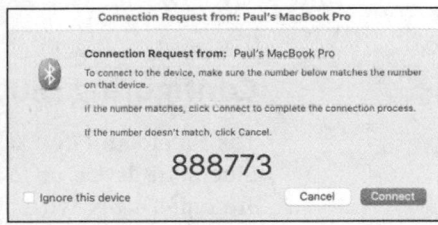

6. **Click the device you want to browse.**

7. **Click Browse.**

8. **Use the browsing dialog that appears to browse the device's folders and files (the ones the device has made available to you, anyway).**

Sending files to a Bluetooth device

If you have some data you want to share with a Bluetooth device, the Bluetooth File Exchange utility is only too happy to help you do it. Here's how it works:

1. **In Finder, choose Go ⇨ Utilities.**

   You can also press Shift+⌘+U. Finder opens the Utilities folder.

2. **Double-click Bluetooth File Exchange.**

   Bluetooth File Exchange displays a file chooser.

3. **If you don't see the file chooser, choose File ⇨ Send File.**

   You can also press ⌘+O.

4. **Choose the file you want to upload and then click Send.**

   The Select Bluetooth Device dialog appears and displays a list of waiting devices.

5. **Click the device to which you want to send the file and then click Send.**

   If your Mac isn't paired with the other device, click the device's Connect button and then follow whatever prompts appear to complete the pairing.

   Bluetooth File Exchange attempts to send the file.

6. **Use the other device's interface to accept the incoming file.**

   For example, you might click Accept if the other device is a Mac configured to display a permission dialog when a Bluetooth device sends a file; see the next section.

Configuring Bluetooth sharing on your Mac

The Bluetooth File Exchange utility is great for browsing and sending stuff to a Bluetooth device or to another Bluetoothed Mac, but what about the other way around? That is, what about getting a Bluetooth device to send things to your Mac? If the Bluetooth device is another Mac, you can crank up Bluetooth File Exchange on that computer and use the techniques from the previous two sections.

However, for any of this to work, you must activate and configure your Mac's Bluetooth Sharing feature. This feature enables other Bluetooth devices to connect to your Mac and specifies what those devices can see and do. To configure how Bluetooth sharing works on your Mac, follow these steps:

1. **Choose ⇨ System Settings or click System Settings on the dock.**

   The System Settings window appears.

2. **Click General.**

3. **Click Sharing.**

4. **Click the Bluetooth Sharing switch on.**

   If macOS asks for a password, enter it and then click Modify Settings.

5. **Click the *i*-in-a-circle (info) to the right of Bluetooth Sharing.**

   The Bluetooth Sharing dialog opens, as shown in Figure 4-10.

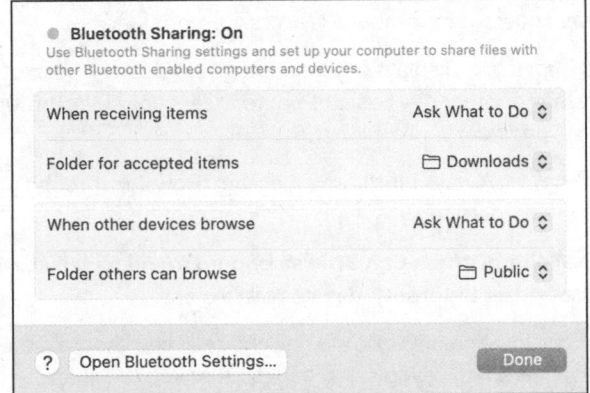

FIGURE 4-10:
Use the Bluetooth Sharing dialog to configure Bluetooth sharing.

6. **Choose one of the following from the When Receiving Items pop-up menu:**

   - *Accept and Save:* Automatically saves any files sent to you through Bluetooth. (I don't recommend this option because someone can send you a malicious application, such as a virus or Trojan Horse, which can wipe out your files when opened.)

   - *Accept and Open:* Automatically saves and opens any files sent to you through Bluetooth. (Again, I don't recommend this option because this — like the preceding option — could automatically run a malicious application sent to your Mac through Bluetooth.)

   - *Ask What to Do:* Displays a dialog that gives you the option of accepting or rejecting a file sent to you through Bluetooth. This option is probably your best choice.

   - *Never Allow:* Always blocks anyone from sending you files through Bluetooth.

7. **Use the Folder for Accepted Items pop-up menu to choose where you want macOS to save the files sent to your Mac via Bluetooth.**

   The default location of Downloads is a good choice. If you choose Other, a chooser dialog appears, letting you navigate to and click a folder where you want to store any files sent to you through Bluetooth.

8. **Choose one of the following from the When Other Devices Browse pop-up menu:**

   - *Always Allow:* Automatically gives nearby Bluetooth devices access to folders you share in Step 9. (I don't recommend this setting because you might never know when someone is accessing your Mac.)

   - *Ask What to Do:* Displays a dialog that gives you the option of accepting or rejecting another device's attempt to access your Mac through Bluetooth. This is probably your best bet.

   - *Never Allow:* Always blocks anyone from browsing through your Mac by using Bluetooth.

9. **Use the Folder Others Can Browse pop-up menu to select which folder on your Mac other Bluetooth devices can access.**

   The default location of Public is a fine choice. If you choose Other, a chooser dialog appears, letting you select a folder that you can share.

10. **Click the close icon or choose System Settings ⇨ Quit System Settings.**

IN THIS CHAPTER

» **Sharing files without having to email them**

» **Accessing files and folder over your network**

» **Sharing a printer on your network**

» **Letting other people see your screen**

» **Controlling another Mac remotely**

Chapter **5**

Sharing Files and Resources on a Network

Many home and small office networks exist for no other reason than to share a broadband internet connection. The designated administrator of such a network attaches a broadband modem to a router, configures the router, sets up a wireless network, and then never thinks about the network again.

There's nothing wrong with this scenario, of course, but there's something that just feels, well, *incomplete* about such a network. Sharing an internet connection is a must for any modern network, but networking should be about sharing so much more: disk drives, folders, documents, music, photos, videos, printers, scanners, and more.

This expanded view of networking is about working, playing, and connecting with your fellow network users. It is, in short, about *sharing*, and sharing is the subject of this chapter. You learn how to access those network resources that others have shared, and you learn how to share your own resources with the network. You also expand your sharing repertoire by learning how to share your printer and how to access printers other network citizens have shared. Finally, you also explore your

Mac's powerful screen-sharing capabilities, which enable people to access your Mac's screen from another network computer and enable you to control another Mac over the network.

Sharing Files and Folders with Folks from Afar

The most common items that people share once they have a network up and running are files and folders. This makes sense because networks are all about collaboration, which means enabling multiple people to work (or play) with stuff you create and vice versa. That stuff exists in the form of files stored in folders, so you can give other people access to some of your Mac's things by sharing either a specific file or by sharing an entire folder. You share files by using AirDrop and you share folders by using your wireless or wired network.

Sharing files by using AirDrop

The most straightforward way to share a file with someone is to send that person a copy of the file. You can do it via email (see Book 2, Chapter 3), text message (see Book 2, Chapter 5), or Bluetooth (see Book 3, Chapter 4). But if the other person is running a Mac, the easiest way to get that file from here to there is via AirDrop, which sends the file "over the air" using a temporary network connection set up between the two Macs.

For AirDrop to work, both Macs must

>> Be on the same Wi-Fi network

>> Have Bluetooth turned on

>> Be within about 30 feet (around 9 meters) of each other

>> Have AirDrop enabled

In that last item, *enabled* means you've configured AirDrop to allow connections from other users. I show you how to configure AirDrop in a moment, but you should know that you have three options:

>> **No One:** You don't allow any AirDrop connections (that is, AirDrop is disabled).

>> **Contacts only:** You allow AirDrop connections only from people who have an Apple ID and that Apple ID's email address (or phone number) is in your

Contacts app. For this to work, both you and the other person must also be signed in to iCloud.

» **Everyone:** You allow AirDrop connections from anyone who meets the requirements I just listed.

To configure AirDrop, macOS gives you three methods: System Settings, Control Center, and the AirDrop window.

Configure AirDrop via System Settings

To configure AirDrop via System Settings, follow these steps:

1. **Click the System Settings icon on the dock (or choose ⌘ ⇨ System Settings).**

The System Settings window appears.

2. **Click General.**

3. **Click AirDrop & Handoff.**

4. **Use the AirDrop pop-up menu (see Figure 5-1) to select the AirDrop option you prefer (No One, Contacts Only, or Everyone).**

For info on the AirPlay settings in this pane, see "Sharing Audio and Video," later in this chapter.

5. **Click the close icon or choose System Settings ⇨ Quit System Settings.**

FIGURE 5-1:
In System Settings, use the AirDrop pop-up menu to configure AirDrop.

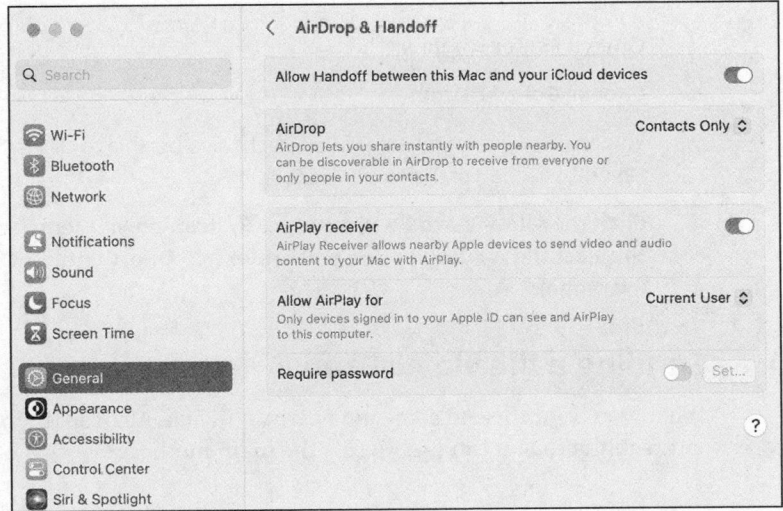

Configure AirDrop via Control Center

To configure AirDrop via Control Center, click Control Center in your Mac's menu bar, click AirDrop to display the window shown in Figure 5-2, and then do one of the following:

>> **Disable AirDrop:** Click the AirDrop switch off.

>> **Enable AirDrop:** Click either Contacts Only or Everyone.

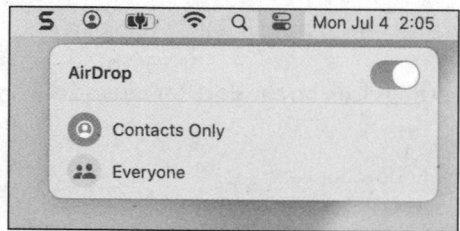

FIGURE 5-2:
In Control Center, click AirDrop to see this window.

TIP You can access the AirDrop settings also from the menu bar. To set this up, open System Settings, click Control Center, click AirDrop, and then click Show in Menu Bar. You can now click the menu bar's AirDrop icon to see the window shown in Figure 5-2.

Configure AirDrop via the AirDrop window

To configure AirDrop via the AirDrop window, follow these steps:

1. **Open a Finder window.**

2. **Choose Go ⇨ AirDrop.**

   You can also press Shift+⌘+R. You might also be able to click AirDrop in the Favorites section of the Finder sidebar.

3. **Click the Allow Me to Be Discovered By drop-down menu (see Figure 5-3) to select the AirDrop option you prefer (No One, Contacts Only, or Everyone).**

Sending a file via AirDrop

When you want to send someone nearby a file via AirDrop, there are a few different techniques you can use. Here's the main method:

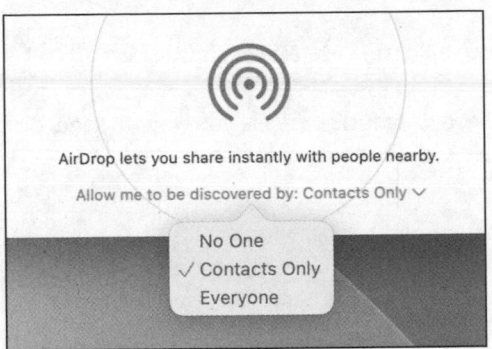

FIGURE 5-3:
In Finder's
AirDrop window,
use the Allow
Me to Be
Discovered By
drop-down menu
to configure
AirDrop.

1. **Open a Finder window.**

2. **Choose Go ⇨ AirDrop.**

   You can also press Shift+⌘+R. You might also be able to click AirDrop in the Favorites section of the Finder sidebar.

   You see the contact photos or other images of the other Mac users who have AirDrop enabled; likewise, they see you only if you have AirDrop enabled. You might also see icons for your other Apple devices, such as your iPhone or iPad; see Figure 5-4.

3. **Choose File ⇨ New Finder Window.**

4. **In the new window, locate the file you want to transfer.**

5. **Drag the file into the AirDrop window and drop it on the icon of the person or device to which you want to transfer the file.**

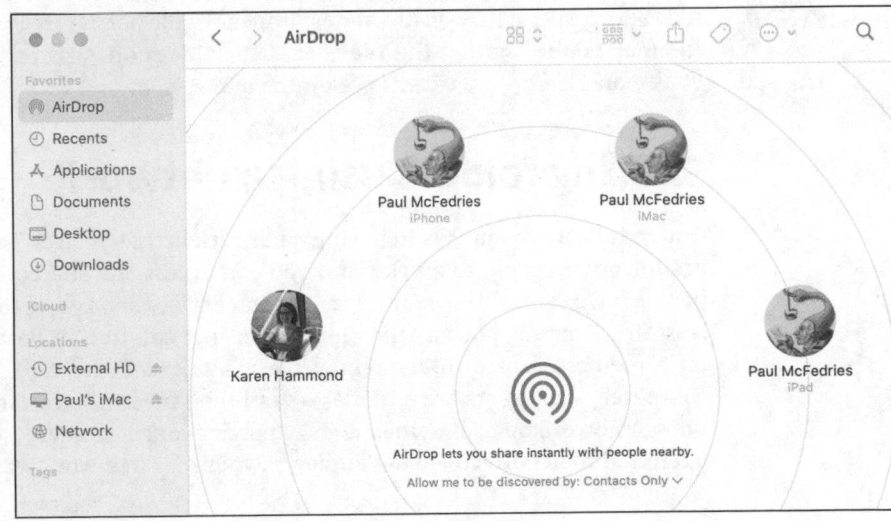

FIGURE 5-4:
Potential
recipients of
AirDrop.

Alternatively, you can also use your Mac's share sheet:

» In any Finder window, right-click the file you want to send, click Share, click AirDrop, and then click the name of the person to whom you want to ship the file.

» In any app that supports sharing, open the file you want to send, click the escaping arrow (share), which is usually found in the app's toolbar or sidebar, click AirDrop, and then click the name of the person to whom you want to send the file.

Receiving a file via AirDrop

AirDrop is a two-way street, meaning that as long as you have AirDrop enables on your Mac, other nearby AirDrop users can send you files, too. When someone attempts to AirDrop you something, you see a notification like the one shown in Figure 5-5. Click Accept if you want to receive the file or click Decline if you don't.

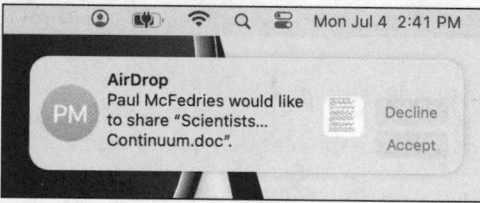

FIGURE 5-5: You see a notification like this when someone tries to AirDrop you a file.

TECHNICAL STUFF

In AirDrop, you don't have to worry about security. AirDrop automatically encrypts files and creates a *firewall* (an almost impenetrable barrier) between your Mac and the Mac you're sharing the file with. Other Macs on AirDrop can only see that you're on AirDrop; they can't peek into your Mac.

Sharing folders using a network

One of the big advantages to having a network is that you can set up shared folders for other people to access, and you can access the shared folders that other people have set up. This feature is so much easier than trying to share data using less direct means, such as the old sneaker-net solution. (That is, place the files on a memory card or other removable media, walk the card over to the other computer — sneakers are optional — and then insert the card in the other computer.) For example, if someone on your network has shared a folder, you can open that folder directly using Finder on your Mac and work with the files.

Sharing data over the network is different from AirDrop in a few ways:

>> With network sharing, you share folders, not individual files.

>> On the network, your Mac doesn't have to be close to the Mac you want to share your stuff with.

>> You have more control over the type of access you want others on the network to have to your shared folder.

>> Your Mac and the Macs you want to share with have to be on the same network, but it can be a wired or wireless network. Also, Bluetooth is not required.

When your Mac is connected to a network, you have the option of sharing one or more folders with everyone else on the network. To share folders, you need to define different permission levels — *privileges* — that allow or restrict what users can do with a folder and the files inside it. The following permission options are available for each computer user and group:

>> **Read & Write:** The user can view, retrieve, edit, and delete files, as well as add files to the folder.

>> **Read Only:** The user can view and open files but can't make any changes to the files or to the folder.

>> **Write Only (Drop Box):** The user can add files to the folder but can't see any files stored in that folder.

>> **No Access:** The user is blocked from accessing files in the shared folder.

You decide which folder(s) to share, who can access that folder, and what access level you want others to have in accessing your shared folder.

Each user on your Mac has their own Public folder, which is created automatically when the user is added, and this folder also comes with a Drop Box folder. By default, any user can add files to and retrieve files from someone else's Public folder (Read & Write privileges). Also, every user can place files in the Drop Box folder (Write Only [Drop Box] privileges), but other users aren't allow to open the Drop Box folder.

Turning on file sharing

The first step to sharing your files over a network is to turn on file sharing. Follow these steps:

1. **Click the System Settings icon on the dock (or choose ⇨ System Settings).**

The System Settings window appears.

2. **Click General.**

3. **Click Sharing.**

4. **Click the File Sharing switch on (if it's not on already).**

macOS enables file sharing.

TIP

If you plan to continue with the next few sections, save yourself a few mouse clicks and leave the Sharing settings onscreen.

Adding a shared folder

Your Mac automatically shares your Public folder (and the Public folder of each user account on your Mac). To share another folder with the network, follow these steps:

1. **Display the Sharing settings.**

See the preceding section, "Turning on file sharing."

2. **Click the *i*-in-a-circle (info) to the right of File Sharing.**

System Settings displays the File Sharing dialog, which displays a list of Public folders on your Mac. If you have more than one user account set up on your Mac, you see the Public folders for each account, as shown in Figure 5-6.

3. **Click + (add) under the Shared Folders list.**

A folder chooser appears.

4. **Locate and then select the folder you want to share.**

5. **Click Add.**

macOS adds the folder to the Shared Folders list.

In the following section, you see how to grant a user privileges to your shared folders.

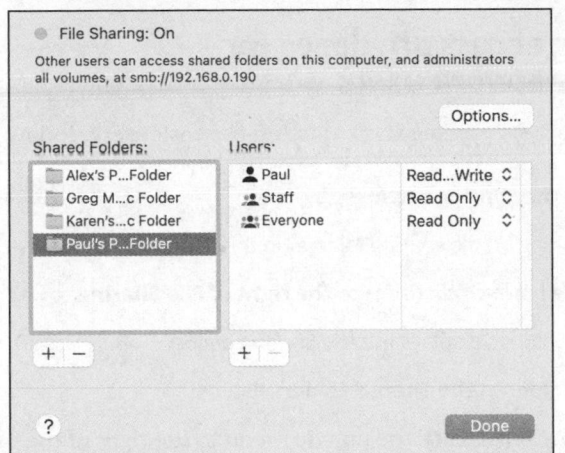

FIGURE 5-6:
The File Sharing
dialog lists your
Mac's public
folders.

REMEMBER

Network mavens tell us that one of the pillars of network security is the *principle of least privilege*. This means you should only share the least that's necessary to get the job done. Don't share an entire folder if the stuff you want to share resides in a subfolder. Don't share a subfolder if you can share a file (say, via AirDrop). Don't provide Read & Write access if Read Only will do. Oversharing can lead to serious problems such as security breaches, file damage, and privacy invasions.

Defining user access to shared folders

After you define one or more folders to share, you can also define the type of access people can have to your shared folders, such as giving certain people the capability to open and modify files and stopping other people from accessing your shared files.

The three types of network users are

- » **Yourself:** Gives you Read & Write access (or else you won't be able to modify any files in your shared folders)

- » **Everyone:** Allows others to access your shared folders as guests without requiring a password

- » **Names of specific network users:** Allows you to give individuals access to your shared folders with a name and a password

If you trust everyone on a network, you can give everyone Read & Write privileges to your shared folders. However, it's probably best to give everyone Read Only privileges and only certain people Read & Write privileges.

Changing access privileges for existing network users

To redefine access privileges for existing network users, follow these steps:

1. **Display the Sharing settings.**

   See "Turning on file sharing," earlier in this chapter.

2. **Click the *i*-in-a-circle (info) to the right of File Sharing.**

   System Settings displays the File Sharing dialog.

3. **Click a folder in the Shared Folders list.**

4. **In the Users list, click the pop-up menu to the right of the user you want to modify, and then choose an access option.**

   Your choices are Read & Write, Read Only, Write Only (Drop Box), and No Access, as shown in Figure 5-7.

5. **Repeat Steps 3 and 4 for each shared folder or user you want to configure.**

6. **Click the close icon or choose System Settings ⇨ Quit System Settings.**

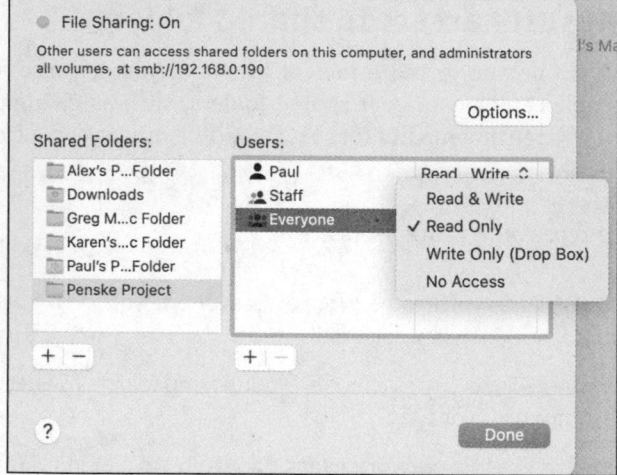

FIGURE 5-7: A user's pop-up menu lets you choose the access privileges for that user.

Giving individuals access to shared folders

The access level you give to the Everyone account for a shared folder means that anyone on the network has that level of access to your files — Read & Write, Read Only, Write Only. You probably want to give Everyone the minimum access (Read Only) to a shared folder and give specific individuals higher levels of access.

To define a username and password to access a shared folder, follow these steps:

1. **Display the Sharing settings.**

   See "Turning on file sharing," earlier in this chapter.

2. **Click the *i*-in-a-circle (info) to the right of File Sharing.**

   System Settings displays the File Sharing dialog.

3. **Click a folder in the Shared Folders list.**

   The Users list enumerates all the people allowed to access this particular shared folder.

4. **Click + (add) under the Users list.**

5. **Click Contacts.**

   Your list of contacts appears.

6. **Scroll through the list and click the name of the person to whom you want to grant privileges and then click Select.**

   The Choose Password dialog appears.

7. **In the Password text box, enter a password.**

   Be careful to note if the caps lock key is or isn't down. This is one area where it matters.

8. **In the Verify text box, reenter the password.**

9. **Click the Create Account button.**

10. **In the dialog that appears, type your Admin password (the one you use to sign in to your Mac) to approve the configuration change and then click Modify Configuration.**

    The person's name appears in the Users list.

11. **Open the Privileges pop-up menu that appears when you click the disclosure arrow to the right of the name you just added to the Users box, and assign access privileges.**

    Your choices are Read & Write, Read Only, or Write Only (Drop Box).

12. **Click Done to close the File Sharing dialog.**

13. **Click the close icon or choose System Settings ⇨ Quit System Settings.**

    macOS also adds the user to the System Settings Users & Groups list as a Sharing Only account.

REMEMBER

Removing accounts from shared folders

If you create an account so that others can access your shared folders, you may later want to revoke that account's access to the folders.

To revoke an account's access to a shared folder, follow these steps:

1. **Display the Sharing settings.**

   See "Turning on file sharing," earlier in this chapter.

2. **Click the *i*-in-a-circle (info) to the right of File Sharing.**

   System Settings displays the File Sharing dialog.

3. **In the Users list, click the user you want to remove.**

4. **Click – under the Users list.**

   A confirmation dialog appears, asking whether you're sure you want to remove the account's access to the shared folder.

5. **Click OK.**

   macOS removes the user from the Users list.

6. **Click Done to close the File Sharing dialog.**

7. **Click the close icon or choose System Settings ⇨ Quit System Settings.**

File sharing in sleep mode

Your Mac can share files even if you set up your Mac to sleep when it's inactive for a certain time. If you want your Mac to wake up when another user on the network wants to access your shared files, follow these steps:

1. **Click the System Settings icon on the dock (or choose ⇨ System Settings).**

   The System Settings window appears.

2. **Click Battery (MacBook) or Energy Saver (desktop Mac).**

3. **For a MacBook, click Options.**

4. **Do one of the following:**

   - *For a MacBook:* Use the Wake for Network Access pop-up menu to select one of the following: Always, Never, or Only on Power Adapter.

   - *For a desktop Mac:* Click the Wake for Network Access switch on.

5. **Click the close icon or choose System Settings ⇨ Quit System Settings.**

Accessing shared folders

You can share your folders with others on a network, and likewise, others may want to share their folders with you. To access a shared folder on someone else's computer, follow these steps:

1. **Open a Finder window.**

2. **Choose Go ⇨ Network.**

You can also press Shift+⌘+K or click Network in the Locations section of the Finder sidebar.

A Network window appears, listing all the computers that offer shared folders, as shown in Figure 5-8.

3. **Double-click the computer you want to access.**

The settings you configured in Sharing come into play based on the user's Apple ID. On that basis, you either get or are denied access.

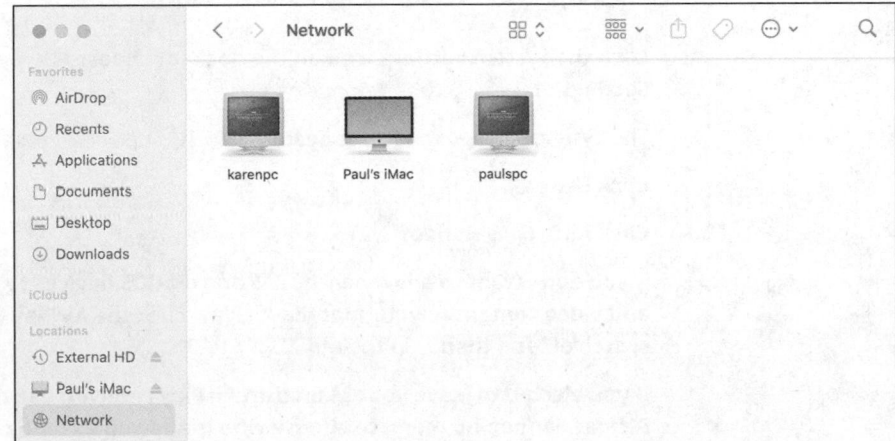

FIGURE 5-8:
The Network window lets you connect to other computers.

REMEMBER

The remote computer's name now appears in the Finder's sidebar, under the Locations heading. When you no longer need access to the computer's shared resources, open a Finder window and click the eject icon that appears to the right of the computer name.

Sharing Audio and Video

Your Mac supports a technology called AirPlay that lets nearby iOS and iPadOS devices send video and audio content to your Mac. So, rather than watching a video on a (relatively) teensy iPhone screen, you (or someone else) can use AirPlay to send that video to your Mac so that it can be watched there. Thankfully, macOS gives you some control over who can do this. You have three choices:

>> **Current User:** Only devices that are signed into your Apple ID are allowed to send AirPlay content to your Mac.

>> **Anyone on the Same Network:** All devices on the same network as your Mac are allowed to send AirPlay content to your Mac.

>> **Everyone:** All nearby devices are allowed to send AirPlay content to your Mac. This is living dangerously, for sure, so if you go this route, you should set up an AirPlay password, as I describe in the steps that follow.

Follow these steps to configure your Mac to use AirPlay:

1. **Click the System Settings icon on the dock (or choose ➪ System Settings).**

   The System Settings window appears.

2. **Click General.**

3. **Click AirDrop & Handoff.**

4. **If you don't want to allow nearby iOS and iPadOS devices to beam audio and video content to your Mac via AirPlay, click the AirPlay Receiver switch off and then skip to Step 7.**

5. **If you elected to leave your Mac as an AirPlay receiver, use the Allow AirPlay For pop-up menu to choose who is allowed to send content to your Mac via AirPlay.**

   As I describe at the beginning of this section, your choices are Current User, Anyone on the Same Network, or Everyone.

6. **If you want to protect your AirPlay with a password (a good idea if you chose Everyone in Step 5), click the Require Password switch on, type the password, and then click OK.**

7. **Click the close icon or choose System Settings ➪ Quit System Settings.**

Sharing Printers

If your Mac is part of a network, one of the big advantages you have is that you can connect a printer to one computer, and the other computers on the network can then use that computer for printing. This feature saves you big bucks because you don't have to supply each computer with its own printer.

REMEMBER

Many printers don't have to be connected to a computer as long as the printer comes with built-in Wi-Fi capabilities. In that case, you connect the printer to your wireless network (your printer's manual will tell you how to do this) and the printer is instantly available to every computer on the same wireless network. Sweet!

Adding a shared network printer

To use a shared network printer, you must first add it to your Mac's list of printers. Follow these steps if the printer is shared on another Mac (see the next section for Windows printers):

1. **Click the System Settings icon on the dock (or choose ⇨ System Settings).**

   The System Settings window appears.

2. **Click Printers & Scanners.**

3. **Click Add Printer, Scanner, or Fax.**

   Your Mac opens the Add Printer dialog, which displays a list of connected printers.

4. **Select the shared printer you want to use.**

   macOS gathers printer information, as shown in Figure 5-9.

5. **Click Add.**

   You can now use a shared network printer.

Adding a shared Windows network printer

If the shared printer you want to use is part of a Windows network, follow these steps to add it to your Mac's list of printers:

1. **Click the System Settings icon on the dock (or choose ⇨ System Settings).**

   The System Settings window appears.

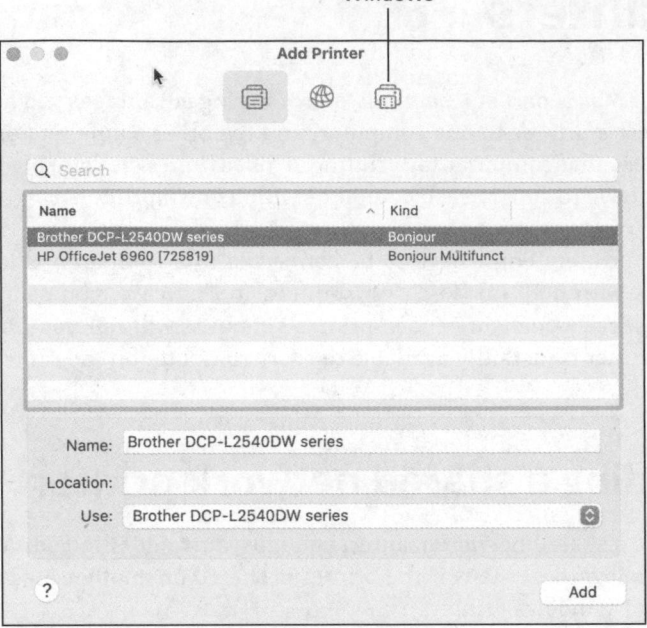

Windows

Add Printer

Q Search

Name		Kind
Brother DCP-L2540DW series		Bonjour
HP OfficeJet 6960 [725819]		Bonjour Multifunct

Name: Brother DCP-L2540DW series

Location:

Use: Brother DCP-L2540DW series

?   Add

FIGURE 5-9:
Click the shared printer you want to use.

2. **Click Printers & Scanners.**

3. **Click Add Printer, Scanner, or Fax.**

   Your Mac opens the Add Printer dialog.

4. **Click the Windows tab (labeled in Figure 5-9).**

5. **Choose the workgroup that contains the computer you want to work with.**

6. **Click the computer with the shared printer you want to add.**

7. **Click Connect and then log on to the Windows computer.**

8. **Click the shared printer you want to use.**

9. **In the Use list, choose Select a Driver to Use and then choose the printer in the list that appears.**

10. **Click Add.**

    You can now use the shared Windows printer.

Sharing your printer with the network

If you have a printer connected to your Mac and you'd generously like other folks on your network to use it, you can share it by following these steps:

1. **Click the System Settings icon on the dock (or choose ⇨ System Settings).**

The System Settings window appears.

2. **Click General.**

3. **Click Sharing.**

4. **Click the Printer Sharing switch on.**

macOS enables printer sharing.

5. **Click the *i*-in-a-circle (info) to the right of Printer Sharing.**

System Settings displays the Printer Sharing dialog, which displays a list of your printers.

6. **Select the check box next to the printer you want to share.**

By default, the Everyone user has Can Print permission, so you don't need to add individual users.

7. **Click Done.**

8. **Click the close icon or choose System Settings ⇨ Quit System Settings.**

Sharing Your Screen

If you're texting with someone who's also using a Mac, you might want to tell the person about a new macOS technique or tell them to modify a setting on their Mac. You could do this using text messages, but it would be much easier and faster if you could somehow operate that person's Mac as if you were there with the person. Surprisingly, Messages lets you do the next best thing: The other person can share their screen, which means not only do you see the other person's Mac but you can also use your mouse and keyboard to control their Mac remotely.

That's pretty awesome, but screen sharing also works the other way. That is, you can invite a person to share your Mac's screen, which enables that person to see what's on your Mac and to control your Mac remotely.

Enabling screen sharing

For you or others to see and work on your Mac from another computer, you need to set up access on your Mac. Follow these steps to do so:

1. **Click the System Settings icon on the dock (or choose ⇨ System Settings).**

   The System Settings window appears.

2. **Click General.**

3. **Click Sharing.**

4. **Click the Screen Sharing switch on.**

   macOS enables screen sharing.

5. **Click the *i*-in-a-circle (info) to the right of Screen Sharing.**

   System Settings displays the Screen Sharing dialog.

6. **Select either of the Allow Access For radio buttons to grant screen sharing privileges to**

   - *All Users,* which allows anyone who sees your Mac on the network or uses the address to access your computer.

   - *Only These Users,* which limits access to the people you add to the list. Click + (add) to add users to the list.

7. **Click the Computer Settings button.**

   A dialog appears enabling you to choose which users may control the screen. Choose one or both of the following options:

   - *Anyone May Request Permission to Control Screen.* Choose this option and anyone you share the screen with can request control of the screen.

   - *VNC Viewers May Control Screen with Password.* Choose this option to enable virtual network computing (VNC) users to control the screen by entering the password you specify in the text field. VNC users access your computer remotely.

8. **Click OK to exit the Computer Settings dialog, and then click Done to close the Screen Sharing dialog.**

9. **Click the close icon or choose System Settings ⇨ Quit System Settings.**

Starting a screen-sharing session with another Mac

After you've enabled screen sharing, you can share your screen with another Mac on the network whose owner has also enabled screen sharing. Sharing a screen is beneficial for educational purposes, such as showing a coworker how to do something. If you've given permission for remote users to control your screen (as I discuss in the preceding section), screen sharing enables the remote user to troubleshoot a problem with your Mac. Screen sharing is also useful for fun things, like sharing a video of your cat preening himself. After enabling screen sharing, a user with permission (again, see the preceding section) can view your screen by doing the following:

1. **Click the Finder icon on the dock and open a new Finder window.**

2. **In the Locations section of the sidebar, click the name of the computer whose screen you want to view.**

   If you don't see the computer in the Locations section, click Network and then double-click the computer in the Network window.

3. **Click the Share Screen button.**

   The other computer's screen appears in a window. The window title bar shows the name of the computer from which the screen is shared. The person sharing the computer can now work on the document or view what is happening on the originating computer.

4. **Choose how you want to interact with the computer that's sharing its screen:**

   You have two options:

   - *Control mode:* You can control the remote Mac with your mouse and keyboard. To enable this mode, choose View ⇨ Switch to Control Mode. You can also click the title bar's control mode icon (mouse pointer inside two concentric circles) or press Option+⌘+X.

   - *Observe mode:* You can only view the screen of the remote Mac. To enable this mode, choose View ⇨ Switch to Observe Mode. You can also click the title bar's observe mode icon (binoculars) or press Option+⌘+X.

   In either mode, the shared screen updates in real time as changes are made on the remote computer.

5. **Choose the desired scaling option:**

- *Zoom In:* Scales the remote shared screen up. Choose View ⇨ Zoom In or click the title bar's scale up icon (magnifying glass with a +).

- *Zoom Out:* Scales the remote shared screen down. Choose View ⇨ Zoom Out or click the title bar's scale down icon (magnifying glass with a –).

- *Actual Size:* Displays the remote shared screen without magnification. Choose View ⇨ Actual Size or click the title bar's actual size icon (magnifying glass with a 1).

6. **To quit screen sharing, choose Screen Sharing ⇨ Quit Screen Sharing.**

Chapter **6**

Maintenance and Troubleshooting

nlike what seems to be the norm with other types of computers (*cough* Windows *cough*), your Mac just works; and it's far less likely to head south on you than most machines out there. However, all computers are complex beasts, and your Mac is as complex as they come. Its excellent design and engineering ensure a mostly trouble-free operation, but it doesn't hurt to do a little preventative maintenance. The techniques addressed in this chapter help ensure that your Mac and the precious data it holds are far less likely to run into trouble.

The good news about Mac problems, if they arise, is that they're relatively rare. The reason for such rarity is a simple one: Application developers and device manufacturers have to build their Mac products only for machines made by a single company. This simplifies things and results in fewer problems — not, however, no problems. As with apps, even in a Mac world, devices sometimes behave strangely or not at all. In this chapter, you also learn some general troubleshooting techniques for hardware woes and also tackle a few specific problems.

Routine Mac Maintenance

Let's get your maintenance chores off to a solid start by examining a few tasks that I describe as *routine,* meaning you ought to perform them regularly to help keep your Mac running smoothly.

Emptying the trash

You might not give a whole lot of thought to the trash icon that's a permanent resident on the right edge of the dock. You delete something, your Mac dutifully tosses it into the trash, and you move on with your life.

However, while you're busy with other things, the trash slowly expands with each new deleted file or folder. After a while, the trash might contain dozens or even hundreds of gigabytes of data. What's the big deal, right? It's just the trash, for goodness' sake! Ah, but the trash is actually a folder on your Mac hard drive. (It's a hidden folder located at /Users/*You*/Trash, where *You* is your username.) So, the more space the trash takes up, the less space you have to store episodes of your favorite shows.

To see just how much space the trash is occupying, follow these steps:

1. **Click the trash icon on the dock.**

   The Trash folder appears.

2. **Choose File ⇨ Get Info.**

   You can also click the gear icon (action) and then click Get Info, or press ⌘+I.

   The Trash Info window appears.

3. **Read the Size value.**

In Figure 6-1, you can see that the trash contains a whopping 34.2 GB of data.

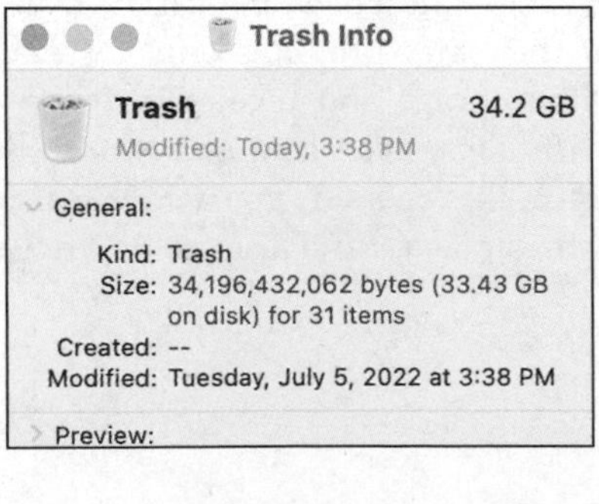

FIGURE 6-1:
The Trash Info window tells you how much hard drive space the trash is currently using.

TECHNICAL STUFF

The sharp-eyed reader might have noticed that in Figure 6-1, the Trash Info window reports 34.2 GB at the top, but the Size value reports "34,196,432,062 bytes (33.43 GB on disk)". What's going on here? First, 34,196,432,062 bytes is approximately 34.2 GB, so that's fine. But why is this 33.43 GB "on disk"? The difference here is a reflection of how files are stored on your Mac's hard drive. Each file is divided into multiple *logical blocks* that are 512 bytes each. Suppose you have a file that contains 513 bytes of data. 512 of those bytes would get stored in one logical block, but the remaining byte would still take up its own full 512-byte logical block. So, in this example, the file would have a size of 513 bytes on disk, but overall it would use up 1,024 total bytes of storage. Repeat this over a large number of files and you can end up with hundreds of megabytes difference and that explains the discrepancy between the two size values shown in Figure 6-1.

So, it makes sense to empty the trash relatively often, perhaps once a month or once every two weeks, depending on how often you delete things. Here's the safe method for taking out the trash:

1. **Click the trash icon on the dock.**

The Trash folder opens.

2. **Examine the Trash files to make sure there's nothing important that you deleted by accident.**

WARNING

Examining the contents of the trash is crucial because once you empty the trash, there's no turning back the clock — all those files are permanently deleted and, unless you have them backed up with Time Machine, there's nothing you can do to get them back.

3. **If you see a file that you don't want deleted, drag the file out of the Trash folder and drop it on the desktop for now.**

After you finish emptying the trash, you can figure out where the rescued file is supposed to go.

4. **Choose Finder ➪ Empty Trash.**

You can also do any of the following:

- Click the Empty button near the upper-right corner of the Finder window.

- Click the action icon and then click Empty Trash.

- Press Shift+⌘+Delete.

Your Mac asks you to confirm.

5. **Click Empty Trash.**

Now, I don't know about you, but after being so careful about making sure I'm not permanently deleting anything important, it bugs me that my Mac asks if I'm sure I want to go through with it. Of course, I'm sure! Fortunately, there are a couple of ways to work around this.

The easiest is to hold down the Option key while you choose Finder ⇨ Empty Trash (or click the Empty button). If your fingers are limber enough, you can also press Option+Shift+⌘+Delete.

A more long-term solution is to tell your Mac not to bother with the confirmation message. Here are the steps to follow to turn off this message:

1. **In any Finder window, choose Finder ⇨ Settings.**

   The Finder Settings window appears.

2. **Click the Advanced button in the toolbar.**

3. **Deselect the Show Warning before Emptying the Trash check box, as shown in Figure 6-2.**

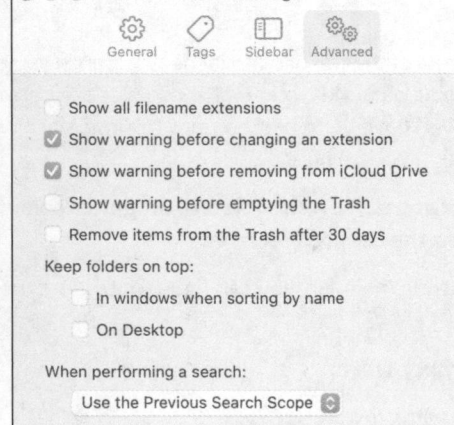

FIGURE 6-2:
To get rid of your Mac's Trash confirmation prompts, deselect the Show Warning before Emptying the Trash check box.

TIP

Rather than try to remember to empty the trash regularly, you can set macOS to do it. In the Advanced tab of the Finder Settings window, select the Remove Items from the Trash after 30 Days check box. Now your Mac will automatically expunge from the trash any item that's been in there for 30 days.

Cleaning up your desktop

The Mac desktop is a handy place to store things, and most Mac users aren't shy about doing just that, so they end up with dozens of icons scattered around the desktop. This isn't a terrible thing, to be sure, but it's not efficient. Once you have more than, say, a dozen icons on your desktop, finding the one you want becomes a real icon-needle-in-a-desktop-haystack exercise.

So, periodically (say once every couple of weeks), you should tidy up your desktop so that you can find things easily and keep the desktop a useful tool. You can do a couple of things:

» **Get rid of any files and folders you absolutely don't need on the desktop:**

- If you're still using the file or folder, move it to the appropriate folder in your user account.

- If you don't need the file or folder anymore, off to the trash it goes.

» **Organize the remaining icons:**

- If you don't care about the order of the icons, click the desktop and then choose View ➪ Clean Up. This lines up all the icons in neat columns and rows based on the desktop's invisible grid.

- If you want to organize the icons by name, click the desktop and then choose View ➪ Sort By ➪ Name (or press Control+Option+⌘+1).

- If you want to apply a tag to related icons, right-click the selection, and then click a tag color. You can then sort the icons by tag: Click the desktop and then choose View ➪ Sort By ➪ Tags (or press Control+Option+⌘+7).

Watching hard drive free space

Although it's true that hard drives are larger than ever these days, it's also true that files are getting larger, too. Music files are almost always multimegabyte affairs; a single half-hour HD TV show can usurp about 1.5GB, and HD movies can be three or four times as large. If you're not careful, it's easy to run out of hard drive space in a hurry.

To prevent that from happening, you should keep an eye on how much free space is left on your Mac's hard drive. One way to do this is to display the Finder status bar by choosing View ➪ Show Status Bar (or press ⌘+/) in any Finder window. Now open any folder on your Mac's hard drive. Finder displays the amount of space available on the hard drive in the status bar at the bottom of the open window.

Another way to check your hard drive's free space is to choose ⇨ System Settings, click General in the sidebar, and then click Storage. At the top of the Storage pane that appears, you see a histogram that shows not only how much free space is available on the hard drive but also the file types that comprise the used space, as shown in Figure 6-3.

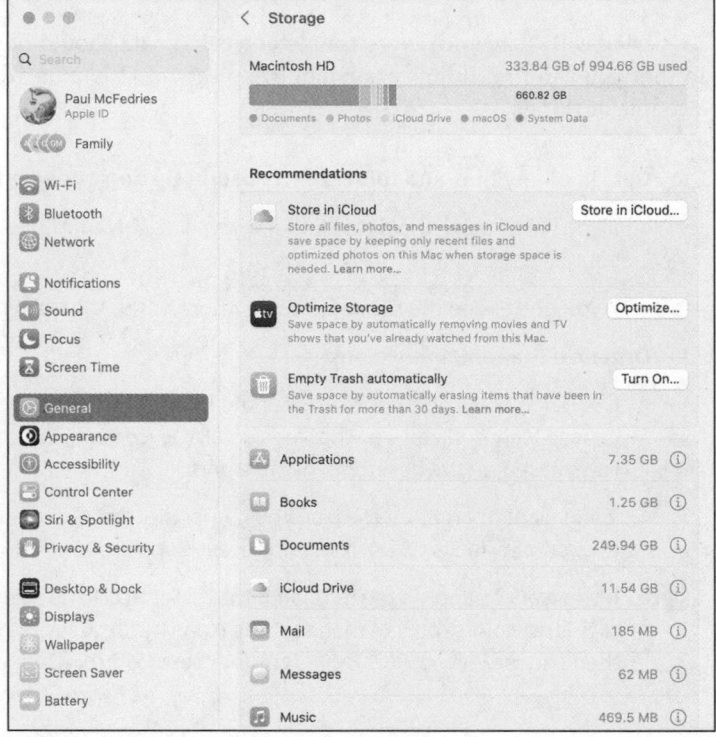

Deleting unneeded files

If you are minding your Mac's hard drive and find that you're running low on free space, you need to start pruning what you no longer need. Sure, you could ramble through your folders willy-nilly and delete a few things here and there, but macOS offers a more robust solution.

First, choose ⇨ System Settings, click General in the sidebar, and then click Storage to display the Storage pane (refer to Figure 6-3). Besides the histogram at the top, the rest of the Storage pane is divided into two sections that you can use to remove stuff from your Mac's hard drive and free up some space:

WARNING

Make sure you have Time Machine running and have at least one full backup completed before you start removing a lot of files from your Mac's hard drive.

>> **Recommendations:** This section includes one or more suggestions that macOS offers for managing and optimizing your hard drive space. The options you see vary depending on the state of your hard drive storage, but you usually get at least the following:

- *Store in iCloud:* Click this button to choose what you'd like to transfer to iCloud. The three options are Desktop and Documents, Photos, and Messages.

- *Optimize Storage:* Click Optimize to configure macOS to automatically remove any movies and TV show episodes that you've already watched.

- *Empty Trash Automatically:* Click Turn On to configure macOS to automatically remove from the Trash folder any items that have been in there for more than 30 days.

>> **Usage:** The rest of the Storage pane is a list of various categories — apps, file types, and other components — that shows the amount of hard drive space that each is using. For each category, you can click the *i*-in-a-circle icon to its right to see a list of the items in that category. From there, you can click an item you no longer need and then click Delete to remove it.

Uninstalling unused apps

To free up some room on your Mac's hard drive, delete any installed apps that you no longer use. The great thing about uninstalling Mac software is that it's just so darn easy: Just drag the app icon from the Applications folder and drop it on the dock's Trash icon. However, the full procedure to reclaim the app's disk space is a bit more involved than that:

1. **In Finder, choose the Applications folder.**

There's a chance the app you want to delete is in the Utilities folder or a folder created by the app's installer, so you may need to open that folder before continuing.

2. **Drag the icon of the app you want to delete and drop the icon on the trash.**

macOS asks for your password to allow the uninstall.

3. **Type your password and then click OK.**

macOS moves the app to the trash.

4. **Click the Trash icon on the dock.**

5. **Right-click the app icon and then click Delete Immediately.**

   macOS asks you to confirm.

6. **Click Delete.**

   macOS removes the app from the trash and frees up the disk space.

REMEMBER Many applications also install files in your user account's Library/Application Support folder or in the Macintosh HD/Library/Application Support folder. Check those locations and delete any folder that belongs to the application you removed.

TIP To navigate to your user account's Library folder, in any Finder window hold down Option and then choose Go ➪ Library. To navigate to the Macintosh HD folder, in any Finder window choose Go ➪ Computer and then open Macintosh HD.

Here's an alternative method that lets your Mac do more of the work:

1. **Choose ➪ System Settings or click the System Settings icon on the Dock.**

   The System Settings window appears.

2. **Click General in the sidebar, and then click Storage.**

3. **Click the *i*-in-a-circle icon to the right of Applications.**

   System Settings displays a list of your Mac's installed apps.

4. **Click the app you want to uninstall and then click Delete.**

   macOS asks you to confirm.

5. **Click Delete.**

   macOS removes the app and frees up the disk space.

Checking the hard drive for errors with First Aid

Hard drives can fall prey to maladies that, although they won't cause the hard drive to push up the daisies, could cause it to behave erratically or even damage files.

For example, your Mac maintains what it calls a Catalog file, which stores the overall structure of the hard drive, including all the folders and files. If that file gets corrupted, it might mean that you or an application can no longer access a folder or file.

You should check your Mac's hard drive for these types of errors every month or so. Here's how:

1. **Click Finder on the dock.**

2. **Choose Applications ⇨ Utilities ⇨ Disk Utility.**

The Disk Utility window appears.

3. **Click Macintosh HD in the list of drives.**

4. **In the toolbar, click First Aid.**

Disk Utility asks you to confirm.

5. **Click Run.**

Disk Utility warns you that your Mac will stop responding during the check.

6. **Say "That's cool" and click Continue.**

Disk Utility begins the check, which takes several minutes.

7. **When the check is complete, click Done.**

Removing login items

When you start your Mac, lots of behind-the-scenes tasks get performed to set up the computer for your use. One of these tasks is that your Mac checks the list of items that are supposed to start automatically when you log in to your user account. These items are usually apps, but they can also be files (in which case macOS opens the file using its associated app), folders, and shared network locations. Appropriately, these items are called *login items*.

Most login items are added by apps because they need some service running right from the get-go, which means that login items are usually quite important. However, not all login items are vital. For example, a login item might be associated with an app you no longer use, or it might open a file or folder that you no longer need at startup.

Whatever the reason, these unneeded login items only serve to slow down your Mac's startup and to consume extra system memory. Therefore, from time to time you should check your user account's login items and remove those you no longer need.

Follow these steps to remove a login item:

1. **Click the System Settings icon on the dock (or choose ⇨ System Settings).**

The System Settings window appears.

2. **Click General.**

3. **Click Login Items.**

   The Login Items pane appears, as shown in Figure 6-4.

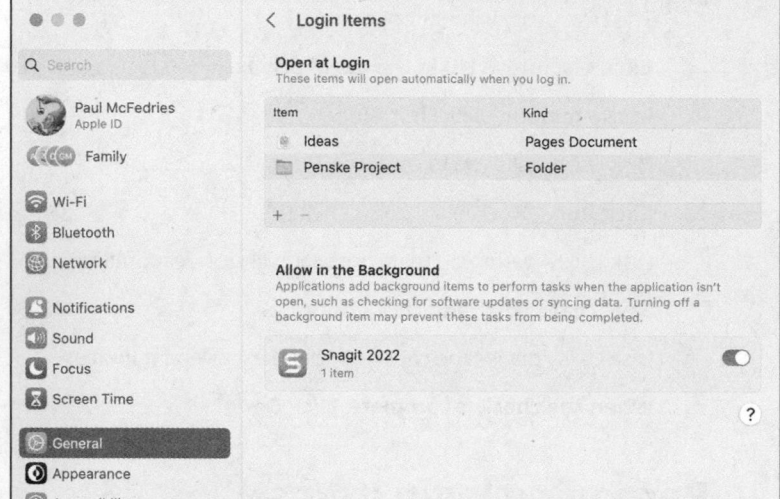

FIGURE 6-4:
The Login Items
pane shows
you the items
that launch
automatically
each time
you log in.

4. **In the Open at Login list of items that open automatically, click the item you no longer need and then click the minus sign (–).**

   macOS removes the login item.

5. **In the Allow in the Background section, click the switch off for any item you don't want to load at login.**

WARNING

   Turn off an app login item only if you're certain you don't need it. Most app login items provide required functionality for the app, so turning off an item might cause the app to behave strangely or crash.

6. **Click the close icon or choose System Settings ⇨ Quit System Settings.**

Cycling your MacBook battery

If you have a MacBook Pro or MacBook Air, your computer comes with an internal battery that enables you to operate the computer without an electrical outlet. The battery also serves as a backup source of power should the electricity fail.

Computing veterans might remember that MacBooks used to have rechargeable nickel metal hydride (NiMH) or nickel cadmium (NiCad) batteries. The NiMH and NiCad types have long been phased out in portable computers because they suffered from a problem called the *memory effect*, where the battery loses capacity if you repeatedly recharge it without first fully discharging it.

The latest MacBooks have rechargeable lithium-polymer batteries, which are lighter and last longer than NiMH and NiCad batteries. Most importantly, lithium-polymer batteries don't suffer from the memory effect.

However, to get the most performance out of your MacBook's battery, you need to cycle it. *Cycling* a battery means letting it completely discharge and then fully recharging it. To maintain optimal performance, you should cycle your Mac's battery once a month or so.

Shutting Down a Crashed App

Apps that always run perfectly may suddenly stop working for no apparent reason, and no matter which keys you press, where you click the mouse, or where you tap the trackpad, nothing happens. Sometimes you might see a spinning cursor (affectionately referred to as the "spinning beach ball of death"), which stays onscreen and refuses to go away until you take steps to unlock the frozen app.

REMEMBER

It's important to understand that I'm talking about a single app crashing, which means that although the app in question is toast, you can still switch to another open app or Finder and continue working. If you can't use *any* open app or clicking anything on the menu bar does nothing, your whole Mac is frozen. To learn how to remedy that more drastic situation, see "Forcing the issue: Making a stuck Mac restart or shut down," later in this chapter.

Sometimes being patient and waiting a few minutes results in the hung-up app resolving whatever was ailing it as though nothing were wrong in the first place. More often, however, the spinning cursor keeps spinning in an oh-so-annoying fashion. To end the torment, you need to *force-quit* the frozen or hung-up app — basically, you shut down the app so that the rest of your Mac can get back to work. To force-quit an app, follow these steps:

1. **Choose ⇨ Force Quit.**

You can also press ⌘+Option+Esc.

macOS displays the Force Quit Applications dialog. Look for the frozen app, which will display *Not Responding* beside it, as shown in Figure 6-5.

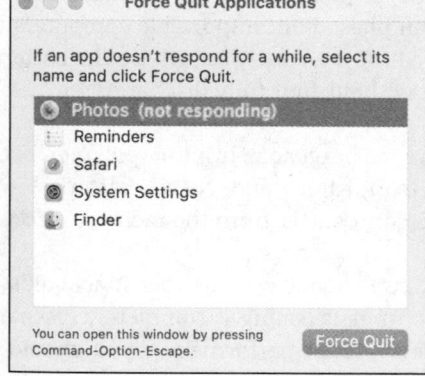

FIGURE 6-5:
Click the lame app and then click Force Quit to put it out of its misery.

2. **Click the non-responsive app and then click Force Quit.**

If Finder isn't responding, click Finder and then click Relaunch.

macOS asks you to confirm.

3. **Click Force Quit.**

If you're rebooting Finder, click Relaunch in the confirmation dialog.

macOS shuts down the frozen app or restarts Finder.

TIP

You can also force-quit a crashed app by right-clicking the app's icon on the dock and then clicking Force Quit from the menu that appears.

General Hardware Troubleshooting Techniques

If you're having trouble with a device attached to your Mac, the good news is that a fair chunk of hardware problems have a relatively limited set of causes, so you may be able to get the device back on its feet by attempting a few tried-and-true remedies that work quite often for many devices. The next few sections take you through these generic troubleshooting techniques.

Basic checklist

If it's not immediately obvious what the problem is, your Mac hardware trouble-shooting routine should always start with these very basic techniques:

>> **Check connections, power switches, and so on:** Some of the most common (and embarrassing) causes of hardware problems are the simple physical things: making sure that a device is turned on; checking that cable connections are secure; and ensuring that insertable devices (such as a USB device) are properly inserted. For example, if you can't access the internet or your network, make sure your network's router is turned on, and make sure that the network cable between your modem and your router (if you have separate devices) is properly connected.

>> **Replace the batteries:** Wireless devices such as keyboards and mice really chew through batteries, so if either one is working intermittently or not at all, always try replacing the batteries to see if that solves the problem.

>> **Turn the device off and then on again:** You *power cycle* a device by turning it off, waiting a few seconds for its internal state to reset (meaning that its capacitors fully discharge or its dynamic volatile memory clears or both), and then turning it back on again. You'd be amazed how often this simple procedure can get a device back up and running. Of course, not all devices have an on/off switch, but this technique works well for devices such as

external displays, printers, scanners, routers, switches, modems, many USB and Thunderbolt devices, and some wireless devices such as mice and keyboards. Many wireless mice have a reset button on the bottom, while some keyboards — notably the Apple Magic Keyboard — have an on/off switch. USB and Thunderbolt devices often get their power directly from the USB or Thunderbolt port. Power cycle these devices by unplugging them and then plugging them back in.

TIP

If you're getting a network error or you can't access the internet, the router may be at fault. Power off the router and then power it on again. Wait until the status lights stabilize and then try accessing the network. If you still can't access the internet, try the same thing with your modem.

>> **Close all apps:** If you have lots of apps going, device drivers (the little programs that enable macOS to communicate with devices, and vice versa) may get weird because there isn't enough memory or other resources. You can often fix flaky behavior by shutting down all your open apps and starting again.

>> **Log out:** Logging out serves to clear the memory by shutting down your apps, but it also releases much of the stuff your Mac has loaded into memory, thus creating a slightly cleaner palette than just closing your apps. To log out, choose ➪ Log Out *User*, where *User* is your Mac username, or press Shift+⌘+Q.

>> **Reset the device's default settings:** If you can configure a device, perhaps some new setting is causing the problem. If you recently made a change, try returning the setting to its original value. If that doesn't do the trick, most configurable devices have some kind of Restore Default Settings option that enables you to quickly return the device to its factory settings.

>> **Upgrade the device's firmware:** Most devices come with *firmware,* a small program that runs inside the device and controls its internal functions. For example, all routers have firmware. Check with the manufacturer to see if a new version exists. If it does, download the new version and see the device's manual to learn how to upgrade the firmware.

>> **Erase your Mac:** As an option of last resort, you can revert your Mac to its factory settings. This means that you completely erase all your Mac's content, settings, apps, and user accounts (and their data). This is a drastic move, so make sure you have a backup of your system (see Book 3, Chapter 1). To erase your Mac, choose ➪ System Settings, click General, click Transfer or Reset, and then click Erase All Contents and Settings. Enter your Mac administrator credentials and click Unlock to open Erase Assistant. Follow the onscreen prompts to erase your Mac.

TIP

I highly recommend erasing your Mac if you're going to sell it or give it to someone else.

Restarting your Mac

If a hardware device is having a problem with some system files, logging off your Mac won't help because the system files remain loaded. By rebooting the system, you reload the entire system, which is often enough to solve many computer problems. You reboot your Mac by choosing ➪ Restart. Click Restart when macOS asks you to confirm (or do nothing and your Mac restarts itself after a minute's delay).

Power cycling your Mac

For problem devices that don't have a power switch — basically, anything inside your Mac, including the display on your iMac or MacBook — restarting your Mac might not resolve the problem because the devices remain powered up the whole time. You can power cycle these devices as a group by power cycling the Mac:

1. **Close all running apps.**

2. **Choose ➪ Shut Down.**

   macOS asks you to confirm.

3. **Click Shut Down.**

4. **After your Mac shuts off, wait for 30 seconds to give all its capacitors (internal doodads that store electric charge) time to discharge.**

5. **Turn the Mac back on.**

Forcing the issue: Making a stuck Mac restart or shut down

If things go seriously awry on your Mac, you may find that you can't do *anything*: Your apps and macOS itself are frozen solid. You can bang away at the keyboard all you want but nothing happens; the mouse pointer doesn't even budge when you move the mouse or slide a finger along the trackpad. That's a major-league lockup you've got there, and your only recourse is to force your Mac to restart or shut down:

>> **Forcing your Mac to restart:** Hold down the Control and ⌘ keys and then press the power button.

>> **Forcing your Mac to shut down:** Press and hold down the power button until the Mac shuts off.

Every once in a great while, you can't even force your Mac to restart or shut down. Meaning you attempt the techniques in this section, your Mac's screen goes black, but it never really shuts down. When that happens, and you have an iMac, Mac mini, Mac Pro, or other desktop Mac that doesn't have an internal battery, your only option is to yank out the power cable.

WARNING

As you might expect, forcing your Mac to restart or shut down doesn't give you any graceful way to close your running apps, so if you have unsaved changes in any open documents, you lose those changes. Therefore, it's a good idea to make sure your Mac is frozen and not just in a temporary state of suspended animation while it's waiting for some lengthy process to finish. If you're not sure, wait five minutes before forcing the restart or shutdown.

Restarting your Mac in safe mode

Login items — apps that run automatically when you log in to your Mac — can cause system problems by using up resources and creating memory conflicts. However, they're not the only behind-the-scenes components that can make your system wig out. Other processes used by your Mac and by your applications can run amok and cause trouble.

To see whether such a process is at the root of your problem, you can perform a *safe boot:* starting your Mac in safe mode, which means that it doesn't load most of those behind-the-scenes components. If the problem persists even in safe mode, you know it's not caused by a hidden process. If the problem does go away, it's a bit harder to deal with because there's no way to disable individual components. You may need to reinstall macOS.

Follow these steps to perform a safe boot:

1. **Choose ⟹ Shut Down.**

   Your Mac asks if you're sure you want to shut down.

2. **Click Shut Down.**

   Your Mac logs you out and then shuts off.

3. **Press and hold down the power button until you see the text *Loading Startup Options*.**

   If you have an Intel-based Mac, press the power button to turn on your Mac, immediately press and hold down the Shift key until you see the login screen with the words *Safe Boot* in the menu bar, and then skip to Step 6.

   After a few seconds, you see an icon for each of your Mac's startup disks (this will usually be just Macintosh HD) and an Options button.

4. **Click Macintosh HD.**

5. **Hold down the Shift key and then click Continue in Safe Mode.**

Your Mac reboots once again, but this time it loads with only a minimal set of components. When you get to the login screen, you see the words *Safe Boot* on the menu bar.

6. **Log in to your Mac.**

Check to see if the problem is still present. If it is, continue with the trouble-shooting techniques in the following sections.

TIP

When you get to the desktop, macOS gives you no indication that it's currently in safe mode, which can be disconcerting. To check that your Mac really did boot into safe mode, choose ⇨ System Settings, click General, click About, and then click System Report to open the System Information utility. In the sidebar, click Software. In the System Software Overview list, check out the value for Boot Mode. If it says *Safe*, you know your Mac is running in safe mode. (If it says *Normal* instead, scratch your head in perplexity and then try running the preceding steps again.)

Starting your Mac using the Recovery app

If you're having trouble starting your Mac, you can boot into Recovery, which is an app that gives you access to various tools that you can use to get your Mac back on its digital feet. When you boot into Recovery, you see a menu with the following tools:

» **Restore from Time Machine:** Enables you to perform a system restore from a Time Machine backup

» **Reinstall macOS *Version*:** Enables you to install a new copy of your current *Version* of macOS

» **Safari:** Launches Safari so you can seek troubleshooting help on the web

» **Disk Utility:** Opens Disk Utility, which you can use to repair or erase a disk

This menu is part of the Recovery app, which you see on the menu bar. The Utilities menu also contains the following tools:

» **Startup Security Utility:** Enables you to set security policies for your Mac's startup disk.

» **Terminal:** Launches a Terminal session, which enables you to change settings via the command line. This one's for experts only!

>> **Share Disk:** Shares your Mac's hard drive with another Mac connected using a USB or Thunderbolt cable. This tool enables you to use the other Mac to troubleshoot your Mac's hard drive.

Here are the steps to follow to boot your Mac into the Recovery app:

1. **If your Mac is running, choose ⇨ Shut Down and then click Shut Down when macOS asks you to confirm.**

2. **Press and hold down the power button until you see the text *Loading Startup Options*.**

   After a few seconds, you see an icon for each of your Mac's startup disks (this will usually be just Macintosh HD) and an Options button.

   If you have an Intel-based Mac, press the power button to turn on your Mac, immediately press and hold down ⌘+R until you see the macOS Utilities dialog, and then skip Step 3.

3. **Click Options and then click Continue.**

   Your Mac boots into the Recovery app.

From here, either click a menu option and then click Continue, or use the Recovery app's menu bar to select a utility to run.

Repairing the hard drive

If your Mac won't start or if an application freezes, it's possible that an error on the main hard drive is causing the problem. To see if this is the case, you need to repair the hard drive using your Mac's Disk Utility app.

How are you supposed to do that if you can't even start your Mac? Good question! The answer is that you need to boot your Mac into the Recovery app (which I explain in the preceding section). You then run Disk Utility from the Recovery app's menu, and that enables you to repair your main hard drive.

REMEMBER

Even if you can start your Mac, you still need to boot to Recovery because you can't repair the main hard drive while it's being used by your Mac.

Follow these steps to repair your hard drive:

1. **Reboot your Mac into the Recovery app.**

   See "Starting your Mac using the Recovery app," earlier in this chapter.

2. **In the main menu, click Disk Utility and then click Continue.**

   Disk Utility opens.

3. **In the sidebar on the left of the Disk Utility window, click the hard drive you want to repair.**

4. **Choose File ➪ Run First Aid.**

   You can also click First Aid in the Disk Utility toolbar.

   Disk Utility asks you to confirm.

5. **Click Run.**

   Disk Utility checks the disk and fixes any problems that it finds.

Ideally, Disk Utility reports that your Mac's hard drive "appears to be OK." In the worst-case scenario, Disk Utility reports that it found errors but can't fix them. In that case, you need to turn to a more heavy-duty solution: a third-party disk repair application. I recommend these two: DiskWarrior (www.alsoft.com) and TechTool Pro (www.micromat.com).

Mac Hardware Problems (and Their Solutions)

The generic troubleshooting and repair techniques covered so far can solve all kinds of problems. However, there are always specific problems that require specific solutions. The rest of this chapter takes you through a few of the most common ones.

Your Mac won't start

Few problems are as frustrating as a Mac that can't get on its feet. Here are some ideas for troubleshooting this most vexing problem:

» **Check your connections:** If your Mac won't even turn on, make sure the power cord is properly connected at both ends. Also, if the power cord is plugged into a power bar or surge protector, make sure that device is turned on.

» **Unplug a desktop Mac:** If a desktop Mac freezes during startup, power it down, unplug the power cord, wait 30 seconds, plug the cord back in, and then try starting the Mac.

» **Remove all nonessential devices:** Disconnect everything from your Mac except the keyboard and mouse. Ideally, replace a third-party mouse and keyboard with the original Apple devices. If your Mac starts successfully, one of the disconnected devices is likely the culprit. Reconnect the devices one at a time, restarting each time you connect another device. If after connecting one of the devices your Mac refuses to start, that last device is the problem.

>> **Try a safe mode boot and then restart:** One of the things a safe mode boot does is delete the cache that your Mac uses for storing fonts to improve performance. If that cache gets corrupted, it could cause startup headaches, so trashing the cache might do the trick.

>> **Repair the hard drive:** A hard drive problem could be causing your startup woes, so boot to the Recovery app device and repair the hard drive (see "Repairing the hard drive," earlier in this chapter).

Your Mac tells you that you don't have enough memory

Macs don't run out of memory very often, but it can happen, particularly if you work with large files or many apps at once and your Mac doesn't have tons of RAM. Here are some things to try if your Mac is low on RAM:

>> **Close large files:** If you have any extremely large files open, try closing them.

>> **Close running apps:** Shut down any apps that you don't need.

TIP

One common cause for low RAM on a Mac is when you have a number of apps running that you don't know about. How can that happen? One way is to think you've shut down an application because you closed that application's window — however, the application remains in memory. Check the dock and see if it shows any running apps that you thought you'd closed. If you see any, right-click the icon and then click Quit.

>> **Log out:** Logging out should help a lot because it shuts down all your open applications and documents.

>> **Restart your Mac:** Restarting your Mac is the ultimate way to clear out RAM and get a fresh start.

Your Mac runs slowly

All Mac users want their Macs to be as speedy as the first day they got them, but sometimes that's not the case. If you find that your Mac has that molasses-in-January thing going, you can try a few things before you consider pulling out your hair.

Sudden slowdown

If the slowdown is a recent and relatively sudden phenomenon, it suggests one of the following remedies:

>> **Shut down some running apps:** It's possible that you have too many apps running, which is causing your Mac to constantly swap data between RAM and the hard drive's virtual memory, which can really slow things down.

>> **Look for a runaway application in Activity Monitor:** In any Finder window choose Go ⇨ Utilities ⇨ Activity Monitor. In the Activity Monitor window, click the CPU tab, and then examine the values in the % CPU column and look for a process that's using up a large percentage of the CPU time. (The processes are sorted by % CPU in descending order, so anything that's gobbling up large chucks of CPU time will appear at the top of the process list.) Here a "large percentage" would mean between over 80 percent. If you see such a process, shut it down (by clicking the process and then clicking the X-in-a-circle on the toolbar).

TIP

Processes often use a big chunk of CPU time temporarily (say, for a few seconds) and then return to normal. So, before shutting down a process, give it a bit of time to see if its CPU hogging is just a temporary thing.

>> **Uninstall a recently installed app:** If the slowdown coincided with a recent app installation, try uninstalling the app by dragging it to the trash.

>> **Repair the hard drive:** Some hard drive file system woes can cause system-wide slowdowns, so try a disk repair to see if that helps fix the problem (see "Repairing the hard drive," earlier in this chapter).

Gradual slowdown

If your Mac has been getting slower gradually, the usual cause is the accumulation over time of apps, widgets, add-ons, and other bric-a-brac that slowly take their toll on system performance. Here are some items to consider when trying to alleviate the slowdown:

>> **Applications:** Installed applications often load files at startup, so they may take up precious resources even when you're not using them. Uninstall any application that you no longer use.

>> **Login items:** Remove as many as you can, as described earlier in the "Removing login items" section.

If your Mac is still sluggish after all this pruning, it's likely that your system just doesn't have enough RAM. If you have a Mac that can be upgraded with more memory, consider taking your Mac to the Genius Bar or your local Mac shop to add more RAM.

Your mouse or keyboard doesn't work

Your mouse and keyboard are your sole connections with your Mac, so if they don't work, you're pretty much stuck. Even if just one of these devices goes on the fritz, using your Mac is next to impossible because few Mac operations can be performed using only one input device. Here are some suggested remedies to try in the face of recalcitrant input devices:

>> **Wait for a bit:** Sometimes it only *seems* as though the mouse or keyboard is stuck when, in fact, it's waiting for some process to finish. Leave the devices be for a bit (particularly the keyboard; banging away on the keys won't solve anything) and then see if they respond.

>> **Disconnect and reconnect:** If you're using a USB mouse or keyboard, disconnect the device, wait a short while (5 or 10 seconds is fine), and then reconnect the device.

>> **Try a different port:** If you're using a USB mouse or keyboard, disconnect the device and then plug it into a different USB port. If the device works now, your USB port may be faulty.

>> **Connect directly to the Mac:** If you're using a USB mouse or keyboard and the device is attached to a USB hub, disconnect the device from the hub and connect it to a USB port on your Mac. If the device works now, your USB hub might be on the fritz.

>> **Try another device:** If you have a spare mouse or keyboard lying around, try connecting it to your Mac. If it works, the original mouse or keyboard is broken.

>> **Turn it on:** If you're using a Bluetooth mouse or keyboard, make sure the device is turned on.

>> **Change the batteries:** If you're using a Bluetooth mouse or keyboard, try a fresh set of batteries.

>> **Pair the device again:** If you're using a Bluetooth mouse or keyboard, try pairing the device and your Mac once again.

>> **Restart:** Rebooting your Mac might just solve the problem.

Your display is garbled

If your display suddenly goes haywire a number of things could be the problem, but the following four are the most common:

>> **It's a temporary glitch:** This is the usual cause of a wonky display, and you solve it by restarting your Mac. Because you can't see the Mac desktop, your mouse is no good to you, so you need to use the keyboard. First press Shift+⌘+Q to log out. If that doesn't work, hold down the Control and ⌘ keys and then press the power button to force your Mac to restart.

>> **For an external display, there's a loose connection:** If your Mac is connected to an external display, check the connection on the Mac end and on the monitor end. If the connector is loose, plugging it in properly should fix the problem right away. If not, turn the monitor off and then turn it back on again.

>> **The display is using improper settings:** If your display somehow gets set to a resolution that it can't handle, you'll see a distorted screen image. To solve this problem, restart your Mac in safe mode, choose ⌘ ➪ System Settings, click Displays, and then use the Resolution pop-up menu to select Default for Display.

>> **The display shows white on black instead of the usual black on white:** This is actually a feature of the Mac's Accessibility settings, and you (or another user) may have turned it on accidentally. Choose ⌘ ➪ System Settings, click Accessibility, click Display, and then click the Invert Colors switch off. If that's not the problem, dark mode might be active. To switch to light mode, choose ⌘ ➪ System Settings, click Appearance in the sidebar, and then click Light.

4
Using Your Mac as a Media Center

Contents at a Glance

Chapter **1**

Tuning In and Listening with Music

What do your Mac and the mullet hairstyle have in common? Both can be described as "business up front, party in the back." When it comes to doing business, your Mac has you covered with apps such as Contacts, Calendar, Pages, Keynote, and Numbers, all of which I describe in detail in Book 5 (titled, appropriately enough, "Taking Care of Business").

But if it's partying you want, well, some would say that's where your Mac *really* shines, thanks to its prowess as a media machine. With apps such as Music, Podcasts, News, TV, Books, and Photos at your service, you have endless ways to waste time, er, I mean, keep yourself entertained and informed.

The chapters here in Book 4 take you on tours of each of your Mac's main media apps. In this chapter, you explore the Music app from Adele to ZZ Top. You travel around the Music window and then get the party started by learning how to listen to your music. You also delve into setting up playlists, either manually or by letting Music's Genius feature do it for you. You also learn how to listen to radio and use the iTunes Store so you can add other media to your Mac — so have your Apple ID handy.

Getting Comfy with the Music App

You use the Music app to play, organize, and stream songs, albums, and playlists. Music also enables you to access the Apple Music service, which with a subscription enables you to enjoy music from Apple's huge library — over 90 million songs as I type these words — and listen to radio by clicking the Radio link in the Apple Music section in the sidebar.

TIP

Apple offers a month-long free trial of Apple Music so you can kick the tires a bit to see if it's worth the subscription fee. As I write this, Apple is also offering six months of free Apple Music when you purchase one of the following audio devices: any AirPods Pro, AirPods (2nd generation and 3rd generation), AirPods Max, HomePod, HomePod mini, Beats Fit Pro, Beats Studio Buds, Powerbeats, Powerbeats Pro, or Beats Solo Pro.

You crank up the Music app by clicking the Music icon (pointed out in Figure 1-1) on the dock. Figure 1-1 shows the Music window that appears and points out a few notable features.

The Music window has three sections: the sidebar, the toolbar, and the content area. The next three sections take a closer look at each feature.

Content area   Toolbar

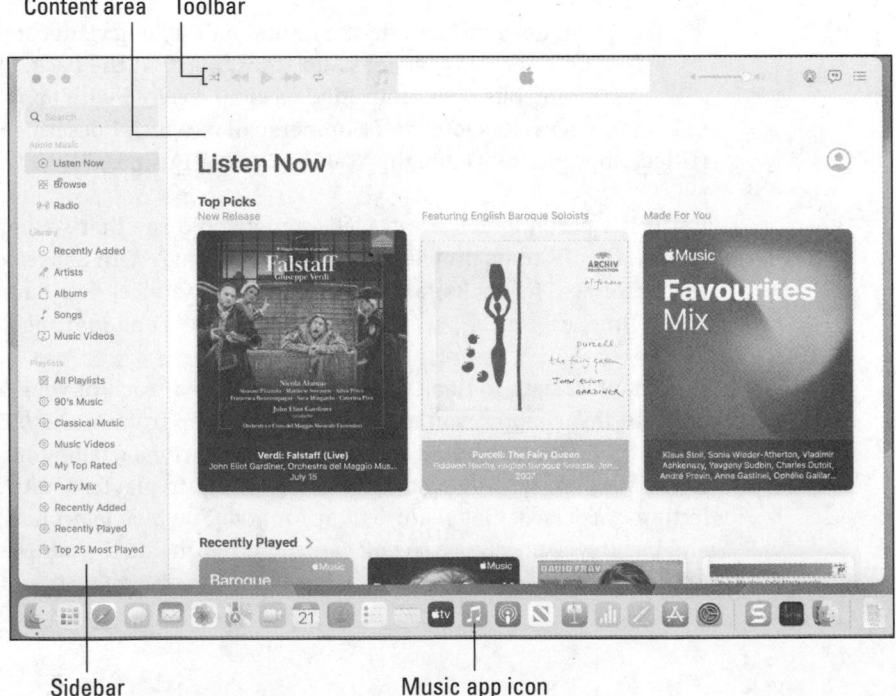

FIGURE 1-1:
Manage your
music from the
Music app.

Sidebar   Music app icon

Touring the sidebar

The sidebar (the pane that takes up the left side of the Music window) is your main Music navigation tool. As you see in Figure 1-1, below the Search box there are three sections to the sidebar: Apple Music, Library, and Playlists. I cover each of these sections next.

Apple Music

Apple Music gives you access to nearly 100 million songs. That's right, 100 million songs, plus curated playlists, song recommendations, and Beats Radio, Apple's streaming music channel with human DJs, sort of like a legacy radio station. You get all this for $9.99 per month or $99 per year, $4.99 per month for college students, or $14.99 per month for a family sharing plan for up to six people. Your first month is free, giving you plenty of time to get hooked on Apple Music before automatic billing kicks in. You can find out more about Apple Music at `www.apple.com/apple-music/`.

TIP

If you want to go all-in with Apple media, consider a subscription to Apple One, Apple's everything-but-the-kitchen-sink collection of services that includes not only Apple Music but also Apple TV+, iCloud+, and Apple Arcade. Prices are $14.95 per month for an individual subscription; $19.95 per month for a family subscription (shared with up to five other people); and $29.95 for a premier subscription that includes News+ and Fitness+ (and can also be shared with up to five other people).

REMEMBER

You'll be married to that subscription price for as long as you want to listen to Apple Music. If you stop subscribing, you'll lose access to music you used to stream and any music you downloaded to your devices through your Apple Music subscription.

The Apple Music section of the sidebar organizes the music in your Apple Music subscription. You have three basic ways of listening to Apple Music:

>> **Listen Now:** Presents Apple Music content based on your listening history. The content area (see Figure 1-1) shows sections such as Top Picks, Recently Played, Made for You, and Stations for You, all of which offer customized music selections based on your previous listening choices. This is the tool to use if you want Apple Music to play music for you using your history.

>> **Browse:** Enables you to peruse Apple Music's nearly 100 million tracks to find new songs and artists. The content area (see Figure 1-2) shows sections such as Everyone's Listening To, New Music, Best New Songs, Daily Top 100, and various genres, curated playlists, and other recommended content from the Apple Music team. While Listen Now is centered on what Apple Music thinks

you're interested in, Browse offers a more general look at music, especially new releases and other new additions to the Apple Music catalog. Just like with Listen Now, when you have a subscription to Apple Music, you can tap any artist, playlist, genre, song, or other listing and play that music whenever you want.

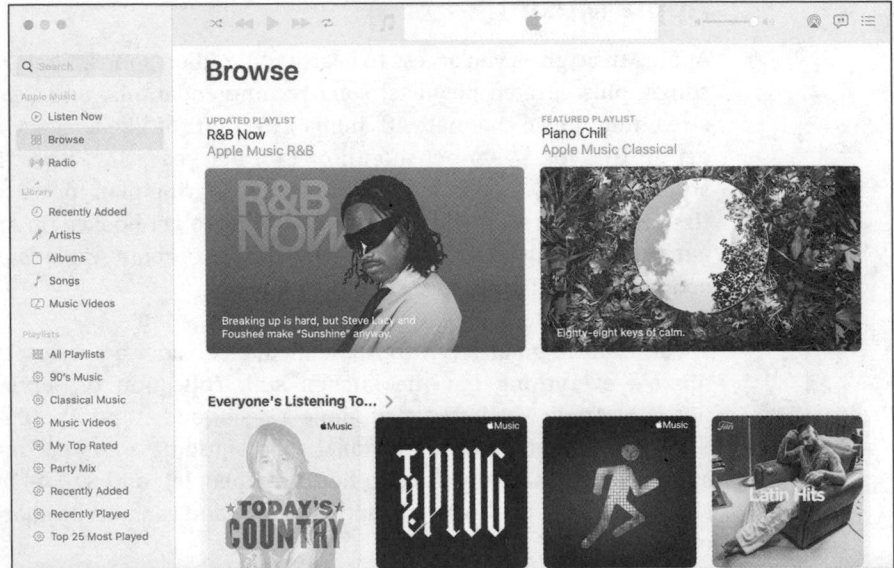

FIGURE 1-2:
Apple Music's Browse section is the place to find new music.

>> **Radio:** Offers access to several streaming music stations. The content area (see Figure 1-3) offers a few suggested stations and sections such as Recently Played, Our Radio Hosts, and Top Stations. The crown jewel in Apple Music's radio collection, and a feature unique to Apple Music, is Apple Music 1, an internet radio station created by humans and with human DJs. Much of the content is created hands-on by Apple's talented staff, with other content created by big and small artists. You can listen to individual shows with distinct flavors helmed by named DJs.

Library

The Library section of the sidebar is where you navigate your own music that you've purchased or imported on your own. The Library section has five items:

>> **Recently Added:** Shows albums and other content you've added to Apple Music recently.

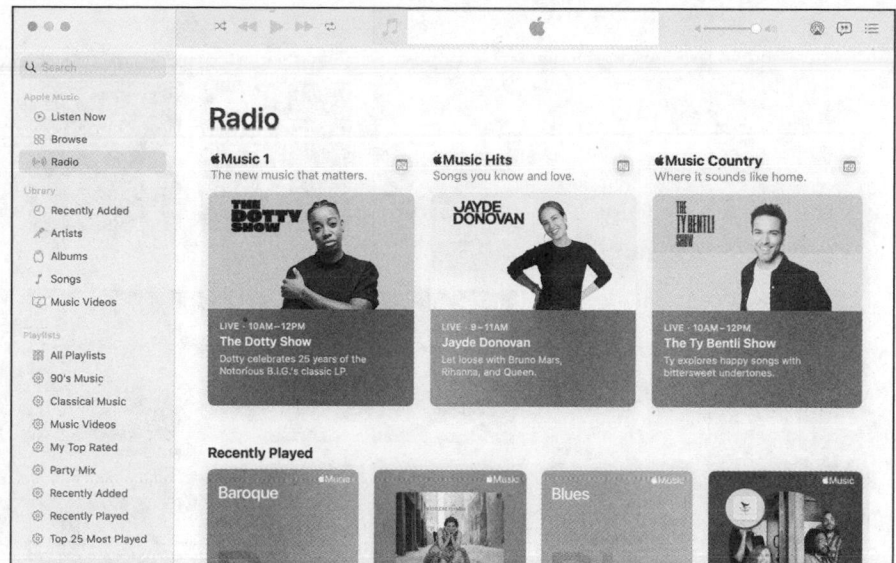

FIGURE 1-3:
Apple Music's Radio section offers live and curated internet radio stations.

>> **Artists:** Shows your music organized alphabetically by the name of each artist in your library. Click an artist to see their albums and tracks.

>> **Albums:** Shows your music organized alphabetically by the name of each album in your library (see Figure 1-4). Click an album to see its tracks.

>> **Songs:** Shows a list of the individual songs from all the albums in your library. The songs are sorted by artist, but you can click the list headers to sort the songs by title, time, album, or genre.

>> **Music Videos:** Shows a thumbnail image from each music video in your library.

Playlists

You can use Music to select a group of songs and store those songs as a *playlist*. When you want to hear that group of songs, just select the playlist rather than having to select each song individually. Maybe you want to make a Sleep playlist, full of classical music to drift off to. Or maybe you want to make a Dinner Party playlist full of the kind of music you like to play for your favorite dinner guests. The possibilities are endless, as you see later in the "Curating Your Music with Playlists" section.

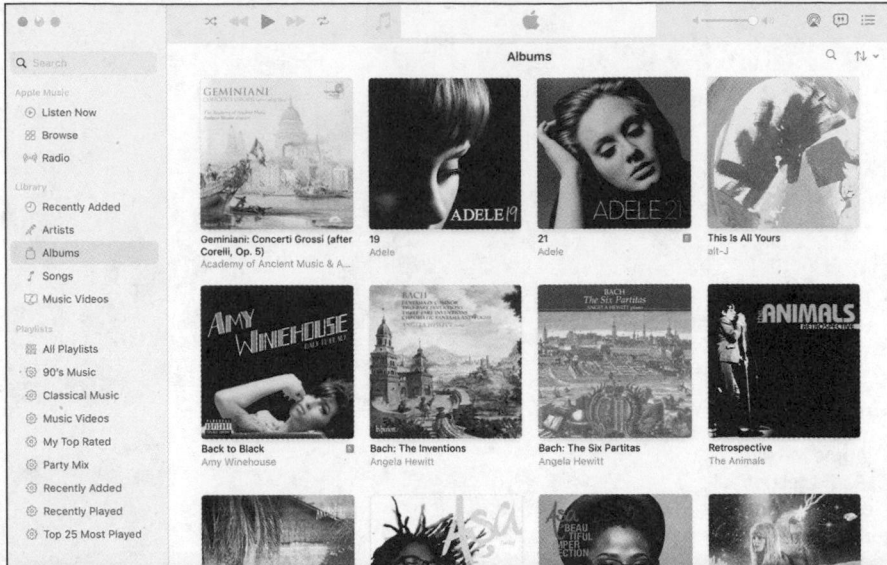

FIGURE 1-4:
The Music app
organizes your
music by artist,
album (shown
here), and song.

Adding a link for iTunes Store

If you want to purchase music from Apple, access to the iTunes Store is a must, but a link to the iTunes Store is a glaring omission from not only the sidebar but also the rest of the Music interface. (You won't miss the link if you plan to listen only to streams via Apple Music.) To add an iTunes Store link to the Music app's sidebar, follow these steps:

1. **Choose Music ⇨ Settings.**

2. **Click the General tab.**

3. **In the Show section, select the iTunes Store check box.**

4. **Click OK.**

   Music adds a Store section and an iTunes Store link to the sidebar, as shown in Figure 1-5.

Finding your way around the toolbar

When you play a track in the Music app, particularly something from your own library, the controls in the toolbar light up and enable you to view, control, and enhance what's playing. As pointed out in Figure 1-6, the toolbar has four main collections of controls:

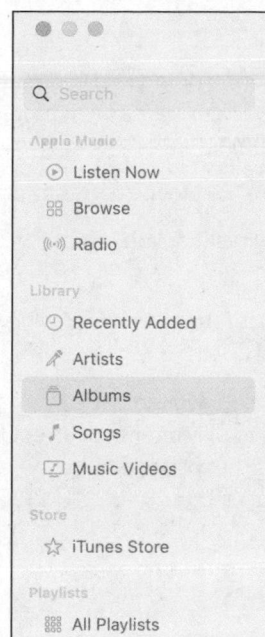

FIGURE 1-5:
You can add
a link to the
iTunes Store to
the Music app
sidebar.

>> **Playback controls:** Control the playback of the current track:

- *Shuffle:* Play the tracks in the current album or playlist in random order.

- *Previous track:* Click once to return to the beginning of the currently playing track; click a second time to navigate to the previous track in the album or playlist. You can also press ⌘+right arrow. To rewind the currently playing track, click and hold down on the control until the track gets back to the position you want.

- *Play/pause:* Click Play to start or resume playback of the currently selected track; click pause to temporarily stop playing the track. You can also press the spacebar to toggle between play and pause.

- *Next track:* Click to navigate to the next track in the album or playlist. You can also press ⌘+left arrow. To fast-forward the currently playing track, click and hold down on the control until the track moves ahead to the position you want.

- *Repeat:* Click once to have Music repeat the current track after it's completed playing; click a second time to have Music start over at the beginning of the current album or playlist after it has played the final track of the album or playlist.

>> **Now playing:** Display info about the currently playing track, including the track name, artist name, and name of the album or playlist.

>> **Volume controls:** Control the playback volume. Drag the slider right to increase the volume (or press ⌘+up arrow); drag the slider left to decrease the volume (or press ⌘+down arrow). Click the left icon to mute the volume; click the right icon to maximize the volume.

>> **Extra buttons:** Access more features related to the currently playing track:

- *AirPlay:* Display a list of available devices that you can use as output devices for the playback.

- *Lyrics:* Display the lyrics (if available) for the currently playing track. You can toggle this pane by pressing Control+⌘+U.

- *Playing Next/History:* Display a pane with two tabs. The Playing Next tab shows a list of the tracks scheduled to play after the current track; the History tab shows a list of the tracks that played before the current track. You can toggle this pane by pressing Option+⌘+U.

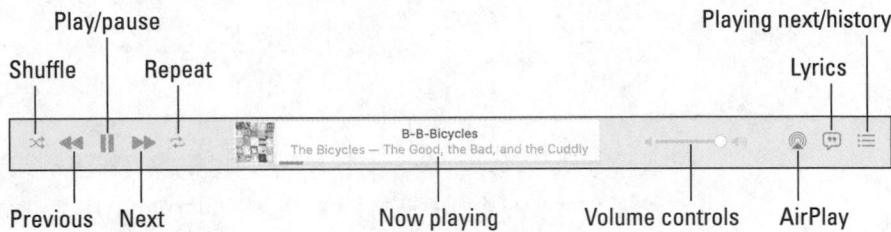

FIGURE 1-6:
The Music app's toolbar tools.

Checking out the content area

To the right of the sidebar, below the toolbar, is a vast piece of the Music app's real estate called the *content area.* What you see in the content area depends on which link you click in the sidebar. For example, Figure 1-1 shows the type of content you see if you click Listen Now under Apple Music. Similarly, Figure 1-4 shows the type of content that appears when you click Albums in the Library section of the sidebar.

Playing Your Music

The Music app turns your Mac into a stereo system and radio. You can play the most common audio files (MP3, WAV, AAC, and AIFF) on your Mac, and you can connect headphones or external speakers to upgrade the playback quality and listening experience.

If you have an Apple Music subscription, you can use the Listen Now, Browse, and Radio commands in the sidebar to access streaming music right away. For your own music library, the process is a bit more complex (which might be why most people just stream music these days):

1. Import some digital audio files into your library.

2. Locate the album, song, or playlist you want to hear.

3. Play the music.

The next three sections expand these steps.

Importing digital audio files

Besides buying audio tracks from the iTunes Store, you might also get digital audio files through the internet or handed to you on a flash drive or an external hard drive. Before you can play any digital audio files in Music, you must first import those files into the app. Here are the steps to follow:

1. **In Music, choose File ⇨ Import.**

   Alternatively, you can press ⌘+O. A file chooser dialog appears.

2. **Navigate to and then select the folder or files you want to import into Music.**

3. **Click Open.**

   Music imports the folder or files.

Alternatively, you can drag and drop one or more digital audio files or a folder of digital audio files. For this to work, you need to set up two Finder windows:

>> In the first Finder window, navigate to your user account folder. Then open the following folders: Music, then Music (yep, Music has a subfolder named Music; no idea why!), then Media, and then Automatically Add to Music.

>> In the second Finder window, navigate to and then select the digital audio files or the folder of digital audio files that you want to import.

With your Finder windows all set up, drag the files or folder from the second Finder window and drop them inside the first Finder window. Music imports the digital audio files and then copies them to the Music\Music\Media\Music folder. (Finder copies the items only if you drag them from an external drive; if the items are located elsewhere on your Mac's hard drive, hold down Option as you drag to copy the items.)

TIP

If you're missing the album art for any of your imported albums, choose File ⇨ Library ⇨ Get Album Artwork, and then click Get Album Artwork when Music asks you to confirm.

TIP

If you have lower-quality audio files from various sources, consider subscribing to iTunes Match. For $24.99 per year, iTunes Match looks at your Music library and upgrades to iTunes Plus quality any songs that you own and that are available in the iTunes Store. Open the iTunes Store (see "Adding a link for iTunes Store," earlier in this chapter), scroll to the bottom of the page, and click the iTunes Match link; then follow the onscreen instructions to subscribe.

Searching your Music library

The Library section of the Music app's sidebar offers several links that enable you to view your music library from different angles: Recently Added, Artists, Albums, Songs, and Music Videos. However, if you have a huge library, it might still take you a ton of time to track down the album or song you want.

Fortunately, Music offers a search feature that's often the fastest way to locate something in the app because you can search by typing some or all of a song or album title or the artist's name. Even better, Music runs the search not only on your library but also on Apple Music and the iTunes Store.

To search Music, follow these steps:

1. **In the sidebar, use the Search text box to enter a search query.**

Enter a word or phrase that represents all or part of a song title, album title, artist name, or playlist name.

2. **Press Return.**

3. **Click where you want Music to search:**

- *Apple Music:* Searches the Apple Music service.

- *Your Library:* Searches the albums, songs, and playlists that you've stored in the Music app.

- *iTunes Store:* Searches the iTunes Store.

Music displays all matches for your query in the content area and organizes the results in various categories, including Top Results, Artists, Albums, Songs, and Playlists. Figure 1-7 shows an example.

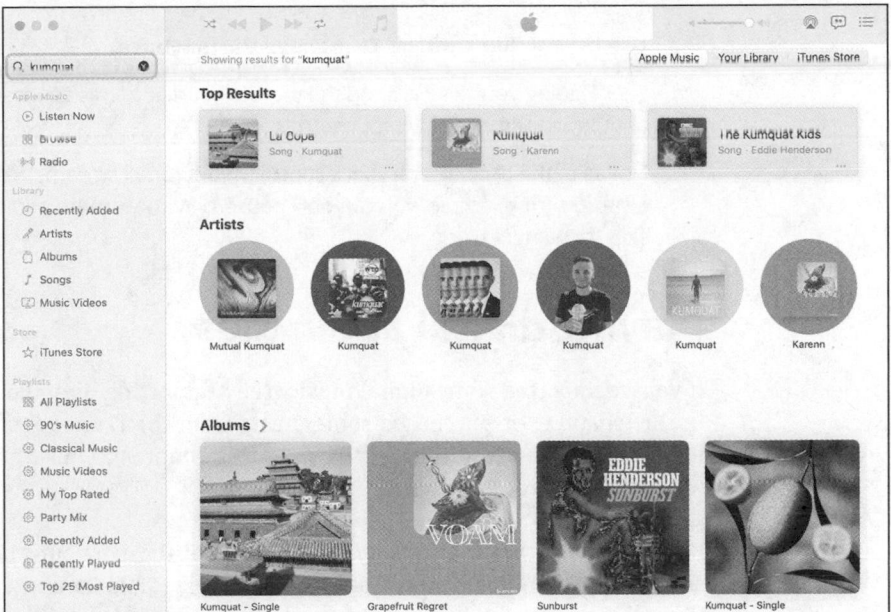

FIGURE 1-7:
Searching
for tunes.

Streaming music

Can you believe you've read this far into a chapter on the Music app but you haven't yet learned how to play music? It's a crime, I know, but it's time to make amends because in this section you learn how to play stuff. Specifically, you learn the basics of playing and controlling streaming music via the Apple Music service. If you don't have a subscription, now's the time to get one; otherwise, skip to the next section to learn how to play music that you've added to your library.

To stream music using the Apple Music service, follow these steps:

1. **In the Music sidebar, click either Listen Now or Browse.**

2. **Locate the album, playlist, or station you want to stream.**

3. **Start the playback:**

   - *Album or playlist:* To play the entire album or playlist, either click the play icon that appears in the lower-left corner of the album or playlist cover or click the album or playlist to open it and then click Play.

   - *Song from an album or playlist:* Open the album or playlist, hover the mouse pointer over the song, then click the play icon that appears to the left of the song title.

   - *Station:* Hover the mouse pointer over the station and then click the play icon that appears in the middle of the station cover.

4. **Use the toolbar controls to manage the playback.**

See "Finding your way around the toolbar," earlier in this chapter, to learn about the toolbar's playback controls.

REMEMBER

Not all of the toolbar's playback controls work for all streams. With a playlist or a station, for example, you can only pause/play the stream and click Next to skip to the next track.

Playing digital audio files

If you've imported some digital music (see "Importing digital audio files," earlier in this chapter) or purchased some music from the iTunes Store (see "Shopping for Music at the iTunes Store," later in this chapter), your Music library will be well stocked and ready to roll.

TIP

Before playing any tracks, you might need to authorize your Mac to play them. If so, choose Account ⇨ Authorizations ⇨ Authorize This Computer, type your Apple ID and click Authorize, type your Apple ID and click Authorize, and then click OK when Music tells you the authorization was successful.

To play an album, playlist, or song, follow these steps:

1. **In the Music sidebar's Library section, click a category, such as Artists, Albums, or Songs.**

If you have any playlists (see "Curating Your Music with Playlists," later in this chapter), you can alternatively click a playlist in the sidebar's Playlists section.

2. **Select the artist, album, or playlist you want to play.**

3. **Start the playback:**

   - *Artist:* To hear all the artist's music in your library, click the play icon that appears to the right of the artist's name. To hear a single album from that artist, hover the mouse pointer over the album cover and then click the play icon that appears. To start with a particular song from that artist, hover the mouse pointer over the song, and then click the play icon that appears to the left of the song title.

   - *Album:* To play the entire album, either hover the mouse pointer over the album cover and click the play icon that appears in the lower-left corner of the album cover, or click the album to open it and then click play.

   - *Playlist:* To play the entire playlist, click the play icon that appears below the playlist info.

- *Song from an album or playlist:* Open the album or playlist, hover the mouse pointer over the song, and then click the play icon that appears to the left of the song title.

4. **Use the toolbar controls to manage the playback.**

   See "Finding your way around the toolbar," earlier in this chapter, to get the 411 on the toolbar's playback controls.

Another way to listen to music is to make a selection of audio files from various artists, albums, or playlists in your library and add them to the Music app's Playing Next list. Follow these steps to try out this technique:

1. **Choose an option from the Library section of the sidebar, such as Songs, Albums, or Artists.**

2. **(Optional) Select the songs you want to play.**

   Click the first song you want to select. You can then ⌘-click more songs to select songs that aren't together or Shift-click the last song to select the first and last song.

3. **Choose when you want the song(s) to play:**

   - To play the song(s) right after the current song, choose Song ⇨ Play Next. You can also right-click any selected song and then click Play Next.

   - To add the song(s) to the end of the Playing Next list, choose Song ⇨ Play Later. You can also right-click any selected song and then click Play Later.

4. **Click the play icon or press the spacebar to start playing your selected audio tracks.**

   The play icon toggles to a pause icon.

5. **To manage the Playing Next list, click the playing next/history icon in the toolbar (labeled previously in Figure 1-6) and make sure the Playing Next tab is selected. Then choose what to do from the following:**

   - *To move a song to a new (higher or lower) position on the Playing Next list:* Click and drag the song to its new position in the Playing Next list.

   - *To see more options:* Click the three dots (. . .) to the right of the song's name. From this list, you can remove a song from the Playing Next list, get Genius suggestions, and much more.

   - *To add similar music:* Click the toggle Autoplay icon (labeled in Figure 1-8) to turn on Autoplay, which uses your Apple Music subscription to augment your Playing Next list with songs that Apple's music algorithm thinks are similar (but are often laughably different).

- *To remove a song from* Playing *Next:* Hover the pointer over a song and then click the red minus sign (–) that appears on the left side.

- *To delete all songs in the Playing Next list:* Click the Clear button.

Toggle Autoplay

FIGURE 1-8:
Turn on Autoplay to add tracks from Apple Music that are similar to those in your Playing Next list.

Fiddling with a few playback settings

Once you import some audio files or start your Apple Music subscription, the Music app's interface offers a reasonably straightforward way to play or stream tunes. There's a good chance you might go your entire Music career without needing to customize the app. However, the Music app does come with a few settings that enable you to tweak how it plays music.

To adjust these playback options, choose Music ⇨ Settings and then click the Playback tab, as shown in Figure 1-9.

Here's a quick look at the audio-related settings in the Playback tab:

>> **Crossfade Songs:** Select this check box to have the next song fade in (gradually increase its volume) while the current song fades out (gradually decreases its volume). You can use the slider to set the total number of seconds for the

crossfade effect. (For example, using the default 6-second crossfade means the effect begins 3 seconds before the end of the current song and ends 3 seconds after the start of the next song.)

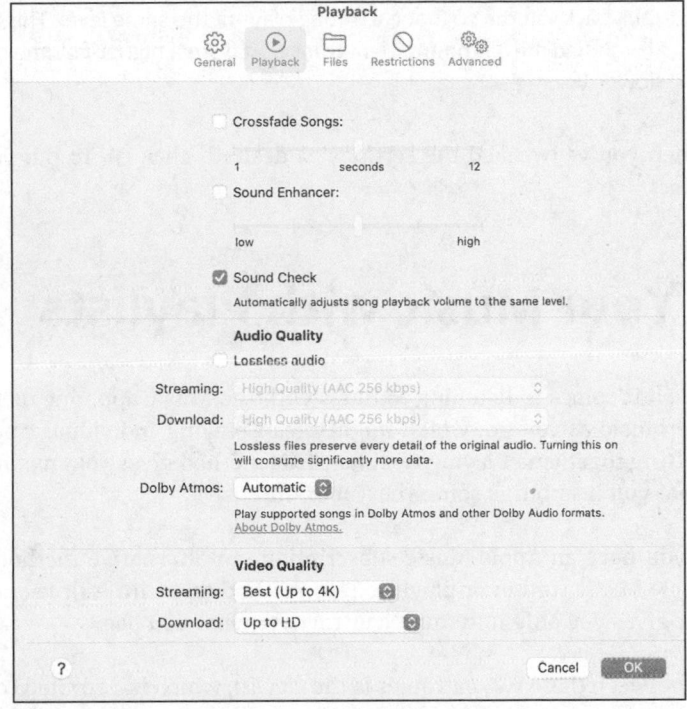

REMEMBER

Crossfading works only if the current song and the next song are from different albums. Music doesn't apply crossfading to tracks from the same album.

>> **Sound Enhancer:** Select this check box to control the perceived depth or wideness of the stereo playback. *Wideness* is an audio geek term that refers to where the sound appears within the listening field: Low wideness means the sound appears in the middle of the field; high wideness means the sound extends out to the left and right of the listening field. Use the slider to set the sound enhancer effect lower or higher, as preferred. (You might want to try tweaking this setting using stereo headphones to get the full effect.)

TIP

If you know what you're doing, you can gain even more control over the playback quality by using the Music app's built-in equalizer. Choose Window ⇨ Equalizer (or press Option+⌘+E) to open the Equalizer window. Select the On check box to turn on the equalizer. Use the pop-up menu to select a preset (such as Dance or Increase Bass) or select Manual and use the frequency sliders (called *faders*) to adjust the volume of each frequency (which run from the lowest bass frequencies on the left to the highest treble frequencies on the right).

>> **Sound Check:** Select this check box to have Music automatically adjust the playback volume so that each song plays at the same level. This is a good idea if you find the all-too-frequent transition from a higher-volume song to a lower-volume song jarring.

When you've tweaked the settings as desired, click OK to put your changes into effect.

Curating Your Music with Playlists

When it comes to listening to tunes with the Music app, one method is to choose the music as you go, which might mean playing individual tracks or albums or putting together a Playing Next list. This method gives you maximum control over what you hear but is somewhat labor-intensive.

If you have an Apple Music subscription, an alternative method is to stream an Apple Music station or playlist. This method takes little time and effort to set up but gives you only minimum control over what you hear.

In between these two extremes is the *playlist,* which is a curated collection of songs that you save in the Music app. Most people use playlists to gather similar music from an artist or a genre or combine tracks that go well with a particular activity, such as a workout, a party, or a chill session. It takes a bit of work to create a playlist, but it's a one-time-only task. Once you've saved the playlist, you can play it any time you like with just a couple of clicks.

Besides this kind of so-called *ordinary* playlist, you can also get the Music app to do most of the work for you by creating smart or Genius playlists. In all, you have the following three playlist options:

>> **Ordinary playlist:** A collection of favorite or related songs that you select manually.

>> **Smart playlist:** A collection of songs that you define by creating rules that specify which tracks to include. For example, you can create rules that match songs by a specific artist, in a specific genre, or with a specific rating. As your audio file collection grows, a smart playlist will automatically include any new songs that match the criteria you defined for that playlist.

>> **Genius playlist:** A collection of songs similar to whatever song you use as the basis for the playlist. That is, when you specify a song as the basis of a Genius playlist, the Music app automatically populates the playlist with songs that are musically similar.

All playlists are shown in the Playlists section of the sidebar.

Setting up an ordinary playlist

If you want total control over which songs are included in a playlist, you need to set up an ordinary playlist. Setting up an ordinary playlist involves two general steps: creating the playlist and then populating the playlist with the songs you want.

Creating an ordinary playlist

To create an ordinary playlist of particular songs you want to play as a group, follow these steps:

1. **In Music, choose File ⇨ New ⇨ Playlist.**

   You can also press ⌘+N.

   A playlist with the default title *Playlist* appears in the content area. The new playlist also appears in the Playlists section of the sidebar.

2. **Type a name for your playlist and then press Return.**

   Music updates the playlist name (both in the content area and in the Playlists section of the sidebar).

3. **In the sidebar, click a Library link.**

   If you know the song you want in your playlist, click the Songs link. If you want one or more songs from a specific artist or album, click the Artists or Albums link, respectively. You can also use the Search box to look for the track you want.

4. **Select the song you want to add to the playlist.**

5. **Choose Song ⇨ Add to Playlist and then click the name of your playlist in the continuation menu that appears.**

   Alternatively, you can drag songs, albums, or artists from the content area and drop them on your playlist in the sidebar's Playlists section.

   Yet another method you can use is to click the three dots (. . .) to the right of the song, album, or artist, click Add to Playlist, and then click the name of the playlist in the continuation menu.

6. **Click the Done button.**

TIP

To make a quick playlist, click the first song, hold down the ⌘ key and click the rest of the songs you want in the playlist, and then choose File ➪ New ➪ Playlist from Selection (or press Shift+⌘+N). Your new playlist appears in the content area with the selected songs. Type a new name for the playlist and press Enter.

Editing an ordinary playlist

After you create a playlist, you can edit it. To add a song to a playlist, right-click the song and from the context menu, choose Add to Playlist ➪ *Playlist Name*. The song you added appears in the playlist.

After you populate a playlist, click its link in the Playlists sidebar, and the playlist appears on the right side of the interface, as shown in Figure 1-10. As you can see, you have many options, including adding a description, playing the songs in order, or shuffling them.

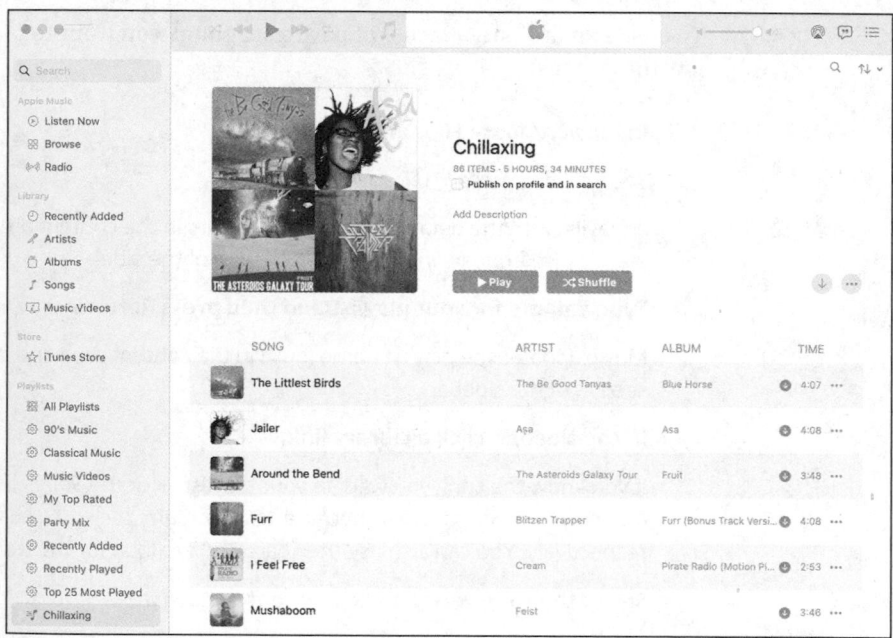

FIGURE 1-10:
Open a playlist to edit it.

You can also perform the following tasks when you have a playlist open:

>> **Rename the playlist.** Double-click the playlist name, type the new name, and then press Return.

>> **Change the order of the songs.** Drag a song up or down in the list and drop it on the position you prefer.

>> **Remove a song.** Right-click the song in the playlist and then click Remove from Playlist. When Music asks you to confirm, click Remove Song.

Deleting a song from a playlist doesn't delete the song from your Music library.

REMEMBER

>> **Delete the playlist.** Click the three dots (. . .) to the right of the playlist's Play and Shuffle buttons, and then click Delete from Library. (You can also right-click the playlist in the sidebar's Playlists section, and then click Delete from Library.) When Music asks if you're sure, click Delete.

Setting up a smart playlist

Manually adding and removing songs from a playlist can get tedious, especially if you regularly add new songs to your Music audio collection. Instead of placing specific songs in a playlist, a smart playlist lets you define specific criteria for the types of songs to store in that playlist, such as songs recorded earlier than 1990, or songs under a particular genre, such as Blues, Country, Hard Rock, or Folk. To create and use a smart playlist, you tag songs, define rules to determine which songs to include, and finally, edit existing playlists.

Tagging songs

To sort your song collection accurately into smart playlists, you can tag individual songs with descriptive information. Most songs stored as digital audio files already have some information stored in specific tags, such as the artist or album name. However, you may still want to edit or add new tags to help smart playlists sort your song collection.

To edit or add tags to one or more songs, follow these steps:

1. **In Music, select the song or songs you want to tag and choose Song ⇨ Info (or press ⌘+I) to display the track information.**

2. **Click the Details tab to display text boxes where you can type or change the song track associated information, rate the songs, or add comments, as shown in Figure 1-11.**

   Alternatively, you can right-click any selected song and choose Get Info from the context menu.

3. **Click a text field and edit or enter information.**

4. **Open the Genre pop-up menu to add or change the song genre.**

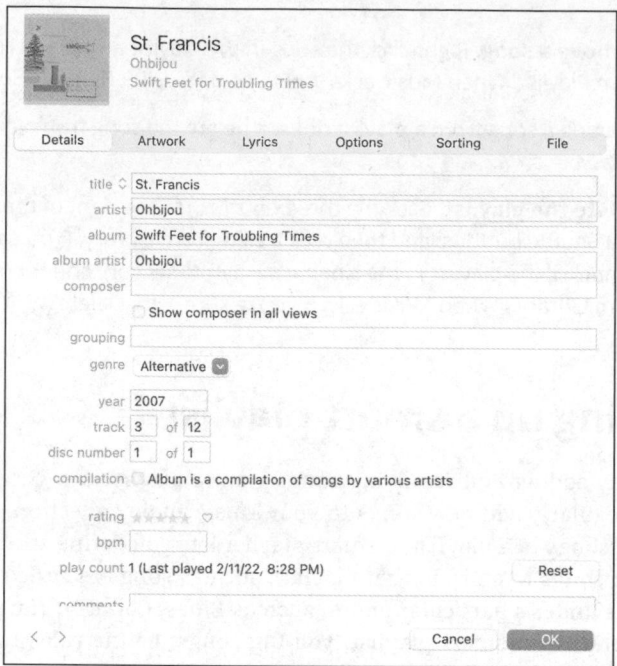

St. Francis
Ohbijou
Swift Feet for Troubling Times

Details   Artwork   Lyrics   Options   Sorting   File

title ⇕ St. Francis
artist Ohbijou
album Swift Feet for Troubling Times
album artist Ohbijou
composer
☐ Show composer in all views
grouping
genre Alternative ⌄

year 2007
track 3 of 12
disc number 1 of 1
compilation ☐ Album is a compilation of songs by various artists

rating ★★★★★ ♡
bpm
play count 1 (Last played 2/11/22, 8:28 PM)   Reset
comments

‹ ›   Cancel   OK

FIGURE 1-11:
Edit or enter tags
to identify a song.

5. **Assign a rating to the songs.**

You can choose a rating from one to five stars or click the heart to love the song.

TIP

You can also love a song by selecting it in your library and then choosing Song ⇨ Love or clicking the heart icon that appears to the left of the song's title. To love an album, open it, click the three dots, and choose Love from the context menu.

TIP

If you want to rate a lot of songs, firing up each song's information window every time is a real time suck. A better way is to configure Music to show the rating stars beside each song. Choose Music ⇨ Settings, make sure the General tab is displayed, select the Star Ratings check box, and then click OK. Now, when you hover the mouse pointer over any song, the rating stars appear, and you can click a star to set the rating just like that. You're welcome!

6. **Click the other tabs, such as Options or Sorting to make additional adjustments to your selected audio files.**

7. **When you finish tagging the songs, click OK to close the dialog and return to the main Music window.**

Creating a smart playlist

Smart playlists use tags to sort and organize your song collection. You can use existing tags that are created for songs automatically (such as Artist and Album), as well as tags you add to your songs to define the type of songs you want that smart playlist to store. A specific criteria for choosing a song is a *rule*.

To create a smart playlist, follow these steps:

1. **In Music, choose File ➪ New ➪ Smart Playlist.**

You can also press Option+⌘+N.

The Smart Playlist dialog appears, prompting you to define a rule for specifying which songs to store in the playlist.

2. **Open the first pop-up menu on the left and choose a category, such as Artist, Genre, or Date Added, for deciding which criteria will be used to automatically add songs to the smart playlist.**

3. **Open the second pop-up menu in the middle and choose an operator.**

The operator determines how Music matches your selection from Step 2 with what you specify in Step 4. The default operator is Contains, but you can also choose Is (for an exact match), Begins With, Is Less Than, and so on. The operators you see in this pop-up list depend on the type of information you selected in Step 2.

4. **Use the text box or third pop-up menu (again, this depends on what you selected in Step 2) to specify what you want Music to match.**

For example, if you selected Genre in Step 2 and Is in Step 3, you might enter Alternative in the text box to match songs in the Alternative genre.

5. **(Optional) Click the plus sign to add another rule to the Playlist, and then repeat Steps 2 through 4 to define the new rule.**

For example, Figure 1-12 shows a smart playlist in progress with rules that specify the Genre as Alternative, the Year (that is, the year the music was published) as less than 2000, and that the song has been loved.

After you add a second rule, the All or Any menu appears next to Match in the first line.

6. **To have Music include a song in the smart playlist only if the song matches every one of your rules, select All in the pop-up menu that appears next to the Match check box.**

To have Music include a song in the smart playlist if the song matches at least one of your rules, select Any in the pop-up menu that appears next to the Match check box.

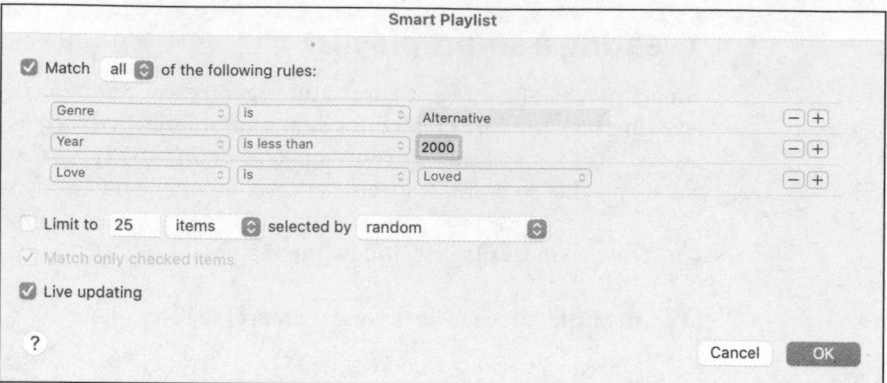

FIGURE 1-12:
You can add multiple rules to your smart playlist.

7. **(Optional) Make other selections in the Smart Playlist dialog:**

   - *Limit To:* Select this check box and enter a number to define the maximum number of (choose one) Items, Minutes, Hours, MB, or GB the smart playlist is allowed to hold. Then choose an option that suits your desired smart playlist criteria from the Selected By pop-up menu.

   - *Live Updating:* Select this check box if you want the smart playlist to update its list of songs automatically each time you add or remove a song from your Music library or change a tag (on a song) used in the rule.

8. **Click OK.**

   Your smart playlist appears in the content area and in the sidebar's Playlists section.

   REMEMBER

   You can differentiate ordinary, smart, and Genius playlists by the icon they use in the Playlists section. Ordinary playlists use an icon that looks like a musical note beside a three-line stave; smart playlists use an icon that looks like a gear; Genius playlists use an icon that looks like orbiting atoms.

9. **Type a name for the smart playlist and then press Return.**

Editing a smart playlist

After you create a smart playlist, you can modify it, such as adding more rules or editing any existing rules. To edit a smart playlist, follow these steps:

1. **In the Playlists section of the sidebar, double-click the smart playlist that you want to edit.**

   The smart playlist appears in the content area of the Music app.

2. **Click Edit Rules.**

   The Smart Playlist dialog appears.

3. **Make any changes to your smart playlist rule(s) and then click OK.**

TIP

If you want to cut to the chase when modifying a playlist, right-click its name and choose Edit Rules from the context menu.

TIP

If you have a lot of playlists, the Playlists list can get pretty crowded. You can streamline your playlist list by filing similar playlists in folders. Choose File ➪ New Playlist Folder. Double-click the folder to rename it with a meaningful name, and then click and drag the playlists you want to file to the folder.

Setting up a Genius playlist

If your guests are already ringing the doorbell and you don't have time to create the background music for your party, you can let Music create a Genius playlist for you with songs Music thinks go well together. A Genius playlist is created based on a song you choose. Genius also suggests new songs for you to purchase that it thinks you'll like based on your purchase history.

Here's how to create a Genius playlist:

1. **In your music collection, click the song you want to use as the basis for your Genius playlist.**

2. **Choose File ➪ New ➪ Genius Playlist.**

   Music creates a new playlist from your music library with songs that Music thinks go well with the song you selected.

   TIP

   Sometimes, instead of creating a playlist, you see a dialog telling you that your chosen song doesn't have enough related songs to create a Genius playlist. Genius seems somewhat limited if you have non-English, classical, obscure, or pre-1960 music. Tagging your songs, as I explain previously in the "Tagging songs" section, can help Genius create playlists because tagging gives Music more information to work with.

   The Genius playlist is automatically named with the song it's based on and saved in the sidebar's Playlist section. Music also displays the playlist in the content area, as shown in Figure 1-13.

3. **Click the pull-down menu under the playlist length to change how many songs you want in your Genius playlist: 25 Songs, 50 Songs, 75 Songs, or 100 Songs.**

TIP

After you add more music to your Music library, choose File ➪ Library ➪ Update Genius to update your Genius playlist.

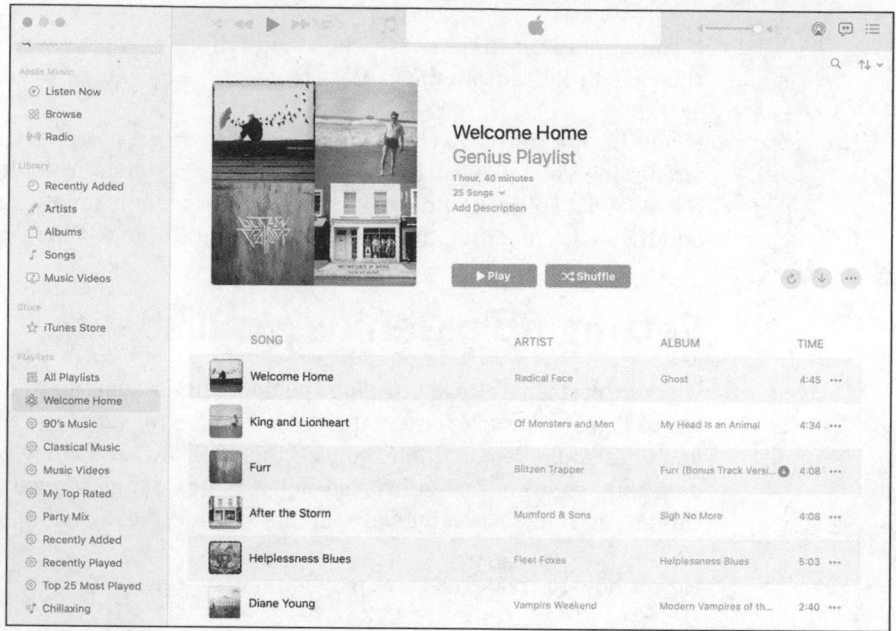

FIGURE 1-13:
Create a playlist like Einstein would create.

TIP

A Genius shuffle is an ad hoc collection of tracks based on what's in your library. To create a Genius shuffle, choose Controls ⇨ Genius Shuffle (or press Option+spacebar), and Music goes to work. Click the playing next/history icon (labeled in Figure 1-6) to see the upcoming songs in the shuffle.

Listening to the Radio

Sometimes you just want to listen to some music for a few hours without having to bother with choosing albums, populating the Playing Next list, or putting together a playlist. The easiest solution is to tune in to a radio station, where it's someone else's job to pick and play the music.

Music offers three types of radio listening:

» **Custom radio station:** A radio station that consists of songs similar to a particular Music item, such as a song or artist. Use the Music interface to display the song, artist, album, or genre (choose View ⇨ As Genres and then click a genre in the list that appears) that you want to use as the basis for your radio station. Click the item's three dot icon (. . .) and then click Create Station.

>> **Apple Music live radio:** A live radio station streamed via your Apple Music subscription. In the Apple Music section of the sidebar, click Radio and then click the play icon for the station you want to hear.

>> **Broadcast radio:** A radio station broadcast over the internet. Music offers two ways to tune in to a broadcast radio station:

- *Via URL:* Use Safari to copy the URL of the radio station. In the Music app, choose File ⇨ Open Stream URL (or press ⌘+U) to display the Open Stream dialog. Paste the URL in the URL field and then click OK.

- *Via search:* In Music, use the sidebar's Search field to search for the radio station you want to hear. You can enter some or all of the station's name, nickname, call sign, or frequency. Click the station once it appears in the search results.

Shopping for Music at the iTunes Store

The iTunes Store offers a plethora of music. Whether you like classic rock or classical music, you can find it at the iTunes Store. You can purchase music and then download it to your Mac and listen to the songs you purchase on other devices.

In this section, I accompany you down the virtual aisles of the iTunes Store. The beauty of the iTunes Store is you don't need a shopping cart, and you can audition the music before you buy it.

TIP

For many purchases, you have to authorize your computer. This helps with copyright issues. You can authorize up to five computers, and you can also de-authorize computers, so don't worry about someone else using your Apple ID if you sell or give away your Mac. Other devices don't count as computers, so your iPad or iPhone aren't part of the five-computer limit. Choose Store ⇨ Authorize This Computer. That's it.

To open the iTunes Store, click the iTunes Store link in the Store section of the sidebar. (Don't see the iTunes Store link? Choose Music ⇨ Settings, select the iTunes Store check box in the General tab, and then click OK.)

With literally millions of digital media files to choose from, the initial impact can be overwhelming, but the iTunes Store organization helps you narrow your choices. When you first open the iTunes Store, the window you see is divided into sections that give you suggestions for different types of music you can purchase (see Figure 1-14).

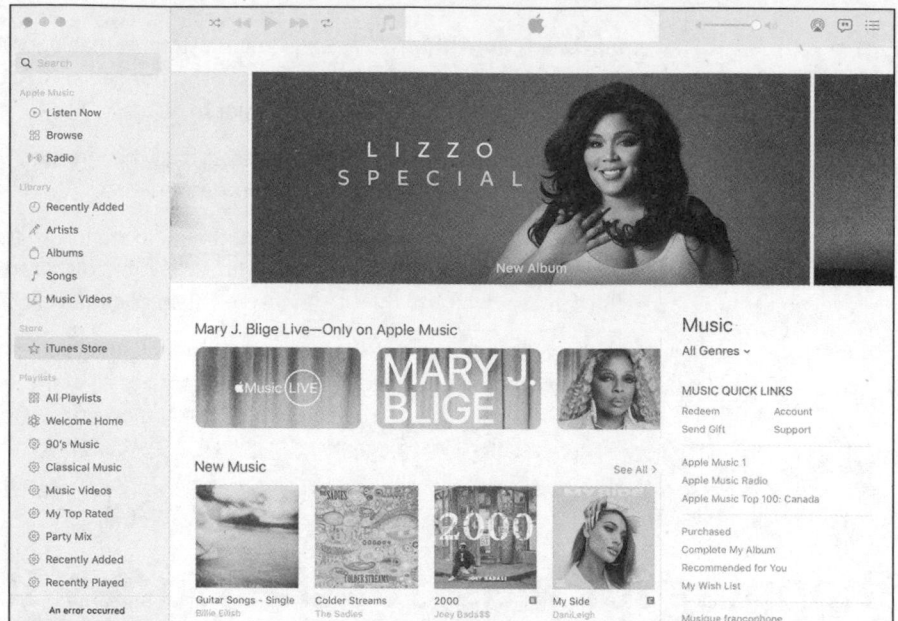

FIGURE 1-14:
Browse the
iTunes Store for
music, music, and
more music.

At the top, you see a banner you can scroll to display new albums. Below the banner you find several sections you can scroll through. On the right side of the store, you see All Genres. Click the disclosure arrow to fine-tune your shopping experience by choosing a genre from the pop-up menu. After choosing a specific genre, the iTunes Store refreshes showing music from your chosen genre.

Down the right side, you see the Music section, which includes several subsections:

» **Music Quick Links:** This subsection is related to your Apple ID/Music account with buttons to access your account, redeem gift cards, send a gift, or request support.

» **Top X:** These subsections are various top-ten lists, such as Top Songs and Top Albums, where you can preview or purchase songs. Click a chart title to see a full display of the list's contents.

TIP

At first glance, it looks like the iTunes Store doesn't offer a search feature. It does, but it's bizarrely hard to find. Click Search in the Music app's sidebar, and then click the iTunes Store tab near the upper-right corner of the window. Now whatever you search for will show results from the iTunes Store.

When you click an icon or name for any type of music from anywhere in the iTunes Store, the information window opens. These are the parts of an information screen, as shown in Figure 1-15:

>> **Buy button:** Click to purchase and download the item. Songs can be purchased singly, or you can purchase the entire album.

>> **Pop-up menu:** Click the drop-down arrow next to the price for a pop-up menu that has options to gift the app to a friend, add it to your own wish list, tell a friend about it, copy the link, or share the album info via Facebook or Twitter.

>> **Songs:** This tab lists all the tracks on the album. The price of the song is listed if you want to purchase an individual song and not the whole album. Hover the mouse pointer over a song and to the left of the song a play icon appears that, when clicked, plays a preview of the song. There's even a Preview All link at the bottom of the song list.

>> **Ratings and Reviews:** Click this tab to see what others have said about this item. Users can give a simple star rating, from zero to five, or write a review.

>> **Related:** Click this tab to see other albums similar to this one.

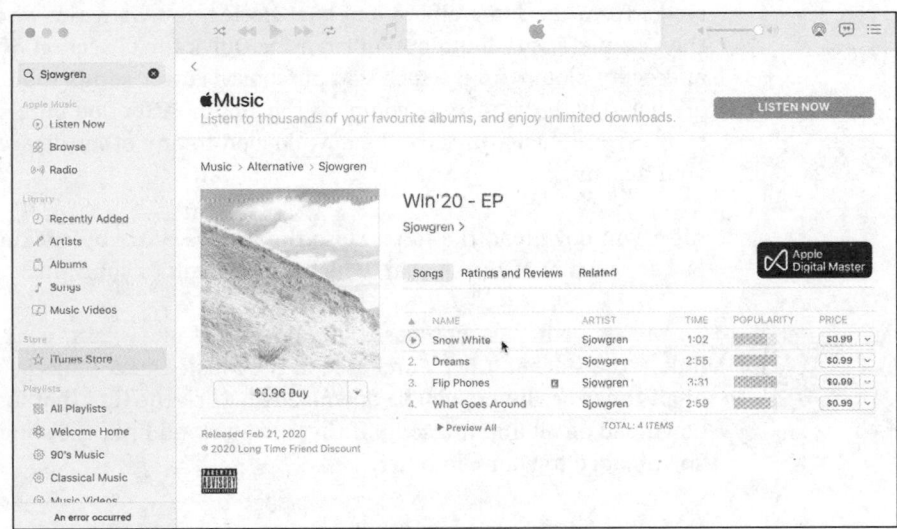

FIGURE 1-15: Information about the album you select is displayed in Music.

When you find something you like, click the Buy button, and the song or album is downloaded to Music on your Mac. If you have other Apple devices (such as an iPad or iPhone), you can sync your Library to other devices by choosing Music ⇨ Settings and then clicking the Sync Library switch on.

REMEMBER

Don't worry if you have to interrupt the download process or it's interrupted unexpectedly. Music remembers the point it reached and will resume downloading when you open the Music app again and have an active internet connection.

Of course, when you buy, you have to pay from your Apple ID account. This happens in either of two ways:

» **Redeem:** You can redeem Apple or Music gift cards, gift certificates, or allowances (more on allowances shortly). Choose Account ➪ Redeem (or click the Redeem link that appears near the bottom of the main iTunes Store page). Either type the code from the gift card or click Use Camera to have the iTunes Store recognize and load the card data using your Mac's camera. The amount of the card or certificate is added to your account.

» **Credit card:** Your credit card information is stored with your account information. You can change your method of payment and even add money to your Apple ID by choosing Account ➪ Account Settings and then clicking Manage Payments.

All songs on Music are currently in iTunes Plus format, which is 256 Kbps AAC without DRM (digital rights management) limitations. Songs cost 69¢, 99¢, or $1.29, and album prices vary depending on the number of songs. If you buy a few songs from the same album and later decide you want the whole album, choose the Complete My Album option from the Quick Links section of the iTunes Store, and every album from which you purchased fewer songs than are on the album are listed with the price to complete the album. After you purchase and download songs from Music, they can be downloaded to any other devices associated with your account.

After you download the item, close the iTunes Store by clicking a button in the Library section of the sidebar, which returns you to your Music library.

TIP

To review your past purchases and download one again, click the iTunes Store link in the sidebar. Click Purchased in the Music Quick Links section to view a list of all tunes or albums you've downloaded. Click the link that looks like a cloud to download an album or a song. If there is no cloud link, the song has already been downloaded to your computer.

Chapter **2**

Enjoying Podcasts, News, and TV

Here we are now, entertain us.

—NIRVANA

t's easy to think of your Mac as a tool for getting things done. And it's certainly true that you can use a Mac to write reports, build budgets, and produce presentations. These are standard-issue tasks in our workaday world. But if you use your Mac *only* to take care of business, you're missing out on a world of Mac-based entertainment and information.

For example, macOS comes with a Podcasts app that enables you to search for, follow, listen to, and manage podcasts. Your Mac also hosts the News app, which gives you access to a wide variety of news sources and stories. Finally, macOS also offers the TV app, which you can use to watch TV series and episodes right from the comfort of your Mac monitor.

In this chapter, you take a walk on your Mac's fun side by diving into the Podcasts, News, and TV apps. You learn how to search for the content you want, start and control the playback of the content, and manage the content. If you believe that all work and no play make Jack and Jill a dull couple, you've come to the right place.

Finding and Playing Podcasts

Podcasts are popular on all devices, including the Mac. They're typically audio programs that are episodic in nature, either because they tell a story or provide information over time or because they're keyed to changing events.

The heart of podcasts on your Mac is the Podcasts app, which enables you to browse podcasts and follow and listen to the shows and episodes that interest you.

To get started, click the Podcasts icon either on the dock (see Figure 2-1) or in Launchpad. The Podcasts window has three sections: the sidebar, the toolbar, and the content area. The next three sections take a closer look at each feature.

Toolbar

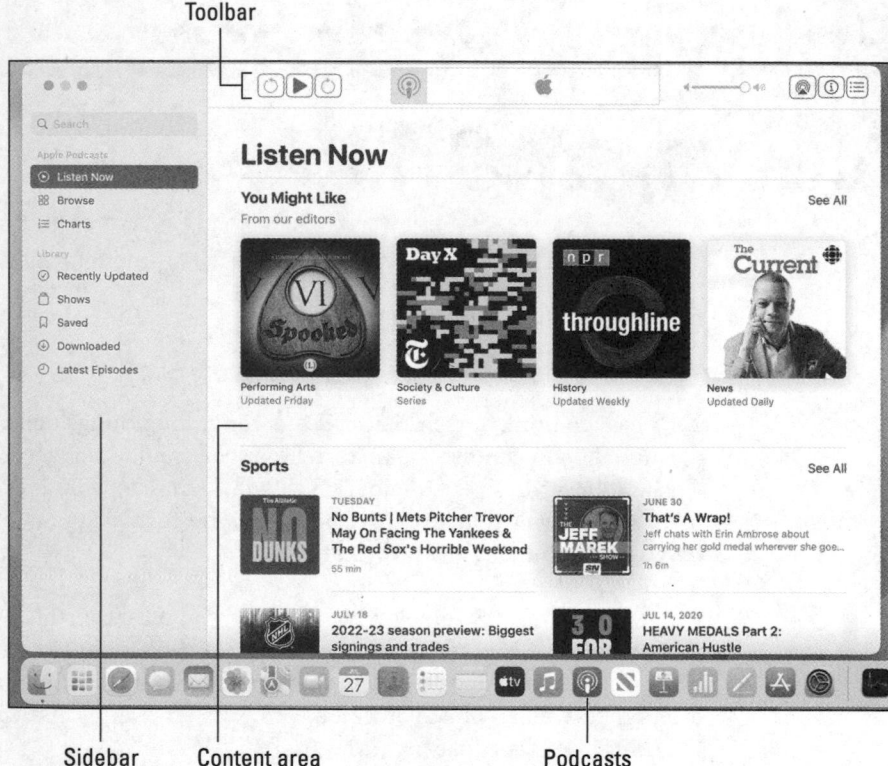

Sidebar   Content area   Podcasts

Examining the sidebar

The sidebar (the pane that takes up the left side of the window) is your main Podcasts navigation tool. As you see in Figure 2-1, below the Search box are two sections to the sidebar: Apple Podcasts and Library. I cover each of these sections next.

Apple Podcasts

Apple Podcasts gives you access to over two million shows and over 60 million episodes. Those are awfully big numbers (and will probably be even bigger by the time you read this), but the Apple Podcasts section of the sidebar can help you find podcast content that interests you:

>> **Listen Now:** Presents Apple Podcasts content based (mostly) on your listening history. The content area (see Figure 2-1) shows sections such as You Might Like, More to Discover, and Channels to Try, all of which offer customized podcast selections based on your previous listening choices.

>> **Browse:** Introduces you to Apple Podcasts' more than two million shows. The content area (see Figure 2-2) displays a couple of featured shows as well as sections such as Subscriber Favorites, New & Noteworthy, and Shows We Love. You also see various genres, curated collections, and other recommended content from the Apple Podcasts team.

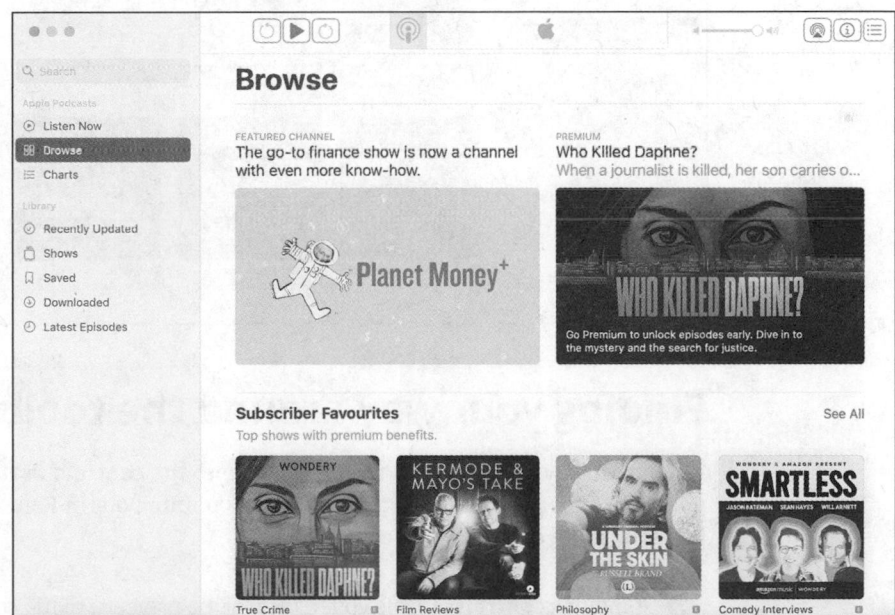

FIGURE 2-2:
The sidebar's
Browse section
is the place for
finding new
podcasts.

Library

The Library section of the sidebar is where you navigate your podcast subscriptions. There are five items in the Library section:

>> **Recently Updated:** Podcasts that have published new episodes recently

>> **Shows:** Podcasts that you're currently following (see Figure 2-3)

>> **Saved:** The podcast episodes you've saved

>> **Downloaded:** The podcast episodes you've downloaded to your Mac so that you can listen to the shows when you're offline

>> **Latest Episodes:** The most recent episodes of the podcasts you follow

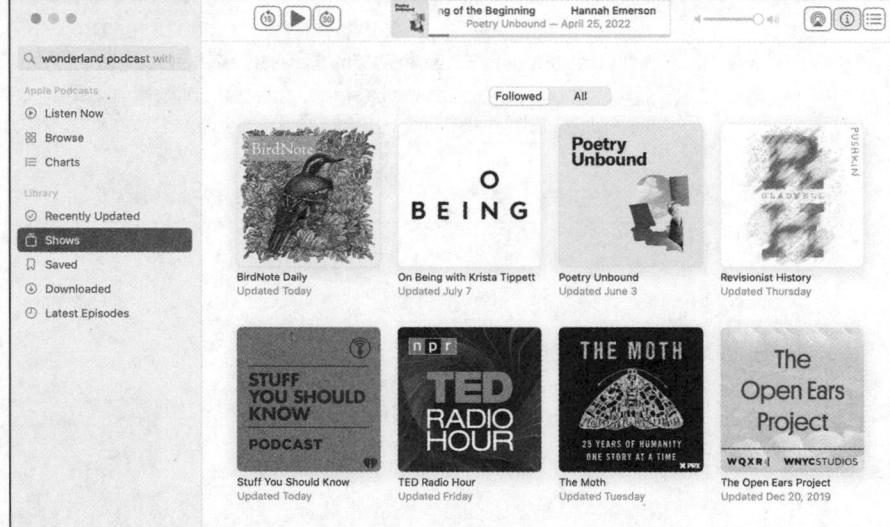

FIGURE 2-3:
The sidebar's Shows link takes you to the podcasts you follow.

Finding your way around the toolbar

When you play an episode in the Podcasts app, the controls in the toolbar become enabled so that you can view and control. As pointed out in Figure 2-4, the toolbar has four main collections of controls:

>> **Playback controls:** Enable you to control the playback of the current episode:

   • *Skip back:* Click to go back 15 seconds. You can also press ⌘+left arrow.

- *Play/pause:* Click the play icon to start or resume playback of the currently selected episode; click pause to temporarily stop playing the track. You can also press the spacebar to toggle between play and pause.

- *Skip forward:* Click to go forward 30 seconds. You can also press ⌘+right arrow.

TIP

You can control the length of time for both the skip back and skip forward icons. Choose Podcasts ➪ Settings and then click the Playback tab. In the Skip Buttons section, use the Forward pop-up menu to select a time interval for the skip forward icon; use the Back pop-up menu to select a time interval for the skip back icon.

Skip back

Skip forward

Playing next

Episode notes

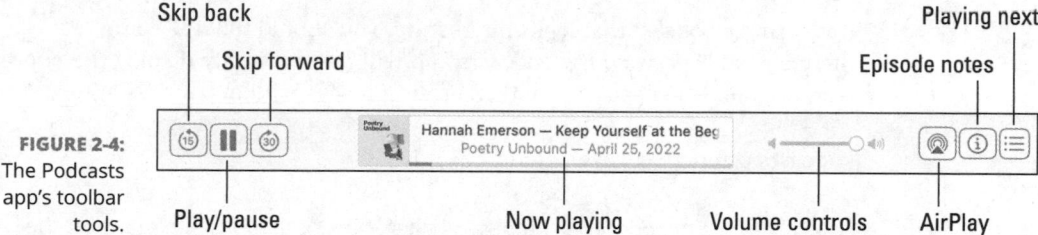

FIGURE 2-4:
The Podcasts app's toolbar tools.

Play/pause

Now playing

Volume controls

AirPlay

>> **Now playing:** Displays info about the currently playing episode, including the episode name, the podcast name, and the episode's original air date.

>> **Volume controls:** Enable you to control the playback volume. Drag the slider right to increase the volume (or press ⌘+up arrow); drag the slider left to decrease the volume (or press ⌘+down arrow). Click the left icon to mute the volume; click the right icon to maximize the volume.

>> **Extra buttons:** Offer more features related to the currently playing track:

- *AirPlay:* Displays a list of available devices that you can use as output devices for the playback.

- *Episode notes:* Displays the background information (if any) that the podcast publisher has created for the episode.

- *Playing next:* Displays a pane that shows a list of the episodes that are scheduled to play after the current episode.

Checking out the content area

The content area (everything to the right of the sidebar and below the toolbar) is the bulk of the Podcasts window. What you see in the content area depends on which link you click in the sidebar. For example, Figure 2-1 shows the type of content you see if you click Listen Now under Apple Podcasts. Similarly, Figure 2-3 shows the type of content that appears when you click Shows in the Library section of the sidebar.

Following a podcast

When you click the Browse link in the left column, the main part of the right window displays podcasts divided into categories. You can also search for specific podcasts by entering a query in the Search text field.

Click a show's thumbnail image to find out more information about that show. After you review a show, you can follow it or listen to recent episodes.

If you find a podcast that looks interesting, you should follow — or *subscribe* — to the podcast. That way, the Podcasts app will automatically display the podcast's recently published episodes in the Latest Episodes window.

Podcasts offers two ways to follow a show:

» If you see the podcast's thumbnail image, hover the mouse pointer over the cover, click the three dots icon (. . .), and then click Follow Show.

» If you're viewing the podcast's info page (see Figure 2-5), click the +Follow button.

FIGURE 2-5:
In a podcast's main page, click +Follow to follow the show.

TIP

If you find a podcast that you'd like to listen to and you can't find it by navigating or searching in the Podcasts app, use Safari to navigate to the podcast's home page. If you see an Apple Podcast icon, great! Click that icon to open the podcast in the Podcasts app. Otherwise, look for an RSS icon and copy that URL, and then return to the Podcasts app and choose File ⇨ Follow a Show by URL (or press Shift+⌘+N). In the Follow a Show by URL dialog, paste the URL into the text field and click Follow.

Reading the News: Extra, Extra, Read All about It!

If you like to (or, in these weird and troubled times, are brave enough to) keep up with current events, you'll love the News app. You can read the latest news, check out news stories by choosing a topic, save stories you like, and peruse articles you've previously read. If keeping abreast of current affairs is your thing, read on.

Reading the daily news

The Apple News app keeps you up to date on current events by including articles from major news sources such as the *Wall Street Journal*, *Los Angeles Times*, CNN Business, and much more. To read the daily news with your cuppa joe or other beverage, follow these steps:

1. **Click the News app icon (pointed out in Figure 2-6) on the dock or in Launchpad.**

   The News app opens showing the top stories for the day. The app is divided into two sections, the sidebar and the content pane, as shown in Figure 2-6.

2. **Click a story you'd like to read.**

   The story opens in the News pane. After you open a story, it's added to your history.

   TIP

   If you see a play icon on an image, click it to watch a video.

3. **Click the back icon (<).**

   News shows the section you were on previously.

4. **Click a category in the sidebar to view articles you're interested in.**

   For example, if you're a sports fan, click Sports in the Suggested by Siri section to view current sports news. Or if you're a foodie, click Food.

5. **To view only the right pane of the interface, click the hide sidebar icon (labeled in Figure 2-6).**

Click the icon again to view the sidebar.

Hide sidebar

News

FIGURE 2-6:
Peruse your daily news in the News app.

REMEMBER

Apple News+ is a subscription service that gives you access to over 300 magazines and newspapers. As of this writing, Apple is offering a 30-day free trial, after which you pay $9.99 per month. You can get News+ also as part of a premier Apple One subscription ($29.95 per month, which also includes Apple Music, TV+, Arcade, iCloud+ with 2TB storage, and Fitness+). To learn more about News+, click the News+ link in the sidebar.

Following a channel or topic

The News app has more news than the average person could consume in a day, and let's face it, some of the news may not appeal to you. You can segregate your favorite types of news by topic and source into neat little links in the Following section of the sidebar. To add a channel or topic to the News sidebar, follow these steps:

1. **Click a link in the sidebar and review the articles.**

2. **When you see an article by a publisher you'd like to follow, right-click the article, click the publisher's name in the context menu, and then click Follow Channel.**

   A window appears with the word *Following* and a check mark. The publisher's name is added to the Following section of the sidebar.

3. **To follow a topic, right-click the topic title in Suggested by Siri, and choose Follow Topic from the context menu.**

   A window appears with the word *Following* and a check mark. The topic is added to the Following section of the sidebar.

To unfollow a channel or topic, in the Following section of the sidebar, right-click the channel or topic and then click Unfollow Channel or Unfollow Topic from the context menu.

TIP

If for some reason you don't want to see news from a specific source or channel, right-click an article by that source or channel, click the publisher's name in the context menu, and then click Block Channel. To learn other ways to restrict content, see the section "Tweaking News content," later in this chapter.

Saving and sharing stories

So much news, so little time. If you're busy but you still like to stay in touch with what's happening in the news, you don't have to read every article that grabs your attention. You can save an article for reading on a rainy day. You can also share an article you think is interesting or would be interesting to a friend.

To save an article, do the following:

1. **In the sidebar, click a section you want to review.**

   The content pane refreshes showing articles in that category.

2. **When you see an article you'd like to save, right-click it and choose Save Story from the context menu.**

   The article is added to the Saved Stories category in the sidebar.

To read a saved story, click Saved Stories in the sidebar and then click the story you want to read.

To remove a saved story, click the Saved Stories link in the sidebar, and then in the News pane, right-click the story and choose Unsave Story from the context menu.

To share a channel or story with a friend, right-click a story in the News pane, and from the context menu, choose Share and then choose an option from the flyout menu. You can share the store via Mail, Messages, Air Drop, Notes, or Reminders.

Tweaking News content

In previous sections, I show you how to read content that's important to you as well as content you like. But let's face it, there are some things you may not want to read (for example, stories with explicit content). To fine-tune the content News makes available for you, do the following:

1. **Choose News⇨Settings.**

   The News Settings window appears.

2. **To limit the amount of content displayed in News today, select the Restrict Stories in Today check box.**

   News displays only stories from channels you follow in Today.

3. **To restrict stories with potentially disturbing content, select the Restrict Stories with Explicit Content check box.**

   News won't show stories with content marked as explicit.

Watching TV on Your Mac

Whether you're an author who spends eight hours or more behind a computer making stuff up or an accountant working on your client's quarterly profit-and-loss statement, you need a break. And the TV app is the perfect source for watching a movie or TV show while you recharge your batteries.

But first you need to launch and navigate the TV app as follows:

1. **Click the TV app icon (pointed out in Figure 2-7) on the dock or in Launchpad.**

   The TV app launches.

2. **Click the Library tab.**

   The Library tab is comprised of a sidebar and the content pane, as shown in Figure 2-7. The sidebar is divided into two sections:

   - *Library:* Enables you to navigate your purchases and rentals

   - *Genres:* Shows the genres of the movies and TV shows you've purchased

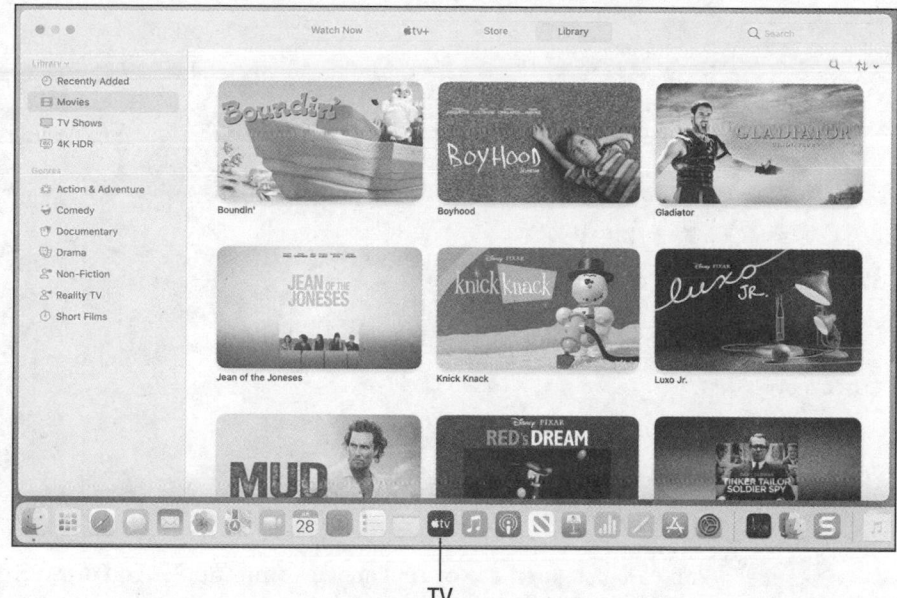

FIGURE 2-7:
It's TV time!

TV

At the top of the interface are two buttons — Watch Now and TV+ — for streaming Apple+ content (if you have a subscription), a Store button to purchase content from Apple, and a button to display your library.

REMEMBER

Apple TV+ is a subscription service that gives you access to hundreds of movies and TV shows, including original Apple programming such as *Ted Lasso* and *The Morning Show*. As of this writing, Apple is offering a seven-day free trial, after which you pay $4.99 per month. (You can also get three free months of Apple TV+ if you purchase certain Apple devices.) You can also get TV+ with any Apple One subscription (starting at $14.95 per month), which also includes Apple Music, Arcade, and iCloud+.

3. Click a link in your Library.

Your options are Recently Added, Movies, TV Shows, 4K HDR, or one of the genres you've purchased.

4. Hover your cursor over a title.

Your options are Play or Download from the Cloud. Click the three-dot icon (. . .) to see more options, as shown in Figure 2-8.

5. Click the play icon to view a movie or TV show.

If you haven't downloaded the movie to your computer, it streams from the Apple Store and begins playing as soon as enough content has downloaded. The movie plays full screen on your computer.

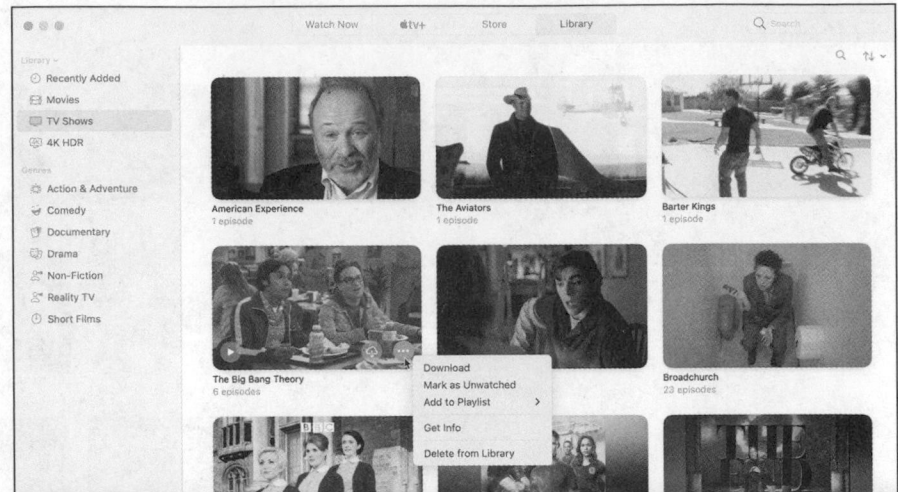

FIGURE 2-8:
Click a movie's
or TV show's
three-dot
icon (. . .) to see
more options.

You can also purchase or rent movies from Apple. You do so from the TV app as follows:

1. **Launch the TV app as outlined in the preceding list.**

2. **Click the Store link at the top of the interface.**

3. **Click the Movies or TV Shows tab.**

   Figure 2-9 shows the Movies section of the Apple Store. At the top of the screen is the featured movie for that section of the store.

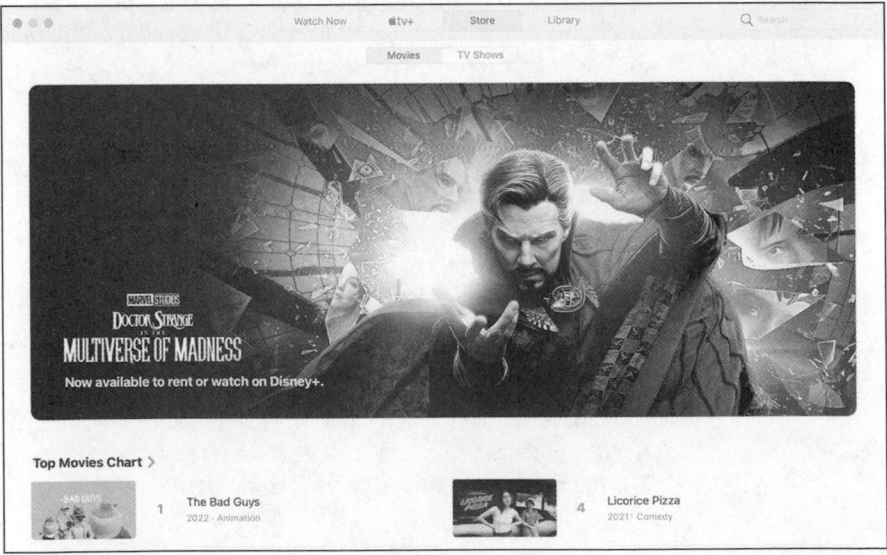

FIGURE 2-9:
Choosing a movie
to buy or rent.

4. **Click a movie or TV show that interests you.**

Information about the movie or show appears in the content pane, as shown in Figure 2-10. The amount of information displayed depends on the show or movie you're considering. Scroll down to see additional information and perhaps play a video trailer.

FIGURE 2-10:
Getting information about a movie.

5. **If you want to watch the movie, do one of the following:**

- *Click Buy.* Click this button to purchase the movie.
- *Click Rent.* Click this button to rent the movie for 24 hours.
- *Click Add to Up Next.* Click this button to add the movie to Watch Now.

After choosing the first or second option, the Sign-in Required dialog appears. If you choose the third option, when you click the movie or show title in Watch Now, the movie or show information appears in the TV pane, and you have the option to buy or rent the movie.

6. **Enter your Apple ID.**

You've purchased or rented the movie.

REMEMBER

The TV app adds purchases to your Library. Unless you choose the option to automatically download TV shows and movies to your computer (choose TV ⇨ Settings ⇨ General and select the Movies and TV Shows check boxes in the Automatic Downloads section), the movie or TV show streams to your computer, which requires an internet connection. If you want to watch a movie anytime and anywhere, choose the option to automatically download Library items to your computer.

Chapter 3

Reading and Listening to Books on Your Mac

When it comes to digital books — or *e-books* as they're usually called — your preferred e-reading device is likely your iPhone or, even better, your iPad with its perfectly sized screen. These portable devices are ideal for settling into a comfy spot to read a page-turner (so to speak) of a novel or some fascinating non-fiction. A reading device that you can hold in your hands is reminiscent of a physical book, so it's the natural way to read e-books.

Then there's your Mac. Many people are surprised to find out that the Mac comes with an app for reading e-books. The idea just seems weird, especially if you have a desktop Mac. Sure, you can rest a MacBook Air or MacBook Pro on your lap to achieve some degree of comfort while reading, but even a notebook Mac seems a tad clunky for easy e-reading.

Still, your Mac does come with the Books app (even if it's a bit harder to find that most other apps), so reading e-books on your Mac is a thing. And if you don't have an iPhone or iPad (or other e-reading device, such as an Amazon Kindle) and want an e-reader, your Mac can fill the role.

In this chapter, you explore the Books app and learn how to use it to purchase e-books in the Book Store, as well as read and manage your e-book collection. But Books also doubles as an audiobook player, so in this chapter you also learn how to use Books to jump on the growing audiobooks bandwagon.

Understanding E-book Formats

If there were one reason why e-books took a long time to take off (in the same way that, say, digital music now rules the planet), it would be because the e-book world started out as hopelessly, headachingly confusing. In the beginning, new formats were announced with distressing frequency and, at its worst, at least two dozen (yes, two dozen!) e-book formats were available.

That situation was bad enough, but it got worse when you considered that some of these formats required a specific e-reading device or program. For example, the Kindle e-book format required the Kindle e-reader or the Kindle app. Similarly, the Microsoft LIT format required the Microsoft Reader program. Finally, things turned positively chaotic when you realized that some formats came with built-in restrictions that prevented you from reading e-books on other devices or programs or sharing e-books with other people.

What the e-book world needed was the simplicity and clarity that comes with having a near-universal e-book format (such as the MP3 format in music). Well, I'm happy to report that one format has emerged from the fray: EPUB. This free and open e-book standard was created by the International Digital Publishing Forum (IDPF; see www.idpf.org). EPUB files (which use the .epub extension) are supported by most e-reader apps and by most e-reader devices (with the Amazon Kindle being the very noticeable exception).

REMEMBER

In spring 2022, Amazon quietly announced that Kindle will begin supporting EPUB files in late 2022.

EPUB is leading the way not only because it's free and nonproprietary but also because it offers the following cool features:

>> Text is resizable, so you can select the size that's most comfortable for you.

>> The layout and formatting of the text are handled by Cascading Style Sheets (CSS). This is an open and well-known standard that makes it easy to alter the look of the text, including changing the font.

>> Text is reflowable. When you change the text size or the font, the text wraps naturally on the screen to accommodate the new character sizes (as opposed to some e-book formats that simply zoom in or out of the text).

>> A single e-book can have alternative versions in the same file.

>> E-books can include high-resolution images right on the page.

>> Publishers can protect book content by adding digital rights management (DRM) support. DRM refers to any technology that restricts the usage of content to prevent piracy. Of course, depending on where you fall in the "information wants to be free" spectrum, DRM may not be cool and may not even be considered a feature.

So, the first bit of good news is that your Mac's Books app supports the EPUB format, which means all the features in the preceding list are available to you.

You can use the Books app to read PDF documents.

The next bit of good news is that the Books app's support for EPUB means that a vast universe of public domain books is available to you. On its own, the Books section of Google Play (https://play.google.com/store/books) offers more than a million public-domain e-books. Several other excellent EPUB sites exist on the web, and I tell you about them, as well as how to get them onto your Mac, a bit later in this chapter.

By definition, public-domain e-books are DRM-free, and you can use them any way you see fit. However, lots of the EPUB books you find come with DRM restrictions. In the case of Apple Books, the DRM scheme of choice is called FairPlay. This is the DRM technology that Apple used on iTunes for many years. Apple phased out DRM on music a while ago but still uses it for other content, such as movies, TV shows, e-books, and audiobooks.

FairPlay means that many of the e-books you download through the Book Store face the following restrictions:

>> You can access your books on a maximum of five computers, each of which must be authorized with your Apple ID account info.

>> You can also read your e-books on a "reasonable number" (Apple's words) of compatible devices that you own, such as your iPhone or iPad.

It's crucial to note the following two restrictions that you trip over with DRM-encrusted e-books:

>> FairPlay e-books don't work on other e-reader devices that support the EPUB format, including the Kobo Libra and the Barnes & Noble NOOK.

>> EPUB-format books that come wrapped in some other DRM scheme do not work in the Books app.

However, remember that DRM is an optional add-on to the EPUB format. Although it's expected that most publishers will bolt FairPlay DRM onto books they sell in the Book Store, it's not required. So, you should be able to find DRM-free e-books in the Book Store (and elsewhere).

Launching the Books App

Unlike many of the apps I've talked about in this book, the Books app doesn't have its own slot on the dock. To launch Books, you have two choices:

>> Open Launchpad and then click the Books icon (labeled in Figure 3-1).

>> Click the search icon (magnifying glass) on the right side of the menu bar, type *Books*, and then click the Books app when it appears in the search results.

Figure 3-1 shows the basic Books window. Any e-books or audiobooks you previously purchased from Apple Books will be automatically shown in Books. Books that have been downloaded to your Mac are accessible from Books. Books that you purchased but didn't download to your Mac have a cloud icon in the right corner of the book icon, which means they're available for download.

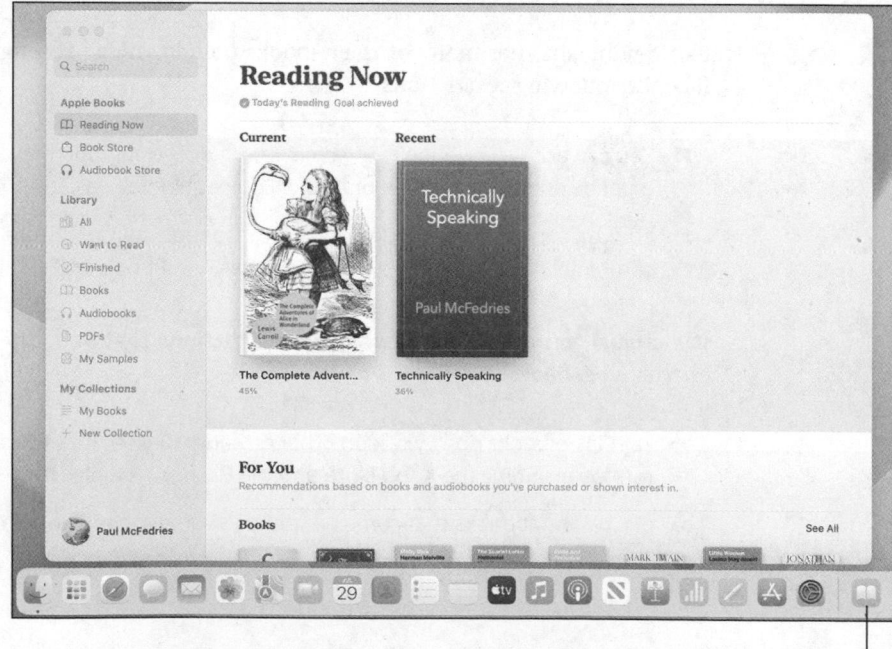

FIGURE 3-1:
Explore the
Books window.

Books icon

Touring the Sidebar

The sidebar (the pane that takes up the left side of the Books window) is your main Books navigation tool. As you see in Figure 3-1, below the Search box there are three sections to the sidebar: Apple Books, Library, and My Collections. I cover each of these sections next.

Apple Books

The Apple Books section of the sidebar organizes the items in your Apple Books subscription. You have three basic ways of navigating Apple Books:

>> **Reading Now:** Shows the e-book you're currently reading, recently read e-books, a few recommendations based on your reading, and a look at some new titles. The Reading Now section is also home to your reading goals:

- *Daily Reading Goal:* The number of reading minutes per day you want to shoot for. To set your daily reading goal, hover the mouse pointer over the Today's Reading chart, click the settings icon (equalizer), enter a number (in minutes per day) in the spin box, and then click OK.

- *Books Read this Year:* The number of books you want to read during the calendar year. To set the number of books you want to read, hover the mouse pointer over the Books Read This Year section, click the settings icon (equalizer), enter a number (in books per year) in the spin box, and then click OK.

>> **Book Store:** Enables you to access the Book Store's huge collection of e-books. See "Browsing the Book Store," later in this chapter.

>> **Audiobook Store:** Enables you to peruse the Audiobook Store's supply of audiobooks. See "Now Hear This: Listening to Audiobooks," later in this chapter.

Library

The Library section of the sidebar is where you navigate the e-books and audiobooks you've purchased or imported on your own. Seven items are in the Library section:

>> **All:** Your complete collection of e-books, PDFs, and audiobooks

>> **Want to Read:** A list of e-books and audiobooks that you've marked that you'd like to read or hear someday

- » **Finished:** The e-books and audiobooks that you've completed

- » **Books:** The e-books that you've purchased or imported (see Figure 3-2)

- » **Audiobooks:** The audiobooks that you've purchased or imported

- » **PDFs:** The PDFs that you've purchased or imported

- » **Samples:** The e-books and audiobooks for which you've asked to view samples

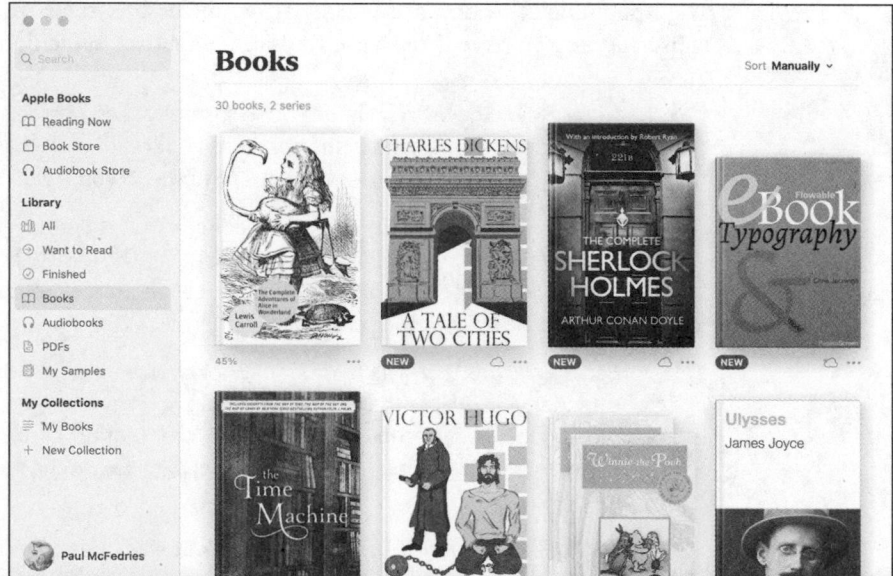

FIGURE 3-2:
The Books app organizes your items by e-books (as shown here), audiobooks, PDFs, and more.

My Collections

You can use Books to select a group of e-books and audiobooks and store those songs as a *collection*. For example, you might want to organize all your mystery novels as one collection and all your 19th-century female writers as another. You can also add a single book to multiple collections.

To create a collection, click New Collection in the sidebar, type a name for the collection, and then press Return. To add a book to this collection, follow these steps:

1. **Use the sidebar's links to locate the book you want to add.**

2. **Click the book's three-dots (...) icon and then click Add to Collection.**

   The Add to Collection dialog appears.

3. **Click the collection to which you want to add the book.**

   Books adds the book to the selected collection.

TIP

Another way to add a book to a collection is to locate it, drag it to the sidebar, and then drop it on the collection.

Browsing the Book Store

The Book Store is the place to go for all your e-book needs, from the latest best-sellers to the timeless classics. The Book Store is home to a massive collection of e-books, most of which you have to buy to read, but a surprising number are free for the downloading.

To browse and shop for e-books, follow these steps:

1. **In the Books sidebar, click the Book Store button.**

   The Book Store opens for business, as shown in Figure 3-3. The Main page shows some featured content at the top, followed by various sections, including New & Trending (the latest and greatest books), For You (recommendations based on your reading habits), Top Charts (a list of top paid books), Coming Soon (books soon to be published), Books We Love (recommendations from the Book Store staff), and Genres.

2. **Click the See All link that appears beside most sections to see the full list of books in that section.**

   You can also navigate sections by clicking the Browse Sections drop-down list near the top-right corner of the Book Store window. This displays a complete list of the Book Store sections, as shown in Figure 3-4. Click the section you want.

   Alternatively, you can type a query into the sidebar's Search text box to find a specific book or genre of books.

3. **Click a book that interests you.**

   The book's the info screen appears (see Figure 3-5) and shows the usual information: title, author, price, ratings, reviews, details (genre, release date, pages, publisher, and more), and related books.

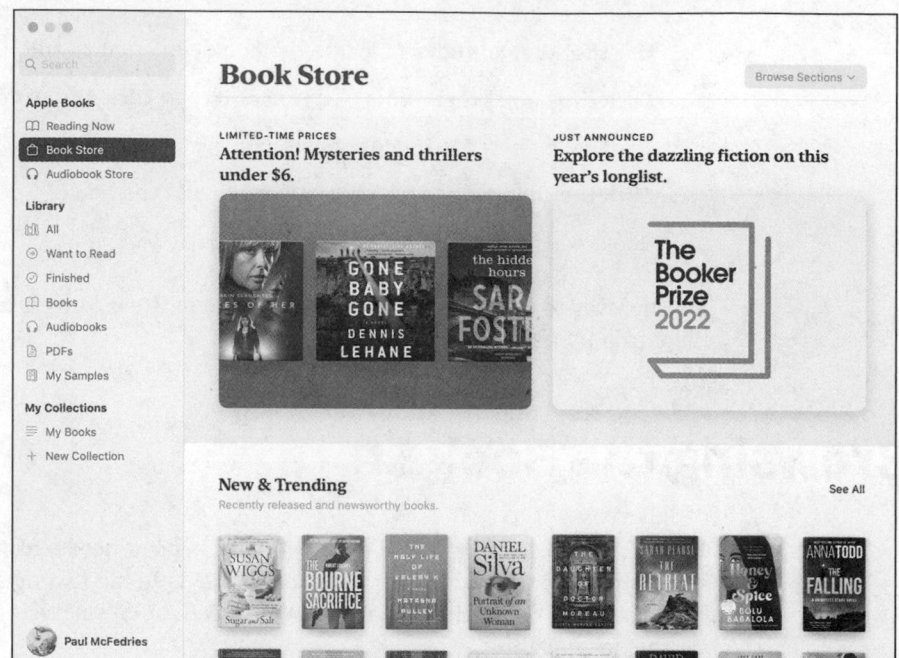

FIGURE 3-3:
The Book Store is
your Mac's local
book shop.

FIGURE 3-4:
Click Browse
Sections to see
all the Book Store
sections.

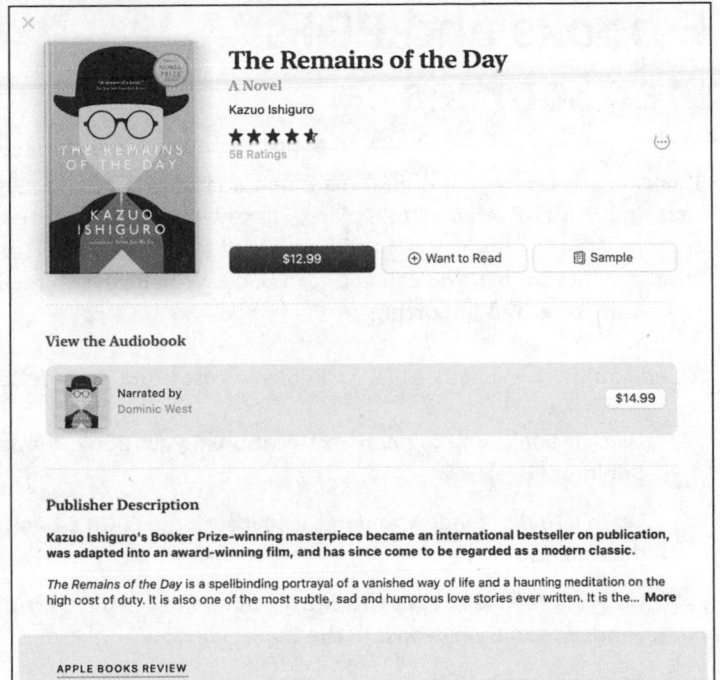

FIGURE 3-5:
The info
screen tells
you everything
you need to
know to make
an informed
purchase.

4. **After you find something you want to try or purchase, click one of the following:**

- *Price:* Click the price button to purchase the book. Enter your Apple ID password in the dialog that appears, and then click Buy to complete the purchase.

- *Want to Read:* Click this button to add the book to your Want to Read list.

- *Sample:* Click this button to download a sample of the book, which then appears onscreen as well as in the sidebar's My Samples area.

As items are downloading, you can continue browsing. After the book down-loads to your Mac, the book has a New or Sample banner across it in your library.

REMEMBER

As long as you sign in to the same Apple ID on all your devices, the Books app syncs purchases from the Book Store across your iOS devices and Macs.

Adding E-books and PDFs from Other Sources

Books neatly keeps your digital reading material such as e-books in the EPUB format and PDFs together in one place. However, the Book Store isn't the only way to populate your library. If you've obtained an EPUB e-book or a PDF document from another source, you can add it to Books. You have two methods you can use: drag-and-drop and importing.

To add an EPUB e-book or PDF to Books via drag and drop, following these steps:

1. **Use the Books app to open any location in your Books library (such as Books or PDFs).**

2. **Open a Finder window and use it to locate the EPUB e-book or PDF document.**

3. **Use your mouse to drag the EPUB e-book file or PDF file from the Finder window, and then drop it in the Books window.**

   Books imports the file.

To import either an EPUB e-book or a PDF that you obtained from sources other than the Book Store, do the following:

1. **Choose File ⇨ Import.**

   A file chooser appears.

2. **Select the EPUB e-book or PDF document you want to import.**

3. **Click Import.**

   Books imports the file.

Reading by Screen Light

After you download one or more books, the joy begins. In the sidebar's Library section, click Books, and then double-click the book you want to read. The book opens in a separate window, as shown in Figure 3-6, usually to the cover but sometimes (as with a sample) to a random page.

TIP

To quickly open a book you recently read, choose File ⇨ Open Recent and select the book you want from the submenu.

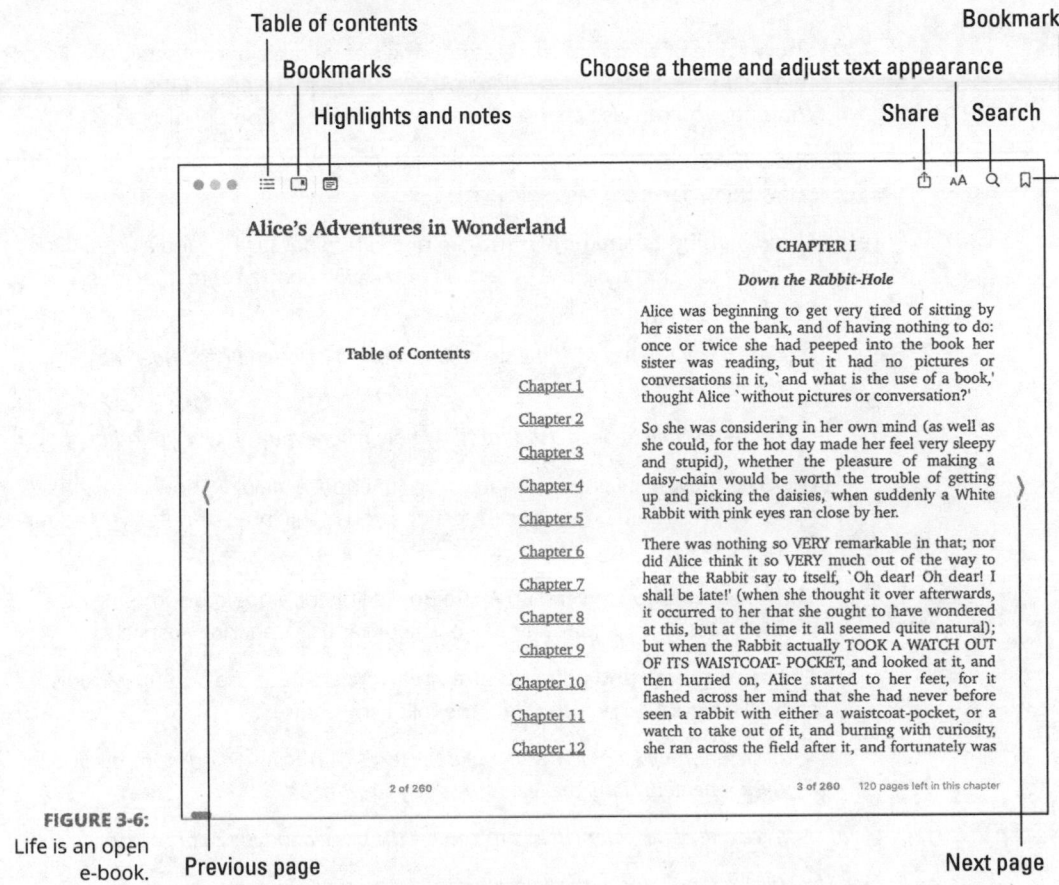

Table of contents

Bookmarks

Highlights and notes

Choose a theme and adjust text appearance

Bookmark

Share   Search

Alice's Adventures in Wonderland

CHAPTER I

Down the Rabbit-Hole

Alice was beginning to get very tired of sitting by her sister on the bank, and of having nothing to do: once or twice she had peeped into the book her sister was reading, but it had no pictures or conversations in it, `and what is the use of a book,' thought Alice `without pictures or conversation?'

Table of Contents

Chapter 1
Chapter 2
Chapter 3
Chapter 4
Chapter 5
Chapter 6
Chapter 7
Chapter 8
Chapter 9
Chapter 10
Chapter 11
Chapter 12

So she was considering in her own mind (as well as she could, for the hot day made her feel very sleepy and stupid), whether the pleasure of making a daisy-chain would be worth the trouble of getting up and picking the daisies, when suddenly a White Rabbit with pink eyes ran close by her.

There was nothing so VERY remarkable in that; nor did Alice think it so VERY much out of the way to hear the Rabbit say to itself, `Oh dear! Oh dear! I shall be late!' (when she thought it over afterwards, it occurred to her that she ought to have wondered at this, but at the time it all seemed quite natural); but when the Rabbit actually TOOK A WATCH OUT OF ITS WAISTCOAT- POCKET, and looked at it, and then hurried on, Alice started to her feet, for it flashed across her mind that she had never before seen a rabbit with either a waistcoat-pocket, or a watch to take out of it, and burning with curiosity, she ran across the field after it, and fortunately was

2 of 260

3 of 260   120 pages left in this chapter

FIGURE 3-6:
Life is an open
e-book.

Previous page

Next page

When you read a book, you can change pages using the following techniques:

>> *Move to the next page:* Move your mouse pointer to the right side of the right page and a right-pointing arrow appears; click that arrow to advance to the next page. You can also press the right arrow key. If you have a trackpad, slide two fingers to the left.

>> *Move to the preceding page:* Move your mouse pointer to the left side of the left page to reveal a left-pointing arrow; click that arrow to display the preceding page. You can also use the left arrow key. If you have a trackpad, slide two fingers to the right.

The toolbar at the top of the screen is bedecked with all kinds of icons (handily labeled in Figure 3-6). Here's what they do:

>> **Show table of contents:** Navigates to the book's table of contents page. From there, click the chapter or section you want to read. To display the table of contents, you can also choose View ⇨ Show Table of Content or press ⌘+T.

>> **Show bookmarks:** See a list of bookmarked pages. (You can also choose View ⇨ Show Bookmarks or press Shift+⌘+D.)

>> **Show highlights and notes:** You can highlight a passage or add a note. Click and drag to select a phrase or section of text. When the contextual menu opens, do one of the following:

- *Click a color to highlight the selected text or click Underline to underline the text.*

- *Click Add Note to open a virtual sticky note where you can type your thoughts.*

Click the show highlights and notes icon (or choose View ⇨ Show Highlights & Notes or press Shift+⌘+N) to see sections you highlighted or notes you added to the book.

>> **Share:** Enables you to send an Apple Books link for a book to someone else via Mail, Messages, AirDrop or any of the other usual sharing suspects.

>> **Choose a theme and adjust text appearance:** Opens the pop-up window shown in Figure 3-7, which offers the following choices:

- *Click the small A or large A to make the text size smaller or larger, respectively. Click repeatedly until the text is the size you want.*

- *Click one of the color choices to change the page and type colors.*

- *Click a font name in the list to change the typeface.*

>> **Search:** Look for a specific word or phrase or jump to a page number. Books offers a list of suggestions as you type. Click the desired item, and Books navigates to it.

>> **Bookmark:** Virtually dog-ear a page so you can find it later.

If you come across an unknown or unusual word, double-click the word and then click Look Up Selection to display the definition of the word in a new window.

To further customize your e-reading experience, choose Books ⇨ Settings, and then click the Reading button to turn on options such as auto-hyphenation and justified text.

TIP

Enhanced or interactive books may have multimedia capabilities, such as clicking a three-dimensional item and then rotating it to view different angles, or watching a video that correlates with the book. These types of books can be read only in Books on Macs and iPads.

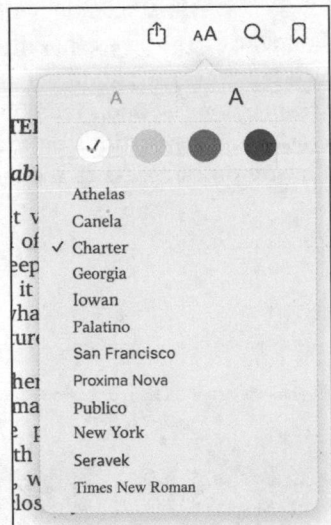

FIGURE 3-7:
Adjust the
typeface style,
size, and color
for comfortable
reading.

WARNING

Some authors have designed their books to work on iOS devices such as the iPad or iPhone. If your computer can't use some of the features exclusive to iOS devices, a warning dialog appears. In spite of the warning dialog, you'll still be able to access many book features. When this dialog appears, click OK and read on.

Now Hear This: Listening to Audiobooks

What do you do if you want to curl up with a good book, but you're driving, working out, cooking, or otherwise doing something that prevents the "curling up" part? Easy: The next best thing to reading a good book is *listening* to one. And, even better, you can use the Books app to browse, buy, and play audiobooks — and performing these tasks is just as straightforward as it is for e-books.

Browsing the Audiobook Store

The Books app maintains a separate Audiobook Store that you can use to peruse a vast collection of audiobooks in genres such as biographies, business, fiction, mysteries, romance, sci-fi, and self-development. To visit the store, click the Audiobook Store link in the sidebar's Apple Books section.

As you can see in Figure 3-8, the Audiobook Store's main page includes a couple of featured audiobooks at the top, followed by sections such as Audiobooks for You (recommendations based on your previous purchases), New & Trending (the latest and greatest audiobooks), Top Audiobooks (the bestseller list), Special Offers (audiobooks on the cheap, including a few freebies), Audiobooks We Love (audiobooks recommended by the Books team), Coming Soon (audiobooks in the pipeline), and Genres. You can also click the Browse Sections button in the top-right corner of the Audiobook Store window for quick access to sections and genres.

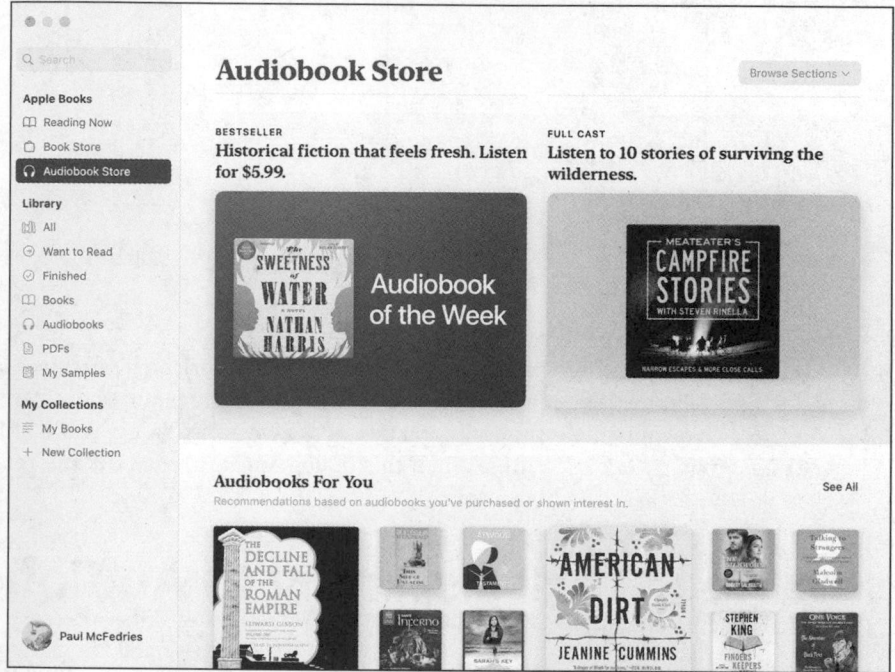

FIGURE 3-8:
The Book app's
Audiobook Store.

If you see an audiobook that piques your interest, click it. The book's info screen appears (see Figure 3-9) and shows the audiobook's particulars, including the title, author, narrator, price, ratings, reviews, details (genre, release date, pages, publisher, and more), and related books.

REMEMBER

Another way to get to an audiobook's info screen is to use the Book Store to open the info screen of the e-book, and then click the View the Audiobook link.

Once you find an audiobook you want to try or purchase, click one of the following:

>> **Price:** Click the price button to purchase the audiobook and download it to your Mac.

>> **Want to Read:** Click this button to add the audiobook to your Want to Read list.

>> **Preview:** Click this button to download and play a sample of the audiobook.

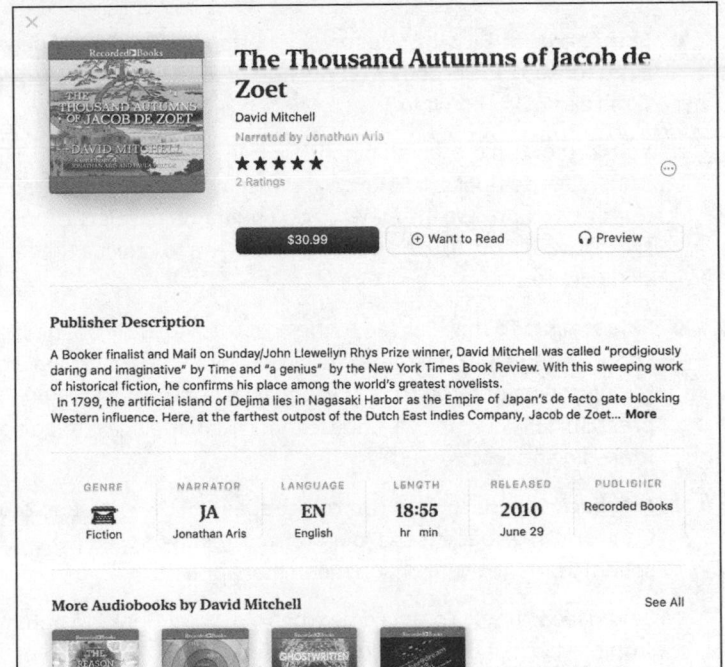

FIGURE 3-9:
The info screen
for an audiobook
is chock full of
useful tidbits to
help you decide
whether to buy
the book.

Listening to and navigating an audiobook

When you're ready to listen to an audiobook you've purchased, click the Audiobooks link in the sidebar's Library section, and then double-click the audiobook. The Books app immediately starts playing the audiobook, which appears in the Now Playing section of the toolbar.

Use the following tools and techniques to control the playback of the audiobook:

» **Play/pause:** Click the play/pause icon in the toolbar. You can also toggle between playing and pausing by pressing the spacebar and by choosing Controls ⇨ Pause and Controls ⇨ Play.

» **Volume:** The controls to the right of the Now Playing area enable you to control the playback volume. Drag the slider right to increase the volume (or press ⌘+up arrow); drag the slider left to decrease the volume (or press ⌘+down arrow). Click the left icon to mute the volume; click the right icon to maximize the volume.

» **Skip back:** Click the skip back icon (to the left of play/pause) to go back 15 seconds. You can also press ⌘+left arrow or choose Controls ⇨ Skip Back.

TIP

» **Skip forward:** Click the skip forward button (to the right of play/pause) to go forward 15 seconds. You can also press ⌘+right arrow or choose Controls ➪ Skip Forward.

You can control the length of time for both the skip back and skip forward icons. Choose Books ➪ Settings and then click the Playback tab. In the Skip Buttons section, use the Forward pop-up menu to select a time interval for the skip forward icon; use the Back pop-up menu to select a time interval for the skip back icon.

» **Skip tracks:** To move ahead to the next track (usually the next chapter), choose Controls ➪ Next Track (or press Shift+⌘+right arrow). To return to the beginning of the current track, choose Controls ➪ Previous Track (or press Shift+⌘+left arrow). Choose that command again to go back to the preceding track.

» **Playback speed:** You can control the speed of the narration by choosing Controls ➪ Playback Speed, then select a relative speed (where 1x is normal speed) from the continuation menu that appears.

» **Set a sleep timer:** To set a time when you want Books to automatically stop playback of the audiobook, choose Control ➪ Sleep Timer, and then select either a time interval (such as 5 minutes or 1 hour) or When Current Chapter Ends.

IN THIS CHAPTER

» Seeing how digital photography works

» Getting your digital images onto your Mac

» Organizing your images

» Taking photos with Photo Booth

» Editing your images in Photos

» Sharing photos with family and friends

Chapter **4**

Picture Perfect: Working with Photos

'm a photographer. My wife is a photographer. All our friends, neighbors, and family members are photographers. You, too, are probably a photographer. How do I know? Because one of the defining characteristics of our modern age is that *everyone* takes photos. Not because everyone wants to be the next Henri Cartier-Bresson or Annie Leibovitz. No, everyone takes photos because everyone carries with them a high-end camera in the form of an iPhone or a similar smartphone. Not only are today's smartphone cameras sophisticated and feature-rich, but they're also incredibly easy to use. Point-and-tap has become the new point-and-shoot.

You can argue that many (most?) people spend far too much time with their phone in front of their face taking pictures and shooting videos instead of enjoying the moment, but let's leave that for another book. The point, really, is that you probably have a huge collection of photos to deal with. Fortunately, that's not a problem because you can use your Mac's Photos app not only for image editing but also for managing and sharing your photos. From start to finish, Photos can take care of organizing your photos so you can focus on taking even more photos. I explain all these tasks in this chapter, but first, I provide a brief introduction — or refresher — on digital photography.

Understanding Digital Photography

A digital photo is one that exists in an electronic format (rather than, say, film). The colors you see in a digital photo come from tiny square pinpoints of light called *pixels,* short for picture elements. The pixels are arranged in rows and columns and the total number of pixels — that is, the number of rows multiplied by the number of columns — is known as the *resolution.*

Today's smartphones and tablets have resolutions measured in *megapixels* — that is, millions of pixels; MP, for short — with modern device cameras capable of producing images with resolutions of 8MP, 12MP, and even more. That's a *lot* of pixels.

Figure 4-1 shows how pixels create an image. The window on the right is a magnified version of the little square pointed out in the window on the left. With the extreme magnification, the right window shows the individual pixels that make up the photo.

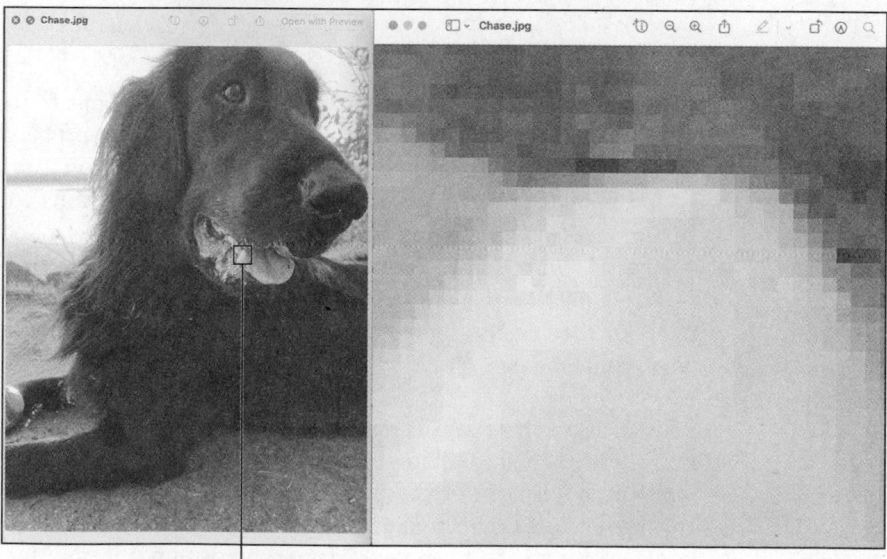

FIGURE 4-1: A digital photo looks smooth (left) but is actually composed of millions of pixels (right).

This area is magnified in the window on the right

One of the prime purposes of high-resolution images is that you can point and shoot and then crop and edit the photo from the very large image you've captured. But try to capture the best image you can and then do a minimal amount of editing.

When you take photos, your digital camera stores those photos in a specific graphics file format. The two most common file formats for capturing digital photographs are

>> **JPEG (Joint Photographic Experts Group):** JPEG is the most common file format because it's recognized by most computers and offers the capability to compress images to shrink the overall file size. (*Compressing* a JPEG file means decreasing the number of colors used in an image, which shrinks the file size but lowers the visual quality.)

>> **RAW:** RAW files are the equivalent of digital negatives. After capturing an image in a camera's RAW format, you can edit it to pixel perfection in Apple's Photos app. Every digital camera manufacturer offers its own RAW file format.

The biggest advantage of RAW files is that they allow for greater manipulation, which is why professional photographers often use RAW files. The biggest disadvantage is that RAW images take up a large amount of storage space, which means that you can't store as many images as photos captured in other formats.

Ultimately, there is no single best file format. If a digital camera lets you save images in different file formats, experiment to see which one you like best. You may prefer one type of file format, such as JPEG, for ordinary use but prefer RAW for special situations that don't require capturing images quickly, such as taking photos of a landscape.

TECHNICAL STUFF

Many cameras also offer the option to capture both RAW and JPEG images at the same time, giving you the best of both worlds. The JPEG images can be used immediately for the web and such, and the RAW images can be used for the special images you want to edit to perfection and print.

Transferring Digital Images to the Mac

To transfer photos from a device — digital camera, mobile phone, scanner, or tablet — to your Mac, you have a couple of choices:

>> You can connect your device to your Mac by using a USB cable or wirelessly using AirDrop or your local network, if your device supports that option.

>> You can pop the flash memory card out of your device and plug it into your Mac's built-in SD card reader (if your camera uses SD cards and if your Mac has the reader) or a third-party card reader that connects to your Mac's USB port.

Except for transferring photos via AirDrop, your Mac treats all the images stored on your device or on the flash memory card as just another external drive from which you can copy photos to your Mac's hard drive (such as into the Photos folder).

When you connect a device to your Mac, it can automatically load an app to retrieve those images. Photos and Image Capture, which both come preloaded on your Mac, can retrieve digital snapshots automatically. In this chapter, I focus on Photos. Use Image Capture if you just want to store photos on your Mac and use a different application to edit them. But most applications such as Adobe Photoshop Elements and Adobe Lightroom can easily import your digital treasures.

If you organize photos in the Photos app, choose it as your default app to retrieve photos from a device. (You can specify another app as the external editor.) If you use a different app to organize your photos, such as Adobe Lightroom, you can make that app your default app. If you use more than one app to organize your photos, you can make Image Capture your default app and then use the Open With command to choose the app you want to use to edit your imported photos, deciding what to use on an image-by-image basis.

Importing photos with the Photos app

The Photos app can import both photos and videos from your camera or phone to your Mac. To import images to Photos, follow these steps:

REMEMBER

1. **Connect your device to your Mac with the appropriate cable (or plug your memory card into your memory card reader).**

   If you're connecting a smartphone or tablet, make sure the device is unlocked.

2. **Launch the Photos app by clicking the Photos icon on the dock (see Figure 4-2) or in Launchpad.**

   The Photos app opens and displays a sidebar and a content pane in which the images appear.

3. **In the sidebar's Devices section, click the device or card that contains the photos you want to import.**

   The images on the device or card are displayed in the content area, as shown in Figure 4-2.

FIGURE 4-2:
Importing a
camera's images
to Photos.

Photos

4. **(Optional) Select Open Photos for This Device.**

If you select this check box, the next time you connect this card or device to your Mac, Photos launches automatically.

5. **Choose an option from the Album pop-up menu.**

The default option is None, which means the imported photos are added to the Library. However, I suggest you choose New Album. This is an important first step to organizing your photo library. If you shoot lots of images, and store them all in the Library, you'll have a hard time finding images even though Photos separates images by the date they were photographed. Let's face it: Scrolling through hundreds of photographs shot on different dates is hard work.

If you heed my sage advice, the New Album dialog appears.

6. **Type a name for your new album, and then click Create.**

To make your life easier (by making your photos easier to find), give the album a name that accurately reflects what the photos represent. If the photos are from a trip to England's Lake District in 2023, a simple name such as Lake District 2023 pretty much tells you everything you need to know.

7. **(Optional) Select the Delete Items after Import check box.**

I suggest you leave this check box deselected unless you're importing images from a phone.

8. **(Optional) Select the photos you want to import by clicking the thumbnail for each photo.**

Unless you're sure you just need a subset of the device photos, it's usually best to import all images. It's hard to judge by looking at a thumbnail whether an image is in focus or whether you like the image.

9. **Import the photos by clicking one of the following buttons:**

- *Import All New Photos:* Imports every photo that you haven't previously imported.

- *Import x Selected:* Imports just the photos you selected (where *x* is the number of images you selected in Step 8).

Photos imports your images.

WARNING

Never yank a memory card out of the card reader port or pull a card reader with a card out of a USB port; doing so may cause your Mac to scramble the data on the memory card. Before physically removing a flash memory card from the port, eject the card safely from your Mac by clicking the Eject button that appears to the right of the flash memory icon in the Finder window sidebar.

Moving photos from other folders into Photos

If you have photos or image files in other folders on your Mac or on an external hard drive or flash drive, follow these steps to bring the photos and images into Photos:

1. **Click the Photos icon on the dock or in Launchpad.**

The Photos app opens.

2. **Choose File ⇨ Import.**

A Finder window opens.

3. **Navigate to the folder that contains the photos you want to import, click the folder, and then click Review for Import.**

Alternatively, open the folder, select individual images by clicking each file you want to import, and then click Review for Import.

After choosing Review for Import, the images appear in the content area. Notice that Photos knows whether an image has already been imported.

4. **Choose an option from the Album pop-up menu.**

I strongly suggest you put the images in a new album as outlined in the preceding section, unless they should be added to an existing album, in which case the album is listed on the pop-up menu.

5. **(Optional) Select the photos you want to import by clicking the thumbnail for each photo.**

Since you have, in a sense, preselected these photos, it's unlikely you'll want to import just a subset of them, but to each their own.

6. **Import the photos by clicking one of the following buttons:**

- *Import All New Photos:* Imports every photo that you haven't previously imported.

- *Import x Selected:* Imports just the photos you selected (where *x* is the number of images you selected in Step 8).

Photos imports your images.

TIP

A fast way to import single photos into Photos is to drag and drop those photos to the Photos icon on the dock or to the Photos app's Library category, which is located in the Photos section of the sidebar.

TIP

If you want to access your photos on all your other devices as well as on the web, tell Photos to upload them to iCloud. This enables you to access the photos on the iCloud site and also makes the photos available on every device signed in to the same Apple ID. Choose Photos ➪ Settings, click the iCloud tab, and select the iCloud Photos check box.

Organizing Your Photo Library

Let's face it: Modern photography is both easy and fun, which is a recipe for shooting hundreds, if not thousands, of images. Why not? But if you just keep adding images to Photos, you end up with a virtual shoebox full of photos with no idea how to find the image of Aunt June that you photographed on Mother's Day in 2016. Earlier in this chapter, I talk a little about organization. But there are a few more things you can do to have a squeaky-clean library in Photos. Yes, the process takes time, but the amount of time pales in comparison to trying to find one treasured image among thousands.

Tagging images

If you get in the habit of tagging images after you import them, they'll be much easier to find later. The secret to tagging (also known as *keywording*) images is to use every conceivable keyword that fits an image. When I import images, I create a keyword for the place the image was photographed or the name of the person in the photography, the type of photography (for example, macro, nature, portrait, or street photography), and any other words that can help describe the image.

REMEMBER

Photos automatically detects scenes, objects, and location types in your photos. For example, if you have lots of photos of beach vacations (lucky you!), you don't have to tag those photos with, say, the terms *beach* or *ocean* or even *palm tree* because Photos automatically detects those whenever they appear in a shot. Automatic detection means that you can search for a term — such as *beach* — and Photos will find all your beach photos even when you don't explicitly add that keyword to the photos.

To add keywords to your images, follow these steps:

1. **Import the images as outlined in the "Transferring Digital Images to the Mac" section, earlier in the chapter.**

   I strongly suggest you create an album for the images.

REMEMBER

2. **Select all the images you just imported.**

   If you imported the photos to an album, select the album from the sidebar's My Albums list, and then choose Edit ⇨ Select All (or press ⌘+A).

3. **Choose Window ⇨ Info.**

   Alternatively, either press ⌘+I or right-click any selected photo and then choose Get Info from the context menu.

   The Info dialog appears.

4. **In the Add a Keyword text field, type a keyword and then press Return.**

   For example, you could start with the name of the place the image was photographed (say, South Beach), and then add a separate keyword for the name of the town (Miami), and a separate keyword for the state (Florida).

5. **Repeat Step 4 to add as many keywords as you need.**

TIP

   If you really like an image, click the heart icon to tag the image as a favorite. You can view these images by clicking the Favorites link in the sidebar.

6. **Click the red close icon.**

   The keywords are applied to the selected images.

While the images you just imported are still in the content area, you can fine-tune your keywords by selecting an individual image or a couple of similar images and adding a keyword. For example, if you're adding keywords to vacation photos and have got some stellar images of Uncle Bob, select those images, right-click, choose Info from the context menu, and add the keyword *Uncle Bob* to them.

TIP

Another option for tagging images is tagging portraits of friends and family with a name. You do this in the Info panel by adding the person's name to the Faces section of the Info window. Any photographs to which you add a person's name appear in the People section of the sidebar.

Using Keyword Manager

Keyword Manager stores all the keywords you've used. You use Keyword Manager to add keywords and to create shortcut keys for keywords.

To display Keyword Manager, choose Window ⇨ Keyword Manager. You can then do the following:

>> **To add a keyword to the list:** Click Edit Keywords, click the plus sign (+), type the new keyword, and then press Return.

>> **To delete a keyword from the list:** Click Edit Keywords, select the keyword, and click the minus sign (–).

>> **To assign a shortcut key to a keyword:** A shortcut key is a letter you press while a photo is displayed to add the keyword to the photo. You have two ways to create a shortcut key for a keyword:

- In Keyword Manager, drag the keyword from the Keywords section to the Quick Group section of the window. Keyword Manager automatically assigns the lowercase version of the keyword's first letter as its shortcut. For example, if the keyword is *Scotland,* the shortcut is *s.*

- Click Edit Keywords, click the keyword, and then click Shortcut. In the text field that appears, type the letter you want to use for the keyword shortcut. For example, if the keyword is South Beach but you've already used *s* as a shortcut, *b* would be a reasonable alternative. Click OK. The keyword is added to the Quick Group section.

When you've finished working in Keyword Manager, click the close icon.

To apply one or more keywords, first select the photo or photos to which you want to apply the keywords. Choose Window ⇨ Keyword Manager, and then for each keyword you want to apply, either click the keyword or press the keyword's shortcut key.

Manually adding information to photos

Your camera or phone automatically adds information to images, such as camera information and GPS data. In this section, I show you how to manually add titles, captions, and other information to your photos. To do so, follow these steps:

1. **Select the photo you want to modify.**

2. **Choose Window ⇨ Info.**

    Alternatively, either press ⌘+I or right-click any selected photo and then choose Get Info from the context menu.

    The Info dialog appears, as shown in Figure 4-3.

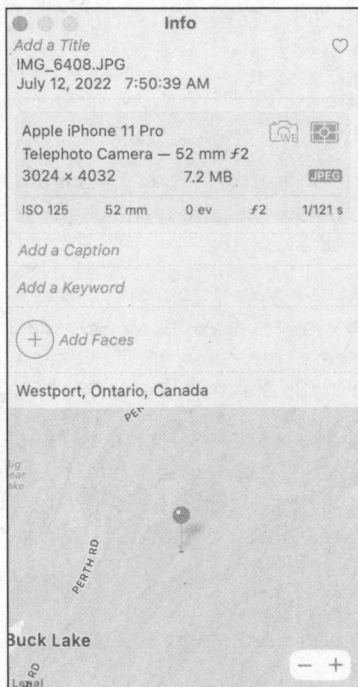

FIGURE 4-3: Add or modify information about a photo.

3. **Edit information for the photo(s) by clicking in the following fields:**

- *Add a Title:* Edit or type a title for the selected photo. If you've selected multiple images, the same title will be applied to all.

- *Add a Caption:* Edit or type a descriptive word or words to describe the photo so you can search for it when you want to find it again. If you've selected multiple images, the same description will be applied to all.

- *Add Faces:* This option is available only if you right-click a full-size image (not a thumbnail). Enter the person's name in the text field, and the image appears in the sidebar's People section.

4. **Click the close icon.**

Creating a smart album

If manually dragging photos in and out of albums is too tedious, you can set up a *smart album* from Photos that will store photos automatically. Follow these steps:

1. **Choose File ⇨ New Smart Album.**

   A dialog appears, asking for a name for your smart album.

2. **In the Smart Album Name text box, type a descriptive name for your album.**

3. **Open the first pop-up menu and choose a criterion, such as Title or Person, or a camera setting like Aperture or Camera Model.**

4. **Open the second and third pop-up menus to refine the criterion you choose in Step 3, such as choosing only photos where the title includes a particular word or phrase.**

   After you define criterion for your smart album, the number of photos that match are listed at the bottom of the dialog.

5. **(Optional) To define another condition, click the plus sign (+) button and repeat Steps 3 and 4.**

   You can add as many conditions to a smart album as you please.

6. **Click OK.**

   Your smart album now stores photos based on your specified conditions. New photos that match the conditions are added to the list.

Organizing albums with folders

Creating albums is a great way to organize your images, but if you're a prolific photographer, you end up with a long list of albums to scroll through to find the one you want. You can make your life a lot easier by creating a folder and then adding albums to that folder. For example, if you organize your vacation photos by creating a new album for each trip you take, you can create a Vacations folder to store all those albums in one place.

To create a folder in which to store your images, follow these steps:

1. **In the Photos sidebar, hover the mouse pointer over My Albums and then click the plus sign (+) that appears.**

   A new folder is added to the My Albums section of the sidebar.

2. **Enter the desired name for the folder.**

3. **Drag albums into the folder.**

   After you organize several albums into a folder, click the disclosure arrow to close the folder.

Deleting photos, albums, and folders

Many times, you'll import photos into Photos and decide that some of those photos aren't worth saving after all. To keep your Photos library from becoming too cluttered, you can delete the photos you don't need.

Besides deleting individual photos, you can also delete albums and folders that contain images you don't want. When you delete an album or a folder (which contains albums), you don't delete the photos; you just delete the folder or album that contains the photos. The original photos are still stored in your Photos library.

Here are the techniques to use to delete stuff in the Photos app:

TIP

>> **To delete a photo from the library:** Locate the photo in your Photos library, click the photo, press the Delete key, and then click Delete when Photos asks you to confirm. If you delete a photo from an album, it's deleted only from that album, not from Photos.

If you just want to delete duplicate photos, the easiest method is to click the sidebar's Duplicates link. The content pane shows all your duplicated photos. It's best here to click the Merge *X* Duplicates link above each set of duplicates (where *X* is the number of duplicates) and then click Merge *X* Duplicates when Photos asks you to confirm. Photos merges the highest-quality elements from the duplicates into a single image.

>> **To delete a photo from an album:** Open the album, click the photo, and then press the Delete key (Photos doesn't ask you to confirm the deletion). Note that when you delete a photo from an album, it's deleted only from that album, not from your library.

>> **To delete an album:** In the sidebar, right-click the album and then click Delete Album. (Alternatively, click My Albums in the sidebar, click the album, and then press Delete.)

>> **To delete a folder:** In the sidebar, right-click the folder and then click Delete Folder. (Alternatively, click My Albums in the sidebar, click the album, and then press Delete.) When Photos asks you to confirm, click Delete.

TIP

If you want to recover your deleted items, press ⌘+Z or choose Edit ⇨ Undo Delete right away. Alternatively, click the sidebar's Recently Deleted link, enter your Mac account password to unlock this folder, right-click the photo you want to restore, and then click Recover.

TIP

If you don't want to delete a photo but you want it out of sight, right-click the image, click Hide 1 Photo from the context menu, and then click Hide when Photos asks you to confirm. The photo will be hidden from view but will still be visible in the Hidden album. If you don't see the Hidden album in the sidebar, choose View ⇨ Show Hidden Photo Album.

To bring your photos out of hiding, click the Hidden link in the sidebar, enter your Mac account password to unlock this folder, right-click the image, and choose Unhide 1 Photo from the context menu. Photos resumes displaying the image.

Mapping your images

If you have a camera or phone that records the location in which the image was photographed as GPS data, you can see where the image was photographed on a map. If your camera or phone does not record GPS data, you can add the location to your image manually.

If your phone or camera records GPS data, right-click the image thumbnail or the full-size image and choose Get Info from the context menu. You can see the location where the image was photographed and other information about the photo (refer to Figure 4-3).

If your phone or camera does not record GPS data with the image's *metadata* (the info the camera stores with the photo), you can map the images as follows:

1. **Select the images you want to map.**

I suggest you do this immediately after importing them.

2. **Choose Window ➪ Info.**

   Alternatively, either press ⌘+I or right-click any selected photo and then choose Get Info from the context menu.

   The Info dialog appears.

3. **In the Location text field, start typing the name of the town.**

   Photos offers a list of suggested locations that match what you've typed so far. You may have to enter the state as well, if the town name is common.

4. **Choose a name from the suggestions list and press Return.**

   A map appears, showing the location of the photos you just mapped.

TIP

If you prefer to hide the location info for one or more photos, select the photos and then choose Image ➪ Location ➪ Hide Location.

Finding images

After you've imported a few thousand images into Photos (which, believe me, will happen sooner than you think), the time will come when you'll want to find a particular image. Yep: It's image needle in a library haystack time.

Fortunately, thanks to the Photos app's scene and object detection and to your judicious use of keywords, titles, and captions, finding the image you want is usually easier than you might think.

To find images, follow these steps:

1. **Click the Library link in the sidebar.**

2. **In the Search text field in the upper-right corner of the window, enter a word or phrase that identifies the image.**

   You can enter a keyword, a location, a location type (such as *lake* or *mountain*), or an object name.

   As you type, Photos shows the matching photos and offers a list of suggested search terms, as shown in Figure 4-4.

3. **Either continue typing or click one of the suggestions.**

   Photos displays the matching images in the content area.

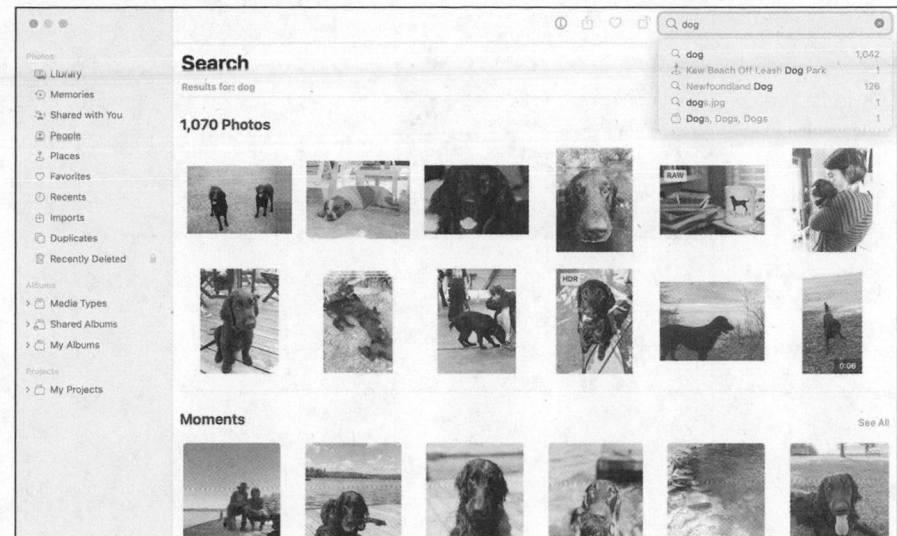

FIGURE 4-4:
Start typing a word or phrase that identifies the image you want and Photos displays matching images and a few search suggestions.

Creating a slideshow

You may be a great photographer, but presentation is everything. To kick up the wow factor several notches, you can create slideshows by following these steps:

1. **In the sidebar, click the item — such as a library folder or an album — that contains the images you want to view as a slideshow.**

   The images are displayed in the content area.

2. **Select the images you want to appear in your slideshow.**

   To select several consecutive images, click the first image, hold down the Shift key, and then click the last image. To select nonconsecutive images, click the first image, hold down ⌘, and click the rest of the images you want in your slideshow.

3. **Choose File ⇨ Play Slideshow.**

   A window appears with slideshow options, as shown in Figure 4-5.

4. **In the Themes tab, click the slideshow theme you want to use.**

   Each time you select an option, Photos automatically runs a preview of the slideshow transitions and music.

5. **(Optional) Click the Music tab and choose a tune from your Music library.**

   If you don't like the theme's default music, you can choose something different.

FIGURE 4-5:
Setting up your
slideshow.

WARNING

If you choose a song from your Music app library, it's probably copyrighted. You're technically not allowed to use copyrighted music in this way, but if the only people you're sharing it with are friends and family, it's probably okay. Just don't share the slideshow on social media, where you could be served a take-down notice for using copyrighted material illegally.

6. **Click the Play Slideshow button to view your handiwork.**

TIP

If you want to create a more advanced slideshow, select the photos you want to include, and then choose File ➪ Create ➪ Slideshow ➪ Photos. In the dialog that appears, use the Slideshow pop-up menu to choose either New Slideshow or an existing slideshow. Type a name for the slideshow, and click OK. In the slide-show project that appears, you can adjust the order of the slides by dragging the thumbnails left or right. You can also apply a different theme, add music, and set up custom timings and transitions.

Capturing Photos with Photo Booth

If your Mac has a built-in FaceTime camera, you can capture photos of yourself (or whoever or whatever is stationed in front of your Mac) by using the Photo Booth application. Photos you snap with Photo Booth are saved as JPEG files in a Photo Booth folder tucked inside your Photos folder.

TIP

To capture photos with Photo Booth, you can plug in an optional external web-cam, such as one of the models sold by Logitech (www.logitech.com) or Microsoft (www.microsoft.com/hardware), or plug in certain camcorders. You can use one of these optional external choices also to conduct live, two-way video chats with friends and family, as I write about in Book 2, Chapter 5.

To capture photos with Photo Booth, follow these steps:

1. **Click the Photo Booth icon from Launchpad.**

The Photo Booth window appears, displaying the image seen through the FaceTime camera as shown in Figure 4-6.

TIP

If you click the Effects button, you can capture a photo by using visual effects (such as fish-eye).

FIGURE 4-6:
Use Photo Booth to capture photos with your Mac's built-in FaceTime camera.

2. **Use the three icons on the lower-left side to choose from three formats:**

- *Four-up photo:* Click the left icon to take four successive photos, just like an old-fashioned photo booth.

- *Single photo:* Click the middle icon to take a single photo.

- *Video:* Click the right icon to record video.

3. **Click the camera icon in the middle of the Photo Booth window.**

   Photo Booth counts down from 3 (in seconds) before capturing your photo. If you choose four-up, Photo Booth snaps four successive shots. If you chose video, Photo Booth begins recording video. Click the camera button again to stop recording video.

   Each captured photo or video appears at the bottom of the Photo Booth window. Click a photo to see it in the Photo Booth viewing pane. Swipe left and right on the trackpad or with the Magic Mouse to move from one photo to the next.

   TIP

   If you hold down the Option key when you click the camera icon, Photo Booth snaps your photo right away without going through the three-second countdown.

4. **(Optional) Click a photo from the preview filmstrip, and then click one of the following choices from the Share pop-up menu:**

   - *Mail or Messages* opens a new message in Mail or Messages (respectively) with your selected photo pasted in the message. Address and send the message as you normally would with either app.

   - *AirDrop* makes your photo available to other AirDrop-capable Macs on the same network. See Book 3, Chapter 4 to learn about AirDrop.

   - *Notes:* Opens a window enabling you to add text for a note with which the image will be saved.

   - *Add to Photos* transfers the photo to your Photos library.

   - *Reminders* creates a new reminder with the photo attached.

   - *Change Contact Picture* enables you to use the selected image as the new photo for your card in the Contacts app.

5. **(Optional) To export your photo to another folder:**

   a. *Choose File ⇨ Export.*

   b. *Click the disclosure triangle next to the Save As field to see Finder.*

   c. *Scroll through the directories and folders to choose the location to which you want to save the image.*

6. **(Optional) To print your photo:**

   a. *Click the photo you want to print in the preview filmstrip.*

   b. *Choose File ⇨ Print.*

   c. *Adjust any necessary settings in the Print dialog that appears, and then click the Print button.*

7. **When you finish snapping and sharing photos, choose Photo Booth ⇨ Quit Photo Booth or press ⌘+Q to exit Photo Booth.**

   Images you export from Photo Booth to Photos are saved in the Photos section of your library.

TIP

You can delete photos you take with Photo Booth as follows:

» **Single image:** In the preview filmstrip, click a photo that you want to delete, and then press the Delete key or click the X in the upper-left corner of the preview image.

» **All images:** To delete all your Photo Booth photos at one time, choose Edit ⇨ Delete All and click OK to confirm your choice.

Editing Photos with Photos

Besides organizing your photos, Photos lets you edit them. Such editing can be as simple as rotating or cropping a photo or as intricate as removing red-eye from a photograph or modifying colors. When your photos look perfect, you might want to go old-school and print hard copies. And, because the JPEG format is universally web-friendly, you can share your photos in a Messages or Mail message, post them on a social network such as Facebook or Twitter, or create a shared Photo Stream on your iCloud account.

First, click any link in your library to see thumbnails of images in that section, and then double-click the photo you want to mess with. Photos opens the image, as shown in Figure 4-7. Here you can perform two basic edits:

» **Rotate the photo:** Click the rotate counterclockwise icon (pointed out in Figure 4-7) to rotate the image 90 degrees counterclockwise. Repeat until the image is right-side-up.

TIP

Sometimes it's faster to rotate the image in the opposite direction. To perform a clockwise rotation, hold down the Option key, which changes the rotate counterclockwise icon to the rotate clockwise icon. Click the icon until the photo is oriented the way you want.

» **Auto-enhance the photo:** Click the auto enhance icon (labeled in Figure 4-7) to have Photos attempt to automatically fix any flaws related to color and contrast.

Auto enhance

Rotate counterclockwise

FIGURE 4-7:
Open a photo to
perform a couple
of basic editing
chores.

If you want to make more substantive edits to an open photo, begin by clicking the Edit button in the upper-right corner of the window. Photos displays the
photo in editing mode, which includes an editing toolbar above the photo and an
editing pane to the right of the photo, as shown in Figure 4-8. Note the icons in
the upper-right side include the rotate counterclockwise and auto enhance icons
I just described.

You can now crop the photo (remove unneeded parts towards the outside edges),
apply a filter, and make many other adjustments, as detailed next.

REMEMBER

You should always crop an image before applying other adjustments. Cropping an
image can change the ratio of tonal values, which can affect the quality of your
other adjustments.

To crop the photo:

1. **Click the Crop tab.**

   The crop tools appear on the right side of the editing window, as shown in
   Figure 4-9.

FIGURE 4-8:
A photo in editing mode.

FIGURE 4-9:
The cropping tools.

2. **Make any of the following changes to the image:**

- If the image is not level, drag the Straighten slider until the image appears straight.

- To rotate the image vertically, drag the Vertical slider. To rotate the image horizontally, drag the Horizontal slider.

- To flip the photo horizontally, click the Flip button.

- If you want the final crop size to conform to a specific aspect ratio (that is, the ratio of width to height), click an option from the Aspect menu. The default option is Freeform, which lets you crop the image willy-nilly. This is usually what you want. However, if you're going to print the image, I suggest you choose an aspect ratio that fits the paper you're going to print it on.

3. **Drag the handles as needed to crop out the portions of the image you don't want.**

   As you drag, a grid appears on your image (see Figure 4-10). This grid enables you to apply the rule of thirds, which means that you make sure a focal point of the photo intersects with a point where the gridlines intersect.

FIGURE 4-10:
Cropping according to the rule of thirds.

4. **When you've finished cropping, exit the Edit pane by clicking Done or continue with the following steps if the image needs some enhancing.**

   If you want to add a filter to the photo, click the Filters tab and then click the filter effect you want to apply.

   Additional adjustments are available on the Adjust tab. Click that tap to display the editing tools shown in Figure 4-11.

FIGURE 4-11:
The Photos app's image adjustment tools.

Most of the options, except Retouch, have an Auto button. I suggest clicking that button to see if you like the results. If you don't, click the disclosure button for the adjustment you applied and tweak the settings. For example, if you press the Auto button to apply a vignette to an image, click the disclosure triangle and you can increase or decrease the strength and change the radius of the vignette.

Many of the adjustments have thumbnail previews of your image with varying degrees of the adjustment (for example, Black and White) applied. If you like the looks of a thumbnail, click it to apply the adjustment to your image.

When you apply an adjustment to an image, the hollow blue dot next to the adjustment name is filled and has a check mark inside. If you don't like the results of a particular adjustment, but don't want to change the others, click the curved arrow to the right of the adjustment name to undo it.

To see how an image looks without an adjustment applied, click the blue circle with a check mark to temporarily remove the adjustment from the image. If you decide you like it, click the blue circle to reapply the adjustment.

You can play with the following adjustments:

» **Portrait:** Adjust the depth of field if the photo was taken in portrait mode iPhone using the Camera app's portrait mode feature.

» **Light:** Lighten or darken a photo.

» **Color:** Adjust the color balance of the image.

» **Black and White:** Convert the image to black and white.

» **Retouch:** Remove sensor dust, or annoying things in your image like the telephone pole growing out of your friend's head. To use this option, click the disclosure triangle, drag the size slider to adjust the size of the brush, click the brush, and then drag over the offending part of your image. Photos attempts to repair it.

» **Red-Eye:** Remove red-eye from photos where the flash reflected off your subject's eyes and made them look red. (This does not work for the weird way animals' eyes often look in photos.) Click the disclosure triangle, drag the size slider to adjust the size of the brush (try to make it the same size as the red-eye you want to remove), click the brush, and then click the red-eye in the photo.

» **White Balance:** Click the Auto button if the whites in your image don't look white.

» **Curves:** Modify tonal areas of your image to enhance the overall look of the photo. Unless you're an experienced enhancer, I suggest letting Photos do the work by clicking the Auto button. Undo the adjustment if you don't like the results.

» **Levels:** Stretch the brightness levels in the shadow and highlight areas of the image. This option is helpful if the image is slightly underexposed. Unless you're an experienced image editor, I suggest you try Auto.

» **Definition:** Add contour and shape to the image. Drag the slider until you photo looks good or click Auto to let Photos figure it out.

» **Selective Color:** Change the hue, saturation, and luminance of individual colors in your image. Use the eyedropper to select a color in the image or click a color swatch. You can get some interesting results using selective color. If you go over the top, you can make this adjustment go away by clicking the blue dot with a check mark in it next to Selective Color.

» **Noise Reduction:** Reduce digital noise in an image. Some people think digital noise looks like film grain. It doesn't. Use this option when you edit a photograph created in dark conditions, such as at night in a dimly lit restaurant.

» **Sharpen:** Enhance an image by increasing the sharpness of images with edges, such as windows. I suggest you click Auto with this adjustment, unless you've sharpened images in other photo-editing applications with good results.

>> **Vignette:** Apply a circular vignette around the image, which draws viewers' attention to the center of the image.

TIP

If your photo ends up looking harsh or garish, and you've dabbled with any option in the Adjust section, click the Reset Adjustments button at the bottom of the Adjust section.

To close the Edit pane, click the Done button.

Sharing Photos

For many people, there's no point in taking photos if they don't share them with others. If you fall in this camp, you can publicize your photos to the world by printing them; posting them on a web page; uploading them directly to Facebook, Twitter, or Instagram; sending them to others via Mail or Messages; or adding them to a shared album via iCloud. In this section, I give you the rundown for sharing in each and every way.

Printing photos

You can print individual photos or groups of photos on your home printer by following these steps:

1. **Click any link in the sidebar to see Images in the content area.**

2. **Hold down the ⌘ key and click each photo you want to print.**

   If you choose multiple images, Photos arranges them to fit the page.

3. **Choose File ⇨ Print.**

   A Print dialog appears.

4. **Click the print styles to the right.**

   The photos appear as they'll be printed.

5. **Choose the printer, paper size, and quality from the pop-up menus.**

6. **Click the Print button.**

Sending photos in a message

If you want to share photos with family members or friends who have an email address or use Messages on a Mac, an iPhone, or an iPad, you can send photos by using the Mail or Messages app. You can send a photo by following these steps:

1. **Click any link in the sidebar to see the images in the content area.**

2. **Hold down the ⌘ key and click each photo you want to send.**

   You can click up to ten photos to send in one email.

3. **Click the arrow-escaping-a-box (share) icon and choose Mail.**

   Your photos appear as attachments in an email message.

4. **In the To text box, enter an email address or addresses, type a subject and a message, and then click Send.**

To send a photo with Messages, follow these steps:

1. **Select the photo you want to send as outlined in Steps 1 and 2 of the preceding list.**

2. **Click the arrow-escaping-a-box (share) icon and choose Messages from the fly-out menu.**

   A new message window appears with your photo attached to it.

3. **Address your message, type an accompanying note, and then click Send.**

REMEMBER

You can also share images via AirDrop, Notes, and Reminders.

Creating a shared album

The Shared Albums feature is part of Apple's iCloud service. If you activate Shared Albums, you can create an album that you can then share with people via iCloud. To make sure that Shared Albums is activated, choose Photos ▷ Settings, click the iCloud tab, and then select the Shared Albums check box.

To share an album with others, do the following:

1. **Click any link in the sidebar to see the images in the content area.**

2. **Hold down the ⌘ key and click each photo you want to share.**

3. **Click the arrow-escaping-a-box (share) icon and choose Shared Albums.**

   The Add to Shared Album dialog appears.

4. **In the Comment area, type a comment if desired.**

5. **Click the New Shared Album button.**

   Later, if you want to add more photos to an album, you can alternatively click the existing shared album at the bottom of the Add a Shared Album dialog.

6. **Type a name for the new shared album.**

7. **In the Invite People box, click the plus sign (+).**

   This opens the Contacts app from which you can choose the people you want to share the album with.

8. **Open the contact and then click the email address you want Photos to use the send the invitation.**

9. **Repeat Steps 7 and 8 until you've added all the people you want to invite to share the album.**

10. **Click Create.**

   The selected photos are copied to the new shared album, which appears in the sidebar under the Shared Albums menu. Photos also sends a message to the people you invited to view that shared album.

TIP

Creating a book, calendar, or similar project is a nice way to organize and view your photos on your computer. To create a new project, hover the mouse cursor over the sidebar's My Projects menu, click the plus sign (+), and choose one of the following options: Book, Calendar, Card, Wall Decor, Prints, Slideshow, or Other. Most of links connect you with the App Store, where you can choose a source to complete your project.

5
Taking Care of Business

Contents at a Glance

Chapter **1**

Managing Contacts

Your Mac comes with a contact management app called (surprise!) Contacts. You use Contacts to store names of people and businesses along with all sorts of information about them: phone numbers; street addresses; virtual addresses, such as those used for email, instant messaging, or websites; social network usernames; and more intimate information, such as birthdays, anniversaries, and relations. Besides storing contact names and related contact information, Contacts can display contact information from more than one source, and it syncs via iCloud with your iOS and iPadOS devices — meaning that if you make a change to contact information on one device or computer, it's automatically updated on all your devices. Contacts also connects with other apps on your Mac so you can open someone's contact card and immediately

» Write and send an email or message to that person.

» Open a FaceTime conversation with that person.

» Display that person's street address in Maps.

If by chance you still send letters or gifts the old-fashioned postal way, you can also print envelopes and mailing labels, and even the entire contacts list directly from Contacts.

Contacts is integrated with the other apps on your Mac that use addresses, including Mail (see Book 2, Chapters 3 and 4), Messages (Book 2, Chapter 5), and Calendar (Book 5, Chapter 2). When you enter or search for a physical or virtual address in those apps, they refer to Contacts. This way, you have to enter contact information only once.

In this chapter, I explain how to set up Contacts by customizing the contact template with fields you use most frequently. Then I outline three ways to enter information: manually, importing data from another contact management app, and syncing with other accounts. In the second half of the chapter, I show you how to set up lists of contacts as well as how to print and export your contacts.

Setting Up Contacts

Contacts acts like an electronic Rolodex (if you can remember such things). You save information about a person in a special container called a *contact card* so you can find that information again.

Each card contains information associated with one contact — be it a person or a company — such as telephone numbers and postal addresses, email addresses, URLs, birthdays, profile usernames, and photos. And most contact information links to something else. For example, click the pin next to an address, and Maps opens to show you a map of that address. Or click the envelope icon next to an email address, and Mail creates a new email message addressed to that person. Click the icon to the right of a URL, and the website opens in Safari. You get the picture.

Viewing your contacts

When you open Contacts by clicking the Contacts icon on the dock (see Figure 1-1) or in Launchpad, the window is divided into two or three columns, as shown in Figure 1-1. From left to right, the first column displays the sidebar, which shows the sources and lists of your contacts. (You can hide this column by choosing View⇨ Hide Lists.) Clicking an item in the sidebar then displays in the second column an alphabetized Contacts list of all contacts in the selected account or list. Click a contact in the Contacts list, and you see its card in the third column.

You have a few options for how the name on a contact card is displayed:

>> **Organize by company name.** When you create a contact card, Contacts assumes that you want to display that card in the alphabetized Contacts list by a person's name. To list a card by company name instead, click the card and choose Card ⇨ Mark as a Company, or press ⌘+\ . (Or, you can select the

Company check box when you're creating a new contact card; I mention this later in the upcoming "Creating a contact" section.) Your chosen card now displays a company name and icon. To change from a company name back to a person's name, choose Card ⇨ Mark as a Person (or press ⌘+\).

>> **Sort by first or last name.** To set whether your cards are sorted by first or last name, choose Contacts ⇨ Settings ⇨ General and then select the sort and display options you prefer.

>> **Change the display name of an individual card.** To change the first name/last name order for one card only, choose Card ⇨ Show First Name Before Last or Card ⇨ Show Last Name Before First. That one card only will change, regardless of the General settings you set.

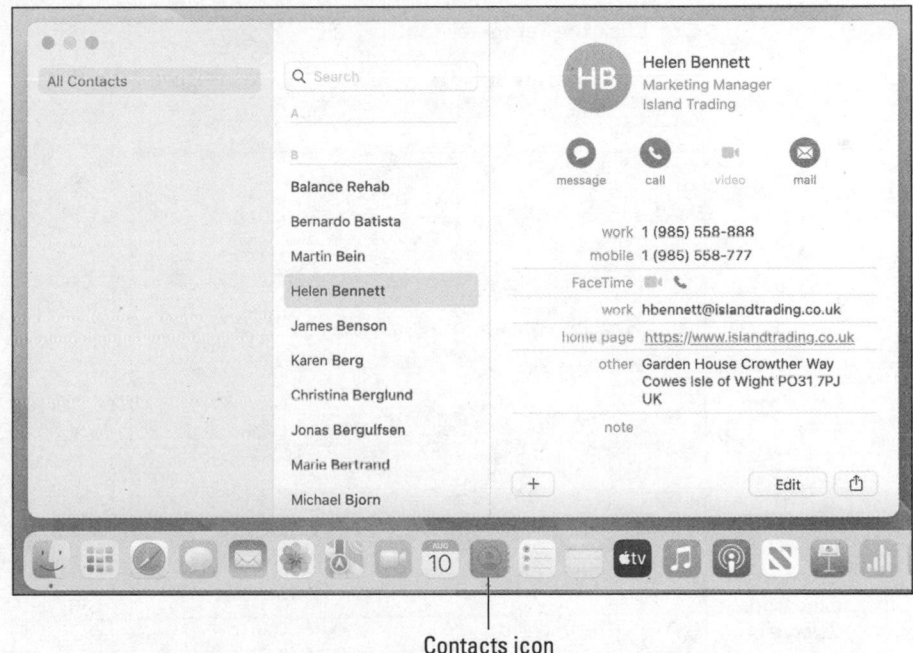

Contacts icon

Managing Contacts

FIGURE 1-1:
From left to right, Contacts displays the sidebar, contacts, and the selected contact card.

TIP

You can view multiple cards by clicking names in the Contacts list, and then choose Card ⇨ Open in Separate Window (or press ⌘+I). Repeat until all the cards you want to see are open. You can view multiple cards by clicking the first card you want to display, and then Shift-clicking the last card you want to display. This technique selects contiguous cards. To select noncontiguous cards, click the first card you want to display and then ⌘+click each additional card you want to display. With your selection made, choose Card ⇨ Open in Separate Window (or press ⌘+I).

Designing your contact card template

Each time you add a new contact, Contacts displays a contact card with blank fields, each of which represents a piece of information to fill in about that person or entity, such as first and last name, company, title, and email address. You may not want or need to store all that information about everyone, so you can define your contact card template to list only the fields you want to use, such as just name and email address. Remember that you can always add more fields to an individual card as needed.

To modify the contact card template, follow these steps:

1. **Choose Contacts⇨ Settings.**

   The Contacts settings appear.

2. **Click the Template tab.**

   The Template settings appear, as shown in Figure 1-2.

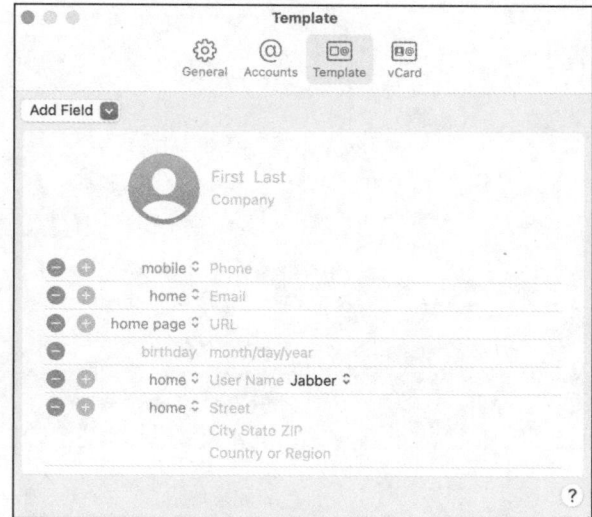

FIGURE 1-2:
Use the Template settings to choose the fields you want on every card.

3. **Remove or add fields as you want:**

   - *To remove a field:* Click the red minus sign to the left of the field and repeat for every field you want to remove.

   - *To add a field:* Click Add Field to open the Add Field pop-up menu (see Figure 1-3) and choose a field to add, such as Job Title or Nickname, repeating for each field you want to add.

TIP

Click the green plus sign next to an existing field to add another field in that category — for example, the plus sign next to Mobile (refer to Figure 1-2) to add a field for another type of phone number, such as Home or Work.

4. **(Optional) Click the label arrow next to the field name to change it or to create a custom field name.**

    For example, the default label for the Phone field is Mobile, but you can click Mobile and then choose another label from the pop-up list, such as iPhone, Home, or Work. If none of the predefined labels turn your crank, click Custom to create your own label.

5. **Click the close icon of the Template settings pane.**

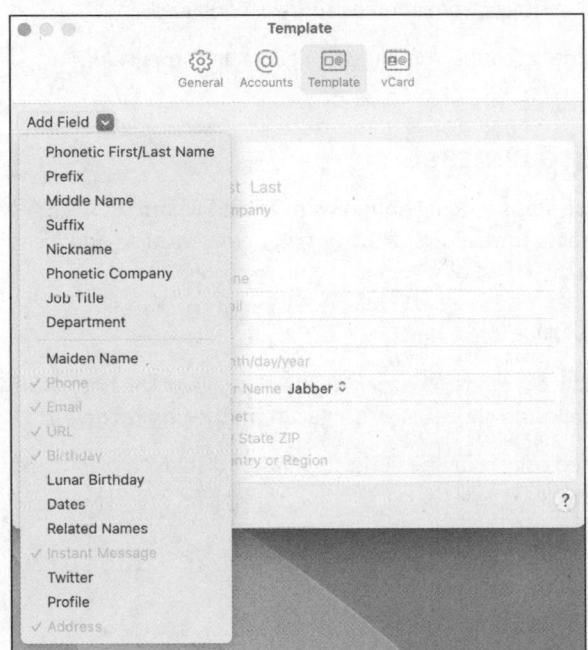

FIGURE 1-3:
The Add Field menu provides more fields you can add to a template.

Now that you've set up the contact card template to your liking, you're ready to enter names and information by creating cards for new contacts.

Adding contacts

Contacts comes with two contact cards: one for Apple, Inc. and one for you. The card that's for you is called My Card, and this contact card always appears at the top of the contacts list. It contains your email address, phone number, street address, photo or representative image, and any other information you want to put on it.

» **To define a different card to represent you:** Click that card and choose Card ➪ Make This My Card.

» **To view your card at any time:** Choose Card ➪ Go to My Card. You can instead click My Card at the top of the contacts list or press Shift+⌘+M.

There are three ways to add contacts, which I explain in the upcoming subsections:

» Create contacts and manually enter information.

» Import contacts from another address book app.

» Add other accounts that include a contacts component.

Creating a contact

Follow these steps whenever you want to add a contact, either when you're populating Contacts for the first time or when you want to add a contact to your existing Contacts.

1. **Choose File ➪ New Card.**

Alternatively, press ⌘+N, or click the plus sign at the bottom of the contact card pane and choose New Contact from the pop-up menu.

The third column of the Contacts window displays a blank card for you to fill in, as shown in Figure 1-4.

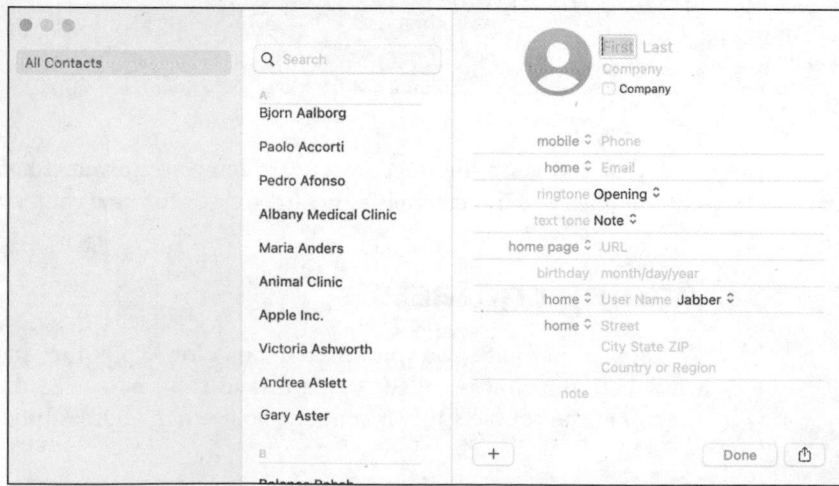

FIGURE 1-4:
Fill out a card to add a contact.

2. **Click the text fields (such as First, Last, or Company) and enter the information you want to save for your contact.**

You don't have to fill every field. And some fields — Birthday, for example — can have just one entry; others, such as those for phone numbers or addresses, can have many entries. When you enter data in the existing field, press Tab to go to the next field. You can also press Shift+Tab to navigate to the previous field.

TIP

When adding information like phone numbers, don't be concerned with the formatting. Just enter the numbers and press Tab, and Contacts formats the phone number for you. For example, if you enter 15555551212, the phone number is displayed as 1 (555) 555-1212.

If you want a contact to be sorted by its business name instead of a person's name, select the check box next to Company.

To change the street address field format, click the street address field name — it's Home, by default — and choose Change Address Format from the pop-up menu. Choose the country for that address, and the card changes to reflect that country's address format.

REMEMBER

When you make changes to a field name or format on a card, the changes apply to that card only. To apply changes to *all* your contact cards, choose Contacts ➪ Settings ➪ Template and make your changes to the template.

3. **(Optional) To add a photo or other image for your contact, follow these substeps:**

  a. *Hover the mouse pointer over the picture button and then click the Edit button that appears. Alternatively, choose Card ➪ Choose Custom Image or press Option+⌘+I.*

  Contacts displays the dialog shown in Figure 1-5.

  b. *Click the type of image you want to add: Memoji, Emoji, Monogram (one or two letters, numbers, or symbols), Camera (the contact's photo, taken with your Mac's camera, if it has one), Photos (an existing photo from your library), or Suggestions (stock images provided by Apple).*

  c. *Select the image you want to use. If you're taking a photo, click the shutter button when your contact is ready.*

  d. *Click Save.*

4. **(Optional) If you want to add a field to this card only, choose Card ➪ Add Field (or click the plus sign at the bottom of the card) and then from the menu, choose a field to add to the card.**

REMEMBER

After you add a field to a card, you need to type information in that field. If you leave the field blank, Contacts removes it when you click Done.

Managing Contacts

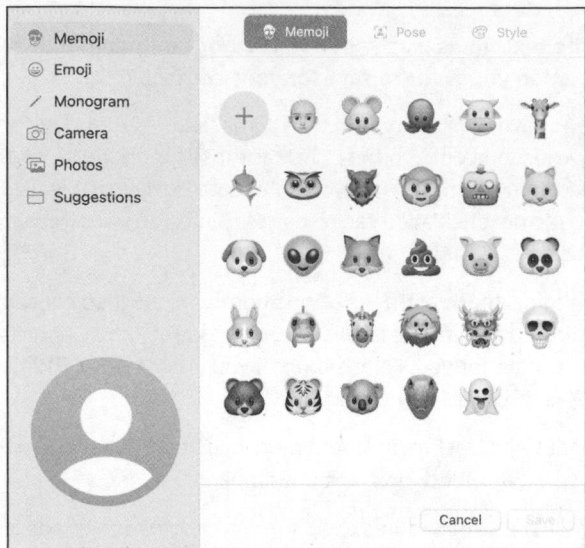

FIGURE 1-5:
Add a photo
to a contact to
connect names
with faces.

5. **To change the label of a field, click the current label and choose from the menu.**

   To forge your own label, click Custom. The Add Custom Label dialog appears. Type in the name you want for the field and then click OK.

6. **Click the Note field (refer to Figure 1-4) and type any additional information that doesn't have an associated field.**

7. **Click the Done button at the bottom of the Contacts window to save your new card.**

TIP

To help you remember how to pronounce names in unfamiliar languages, Contacts has a Phonetic First/Last Name field and a Phonetic Company field. And the Related Names field gives you a place to enter the name of a contact's spouse, child, or assistant. Click the field name to reveal a pop-up menu of options.

Importing contacts

If your contacts are already in another app, there's no need to retype all that data. Just import the data into Contacts. Contacts understands the following four file formats:

» **vCard:** Standard file format used to store contact information; used by apps on different types of computers.

» **LDIF:** Standard data interchange file format.

TECHNICAL STUFF

LDIF stands for Lightweight Directory Access Protocol (LDAP) Data Interchange Format.

>> **Text file:** Tab-delimited or comma-separated value (CSV) format; comes from a database, spreadsheet, or contact app.

>> **Contacts Archive:** Standard Contacts file format useful for transferring data between Macs with Contacts. Contacts can also read archive files from the Address Book app, the predecessor to the Contacts app.

To import a contact's data file into Contacts, follow these steps:

1. **Choose File ⇨ Import.**

   A file chooser dialog appears.

2. **Select the file you want to import and then click Open.**

   If you import a CSV list, a dialog with the standard card template appears, listing the fields that will be imported.

3. **Accept or review duplicate cards:**

   - *To automatically accept duplicates:* Click Import.

   - *To see duplicates and resolve differences between the two:* Click Review Duplicates.

4. **Click Next.**

   The new contacts are imported and appear in a smart list named Last Import. You can review all contacts in this list and edit and delete them as needed until you import additional contacts (at which point Contacts creates a new Last Import smart list to hold the latest imported contacts).

TIP

If you're importing a text or CSV file, make sure that the correct field labels are associated with the data being imported. You can change the field labels if necessary.

When the import is finished, Contacts contains the new contact cards.

TIP

In apps that use the vCard format, you can export the contents to a vCard file and then email the file to yourself. Save the attached vCard file and then double-click it to import the contact into Contacts automatically without having to bother with the preceding steps.

Your newly imported contacts will appear in both the All Contacts list and the Last Import list under the sidebar's Smart List heading.

Accessing contacts from another device or server

I explain iCloud syncing in Book 1, Chapter 3, but it deserves attention here as well. If you have a mobile phone and keep contact information on a cloud server (such as iCloud or Google) or a social network (such as Facebook or LinkedIn), you can add that information to Contacts on your Mac, too.

Likewise, you may have access to address books on network servers — perhaps, the company directory at your place of employment. By adding the cloud or remote account information to Contacts, you can access the information.

REMEMBER

Because the data is in a *remote* location (not on your Mac), you need to be online or on the network to access the information, and you may or may not have editing privileges.

To add an account, follow these steps:

1. **Choose Contacts ⇨ Add Account.**

2. **Complete one of the following step lists:**

(a) *Select the radio button next to the service you want to add, such as Google (see Figure 1-6), and then click Continue.*

(b) *Type in your username and password.*

Your account is verified.

(c) *Select the Contacts radio button (if it isn't already) selected and then click Done.*

Or

(a) *Select the Other Contacts Account radio button and then click Continue.*

(b) *Choose CardDAV or LDAP from the pull-down menu.*

(c) *Enter the requested information.*

You may have to ask the network administrator or a techie in your group for the information.

(d) *Click Sign In.*

Your access is verified.

That account is added to the Accounts list (choose Contacts ⇨ Settings and then click the Accounts tab).

TIP

When you access multiple accounts, Contacts does its best to merge cards from different accounts onto one card. When a contact card contains information from more than one account, at the very bottom of the card you see a Cards field, which lists the accounts the card references.

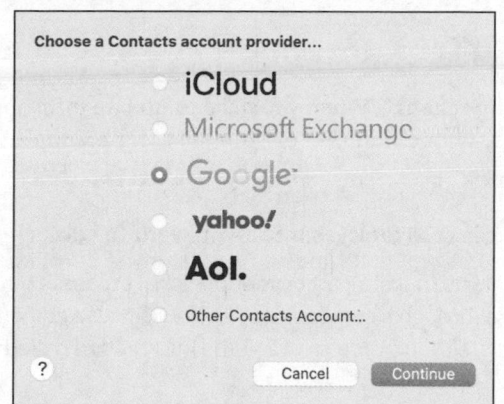

FIGURE 1-6:
Add an account to access address books stored on cloud or remote servers.

Messing with Your Contacts

There's no reason to add names and numbers to Contacts if you don't plan to use them. In this section, I explain all the different things you can do with Contacts: how to search for a number, edit a card when contact information changes, and create lists to make it easier to communicate with many people at once.

Searching contacts

The more contact cards you store in Contacts, the harder it is to find a particular contact you want. Instead of scrolling through every contact card to locate a certain one, you can search for specific contacts by following these steps:

1. **In the sidebar, click All Contacts or click the list you want to search.**

2. **Click the search text field above the contacts list.**

3. **Type a word or phrase that you want to find, such as a person's name or the company that person works for.**

   The app displays a list of contacts that match the text you typed.

4. **Click a contact to display the card for that person or company.**

TIP

To search for the occurrence of a contact's name on your Mac, right-click the name of the contact in the contacts list and choose Spotlight from the shortcut menu.

Editing a card

Life is dynamic; things change. When you need to update information on a card — a change of address, phone number, or company, for example — edit a card by following these steps:

1. **Find and open the card for the contact you want to edit.**

TIP

   You can edit contacts that are part of your personal accounts but probably not those you access through a company server. You can also add information to LinkedIn contacts, although you can't edit the information pulled from the contact's profile.

2. **Click the Edit button at the bottom of the window.**

   Contacts displays not only all the fields that contain information but also the other (empty) fields in your contact card template.

3. **Do one of the following:**

   - Click the field in which you want to edit information, such as an out-of-date email address or phone number. The existing information is highlighted, and you can type the updated information to replace the existing information.

   - Click an empty field and enter new information.

   - Click the plus sign at the bottom of the page and select a field you want to add from the menu. (Click More Fields if you don't see what you're looking for and then choose from the continuation menu.) Type in the new information in the added field.

   - Click the white-on-red minus sign to delete the contents of a field.

   If you delete the contents of a field by mistake, press ⌘+Z right away.

4. **Repeat Step 3 to add additional fields or make additional edits.**

5. **Click the Done button.**

   Contacts saves the updated contact information.

TIP

You can add or edit notes in the Note field without being in Edit mode. Just click in the Note field and type what you want.

Deleting a contact

Alas, people come and go in your life. For those who go, you probably don't want their cards cluttering your contacts list. When it's time for a little housekeeping, prune the contact cards you don't need any more.

REMEMBER

You can delete only those contacts that are stored directly on your Mac or accounts that you access directly, such as via iCloud or Google. For example, you can't delete contacts on your company's server.

To delete someone from Contacts, click the person's card and choose Edit ⇨ Delete Card, or press Delete. When Contacts asks you to confirm the deletion, click Delete to make it so. If you accidentally delete a contact, press ⌘+Z or choose Edit⇨ Undo to restore it.

TIP

To choose multiple contacts to delete, begin by clicking the first card you want to remove. To add nonconsecutive cards to the selection, hold down the ⌘ key and click at will; to select consecutive cards, hold down the Shift key and click the last of the cards you want to include in the selection.

Making a list (and, optionally, checking it twice)

To help organize the contacts you've stored in the Contacts app, you can create lists of people. For example, you might have one list for your co-workers, another for friends, yet another for family members, and one for your what-happens-in-Vegas-stays-in-Vegas gang. For greater convenience, you can even store the same contact in multiple lists. Although you don't have to use lists, this feature can help you manage your list of important contact cards. It's also a great way to send emails to multiple people at once because you can address the message to the list instead of typing each address separately.

Contacts initially contains one list named All Contacts which, as the name implies (or, really, states clearly), stores all the contacts you've added to the app. Even when a contact is assigned to another list, the contact remains in All Contacts.

REMEMBER

If your Mac is signed in to a network account server, you may see a second list: Directories. The Directories list contains a list of contacts of everyone signed in to that network's directory. If you're using a Mac at home without a network account server, you won't see the Directories list.

Adding and populating a list

You can create as many lists as you want, but for lists to be useful, you need to add contacts to that list. To create a new list, follow these steps:

1. **Choose File ⇨ New List.**

Alternatively, press Shift+⌘+N, or click the plus sign at the bottom of the screen and choose New List from the pop-up menu.

Managing Contacts

Contacts creates the new list and adds it to the sidebar with the default name *untitled list*.

2. **In the sidebar, replace *untitled list* with a more descriptive name, and then press Return.**

3. **In the sidebar, click All Contacts to see all the contacts stored in the app.**

   If the contact you want is stored in an existing list, you can alternatively click that list in the sidebar.

4. **Display the contact you want to add to your new list.**

TIP

   To add multiple contacts, begin by clicking the first one you want to add. To include nonconsecutive cards in the selection, hold down the ⌘ key and click each of the other contacts; to add consecutive contacts, hold down the Shift key and click the last of the contacts you want to include in the selection.

5. **Drag the contact (or any selected contact) over to the sidebar and drop it on the name of the list you just created.**

   Your chosen contact appears in your newly created list and in the All Contacts list.

6. **Repeat Steps 4 and 5 as needed until you've populated your new list.**

TIP

To see the lists to which a contact belongs, click that person's card in the contacts list and then hold down the Option key. In the sidebar, Contacts highlights the lists that contain that contact.

Creating a list from a selection of contacts

Rather than first creating a list and then filling it with selected folks, you can also work the other way around. That is, you can select the list members first, and then add them all to a new list. To create a new list from a selection of contacts, follow these steps:

1. **In the sidebar, click All Contacts.**

   If the contacts you want to work with are stored in an existing list, you can alternatively click that list in the sidebar.

2. **Click the first contact you want to include in the selection.**

3. **Select the rest of the contacts you want to include in your new list:**

   - *To select nonconsecutive contacts:* Hold down the ⌘ key and click each of the rest of the contacts you want to store in the list.

   - *To select consecutive contacts:* Hold down the Shift key and click the last of the contacts you want to store in the list.

4. **Choose File ⇨ New List from Selection.**

   The list appears in the sidebar list with the default moniker *untitled list.*

5. **Type a more descriptive name for your list, and then press Return.**

   Your list now contains the contacts you selected in Steps 2 and 3.

TIP

To send an email to every contact included in a list, right-click the list in the sidebar and then click Send Email to "*List*" (where *List* is the name of the list).

Editing a distribution list

Say you have more than one phone number, email, or street address for the same person. To choose which fields to use for each contact in a list, edit the distribution list. For example, you can choose the same type of address for all members of the list — for example, using the work address — or you can select the information for each member of the list. Follow this procedure:

1. **Choose Edit⇨ Edit Distribution List.**

   Contacts opens a dialog that contains your lists.

2. **Select the list you want to edit.**

3. **Click the column header to open a pop-up menu that lets you choose which type of data you want to manage: Email, Phone, or Address.**

4. **Select the corresponding information you want to use for each member who has more than one entry.**

Adding contacts automatically with smart lists

Adding contacts manually or selecting them for a list is fine, but what if you frequently add and delete contacts? Doing all this manually can get old. To keep your list's contacts accurate and up to date more easily, you can use the smart lists feature.

With a smart list, you set up one or more conditions that define the types of contacts you want to store in the list. The set of conditions you use to match contacts is called a *rule*. For example, you could create a smart list from any one of the following rules:

>> The Company field is a specified name.

>> The Email field contains a specified domain name.

>> The State field is a specified state or province and the City field is a specified city or town.

Whatever rule you use, Contacts automatically populates the smart list with all the cards that match the conditions. And as your contact data changes, Contacts automatically updates the smart list to reflect those changes.

To create a smart list, follow these steps:

1. **Choose File ⇨ New Smart List, or press Option+⌘+N.**

   Contacts displays a dialog that enables you to define your smart list with a name and a rule consisting of one or more conditions.

2. **In the Smart List Name text box, type a name for your smart list.**

   Now you need to define the smart list rule, which consists of one or more conditions. Most conditions take the following general form:

   field operator value

   where *field* is the contact card field you want to search, such as Name, Company, or City (you can also choose Card to represent every field in the contact card); *value* is the *field* content that you want to match; and *operator* is how you want Contacts to match the *field* and *value*.

   For example, for most fields, the default operator is the keyword Contains, which means Contacts matches cards where *field* includes *value*.

3. **In the first pop-up menu, choose a field (or Card for the entire card). You can also click Other to open a menu that lets you choose a few other field types.**

4. **In the second pop-up menu, choose the operator you want to use.**

5. **In the text box to the right of the operator menu, enter the field value you want to match.**

   For example, if you want to create a smart list for people who work for a certain company, choose Company in the field pop-up menu, choose Is in the operator pop-up menu, and then type the company name in the text box.

REMEMBER

Although most conditions use the *field operator value* format, date fields (such as Birthday and Anniversary) use a slightly different format: *field operator value unit*, where *unit* is Days, Weeks, Months, or Years. For example, to create a smart list that contains each contact who has a birthday coming up in the next two weeks, you'd choose Birthday in the field pop-up menu, Is In the Next in the operator pop-up menu, type **2** in the value text box, and choose Weeks in the unit pop-up menu, resulting in the condition Birthday is in the next 2 weeks (see Figure 1-7).

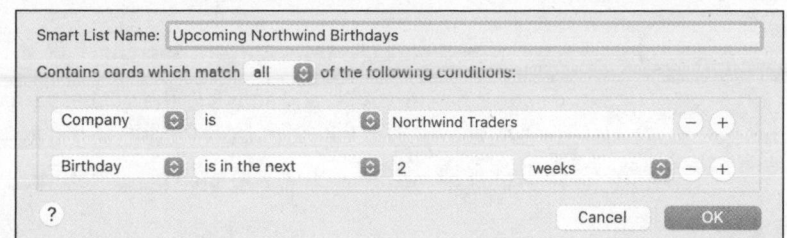

FIGURE 1-7:
You can specify two or more conditions to define your smart list.

6. **(Optional) To add another condition to your rule, click the + button to the right of the current condition and then repeat Steps 3 through 5.**

   Figure 1-7 shows a smart list rule with two conditions added.

   If you create additional conditions and later decide you don't want one of them, you can remove that condition by clicking the minus sign that appears to the right of the condition.

7. **(Optional) If your smart list rule contains two or more conditions, Contacts adds a pop-up menu just below the Smart List Name text box (refer to Figure 1-7). Use that pop-up menu to select one of the following:**

   - *All:* Tells Contacts to add a card to the smart list only if the card matches every one of the conditions.

   - *Any:* Tells Contacts to add a card to the smart list if the card matches one or more of the conditions.

8. **Click OK.**

   Contacts creates the smart list and adds it to the sidebar's Smart Lists section.

Creating a smart list from search results

Defining the conditions for storing names automatically in a smart list can be cumbersome when you aren't quite sure whether the defined rule will work exactly the way you want. As an alternative, you can search for the types of contacts you want to store, and then create a smart list based on your search results. Using this approach, you can see exactly which types of contacts will appear in your smart list.

To create a smart list from search results, follow these steps:

1. **Click All Contacts, and in the search text field, type the text you want to find (such as the name of a company, a last name, or part of an email address), and press Return.**

   The contacts list shows the cards that Contacts found based on the text you typed in.

2. **Choose File ➪ New Smart List from Current Search.**

   Contacts creates a new smart list and adds it to the sidebar's Smart Lists section. The default name for the smart list is the search text you typed.

3. **Edit the smart list name, if needed, and then press Return.**

TIP

You can edit a smart list by right-clicking the name and then clicking Edit Smart List.

Deleting a list or a list contact

If you create a list and no longer need it, you can delete it. When you delete a list, you delete only the list container; you don't delete any contact cards stored in that list. To delete a list, click the list in the sidebar, choose Edit ➪ Delete List, and then click Delete when Contacts asks you to confirm.

You can delete a contact from a regular list (that is, not a smart list) by selecting the list, clicking the contact you want to delete, choosing Edit ➪ Delete Card, and then clicking Remove from List in the dialog that appears.

Sharing Your Contacts

Sometimes you may need to share contact information with others. Contacts makes it easy to share one card or a list in the vCard format. A *vCard* is a standard format that many apps use to store contact information. When you share contact data as a vCard, the information can be imported or viewed by another app and computer, such as a Windows PC running Outlook.

Sending one contact at a time

To share a single card, select the card in the contacts list, click the Share button in the bottom-right corner of the contact card, and then select one of the following:

» **Mail:** Opens a blank email message that contains a vCard attachment. Address the message to one or more recipients, add a subject line and some message text, and then click Send.

» **Messages:** Opens a blank text message with a vCard attachment. Address the message and click Send.

- >> **AirDrop:** Enables you to send the vCard via AirDrop to nearby Macs or Apple devices that have AirDrop turned on.

- >> **Notes:** Adds the contact information as a note in the Notes app. This stores the information in iCloud and is also available on other devices that are linked to your computer, such as your iPhone.

- >> **Edit Extensions:** Opens the Select Extensions for Sharing with Other dialog, enabling you to select other extensions to include in the sharing menu.

If you want to send your own card, choose Card ⇨ Share My Card and then choose one of the following options from the submenu:

- >> **Email My Card:** Opens a blank email message that contains a vCard attachment. Address the message to one or more recipients, add a subject line and some message text, and then click Send.

- >> **Message My Card:** Opens a blank Messages message with a vCard attachment. Address the message and click Send.

- >> **AirDrop My Card:** Enables you to send the vCard via AirDrop to nearby Macs or Apple devices that have AirDrop turned on.

Exporting multiple cards

You have three choices for sharing multiple cards from Contacts:

- >> Export contact data in the vCard format, which most contact management apps can import.

- >> Export as an archive, which most Macs can display.

- >> Export as a PDF, which most computers and hand-held devices can display.

Consider both the recipient's computer system and how the data will be used when exporting the cards. After the file is imported to another contact management app, either from the vCard or archive format, it can be edited. However, a PDF file is an image of the data, so it can be viewed or printed, but the data can't be edited.

WARNING

When exporting contacts for use in another app, the app you're importing may not recognize every detail for the contact, such as a person's picture or notes you've added to a person's contact card.

Whichever file type you choose, the process is as follows for exporting contacts from Contacts:

1. **Select the cards you want to export by doing one of the following:**

   - Click All Contacts.

   - Click a list.

   To quickly export a list, right-click a (non-smart) list name and choose Export List vCard.

   - In the contacts list, select the first card you want to export. To include nonconsecutive cards in the selection, hold down the ⌘ key and click each of the other cards; to add consecutive cards, hold down the Shift key and click the last of the cards you want to include in the selection.

2. **Choose the file type to which you'd like to export the contacts.**

   - *To export as a PDF:* Choose File ⇨ Export as PDF.

   - *To export as a vCard or an archive:* Choose File ⇨ Export, and then choose Export vCard or Contacts Archive from the submenu.

   A Save As dialog appears.

3. **Type a descriptive name for your file in the Save As text box.**

4. **Choose the location to store your file; this can be an external drive or a folder on your Mac.**

5. **Click Save.**

   You can then treat the file as you would any other file you want to share: Send it to someone as an email attachment; copy it to a flash drive; or upload it to a cloud server, such as Dropbox.

Although your best bet for backing up Contacts is using iCloud, as explained in Book 1, Chapter 3, you can also use one of the sharing options to create a backup that you store on an external drive, a network share, or a remote storage server.

Printing your contacts

You can export contacts to a PDF file (as I describe in the preceding section) and then print the document, or you can print directly from Contacts. In addition to printing in list form, Contacts lets you print all or some of your contact information in different formats, such as mailing labels or cards that you can carry with you. To print your contacts, follow these steps:

1. **Use one of the following methods to select the cards you want to print:**

   - Click a single contact card.

   - For multiple, nonconsecutive contacts, click the first contact, hold down the ⌘ key, and click each of the other contacts you want to print.

   - For multiple, consecutive contacts, click the first contact, hold down the Shift key, and then click the last contact you want to print.

   - To print all contact cards stored in a list, click the list name and then choose Edit ⇨ Select All or press ⌘+A.

2. **Choose File ⇨ Print.**

   A Print dialog appears, as shown in Figure 1-8.

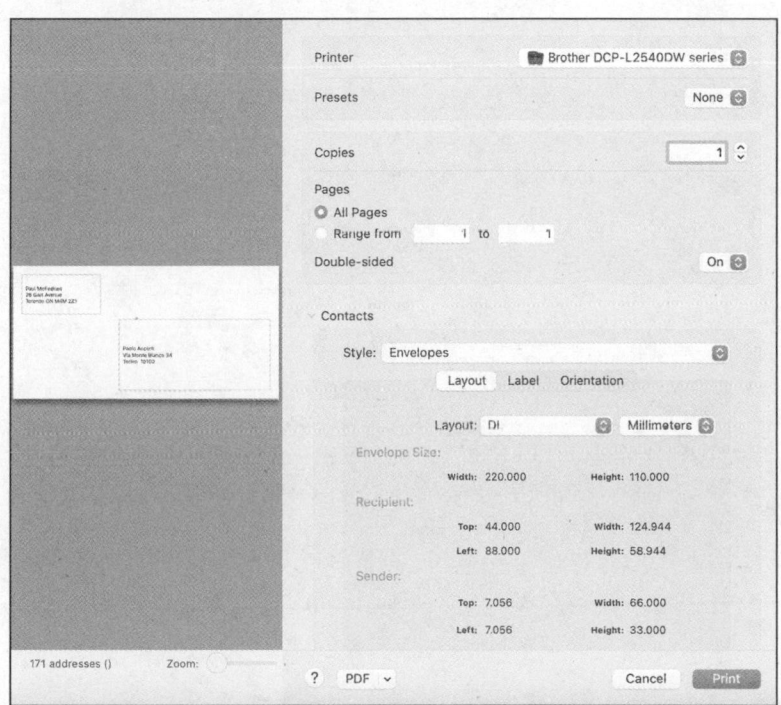

FIGURE 1-8:
Use the Print dialog to choose how you want to print the selected contacts.

3. **Click the Style pop-up menu and choose one of the following:**

   - *Mailing Labels:* Prints names and addresses on different types of mailing labels

   - *Envelopes:* Prints names and addresses on envelopes fed into your printer

   - *Lists:* Prints your contacts as a long list

WARNING

REMEMBER

Make sure you have the right media in your printer for the option you choose in Step 3.

Depending on the style that you choose in this step, you may need to pick additional options, such as defining the specific size of your mailing labels or choosing whether to print names in alphabetical order. You can also adjust other settings and options, such as number of copies and the font you want to use for your printed output.

4. **Click Print.**

   Contacts prints the selected cards.

Chapter **2**

Tracking Events and Tasks

t least a billion books are out there telling you the secret of getting your act together and your life organized. I'm going to save you a big chunk of cash by telling you that secret right here and now: Remove all the stuff swirling around your brain — all those appointments and assignments, all those errands and events, all those to-do lists and tasks — by recording them using some kind of system that will help to remind you to get everything done at the appropriate time.

Yep, that's it. When you have all those things cluttering your mind, you're in a constant state of stress and anxiety because it all feels like too much and you're constantly playing catch-up because of things you missed or forgot. Ah, but off-load everything into a system that both records them and reminds you to do them, and suddenly anxiety gives way to peace and stress makes way for relaxation.

So, what "system" am I talking about here? The time-management gurus would be happy to sell you an expensive and complicated scheme, but you don't need anything like that. Instead, you can rely on two tools that come free with your Mac: Calendar and Reminders. Both are designed not only to record all your upcoming events and tasks but also to remind you when they're happening or due, so you can get on with the far more important business of living your life. In this chapter, you explore both Calendar and Reminders and learn how they can help you keep your affairs in order and your sanity intact.

Getting Acquainted with Calendar

You use the Calendar app to record future activities, which could be a doctor's appointment, a business meeting, a lunch date, or your kid's soccer practice. Whatever the activity, Calendar refers to it as an *event*.

You get the Calendar app on the desktop by clicking the Calendar icon on the dock (see Figure 2-1) or in Launchpad. The bulk of the Calendar screen is taken up by a large calendar that shows the current month and marks the current date with a red circle (see Figure 2-1).

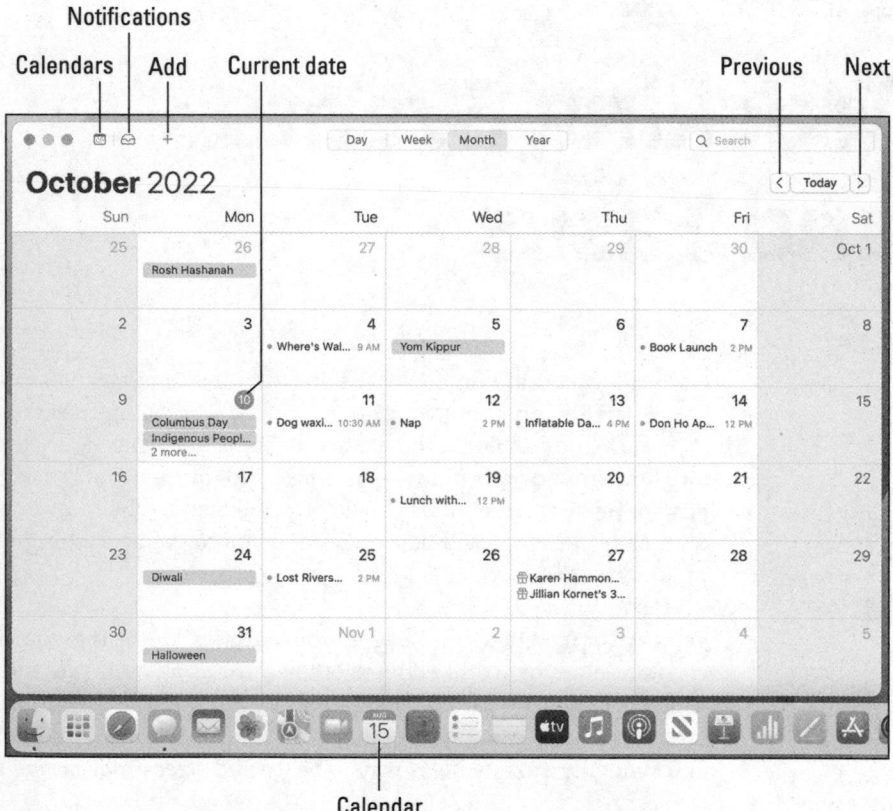

FIGURE 2-1:
Use the Calendar app to record your upcoming events.

Getting to know the Calendar toolbar

The toolbar at the top of the Calendar window displays the following items, as shown in Figure 2-1:

>> **Calendars:** Toggles the Calendar list sidebar on and off (see "Working with Multiple Calendars," later in this chapter).

>> **Notifications:** Toggles the Notifications sidebar on and off. The Notifications sidebar shows your event invitations (see "Responding to event invitations," later in this chapter).

>> **Add (+) icon:** Adds an event to your calendar (see "It's a Date: Creating an Event," later in this chapter).

>> **Views:** Gives you access to the four Calendar views: day, week, month (shown in Figure 2-1), and year. (See "Switching Calendar views," next).

>> **Search:** Enables you to find events based on the text you type in the search field (see "Searching for an event," later in this chapter).

>> **Today:** Takes you to the current day in the view you're using. The arrows to the left and right move one unit (day, week, month, or year, depending on the current view) into the past or into the future (respectively) from the displayed date.

Switching Calendar views

Calendar offers four views that determine how your events appear in the calendar and the level of detail the calendar shows for each event:

>> **Day:** Shows the selected day's upcoming events on the left; on the right, you see a mini-month calendar and a summary of the day's first event (refer to Figure 2-2). This view offers the most detail for your events.

>> **Week:** Displays a week-at-a-glance version of your calendar, as shown in Figure 2-3. A column for each day is divided into hours, with each event taking up its allotted time slot. The longer the event, the more detail you see.

>> **Month:** Shows a month-at-a-glance with as much of the text of your events as possible on each day (see Figure 2-1).

>> **Year:** Displays the entire year in one pane, as shown in Figure 2-4. This view doesn't show anything about your scheduled events. However, you can click a date to see a pop-up list of the appointments for that day (as demonstrated in Figure 2-4). You can also double-click a date to open that day's events in day view.

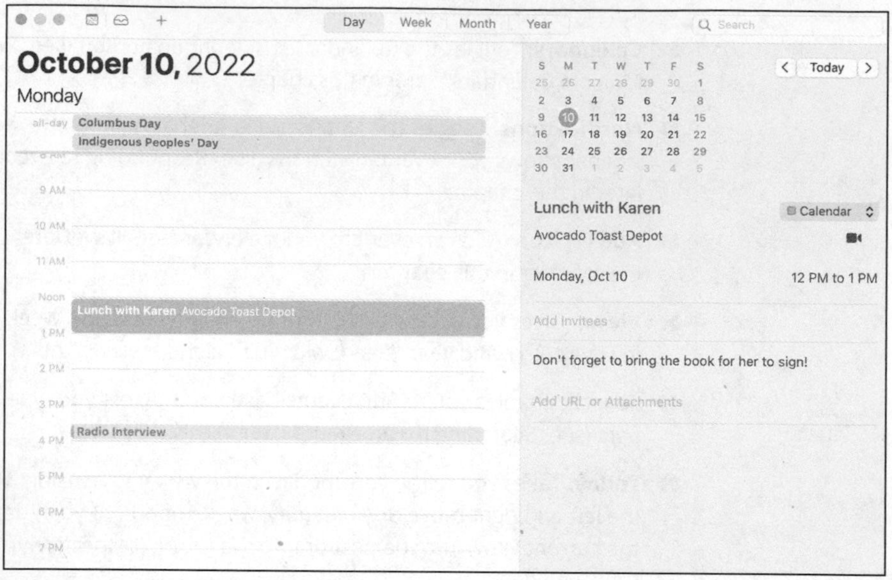

FIGURE 2-2:
For maximum
event detail,
switch to
day view.

FIGURE 2-3:
A calendar in
week view.

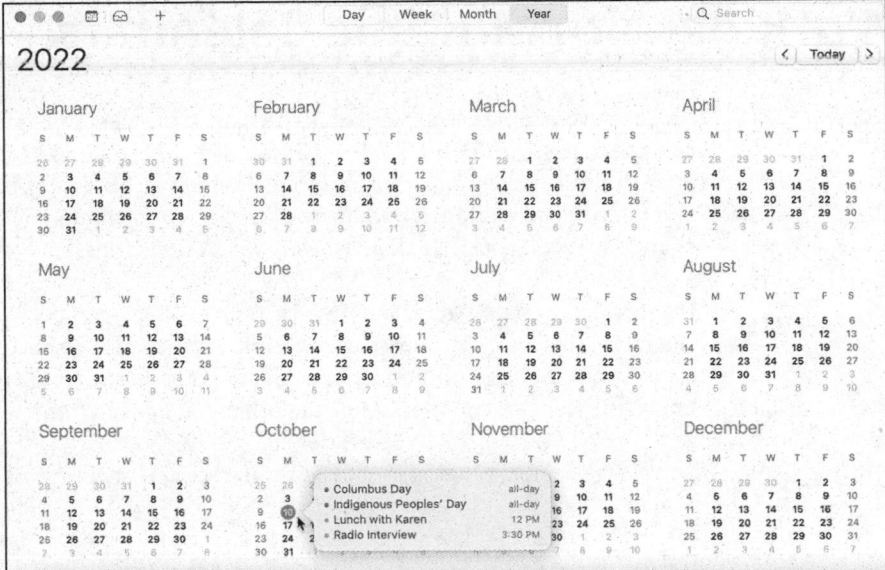

FIGURE 2-4:
Click a day in year view to see that day's events.

Navigating the calendar

You can move from one view and date to the next in the following ways:

» **Mini-month:** In day view, click a date in the mini-month to display that date in day view.

» **Month:** Double-click a date in month view to open that date in day view. You must double-click the actual day number; if you double-click in the space, a new event is created.

» **Week:** Double-click a date — again, the actual day number — in week view to open that date in day view.

» **Year:** Double-click a date in year view to open that date in day view. Double-click a month in year view to open that month in month view.

» **Previous:** Click this button (pointed out in Figure 2-1) or choose View ⇨ Previous (⌘+left arrow also works) to navigate to the previous item in the current view (for example, the previous month if you're in month view).

» **Next:** Click this button (pointed out in Figure 2-1) or choose View ⇨ Next (or ⌘+right arrow) to navigate to the next item in the current view (for example, the next week if you're in week view).

Working with Multiple Calendars

One of the welcome conveniences of the Calendar app is that it enables you to view calendars from different sources simultaneously. Calendar accesses and manages multiple calendars from multiple sources or accounts, including your Mac and your iCloud account as well as online accounts where you keep (and perhaps share) calendars, such as Google or Microsoft Exchange.

TECHNICAL STUFF

Due to ongoing concerns about privacy and the sharing of personal data, the list of calendars that you can view in the Calendar app changes over time, so check what options are available to you as you set up your calendars. Look for information under the Help tab in Calendar or the other calendars in which you're interested.

You can also import calendar data from another calendar or time management app.

When you click the Calendars icon on the toolbar (refer to Figure 2-1) or choose View ⇨ Show Calendar List, the Calendars list sidebar appears on the left side of the Calendar window and displays the accounts you have activated. The calendars from each account are listed below its name.

When a calendar's check box is selected in the Calendars list, it means you see that calendar's events. To hide that calendar's events, deselect its check box.

In the next few sections I explain how to create a calendar on your Mac or from iCloud as well as how to add calendars from other sources by accessing the associated accounts.

Creating a new calendar

Calendar opens with a default calendar to get you started. In the Calendars list, you might see an On My Mac heading with Calendar listed under it. If you turned on Calendar in iCloud, you see iCloud — and any calendars you created on another device that uses the same iCloud account — in the Calendars list. You may want or need to create additional calendars for other purposes. To create a new calendar, follow these steps:

1. **Choose File ⇨ New Calendar (or press Option+⌘+N).**

    If you don't have other accounts, that's all you have to do for now, so skip to Step 3.

2. **In the displayed continuation menu, click On My Mac (or iCloud, if you use iCloud) or one of the remote servers where you keep calendars (if you use remote servers).**

    An *Untitled* calendar appears in the Calendars pop-up list.

3. **Type a descriptive name for your calendar and then press Return.**

4. **Make sure your new calendar is selected in the Calendars list and then choose Edit ⇨ Get Info (or press ⌘+I).**

   Calendar displays an Info dialog for your new calendar.

5. **Click the color pop-up menu (it's just to the right of the Name text box) and click the color you want Calendar to apply to events you add to this new calendar.**

6. **Click OK.**

   Your new calendar is ready to store events.

TIP

The position of your new calendar (or any calendar, for that matter) in the Calendar list sidebar isn't set in stone. To move a calendar within its section, simply drag and drop it.

Adding calendars from other accounts

If you use a service that comes with a calendar component (such as Google or Yahoo!), you can add that calendar to the Calendar app. You can also add CalDAV or Exchange accounts, which are the formats most often used for shared corporate calendars. Events that you create or change at work with your company's calendar application, or events you create or change by using your Google or Yahoo! account, are added automatically to your calendar, and vice versa.

To add a calendar from another account, follow these steps:

1. **Choose Calendar ⇨ Add Account.**

   The Choose a Calendar Account Provider dialog appears.

2. **Do one of the following:**

   - *Select the radio button next to the account you want to add (such as Google, as shown in Figure 2-5) and then click Continue. Type your username (it may be an email address) and password, and then click Create or Continue to verify your account. Click the switch next to Calendar on, if necessary, and then click Done.*

   - *Select the radio button next to Other CalDAV Account and then click Continue. Choose the account type from the pull-down menu: Automatic, Manual, or Advanced. (I suggest leaving Automatic selected.) Type the email address and password you use to access this calendar. Click Sign In to verify your account.*

   That account is added to the Calendars list, and your online calendar's events appear in your Calendar window.

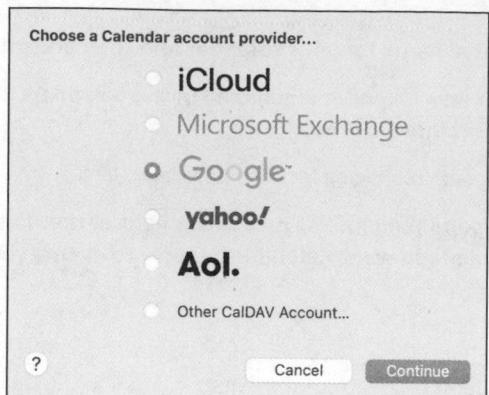

FIGURE 2-5:
Adding Calendars
from other
accounts takes
just a few clicks.

3. **After the account is set up, choose Calendar ⇨ Settings and then click the Accounts tab.**

4. **Click the name of the account you added.**

5. **From the Refresh Calendars pull-down menu, choose the interval at which you want Calendar to retrieve information from the account or update information you add on the server, as shown in Figure 2-6.**

   If you select a specific time interval — such as Every Minute or Every 15 Minutes — Calendar checks the server at the specified time interval and fetches changes or sends changes you made. Alternatively, you can click Manually to refresh the calendar yourself when you want to, by choosing View ⇨ Refresh Calendars.

6. **Click the close icon.**

REMEMBER

When you use iCloud or another account–based online calendar (such as Google or Yahoo!), you can sign in to the same account, or accounts, on your smartphone, tablet, or from another computer. Your calendars are always at your fingertips.

Subscribing to online calendars

Another source of calendars for Calendar are those you can subscribe to online, such as a calendar of holidays, sports team schedules, bridge tournaments, or new movie releases. Calendars you subscribe to appear under the Other category in the Calendars list. Events that appear in these calendars are added, deleted, and modified by whoever maintains the online calendar, which you can view but not change.

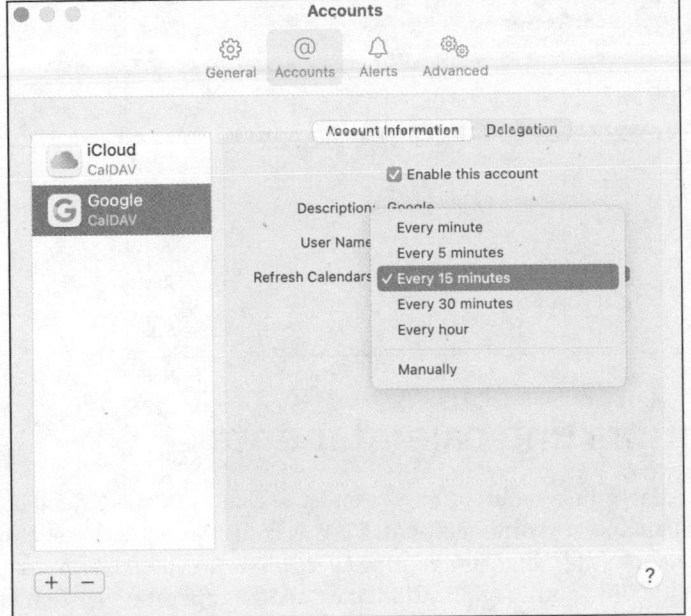

FIGURE 2-6:
Choose how
often you
want Calendar
to refresh
information for
each account.

To subscribe to an online calendar

1. **Choose File ⇨ New Calendar Subscription (or press Option+⌘+S) to open the URL dialog.**

2. **Type the website URL for the calendar you want to subscribe to.**

   For example, the link to a U.S. Holidays online calendar is `https://p06-calendars.icloud.com/holiday/US_en.ics`.

3. **Click the Subscribe button.**

   Calendars display an Info dialog for the calendar, as shown in Figure 2-7.

4. **Adjust the settings (such as the calendar color and refresh interval) to taste and then click OK.**

   The name appears in the Calendars list under Other, and the calendar's events appear in the Calendar window.

TIP

Visit iCalShare (`www.icalshare.com`) to find calendars you can subscribe to.

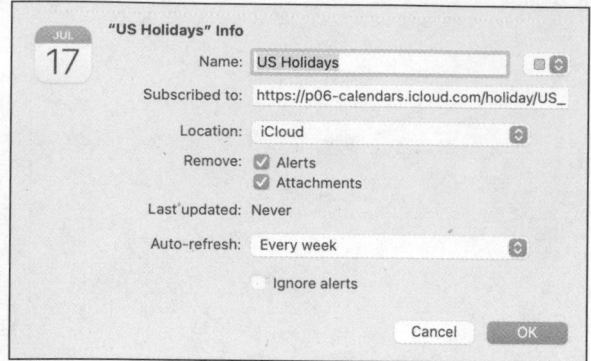

FIGURE 2-7:
You can subscribe
to an online
calendar.

Importing calendar data

Earlier, I talk about adding calendar accounts to the Calendar app (see "Adding calendars from other accounts"). This is the easiest way to get other calendar app data into the Calendar app. However, what can you do if you store calendar information in another application or on another operating system and you're not able to add that data as a new account?

In this case, you can export that data as a Calendar file or a vCalendar (.vcs) file, and then import that file into Calendar. If you're using Microsoft Outlook, save your calendar information as a separate file (as opposed to exporting it), and then import that file into Calendar.

After you save calendar data from another application, you can import that file into Calendar by following these steps:

1. **Choose File ➪ Import.**

   A file chooser dialog appears.

2. **Click the drive or folder or both that contains the file you want to import.**

3. **Click the file you want to import and then click Import.**

   Calendar imports your chosen calendar file's data. You can then rename the calendar if you want, and add events or edit existing ones, as explained just a bit further along in this chapter.

Renaming, merging, and deleting calendars

At any time, you can rename a calendar or group, whether it's on your Mac or on one of the online services (such as iCloud, Google, and Yahoo!). The name of a calendar or group is for your benefit and has no effect on the way Calendar works. To rename a calendar or group, double-click a calendar or group name, which opens the name in a text box. Type a new name and press Return.

If you have events split between two calendars, you might later decide that those two calendars should be a single calendar. In that case, you should merge the two calendars, which means that Calendar moves all the events from calendar A to calendar B and then deletes calendar A. To perform a merge, right-click the calendar you no longer want to keep, click Merge, and then use the continuation menu to click the calendar into which you want to merge the events. When Calendar asks you to confirm, click Merge.

If you no longer need a particular calendar or group, click the one you want to delete and choose Edit ⇨ Delete. If you have any events stored on a calendar, a dialog appears, asking whether you really want to delete that calendar. Click Delete. If you delete a calendar by mistake, choose Edit ⇨ Undo or press ⌘+Z before you perform any other action in Calendar.

WARNING

When you delete a calendar, you also delete any events stored on that calendar. There's no way to restore those events, so make sure you really want to delete the calendar.

It's a Date: Creating an Event

Got a date and you can't be late? Perhaps it's coffee with an old friend or lunch with an old flame. Whatever the rendezvous, you can add it to Calendar so you won't forget or schedule a conflicting activity at that time.

Some common types of events are meetings, appointments with clients, times you need to pick up someone (such as at the airport), or recreational time (such as a concert or a two-week vacation).

You can create two types of events in Calendar:

>> **Regular event:** An event that occurs on a specific date at a specific time (such as a dentist appointment or a breakfast meeting).

>> **All-day event:** An event that occurs on a specific date but with no set time (such as a birthday or vacation day).

Creating a regular event

If an event occurs on a set date at a set time, it's a regular event that you can add to your schedule using Calendar. To create an event, start by deciding which calendar to store the event in, and then be sure you know the event's starting date and time and duration (or ending time). You also have options to create an event alert, make the event repeat, and invite others to the event.

There are two types of regular events:

» **Quick event:** Enables you to quickly type a date, a time, and an event without much description, such as "dinner with Shaquille, Friday at 7 pm."

» **Detailed event:** Enables you to specify complete event info, including the calendar, location, alerts, recurrence, travel times, and other helpful information to get you to the right place at the right time.

Setting up a quick event

Follow these steps to forge a quick event:

1. **Click + (add event) on the toolbar (refer to Figure 2-1).**

   Alternatively, choose File ⇨ New Event or press ⌘+N.

   Calendar displays the Create Quick Event pop-up.

2. **Use the text box to type a phrase that defines your event.**

   Calendar understands common phrases, such as "dinner on Tuesday" or "staff meeting next Thursday from 9 a.m. to 1 p.m." Calendar uses the current date as the point of reference, and the default duration for an event is one hour. "Breakfast" or "morning" starts at 9:00 a.m. "Lunch" or "noon" begins at 12:00 p.m. "Dinner" or "night" starts at 8:00 p.m.

3. **Either click the suggested event (see Figure 2-8) or press Return.**

   Calendar adds the quick event.

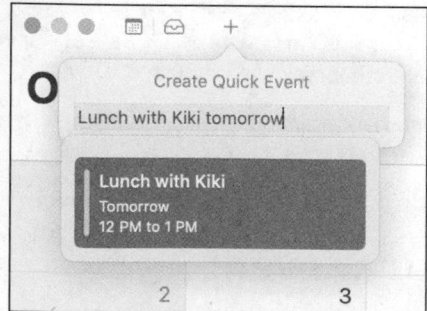

FIGURE 2-8:
Creating a
quick event.

Setting up a detailed event

Follow these steps to define a detailed event that includes the event name, calendar, start time, and stop time, as well as optional details such as the event location, URL, notes, reminders, and recurrence:

1. **Using your preferred view, display the date on which the event occurs.**

2. **Use one of the following techniques to begin the event definition:**

   - **Day view:** Double-click the time you want the event to begin. Or click and drag from the starting time to the ending time.

   - **Week view:** Under the date on which the event occurs, either double-click the time the event begins or click and drag from the starting time to the ending time.

   - **Month view:** Double-click the date of the event. Calendar begins a default event that starts at 9:00 a.m. and lasts for an hour.

   Calendar displays a pop-up window like the one shown in Figure 2-9.

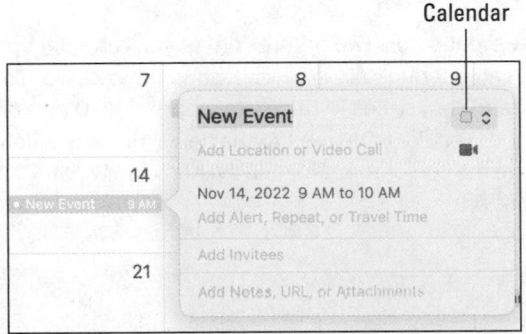

FIGURE 2-9:
Calendar begins by creating a barebones event.

3. **Replace the default *New Event* text with a descriptive title for your event.**

   At this point, your event has a proper title, starting and ending times, and has been assigned to a calendar (the color of which appears in the Calendar control, labeled out in Figure 2-9). If that's good enough for you (and for many events it will be), click outside the pop-up window and skip the rest of these steps, all of which are optional.

4. **To assign the event to a particular calendar, click the Calendar pop-up menu (labeled in Figure 2-9) and choose the calendar.**

5. **To specify a named location or address for the event, click the Add Location text box and start typing the name or address, and then click the location when it appears in the search results.**

6. **If the event is a scheduled FaceTime call, click the video camera icon.**

Calendar creates a new FaceTime link. You can click the FaceTime button to see the link, share it with other people, and open the link.

7. **To modify the event's starting and ending dates or times or both, click the date and time in the pop-up window to expand the options and make your changes.**

8. **If the event repeats on a regular schedule, you can add all those events at once by specifying the recurrence interval:**

a. *Click the Repeat pop-up menu and choose an option, such as Every Day, Every Month, or Custom.* If you choose Custom, a dialog like the one shown in Figure 2-10 appears, letting you define specific days for the recurring event, such as every Monday or the first Wednesday of every month.

b. *If you chose Custom, specify your custom recurrence interval and then click OK.*

c. *Click the End Repeat pop-up menu to choose when the repeating should stop:* Never (if you want the event to repeat in perpetuity), After (the number of times you want the event to repeat), or On Date (the date on which the repetition should stop).

TIP

If a particular event occurs two or three times, you can set it up as a repeating event or you can just duplicate it, which is sometimes easier. To duplicate an event, click it and choose Edit ⇨ Duplicate, or press ⌘+D (or hold down the Option key and then drag the event to the new time slot). When the duplicate appears, move the cursor to it, drag the event to a new date, and then release the mouse button.

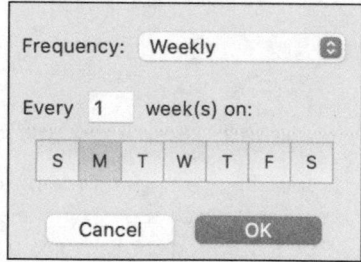

FIGURE 2-10:
You can define a custom interval for a recurring event.

9. **If you want to specify the travel time to the event, click the Travel Time pop-up menu and then click a specific time value (such as 30 Minutes or 1 Hour) or click Custom to enter a custom time value in minutes or hours.**

TIP

After you add the event, Calendar includes the travel time as part of the event's block in the calendar. (If you don't see travel time reflected in the calendar, choose View ⇨ Show Travel Time.) Taking traveling time into account helps you avoid scheduling appointments too close together.

10. **If you want Calendar to remind you when an event is coming up, follow these substeps to set up one or more alerts:**

  a. *Click the Alert pop-up menu and click when you want Calendar to let you know about the upcoming event.* For example, you can choose At Time of Event, 30 Minutes Before, or 1 Day Before. You can also choose Custom to display the dialog shown in Figure 2-11. Only perform substeps b through d if you choose Custom.

FIGURE 2-11:
You can define a
custom alert for
an event.

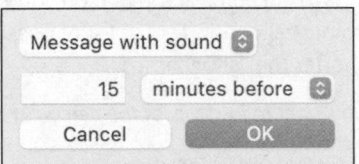

FIGURE 2-11: You can define a custom alert for an event.

  b. *Use the top pop-up menu to select how you want to receive the alert:*

  - Message with Sound: The default option displays a notification message with the default Calendar alert sound.

  - Email: If you have more than one address, choose the one (from the pop-up menu) you want the alert sent to.

  - Open File: This option opens the Calendar app. To open a different file, such as a report that you can review for an upcoming meeting, choose Other in the pop-up menu below the alert type menu and then scroll through the directories and folders of your Mac to select the file you want to open and then click Select.

  c. *Define the alert time by selecting a unit in the right pop-up menu (such as Minutes Before, Hours Before, or Days Before), and then using the left text box to type a numeric value.*

  d. *Click OK.*

  e. *(Optional) Add another alert by hovering the mouse pointer over the existing alert and then clicking the plus button that appears to the right.* An additional alert can be useful. For example, if the alert is for a business meeting, being alerted a day before lets you get your ducks in a row by preparing. A second alert an hour before the meeting enables you to make last-minute preparations.

11. **If you want to add extra info to the event definition, click the Add Notes, URL, or Attachments area.**

The Add Notes, Add URL, and Add Attachment fields appear:

  - *Add Note:* Click inside the text box and type any additional notes about your event.

- *Add URL:* Click inside the text box and type or paste a website address relevant to your event, such as a restaurant's website for an upcoming dinner.

- *Add Attachment:* Click to open a file chooser dialog. Select a file to attach to the event (such as a business presentation that you need to give at the event), and then click Open.

12. **If you want to invite people to your event:**

   a. *Click Add Invitees and begin typing a name.* If the person you want to invite is in Contacts, Calendar automatically shows you a list of possible matches. The more you type, the shorter the list becomes.

   b. *When you see the person you want to invite, click the person's name.*

   c. *Repeat Steps a and b until you add all your invitees.*

TIP

   If you created one or more groups in Contacts, start typing the name of the group in the Add Invitees window. Click the name of the group to invite all members of the group to your event.

   d. *Click Send.* An invitation is sent to all invitees using the Calendar or ICS file format. If an invitee has Calendar or another calendar application associated with the email address, the invitation is sent directly to Calendar or the calendar application.

TECHNICAL STUFF

   ICS is the standard file type for exchanging calendar information. Calendar, Outlook, Google Calendar, and Calendar (on iPhones and iPads) support the ICS standard. When you send or receive an email with an invitation attached, the invitation probably has the .ics filename extension. To add the event automatically to Calendar or the calendar application currently in use, you or the recipient simply click that attachment in the email message.

   The recipients have the option to respond with Yes, No, or Maybe. You receive an email when recipients respond: A white check mark in a green circle appears next to the recipients who accept, a question mark in an orange circle indicates a Maybe response, and a red circle-with-slash means the recipient declined the invitation.

13. **If you didn't follow Step 12 (which closes the event pop-up window after you click Send), click outside the event pop-up window to close it.**

Creating an all-day event

Some events don't really have specific times that you can pin down. These include birthdays, anniversaries, sales meetings, trade shows, conferences, and vacations.

What all these types of events have in common is that they last all day: in the case of birthdays and anniversaries, literally so; in the case of trade shows and the like, "all day" refers to the entire workday.

Why is this important? Well, suppose you schedule a trade show as a regular appointment that lasts from 9 a.m. to 5 p.m. When you examine that day in Calendar, you see a big fat block that covers the entire day. If you also want to schedule meetings that occur at the trade show, Calendar lets you do that, but it shows these new appointments "on top" of this existing trade show event. This makes the schedule hard to read, so you might miss an appointment.

To solve this problem, configure the trade show (or whatever) as an all-day event. Calendar clears it from the regular schedule and displays the event separately, near the top of the calendar when it's in day or week view. Here are the steps to follow to create an all-day event:

1. **Using your preferred view, display the date on which the event occurs.**

2. **Use one of the following techniques to begin the event definition:**

   - **Day view:** Double-click anywhere inside the All-Day area at the top of the schedule.

   - **Week view:** Under the date on which the event occurs, double-click anywhere inside the All-Day area at the top of the calendar. If the event lasts multiple days, click and drag across the All-Day field for each day of the event.

   - **Month view:** Double-click the date of the event. If the event lasts multiple days, click and drag across each day of the event. Calendar begins a default event that starts at 9:00 a.m. and lasts for an hour. (Don't worry, you convert this default event to an all-day event in Step 4.)

   Calendar displays a pop-up window like the one shown earlier in Figure 2-9.

3. **Replace the default *New Event* text with a descriptive title for the all-day event.**

4. **If you used month view to start the event, click the date and time in the pop-up window to expand the options and then select the All-Day check box.**

5. **Fill in the rest of the event details as needed.**

   Calendar adds the event to the date's All-Day field at the top of the calendar (in day view or week view).

Editing an Event

Sometimes a title, time, and date are enough descriptors for an event. Other times, you want to add more information, or something changes and you have to modify the location or the date or time of an event. To make any change to an existing event, you can edit that event.

Tweaking an event's times using drag-and-drop

TIP

You can quickly change the start time or end time or both of a regular event by using the mouse or trackpad:

>> **To change the start time:** In day view or week view, move the mouse pointer to the top edge of the event block in the calendar (the pointer changes to a two-way-pointing arrow with a horizontal bar), and then drag the top edge up (for an earlier start time) or down (for a later start time).

>> **To change the end time:** In day view or week view, move the mouse pointer to the bottom edge of the event block in the calendar (the pointer changes to a two-way-pointing arrow with a horizontal bar), and then drag the bottom edge up (for an earlier end time) or down (for a later end time).

You can also use your mouse or trackpad to move an event to a new time or even a new date:

>> **Day view:** Drag the event up or down and drop it on the new time.

>> **Week view:** Drag the event up or down (to change the time) or left or right (to change the date) and drop it on the new time or date or both.

>> **Month view:** Drag the event and drop it on the new date. In this case, Calendar changes the event's date but not its times.

TIP

If you have to move the event to a date several weeks (in week view) or several months (in month view) away, it's easier to change the dates manually using the event editing dialog, as I describe in the next section.

Changing the details of an event

As the Buddha said, everything is impermanent, so it's almost inevitable that after you create an event, *something* about that event will change. Perhaps it's now at a new location or the date has been moved up a week. Whatever the reason, editing an event lets you change any event detail, including the title, calendar, date, time, alerts, and recurrence.

To edit an existing event, follow these steps:

1. **Double-click the event you want to modify.**

Alternatively, click the event and choose Edit ⇨ Edit Event or press ⌘+E.

The event editing dialog appears.

2. **Make your changes to the event's details, as needed.**

Remember that if you want to change the event's All-Day status, the starting or ending dates or times, the recurrence interval, the travel time, or the alerts, you need to first click the current date and time to display the controls.

For the details on working with the above fields as well as changing the calendar, adding invitees, and adding notes, a URL, or attachments, see "Setting up a detailed event," earlier in this chapter.

3. **When you're done, click outside the event editing dialog to close it and save your changes.**

Responding to event invitations

If someone sends you an event invitation, you see a notification and the invitation appears in the Notifications sidebar (click the toolbar's Inbox icon or choose View ⇨ Show Notifications). The number that appears beside the Inbox icon indicates the number of invitations you have. A badge also appears on the Calendar icon on the dock, and that badge's number also indicates the number of invitations you have in your Inbox.

When you click the Inbox, the invitations appear, as shown in Figure 2-12. Click Accept if you want to attend the event; click Decline if you prefer to skip it; or click Maybe if you're not sure right now. Calendar notifies the sender of your response. If you click Accept, the event is added to your calendar.

Deleting an event

When you no longer need to remember an event, you can delete it. Just click it and choose Edit ⇨ Delete or right-click the event and choose Delete from the context menu. You may get a warning message if the event has attachments or invitees. If you delete an event by mistake, press ⌘+Z or choose Edit ⇨ Undo right away to retrieve your event.

FIGURE 2-12:
Open the
Notifications
sidebar to see
and respond
to your event
invitations.

REMEMBER

If you delete an event with invitees, you don't have to notify them. The Calendar app sends an email to each invitee, letting them know the event has been cancelled.

Keeping Your Events Organized

Storing events is useful only if you can readily view upcoming events so you can prepare for them (and not forget about them!). To help you find and view events, Calendar offers several different methods that include using colors to identify different types of events and letting you search for a specific event by name.

Color-coding events

Many new Calendar users make the mistake of dumping every new event in a single calendar (usually the one with the unhelpful name Calendar). That can make Calendar much harder to use because events in a calendar reflect the color you assigned to the calendar. That means you can easily end up with a sea of, say, blue events, which doesn't help you differentiate those events in any way.

A better way is to designate a different color for each calendar and then assign each event to the appropriate calendar. So, for example, if you assign the color blue to your Personal calendar and the color green to your Work calendar, you can quickly identify which events on your calendar are personal (blue) or work-related (green).

TIP

Use contrasting colors for multiple calendars to make it easy to tell which events belong to which calendar.

Selectively hiding events

Normally, Calendar displays all events, color-coding them so you can tell which events belong to which calendars. However, if you have too many events, you may find mixing personal and work events too confusing. If you want to see only events stored on a specific calendar (such as the Personal or Work calendar), you can hide the events stored on other calendars.

To hide events stored on a calendar, choose View ➪ Show Calendar List (or click the Calendars icon in the toolbar; see Figure 2-1) to open the Calendar List sidebar, and then deselect the check box of that calendar. When you're ready to view that calendar's events again, display the Calendar List sidebar and select the calendar's check box.

Checking today's events

Probably the most important events you need to keep an eye on are the ones you've scheduled for today. To see everything on your schedule for today, click the Today button near the top-right corner of the Calendar window. You can also choose View ➪ Go to Today or press ⌘+T.

Checking events on a specific date

Sometimes you may need to know whether you have any events scheduled on a certain date. To check a specific date, choose View ➪ Go to Date (or press Shift+⌘+T) to open the Go to Date dialog, select the date you want, and then click Show; alternatively, double-click the date in one of the calendar views.

REMEMBER

The month view can show you the events scheduled for a particular date, but the day and week views can show you the specific times of your events for that day.

Searching for an event

If you scheduled an event several days ago, you may forget the exact date of that event. To help you find a specific event, Calendar lets you search for it by typing all or part of the information stored in that event, such as the event name, the attendee names, or any notes you stored about the event.

To search for an event, follow these steps:

1. Click the search text box in the upper-right corner of the Calendar window.

2. **Type as much text as you can remember about the event you want to find, such as an attendee's name or the location of the event.**

   As shown in Figure 2-13, Calendar displays a list of results that match your search text as well as a drop-down menu that you can use to specify the type of search you want to perform.

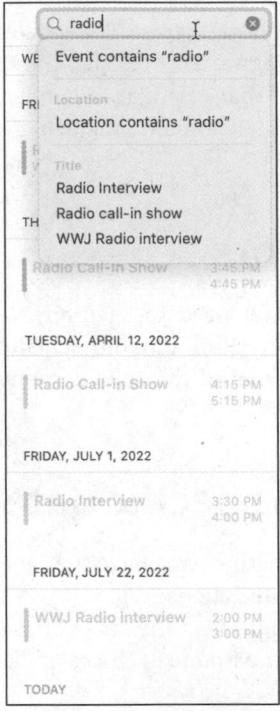

FIGURE 2-13:
You can search
for events and
specify the type
of search to run.

3. **Click the type of search you want to run:**

   - *Event Contains* search text: Searches the entire event info for your search text.

   - *Location Contains* search text: Searches just the event locations for your search text.

   - *Title:* Displays a list of events where the title includes your search text. Click one of the titles to search for events that match the title.

   The Calendar application displays a list of events that match the search type you chose, with events yet to come in bold. The list appears in a column on the right of the calendar window, as shown in Figure 2-13. If you have a recurring event, every instance that matches the search will appear. If the event you seek is on a hidden calendar (one that isn't selected), its contents won't appear in the search.

4. **Double-click an event from the list.**

Your chosen event appears.

5. **Click X (clear) in the search text box to remove the list of matching events.**

Exporting Calendar data

To share your calendars with other applications (even those running on other operating systems, such as Windows or Linux), you need to export your Calendar file by following these steps:

1. **Choose File ⇨ Export ⇨ Export.**

A dialog appears, giving you a chance to choose a filename and location to store your Calendar data.

2. **In the Save As text box, type a name for your file.**

3. **Choose the location to store your file by clicking the Where pop-up menu or by clicking the disclosure arrow to expand the window and view the directories and folders on your Mac.**

4. **Click Export.**

Sharing your calendars

You can print your calendar and give a copy to people, but an easier way to share is to give others access to your calendar online. Your calendar will be a read-only file; the people who have access can view your calendar but can't change it. To share your calendar, follow these steps:

1. **Click the Calendar icon to open the Calendar List sidebar (or choose View ⇨ Show Calendar List).**

2. **Click the calendar you want to share.**

You can share calendars from only On My Mac or iCloud.

3. **Choose Edit ⇨ Publish for a calendar on your Mac. Or, if you want to publish a calendar that's on iCloud, choose Edit ⇨ Share Calendar.**

4. **For calendars on your Mac, you can type a name for your calendar that will help those who have access understand what the calendar represents.**

   This name is for only the shared calendar; it doesn't change the name of the calendar in Calendar.

   Shared iCloud calendars use the name they have in Calendar, so you should give your calendar a recognizable name.

5. **Do one of the following to publish your calendar:**

   - *For calendars on your Mac*: Type the URL web address of the server along with your login and password in the related fields. Select the options you want from the check boxes at the bottom of the dialog. Then click the Publish button.

   - *For calendars on iCloud*: If the people you want to share your calendar with are in Contacts, type the names and then choose the correct email addresses from the matches that appear. Otherwise, type the email addresses of the people you want to share the calendar with.

   Choose Window ➪ Contacts to display your contacts. Move the Contacts window so that it and the Share dialog are visible. You can now drag-and-drop contacts you want to share a calendar with from the Contacts window into the Share dialog.

   If you want to make the calendar public, select the Public Calendar check box. To send folks a link to subscribe to your public calendar, click the share icon and then choose how you want to send the link (such as Mail or Messages).

6. **Click Done.**

Getting Things Done with Reminders

The Calendar app is an excellent tool for tracking appointments, meetings, and other events. By adding an alert to an event, you get a digital click on the shoulder to remind you when and where your presence is required.

However, our days are littered with tasks that could be called *subevents*. These are things that need to be done at a certain point during the day, but don't rise to the level of full-fledged events: returning a call, taking the laundry out of the dryer, turning off the sprinkler. If you need to be reminded to perform such a subevent, it seems like overkill to crank out an event using the Calendar app.

Fortunately, macOS offers a better solution: the Reminders app. You use this app to create *reminders,* which are simple nudges that tell you to do something, to be somewhere, or whatever. These nudges come in the form of Notification Center banners that appear on your screen at a time you specify, when your (portable) Mac reaches a particular location, or when you send a text message to someone. If you have an iCloud account, you can sync your reminders between your Mac, iPhone, and iPad.

Setting a reminder for a specific time

Here are the steps to follow to set up a reminder that alerts you at a specific time:

1. **Click Reminders on the dock (see Figure 2-14) or in Launchpad.**

   The Reminders app appears.

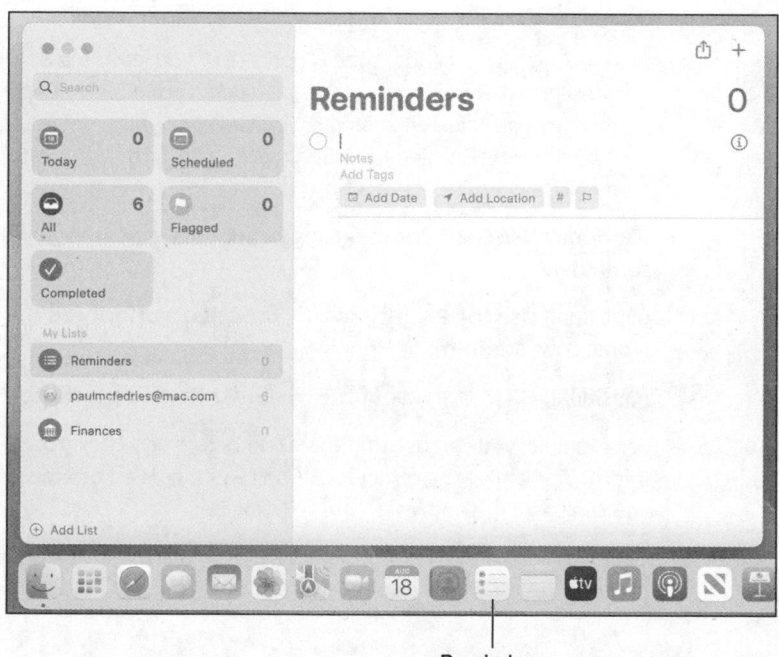

FIGURE 2-14:
A fresh reminder ready to be defined.

Reminders

2. **Click the list you want to use to store the reminder.**

   This list will be the one named Reminders (at least at first; see "Creating a list," later in this chapter).

3. **Choose File ⇨ New Reminder.**

You could also click + (new reminder) in the upper-right corner of the window, press ⌘+N, or click anywhere in the empty space below the list of reminders (which will be empty if you're just starting out with Reminders).

The Reminders app creates a new reminder, as shown in Figure 2-14.

4. **Type the reminder text.**

5. **Click the *i*-in-a-circle (more info) that appears on the right side of the new reminder.**

6. **Select the On a Day check box, click the displayed date, and then use the calendar that pops up to set the date of the reminder.**

The default date for a new reminder is today, so you need to pop up the calendar only if you want your reminder on another date.

7. **Select the At a Time check box and then use the controls that appear to set the time of the reminder.**

REMEMBER

Setting a specific reminder time is optional. If you leave the At a Time check box deselected, Reminders creates an *all-day* reminder that appears at 9 a.m. on the date you selected in Step 6. You can change the default all-day reminder time by choosing Reminders ⇨ Settings and then choosing your preferred time in the All-Day Reminders section.

8. **(Optional) Use the Repeat setting to set up a repeat interval for the reminder.**

9. **(Optional) Use the Priority setting to assign a priority to the reminder: None, Low, Medium, or High.**

10. **(Optional) Fill in the rest of the reminder fields as needed.**

For example, you can use the Notes text box to add background text or other information about the reminder. If the reminder is associated with a web page, you can paste the address in the URL text box.

11. **Click anywhere in the empty space below the list of reminders.**

Reminders saves the reminder.

Setting a reminder for a specific location

Getting an alert at a specific time is the standard way of working with reminders, but the Reminders app supports a second type of criterion: location. That is, when you specify a location for a reminder, the app sets up a *geo-fence* — a kind of virtual border — around that location. When your Mac crosses that geo-fence (this assumes you have a notebook Mac that you can take with you; if you're using iCloud to sync events with your other devices, your iPhone or iPad will also trip the alert when it crosses the geo-fence), the associated reminder appears on your screen. So, for example, if you're on your way to a meeting with a client, you could create a reminder that includes notes about the meeting or the client, and then specify the meeting location as the criterion.

Here are the steps to follow to set up a location-based reminder:

1. **Click the list you want to use to store the reminder.**

2. **Choose File ⇨ New Reminder.**

   Alternatively, click + (new reminder) in the upper-right corner of the window, press ⌘+N, or click anywhere in the empty space below the list of reminders.

   The Reminders app creates a new reminder.

3. **Type the reminder text.**

4. **Click the *i*-in-a-circle (more info) that appears on the right side of the new reminder.**

5. **Select the At a Location check box.**

6. **Use the Enter a Location text box to specify the name or address of the location you want to use, and then click the location when it appears in the search results.**

   Alternatively, you can click Current Location to use your present whereabouts.

7. **Specify when you want your Mac to display the reminder:**

   - *Arriving:* Select this option to have the reminder appear when your Mac first comes within range of the location.

   - *Leaving:* Select this option if you prefer to see the reminder when your Mac goes out of range of the location.

8. **Follow Steps 8 through 11 from the "Setting a reminder for a specific time" section to fill in the reminder details.**

Setting a reminder for when you message someone

Have you ever said to yourself, "I must remember to mention X the next time I text so-and-so" and then, when you finally do text that person, you completely forget to include any mention of X? I suspected as much.

Well, I'm happy to report that those incidents are now in your past because you can create a reminder that pops up the next time you send a text to someone using the Messages app. Here's how to set it up:

1. **Click the list you want to use to store the reminder.**

2. **Choose File ⇨ New Reminder.**

   Alternatively, click + in the upper-right corner of the window, press ⌘+N, or click anywhere in the empty space below the list of reminders.

   The Reminders app creates a new reminder.

3. **Type the reminder text.**

4. **Click the *i*-in-a-circle that appears on the right side of the new reminder.**

5. **Select the When Messaging a Person check box.**

6. **Use the Add Contact text box to start typing the name of the person, and then click the person when they appear in the search results.**

7. **Follow Steps 8 through 11 from the "Setting a reminder for a specific time" section to fill in the reminder details.**

Creating a list

The Reminders app comes with a default list named Reminders. That list might be all you ever need, but you can also create a list. For example, you might want to keep your personal and business reminders separate.

Whatever the need, feel free to create your own list by following these steps:

1. **If the Reminders app isn't currently displaying the sidebar, choose View ⇨ Show Sidebar, or press Option+⌘+S.**

   The Reminders app displays the sidebar.

2. **Choose File ⇨ New List.**

   You can also click Add List at the bottom of the sidebar or press Shift+⌘+N.

   Reminders opens a dialog for defining your new list, as shown in Figure 2-15.

3. **Use the Name text box to type a name for your list.**

4. **Click the color you want to use for the list.**

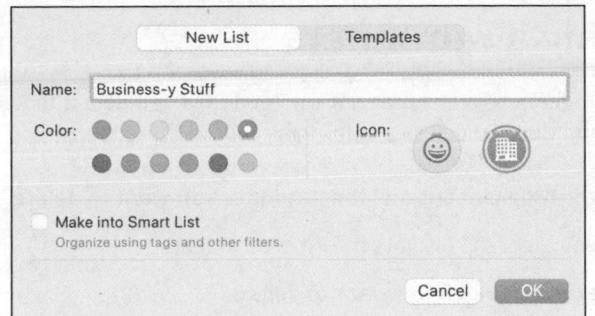

5. **In the Icon section, click a button to select either an emoticon (left) or an icon (right) to represent your list.**

6. **Click OK.**

   The Reminders app adds the list.

Completing a reminder

When a reminder is complete, you don't want it lingering in the Reminders list (or whatever list it's in), cluttering the screen and making it hard to look through your remaining reminders. To avoid that, once the reminder is done, select the radio button beside it. This tells Reminders that the reminder is complete, and the app immediately moves it to the Completed list.

Alternatively, when the reminder notification appears (see Figure 2-16), click Options and then click Complete. (You can also postpone the reminder by clicking one of the Remind Me commands.)

TIP

To see your completed reminders, click the Completed item in the Reminders app sidebar or choose View ⇨ Show Completed.

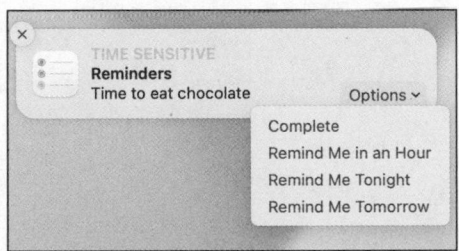

FIGURE 2-16:
In the reminder
notification, click
Options and
then Completed
to mark the
reminder as
done.

Deleting a reminder

If you no longer need a reminder, it's a good idea to delete it to keep your reminder lists neat and tidy. To delete a reminder, follow these steps:

1. **Click the list that contains the reminder you want to delete.**

The Reminders app displays the list's reminders.

2. **Select the reminder you want to delete.**

3. **Choose Edit ⇨ Delete.**

Alternatively, either press Delete or right-click the reminder and then click Delete in the shortcut menu.

Reminders deletes the reminder.

Setting the default Reminders list

The default list is the one that Reminders uses when you don't specify a particular list when you create a reminder. If you have a particular list you'd prefer to use as the default, follow these steps to set it:

1. **Choose Reminders ⇨ Settings.**

The Settings dialog appears.

2. **Use the Default List pop-up menu to select the list you want to use as the default.**

3. **Click the red close icon.**

Chapter **3**

Crafting Fancy-Schmancy Documents with Pages

I f you just want to bang out a quick to-do list or get down a few of the thoughts buzzing around in your brain, you could use the Notes app or even Mail to send yourself a message. But at some point, you're going to want to create something more substantial. It might be a letter, a memo, a résumé, or a report. It might be something fancy such as business cards, a flyer, or a poster. Or it might be something that's both fancy and schmancy, such as a newsletter, a brochure, or a birthday card.

Okay, I hear you saying, "But surely I need some kind of high-end and prohibitively expensive page-layout app to do most of that?" First, stop calling me Shirley.

Second, nope, you don't need anything of the sort because you have everything you need already installed — and therefore free — on your Mac. I'm talking here about the Pages app, which can handle almost any word-processing or page-layout chore you throw at it: everything from a quick memo all the way up to that novel or cookbook you've always wanted to write.

In this chapter, you learn everything you need to know to use Pages to compose whatever type of document you want. You explore Pages' powerful templates; learn how to enter, edit, and format text; delve into styles; master non-text elements such as images, shapes, charts, and tables; and investigate Pages' document-related features.

Getting a Head Start with Document Templates

To help you start writing, Pages offers a variety of document templates, each of which contains a prefab layout with suggested or placeholder text (of the *lorem ipsum* variety) and often extra goodies such as images and tables. When you create a document from a template, much of the work has already been done. Sweet! All you have to do is enter text (or replace the *lorem ipsum* placeholder text) and customize the appearance of the template to suit your taste. You're way ahead of the game because you don't have to create everything from scratch. The following sections tell you how to get started.

Creating a document from a template

Pages offers more than 100 templates, which are organized into categories such as Reports, Letters, Flyers & Posters, and Newsletters. (That's a lot of templates, true, but you can find many more on the web. I give suggestions for websites to visit in Book 5, Chapter 6.)

Some templates, such as those for reports or letters, are designed mostly for writing (relatively) plain and simple documents, with the emphasis on content. In these templates, you type continuous text directly on the page in the document and can insert images or charts. Other templates, such as flyers or newsletters, are designed for mixing text and graphics when content and presentation have almost equal importance. The text in these templates goes into text boxes rather than the page itself. When choosing a template, you want to select one that's closest to the type of document you want to create.

WARNING

After you create a document by using a template, you can't switch the document to another template. If you want to use a different template, you have to create a document from that template.

To create a document from a template, follow these steps:

1. **Click the Pages icon on the dock (see Figure 3-1) or in Launchpad.**

If you've previously created documents in Pages, they appear in a file chooser dialog when you launch the application. If you see the file chooser, click Cancel.

2. **Choose File⇨New (or press ⌘+N).**

The Choose a Template dialog appears, displaying different templates you can choose, as shown in Figure 3-1.

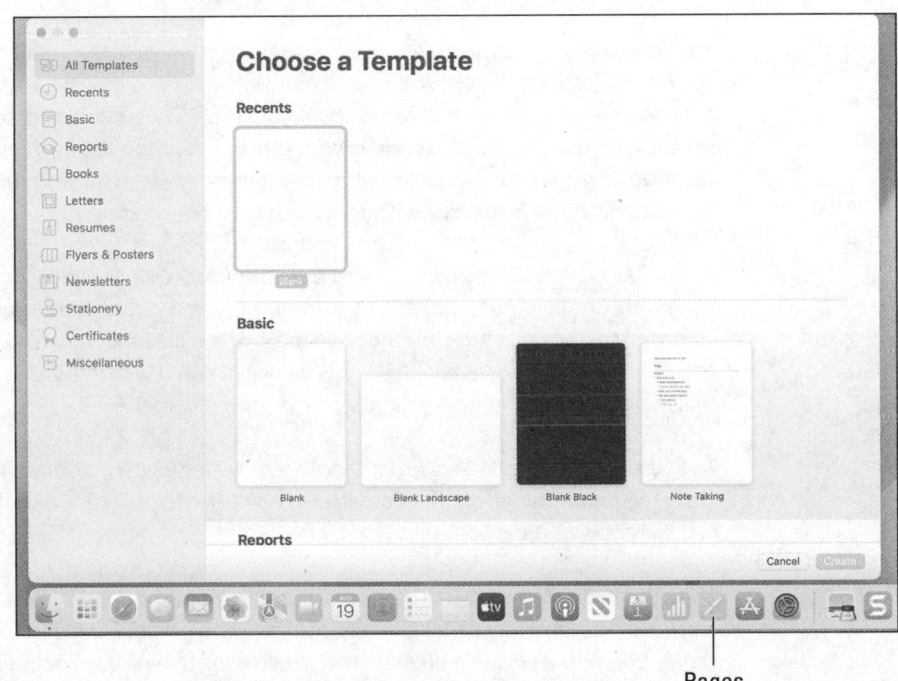

FIGURE 3-1:
Pages provides various templates to help you create a document quickly.

Pages

3. **To narrow your choices, click a template category in the list on the left.**

4. **Select the template you want to use.**

If you want to start from scratch (that is, with no predefined text or formatting), click one of the blank templates in the Basic category: Blank, Blank Landscape, or Blank Black, whichever best suits the type of document you want to create.

5. **Click the Choose button.**

   Or double-click the thumbnail for the template you want to use.

   Pages opens your chosen template as a new, untitled document.

6. **If you're sure you want to continue using this new document, choose File ⇨ Save (or press ⌘+S).**

   The Save As dialog opens. Type a name for your document and choose the folder where you want to store it. Pages supports versions, which keep a running backup of your document each time you change it. (I explain this feature in Book 1, Chapter 4, and Book 3, Chapter 1.)

TEXT ON A PAGE VERSUS TEXT BOXES

You can quickly and easily create colorful documents on your Mac, but choosing the correct template can be confusing. For example, if you have to write a 100-page report, choose a report template that uses continuous text — not a newsletter template, which uses text boxes. Likewise, to publicize your garage sale, choose a flyer template, which will have only one box on a page, not a letter template, which will let you have continuous text that flows across several pages.

In continuous text (also known as word-processing) documents, you type directly on a page with, um, continuous text. You can insert photos or tables if you want, but they complement the text and aren't the main focus of the document. In documents with text boxes (also known as *page layout*), you have to create a text box first and then place that text box somewhere on your page.

The advantage of continuous text is that Pages creates pages automatically while you type. The disadvantage of this approach is that it's harder to define exactly where the text will appear on the page.

The advantage of using text boxes is that you can move those text boxes anywhere on a page (or to a different page). The disadvantage of typing text in text boxes is that they can display only a limited amount of text. If you need to type a larger chunk of text, you may need to link text boxes so that when your text overflows one text box, it flows automatically into another one.

Another difference between continuous text and text box documents is that you must manually add or delete pages when you use a template with text boxes. To add a page, choose Insert ⇨ Page; to delete a page, select it and choose Edit ⇨ Delete. With a continuous text template, Pages adds pages automatically while you type and deletes pages as necessary when you delete text.

Replacing placeholder text

Nearly every template (except for the blank templates) contains placeholder text, which is a variety of the *lorem ipsum* pseudo-Latin that's been used in typesetting as dummy text since the sixteenth century. The *lorem ipsum* is there to show you what the document looks like when it has a full complement of text. Your job is to replace the *lorem ipsum* with your own text. To change placeholder text in a template, follow these steps:

1. **Select the placeholder text you want to change:**

   - *If the placeholder text is in a regular paragraph:* Click anywhere inside the paragraph.

   - *If the placeholder text is in a text box:* Double-click anywhere inside the text box.

   Pages selects the placeholder text you clicked or double-clicked, as shown in Figure 3-2.

2. **Type any new text you want to replace the placeholder text.**

FIGURE 3-2:
To replace place-holder text, select it and type new text.

Replacing placeholder photos and graphics

Many templates display placeholder photos and graphics. Unless you happen to like the image included with a template, you'll probably want to replace it with one of your own. Here I explain how to place photos from Photos; how to place images from other places on your computer; and how to insert a chart or table from Numbers, Apple's spreadsheet application.

Inserting photos from Photos

These steps work with both templates and blank documents to add or replace photos in Pages documents with photos from the Photos app:

1. **Use one of the following techniques to get started, depending on whether you're replacing a placeholder image or inserting a new image:**

   - *To replace a placeholder image:* Click the photo icon in the lower-right corner of the placeholder image.

   - *To insert a new image at the current cursor position:* In the Pages toolbar, choose Media ➪ Photos.

   A media browser dialog appears, as shown in Figure 3-3.

FIGURE 3-3:
Use the media browser to insert the photo you want to use in your document.

2. **Click the Photos tab, if it's not selected already.**

3. **In the sidebar on the left, click a folder, a media type, or an album.**

   This narrows your choices and makes it easier to find the photo you want to add to your document.

4. **Click the photo you want to insert.**

   Pages replaces the placeholder image with the photo you choose from the media browser. In the next section, I explain how to manipulate photos in your documents.

Moving and resizing a photo

After you place a photo in a document, you can move or resize it.

To move a photo, follow these steps:

1. **Drag the photo.**

   If your document has continuous text, the paragraphs shift while you move the image so that the text runs before and after the image. If you're using a document with text boxes, the image moves directly over the text box.

2. **Drop the photo in the position you prefer.**

To resize a photo, follow these steps:

1. **Click the photo you want to resize.**

   Handles appear around your chosen picture.

2. **Move the pointer to a handle until the pointer turns into a two-way pointing arrow.**

3. **Drag the handle to resize your photo.**

   You can also hold down the Option key and drag the handle to resize the photo around its midpoint.

   As you drag, note that the photo maintains its original aspect ratio. Also, any surrounding text wraps around the photo as the size changes.

TIP

   Whether text wraps around the photo depends on the Text Wrap setting. Click the photo and then in Format Inspector on the right, click the Arrange tab. Use the Text Wrap pop-up list to select how you want text to wrap with respect to the image: Automatic, Around, Above and Below, or None.

4. **Release the mouse button or lift your finger from the trackpad when you're happy with the new size of the photo.**

Inserting other images

If the image you want to insert isn't stored in Photos, do the following:

1. **Choose Insert ⇨ Choose (or press Shift+⌘+V).**

   A file chooser dialog opens.

2. **Locate and then select the image you want to insert.**

3. **Click Insert.**

   Pages adds the image to your document.

4. **(Optional) To use your inserted image to replace a placeholder image, click the placeholder image, press Delete, and then drag the inserted image to the placeholder location.**

TIP

You can also modify and mask images. I show you how to handle these tasks in Book 5, Chapter 6.

Inserting a chart or table from Numbers

You can insert a chart or table from a Numbers file into a Pages document. (Numbers is Apple's spreadsheet app, which I explore in Book 5, Chapter 5.) Alternatively, in the later section, "Crafting Charts and Tables in Pages," I explain how to create a chart or table directly in Pages.

Here are the steps to follow to insert a Numbers chart or table into a Pages document:

1. **Open the Numbers document that has the chart or table you want to insert.**

2. **Select the chart or table you want to insert.**

3. **Choose Edit ⇨ Copy or press ⌘+C.**

4. **Return to your Pages document.**

5. **Position the insertion point at the position in the document where you want the chart or table to reside.**

6. **Choose Edit ⇨ Paste or press ⌘+V.**

7. **Drag the selection handles to resize the placeholder as needed to accommodate the table or chart.**

Inserting pages or sections

In continuous text documents, no matter how much text you type, pages are added. Each page has the same layout, although some elements may be slightly changed. For example, when a second page is added to a letter, it has reduced header information (such as a smaller logo) and a page number instead of the address in the footer. In some documents, you may want to manually add a page break or create a section that has different margins than the rest of the document or begins a new chapter. For example, a financial report may have a cover page as one section, a table of contents for the second section, and third section containing descriptive text with charts and graphs.

To insert a page into your document, follow these steps:

1. **Place the cursor at the position where you want the current page to end and the inserted page to begin.**

   Most of the time, you'll want to insert the new page right after a particular page in the document, in which case you'd place the cursor at the end of that existing page.

2. **Choose Insert ➪ Page Break.**

   Alternatively, press ⌘+Return or click the toolbar's Insert button and then click Page Break.

   Pages starts a new page and moves the text after the cursor to the top of that page.

TIP

To add a full blank page at the current cursor position, click the toolbar's Add Page button. This is different than adding a page break in that Pages inserts a blank page and then moves the text after the cursor to the top of the next page.

You can add a new *section* to a document at any time without affecting the existing pages. Or, add a *section break* within an existing page, and then anything after the section break will move to the new section.

To add a new section to the end of your document, choose Insert ➪ Section.

To add a section break, do the following:

1. **Place the cursor at the beginning of the text you want to move to the new section.**

2. **Choose Insert ➪ Section Break.**

   The new section begins with the text that comes after where you placed the cursor.

Moving around your document

To see all the pages of your document, choose View ⇨ Page Thumbnails from the toolbar or the menu bar. A left sidebar opens, showing thumbnails of the pages or sections in your document, as shown in Figure 3-4. When you click a thumbnail, a colored background surrounds all the pages in the same section. The first page of a section is flush left, and subsequent pages in the section are indented to the right.

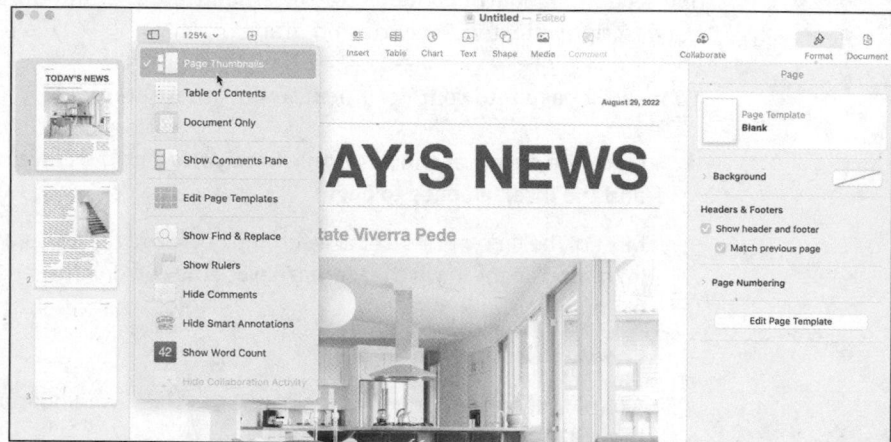

FIGURE 3-4:
Thumbnails show you all the pages in your document.

TIP

To hide page thumbnails, choose View⇨ Document Only.

The page thumbnails not only show you how many pages are in a section but also enable you to jump from one page to another. Just click a thumbnail to move to that page.

Two other tools help you manage your document:

» **Zoom:** In the toolbar, click the Zoom pop-up menu, which lets you zoom in or out of your document to views that range from 25 to 400 percent. You can also choose to view one or two pages side by side at a time or to Fit Width or Fit Page. After you view two pages, Fit Spread is an option on the Zoom menu.

» **Word count:** Choose View ⇨ Show Word Count (or press Shift+⌘+W) to display (at the bottom center) the number of words in your document.

TIP

Choose View ⇨ Hide Word Count (or press Shift+⌘+W) to remove the word count from view.

Messing Around with Text

Text can appear directly on a page or inside a text box. Although you type text directly on a page in continuous text documents (such as those created with the Blank template, letters, or reports), you can add text boxes and type text inside those text boxes. You might choose this approach when you want to insert a sidebar or a pull quote. In some templates, such as newsletters, posters, and business cards, you can type text *only* inside text boxes.

TIP

In many ways, text boxes behave like other objects placed in your document, such as photos or charts, and have a few different options than continuous text. I explain adding text boxes later in this chapter in the "Creating a text box" and "Moving a text box" sections.

Either way, after you type your text, you probably want to make some changes. In the following subsections, I explain how to edit, format, and adjust the spacing of your text.

Editing text

Whether you're typing text directly on a page or inside a text box, you can edit text by adding, deleting, or rearranging it as follows:

>> **Adding text:** To add text, place the cursor where you want the new text to appear, click, and then type away.

>> **Deleting text:** You can delete text in three ways:

- *Move the cursor to the right of the characters you want to erase and press Delete.* The Delete key appears to the right of the +/= key.

- *Select text and press Delete.* Select text by holding down the Shift key and moving the cursor with the arrow keys or by clicking and dragging the mouse over the text to select it, and then press Delete.

- *Move the cursor to the left of the characters you want to erase and press Forward Delete.* The Forward Delete key appears under the fn key on full-size Mac keyboards. With smaller Mac keyboards, you can mimic Forward Delete by pressing fn+Delete.

>> **Rearranging text:** After you write some text, you may need to rearrange it by copying or moving chunks of text from one location to another. You can copy and move text between two text boxes or from one part of a continuous text page to another part of the same page — or to another page.

To copy and move text, you can use the Cut, Copy, and Paste commands on the Edit menu, but you might find it quicker to select and drag text with the mouse. Simply select the text you want to move, and then drag it to a new location. Release the mouse button or lift your finger from the trackpad to finish moving your text.

If you want to copy text, hold down the Option key while dragging the selected text.

REMEMBER

Formatting text

The text styles and images you choose for your document create the tone of what you want to communicate — businesslike, fun, weird, and so on. You can format text by using fonts, effects (such as bold), sizes, and colors. (Later in this chapter, in the "Faster Formatting with Styles" section, I tell you how to apply formatting in a different way.)

To give you fast access to the formatting options, Pages displays a Format pane (see Figure 3-5) down the right side of the Pages window. To view (or hide) the Format pane, click the Format button on the toolbar or choose View ⇨ Inspector ⇨ Format.

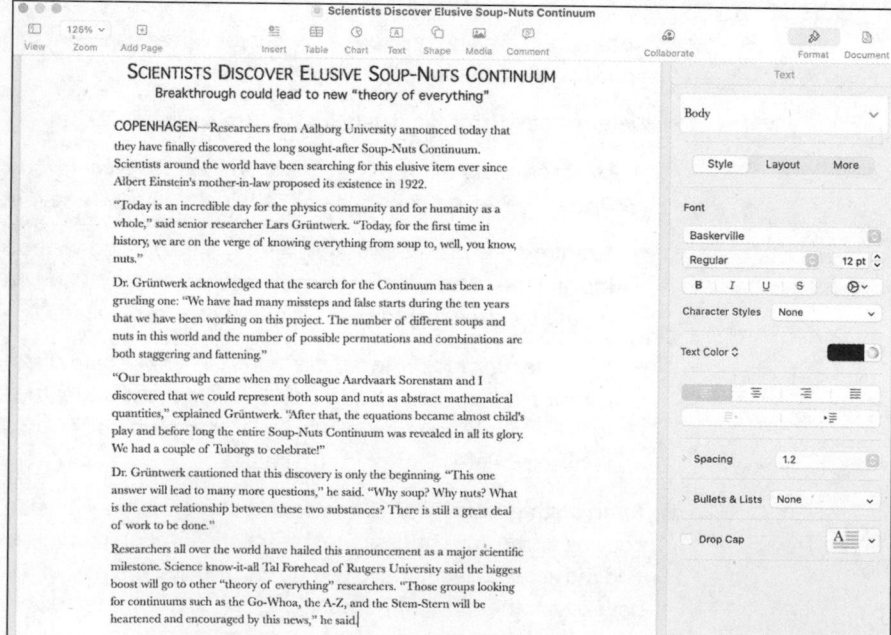

FIGURE 3-5: Use the Format pane to choose fonts, effects, sizes, text spacing, and alignment.

Select the text you want to format and then click the Style tab of the Format pane. Then, in the Font section, do any of the following:

>> **Click the font family.** (It's Baskerville in Figure 3-5.) Then choose a typeface from the menu that appears. Pages has what-you-see-is-what-you-get (affectionately known as WYSIWYG and pronounced "wizzy-wig") menus so you see what the font looks like in the pop-up menu.

>> **Click the typeface.** (It's Regular, in Figure 3-5.) Then choose a typeface, such as Italic or SemiBold. You can also click the buttons below this menu or make a selection from the Character Styles pop-up menu.

>> **Click the size arrows or type a number for the size you want.** (The size is 12 pt in Figure 3-5.)

>> **Click the color swatch or picker.** A color menu appears when you click the swatch, or a choice of color pickers appears when you click the color circle next to the swatch. Click a color to change the color of your selected text. If you're working with the color picker, choose a different color picker by clicking an icon at the top of the dialog.

TIP

For more info on choosing colors, see Book 5, Chapter 4, where I tell you how to use these tools in Keynote. The color tools are similar in Pages and Keynote.

>> **Click the gear button to open the Advanced Options menu, as shown in Figure 3-6.** Use the pop-up menus to fine-tune character spacing, ligatures, and capitalization, or to add a background color. If you select the Shadow check box, additional menus appear to adjust how your selected text will be shadowed.

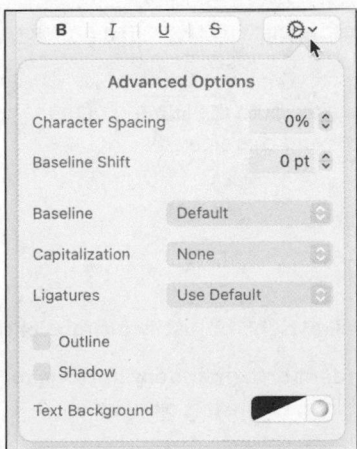

FIGURE 3-6: Use Advanced Options to fine-tune your text.

TIP

To adjust text in a text box, select the desired text, and then click the Text tab of the Format pane. For example, if the text box has a header, click the text to select it and then change the format. Any other text in the text box is unchanged.

Adjusting line spacing, justification, and margins

You can change how characters look by playing with the font, but you can also change the way a block of text looks by changing how it's spaced on the page. In concrete terms, this means changing the

>> **Alignment:** Define how text aligns within the left and right margins, in text boxes, and also between the top and bottom.

>> **Spacing:** Define how close together lines in a paragraph appear and how much space is between paragraphs.

>> **Margins:** Define the left and right boundaries that text can't go past.

Changing alignment

The Pages tools that adjust alignment of your selected text are in the Alignment section in the Style tab of the Format pane, as follows:

>> **Align Left:** Text appears flush against the left margin but ragged along the right margin.

>> **Center:** Each line of text is centered within the left and right margins so that text appears ragged on both left and right margins.

>> **Align Right:** Text appears flush against the right margin but ragged along the left margin.

>> **Justify:** Text appears flush against both the left and right margins, but extra space appears between words and characters.

To align text, follow these steps:

1. **Select the text you want to modify.**

2. **Click the align left, center, align right, or justify buttons of the Format pane.**

3. **(Optional) Click the left outdent or right indent buttons to move the selected text about half an inch to the left or right.**

   The left outdent button is active only after you indent the selected text. Click the buttons more than once to further indent or outdent.

Changing line spacing

Line spacing used for most purposes typically varies from 0.5 to 2.0. (A value of 1.0 is single spacing, and a value of 2.0 is double spacing.) To change line spacing, follow these steps:

1. Select the line or lines of text you want to modify.

2. Click the disclosure arrow next to Spacing to display the spacing options, as shown in Figure 3-7.

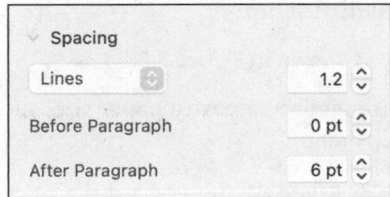

FIGURE 3-7: Use the Format pane's Spacing options to adjust the line spacing.

3. Open the pop-up menu on the left and choose Lines if it isn't selected.

4. Click the up and down arrows for the spacing field to the right of the pop-up menu to change the line spacing value, or enter a value, such as 1.5.

5. (Optional) Choose one of the other options from the pop-up menu and then choose a value accordingly:

- *At Least:* Sets a minimum of points for each line. This should be a minimum of the font size. For example, if you use a 10-point (pt) font, a 10 pt spacing is equal to a single-spaced paragraph.

- *Exactly:* Sets the points to the exact number you choose.

- *Between:* Sets the number of points for the space between lines of text. The minimum is 1 pt and is equal to single spacing. A value equal to your font points creates double-spacing.

TIP

The changes to your selected text occur immediately so you can try different solutions and see the effect they have on your text.

6. Click the up and down arrows next to the value fields for Before Paragraph and After Paragraph to set the amount of blank space that occurs there.

Defining margins for the entire document

A document's *margins* are the blank spaces that appear to the left and right of the page text, and above and below the page text.

REMEMBER

The margins apply only to a document with continuous text. Documents that use only text boxes are limited by the edges of the page.

To define the margins for the whole document, do the following:

1. **Click the Document button on the far right side of the toolbar or choose View ⇨ Inspector ⇨ Document Setup.**

2. **Click the Document tab, as shown in Figure 3-8.**

3. **In the Printer & Paper Size section, choose a paper size, such as US Letter or Legal, from the pop-up menu.**

4. **(Optional) Change the page orientation.**

5. **In the Document Margins section, use the Top, Bottom, Left, and Right text boxes to type the values you want for your document margins.**

   Or use the up and down arrows in each control to choose a value.

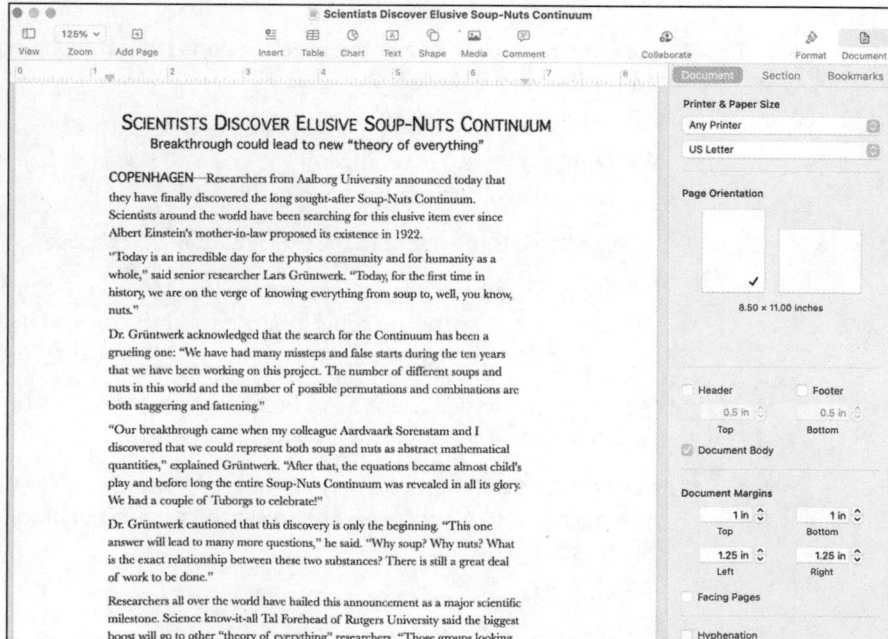

FIGURE 3-8: Set the margins for the entire document.

TIP

To set the units of measure for your rulers, choose Pages ⇨ Settings and then click Rulers. Use the pop-up menu next to Ruler Units to choose Inches, Centimeters, or Points.

Defining margins for a portion of text

To define the left and right margins of a portion of text — say a long citation from a book — you can use the ruler, which appears at the top of the Pages window when you choose View ⇨ Show Ruler (or press ⌘+R). The ruler lets you define an exact location for your margins, such as placing the left margin exactly 1.5 inches from the left edge of the page.

To define the left and right margins of selected text, follow these steps:

1. **Select the text you want to modify.**

2. **Drag the left margin marker (see Figure 3-9) left or right along the ruler and drop it on the new position.**

   The left margin marker is the orange triangle that appears on the left side of the ruler. If only the first lines of your paragraphs move, you've selected the indent marker, which is at the very top of the left margin marker; grab the left margin marker from the bottom.

3. **To indent the first line of a paragraph or paragraphs in your selected text, drag the indent marker to a new position on the ruler.**

   The indent marker is the thin rectangle that appears on top of the left margin marker. Figure 3-9 shows the left and right margin markers and the indent marker.

   If you drag the left margin marker after you move the indent marker, the indent marker moves with the left margin marker; dragging the indent marker, however, moves the indent marker by itself.

4. **Drag the right margin marker to a new position on the ruler.**

   The right margin marker is the orange triangle that appears on the right side of the ruler.

TIP

To establish precise indent measurements for the first lines of paragraphs and also for the left and right margins of your selected text, click the toolbar's Format button, click the Layout tab, and then click the disclosure arrow next to Indents. Use the First, Left, and Right controls to set your precise markers.

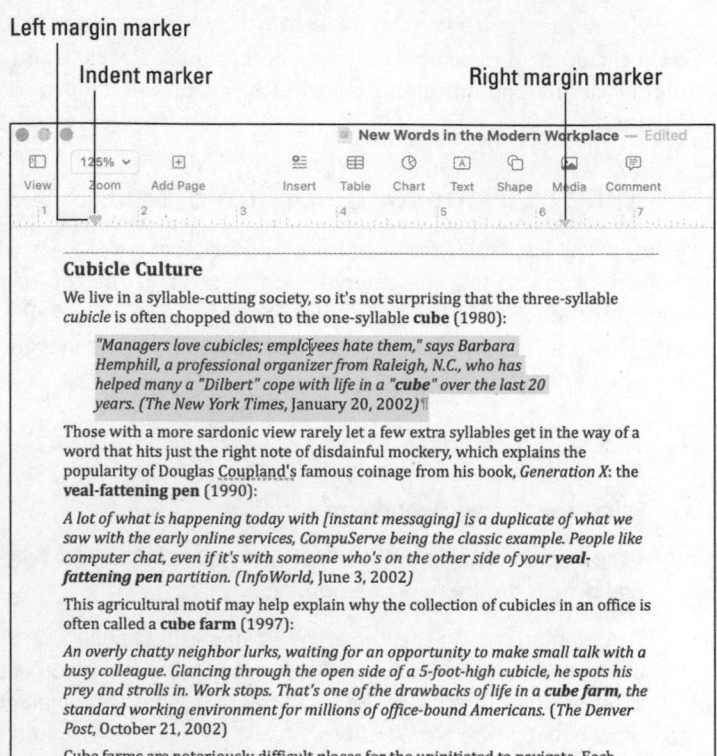

Left margin marker

Indent marker

Right margin marker

FIGURE 3-9:
Adjust paragraph
margins and set
first-line indents.

Adding tab stops

Documents look much better if they're properly indented and if their parts line up like soldiers on parade. One easy way to do this is to use tab stops whenever you need to create some room in a line. A *tab stop* (usually shortened to just *tab*) is a ruler marker that defines how far Pages shifts the cursor to the right when you press the Tab key. You can set a tab stop for the entire document or for a subset of the text, such as a paragraph.

Tabs are useful because they're meticulously precise. When you press the Tab key, the cursor leaps ahead to the next tab stop, no more, no less. (If you don't have any tab stops set, pressing Tab moves the cursor ahead half an inch.)

Pages lets you set four kinds of tabs:

>> **Left:** Text lines up with the tab on the left. This type of tab appears on the ruler as a right-pointing triangle.

>> **Center:** Text is centered on the tab. This type of tab appears on the ruler as a diamond shape.

>> **Right:** Text lines up with the tab on the right. This type of tab appears on the ruler as a left-pointing triangle.

>> **Decimal:** Numbers line up with the tab at their decimal places. This type of tab appears on the ruler as a circle.

To set one or more tab stops, follow these steps:

1. **Click anywhere in the paragraph to which you want the tab stops to apply.**

   If you want to apply the tab stops to multiple paragraphs, select some text in each paragraph.

2. **Click the Format icon on the toolbar or choose View ⇨ Inspector ⇨ Format.**

3. **Click the Layout tab.**

4. **Click the disclosure arrow next to Tabs.**

   The Tabs controls appear.

5. **(Optional) Click in the Decimal Character field if you plan to use the tab to align numbers by their decimal separators.**

   For example, you could change a period to a comma if you're creating a European document.

6. **Enter a value or click the up and down arrows to choose a value in the Default Spacing field.**

   The default spacing refers to the amount of space that Pages creates between each tab stop, starting from the left margin marker. Using 0.5 inches as the default spacing, for example, means that Pages creates the first tab stop 0.5 inches from the left margin. Add a second tab stop and it appears 1 inch from the left margin.

7. **Click the plus button at the bottom of the Tabs section.**

   Pages adds a tab stop to the table, as shown in Figure 3-10.

8. **Configure the tab stop as follows:**

   (a) *Click the number under Stops and indicate a precise position for the tab.*

   (b) *Click the type of tab you want in the menu under Alignment: Left, Center, Right, or Decimal.*

   (c) *Choose a Leader style from the pop-up menu: none, dashes, dots, a line, or arrows.* Pages fills the gap to the tab stop with the character you choose.

   If you want to delete a tab, click the tab and then click the minus sign.

Tab stop

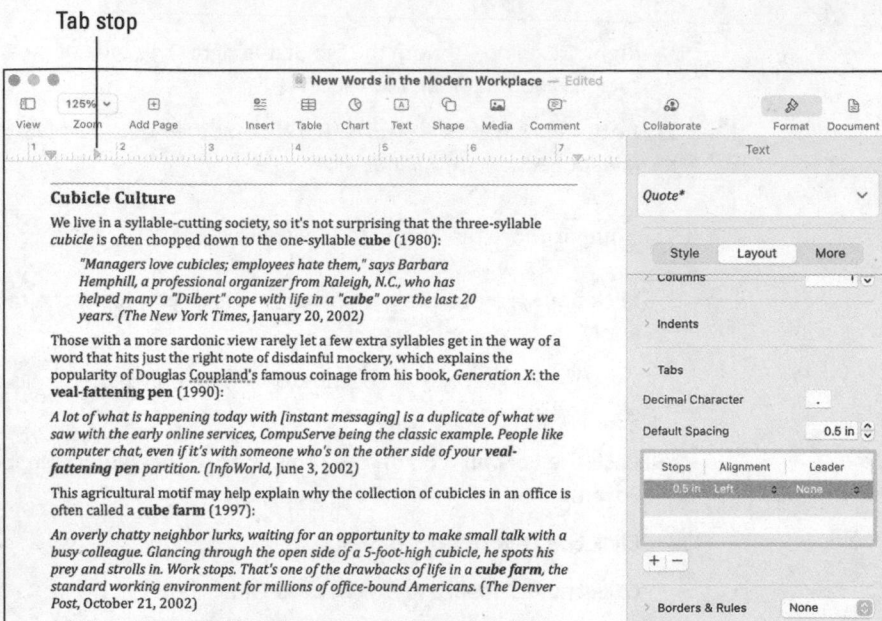

FIGURE 3-10:
A tab stop added
to a document.

TIP

As you add tab stops in Tabs section of the Layout tab, note that the tabs appear on the ruler in the specified position, as pointed out in Figure 3-10. (Not seeing the ruler? Choose View ⇨ Show Ruler or press ⌘+R.) Happily, you can use the ruler as a faster method to create tab stops. As usual, click inside the paragraph you want to work with (or select multiple paragraphs); then move the mouse pointer into the ruler, point at the position where you want your tab stop, and click. A tab stop appears instantly. If the tab isn't quite in the right spot, just drag it to the left or right. To change the tab type, double-click the tab until you get the one you want. To get rid of a tab, drag it off the ruler.

Adding headers and footers to a continuous text document

The *header* is the space between the top of the document text and the bottom of the top margin. Similarly, the *footer* is the space between the bottom of the document text and the top of the bottom margin.

The header and footer are where you usually place the date, page number, or document title; they contain information that repeats on each page. As with margins, documents that use text boxes don't have headers or footers.

REMEMBER

If you use a template, the headers and footers are predefined, but that doesn't stop you from changing them.

Here's how to use headers and footers:

1. Click the Document button on the toolbar.

Or choose View ⇨ Inspector ⇨ Document Setup.

2. Click the Document tab (refer to Figure 3-8).

3. Select the Header check box, the Footer check box, or both.

Text boxes for one or both will be added to your document.

4. Choose how far from the edge of the page you want the header and footer to appear; type a number or use the up and down arrows.

The header or footer text box moves according to the value you set. The top and bottom margins must be greater than the header and footer distance; otherwise, the document text will cover the header and footer. If you modify the header and footer distance, you usually need to modify the document margins.

5. In the Document Margins section, enter a value in the Top and Bottom text fields, or use the arrows to specify each margin.

If your header is 1 inch, your top margin should be at least 1.5 inches. The header will begin 1 inch from the top of the page, and the main text — also known as the *document body* — will begin 1.5 inches from the top of the page or .5 inch below the header.

6. Leave the Document Body check box selected.

Deselecting this box will convert your document to a page layout (text-box-only) document and may cause you to lose some of your work.

7. Move the pointer near the top or bottom of the page, more or less where the header or footer should be, until an empty box appears, as shown in Figure 3-11.

8. Click in the empty box.

The cursor flashes in the empty box.

There are actually three text boxes — one on the left, one in the center, and one on the right. You can enter distinct information in each and press Return independently in each one so that text appears on different lines. Press Tab to jump from one box to the next.

9. Type the text that you want to display at the top or bottom of each page.

Format the text as you would any other text, setting the typeface, size, and style or choosing a style associated with the template.

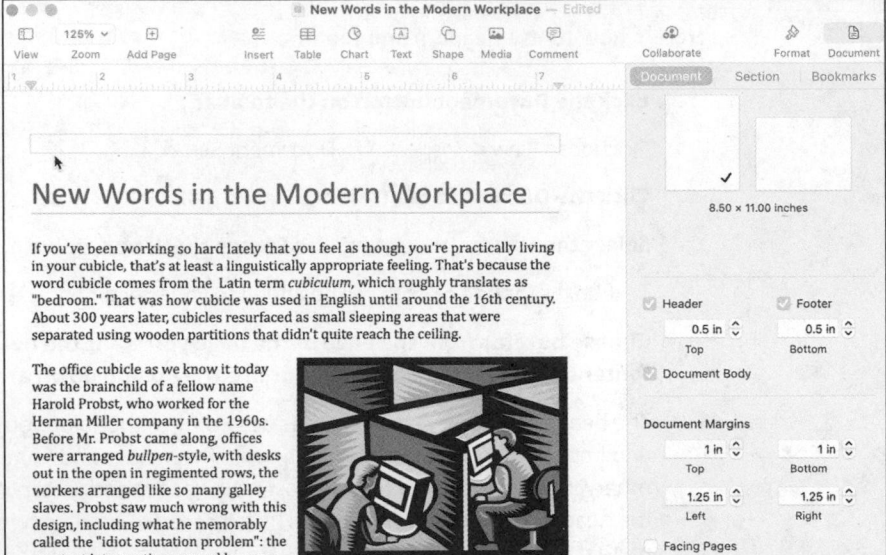

FIGURE 3-11:
Move the mouse pointer to the header position to display the text box.

10. **To add the date or page number automatically, position the cursor where you want the text to appear, click the menu bar's Insert command, and then click Page Number, Page Count, or Date & Time.**

   To format the Date & Time, double-click the inserted text. A window opens, as shown in Figure 3-12, where you can then use the Choose Date Format pop-up menu to choose your preferred date format.

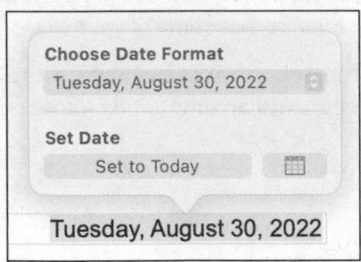

FIGURE 3-12:
Double-click the inserted date and time to choose a format.

   To format the page numbers, click the toolbar's Document button, click the Section tab, and then click the Format pop-up menu to choose the number style (Arabic, Roman, or letters).

If your document has multiple sections that you want numbered separately, click the first page of a section in the Page Thumbnails, click the toolbar's Document button, and then click the Section tab. Select the Start At radio button (which automatically deselects the Continue from Previous Section radio button) and then type the page number with which you want the section to begin, as shown in Figure 3-13.

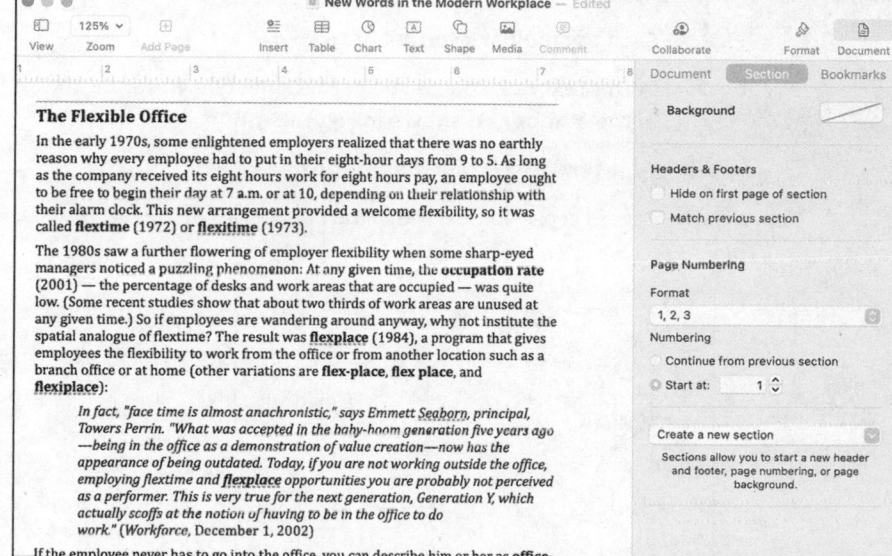

FIGURE 3-13: Specify headers and footers and page numbering for sections as well as the entire document.

If you don't want headers to appear on the first page — for example, you create a report that has a cover page — click the Document button on the toolbar and then click the Section tab. Select the Hide on First Page of Section check box.

Corralling Text into Text Boxes

As I mention earlier, text boxes hold text that you can place anywhere on a page (even in the middle of other text). You can create and place text boxes on any Pages document, whether created from a blank document or a template.

Creating a text box

When you create a text box, other text will wrap around it, making a text box an ideal candidate when you want to create a sidebar in a document. To create a text box, follow these steps:

1. **Click the Text icon on the toolbar or choose Insert ⇨ Text Box.**

   A text box appears on the page.

2. **Click the toolbar's Format button.**

3. **In the Text tab, choose the paragraph style you want to use for the text in the text box, as shown in Figure 3-14.**

4. **Type new text inside the text box.**

   Pages keeps your text within the boundaries of the text box.

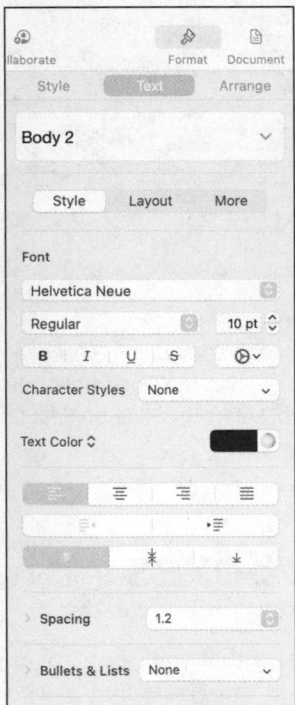

FIGURE 3-14: Choose the text style for your new text box.

Moving a text box

After you create a text box, you can move it. Move the mouse pointer anywhere within the text box and then drag the text box to a new location, even to a different page. If the new location is a long way off in a lengthy document, dragging the text box all the way to this position might be a hassle. Instead, you can click the text box, choose Edit ⇨ Cut, click the destination page in the Pages pane (choose View ⇨ Show Thumbnail Pages if you don't see it), and then choose Edit ⇨ Paste to place your text box on the selected page.

Resizing a text box

Sometimes a text box is too large or small for the text you type inside. To fix this problem, resize the text box:

1. **Click anywhere inside the text box.**

   Pages displays square resizing handles on the corners and in the middle of each side.

2. **Move the pointer to a handle until the pointer turns into a two-way arrow.**

3. **Drag a handle to resize the text box.**

   Drag the handles on the top or bottom to resize the text box vertically (that is, make it taller or shorter); similarly, drag the handles on the left or right side to resize the text box horizontally (that is, make it wider or narrower). Handles on the corners resize proportionally in both directions, making the overall box bigger or smaller. You can also hold down Option and drag any handle to resize the text box around its midpoint.

Uniting text boxes

If you type more text than a text box can display, you see a clipping indicator icon, which appears as a plus sign inside a square at the bottom of the text box. When you see the clipping indicator icon, you have three choices:

>> **Make the text smaller:** You can reduce the font size until the text fits inside the box. However, you might make the text too small to read and the smaller text might look odd compared to the normal-size text around it.

>> **Enlarge the text box.** You can resize the text box so it can display more text, as I describe in the preceding section. This may not always be practical because your page layout may not accommodate an expanded text box.

>> **Unite two text boxes.** If you can't resize the text box to show all the text, create another text box (say, on the next page). Click one of the text boxes, click the toolbar's Format button, and then click the Arrange tab. Hold down Shift and click the other text box so that both text boxes are now selected. Click the Unite button that appears at the bottom of the Arrange tab. The two text boxes come together and your text flows from one to the next.

Depending on how much text you have, you can (and may need to) unite three or more text boxes.

If two text boxes overlap, select them and then select the Arrange tab of the Format pane. You can then intersect the text boxes (click the Intersect button), subtract one text box from another (click the Subtract button), or exclude one text box from another (click the Exclude button).

Faster Formatting with Styles

You can save time and effort when formatting your Pages documents by taking advantage of Page's predefined styles. A *style* is a collection of formatting options, such as fonts, colors, borders, shading, and alignment. When you apply a style to some text, Pages applies all of the style's formatting at once.

Why is this a big deal? It's not if you apply formatting once and move on with your life. But it is a very big deal if, like most of us, you have a set of formatting options that you apply repeatedly. For example, you might format the title of each document with 30-point bold Helvetica Neue. That'd fine the first few times, but after applying the same formatting for the tenth or twentieth time, it gets old. Instead, you can package all those formatting options into a style and apply the style whenever and wherever you need it with just a few of mouse clicks.

The Pages templates come with a few preset styles that you can use right out of the box. These styles include Title (for the document's main title), Subtitle (for the document's subtitle, if it has one), Heading (for each main heading in the document), and Body (for the regular document text). However, you're free to create your own formatting styles, too. By using both preset and custom styles, you can format text quickly and consistently with minimum effort.

The following are the types of styles you can apply in your Pages documents:

>> **Paragraph styles:** Affect an entire paragraph (or all the paragraphs you select).

>> **Image styles:** Affect inserted images, applying special effects, borders, fill, and shadows.

>> **Text box styles:** Affect all the text inside a text box. Rather than styling all the text, you might prefer to style individual paragraphs in the text box. That's perfectly fine — you just have to follow the instructions for paragraph styles (see "Taking advantage of paragraph styles") and make sure that you select the text box paragraph you want to style.

Taking advantage of paragraph styles

When you're working with text — whether it's continuous text or text box text — you can apply a preset style, modify an existing style, or create a style, as the next few sections show.

Applying a preset paragraph style

To apply a preset paragraph style to some text, follow these steps:

1. **Click anywhere in the paragraph to which you want apply the style.**

   To apply the style to multiple paragraphs, select some text in each paragraph.

2. **Click the Format button on the toolbar.**

3. **If you're working with text in a text box, click the Text tab.**

4. **Click the disclosure arrow at the top of the Format pane to open the Paragraph Styles menu, as shown in Figure 3-15.**

5. **Choose the style that you want to use for your selected text.**

   Pages formats your selected text.

TIP

In Figure 3-15, note the continuation arrow to the right of the Title style. Clicking that arrow displays a continuation menu that contains commands including Rename Style (to give the style a new name) and Delete Style (to remove the style). You can also click Shortcut to assign a hot key (F1 through F8); that way, when you want to apply the style, instead of using the Format pane, you can select the text and press the shortcut key associated with the style.

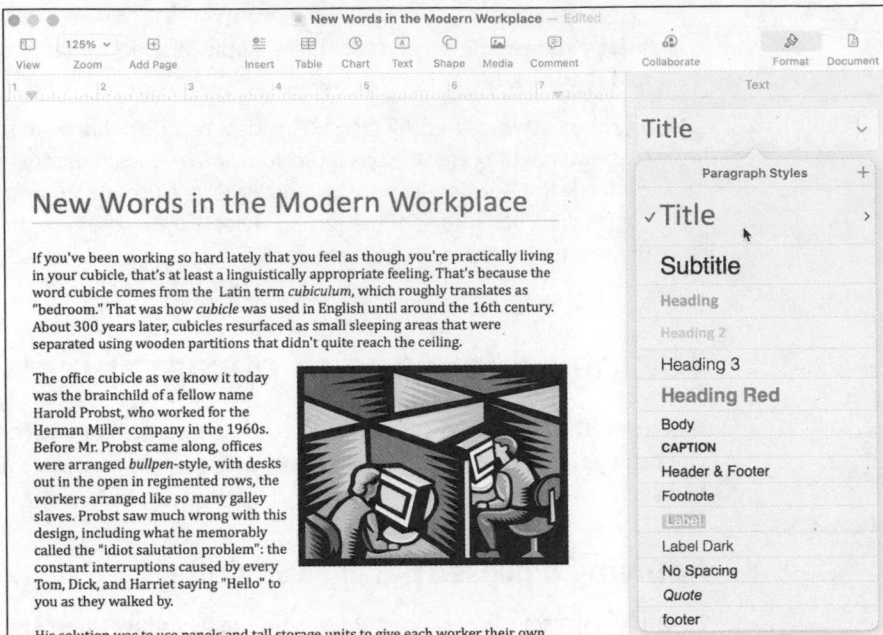

FIGURE 3-15:
The Paragraph
Styles menu lists
the existing styles
available in the
document.

Modifying a preset paragraph style

To modify an existing paragraph style and apply the modified style to some text, follow these steps:

1. **Click anywhere in the paragraph to which you want apply the style.**

   To apply the style to multiple paragraphs, select some text in each paragraph.

2. **Apply the style using the Paragraph Styles menu, as I describe in the preceding section.**

3. **Use the Font tools (as I explain in the earlier section "Formatting text") to make changes to the paragraph style.**

   When you modify an existing text style, an asterisk appears to the right of the style name.

4. **Click Update to the right of the style name.**

   Pages updates the style with your new formatting.

Creating a paragraph style

To create a paragraph style and apply the new style to some text, follow these steps:

1. **Click anywhere in the paragraph to which you want apply the new style.**

   To apply the new style to multiple paragraphs, select some text in each paragraph.

2. **Display the Paragraph Styles menu, as I describe in the "Applying a preset paragraph style" section.**

3. **Click the plus sign next to Paragraph Styles.**

   A new style is added to the menu with the name of the original style followed by the number 1. The name is highlighted, allowing you to type a new name.

4. **Type a name for the new style and press Return.**

5. **Use the Font tools (as I explain in the earlier section "Formatting text") to set the formatting options for the new the paragraph style.**

6. **Click Update to the right of the style name.**

   Pages updates the style with your new formatting.

Applying an image style

To apply a style to an image, follow these steps:

1. **Click the image you want to modify.**

2. **Click the toolbar's Format button.**

3. **Click the Style tab and then click one of the Image Styles, as shown in Figure 3-16.**

   Pages formats your selected image with the style. If you don't want to create a new image style, skip the rest of these steps.

4. **Use the following tools to make changes to the image style. Click the disclosure arrow to the left of the Border and Shadow tool to reveal the available options:**

   - *Border:* Surrounds your image with a line or picture frame; define the width, color, and scale of your choice. If the image already has a border, you use this tool to modify it.

   - *Shadow:* Creates one of three types of shadows — Drop, Contact, or Curved — behind the entire image. Blur, offset, and opacity settings add more special effects.

   - *Reflection:* Adds a mirrored effect of your image under it.

   - *Opacity:* Affects the entire image and changes the intensity of all components — the text, fills, and borders. This is a good tool if you want to use the image as a backdrop behind text.

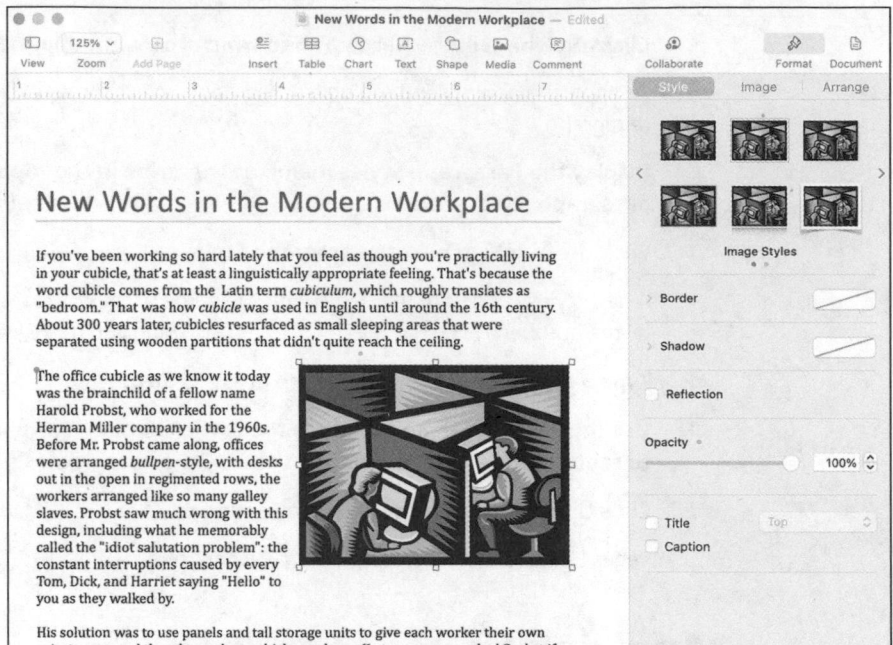

FIGURE 3-16:
Use the Style tab
to apply a style
to the selected
image.

5. **Click the right triangle to open a second Image Styles chooser, and then click the plus sign to create a new image style.**

   A new style is added to the chooser and the thumbnail shows the effects you selected in Step 4.

Applying a text box style

When you create a text box, you can apply a paragraph style to the text (as I explain in the earlier section, "Taking advantage of paragraph styles"), and you can format the box itself, adding a background fill color, border, and shadow. To format the box itself with a style, follow these steps:

1. **Click the text box you want to modify.**

2. **Click the toolbar's Format button.**

3. **Click the Style tab.**

4. **Click one of the thumbnails in the Shape Styles section to apply a preset style to the text box.**

   Pages formats your selected text box with the style. If you don't want to create a text box style, skip the rest of these steps.

5. **Use the Fill, Border, Shadow, and Opacity tools to make changes to the image style.**

   - *Fill:* Styles the text box background with a color, a gradient, or an Image.

   - *Border:* Surrounds your text box with a line or picture frame; define the width, color, and scale of your choice.

   - *Shadow:* Adds one of three types of shadows — Drop, Contact, or Curved — behind the entire text box. Blur, offset, and opacity settings add more special effects.

   - *Reflection:* Adds a mirrored effect of your text box under it.

   - *Opacity:* Affects the entire text box and changes the intensity of all components — the text, fills, and borders.

6. **Click the right triangle to open a second Shape Styles chooser, and then click the plus sign to create a text box style.**

   A new style is added to the chooser and the thumbnail shows the effects you selected in Step 5.

Crafting Charts and Tables in Pages

As I mention earlier in this chapter, you can insert charts and tables directly from Numbers, which is great when you already have the charts and tables prepared or if you have complex data that's easier to work with in Numbers. If you're starting from scratch, it may be quicker to build your chart or table directly in Pages.

Adding a chart

You use a *chart* to graphically represent data. Sometimes presenting your information as a chart makes your information easier to understand. To that end, Pages offer more than 20 chart types, from 2D column, line, and pie charts to 3D bar and area charts.

To add a chart to a Pages document, follow these steps:

1. **Position the cursor where you want the new chart to appear.**

2. **Choose Insert ⇨ Chart or click the toolbar's Charts button, and then choose the type of chart you want to create.**

   A default chart appears.

3. **Click the Edit Chart Data button at the bottom of the chart.**

The Chart Data editor appears, as shown in Figure 3-17.

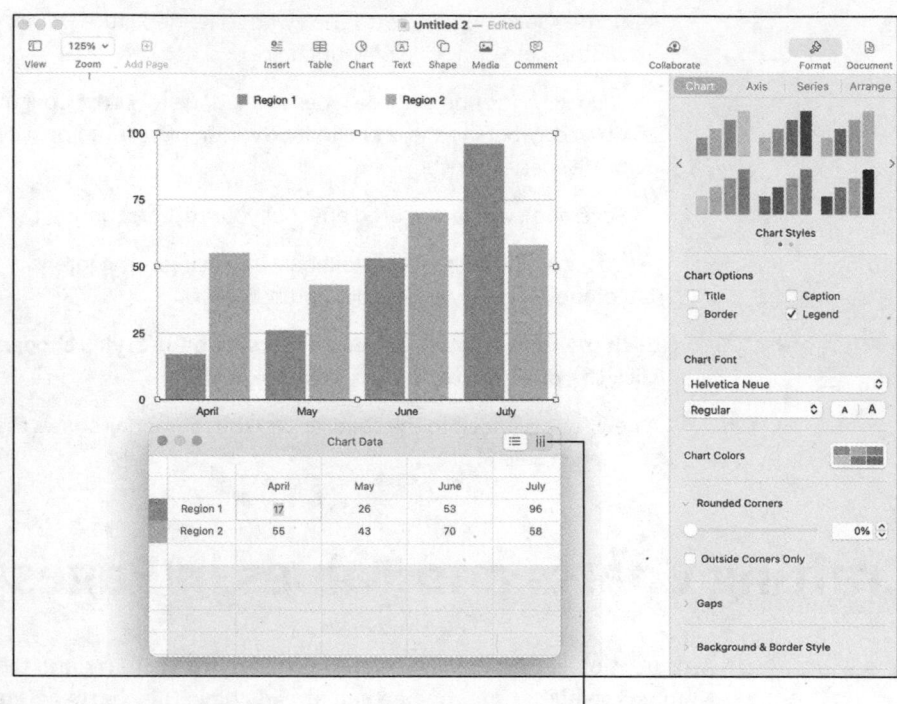

FIGURE 3-17:
Enter the data
you want to dis-
play in the Chart
Data editor.

Plot columns as series

4. **For each row and column field header in the Chart Data editor, double-click the header to select the placeholder text and then type the header you want on your chart.**

The new row headers appear in the chart as the data series and the new column headers appear in the chart as the data categories.

TIP

If you prefer to have the columns as the series and the rows as the categories, click the plot columns as series icon (labeled in Figure 3-17).

TIP

Rather than double-clicking each cell you want to modify, you might find it easier to press Tab to move one cell to the right, Shift+Tab to move one cell to the left, or Return to move one cell down, and then type the text or value you want.

5. **For each cell below and to the right of the headers, double-click the cell and then type the number value you want in the cell.**

As you modify the cell data, Pages updates the chart to reflect the new values.

6. **Click the toolbar's Format button to open the Format pane and then click the following tabs to choose how you want the data to appear:**

- *Chart:* Change the chart's color scheme (Chart Styles), typeface, and size; add gaps between columns; add backgrounds, borders, and shadow; and even change the chart type.

- *Axis:* Edit the axis options and value labels on the axis.

- *Series:* Edit value labels on the bars and add trendlines.

- *Arrange:* Wrap text around the chart and align and distribute its position among other objects on your document, such as text boxes and images.

TIP

See Book 5, Chapter 5, where I present Numbers. Read that chapter for detailed instructions about formatting charts.

To remove a chart, click it and press Delete.

Adding a table

A *table* comprises rows and columns of related information where each column represents an information category (such as name, phone number, or address) and each row represents an example of the table data (such as a customer or contact with a specific name, phone number, or address). The intersection of a row and a column is a *cell* and you input your data in the table cells.

Tables in Pages are *calculable*, which means that you can write formulas or insert functions in much the same way you would in Numbers.

These are the steps for adding a table to your document:

1. **Position the cursor where you want the new table to appear.**

2. **Choose Insert ⇨ Table and then click the type of table you want.**

   Choose Headers if you want to add both row and column headers to the table; choose Basic if you want just column headers; choose Plain if you want no headers; or choose Sums if you want to create totals for each column.

   Alternatively, click the toolbar's Table button to display a chooser that offers several pages of table styles. Use the right and left arrows to find the style you want, and then click that style.

   Pages adds a blank table to your document, as shown in Figure 3-18.

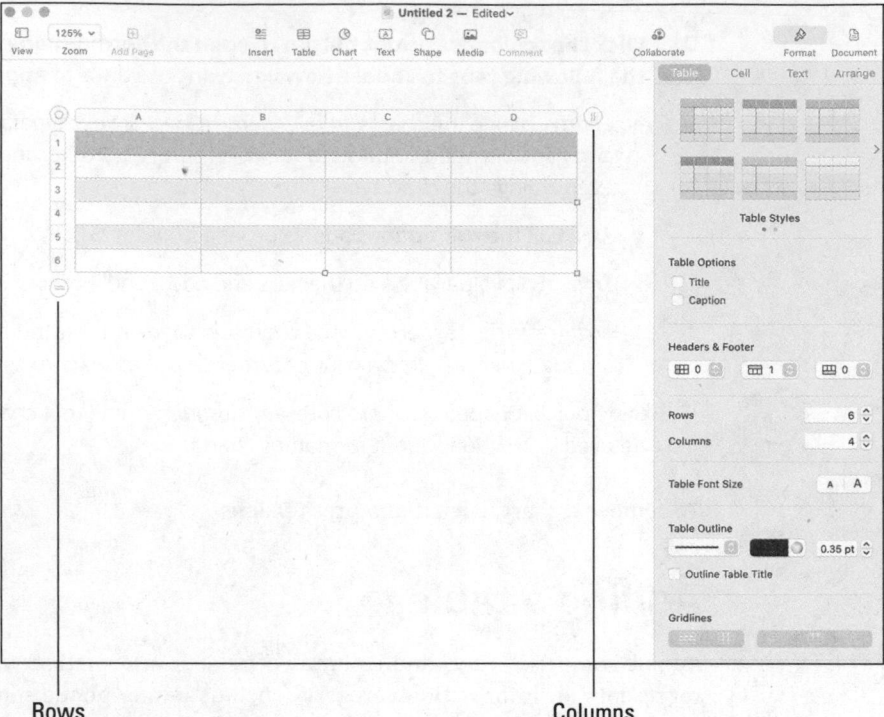

FIGURE 3-18:
A blank table
added to a Pages
document.

Rows   Columns

3. **Resize any column's width by moving the mouse pointer over the right border of the column's header until the pointer becomes a double-headed arrow and then dragging right or left until the column is the width you prefer.**

You can resize any row's height by moving the mouse pointer over the bottom border of the row's header until the pointer becomes a double-headed arrow and then dragging down or up until the row is the height you want.

4. **To add rows to your table, you have three choices:**

- *To add a single row to the end of the table:* Click the bottom-right cell and then press Tab.

- *To change the total number of rows:* Click the Rows button (labeled in Figure 3-18) and then use the control that appears to set the total number of rows you want.

- *To insert a new row:* Click any cell in the row above or below which you want to insert the new row, choose Format ➪ Table, and then click either Add Row Above or Add Row Below.

5. **To add columns to your table, you have two choices:**

- *To change the total number of columns:* Click the Columns button (labeled in Figure 3-18) and then use the control that appears to set the total number of columns you want.

- *To insert a new column:* Click any cell in the column to the left or right of which you want to insert the new column, choose Format ⇨ Table, and then click either Add Column Before or Add Column After.

6. **Click the toolbar's Format button and then click the tabs to edit the table as follows:**

- *Table:* Change the table color and layout scheme (Table Styles), and use the menus to set the number of header rows and columns and footer rows, select the table font size, and add a table outline and grid lines.

- *Cell:* Select all the cells or a portion of them and then choose the data format you want to use to fill the cells and add a fill and a border to the cells.

TIP

  To select a column of cells, click its header. To select a row of cells, click its number.

- *Text:* Edit the font and text alignment. Alternatively, you can select a preset style by clicking the disclosure button to the right of the style and then choosing one from the menu.

- *Arrange:* Wrap text around the table and align and distribute its position among other objects on your document, such as text boxes and images.

7. **Set up functions and conditional formats by entering numerical data in a row or column of cells.**

  Type an equal sign (=) to open the Functions pane and then assign a function — for example, sum or average — to the cell at the bottom of a row, or end of a column.

TIP

  See Book 5, Chapter 5, where I present Numbers. Read that chapter for detailed instructions about formatting tables and writing formulas and using functions.

Adding shapes

Shapes add interest to your documents and make a good alternative to using a background fill and border for your text. For example, you can create an interesting shape and then place a text box over it. (See the later section, "Arranging objects," to learn about positioning the two.) So rather than have a boring rectangle of text with a colored background, you can have, say, a polygon with the text on it. If you use the Wrap Text tool that follows the contours of the shape, your text takes on the polygon shape, too.

With your document open to the page where you want to insert a shape, follow these steps:

1. **Click the toolbar's Shape button.**

   Pages displays the Shape pop-up window, as shown in Figure 3-19.

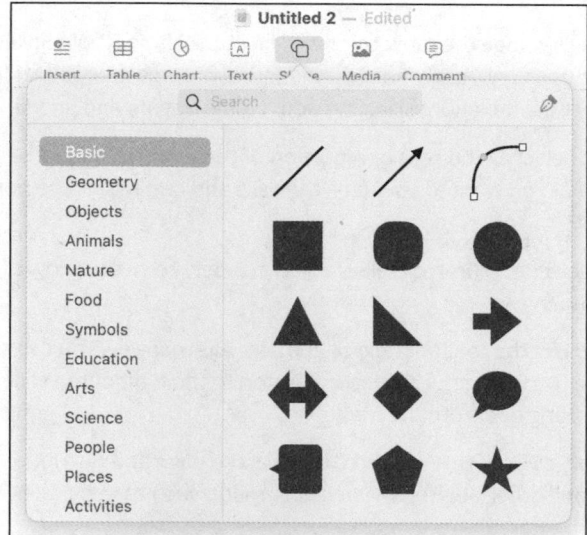

FIGURE 3-19:
Pages offers many different shape types to add to your documents.

2. **Click a shape category.**

3. **Click the shape you want.**

   Your selected shape appears on the page with active resizing handles.

   Alternatively, you can choose Insert ⇨ Shape and then choose a shape from the flyout menu.

4. **Click the shape and grab a *resizing handle* — one of the squares on the box that surrounds the shape — to enlarge or reduce the shape to the size you want.**

5. **Modify the shape.**

   Many shapes have green grabber dots that you drag to change the shape or size of the shape. Hover the cursor over one of the green dots until it changes from an arrow to a plus sign, and then drag to see how the shape changes. For example, dragging clockwise or counterclockwise on the star or polygon increases or decreases the number of points on the star and the number of sides on the polygon. The grabber dot on the quote bubble or square moves the direction of the angle that points to another object.

If the shape you're using doesn't have green grabber dots, choose Format ⇨ Shapes and Lines ⇨ Make Editable. Red dots appear around the shape. Grab a dot and drag it to change the default shape. When you're done folding, spindling, or mutilating the shape, click outside it to apply the changes. (If you go too far when you fold, spindle, or mutilate the shape, press ⌘+Z as needed to reverse your changes.)

6. **Drag the shape to better position it on the page.**

7. **Click the shape, click the toolbar's Format button, and click the Style tab in the Format pane.**

8. **Click the options you see to choose a different shape style.**

   From the Format pane, you can also change the fill, add a border, add a drop shadow to the shape, or add a reflection.

TIP

To add text to your shape, click the shape and begin typing.

Bringing your objects to heel

It's not uncommon to have multiple shapes, text boxes, images, and charts in a single document, but having multiple objects kicking around can lead to problems.

For example, when you add a second object to a document, that second object resides in a higher layer (metaphorically speaking) than the first. To see this for yourself, move the second object over the first and note that the second object now sits in front of the first. Nothing wrong with that, necessarily, but sometimes one object hides another and you tear out significant clumps of hair trying to find the hidden item.

Also, once you have several objects near each other, your document can start to look messy if those objects are placed willy-nilly on the page.

To help save your sanity (not to mention your hair), you have the following ways of bringing your objects under control:

>> **Group objects:** Bind two or more objects so that Pages treats them as a single object. For example, when you move a group, Pages moves all the objects in a group at the same time.

>> **Arrange objects:** Control which objects appear in front of or in back of your other objects.

>> **Align objects:** Organize objects in relation to each other by lining up their left, right, top, or bottom sides.

>> **Distribute objects:** Evenly space three or more objects between the two farthest objects.

Grouping objects

Follow these steps to combine multiple objects into a group that Pages treats as a single object:

1. **Select the objects that you want to arrange.**

To select multiple objects, click the first object, hold down the Shift key, then click each of the other objects you want in the selection.

2. **Choose Arrange ⇨ Group.**

The objects stay together and move together.

You can also group the selected objects by clicking the toolbar's Format button, clicking the Arrange tab, and then clicking Group.

If you need to edit individual objects in a group, first ungroup the objects by selecting the group and then choosing Arrange ⇨ Ungroup. After you edit one or more objects that were in a group, you can then regroup them by following the steps in this section.

Arranging objects

By default, each new object you add to a document sits in a layer that's in front of all the other existing document objects. Somewhat surprisingly, you can fiddle with these layers in two ways:

>> **Move an object to a lower level:** You can send an object back one level or all the way back to the lowest level.

>> **Move an object to a higher level:** You can send an object forward one level or all the way forward to the highest (front) level.

To control the layer in which an object resides, follow these steps:

1. **Click the object that you want to arrange.**

2. **On the Arrange menu, select one of the following commands:**

   - *Bring Forward:* Raises the object one level. You can also press Option+Shift+⌘+F.

   - *Bring to Front:* Raises the object to the top level. You can also press Shift+⌘+F.

   - *Send to Back:* Lowers the object to the bottom level. You can also press Shift+⌘+B.

   - *Send Backward:* Lowers the object one level. You can also press Option+Shift+⌘+B.

TIP

You can arrange the selected object also by clicking the toolbar's Format button, clicking the Arrange tab, and then selecting an arrange icon: back, front, backward, or forward.

Aligning objects

To align your document objects, do the following:

1. **Select the objects that you want to align.**

   To select multiple objects, click the first object, hold down the Shift key, and then click each of the other objects you want in the selection.

2. **Choose Arrange ⇨ Align Objects.**

3. **Select one of the following commands:**

   - *Left:* Aligns the left edges of the selected objects with the left edge of the leftmost object.

   - *Center:* Calculates the horizontal midpoint of all the selected objects (that is, halfway between the left edge of the leftmost object and the right edge of the rightmost object) and aligns the objects on that midpoint.

   - *Right:* Aligns the right edges of the selected objects with the right edge of the rightmost object.

   - *Top:* Aligns the top edges of the selected objects with the top edge of the topmost object.

   - *Middle:* Calculates the vertical midpoint of all the selected objects (that is, halfway between the top edge of the topmost object and the bottom edge of the bottommost object) and aligns the objects on that midpoint.

   - *Bottom:* Aligns the bottom edges of the selected objects with the bottom edge of the bottommost object.

TIP

You can align the selected objects also by clicking the toolbar's Format button, clicking the Arrange tab, and then selecting an alignment from the Align drop-down menu.

Distributing objects

To distribute your document objects, do the following:

1. **Select the objects that you want to distribute.**

   To select multiple objects, click the first object, hold down the Shift key, and then click each of the other objects you want in the selection.

2. **Choose Arrange ⇨ Distribute Objects.**

3. **Select one of the following commands:**

   - *Horizontally:* Distributes the selected objects so they're spaced evenly horizontally.

   - *Vertically:* Distributes the selected objects so they're spaced evenly vertically.

   - *Evenly:* Distributes the selected objects so they're spaced evenly both horizontally and vertically.

TIP

You can distribute the selected objects also by clicking the toolbar's Format button, clicking the Arrange tab, and then selecting a value from the Distribute drop-down menu.

Locking objects

When you lock one or more objects or groups, you can't move, delete, or edit the locked items. To lock an object, a selection of objects, or a group, follow these steps:

1. **Select the objects that you want to lock.**

   To select multiple objects, click the first object, hold down the Shift key, and then click each of the other objects you want in the selection.

2. **Choose Arrange ⇨ Lock (or press ⌘+L).**

TIP

   If the Lock command is disabled, display the Format pane, click the Arrange tab, and then click Stay on Page.

   Pages locks the selected objects.

   To unlock the objects, choose Arrange ⇨ Unlock (or press Option+⌘+L).

TIP

You can lock the selected objects also by clicking the toolbar's Format button, clicking the Arrange tab, clicking Stay on Page, and then clicking Lock. To unlock items, click Unlock in the Format pane.

Wrapping text around an object

When you insert a text box, photo, or chart inside continuous text or a text box, it sits on top of the existing text. To neatly separate the text and object, you want to *wrap* the text around the object. Follow these steps:

1. Click the object, be it a text box, photo, or chart.

2. Click the toolbar's Format button.

3. Click the Arrange tab, as shown in Figure 3-20.

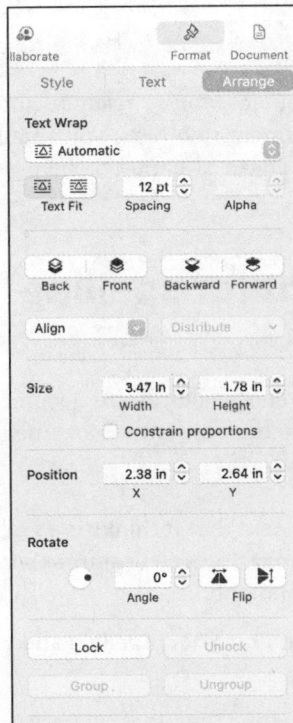

FIGURE 3-20:
The text wrapping options are located on the Arrange tab of the Format pane.

4. Click the Text Wrap pop-up menu and choose one of the following:

- *Automatic:* Pages determines the best distribution for the object in the text.

- *Around:* The text surrounds all sides of the object.

- *Above and Below*: The text appears above and below the object, but the spaces to the left and right are clear.

- *Inline with Text:* The bottom edge of the text box is aligned with the next line of text in the document.

- *None:* The object sits on top of the text.

5. **If you select any of the choices in Step 4 except None or Inline with Text, do the following:**

   a. *Click one of the Text Fit buttons to have the text create a rectangle around the object (left button) or flow around the contours of the object (right button).*

   b. *Type in the Spacing field or use the up and down arrows to indicate the amount of space between the object and the text.*

Polishing Your Document

When you finish designing your document, you're ready to show it to the world. Of course, before you show your document to others, you should proofread it for grammar and spelling. Fortunately, Pages is happy to help you check a document's spelling and grammar.

Checking a document for spelling and grammar gaffes

Pages can spell-check and grammar-check your entire document, including text trapped in text boxes and shapes. To check an entire document for spelling and grammar slip-ups, follow these steps:

1. **If you also want Pages to flag any text that it thinks is a grammar error, choose Edit ➪ Spelling and Grammar ➪ Check Grammar with Spelling to put a check mark next to that command.**

2. **Choose Edit ➪ Spelling and Grammar ➪ Show Spelling and Grammar (or press ⌘+:).**

   If, instead, you choose Edit ➪ Spelling and Grammar ➪ Check Document Now (or press ⌘+;), Pages underlines words it thinks are misspelled, but it doesn't offer any suggestions.

   The first instance of a misspelled word is highlighted and the Spelling and Grammar dialog appears.

3. **Click one of the following:**

- *Change:* Changes the misspelled word with the word selected in the list box. This option is not available if the word was not found in the Pages dictionary.

- *Find Next:* Looks for the next misspelled word.

- *Ignore:* Skips the misspelled word.

- *Learn:* Stores the selected word in the Pages dictionary.

- *Define:* Launches your Mac's Dictionary application and displays the word's definition in the Dictionary's main window.

- *Guess:* Offers best-guess word choices.

4. **Repeat Step 3 until you've checked the entire document, and then click the red close icon of the Spelling dialog to make it go away.**

TIP

By default, Pages checks your spelling while you type. When Pages identifies a misspelled word, it underlines it with a red dotted line. If you right-click any word underlined with a red dotted line, Pages displays a shortcut menu of correctly spelled words that you can choose. If you want to turn off spell-checking while you type, choose Edit ⇨ Spelling and Grammar ⇨ Check Spelling While Typing to clear the check mark for this command.

REMEMBER

Proofreading your document is a good idea, even after spell-checking, because the spell checker only makes sure that the word is correctly spelled. If you type, "I have to dogs" when you really meant to type, "I have two dogs," the spell checker isn't going to flag that.

Finding and replacing text

Pages can also find and replace words or phrases. Say you're writing an article about a person named Swanson, only to realize that just before you send the article to your editor that the name is spelled Swansen. Pages will search your entire document and replace Swanson with Swansen. To find and replace a word or phrase, do the following:

1. **Choose Edit ⇨ Find ⇨ Find (or press ⌘+F).**

   The Find dialog opens.

2. **In the Find field, type the word or phrase you want to find.**

   Pages displays the number found to the right of the word you type. The default option for this command is to find text. The next step shows you what you need to do to replace text along with two other useful options.

3. **Click the disclosure arrow to the right of the gear icon and choose Find and Replace.**

   There are two additional options on this menu.

   - *Whole Words:* Select this option to ignore whole words that contain your text. If, for example, you search for *place* and select this option, *placemat* or *placement* won't be highlighted.

   - *Match Case:* Select this option to have Pages distinguish uppercase and lowercase letters and find text *exactly* as you type it.

4. **In the Replace field, type the word or phrase you want to replace the found text with.**

   Pages highlights the word you want to find.

5. **Click Replace All to replace all instances of the old word with the new word. Or click Replace & Find to replace this instance of the word and find the next instance of the word or phrase, and then click one of the following:**

   - *Replace:* Click this option to replace the old word with the new one. You have to click Next to highlight the next occurrence.

   - *Replace All:* This is the only option if you choose Replace for the first instance of the word or phrase that Pages finds.

   If you choose Replace & Find, you can examine each instance of the word or phrase you asked Pages to find. If you don't want to replace an instance of the word, click the right arrow to advance to the next instance of the word or the left arrow to review the previous instance.

Exporting to a Different File Format

Chances are that you'll want to share your document electronically, too. However, as much as you love your Mac and Pages, not everyone uses the same types of computers or applications. Don't let that stop you from sharing your document files, though, because Pages can export files in diverse formats.

Although Pages saves documents in its own proprietary file format when you choose File ➪ Save, if you want to share your Pages documents with others who don't have the Pages application, you can use one of the following file formats:

- **PDF:** Saves your document as a series of static pages stored in the PDF file format that can be viewed (but not necessarily edited) by any computer with a PDF viewing application.

- **Word:** Saves your document as a Microsoft Word file, which can be opened by any word processor that can read and edit Microsoft Word files.

- **EPUB:** Saves your document in a format that can be read in Books on an iPad or iPhone as well as on many electronic readers.

- **Plain Text:** Saves your document as text without any formatting or graphic effects.

- **Rich Text Format:** Saves your document as an RTF, which can be opened by most word-processing programs.

- **Pages '09:** Saves your document a Pages '09 document. If you're sharing your document with someone who hasn't upgraded their version of Pages for a long time (since 2009!), this is a way to be sure they can access your document.

REMEMBER

The PDF file format preserves all formatting, but it doesn't let anyone edit that file unless they use a separate PDF-editing application, such as Adobe Acrobat Pro. If someone needs to edit your document, the Word option preserves Pages documents well. The Plain Text option is useful only if you can't transfer your Pages document to another application as a Word file.

To export a Pages document, follow these steps:

1. **Choose File ➪ Export To and then click the file format you want to use for the exported file.**

   A dialog appears. The document will be exported with the original filename.

2. **Modify whatever options are presented for the file format you chose, and then click Next.**

   Each format has different options. For example, if you export to EPUB, you have cover options, layout options, and so on. You can require a password to open the document if you export to Word, PDF, or Pages '09.

   The file folder chooser dialog appears.

3. **Select the folder where you want to store your document.**

4. **Click Export.**

   Pages exports your document to the file format you chose.

REMEMBER

When you export a document, your original Pages document remains untouched in its original location.

You can also share your documents as Mail or Messages attachments or make them available on iCloud or AirDrop, not to mention social-networking sites. See the end of Book 5, Chapter 4, to learn about sharing with Keynote. Sharing works the same for Pages as for Keynote.

IN THIS CHAPTER

» Creating a presentation

» Adding, editing, and formatting text

» Working with shapes, charts, and tables

» Inserting photos and movies

» Changing the order of slides

» Using transitions and effects

» Customizing themes with layouts

» Giving a presentation

Chapter **4**

Producing Persuasive Presentations with Keynote

I f you have to present information at a gathering — it could be a sales meeting, a staff get-together, a night-school class, a community meetup, or an industry conference — you don't want to be standing at the front of the room or on the stage naked. I don't mean *naked* naked, of course; I'm talking about giving your audience something to look at besides you. I'm talking, in short, about a *presentation*, which is a collection of slides, each of which has some related info.

That might sound like a lot of work, but your Mac has your back on this one in the guise of the Keynote app. Keynote is designed to help you quickly produce professional-looking presentations that you'll be proud to show, whether your gig is a school project or an actual keynote address. Keynote's ready-made themes get your presentations up and running quickly, and you can spice up your presentation with images, tables, charts, and audio and visual effects, from play-ing music and movies to showing visually interesting effects — stuff like text sliding across the display or dissolving into nothingness. Such effects help get your point across and hold an audience's attention. As you learn in this chapter, it's all just a few clicks away.

This chapter covers the Keynote basics: working with themes and slide layouts, replacing placeholder text and media with your text and media, and adding charts, tables, and animation. At the end of the chapter, I give you tips for practicing your presentation and tell you about the options you have for running the presenta-tion without even being present. When you're up to speed on the basics, check out Book 5, Chapter 6, which shows you some nifty Keynote tricks.

Getting Your Presentation Off the Ground

A Keynote presentation consists of one or more slides, where each slide typically displays information to make a single point. Most slides contain text (usually in the form of a bulleted list; see Figure 4-1) and perhaps an image or two, but a slide can also include shapes, a chart, a table, some audio, and even a video.

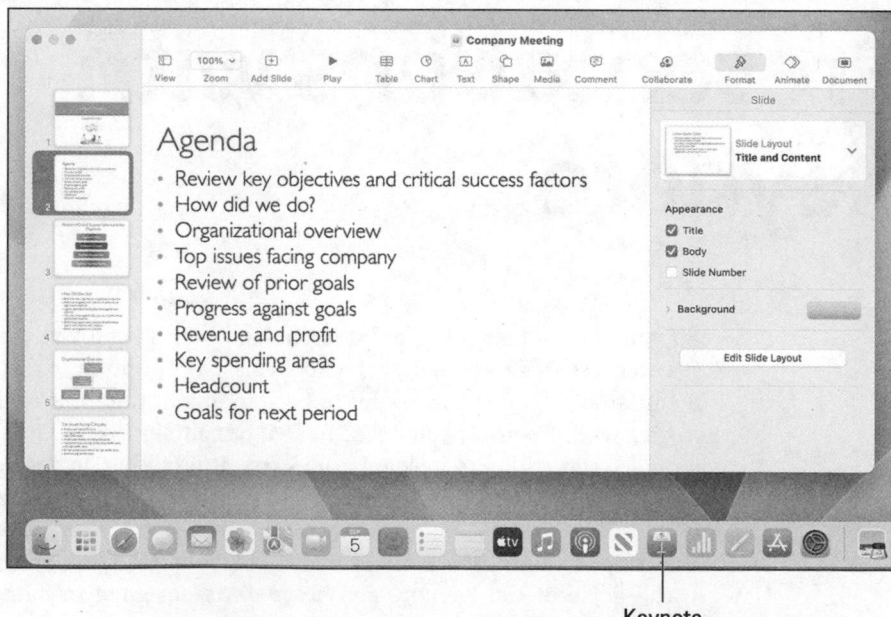

FIGURE 4-1:
Use a theme to get your Keynote presentation off to a rousing start.

Keynote

To make your presentation even more interesting to watch, you can add *transition* effects, which appear when you switch from one slide to another. To emphasize the information on a particular slide, you can add individual visual effects, known as *builds*, to specific items, such as making text rotate or making a graphic image glide across the screen and halt in place.

I explain how to add all these embellishments to your presentation in the sections that follow. But first, here are the general steps you'll follow to create a presentation in Keynote:

1. **Launch the Keynote app by clicking its icon on the dock (pointed out in Figure 4-1) or in Launchpad.**

2. **Choose File ⇨ New and then pick a theme to use for your presentation.**

3. **Create one or more slides.**

4. **Type text or place graphics and images on each slide.**

5. **(Optional) Add an audio or video file to each slide.**

6. **(Optional) Add visual effects to animate an entire slide or just the text or graphics that appear on that slide.**

7. **Save your presentation.**

Choosing a theme and saving your presentation

A presentation consists of multiple slides. Although a black-and-white presentation can be elegant in a retro sort of way, color helps attract and keep your audience's attention. To make the creation of your presentation easier, Keynote provides *themes* that give your slides a consistent appearance, such as the font, size, style, and background color. Within each of the 28 themes (as of this writing), there are multiple *slide layouts*, which are templates for your slides. Each slide layout in a theme defines the look of each slide you create based on the layout. I explain how to work with and create slide layouts in the section "Editing Slide Layouts to Customize Themes," later in this chapter. Most themes have the following slide layouts:

>> Title, top or center

>> Title and subtitle

>> Title and bullets

>> Title, bullets, and photo

>> Bullet list

>> Photo (horizontal, vertical, three-up, or full-slide photo)

>> Quote

>> Blank

Each theme offers a standard and wide (HD) format. Make sure you decide which you want to use before creating your presentation.

TIP

If you want to create a presentation without using a theme — say you want your presentation to reflect your corporate color scheme and font family — pick a simple theme, such as Basic Black or Basic White, to start so you have multiple slide layouts to which you can apply your desired color scheme, fonts, and so on.

To pick a theme, follow these steps:

1. **Choose File ⇨ New (or press ⌘+N).**

The Choose a Theme dialog opens, as shown in Figure 4-2.

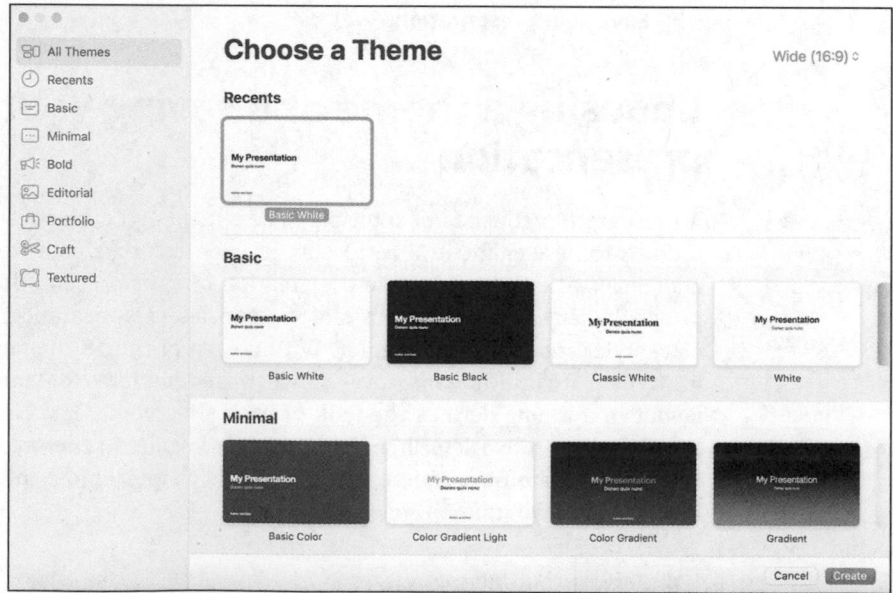

FIGURE 4-2:
Keynote provides
a variety of
themes for your
presentations.

2. **Choose the slide format from the drop-down list near the top-right corner of the dialog: Standard (4:3) format or Wide (16:9) format.**

Standard size slides echo traditional, squarish 35mm slides and work well if you connect a projector to your Mac. Choose the Wide format when you plan to connect your Mac to a wide-screen HD monitor. If you're not sure which you'll be using, choose Wide because most projectors can accommodate wide and you don't risk having blank spaces to the left and right of your slides when projected on a wide-screen monitor.

3. **Click the theme you want to use.**

4. **Click Create.**

   Keynote creates the first slide of your presentation, using your chosen theme. At this point, you can add text, graphics, audio, or video to the slide or you can add new slides.

5. **Choose File ⇨ Save.**

   A Save As dialog opens.

6. **Type a name for your presentation.**

7. **Type any tags you want to attach to the file or choose existing ones from the pop-up menu.**

   You can use tags to find files in Spotlight Search.

REMEMBER

8. **Click the Where pop-up menu and choose a destination for your file.**

   You can save the presentation to a folder on a hard drive, an external hard drive, iCloud Drive, or your Keynote folder in iCloud.

9. **Click Save.**

TIP

If, after saving a file or opening an existing file, you want to move the presentation from your Mac to iCloud or vice versa, or to an external disk or flash drive, choose File ⇨ Move To and then select the new location from the Where pop-up menu. This action removes the presentation from its original location and places it on the new one.

Opening an existing file

If you're working on a document on one source, such as your Mac, and you want to open a document from another source, such as iCloud or an external drive, choose File ⇨ Open, and choose one of the following locations:

>> **Keynote:** You find Keynote listed as a subfolder of iCloud on the sidebar of the Finder window. Choose this option, click the file you want to work on and then click Open.

>> **iCloud Drive:** You find your iCloud drive on the left sidebar of the Finder window. After choosing this option, click one of the documents in the list, and

then click Open. (You need an internet connection to work on iCloud documents.)

>> **From your Mac or external drive:** From the Where pop-up menu, scroll through the directories and folders to find an existing document you want to work on, click it, and then click Open.

You can also use Keynote to open a presentation created in another presentation app, and then use it as is, make changes, and even save it as a Keynote file. To open a non-Keynote presentation, such as Microsoft's PowerPoint, drag the file you want to open over the Keynote icon on the dock or follow the steps outlined in the preceding paragraphs.

Finding your way around Keynote

After you create a presentation, the Keynote slide editor window opens in navigator view, as shown in Figure 4-3. Across the top of the Keynote window, you see the toolbar, which holds icons for the most frequently used functions. Below the toolbar, on the right side of the window, is the Format pane, which has controls for formatting the text and objects on your slides. I explain both toolbar and Format pane functions throughout this chapter.

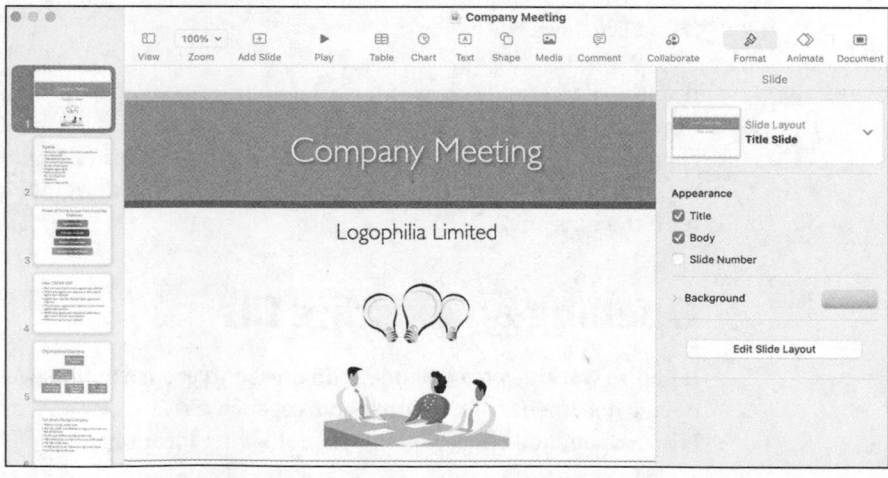

FIGURE 4-3: Navigator view gives you an overview of your presentation while working on a specific slide.

The window can have between one and three panels in the four available views. To switch to a different view, choose the View icon on the Keynote toolbar or click View on the menu bar, and then choose Navigator, Slide Only, Light Table, or Outline.

This is what you see in each view:

» **Navigator:** Useful for editing individual slides and manipulating all the slides in an entire presentation. Referring to Figure 4-3, you can see that thumbnails of your slides are displayed in the slide navigator in the left pane, the slide you're editing is in the center panel, and the Format pane is on the right. To edit your presentation in this view, choose View ⇨ Navigator or click the toolbar's View icon and then click Navigator.

» **Slide only:** Useful for editing the text and graphics of a single slide. The slide navigator pane closes, but you still have all the formatting tools available in the Format pane. To edit your presentation in this view, choose View ⇨ Slide Only or click the toolbar's View icon and then click Slide Only.

» **Light table:** You see all your slides together, as shown in Figure 4-4. You can click and drag slides to a new position or change the slide layout by choosing a new one from the Format pane. Move the slider at the bottom of the left pane to show more, but smaller, slides or fewer, larger slides. When you double-click a slide in light table view, it opens in the most recent of the three other views you used. This view is particularly useful for manipulating a large number of slides in a presentation. To edit your presentation in this view, choose View ⇨ Light Table or click the toolbar's View icon and then click Light Table.

In both navigator and light table views, slides with audio or movie media have three empty circles in the lower-left corner of the slide thumbnail image.

TIP

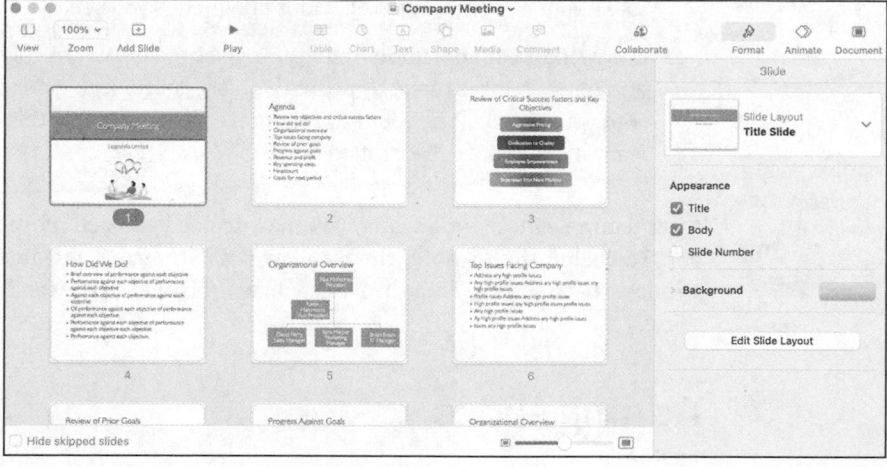

FIGURE 4-4:
Light table view
displays slides
in rows and
columns for easy
rearranging.

>> **Outline:** Similar to navigator view, but instead of seeing thumbnail images in the slide navigator, you see the text of each slide, which you can edit, and the edits are reflected on the slides. Choose Keynote ⇨ Settings ⇨ General to choose the font size you want to use in outline view. To edit your presentation in this view, choose View ⇨ Outline or click the toolbar's View icon and then click Outline.

Besides the presentation views, you can choose additional items you may want to see in the window. Choose the toolbar's View button and then choose from these options:

>> **Show/Hide Rulers (not available in light table view):** Toggles the display of the rulers. Use the rulers as a reference when working with objects on your slide.

>> **Show/Hide Comments:** Toggles the display of comments. Showing comments is useful if other people comment on your presentation before or after you give it.

>> **Show/Hide Presenter Notes (not available in light table view):** Toggles the display of presenter notes. Presenter notes are notes you can view when giving your presentation. You see the notes on your computer below the slide preview, which helps you remember what you want to say, but the projected presentation displays only your slides. When you select Show Presenter Notes, you can type your speech or reminders on each slide.

To change the font or create a list format of notes, click the Presenter Notes section, and then click the Format icon in the toolbar (refer to Figure 4-3); make your choices from the buttons and menus you see.

>> **Show/Hide Collaboration Activity:** Toggles the display of edits, additions, and other changes made by people who are collaborating on the presentation with you. See "Sharing your Keynote presentation," later in this chapter, to learn more about collaboration.

TIP

After using Keynote for a while, you may decide you need more icons on the tool-bar. To customize Keynote, choose View ⇨ Customize Toolbar, and then from the window that appears, drag the icons you want to add to the toolbar, and drop them there.

Adding slides

When you create a presentation, Keynote populates it with a single slide. Now it's certainly possible that getting across a sufficiently succinct idea might require just a single slide. If so, awesome: You can leave work early today. However, it's far more likely that giving your ideas their due requires multiple slides. In that case, feel free to add as many slides as you think necessary (or you think your audience can sit through). Keynote lets you slip new slides into a presentation in three ways: adding a blank slide; adding a slide with a predefined layout; and duplicating an existing slide.

Adding a blank slide

To add a blank slide to a presentation, do one of the following:

» Choose Slide ⇨ New Slide (or press Shift+⌘+N). The new blank slide appears at the end of the presentation.

» Right-click a slide thumbnail in the left panel and choose New Slide. The new blank slide appears after the slide you clicked.

» Click a slide in the navigator or light table view, click the toolbar's Add Slide icon, and then click Blank. The new blank slide appears after the slide you clicked.

» Click a slide in the navigator or light table view and press Return. The new blank slide appears after the slide you clicked.

Adding a slide with a predefined layout

Each Keynote theme has a selection of slide layouts that you can use to build your presentation. When you use a slide layout, you need only insert your text and images in the existing placeholders, and that makes presentation creation a snap. The slide layout structures are more or less the same for each theme, but the colors, style, and fonts that have been applied make each theme different.

To create a slide with a slide layout, follow these steps:

1. **Click the slide after which you want the new slide to appear.**

2. **In the Keynote toolbar, click Add Slide.**

Keynote displays the Add a Slide menu, as shown in Figure 4-5.

3. **Click the slide layout you want.**

You can change the slide layout later, even after you add your own text and images — I tell you how in just a bit.

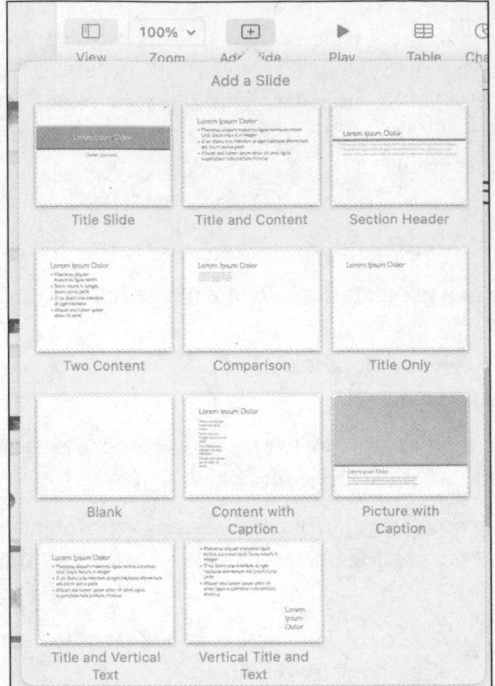

FIGURE 4-5:
The Add a Slide
menu shows you
all available slide
layouts.

Duplicating slides

Making duplicate slides is helpful if you want to use the same header or layout on multiple slides. Even if you use slide layouts, you may tweak them and want to duplicate your efforts. Here's how:

>> **Duplicate one slide.** Click the slide you want to duplicate and choose Edit ⇨ Duplicate Selection. You can also press ⌘+D or right-click the selected slide and then click Duplicate. The duplicate slide appears immediately after the original.

>> **Duplicate multiple slides.** Select the slides you want to duplicate and choose Edit ⇨ Duplicate Selection. You can also press ⌘+D or right-click any selected slide and then click Duplicate. The duplicate slides appear after the last selected slide.

TIP

To select multiple consecutive slides, click the first slide you want to duplicate, hold down the Shift key, and then click the last slide you want to duplicate. To select multiple nonconsecutive slides, click the first slide, and then hold down the ⌘ key as you click the other slides you want in the selection.

TIP

If you want to create a duplicate of your entire presentation, choose File ⇨ Duplicate (or press Shift+⌘+S).

Manipulating Text

Whether it's a title, subtitle, bulleted list, quote, or descriptive paragraph, text on a slide is written in a text box — although the box borders can be invisible. Most slides contain at least one text box that holds the title of the slide. Other text may be free flowing or even a bulleted list inserted with an image.

Entering text

With the exception of the Blank slide layout, each slide layout has one or more text placeholders in text boxes (along with, in some cases, a media placeholder, depending on the layout you choose). You replace the text placeholders with your own words, as outlined in the following steps:

1. **Open the slide that you want to edit or create a slide using one of the methods outlined in the "Adding slides" section.**

   Your chosen slide appears.

2. **Double-click the placeholder text that appears in the title, subtitle, or body text box.**

   The placeholder text disappears.

3. **Type your text.**

   If you're entering text in a bulleted list placeholder, press Return after each item to create a new item. To indent a bullet (and thus create a sub-bullet), press Tab at the beginning of an item.

   The text style matches that shown in the placeholder text.

Inserting text boxes

Even when you work with a slide layout that contains text boxes, you can add your own text boxes as needed. Here's how it's done:

1. **Display the slide where you want to place the text box.**

2. **Choose Insert ⇨ Text Box.**

   Alternatively, click the toolbar's Text button.

   Keynote adds a text box to the slide.

3. **Click the toolbar's Format button, click the Style tab in the Format pane, and then click the text box style you want to use.**

4. **Drag the text box to the position you want on the slide.**

5. **To resize the text box, drag the resizing handles (the small boxes on the corners and in the middle of each edge).**

6. **Double-click the word *Text* to erase it.**

7. **On the Format pane, click the Text tab, and then choose Body from the list of styles.**

   If you want your text to be a bulleted list, display the Format pane, click the Text tab, and then click the Bullets & Lists drop-down menu and select Bullets.

8. **Type the text you want on your slide.**

If you want to delete a text box, click it once and then press the Delete key.

Editing text

To edit text that you've already entered, you have two choices:

>> **In outline view:** Select the slide you want to edit in the slide navigator, as shown in Figure 4-6, and then edit the text. You can change the titles and add and delete bullets. Select a bulleted item and click and drag it by the bullet to move it up or down in the list or move it to another slide. Double-click the slide icon to collapse and hide the text.

>> **In navigator or slide only view:** Double-click a word to highlight and change it. Or click and drag to select blocks of text you want to edit and then make the changes you want.

To ensure that you don't give a presentation filled with typos and misspelled words, check the spelling in your presentation by choosing Edit ➪ Spelling and Grammar ➪ Check Spelling While Typing.

Formatting text and text boxes

Themes have predefined fonts, font sizes, and colors that create a coordinated design throughout the presentation and, quite frankly, make creating a presentation a snap. Nonetheless, you can format the text if you want by changing fonts, font sizes, or colors.

Use fonts and colors sparingly. Using too many fonts or colors can make text harder to read. When choosing text colors, make sure that you use colors that contrast with the slide's background color. For instance, light yellow text against a white or light-colored background is nearly impossible to read.

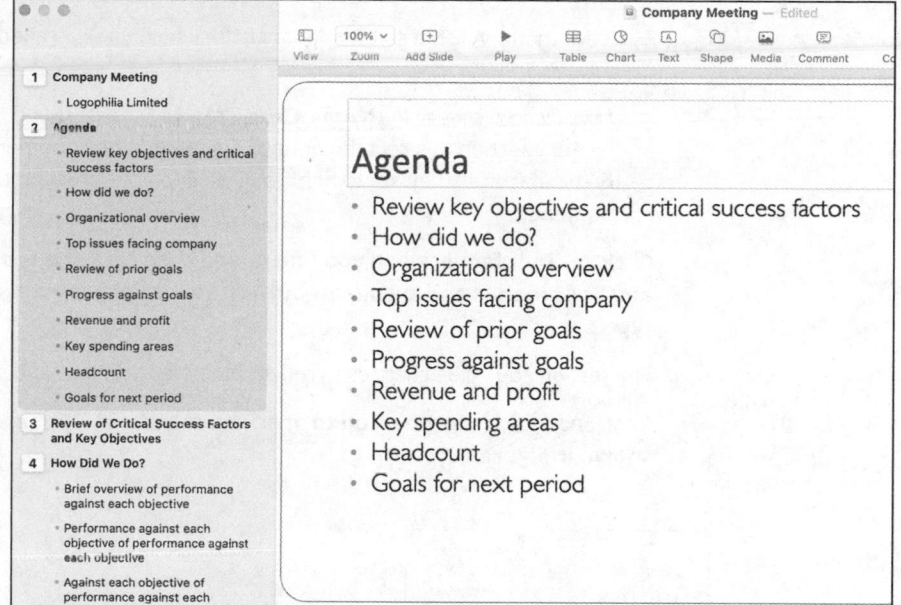

FIGURE 4-6:
Edit text in the
slide navigator in
outline view.

TIP

Any time you want to edit or change the style of an object — be it text, a shape, photo, chart, or table — click the object, and then click the toolbar's Format button. In the Format pane, click the tabs to see the editing and style options you can apply to the selected object. See the following sections for more details on formatting fonts, paragraphs, bullets, and backgrounds.

Changing fonts

Most likely, you've changed fonts in other programs, and the procedure in Keynote is similar. If you'd like to select a different font, change the font size, or change the font color, follow the instructions here.

TIP

Changing a font on a slide will change only that slide. If you want to make the same change to all slides in your presentation, you must change the slide layout, and I dedicate a section to that topic further along in this chapter (see "Editing Slide Layouts to Customize Themes").

After you've selected the text, you can edit fonts with the Format menu or follow these steps:

1. **In the Format pane, click the Text tab and then click the Style button.**

2. **Do one of the following:**

   - *If you want to use a different font style that's part of your chosen theme:* Click the disclosure triangle next to the sample font to open the Paragraph

Styles menu. A list of styles appears from which you can choose a different one.

- *If you want to change the typeface, size, or style:* Scroll through the menus in the Font section to select the options you want. The Font menu shows the typefaces as they are to help you imagine your presentation using that font.

3. **Click the font family when you find it, and then click the Typeface, Size, and Style menus and alignment buttons to make those changes to your type.**

   The text on your slide changes to reflect the typeface, style, and size.

4. **(Optional) Click the gear icon to open the Advanced Options menu, as shown in Figure 4-7.**

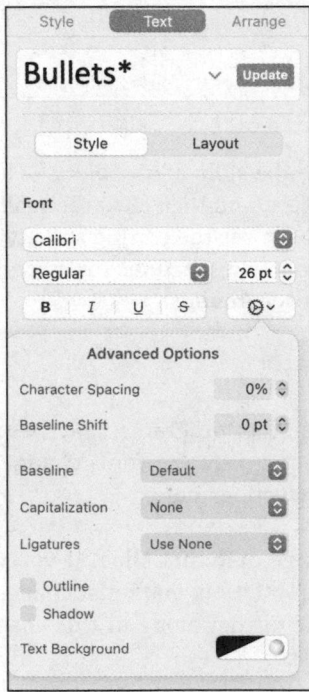

FIGURE 4-7:
The Text section of the Format pane lets you modify text.

5. **(Optional) Choose an option from the Text Color pop-up menu, and then click the Colors icon to change the color of the font.**

   The first option lets you choose a different option, such as a gradient fill or an image fill. The color swatch opens a chooser that displays colors used in the theme. The color wheel icon next to the color swatch opens the color wheel, as shown in Figure 4-8. Here's how to choose colors in the color wheel.

a. *Click the color picker you prefer: Color Wheel (the default), Color Sliders, Color Palettes, Image Palettes, or Pencils.* The color pickers give you different ways to choose colors. Click through to see which you're most comfortable using.

b. *Click the desired color in the color picker that appears in the Text Color window.*

c. *(Optional) In the color wheel, make the color lighter or darker by dragging the slider on the right side up and down.*

d. *(Optional) In any of the color pickers, adjust the opacity by dragging the Opacity slider left to decrease opacity or right to increase opacity or by typing a precise percentage in the text box to the right.*

e. *When you have a color you like, drag the color from the color box at the top to the color palette at the bottom. Your color is saved in the palette for future use.*

f. *Click the red close icon or choose View ⇨ Hide Colors.*

Keynote immediately uses your chosen color to color the text you selected. You can play around until you find a color you like.

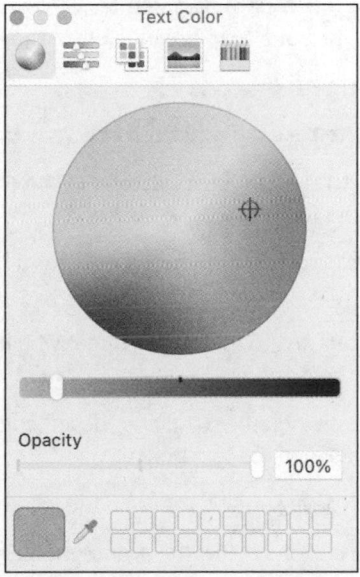

FIGURE 4-8: The Text Color window lets you choose a text color.

The name in the Paragraph Styles menu changes to reflect the new settings you choose, and an asterisk appears next to the name along with an Update button (refer to Figure 4-7). You can take the following actions:

≫ **Click Update.** All slides that use that layout will reflect the changes you made.

>> **Click the name in the Paragraph Styles menu.** Choose the original style from the menu to revert to that style or click the plus sign (+) at the top of the Paragraph Styles window to add the edited style as a new style. The latter option opens an editable text field in the Paragraph Styles window into which you type the name of the style. The new style is added to the paragraph styles menu for future use.

WARNING

Fonts aren't part of your presentation, but they reside on the computer from which you give the presentation. If you intend to use your presentation on a different computer, make sure that the fonts in your presentation are installed on the other computer, or Keynote will choose what it considers the closest font. So not only could the substitute font be ugly, but words may not fit in text boxes and may be cut off or dropped to a second line that could push lower text off the slide. If you use symbols or special characters, and they aren't available in the substitute font, they'll be replaced by a different symbol or an empty square.

Formatting paragraphs

Keynote considers even a single line a paragraph as far as formatting alignment and vertical spacing of the text in your text boxes. Select the text you'd like to modify and follow these steps:

1. **On the Format pane, click the Text tab and then the Style button.**

2. **Click the horizontal and vertical alignment buttons in the Alignment section and choose one of the following**

   - *Left Alignment* (default): Text is aligned on the left and has a ragged edge on the right.

   - *Center Alignment:* Moves your text to the center, but any bullets you have remain at the left edge of the text box.

   - *Right Alignment:* Aligns your text on the right, and the left edge is ragged; bullets remain on the left edge of the text box.

   - *Justified:* Adjusts the text to have straight edges on the left and right.

   - *Minor adjustment:* The two buttons below the alignment buttons shift the bullet and text one space at a time to the left or to the right.

   - *Upper Alignment:* Moves the text to the top of the text box.

   - *Middle Alignment:* Moves the text to the middle of the text box.

   - *Lower Alignment:* Moves the text to the bottom of the text box.

GIVING YOUR PRESENTATION THAT SOMETHING EXTRA

Capitalizing whole words or phrases in your presentation, especially in titles, is EYE-CATCHING. With Keynote, you don't have to use Caps Lock and retype everything if you change your mind. Choose the text to which you want to add pizzazz and then choose Format ⇨ Font ⇨ Capitalization (or choose Capitalization in the Advanced Options window), then choose one of the following:

- **None:** The default option. You create a capital letter by holding down the Shift key and then pressing the letter you want to capitalize.

- **All Caps:** Capitalizes all the letters in your selected text.

- **Small Caps:** Capitalizes all the letters in your selected text — but in a small size. Any letters you type while holding the Shift key will be big capital letters.

- **Title Case:** Capitalizes the first letter of each word in your selected text, except articles, conjunctions, and short prepositions.

- **Start Case:** Capitalizes the first letter of each word in your selected text, including articles, conjunctions, and prepositions.

You can also create a new text box and choose one of the previous capitalization options to apply the desired capitalization to any text you type.

If your text is just a little too long for the space it's in, you can scrunch it together, just barely, so that it fits without using a smaller font size. Choose Format ⇨ Font ⇨ Character Spacing ⇨ Tighten. For more precision, choose Character Spacing in the Advanced Options window and pick a specific percentage to tighten. If the typeface has a condensed variant, choose that for the best results.

3. **To change the vertical spacing between the lines of your text:**

   a. *Click the disclosure triangle next to Spacing to see the menus shown in Figure 4-9.*

   b. *Choose the distance you want between the lines and before and after paragraphs, if your text box has more than one paragraph.*

TIP

Text boxes adjust to the amount of text you type, so if you type more text than space allows, the text box grows as much as it can and then the font size begins to shrink to accommodate the text; delete text, and the font size grows again.

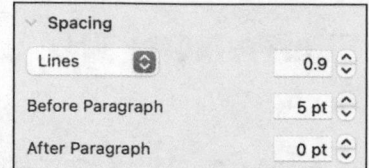

FIGURE 4-9:
Choose the
distance between
lines with the
spacing menu.

Formatting bullets

As I mention earlier in this chapter, themes come with predefined fonts, colors, styles, and bullets as part of the package. But Keynote offers such a variety of bullets, you may want to have some fun and change them. Select the text and follow these steps to change bullets:

1. **On the Format pane, click the Text tab and then the Style button.**

2. **Click the disclosure triangle next to Bullets & Lists.**

Keynote displays the options shown in Figure 4-10.

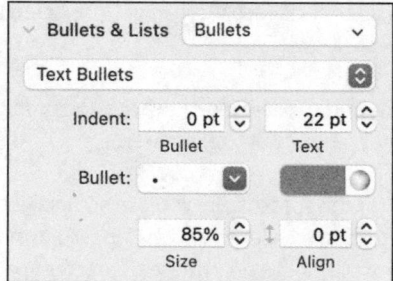

FIGURE 4-10:
Choosing a
style for your
bulleted list.

3. **Use the Bullets & Lists drop-down menu to choose one of these options:**

- *Bullet:* Creates a standard bullet (a period) before each item on your list.

- *Image:* Creates an image bullet before each item on your list. This option opens the Image Bullets menu from which you can select an image and specify the image size and alignment. You also have the option to use a custom image.

- *Lettered:* Creates a letter before each item in your list, starting with A. This option opens a menu from which you can choose the letter style and the letter shown before the first item in your list.

- *Numbered:* Creates a number before each item in your list starting with 1. This option opens a menu from which you can choose the number style and the number shown before the first item in your list.

4. Click the next menu to choose the bullet style: No Bullets, Text Bullets, Image Bullets, or Numbers.

5. Use the other pop-up menus to make adjustments; menus differ slightly from one list style to another:

- *Bullet/Number Indent:* Adjusts the distance from the outer edge of the text box and the bullet. The text moves with the bullet.

- *Text Indent:* Adjusts the distance from the outer edge of the text box and the text. The greater the difference between the bullet indent and the text indent, the farther the text is from the bullet.

- *Align:* Sets the vertical position of the bullet in relation to the text.

- *Size:* Alters the size of the bullet.

- *Color/Image:* Lets you edit the color of text or number bullets and the icon used for image bullets.

- *Numbered bullets:* Lets you choose from Arabic, Roman, and outline format, with and without parentheses.

Changing backgrounds and borders

A text box can have a background color that's different from the slide background or the box may be outlined by a border or frame. Again, the preset styles are in keeping with the theme you choose, but if you want to change them or you're creating a custom theme, select the text box and follow these steps:

1. On the Format pane, click the Style tab.

Keynote display the text box style options, as shown in Figure 4-11.

2. Click the disclosure triangles next to each option and then make your selections from the pop-up menus.

Choose from the preset style at the top of the Format pane, which formats the background of the cell and text, or choose an option from the pop-up menus. You see a preview of your choices on the slide:

- *Fill:* Puts a color, gradient, or image behind your text. Depending on the choice, you're presented with tools for choosing the color, the spectrum and direction (gradient), and scaling (image).

- *Border:* Surrounds your text with a line and picture frame; define the width, color, and scale of your choice.

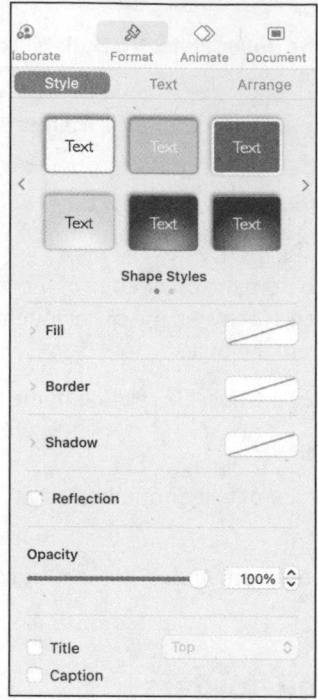

FIGURE 4-11:
Fills, borders, and shadows make text boxes stand out.

- *Shadow:* Creates one of three types of shadows — Drop, Contact, or Curved — behind the entire text box. Blur, offset, and opacity settings add more special effects. If you choose the Curved option, you can specify whether the shadow appears on the left side, bows inward, or bows outward.

- *Reflection:* Adds a mirrored effect of your text box under it. After choosing this option, you specify how visible the reflection is.

- *Opacity:* Affects the entire text box and changes the intensity of all components: the text, fills, and borders and reflections.

Adding Shapes, Charts, and Tables

One basic principle of a good presentation is giving the audience something interesting to look at. Over the next few sections, I take a look at the various visual-aid options offered in Keynote, including shapes, charts, and tables.

Inserting predefined shapes

Shapes can help draw your viewers' eyes to the thing you want them to notice. An arrow can connect your first point to your second; a star makes a key success stand out visually. Keynote comes with 3 types of lines (straight, arrow, and curved); 12 ready-to-go basic shapes that you can stretch, shrink, and twist to get the shape you need; and dozens of ready-to-use shapes in categories such as animals, food, and people. If you're an artistic type, you might want to try the tool for drawing your own shape.

Follow these steps to insert a shape on your slide:

1. **Create a new slide or select the slide on which you want to insert the shape.**

2. **Click the toolbar's Shape button.**

Keynote displays the pop-up window shown in Figure 4-12.

Draw with the pen tool

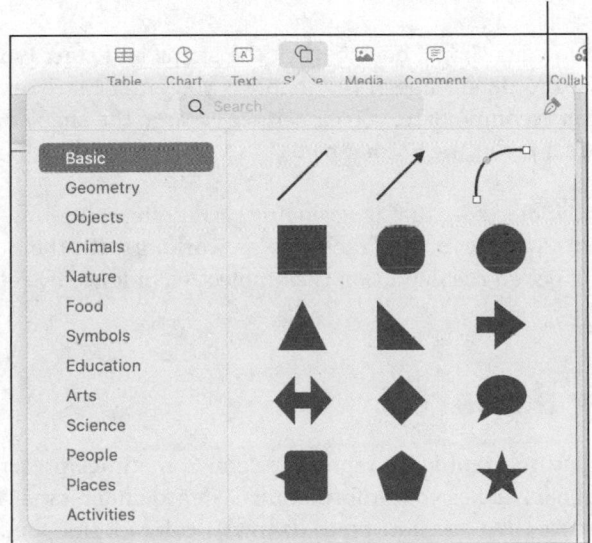

FIGURE 4-12:
Keynote offers dozens of shapes to add to your presentation.

3. **Click a category on the left, and then click the shape you want.**

TIP

If you want to draw your own shape, click the draw with the pen tool icon (labeled in Figure 4-12). Click where you want to start. Move the pointer to where you want to change direction, and then click to place a vertex; repeat until your shape is complete, and then double-click to stop drawing. To curve a line, drag the handle that appears in the middle of the line after you set it.

Your selected shape appears on the slide with active resizing handles.

4. **Use the resizing handles — the squares on the box that surrounds the shape — to enlarge or reduce the shape to the size you want.**

   All shapes have eight resizing handles. Drag a corner handle to resize the width and height of the shape simultaneously. Hold down the Shift key while dragging a corner handle to resize the shape proportionately. Drag a handle for the top center or bottom center to change the height of the shape. Drag a handle from the left center or right center to change the width of the shape.

5. **Drag the shape to where you want it on your slide.**

   Be sure to position the mouse pointer in the interior of the shape when dragging, not on any edge of the shape.

6. **To make changes to the shape:**

   a. *Select the shape (if it's not selected already), click the toolbar's Format button, and then click the Style tab in the Format pane.*

   b. *Use the Style tab options to change the color of the shape or add special effects such as fill, shadow, and borders to the shape.*

TIP

To add text to your shape, double-click the shape and start typing. As you type, the text wraps to the outline of the shape. If you enter more text than the size of the shape can accommodate, you can either enlarge the shape or change the font size in the Text tab of the Format pane.

REMEMBER

Working with objects — that is, grouping, arranging, aligning, distributing, and locking them — in Keynote is the same as working with them in Pages. Therefore, you can get all the details on these object techniques by referring to Book 5, Chapter 3.

Adding a chart

You use a *chart* to graphically represent data. Sometimes presenting your information as a chart makes your information easier to understand. To that end, Keynote offer more than 20 chart types, from 2D column, line, and pie charts to 3D bar and area charts.

To add a chart to your presentation, follow these steps:

1. **Create a slide or select the slide on which you want to insert the shape.**

2. **Choose Insert ⇨ Chart or click the toolbar's Charts button, and then choose the type of chart you want to create.**

   A default chart appears.

3. **Click the Edit Chart Data button at the bottom of the chart.**

   The Chart Data editor appears.

4. **For each row and column field header in the Chart Data editor, double-click the header to select the placeholder text and then type the header you want on your chart.**

   The new row headers appear in the chart as the data series and the new column headers appear in the chart as the data categories.

TIP

   If you prefer to have the columns as the series and the rows as the categories, click the Plot Columns as Series button in the upper-right corner of the Chart Data editor.

TIP

   Rather than double-clicking each cell you want to modify, you might find it easier to press Tab to move one cell to the right, Shift+Tab to move one cell to the left, or Return to move one cell down, and then type the text or value you want.

5. **For each cell below and to the right of the headers, double-click the cell and then type the number value you want in the cell.**

   As you modify the cell data, Keynote updates the chart to reflect the new values.

6. **Click the toolbar's Format button to open the Format pane and then click the following tabs to choose how you want the data to appear:**

   - *Chart:* Change the chart color scheme (Chart Styles), the typeface, and the size; add gaps between columns; add backgrounds, borders, and shadow; and even change the chart type.

   - *Axis:* Edit the axis options and value labels on the axis.

   - *Series:* Edit value labels on the bars and add trendlines.

   - *Arrange:* Wrap text around the chart and align and distribute its position among other objects on your document, such as text boxes and images.

TIP

   See Book 5, Chapter 5, where I present Numbers, for detailed instructions about formatting charts.

To remove a chart, click it and press Delete.

Adding a table

A *table* comprises rows and columns of related information, where each column represents an information category (such as name, phone number, or address) and each row represents an example of the table data (such as a customer or contact with a specific name, phone number, or address). The intersection of a row and a column is a *cell*, and you input your data into the table cells.

Tables in Keynote are *calculable*, which means that you can write formulas or insert functions in much the same way you would in Numbers.

These are the steps for adding a table to your document:

1. **Create a new slide or select the slide on which you want to insert the shape.**

2. **Choose Insert ⇨ Table and then click the type of table you want.**

   Choose Headers if you want to add both row and column headers to the table; choose Basic if you want just column headers; choose Plain if you want no headers; or choose Sums if you want to create totals for each column.

   Alternatively, click the toolbar's Table button to display a chooser that offers several pages of table styles. Use the right and left arrows to find the style you want, and then click that style.

   Keynote adds a blank table to your document.

3. **Resize any column's width by moving the mouse pointer over the right border of the column's header until the pointer becomes a double-headed arrow and then dragging right or left until the column is the width you prefer.**

   You can resize any row's height by moving the mouse pointer over the bottom border of the row's header until the pointer becomes a double-headed arrow and then dragging down or up until the row is the height you want.

4. **To add rows to your table, you have three choices:**

   - *To add a single row to the end of the table:* Click the bottom-right cell and then press Tab.

   - *To change the total number of rows:* Click the rows icon (two horizontal lines in a circle, at the bottom left of the table) and then use the control that appears to set the total number of rows you want.

   - *To insert a new row:* Click any cell in the row above or below which you want to insert the new row, choose Format ⇨ Table, and then click either Add Row Above or Add Row Below.

5. **To add columns to your table, you have two choices:**

   - *To change the total number of columns:* Click the columns icon (two vertical lines in a circle, at the top right of the table) and then use the control that appears to set the total number of columns you want.

- *To insert a new column:* Click any cell in the column to the left or right of which you want to insert the new column, choose Format ➪ Table, and then click either Add Column Before or Add Column After.

6. **Click the toolbar's Format button and then click the tabs to edit the table as follows:**

   - *Table:* Change the table color and layout scheme (Table Styles), and use the menus to set the number of header rows and columns and footer rows, select the table font size, and add a table outline and grid lines.

   - *Cell:* Select all the cells or a portion of them and then choose a data format you want to use to fill the cells and add fill and border to the cells.

   To select a column of cells, click its header. To select a row of cells, click its number.

   - *Text:* Edit the font and text alignment. Alternatively, you can select a preset style by clicking the disclosure button to the right of the style and then choosing one from the menu.

   - *Arrange:* Wrap text around the table and align and distribute its position among other objects on your document, such as text boxes and images.

7. **Set up functions and conditional formats by entering numerical data in a row or column of cells.**

   Type an equal sign (=) to open the Functions pane and then assign a function — for example, sum or average — to the cell at the bottom of a row or the end of a column.

   See Book 5, Chapter 5, where I present Numbers, for detailed instructions about formatting tables and writing formulas and using functions.

TIP

Adding media files

Text by itself can be as monotonous and confusing to read as the flight arrival and departure displays at an airport. Adding sound, still images, and movies makes your presentation appealing and communicative. Sound can be an audio recording of a song stored in Music, photos can be digital photographs stored in Photos, and movies can be short video clips.

Adding sound

You can add any audio file stored in Music or stored on your computer to a slide in your presentation or to the entire presentation.

Adding sound to a slide

To add sound to a slide, follow these steps:

1. **Display the slide on which you want to add an audio file.**

2. **Click the toolbar's Media button and then click Music.**

   A media chooser dialog appears with the Music tab displayed.

   Your Music library is displayed, as shown in Figure 4-13. You can choose a song from the library or from a playlist.

FIGURE 4-13:
The browser lets you choose an audio file from Music.

3. **Click the library, playlist, or folder where your audio resides.**

   The available files from which you can choose are displayed.

4. **Click the audio file you want to use and then close the Chooser dialog.**

   Keynote displays an audio icon directly on your slide to let you know audio is inserted here. If desired, you can drag the icon to a different location.

5. **Select the toolbar's Format button, and then select the Audio tab in the Format pane.**

6. **Set the following audio options, as preferred:**

   - *Replace:* Click to change the audio with a different file.

   - *Controls:* Play the audio file.

- *Volume:* Set the playback volume.

- *Edit Audio:* Click this disclosure arrow to display the trim control, which you can use to cut from the beginning and the end of the audio file so that only a portion plays with your slide.

- *Repeat:* Choose whether you want the audio file to keep playing after it ends. Choose None for no repeat; Loop to have the audio start over from the beginning; or Loop Back and Forth to have the audio play backward, then forward again, and so on.

- *Start Audio on Click:* When this check box is selected (the default), you click anywhere on the slide to start playback; if you deselect this check box, Keynote starts the audio automatically as soon as you navigate to the slide in your presentation.

- *Play Audio Across Slides:* When this check box is selected (the default), Keynote continues the audio playback even when you transition to the next slide; if you deselect this check box, Keynote stops the audio as soon as you navigate to the next slide in your presentation.

Adding a presentation soundtrack

To add soundtrack audio that plays during the entire slideshow, do the following:

1. **Click the toolbar's Document button.**

   Keynote displays the Document pane.

2. **Click the Audio tab, shown in Figure 4-14.**

3. **Click the plus sign (+)at the bottom right of the Soundtrack section.**

   The media browser opens, displaying your Music library and playlists.

4. **Click the audio you want to use as the presentation soundtrack.**

   Keynote closes the media browser and adds the audio to the Soundtrack list.

5. **Choose the Soundtrack section's pop-up menu to choose one of the following:**

   - *Play Once:* The track stops playing if the audio ends before the presentation is over.

   - *Loop:* Plays the audio again from the beginning if the track ends before the presentation is over.

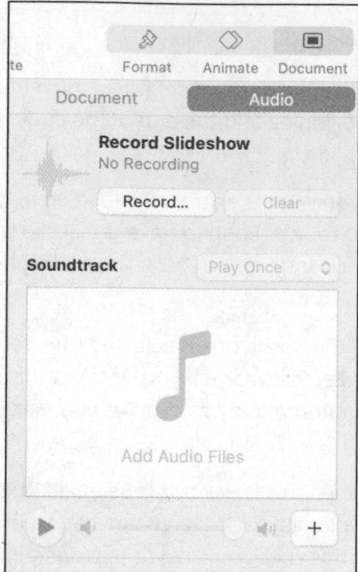

FIGURE 4-14:
Use the Audio tab to add a soundtrack that plays during your entire presentation.

TIP

You can use multiple audio files as your presentation soundtrack by repeating Steps 3 and 4 as often as needed. The audio files will play in the order in which they appear in the Soundtrack list. You can change their order by dragging them to different locations in the Soundtrack list.

TIP

You can add voiceover to accompany your presentation so when people view it without you they have the benefit of hearing what you want to say about each slide. In the Document pane's Audio tab, click Record (or choose Play ➪ Record Slideshow). If your Mac asks you to permit Keynote to use your microphone, be sure to click OK. Keynote starts the presentation and begins the recording. Deliver your slide spiel, click the right arrow to move to the next slide, and repeat until you're done. Press the Esc key when you finish. Choose Play ➪ Play Slideshow to hear how you did.

Adding photos or movies

If you store digital photos or video in Photos, you can place a photo or video file on any slide in a Keynote presentation by following these steps:

1. **Create a slide or click the slide where you want to insert a photo.**

2. **Use of the following techniques to get started, depending on whether you're replacing a placeholder image or inserting a new image:**

- *To replace a placeholder image:* Click the photo icon in the lower-right corner of the placeholder image.

- *To insert a new image:* In the Keynote toolbar, choose Media ➪ Photos.

Your Photos library is displayed in the media browser.

If you want to add a movie instead of a photo, click the media browser's Movies tab.

The media browser displays all the pictures or movies stored in Photos. Click an album or event to narrow your choices and more easily find the image or movie you want.

3. **Click the photo or movie you want and then close the media browser dialog (if Keynote doesn't close the media browser automatically).**

If your slide doesn't include a media placeholder, the photo or movie fills your slide. Resize the photo or movie by clicking it and then dragging the resize handles. Click and drag to position the photo or movie where you want it.

If your slide does include a media placeholder, the photo or movie fills the placeholder box, maintaining any border, shadow, and fill styles.

4. **Edit the photo or movie by clicking it and then clicking the toolbar's Format button. Click the tabs as follows:**

- *Style:* Offers menus to choose one of the predefined image styles associated with the theme or change the borders, shadows, opacity, and reflection in the same way as explained for text boxes.

- *Image:* Gives options for replacing the photo, masking and adjusting it, which I explain in Book 5, Chapter 6.

- *Movie:* Lets you replace the movie, adjust the volume, trim the movie, and choose the *poster frame* (the frame displayed in your presentation). You can also select or deselect Start Movie on Click. When deselected, the movie will begin as soon as the slide appears in the presentation; when selected, press the spacebar or click the movie to start playback.

TIP

If the movie you add to your presentation has a black frame at the start, click Edit Movie in the Edit Movie section of the Format pane's Movie tab, and then drag the Poster Frame slider until you see the frame you want displayed in your presentation.

- *Arrange:* Gives you the option to arrange where the media appears in the stacking order.

TIP

If you plan to use your presentation on a different computer, choose Keynote ➪ Settings ➪ General. Next to Saving, make sure the Copy Audio and Movies into Document check box is selected so your media files are part of the presentation.

Rearranging Slides

Keynote displays slides in the order in which they appear in the navigator, outline, or light table view. In navigator and outline view, the top slide appears first, followed by the slide directly below it, and so on, whereas in light table view, they're arranged left to right in a grid. After you create two or more slides in a presentation, you may want to move a slide to an earlier or later position.

To move one or more slides in a presentation, follow these steps:

1. **Pull down the View menu and choose either Navigator or Outline (to display the slides vertically in the slide navigator pane) or choose Light Table (to display slides in rows and columns).**

2. **Select the slide or slides you want to move.**

   To select multiple, consecutive slides, click the first slide you want to duplicate, hold down the Shift key, and then click the last slide you want to duplicate.

   To select multiple, nonconsecutive slides, click the first slide, then hold down the ⌘ key as you click the other slides you want in the selection.

3. **Drag any selected slide to the new position.**

   TIP

   If you decide against moving the slides while you're mid-drag, press Esc to bail out of the operation.

   In light table view, Keynote moves slide icons out of the way to show you where your moved slides will appear, but a grayed rectangle remains in the original positions until you release the mouse button or lift your finger from the trackpad.

Creating a group of slides

If you have a presentation with a large number of slides, it can be hard to discern the overall organization of the presentation based on the limited number of slides displayed in the slide navigator pane. (Yep, you can get more of a bird's-eye view using the slide table, but you can't use that view when you're editing a slide.)

Fortunately, most large presentations have sequences of related slides. In a budget presentation, for example, you might have several slides related to revenue and several slides related to expenses. Having a run of related slides is useful because Keynote enables you to group those slides, which then become, in a sense, sub-slides of the first slide in the group. You can then *collapse* the group, which means that Keynote displays only the group's first slide in the slide navigator pane. Create a group for each of your presentation's related-slide sequences, and soon your presentation's overall organization becomes clear even in the limited space of the slide navigator pane.

Once you have a group of slides, Keynote enables you to work with the group as follows:

>> You can expand the group so that all its slides appear in the slide navigator pane. The slides appear slightly indented from the first slide to indicate that they're part of a group.

>> When a group is collapsed, you can drag the group to a new position within the presentation without losing the order of the individual slides in the group.

To create a group, follow these steps:

1. **Choose View ⇨ Navigator.**

2. **Click the slide that you want to use as the first of the group.**

This is the slide that will remain visible in the slide navigator pane.

3. **Hold down Shift and then click the last slide you want in the group.**

Keynote selects all the slides between (and including) the first and last slide.

4. **Press Tab.**

You can also drag any selected slide slightly to the right.

A disclosure arrow appears next to the first slide in the group, and subsequent slides are indented. For example, in Figure 4-15, Slide 3 is the first slide of the group, so it has the disclosure arrow to its left; slides 4 through 7 are in the group, they so appear indented from slide 3.

TIP

In case you're wondering, yes, it's possible to create a *subgroup* (that is, a group within a group). Within an existing group, click the first slide you want to include in your subgroup and then press Tab. Keynote indents the slide a bit farther to the right and adds a disclosure arrow to the slide above. Repeat for subsequent slides until your subgroup is complete.

Clicking the disclosure arrow opens and closes the group.

To remove a slide from a group, click the slide, and then press Shift+Tab (you can also drag the slide to the left).

Disclosure arrow

First slide of the group

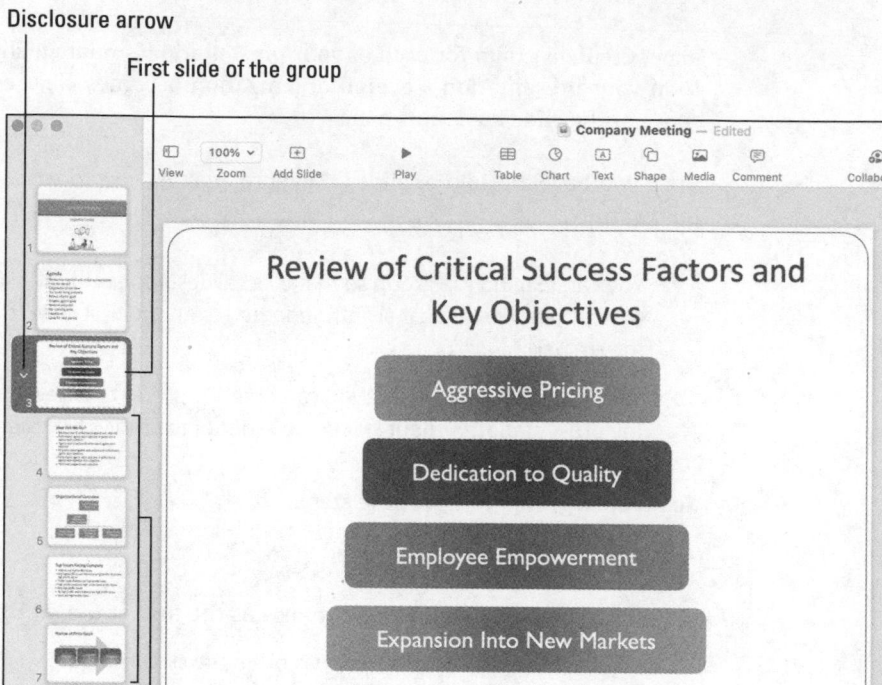

FIGURE 4-15:
In a group of slides the first slide (slide 3 here) has a disclosure arrow and the subsequent slides (4 through 7 here) are indented.

The rest of the group's slides appear indented

Deleting a slide

Eventually, you may find that you don't need a slide anymore. Deleting a slide is easy, and deleting a slide group is, perhaps, too easy.

WARNING

In groups, if you delete the head slide when the group is closed, the entire group is deleted. If you delete the head slide when the group is open, only that slide is deleted; slides in the group or subgroups move one step to the left.

To delete a slide, go to the navigator, outline, or light table view, select the slide that you want to delete, and then do one of the following:

>> Press Delete.

>> Choose Edit ⇨ Delete on the menu bar.

>> Right-click the slide and choose Delete.

TIP

If you delete a slide by mistake, immediately choose Edit ⇨ Undo Delete (or press ⌘ +Z).

Skipping a slide

You may use the same presentation multiple times but with different audiences or time allowances, so you may not want to use every slide every time. You can suppress slides without deleting them, which gives you the flexibility of using the same presentation in different settings.

To skip a slide, go to the navigator, outline, or light table view, select the slide you want to skip, and then choose Slide ⇨ Skip Slide. (You can also press Shift+⌘+H or right-click the slide and then click Skip Slide.) Keynote collapses the slide to a horizontal line in navigator view; hides the slide number in outline view; and grays out the slide in light table view.

To add a skipped slide back into the presentation, select the slide and then choose Slide ⇨ Unskip Slide (you can also press Shift+⌘+H or right-click the slide and then click Unskip Slide).

Creating Transitions and Effects

To make your presentations visually interesting, you can add transitions and effects. *Slide transitions* define how a slide appears and disappears from the display. *Text and graphic effects* define how the text or graphic initially appears on or disappears from the slide and how it moves around a slide. You can also add hyperlinks to your presentation.

Creating a slide transition

To create a slide transition, follow these steps:

1. **Choose View ⇨ Navigator.**

2. **In the slide navigator pane, click the slide that you want to animate with a transition.**

3. **Click the toolbar's Animate button to open the Transitions pane.**

4. **Click the Add an Effect button to see the Effects menu (as shown in Figure 4-16).**

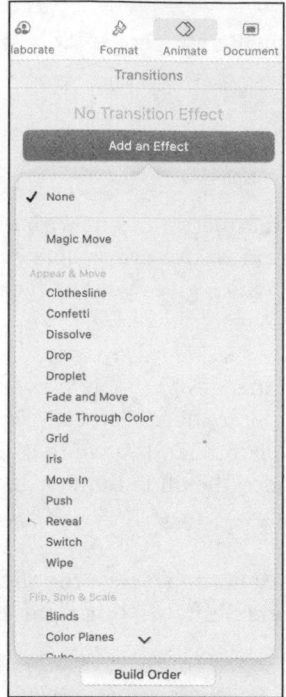

FIGURE 4-16:
Use the
Transitions menu
to choose a
transition.

5. **Choose an effect that piques your curiosity.**

Depending on the transition effect you choose, you may need to define other options, such as the direction or duration of your transition.

The Magic Move effect lets you add animation to your presentation without hiring a designer. It animates an object, moving it from its location on one slide to a new location on the next slide. The object must be the same on both slides. Place the object at the starting point on the first slide and then on the end point on the second slide. The Magic Move feature moves the object when the slide transitions from the first slide to the second slide.

A preview of your transition in action appears in the central slide pane.

REMEMBER

Transition options vary depending on the effect you choose. You choose options such as the direction from which the transition begins, the duration of the transition, and how the transition starts from pop-up menus.

Click the Change button to use a different transition or add another one; choose None in the Effects pop-up menu to remove a transition.

TIP

6. **Click the toolbar's Animate button to close the Transitions pane.**

Creating text and graphic effects

Sometimes you want your bullets to show up one at a time. Instead of creating separate slides — the first with one bullet, the second with two bullets, the third with three, and so on — create your slide with the bullets you want, and then define how Keynote builds your slide during your presentation. Keynote offers three ways to create text and graphic effects in over 25 types of transitions:

>> **Build In:** Defines how text and graphics enter a slide. (If you choose the Build In transition, initially, the text and graphics won't appear on the slide.)

>> **Action:** Defines how text and graphics move on a slide.

>> **Build Out:** Defines how text and graphics exit a slide.

Creating builds

To define an effect for text or graphics, follow these steps:

1. **Choose View ⇨ Navigator.**

2. **In the slide navigator pane, click the slide that contains the text or graphic you want to display with a visual effect.**

3. **Click the text or graphic you want to animate, such as a text box with a bulleted list, a table, or a chart.**

4. **Click the toolbar's Animate button.**

5. **Click the Build In tab or the Build Out tab.**

6. **Click Add an Effect and choose an effect from the pop-up menu.**

7. **Set the Delivery options to build your bullet list, chart, or table, one item at a time.**

   Delivery options vary depending on the effect you choose. The options you specify determine how each bullet from a list is delivered during the presentation or how an individual word is delivered.

8. **Click Preview to see how the build will be displayed during your presentation.**

9. **Click Change and use the pop-up menu to use a different effect or remove the effect (by clicking None at the top of the list).**

10. **(Optional) Click another object and assign a build to that object as in Steps 6 and 7.**

11. **(Optional) Follow these substeps to modify the order in which the builds occur:**

   a. *Click the Build Order button to open the Build Order window (see Figure 4-17).*

   b. *Click and drag the objects in the list to set the order they'll be added to the slide.*

   c. *Click an object, and then in the Build In section of the Animate pane, choose when to start the builds and the delay between each object.*

   d. *Click Preview to see how the builds will look during your presentation.*

   e. *Click the close icon to exit the Build Order window.*

12. **Click Animate in the toolbar to close the Builds pane.**

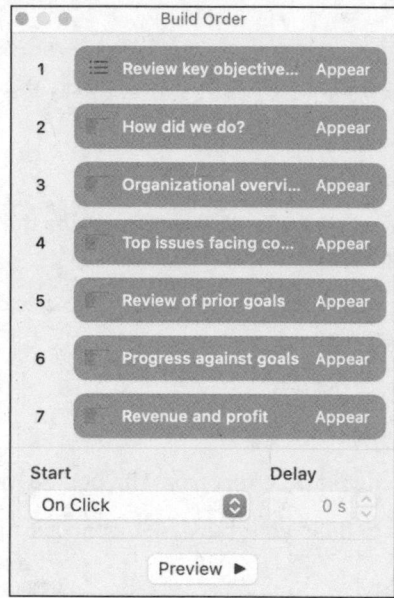

FIGURE 4-17:
Builds are a great way to show information one piece at a time.

Making text and graphics move on a slide

If you choose the Action button for text or graphics, you can choose the move effect, which lets you define a line that the text or graphic follows as it moves across a slide. To define a line to move text or graphics on a slide, follow these steps:

1. **Follow Steps 1 through 4 in the preceding section for creating builds.**

2. **Click the Action tab.**

3. **Click Add an Effect.**

4. **Choose Move from the Effect pop-up menu.**

Keynote displays a red line that shows how your chosen text or graphic will move, as shown in Figure 4-18.

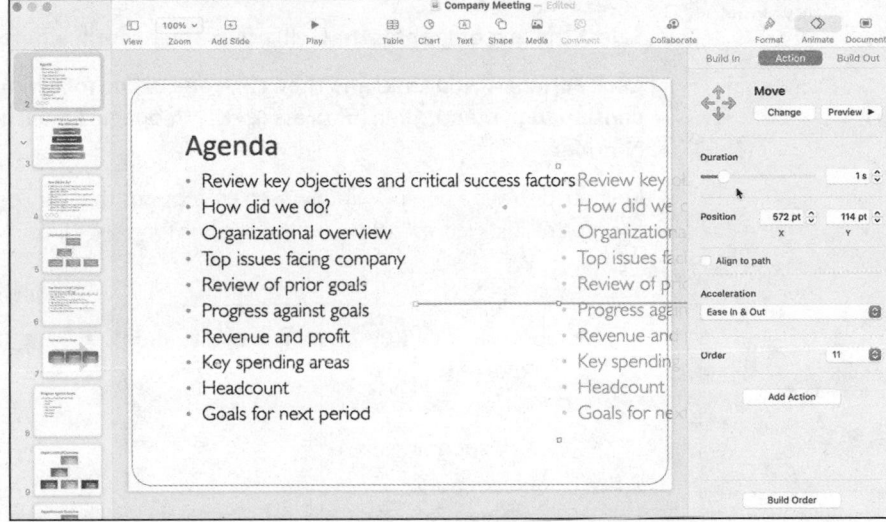

FIGURE 4-18:
Keynote displays
the path
connecting text
or graphics
on a slide.

5. **(Optional) Click and drag the handle at the beginning or end of the red line to move the line or change its length.**

Moving the red line changes the direction your chosen text or graphic moves. Changing the line length determines how far your chosen text or graphic moves.

6. **(Optional) To add another action to the same object, click the Add Action button and repeat Steps 4 and 5.**

REMEMBER

The Action feature moves an object or text on a slide. The Magic Move feature animates objects or text from one slide to the next during the slide transition.

Adding hyperlinks to your presentation

Like links in a web page, hyperlinks in your presentation connect to another point in the presentation, connect to a website, or open an outgoing email message. They're particularly useful for creating presentations that a viewer will watch alone — say, at a kiosk or even on your website. You don't have to be present for the viewer to see your presentation. Hyperlinks are also helpful if you want to access media stored remotely, such as a video that would take up storage on your computer.

Here's how to create a hyperlink:

1. **Choose View ⇨ Navigator.**

2. **Click the slide that contains the text or graphic that you want to use as the departure point for the hyperlink.**

3. **Select the text or graphic that will act as the hyperlink button.**

4. **Click Format ⇨ Add Link, and then click one of the following from the continuation menu: Slide (or press ⌘+K), Webpage, Email, or Phone Number.**

Keynote displays a pop-up window with link options that vary depending on the type of link. Figure 4-19 shows the options for a slide link.

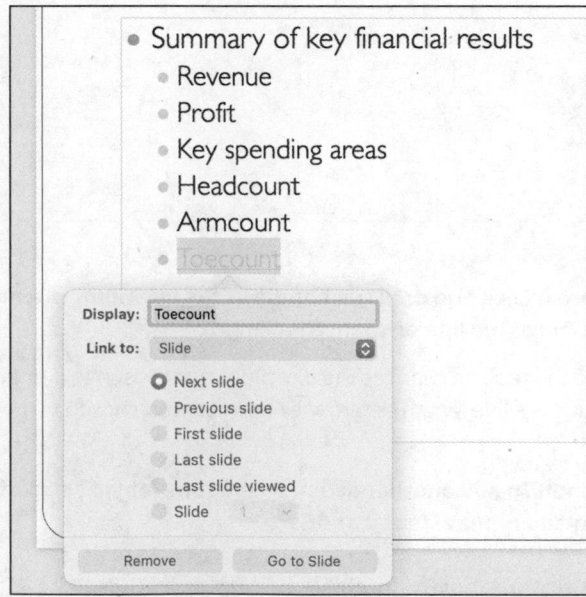

FIGURE 4-19:
The options available for a slide link.

5. **Configure the options for the link:**

- *Slide:* Select the radio button for the linked slide, or select Slide and then fill in the slide number.

- *Webpage:* Use the Link text box to type or paste the address of the linked web page.

- *Email:* Use the To text box to type the address to whom the message should be sent; use the Subject text box to type the message's subject line.

- *Phone Number:* Use the Number text box to type the phone number.

TIP

You can also create a link that exits the presentation. In the link pop-up window, use the Link To pop-up menu to select Exit Slideshow. Clicking the hyperlink will close the presentation.

6. **Click outside the pop-up window to finalize the link.**

To make changes to a hyperlink, click the link and then click Edit. To delete a hyperlink, click the link, click Edit, and then click Remove.

Editing Slide Layouts to Customize Themes

Instead of tweaking a slide layout and then duplicating the slide or duplicating a whole presentation and then redoing the text and images, you can make changes to the slide layout or create a Keynote theme. *Slide layouts* are the templates used to create new slides. When you change a layout, you can then update all slides that use that layout in the presentation. Changes you make to slide layouts in a presentation affect only that specific presentation. See the tip after these steps about how to create a new theme. To edit slide layouts, follow these steps:

1. **In any view, choose View ⇨ Edit Slide Layouts.**

   If you see a dialog warning you that "Editing a slide layout may change slides based on that layout," click Edit Slide Layouts to proceed.

   The first slide layout appears. In the same view, you see the slide layout and the format tools. I find navigator view easiest for editing layouts because you can see all the slide layouts in the left panel.

2. **Click the layout you want to edit.**

3. **Click the part you want to change (text or image), and then make the changes you want in the Format pane.**

   For example, you can simply choose a different predefined style for that placeholder by clicking the menus in the Format pane, or you can change the font itself, the color, size, and alignment.

   For text, you can also add new styles to the list or rename or delete existing styles, and then use those new or renamed styles on subsequent slide layouts. Click text on any slide, and then click the Text tab in the Format pane. Click the text name to open the paragraph styles menu and then click the plus sign at the top to add a new style or click a style to delete or rename it, as shown in Figure 4-20.

   For text boxes or image placeholders, you can change the borders and shadows. Click and drag to change the position of placeholders.

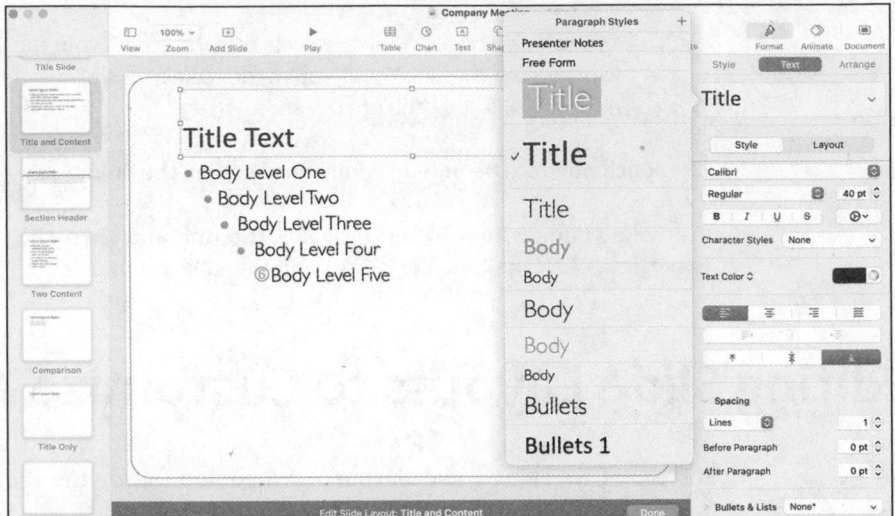

FIGURE 4-20:
Create your
own slide layout
layouts.

4. **Repeat Steps 2 and 3 for other slide layouts.**

5. **Rename the layout by double-clicking the layout name in the slide navigator and typing a new name.**

6. **Create a new slide layout by clicking the existing slide layout you want to use as the basis for the new layout, right-clicking any existing layout, and then choosing New Slide Layout from the context menu.**

   For example, if you frequently use a specific type of chart, you could add a slide layout to the theme you use most often and insert a chart on that slide layout.

   The new slide layout appears below the slide from which it was created, with the default name appended with *copy*. Edit the layout as shown in the previous steps; if you want, rename it.

7. **Click Done when you finish.**

TIP

To make your own personalized theme, create a presentation from a plain theme or one that's similar to the end result you want. Edit the slide layouts, choose File ⇨ Save Theme, click Add to Theme Chooser, type a name for the theme, and then click Create. If you're creating a theme you'll use often, consider putting your company name or logo in the theme so it's one less task you have to do when creating presentations.

Polishing Your Presentation

When you finish adding and modifying the slides in your presentation, you need to show your presentation to others. You may give a presentation in person or post it on YouTube or your website so people can view it at their leisure.

Previewing a presentation

After you finish creating a presentation, you need to preview it to see how it looks and, if needed, edit it to fine-tune it. The slide order or visual effects may have looked good when you put your presentation together, but when you view it in its entirety, you may suddenly notice gaps or repetitions. To view a presentation, follow these steps:

1. **In the navigator, outline, or light table view, click the first slide you want to view.**

   If you click the first slide of your presentation, you'll view your entire presentation. If you click a slide in the middle of your presentation, your slideshow begins from that slide and proceeds until it reaches the last slide.

2. **Click the toolbar's Play button or choose Play ⇨ Play Slideshow on the menu bar.**

   Pressing Option+⌘+P also works.

   The slide you chose in Step 1 appears.

3. **When you're ready to view the next slide, click the mouse button or trackpad, press the spacebar, or use the right arrow key.**

   If needed, note that pressing the left arrow key takes you back a slide.

4. **Repeat Step 3 as needed to run through your entire presentation.**

   Press Esc if you want to stop viewing your presentation before reaching the last slide.

5. **When you reach the last slide of your presentation, click the mouse button or trackpad, or press the spacebar, to exit your presentation.**

TIP

If you don't want to click through the presentation, click the toolbar's Document button, click the Document tab, and then choose Self-Playing in the Presentation Type pop-up menu.

Rehearsing a presentation

Previewing a presentation lets you make sure that all the slides are in the right order and that all effects and transitions work as you expect. Before giving your presentation, you may want to rehearse it and let Keynote approximate how much time you spend on each slide.

Rehearsing can give you only a general estimate of the time needed to give your presentation. In real life, various conditions — for example, an impatient audience sitting in a stuffy conference room where the air conditioning suddenly breaks down — may make you nervous or speed up your timing.

To rehearse a presentation, follow these steps:

1. **In the navigator, outline, or light table view, click the first slide you want to view.**

2. **Choose Play ➪ Rehearse Slideshow.**

Keynote displays the first slide.

3. **Click the Tools button in the upper-right corner.**

Keynote displays the presentation tools, as shown in Figure 4-21. Use the check boxes to display (when selected) or hide (when deselected) the parts of the presentation you want to see. In particular, I recommend selecting the Clock check box, which enables you to see how much time has elapsed.

To add presenter notes, click in the Presenter Notes text box shown in Figure 4-21, and enter some notes as a prompt of what to say to your audience. Presenter Notes are a huge benefit the first time you present your handiwork to a live audience, especially if you're not a seasoned public speaker.

4. **Practice what you're going to say when presenting each slide and press the spacebar or click the mouse button to advance to the next slide.**

Preparing for your big event

When the day arrives to give your presentation, Keynote has some tools to help you then, too. As long as your presentation will be presented with a second projection system — that is, not viewed directly on your Mac while you're giving it — you can enable the presenter display, which lets you display your notes and stopwatch next to your slides on your Mac while the audience sees only your slides.

The presenter display is enabled by default, but you can follow these steps to make sure:

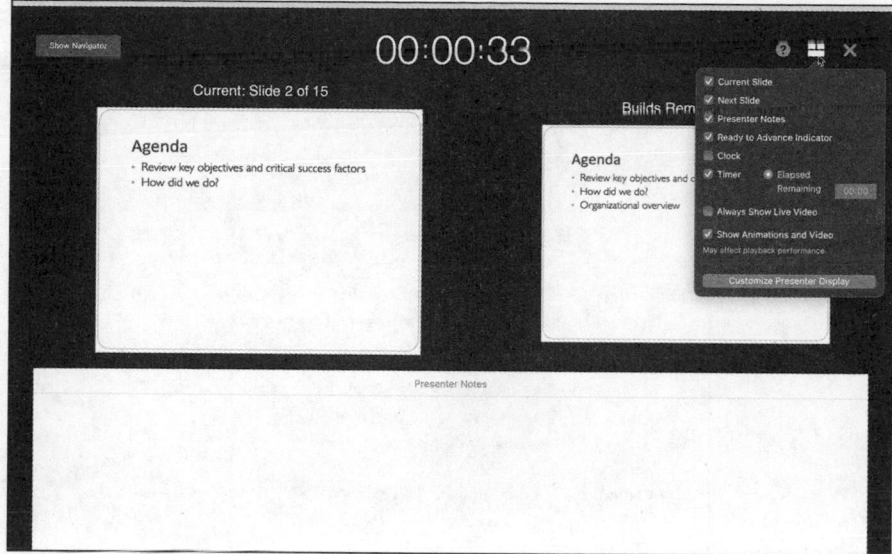

FIGURE 4-21:
Keynote can track how much time you spend on each slide.

1. **Choose Keynote ⇨ Settings.**

2. **Click the Slideshow tab.**

3. **Select Enable Presenter Display in Full Screen.**

   When your computer is connected to a projection system, you see the presenter display (refer to Figure 4-21).

4. **Select the items you see onscreen, such as the pointer, in the Interacting section as shown in Figure 4-22.**

5. **Click the red close icon on the Settings window.**

Controlling your presentation remotely

If you're a social person who likes to mingle with the attendees while giving a presentation, you'll be happy to know that you can use your iOS device to control your presentation while you're off fraternizing with your audience. To play your presentation remotely:

1. **On your iPhone, install the iOS version of Keynote from the App Store.**

2. **On your Mac, choose Keynote ⇨ Settings, and click the Remotes tab.**

3. **Select the Enable check box.**

   You still need the Settings dialog, so don't close it just yet.

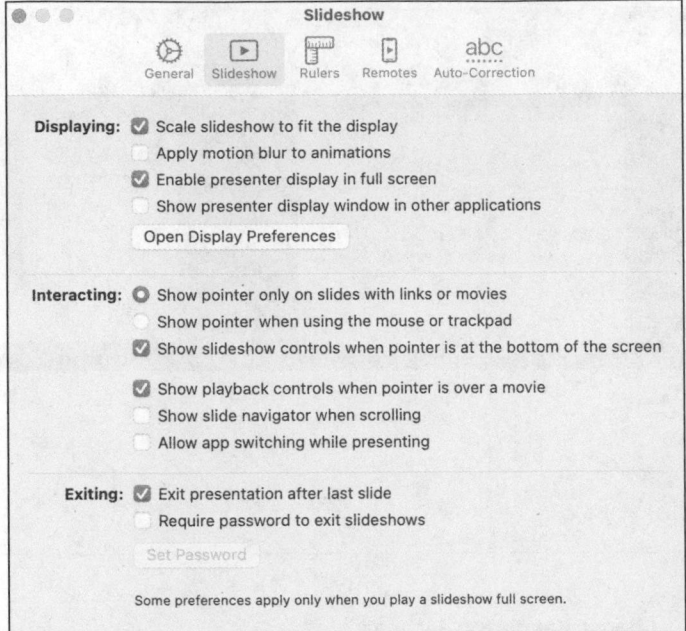

FIGURE 4-22:
Choose how
you want to
interact with your
presentation.

4. **Launch Keynote on your iOS device, and then tap the Remote icon in the upper-right corner of the interface.**

   A window appears telling you that your device can be used to remotely control Keynote presentations.

5. **Tap Continue.**

   Your iOS device asks if Keynote is allowed to find and connect to devices on your local network, as shown in Figure 4-23.

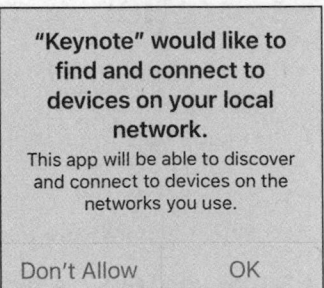

"Keynote" would like to find and connect to devices on your local network.

This app will be able to discover and connect to devices on the networks you use.

Don't Allow   OK

FIGURE 4-23:
Your iOS device
will ask if it's cool
that Keynote look
for devices
(in this case, your
Mac) on your
network.

6. **Tap OK.**

   A pulsing blue dot appears.

7. Tap the blue dot.

On your Mac, the Settings dialog's Remotes tab refreshes and you now see your iOS device in the list, as shown in Figure 4-24.

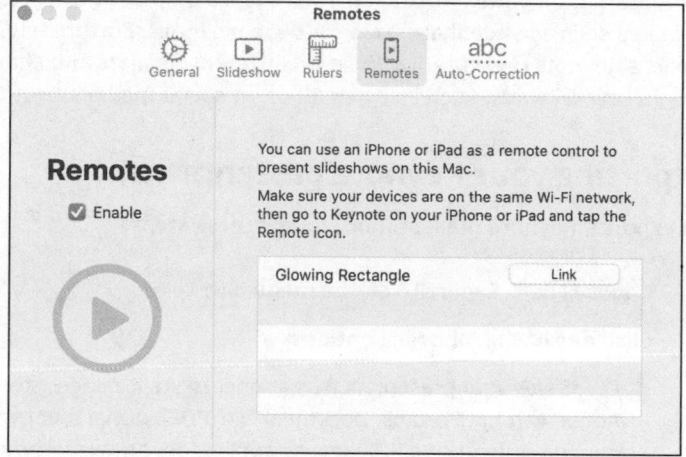

FIGURE 4-24: Linking an iOS device to use as a remote control.

8. Click Link.

A four-digit verify code appears on your Mac and iOS device.

9. Make sure that the code is the same on both devices, and then click Confirm on your Mac.

Your iOS device is linked to your Mac and can be used to play your presentations remotely.

10. Click the red close icon to exit the Settings dialog.

To play a presentation remotely, your Mac and iOS device must be connected wirelessly to a Wi-Fi network. After you launch Keynote and open your presentation, launch Keynote on your iOS device and a huge green play icon appears in the middle of your screen. Tap the play icon and, as long as you don't wander too far from your Mac, you can controls your slides while you horse around with your audience.

TIP

If you use an Android or Windows handheld device, check out remote control apps in their stores too.

Letting others run your presentation

When you give a presentation, you'll probably do it directly from your Mac. However, there may come a time when you need to save your presentation to run on a different type of computer or you want to give others the opportunity to see your presentation on your website, on YouTube, or on one of the presentation sharing websites such as SlideShare (www.slideshare.net). Fortunately, Keynote lets you *export* a Keynote presentation in seven different formats and share your presentation in several ways, such as by email or on social media sites.

Exporting your Keynote presentation

To export a Keynote presentation, follow these steps:

1. **Choose File ⇨ Export To on the menu bar.**

2. **Click one of the following options:**

   - *PDF:* Saves your presentation as a series of static images stored in the Adobe Acrobat Portable Document File (PDF) format that can be viewed by any computer with a PDF viewing application. Any visual or transition effects between slides will be lost.

   - *PowerPoint:* Saves your presentation as a PowerPoint file that you can edit and run on any computer that runs PowerPoint. (Certain visual effects and transitions may not work in PowerPoint.)

   - *Movie:* Saves your presentation as a movie that can play on a Windows PC or Mac computer that has the free QuickTime player. This movie preserves all transitions and visual effects.

   - *Animated GIF:* Saves your presentation as a GIF image that plays your presentation.

   - *Images:* Saves each slide as a separate graphic file.

   - *HTML:* Saves each slide as a separate web page. Any visual or transition effects between slides will be lost.

   - *Keynote '09:* Saves your presentation as a file that's compatible with older versions of Keynote.

TIP

If you want to preserve your visual effects and transitions, save your presentation as a movie, which also allows you to play your presentation on a TV connected to an iOS device. If you want to preserve and edit your presentation on a Mac or Windows PC running Microsoft PowerPoint, save your presentation as a PowerPoint file.

The Export Your Presentation dialog opens and displays the tab that corresponds to the command you selected in Step 2. For example, if you choose the Movie command, you see the Movie tab, as shown in Figure 4-25.

Depending on the option you choose in Step 2, you may see additional ways to customize your presentation.

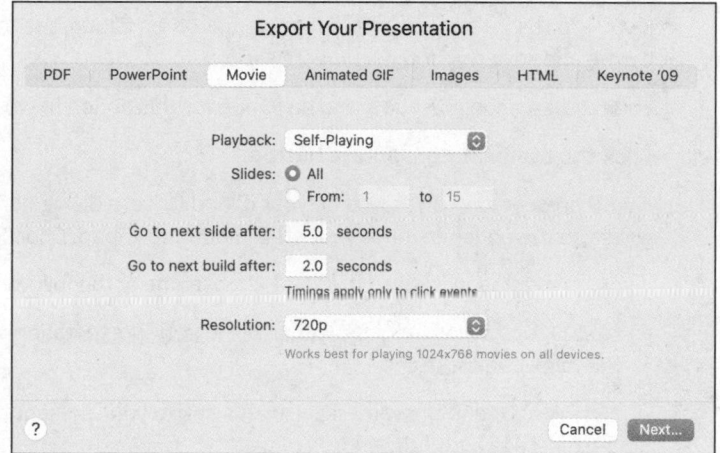

FIGURE 4-25:
Keynote displays the tab that corresponds to the export format you selected.

3. **Click Next.**

   A folder chooser dialog appears.

4. **Select the folder where you want to store your exported presentation.**

   You may need to switch drives or folders until you find where you want to save your file.

5. **Click Export.**

REMEMBER

When you export a presentation, your original Keynote presentation remains untouched in its original location.

Sharing your Keynote presentation

You have two ways to share your presentation: Save the presentation to your iCloud.com storage and then share the link, or share the presentation file. Sharing the presentation file (via email, say) is problematic because if you want multiple people to work on the file, you'll need to send out multiple copies of the file and manage multiple emails. It's much easier and more efficient to enable your collaborators to work on a single copy of the presentation via an iCloud.com link.

When you share the link, you can configure the share to allow anyone who opens the presentation to make changes to it, and those changes will be seen by you and by your other collaborators.

Here's how you can share your presentation via iCloud:

1. **Make sure you've saved your presentation on iCloud.**

   If you aren't sure how to save your presentation on iCloud, see the "Choosing a theme and saving your presentation" section.

   Your presentation must be saved on iCloud for this option to work.

REMEMBER

2. **Click the toolbar's Collaborate button.**

   If your presentation isn't saved on your iCloud Drive, a dialog notifies you and gives you the option to move your presentation to iCloud. Choose this option.

   If your presentation is saved to iCloud, choose one of the following options:

   - *Mail:* Opens a new message with a link to your presentation. Address the message and click Send.

   - *Messages:* Opens a new message with a link to your presentation. Address the message and click Send.

   - *Copy Link:* Places the link on the clipboard so you can paste it somewhere else, such as on your website or in another presentation.

   - *AirDrop:* Give you the option to collaborate with other people on your network who have AirDrop enabled.

3. **Set the following options for the shared presentation:**

   - *Who can access:* Choose an option from the pop-up menu. Your choices are Only People You Invite or Anyone with the Link.

   - *Permission:* Choose an option from the pop-up menu. Your choices are Can Make Changes or Can View Only.

4. **Click Share.**

5. **Share the presentation according to the option you selected in Step 2 (such as sending an email or text or copying the link to a social media post).**

Click the toolbar's Collaborate button and then click Share Settings to see the link as well as who else is editing it. To remove the link from any place that you've shared it, click the Stop Sharing button.

TIP

REMEMBER

For more tips on using Keynote, go to Book 5, Chapter 6.

Chapter 5

Crunching with Numbers

A *spreadsheet* is a document designed to work with numbers. You can use a spreadsheet to store numeric data, but most spreadsheets come into their own when you create special entries called *formulas* that calculate results. Formulas can be as simple as adding two or more numbers and as complex as calculating the monthly payment for a loan given the principal, interest rate, and term.

Your Mac comes with a spreadsheet app called (appropriately, if uninspiringly) Numbers, which lets you not only store and calculate numeric values but also add text (either as data or to help describe what the spreadsheet does), dates, and times. To make calculations easier, Numbers also comes with hundreds of predefined functions that encapsulate complex calculations in areas such as finance and statistics. For your right brain, Numbers enables you to visualize your data using a wide variety of charts.

In this chapter, I explain the parts of a spreadsheet and how to create a spreadsheet or open an existing spreadsheet created in a different application. I show you how to work with your data on a spreadsheet, including setting up tables, entering data, and using formulas. I give you some tips for personalizing a spreadsheet to make it aesthetically pleasing. At the end of the chapter, I go over sharing your spreadsheet, even if the person you want to share with doesn't use Numbers.

Touring the Numbers Window

The Numbers window is divided into two main sections: the sheet and the Format/Organize pane. You can place data, tables, formulas, charts, and even graphics and media on the sheet. The Format pane is where you apply styles and color to the fonts and data you select in the worksheet, and the Organize pane is where you establish criteria to sort data on tables. Following are other things you can see on the Numbers window:

>> **Toolbar:** Across the top is the toolbar, which has buttons for frequently performed tasks.

TIP

To customize the Toolbar to suit your working preferences, choose View ➪ Customize Toolbar. From the window that appears, drag your favorite buttons to the toolbar and drag the buttons you never use off the toolbar.

>> **Sheet tabs:** As you add new sheets to the file, tabs appear across the top, which you click to move from one sheet to another.

>> **Row numbers and column letters:** These identify each row and column in the sheet. The row numbers (1, 2, 3, and so on) are on the left, while the column letters (A, B, C, and so on) are just below the sheet tabs.

A sheet may have zero or more *tables*, which are distinct grids comprising one or more rows and one or more columns. The intersection of a row and column is a *cell*, and that's where you type and store numbers, text, and formulas, as shown in Figure 5-1. A cell has the coordinates of the column and row. For example, E4 (pointed out in Figure 5-1), is the intersection of the fifth column (E) and the fourth row (4).

Besides the mundane but fundamental cells that form the backbone of any spreadsheet, you can also place the following eye-catching (and useful) items in your sheets by clicking the buttons on the toolbar, as shown in Figure 5-2:

>> **Insert:** Add a formula or function to a cell.

>> **Table:** Insert a *table,* which consists of rows and columns that can contain words, numbers, calculated results, or a combination of these types of contents.

>> **Chart:** Insert a *chart,* which displays a visual representation of the data stored in a table. Common types of charts are line, bar, pie, and column. With Numbers, you can build two-axis and mixed charts as well as 2D, 3D, and interactive charts.

Row headings

Add a sheet   Sheet tabs   Active cell   Column headings

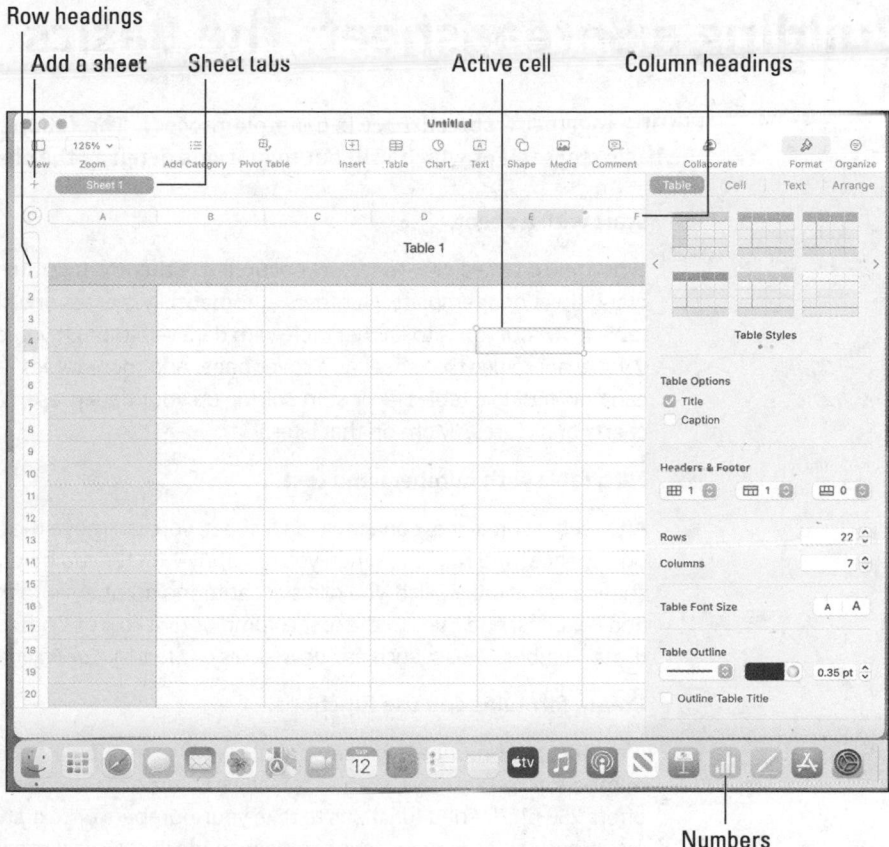

FIGURE 5-1:
The parts of a
Numbers window
and sheet.

Numbers

>> **Text:** Insert a text box, which enables you to type and store text independent of the rows and columns in a table.

>> **Shape:** Insert a shape to add pizzazz to your sheet.

>> **Media:** Insert photos, music, or movies to your sheet.

>> **Comment:** Insert a comment, which when you share your spreadsheet enables others to give you feedback without changing the sheet itself.

FIGURE 5-2:
A sheet can have
tables, charts,
text boxes, and
images.

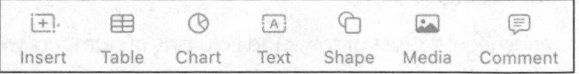

Building a Spreadsheet: The Basics

Putting together a spreadsheet is a simple process. The following list points out the basic steps (all of which I fill out in glorious detail as the chapter progresses):

1. **Start with a sheet.**

   When you create a new Numbers document, either from scratch by choosing a blank sheet or a template, Numbers automatically creates one sheet with one table in it. Your job is to fill that table with data — although you could delete it if you want to use that sheet as a cover page. Add more tables — yes, a sheet can hold multiple tables — or start spicing up your data presentation with charts or pictures. (More on that later.)

2. **Fill a table with numbers and text.**

   After setting up at least one table on a sheet, you can move the table around on the sheet and resize it. When you're happy with the table's position on the sheet and the table's size, you can start entering numbers into the table's rows and columns. Add titles to the first column or first row or both to identify what those numbers mean, such as *August Sales* or *Monthly Car Payments*.

3. **Create formulas and use functions.**

   After you enter numbers in a table, you'll want to manipulate one or more numbers in certain ways, such as totaling a column of numbers. Numbers offers 250 predefined functions to take your numbers or text and calculate a result, such as how much your company made in sales last month or how a salesperson's sales results have changed.

   REMEMBER

   You can perform calculations in Numbers in two ways: Write your own formulas or use the predefined functions, which usually require one or more variables to calculate a result. Both formulas and functions are mathematical expressions that calculate useful results. (And, just to be clear, it's fine to use one or more functions in your custom formulas.)

4. **Visualize data with charts.**

   Just glancing at a dozen numbers in a row or column might not show you much of anything. By turning numeric data into a line, bar, or pie chart, Numbers can help you spot trends in your data.

5. **Polish your sheets.**

   Most spreadsheets consist of rows and columns of numbers with a bit of descriptive text thrown in for good measure. Although functional, such spreadsheets are boring to look at. That's why Numbers also offers extensive formatting options that can make everything easier to read and more pleasant to look at.

Creating a Spreadsheet with Your Bare Hands

To help you create a spreadsheet, Numbers provides dozens of templates that you can use as-is or modify. Templates contain preset tables with formulas, which calculate the task at hand. For example, in the Personal Savings template, you enter your goal, the length of time for your investment, and the interest rate, and then the template calculates how much you have to save each month to reach your goal. Changing the values changes the results.

Templates also have predefined font styles and color schemes. You can alter anything you want in a template — tables, charts, colors — but finding a template that's close to what you want to do gives you a head start. That way, you don't have to spend time designing and can concentrate on your numbers, formulas, and other data.

TIP

If you prefer, use the Blank template to create a spreadsheet (one sheet with one table) from scratch. If you design a particularly useful spreadsheet, you can save it as a custom template (by choosing File ⇨ Save as Template).

Creating a spreadsheet with a template

To create a spreadsheet based on a template, follow these steps:

1. **Click the Numbers icon on the dock (refer to Figure 5-1), if you haven't launched the app already.**

2. **Choose File ⇨ New.**

   The Choose a Template window appears, as shown in Figure 5-3.

3. **Click a template category in the list on the left (or click All Templates if you want to see all currently available templates).**

4. **Click the template you want to use and then click Create.**

   Choose a template that's closest to what you want to do, such as a schedule or a personal budget.

   Numbers opens your chosen template.

REMEMBER

If you want to start with a blank spreadsheet, click Blank, which is the first template under Basic.

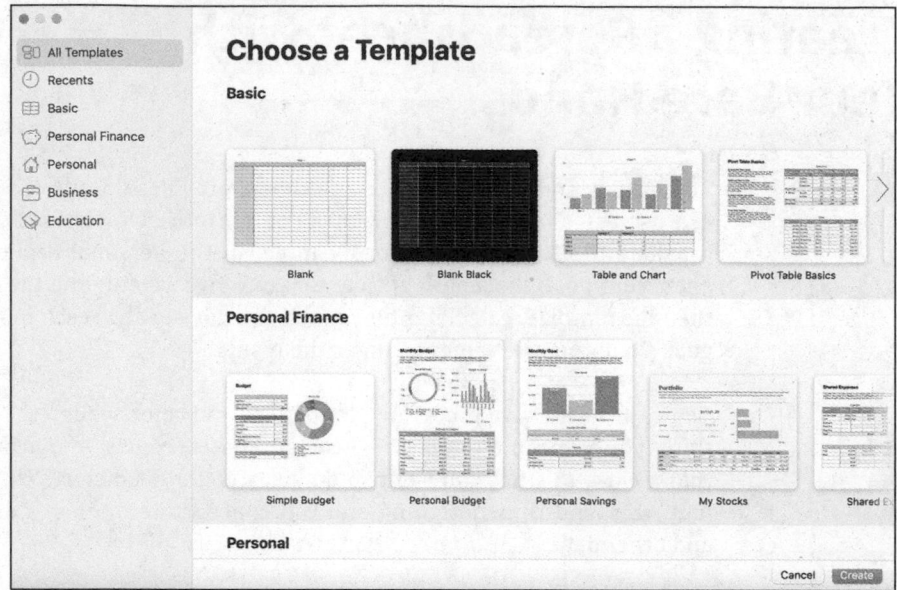

FIGURE 5-3:
Templates are organized in categories, such as Personal or Business.

5. **Choose File ➪ Save.**

   The Save As dialog opens.

6. **Type a name for your spreadsheet and save it.**

   Save the file to a folder on your Mac, to your iCloud Drive, or to the Numbers folder on your iCloud Drive.

Opening an existing file

To open a previously saved Numbers file, do one of the following:

REMEMBER

» Choose File ➪ Open, click Numbers in the iCloud section of the sidebar, click one of the documents in the list, and then click Open.

   You need an internet connection to work on iCloud Drive documents.

» Choose File ➪ Open, browse the folders on your Mac or external drive in which the document is stored, select the desired document, and then click Open.

» Choose File ➪ Open Recent and choose a file from the flyout menu.

You might have spreadsheets that were created in a different application (such as Microsoft Excel), or you may have raw data that you want to bring into Numbers (such as comma-separated value [CSV] or tab-delimited text). You can open the file in Numbers, and Numbers will create sheets and tables with the data supplied. To open a non-Numbers file, drag the file you want to open over the Numbers icon on the dock or choose File ➪ Open, select the file, and then click Open.

Messing Around with Sheets

Every Numbers spreadsheet has at least one sheet, although you can have many. A sheet acts like a (nearly) limitless page where you store the tables, charts, and other objects that your spreadsheet model requires. You want to use sheets to organize the information in your document, such as using one sheet to hold January sales results, a second sheet to hold February sales results, and a third sheet to hold a line chart that shows each salesperson's results for the first two months.

To help organize your sheets, Numbers stores their names in the tabs at the top of the sheet. Clicking the disclosure arrow on the right end of a sheet tab opens a list of all tables and charts stored on that particular sheet, along with options for copying, deleting, or renaming the sheet, as shown in Figure 5-4.

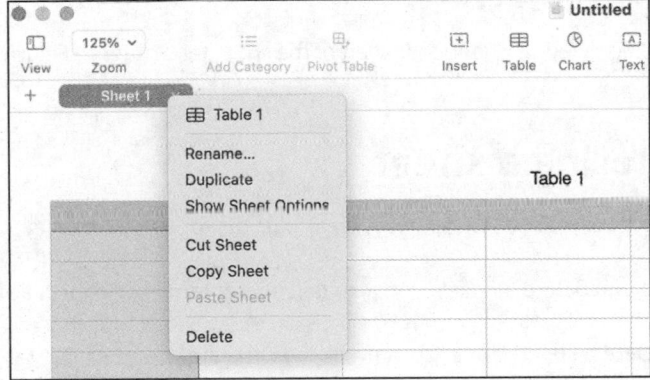

FIGURE 5-4:
View a sheet's elements.

To view the contents of a specific sheet, click that sheet's tab name in the row of tabs just below the toolbar. To view a particular table or chart, find the sheet that contains that table or chart, and then click the table or chart.

Renaming a sheet

By default, Numbers supplies sheets with unhelpful names such as Sheet 1 and Sheet 2. Your spreadsheet will be much easier to navigate if you give each sheet a descriptive name that tells you (or anyone examining your spreadsheet) what the sheet contains.

To rename a sheet, follow these steps:

1. **Move the mouse pointer over the tab of the sheet you want to rename.**

   Numbers displays the sheet's disclosure arrow on the right side of the tab.

2. **Click the disclosure arrow and then click Rename.**

   Numbers opens the sheet name for editing.

3. **Type the new sheet name.**

4. **Press Return.**

Adding a sheet

You can always add another sheet. When you add a sheet, Numbers creates one table on that sheet automatically. To add a sheet, choose one of the following:

» Choose Insert ➪ Sheet from the menu bar.

» Press Shift+⌘+N.

» Click + (add a sheet) to the left of the sheet tabs (refer to Figure 5-1).

Deleting a sheet

If you need a sheet to go away, clear out, disappear, whatever, you can delete it.

WARNING

When you delete a sheet, you also delete any tables or charts stored on that sheet.

To delete a sheet, hover the cursor over the right end of the tab for the sheet you want to delete. Click the disclosure arrow when you see it, and then choose Delete from the pop-up menu (refer to Figure 5-4).

Adding or removing a table

As I mention earlier, a sheet can hold one or more tables, and the data you put in a table can be used on its own or as the data source for a chart you add to the sheet. When you add a table, it uses the color scheme and the typefaces associated with the template you're using. But the table is empty, so you have to input the data.

To add a table, follow these steps:

1. **Click the tab for the sheet where you want to insert the table.**

2. **Click the toolbar's Table button on the toolbar and click the left and right arrows to flip through the color selection.**

3. **Click the table you want.**

   The table appears on your spreadsheet.

TIP

To remove a table, click the select table icon (labeled in Figure 5-5) and then press Delete.

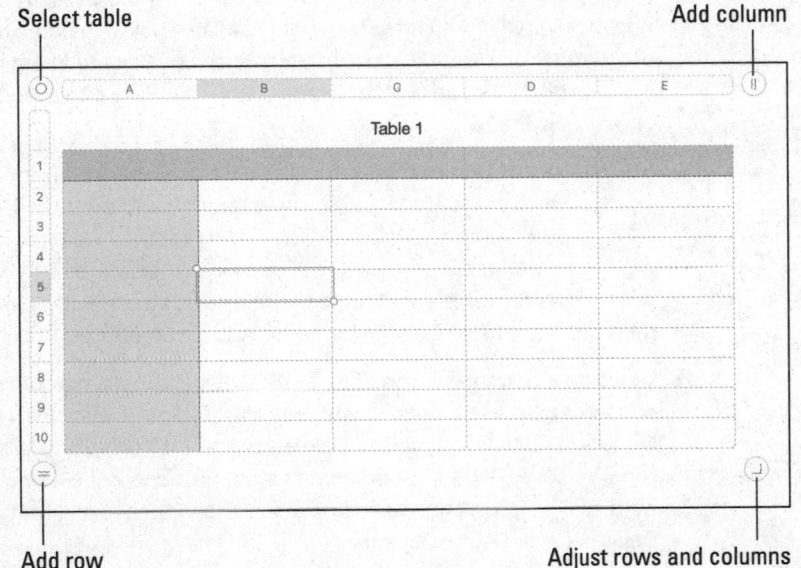

FIGURE 5-5: Click the Select Table button to, well, select the table.

Adding and removing rows and columns

You have a variety of options for adding and removing rows and columns in your table:

>> **Adding a row:** Click the add row icon (labeled in Figure 5-5) to add a row to the bottom of the table.

>> **Adding a column:** Click the add column button (labeled in Figure 5-5) to add a column to the right of the table.

>> **Adjusting the number of rows and columns simultaneously:** Click inside the table and then drag the adjust rows and columns icon (pointed out in Figure 5-5). Drag down to add rows; drag up to remove rows; drag right to add columns; and drag left to remove columns.

TIP

Click the table and then click the select table icon in the upper-left corner (pointed out in Figure 5-5). Drag the handles around the edges to resize the table. This action doesn't add rows and columns; it proportionally changes the table size.

TIP

To move a table to a new position in the sheet, click the table and then drag the select table icon until the table is where you want it.

>> **Inserting a row in the table:** Click a cell anywhere in the row above or below which you want to add the new row, and then choose either Table ➪ Add Row Above or Table ➪ Add Row Below. You can also hover the mouse pointer over the number of the row before or after which you want to insert the new row, click the disclosure arrow that appears, and then click either Add Row Above or Add Row Below.

>> **Inserting a column in the table:** Click a cell anywhere in the column before or after which you want to add the new column, and then choose either Table ➪ Add Column Before or Table ➪ Add Column After. You can also hover the mouse pointer over the letter of the column before or after which you want to insert the new column, click the disclosure arrow that appears, and then click either Add Column Before or Add Column After.

>> **Deleting a row or column:** Click a cell anywhere in the row or column you want to delete, and then choose either Table ➪ Delete Row (or press Option+⌘+Delete) or Table ➪ Delete Column (or press Shift+⌘+Delete). You can also hover the mouse pointer over the number of the row or column you want to delete, click the disclosure arrow that appears, and then click either Delete Row or Delete Column.

TIP

Delete multiple columns or rows by highlighting those column or row headings, and then choosing either Table ➪ Delete Columns or Table ➪ Delete Rows.

If you click the disclosure arrow of column A or B or row 1 or 2, you also have choices to insert header rows or columns or to convert the selected row or column into a header row or column. (See the "Inserting headers and resizing rows and columns" section for more information.)

>> **Adjusting row height:** Move the mouse pointer over the bottom edge of the row heading until the pointer becomes a double-sided arrow, and then drag the edge up (for a shorter row) or down (for a taller row). You can also click the row heading disclosure arrow and then click Fit Height to Content to adjust the height of the row to accommodate its tallest item.

>> **Adjusting column width:** Move the mouse pointer over the right edge of the column heading until the pointer becomes a double-sided arrow, and then drag the edge left (for a narrower column) or right (for a wider column). You can also click the column heading's disclosure arrow and then click Fit Width to Content to adjust the width of the column to accommodate its widest content.

Selecting table items

Before you can format anything in a Numbers table, you need to select the cells, rows, or columns you want to work with. Here are the techniques to use:

>> **Selecting cells:** Click a cell to select it; drag the mouse pointer through multiple rows or columns or both to select a range of cells; click the first cell you want to select and then hold down Shift and click the last cell of the range you want to select; or click the first cell you want to select and then hold down ⌘ and click the other cells you want in the selection.

REMEMBER

The selected cell is sometimes called the *active cell,* and Numbers marks the active cell by drawing a temporary border around it (refer to Figure 5-1). If you select a range of contiguous cells, Numbers draws a temporary border around the outer edges of the range.

>> **Selecting rows:** Click the row's number to select the entire row; drag the mouse pointer through multiple row numbers to select those rows; or select the first row you want to use, hold down ⌘, and then click the number of each of the other rows you want in the selection.

>> **Selecting columns:** Click the column's letter to select the entire column; drag the mouse pointer through multiple column letters to select those columns; or select the first column you want to use, hold down ⌘, and then click the letter of each of the other columns you want in the selection.

TIP

You can also choose Table ⇨ Select and then use the commands in the continuation menu to perform more specific selections. For example, clicking the Extend to Last Value in Column command creates a cell selection from the currently selected cell to the last occupied cell in the column.

Changing the appearance of a table

Click the toolbar's Format button to open the Format pane and see the tools you can use to edit the appearance of your table. Select the cells, rows, or columns you want to edit, and then click the tab of the Format pane corresponding to what want to change:

>> **Table:** Adjust the color, font size, grid lines, and number of header and footer cells. These changes affect the entire table.

>> **Cell:** Make changes to the cells, rows, or columns you select either singly or in multiples. Define how the data is formatted, such as currency or percentage, and assign fill and border colors and styles.

>> **Text:** Define the text color, style, and alignment of text in selected cells, rows, or columns.

>> **Arrange:** Reposition the table in relation to other objects on the sheet or align it on the sheet itself.

Inserting headers and resizing rows and columns

Headers are the first rows and columns of your table (typically row 1 and column A), where you usually type the names of the rows and columns. Footers are the final rows of the table, where you can repeat header names in particularly large tables. You can have header rows and columns that span up to five rows or columns, which is a handy way to use titles and subtitles for each row or column. Another way to insert header rows and columns is the following:

1. **Click the table, click the Format button on the toolbar, and then click the Table tab of the Format pane.**

2. **In the Headers & Footer section, use the pop-up menus to choose the number of row and column headers and column footers you want, up to five for each.**

3. **To make your header rows and columns stay put while you scroll through the rest of your table, click Freeze Header Rows/Columns in the pop-up menu.**

To insert header rows or columns after you already have data in your table, follow these steps:

1. **Click a cell in one of the header rows or columns, either before or after where you want to insert another header row or column.**

2. **Click the Table menu and choose from the following:**

   • *Add Header Row Above:* Inserts an additional header row directly above the selected cell

- *Add Header Row Below:* Inserts an additional header row directly below the selected cell

- *Add Header Column Before:* Inserts an additional header column to the left of the selected cell

- *Add Header Column After:* Inserts a new column to the right of the selected cell

To emphasize the header rows and columns and footers and make them stand out from the contents of the table, you can outline single cells — or the entire row or column — with a border or fill the cells with a background color or both. Select the cells you want to emphasize and then do the following:

1. **Click the Cell tab in the Format pane (click the Format icon on the toolbar if you don't see the Format pane).**

2. **Click the disclosure arrow next to Fill to add a background color to the headers or footers.**

   a. *If the cell is not filled, choose an option from the Color Fill pop-up such as Gradient. Choose an option from the Fill pop-up menu.* If the cell is filled with a color or gradient, go to Step b.

   b. *Click the color swatch to choose a standard color or click the button next to the swatch to open the color pickers and choose a color from the color wheel.* If the cell is filled with a gradient, you have two color swatches, one for the first color of the gradient and one for the second.

3. **Click the disclosure arrow next to Border Style and choose your border options.**

   a. *Click the Border button and choose a border style.*

      If you select one cell in the table and then choose the four-sided border, the four sides of that one cell will have the border.

      If you select several cells, and then choose the four-sided border, the border surrounds the group but the lines between the cells remain unchanged.

      If you want to add a border around all the selected cells, choose the border style that has both the outline and the inner lines emphasized.

   b. *Click the Border Styles button and choose an option from the pop-up menu.* The options in this menu determine the width and color of the border based on the table style you choose for the table.

   c. *Click the pop-up menu below the Border Styles section and change the border style from line to dash or dot.*

d. *Use the up and down arrows below the pop-up menu from Step c to change the thickness of the border.*

e. *Click the color swatch to choose a standard color or click the button next to the swatch to open the color pickers and choose a color from the color wheel.*

Populating Tables with Data

Now you get into the number–crunching part of Numbers. You need to know about the types of data you can store inside a table: numbers, text, dates, times, and formulas.

I give you details about working with each type of data in the next few sections. However, in summary, to type anything into a table, follow these steps:

1. **Select the cell in which you want to enter the data.**

You usually select a cell by clicking it. However, if the current active cell is in the same table, you can also select a cell by pressing the arrow keys.

2. **Type a number, text, a date, a time, or a formula.**

- For a number, feel free to add a currency symbol (such as $), a thousands separator (such as a comma), a percentage symbol (%), or a decimal point, as needed.

- For a date, enter the day, month, and year values using a format that's recognized where you live. In the United States, for example, you could enter a date as August 23, 2023 or 08/23/2023 (to name just two).

- For a time, enter the hour, minute, and second values using the *hh:mm:ss* format, followed optionally by AM or PM (for example, 9:15:30 AM). If you leave off the AM/PM, Numbers interprets the time using the 24-hour clock, so 9:15:30 is interpreted as 9:15:30 AM, while 21:15:30 is interpreted as 9:15:30 PM.

- For the on crafting formulas, see the section "Building formulas to calculate results," a bit later in this chapter.

3. **Press Return.**

Numbers completes your data entry and shifts the active cell to the cell below. If you'd rather complete the entry and have the active cell shift to the right, press Tab instead of Return. You can also complete the entry by pressing any arrow key (in which case the active cell shifts in the arrow direction) or you can click the cell into which you want to type the next entry.

4. **Repeat Steps 2 and 3 for each item you want to add to the table.**

TIP

When you're typing text in a cell, you occasionally need to enter that text on multiple lines. To create a new line while you're typing text in a cell, press Shift+Option+Return. As you enter new lines, the height of the cell increases to accommodate the new text.

TIP

After you complete a cell entry, you can double-click the cell to edit its contents.

Applying a data format

When you type a number in a cell, if you don't include extra features such as a currency symbol or thousands separator, the number will look plain — 74983 or 60.95. To make numbers like these easier to read and more meaningful, you should apply a data format to them. For example, the number 74,983 is easier to read than 74983. Similarly, the number 60.95 could refer to anything, but if you use a data format that makes the number appear as $60.95, your number now clearly represents a dollar amount.

Numbers comes with several predefined data formats. For example, for a currency value, you can apply the Currency data format, which enables you to specify the currency symbol, the number of decimal places, and a thousands separator. You can also create custom data formats if none of the predefined data formats is quite right for your needs.

To apply a data format to one or more cells, follow these steps:

1. **Select the cell or cells to which you want to apply the data format.**

REMEMBER

If you select empty cells, Numbers remembers the assigned data format and automatically applies that data format to entries you type in those cells in the future.

2. **Click the toolbar's Format button and then click the Cell tab of the Format pane.**

3. **Use the Data Format pop-up menu to choose how you want the data to appear, as shown in Figure 5-6.**

Each choice has options that appear in the Format pane:

- The numeric choices have submenus with further choices, such as how many decimals or the currency symbol.

- When cells are formatted as Text, numbers have no numeric values. This option is useful for typing zip codes and phone numbers.

- The Date & Time and Duration choices offer formatting options such as spelling out the month or using a number.

Crunching with Numbers

- The next set of choices — from Checkbox down to Pop-up Menu — are neither numeric nor text but instead let you create data-entry cells that require an action, such as clicking to place a check mark in the box, or limit your choices, such as a pop-up menu.

- To define your own data format, click Create Custom Format and use the dialog that pops up to enter a data format name, the data type (Number, Date & Time, or Text), and the custom format (the specifics of which depend on the data type).

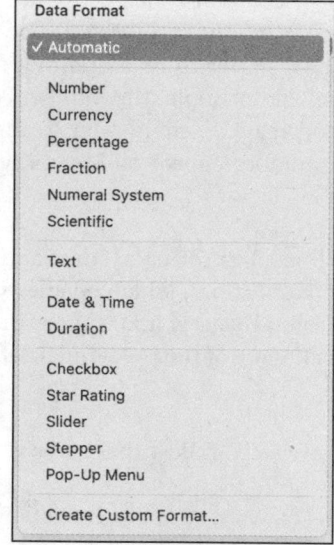

Formatting table data

You can make your tables easier to read and more eye-catching by applying formatting — including colors, backgrounds, borders, and fonts — to the cells.

To format one or more cells, follow these steps:

1. **Select the cell or cells you want to format.**

REMEMBER

If you select empty cells, Numbers remembers the assigned formatting and automatically formats any data you enter in those cells in the future.

2. **Click the toolbar's Format button to open the Format pane.**

3. **Click the Cell tab.**

4. **To add a background color or border or both to your cells, use the Fill and Border options (click the Fill disclosure arrow to see the background color options). Choose the options you want from the pop-up menus, as shown in Figure 5-7.**

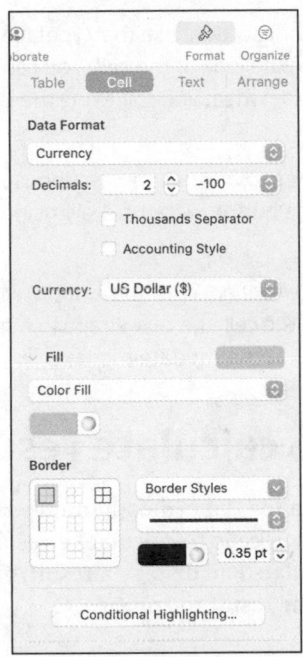

FIGURE 5-7:
Add background colors and borders to cells.

The cells automatically change as you try different effects:

- *Fill* puts a color, a gradient, or an image behind characters typed in the cell. Depending on the choice, you're presented with tools for choosing the color, the spectrum and direction (gradient), and scaling (image).

- *Border* surrounds your cell(s) with a line; define the width and color and choose whether you want a border around each cell or around the group of cells or only on one side or in between.

- In either section, use the colors icon — which consists of a solid color block and a color wheel — to change the color of the fill or border. Clicking the solid color block opens a drop-down palette that displays colors used in the theme; clicking the color wheel opens a Color window that offers several methods to specify a custom color.

5. **To format the style of the characters in the selected cell(s) — whether they're formatted as numbers, text, or data entry — click the Text tab in the Format pane and then the Style button. Then do the following:**

- *To use a different font in the theme:* Click the Paragraph Styles menu and choose a different font.

- *To change the font style:* In the Font section, use the Typeface, Size, and Style menus and buttons to fine-tune the look of the cell. You can also change the font color by clicking the color wheel and following the steps mentioned previously.

- *To choose how you want your text to appear in the cell:* Choose an option from the alignment buttons. The button with the A aligns numbers to the right and text to the left.

- *Accept the default Wrap Text in Cell option.* With this option, when the text you enter exceeds the width of the cell, the text wraps to a new line and the height of the cell changes to accommodate the text.

Building formulas to calculate results

The main purpose of a table is to use the data (mostly numbers, but also sometimes text, dates, or times) you store in cells to calculate a result, such as adding a row or column of numbers. To calculate and display a result, you need to store a formula in the cell where you want the result to appear.

Numbers provides three ways to create a formula in a cell:

>> Using the Quick Formula feature

>> Typing the formula directly in the cell

>> Using one of Numbers' predefined functions

Using Quick Formula

To help you calculate results in a hurry, the Quick Formula feature offers a variety of formulas that can perform common calculations. Given a range of cells with numeric values, the following Quick Formula calculations are available:

>> **Sum:** Adds the numbers

>> **Average:** Calculates the arithmetic mean of the numbers

>> **Minimum:** Displays the smallest of the numbers

>> **Maximum:** Displays the largest of the numbers

>> **Count:** Displays the number of cells (applies to any data type, not just numbers)

>> **Product:** Multiplies the numbers

To use a Quick Formula, follow these steps:

1. **Click the empty cell at the bottom or to the right of cells that contain the numbers you want to work with.**

2. **Choose Insert ⇨ Formula.**

3. **From the flyout menu, choose Sum, Average, Minimum, Maximum, Count, or Product.**

   Numbers displays the result in the cell you selected in Step 1.

Typing a formula

Quick Formula is handy when it offers the formula you need, such as when you add rows or columns of numbers with the Sum calculation. Often, however, you need to create your own formula.

Every formula consists of three parts:

>> **Equal sign (=):** Always appears at the start of the formula; it tells Numbers to treat what follows as a formula.

>> **Operands:** Specifies the input values that the formula uses for its calculations. An operand can be any of the following:

- *Literal value:* A number, date, time, or text value.

- *Cell reference:* The address of a single cell, such as A1 or D10.

- *Range reference:* The coordinates of a group of contiguous cells. A range reference uses the format *UL:LR,* where *UL* is the cell address of the upper-left corner of the range and *LR* is the cell address of the lower-right corner of the range. A1:D10 and C5:C100 are examples of range references.

- *Function:* A predefined Numbers function and any arguments it requires. Numbers uses the function result in the formula.

>> **Operators:** Tells Numbers which operations the formula should perform on the operands. For example, the arithmetic operators are addition (+), subtraction (–), multiplication (*), and division (/).

A typical formula looks like this:

```
=A3 * 0.08
```

This formula tells Numbers to take the number stored in cell A3 and multiply it by the literal value 0.08 (this might be a sales tax calculation, for example).

To build a formula, follow these steps:

1. **Click (or use the arrow keys to highlight) the cell where you want the formula results to appear.**

2. **Type =.**

   The formula editor appears over the selected cell, as shown in Figure 5-8.

   TIP

   You can move the formula editor if you move the pointer to the left end of the formula editor. When the pointer turns into a hand, drag the formula editor to a new location so it doesn't hide the cell you're working on.

Accept changes and close

Cancel changes and close

	A	B	C	D	
		Product Inventory			
1	Product	Cost Price	Inventory	Total Cost	
2	Northwind Traders Chai	13.50	· f_x ~		⊗ ⊘
3	Northwind Traders Syrup	7.50	50		
4	Northwind Traders Cajun Seasoning	16.50	0		
5	Northwind Traders Olive Oil	16.01	15		
6	Northwind Traders Boysenberry Spread	18.75	24		
7	Northwind Traders Marmalade	60.75	8		
8	Northwind Traders Dried Pears	22.50	32		
9	Northwind Traders Curry Sauce	30.00	30		
10	Northwind Traders Walnuts	17.44	40		

FIGURE 5-8:
When you start a formula by typing =, Numbers instantly displays the formula editor pop-up over the cell.

3. **Enter an operand.**

   For example, if the operand is a cell, you can click that cell and Numbers automatically adds the cell reference to your formula. In most cases Numbers enters a descriptive cell reference based on the text at the top row and first column of the table. For example, if I were to click cell B2 in Figure 5-8, Numbers would enter Cost Price Northwind Traders Chai into the formula. If your sheet doesn't include column or row titles, Numbers enters the cell address (such as B2).

Selecting a range of contiguous cells automatically adds that range reference to the formula.

TIP

4. **Type an operator, such as * for multiplication or / for division.**

For easier formula reading, it's common to add a space between each operand and operator. Numbers ignores the spaces when calculating the formula result.

TIP

If your formula entirely (or mostly) involves adding cell values, a fast way to build the formula is to enter those values by clicking each cell in turn. As you click, Numbers automatically adds an addition operator (+) between each cell reference.

5. **Repeat Steps 3 and 4 until your formula is complete.**

6. **When you're done, click the green check mark (accept changes and close), labeled in Figure 5-8).**

Numbers displays the formula result in the cell. To see the formula itself, select the cell and examine the formula bar that appears at the bottom of the Numbers window.

TIP

For a fast way to calculate values without having to type a formula in a cell, use instant calculations. Select two or more cells that contain numbers, and you can see the results in the instant calculations results along the bottom of the Numbers window, as shown in Figure 5-9. You can change the types of results you see in the instant calculations results by clicking the gear icon in the bottom right and then selecting the functions you want to see from the pop-up menu.

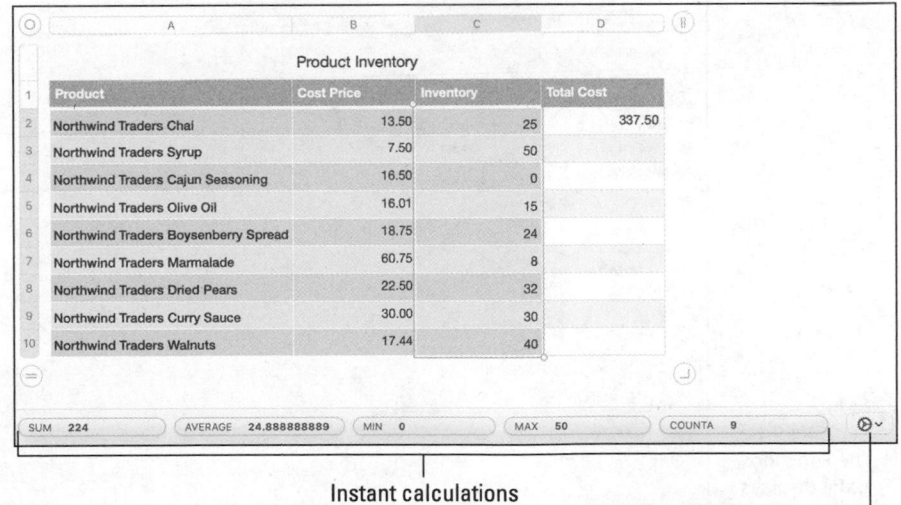

Crunching with Numbers

FIGURE 5-9:
Instant calculations can show results without typing a formula first.

Instant calculations

Choose which functions to show

Using functions

Typing simple formulas that add or multiply is relatively straightforward. However, many calculations can get more complicated, such as trying to calculate the amount of interest paid on a loan with a specific interest rate over a defined period.

To help you add many commonly used calculations to your formulas, Numbers provides a library of 250 *functions*, which are prebuilt formulas that you can plug into your table and then define what data to use.

To use a function, follow these steps:

1. **Click (or use the arrow keys to highlight) the cell where you want the function results to appear.**

REMEMBER

Most functions calculate their results by using one or more input values called *arguments*. You can insert an argument directly into a function as a literal value, but most of the time the argument values will be in other cells of the table, in which case you enter the cell addresses as the function arguments. Therefore, to ensure that your function returns a correct result, make sure you've entered all required values in your table.

2. **Press the equal sign (=) key.**

The formula editor appears, and the Functions pane opens, as shown in Figure 5-10.

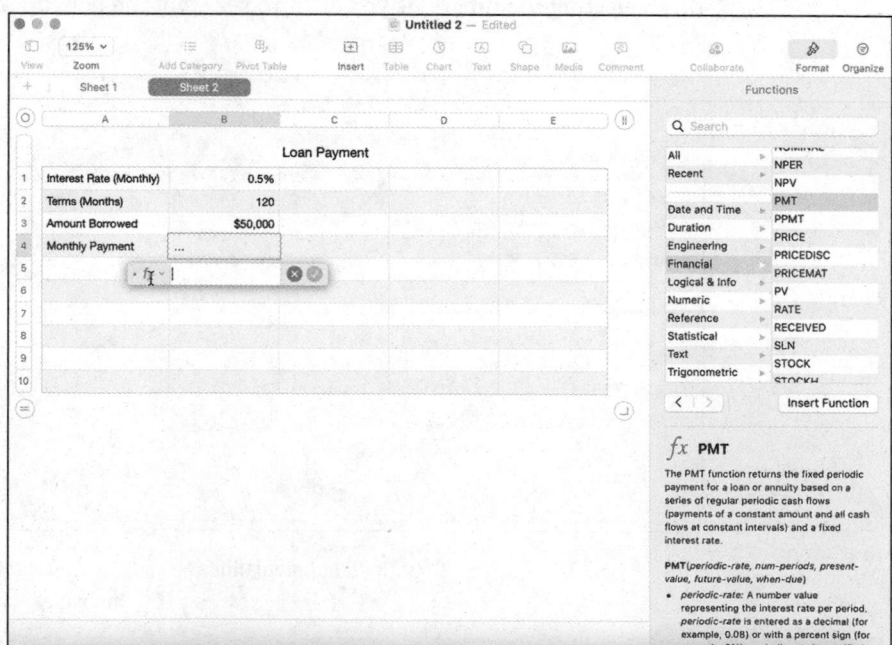

FIGURE 5-10: The Functions pane displays all available functions in Numbers.

3. **Choose the type of function you want from the left column (or click All), and then scroll through the functions on the right and click the one you want to insert.**

A definition for the selected function is shown at the bottom of the pane, along with an explanation of the types of data needed to complete the operation and an example of how it works.

4. **Click the Insert Function button.**

The formula editor now contains your chosen function and you see a placeholder for each function argument.

5. **For each placeholder, click the placeholder name, and then either type a literal value or click the cell you want to use as the argument value.**

TIP

Placeholders that have a dark gray background indicate required arguments, so you must enter a value for those placeholders. Placeholders that have a light gray background indicate optional arguments.

Figure 5-11 shows the PMT function in the process of being added to cell B4. The first three arguments are required and so have been filled in with the cell addresses B1, B2, and B3. The final two arguments are optional and can be ignored.

6. **Fill in the rest of your formula, as needed.**

7. **Click the green check mark (accept changes and close).**

Numbers shows your formula result in the cell.

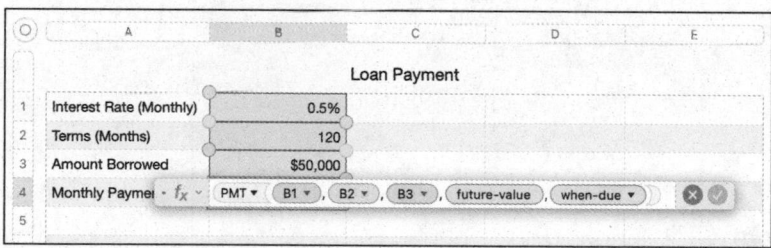

FIGURE 5-11:
The PMT function being added to cell B4.

REMEMBER

When you're dealing with financial values, amounts that you pay out (such as a monthly loan payment) are negative values, while amounts you receive (such as the loan principal) are positive values.

Conditionally formatting data-entry cells

You can set a *conditional highlight* so that if your data meets a certain criterion or condition, Numbers will highlight the number or text in a color you want. Say you create a spreadsheet to track office supply inventory, and you want to know when you have fewer than five black pens. Set the conditional formatting of the cell to "less than or equal to 5." Then, when there are five or fewer pens, the cell changes color. Now, at a glance, you see pertinent information. To use conditional formatting, follow these steps:

1. **Select the cell(s) where you want to use conditional formatting.**

2. **Click the Format button on the toolbar, and then click the Cell tab of the Format pane.**

3. **Click the Conditional Highlighting button at the bottom of the pane.**

   You may have to scroll to find it.

4. **Click the Add a Rule button.**

   The Choose a Rule window opens, as shown in Figure 5-12.

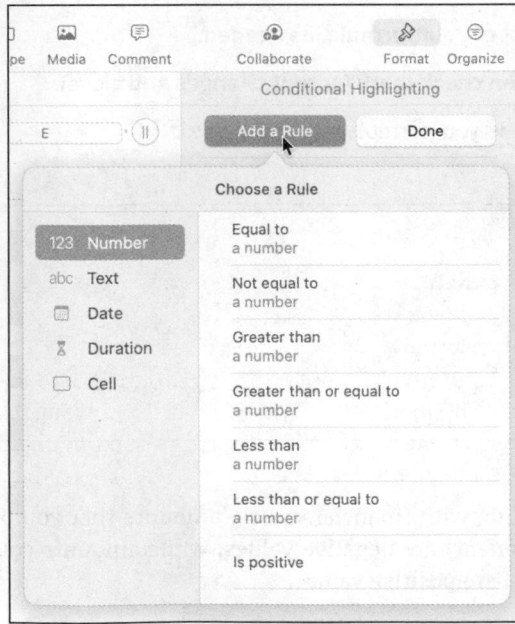

FIGURE 5-12:
You set up conditional formatting by adding rules that define when Numbers highlights the cells.

5. On the left side of the window, click a rule category that corresponds to the type of data you're working with (such as Number or Text).

Numbers displays a list of the available rules in that category.

6. Click the rule you want to use.

A field appears where you can type a value.

- *If you want to refer to another cell:* Click the oval button on the right end of the field and type a cell reference. Or click the cell in your sheet, and its reference appears in the field.

- *To change the value:* Click in the field and press the Delete key, and then type another value or enter a different cell reference.

7. Click the pop-up menu to format how you want the data highlighted.

The sample box shows how the cell will appear if the data in it meets the conditional rule you set.

8. (Optional) To add another rule, repeat Steps 4–6.

9. (Optional) To delete a rule, click the trash icon to the right of the rule name.

10. (Optional) To rearrange the order of the rules, hover the cursor to the left of the rule name and click and drag the rearrange icon (three horizontal lines).

11. Click Done.

Sorting data

When you enter your data, you don't always do so in the order you want to see it. For example, to track invoices, you create a column for each piece of data, such as invoice number, date of purchase, customer name, and total, and then you enter the data from a stack of invoices so each row holds the data for one invoice. You might enter the data by invoice number first but then want to sort by customer name to see which customers have more than one outstanding invoice or by total to see who spent the most. You can sort the data by one of those columns in two ways:

» **Ascending:** Sorts letters from A to Z, numbers from 0 to 9, and dates and times from earliest to latest.

» **Descending:** Sorts letters from Z to A, numbers from 9 to 0, and dates and times from latest to earliest.

Here's how you sort data:

1. **Click anywhere inside the table you want to sort or select a group of cells you want to sort.**

2. **Hover the cursor over the letter of the column that you want to use as the basis of the sort.**

   A drop-down arrow appears to the right of the column letter.

3. **Click the drop-down arrow to open the pop-up menu.**

4. **Select Sort Ascending or Sort Descending to establish the order in which you want the data.**

   Numbers will sort your data by the column you chose.

TIP

By default, Numbers sorts the entire table when you sort a column. To choose different sort options, click the Organize button on the toolbar to display the Organize pane, and then click the Sort tab. (You can also click any column letter's drop-down arrow and then click Show Sort Options.) From here, you can choose to sort only selected rows, add a column, sort by categories, and so on. The available options differ depending on the content of your table.

Deleting data

If you ever want to delete data in a cell, you can do so in two ways:

» Delete data but retain any formatting you've applied to the cell.

» Delete both the cell's data and its formatting.

To delete data but retain any applied formatting, follow these steps:

1. **Select one or more cells that contain the data you want to delete.**

2. **Press Delete or choose Edit ⇨ Delete from the menu bar.**

To delete both data and formatting in cells, follow these steps:

1. **Select one or more cells that contain data and formatting you want to delete.**

2. **Choose Edit ⇨ Clear All from the menu bar.**

Visualizing data with a chart

A *chart* is a graphical representation of the data in a table. Before you add a chart to your sheet, create a table and enter the data you want the chart to represent. Then, do the following:

1. **On the table where you input the data for your chart, select the data, including row and column headers.**

2. **Click the toolbar's Chart button.**

You can also choose Insert ⇨ Chart and then skip to Step 5.

3. **Click a tab for the type of chart you want: 2D, 3D, or Interactive.**

4. **Click the left and right arrows to flip through the color selection.**

5. **Click the chart you want.**

The chart with your data appears on your sheet.

If the data is on one sheet but you want to place the chart on another sheet, do the following (you can use these steps also to create charts on the same sheet, if you want):

1. **Click that sheet where you want to place the chart.**

2. **Insert an empty chart:**

- *Click the toolbar's Chart button and then click the chart you want.*

- *Choose Insert ⇨ Chart and then click the chart you want.*

3. **Click Edit Data References at the bottom of the chart.**

4. **Click the sheet that holds the data.**

5. **Select the cells, including row and column headers, containing the data you want in the chart.**

6. **Click the Done button in the lower-right corner of the Numbers window.**

The data selected from the table flows into the chart on the other sheet.

TIP

Interactive charts are created the same way as 2D or 3D charts. Here's the difference. Rather than displaying, for example, eight columns that represent two types of data for four months, you see two columns at a time, and clicking the playback arrows animates the data.

After you have a chart added to a sheet, Numbers offers quite a few options for customizing and formatting the chart to your liking. Click the chart to select it, click the toolbar's Format button, and then go through the tabs of the Format pane to edit the appearance and position of the chart and data:

» **Chart** gives you tools for changing the colors and fonts of the chart, as well as adding special effects such as shadow or opacity, a title, and a legend. At the bottom of the panel is the Chart Type menu. Click it to change to a different type of chart; any data you entered will appear in the new chart type.

» **Axis** (all but pie charts) lets you name the axes and change the scale. Here you also find the menus for defining the value labels with percentage, currency, or others.

» **Series** (all but pie charts) offers menus for naming value labels.

» **Wedges** (only pie charts) shows check boxes and menus for adding labels and defining the value data format. With the slider bars, you can move the labels off the chart itself and separate the pieces of the pie by setting a greater distance from the center.

» **Arrange** lets you reposition the chart in relation to other objects on the slide or align it on the sheet itself. This doesn't change parts of the chart.

» **Axis/Wedge Labels** lets you can define the label (number, percentage, and so on) and also change the font family, size, style, and color. Double-click any text on the chart, and the Axis or Wedge Labels tab appears in the Format pane.

Renaming tables and charts

Numbers gives each table and chart a generic name, such as Table 1 or Chart 3. To help you better understand the type of information stored on each sheet, use more descriptive names, especially when adding multiple tables and charts. The table and chart names appear when you click the drop-down arrow on the sheet tab.

Before you rename a table or chart, make sure that Numbers is displaying the table or chart title:

» **Table:** Click inside the table, click the toolbar's Format button, click the Table tab, and then select the Title check box.

» **Chart:** Click inside the chart, click the toolbar's Format button, click the Chart tab, and then select the Title check box.

To rename a table or chart, double-click the title placeholder text to open the text for editing, then type a new name for the table or chart.

Sharing Your Spreadsheet

You put a lot of effort into making your spreadsheet presentable. When you're ready to present it, you can share your spreadsheet with others by exporting it or by using your Mac's standard-issue share options.

Exporting a spreadsheet

When you choose File ⇨ Save, Numbers saves your spreadsheet in its own proprietary file format. If you want to share your spreadsheets with others who don't have Numbers, export your spreadsheet into another file format by following these steps:

1. **Choose File ⇨ Export To.**

Numbers displays a continuation menu.

2. **Click one of the following formats:**

- *PDF:* Saves your spreadsheet as a series of static pages stored in the Adobe Acrobat Portable Document Format (PDF) that can be viewed by any computer with a PDF-viewing application.

- *Excel:* Saves your spreadsheet as a Microsoft Excel file, which can be opened and edited by any spreadsheet app that can read and edit Microsoft Excel files.

- *CSV:* Saves your spreadsheet in comma-separated value (CSV) format, which is a universal format that preserves only data but not the charts or pictures you've stored on your spreadsheet.

- *TSV:* Saves your spreadsheet in tab-separated value (TSV) format, which saves data in a tabular structure that can be interpreted by spreadsheet applications that can reconstruct a spreadsheet using tab-separated values.

- *Numbers '09:* Saves your spreadsheet as a file compatible with the version of Numbers released in 2009 (as well as earlier versions).

REMEMBER

The PDF file format preserves formatting 100 percent, but you need extra software to edit it. Generally, if someone needs to edit your spreadsheet and doesn't use Numbers, choose File ⇨ Export To ⇨ Excel. The CSV option is useful only for transferring your data to another application that can't read Excel files.

Numbers opens the Export Your Spreadsheet dialog and displays the tab for the format you chose. If you want, you can switch to another format by clicking the corresponding tab.

3. **Select the data format options, which vary depending on the selected format.**

   For example, if you're exporting to an Excel file, you can choose whether Numbers creates an Excel worksheet for each sheet in your Numbers file or for each table.

4. **If you want to add a password to open the document, select the Require Password to Open check box (all except CSV).**

5. **Click Next.**

   A chooser dialog appears, where you enter a name and specify a location to save your exported spreadsheet.

6. **In the Save As text box, enter a name for your exported spreadsheet.**

7. **Click the folder where you want to store your spreadsheet.**

8. **Click Export.**

REMEMBER

When you export a spreadsheet, your original Numbers spreadsheet remains untouched in its original location.

Sharing files directly from Numbers

You have two more ways to share your spreadsheet:

» **Upload the spreadsheet to iCloud.com and then share the link.** When you share the link, anyone who opens it can make changes to it, and those changes will sync to your Mac and iOS devices that access the spreadsheet.

» **Share the spreadsheet file itself (say, via email).**

Either way, when you share the link or spreadsheet, all the sheets contained in the spreadsheet are included.

Here's how you can share your presentation:

1. **Choose Share ➪ Send a Copy, and then choose one of the following options from the flyout menu:**

   - *Mail:* Send a copy of your spreadsheet via email.

   - *Messages:* Send a copy of your spreadsheet via Messages.

   - *AirDrop:* Send a copy of your spreadsheet via AirDrop.

All these choices open a dialog that lets you send the spreadsheet as a Numbers file or as a PDF, Excel, CSV, or TSV file.

2. **Choose the tab of the file type you want to use for the shared document.**

3. **Select the data format options, which vary depending on the selected format.**

4. **Click Next.**

   The file is converted if you chose an option other than Numbers.

5. **Type the address(es) to which you want to send the spreadsheet, and then click Send.**

   For AirDrop, a file is created that other people on your local network with Macs using AirDrop can see and access. See Book 3, Chapter 4 to learn more about AirDrop.

REMEMBER

You can use Numbers also to collaborate with others, a task I show you in Book 5, Chapter 6.

IN THIS CHAPTER

» **Collaborating with others on a document**

» **Inserting photos, movies, and music in your documents**

» **Copying and pasting into your documents**

» **Editing photos**

» **Making comments in your documents**

» **Tracking down third-party templates**

Chapter **6**

Getting More Out of Pages, Keynote, and Numbers

One of the traits that makes Apple's flagship productivity applications — Pages, Keynote, and Numbers — so attractive (besides coming free with your Mac!) is their long list of similarities. From the way the windows are arranged to the way the menus are organized to the large collection of shared tools, once you've worked with one of these apps, getting up to speed on the others is much easier.

I talk about some of these shared features in the past three chapters, but this chapter is devoted to a few tools and techniques common to all three apps. In the pages that follow, you explore quite a few useful features that work the same whether you're writing a résumé in Pages, preparing a presentation in Keynote, or building a budget in Numbers. These features include collaborating with other folks on a document; adding pictures, audio, and video to a document; the basics of copying and pasting stuff; some useful photo-editing techniques; adding comments to a document; and finding interesting and useful document templates online.

Collaborating with Colleagues

In today's team-oriented business world, most documents of any import are the products of multiple hands. One person might create a document, but then lots of people get their proverbial two cents in by making actual or suggested edits to improve (you hope!) the document.

In the past, getting others to work on your document often involved sharing a copy of the document via email. Unfortunately, if you sent the document to six people, you got back six different versions with six different edits or suggestions and you had to then spend an inordinate amount of time incorporating those edits and suggestions into the original. Too much work!

The collaboration process is similar to (and simpler than) other collaboration processes you may have encountered. The basic process follows:

1. You *create* a document.

2. Using your internet connection, you *invite* one or more other people to collaborate on the document.

3. You or any of your invitees *edit* the document, and the others see those changes.

That's the basic outline.

REMEMBER

To set up a document for collaboration, you must have an internet connection and an iCloud account. The person you're sharing with doesn't need iCloud or even a Mac for basic viewing and some editing of the document, but an internet connection is a must.

As you see in the following steps, you can use some additional options, but "create, invite, edit" is the basic process. Here are the details:

1. **In Pages, Keynote, and Numbers, create or open the document on which you want to collaborate with others.**

2. Click the toolbar's Collaborate button.

If your document isn't already in iCloud, a dialog shows up to prompt you to move it there. If you don't see this dialog (because your document already resides in iCloud), skip to Step 4.

3. Click Move to iCloud.

The Share File dialog appears, as shown in Figure 6-1.

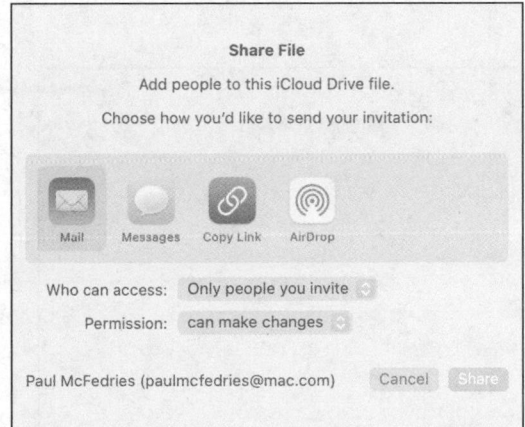

FIGURE 6-1:
Use the Share File dialog to specify how you want to send your invitation.

4. Click the method you want to use to invite your collaborators:

- *Mail:* Sends the invite in an email message
- *Messages:* Sends the invite in a text message
- *Copy Link:* Copies the share link so that you can paste it elsewhere, such as in a blog or social media post
- *AirDrop:* Sends the invite wirelessly to another Mac user or someone who's using an iOS device

The following steps assume that you clicked Mail to invite collaborators via email.

5. Use the Who Can Access pop-up menu to determine who can access the shared document.

If you choose Only People You Invite, just your invitees are allowed to access the online document. If, instead, you choose Anyone with the Link, anyone who loads the document's online address in their web browser can access the document. Choose Anyone with the Link if you want to enable your invitees to invite others by sharing the link.

6. **Use the Permission pop-up menu to determine what your collaborators can do with the shared document.**

Select Can Make Changes if you want your collaborators to be able to edit the document and make other changes; select Can View Only if you don't want your collaborators to edit the document.

7. **Click Share.**

A Mail window opens where the title of your document is the subject and the message body includes a link to the document, as shown in Figure 6-2.

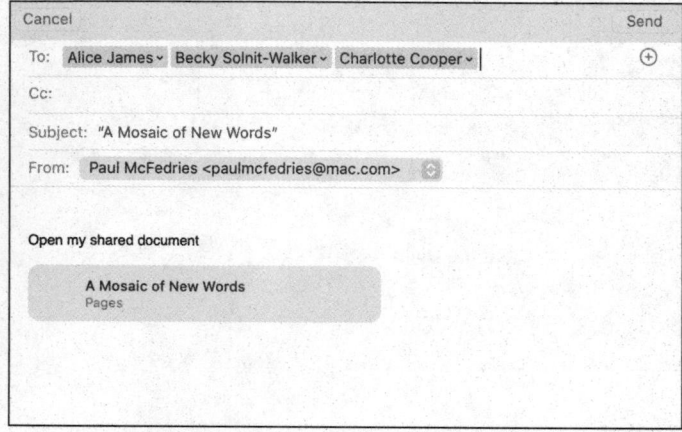

FIGURE 6-2: Sending the document to your collaborators.

8. **Add the email address of each person that you want to collaborate on the document, and then click Send.**

Your invitation is sent and you're returned to the document, where you now see *Shared* to the right of the document name.

When a collaborator receives an invitation, they click the document link to open the document in iCloud using the online version of the document's native app (Pages, Keynote, or Numbers). If you gave the collaborator permission to make changes, an invitee can then make whatever edits and other changes they see fit. When that person saves the document, it's saved to iCloud with their changes. The next time you or another collaborator opens the document, the changes made by the first collaborator are there to behold. For Numbers or Pages, if someone else is currently working on the document, you see an extra cursor for that person, which will move as that person moves around the document. You'll even see that person's changes (assuming they have the requisite permission) in real time. In Numbers, you can see who's with you in the file by hovering the mouse pointer over the cursor until the person's name appears in a pop-up banner.

As the document owner, you can choose File ⇨ Revert To ⇨ Browse All Versions to see all versions of the document tiled in a manner similar to viewing a Time Machine backup. You can click through the versions, download and view them, and if desired, restore the document to a previous version.

Inserting Media from Other Sources

Because documents are often shared electronically and viewed on a computer, media can be a fun — and informative — addition to any kind of document. A song might seem an odd addition to a spreadsheet, but a sound effect that screams "Wow!" when sales totals are over the top can be a way to compliment your sales team. I show you how to insert photos, movies, and music from Music and Photos into your newsletters, presentations, and spreadsheets in Book 5, Chapters 3, 4, and 5, respectively, but you can also add media from other sources by following these steps:

1. **In any of the Apple apps — Pages, Keynote, or Numbers — choose Insert ⇨ Choose.**

   A file chooser dialog opens.

2. **Browse the directories and folders until you find the file you want to insert.**

   If the file is on a flash drive or another external drive, click that drive in the Devices section to see files stored there.

3. **Select the file.**

4. **Click Insert.**

   The media file is inserted in your document.

REMEMBER

Audio and video can be truly appreciated only in electronically distributed documents — they don't do much for printed matter.

TIP

You can insert a supported file also by opening an Apple application such as Photos or Music on the same desktop where you're working on Pages, Keynote, or Numbers, dragging a supported file such as an image or audio file, and dropping it into Pages, Keynote, or Numbers.

Copying and Pasting

Two of the most helpful functions when working with documents on computers are copy and paste. In Pages, Keynote, or Numbers, you can copy just about any text, image, object, table, or chart and then paste it somewhere else in the same document, in a new document in the same app, or in a different app. Here are the few simple steps it takes:

1. **Click the item you want to copy.**

2. **Choose Edit ⇨ Copy or press ⌘+C.**

3. **Go to the place you want to insert the item you copied.**

4. **Choose Edit ⇨ Paste or press ⌘+V.**

TIP

- If the item you copied is formatted, choose Edit ⇨ Paste and Match Style.

- If you copied cells from Numbers that contain formulas, choose Edit ⇨ Paste Formula Results to paste the results instead of the formulas.

Modifying Photos

Pages, Keynote, Numbers, and Preview provide some quick and easy ways to modify the appearance of a photo:

» **Masking:** Masking lets you display just a portion of an image, such as an oval or star-shaped area. Masking hides the other parts of the image; if you unmask an image, you see the whole thing again. This process is different from cropping, which cuts off the portion of the image you don't want.

» **Instant Alpha:** Instant Alpha lets you make part of an image transparent, enabling the background of your document to show through.

» **Adjust image:** You can adjust contrast, exposure, and sharpness to make a photo look its best.

Masking a photo

A mask acts like a cookie cutter that you plop over a photo to save anything inside the cookie-cutter shape but hide anything outside the shape. Pages, Keynote, and Numbers provide a variety of shaped masks, such as ovals, stars, arrows, and triangles. For example, in your school newspaper you could put the face of a sports winner in a star shape.

To apply a mask to a photo, follow these steps:

1. **Click the photo you want to mask.**

2. **Choose Format ⇨ Image ⇨ Mask with Shape, and then choose a shape from the flyout menu, such as Oval, Diamond, or Star.**

   You can also click the toolbar's Format button, click the Image tab, and then click Edit Mask.

   Your chosen mask appears over your photo, as shown in Figure 6-3 (which demonstrates the oval shape). The parts of the image outside the mask are dimmed. An editing tool appears at the bottom of the image.

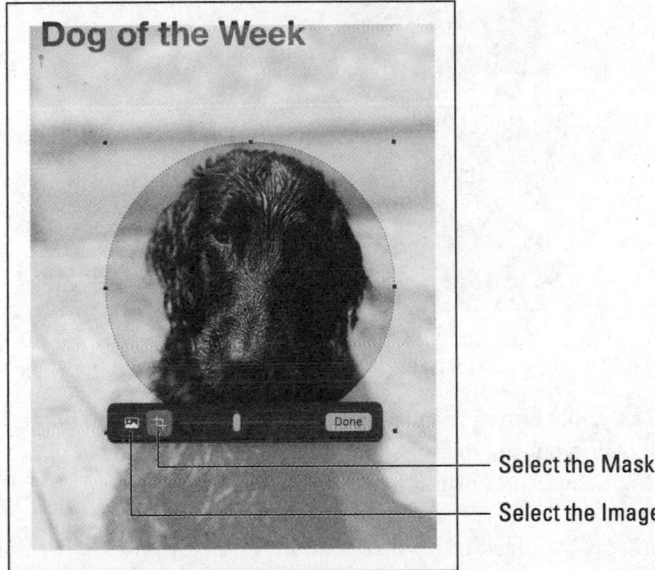

FIGURE 6-3:
Use a mask to save a portion of a photo.

Select the Mask

Select the Image

3. **(Optional) Resize the photo or the mask or both.**

   - *Photo:* Click the select the image icon (labeled in Figure 6-3) on the editing tool and then resize the photo with the slider or the photo's sizing handles.

   - *Mask:* Click the select the mask icon (labeled in Figure 6-3) on the editing tool to resize the mask with the mask's sizing handles.

   Holding down the Shift key while dragging a mask handle retains the mask's aspect ratio (that is, the ratio of width to height). You can also hold down the Option key and drag a mask handle to resize the mask from the center point.

TIP

4. **To choose which part of the picture appears within the mask, drag the image until the part you want to show is inside the mask.**

TIP

You move the photo to position it within the mask: You don't move the mask over the photo.

5. **Click the Done button or click outside the image.**

The mask is applied to your photo, as shown in Figure 6-4.

Dog of the Week

FIGURE 6-4:
View the masked photo.

WARNING

You can apply only one mask at a time to a photo. If you want to apply a different mask over a photo, you must remove the first mask by clicking the masked photo and then choosing Format ⇨ Image ⇨ Reset Mask.

TIP

If you apply a mask to an image and are not satisfied with the results, click the masked photo and then choose Format ⇨ Image ⇨ Edit Mask.

Making parts of a photo transparent

With the Instant Alpha feature, you can create interesting visual effects by turning one or more regions of a photo transparent so that the document background shows through. This process differs from cropping, which is when you lop off unwanted portions of the photo.

To make one or more regions of a photo transparent, follow these steps:

1. **Click the photo you want to modify.**

2. **Choose Format ⇨ Image ⇨ Instant Alpha from the menu bar.**

You can also click the toolbar's Format button, click the Image tab, and then click Instant Alpha.

A dialog appears over your photo, telling you how to use the Instant Alpha feature, as shown in Figure 6-5. In this example, text (the document's title and subtitle) is behind the upper-right corner of the photo. I want to use Instant Alpha to make the sky transparent and allow the text to show through.

Click a color to make it transparent.
Drag to make similar colors transparent.   Reset   Done

FIGURE 6-5:
A photo ready for the Instant Alpha treatment.

3. **Specify the region of the image that you want to make transparent:**

   - *If the region is a solid color:* Click anywhere within that region.

   - *If the region is a gradient of very similar colors (such as the sky in the photo shown in Figure 6-5):* Position the mouse pointer within the region, drag the pointer through the gradient, and then release when Instant Alpha selects the entire region.

   Instant Alpha turns the selected region transparent.

4. **Repeat Step 3 until you've added transparency to all the regions you want to hide.**

TECHNICAL STUFF

A common use of Instant Alpha is to eliminate a background and make the main subject stand out, maybe even then paste it over a different background. Instant Alpha uses color to identify the part you want to eliminate, so when you're dealing with a color gradient, you may have to do Step 3 more than once to eliminate more parts. Instant Alpha highlights all parts of your photo that are similar in color to the area that you're dragging across.

5. **Click Done to save the changes.**

    Instant Alpha makes the selected regions transparent and the underlying document content appears, as shown in Figure 6-6.

FIGURE 6-6: The photo from Figure 6-5 with the sky removed using Instant Alpha.

TIP

You can use the Instant Alpha feature multiple times to remove different colors from the same photo. If you make a mistake, choose Edit ➪ Undo Instant Alpha on the menu bar or press ⌘+Z.

Using Adjust Image

Another way to tweak your photos is to choose View ➪ Show Adjust Image, which opens the window shown in Figure 6-7. Use the sliders to adjust contrast, exposure, sharpness, and other aspects of your photo. Click the Enhance button if you want the Adjust Image tool to auto-correct the image (as I did in Figure 6-8). You see the effects immediately in your image and need only click the red close button to accept them. Click the Reset Image button if you don't like the changes you made; doing so returns your image to its original state.

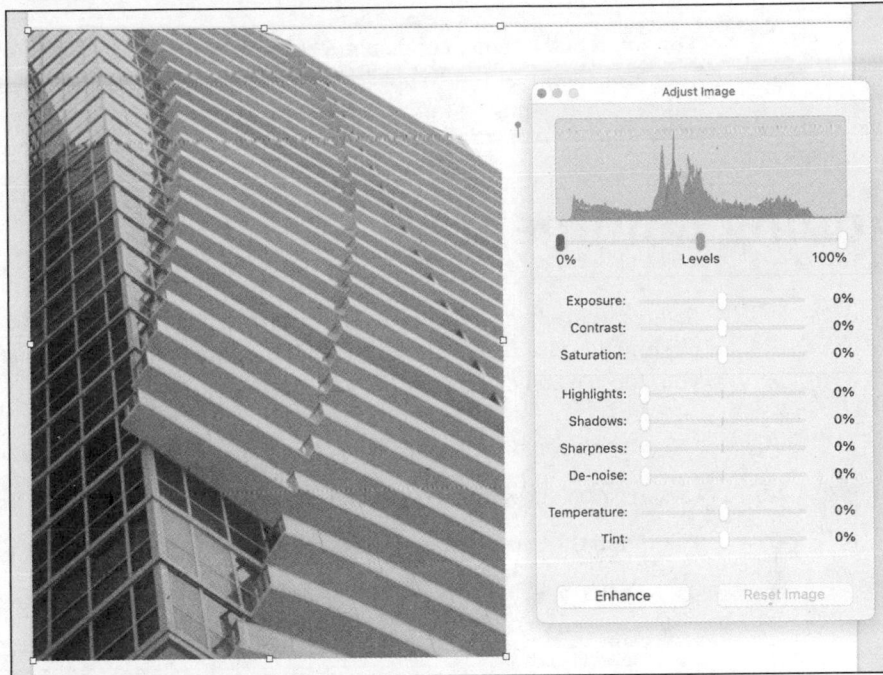

FIGURE 6-7:
Use Adjust Image
to tweak photos.

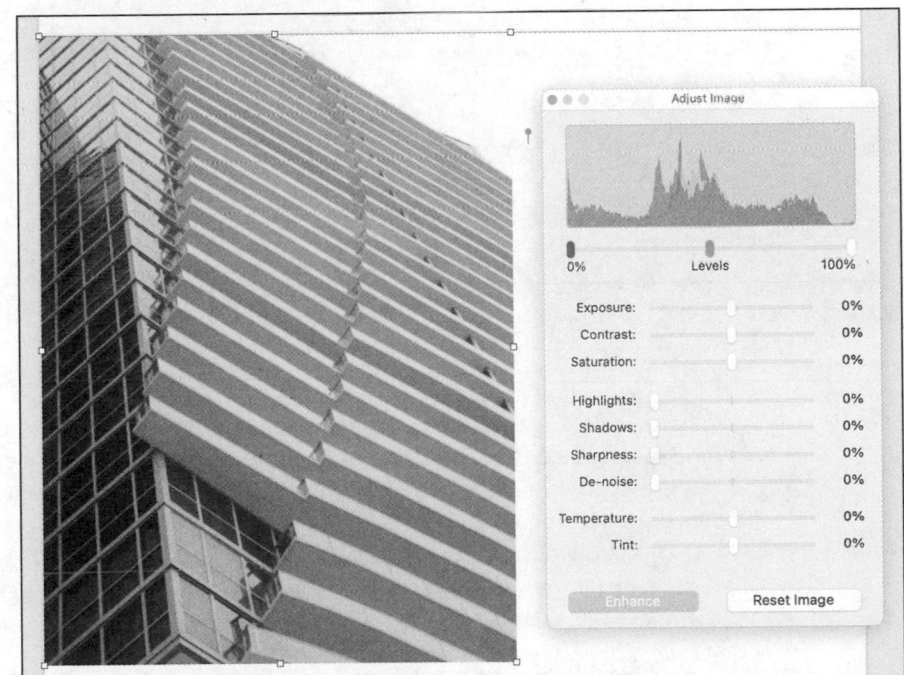

FIGURE 6-8:
For an easy fix to
less-than-perfect
photos, click the
Enhance button.

CHAPTER 6 **Getting More Out of Pages, Keynote, and Numbers** 729

TIP

For some quick fixes, you can click the toolbar's Format button, click the Image tab, and then use the Exposure and Saturation sliders to adjust the photo. The Image tab also has Enhance and Reset buttons.

Adding Comments

Comments are like sticky notes in your document. You can leave notes for yourself or someone else reading your document, and other people can leave comments for you, too. To add comments, do the following:

1. **In an open document, click the Comment icon on the toolbar.**

A virtual sticky note appears on your document.

2. **Type the comment you want to make, as shown in Figure 6-9.**

3. **Click Done.**

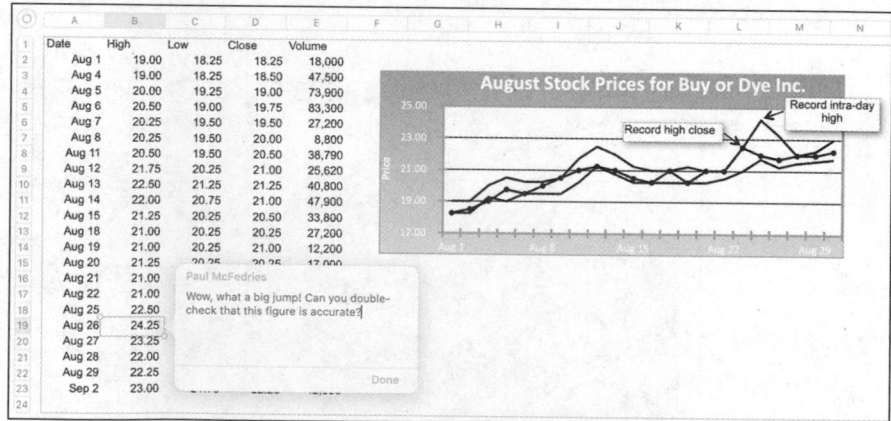

FIGURE 6-9:
Add comments
as reminders or
notes.

That's it. In Pages, a colored square appears in the document to indicate where you inserted a comment, while in Keynote and Numbers, your comment remains on the window, unless you hide it as explained next. To manage your comments, try these techniques:

» **Edit:** Click the comment (in Pages, click the icon in the document to open it) and edit or add more to it.

» **Hide or display:** Choose View ⇨ Comments (Comments and Changes in Pages) ⇨ Hide Comments to hide all comments. (This won't delete them.)

Choose View ⇨ Comments/Comments and Changes ⇨ Show Comment to see them again.

» **View additional comments:** Choose View ⇨ Comments (Comments and Changes in Pages) ⇨ Show Next Comment (Show Next Comment or Change in Pages), or Choose View ⇨ Comments (Comments and Changes in Pages) ⇨ Show Previous Comment (Show Previous Comments and Changes in Pages).

» **View the Comments pane:** Choose View ⇨ Show Comments Pane.

» **Delete:** Open the comment and click Delete.

» **Reply:** If you're collaborating with others and you add a comment to a document, others can respond by opening the comment and clicking Reply.

TIP

To track whose comments belong to whom, you — and other people with whom you share documents and who make comments on your documents — can add an author name to the comments. For each commenter, choose *App Name* ⇨ Settings ⇨ General and type a name in the Author field. As extra ID help, choose View ⇨ Comments (Comments and Changes in Pages) ⇨ Author Color to assign a color to each comment author.

Finding More Templates

If the standard templates and typefaces offered in Pages, Keynote, and Numbers don't satisfy your creative needs, you might want to turn to one of several third-party software developers who offer free or for-fee templates that work with these applications. I list a few here, but make sure to check out the App Store and search the internet for others.

» **Graphic Node** (www.graphicnode.com**):** Offers still and motion themes and animations

» **KeynotePro** (www.keynotepro.com/index.aspx**):** Sells stylized templates for traditional presentations and kiosks

» **Keynote Themes Plus** (http://www.keynotethemesplus.com/home.html**):** Produces high-definition themes and presentations

» **StockLayouts** (www.stocklayouts.com**):** Provides free and paid Pages templates are available in various formats and specific to different industries such as health care, sports, and education

Index

About the Author

Paul McFedries has been a technical writer for 30 years and has been using Macs since the 1980s (yes, there were Macs in the world even way back then). He has written more than 100 books that have sold more than four million copies throughout the solar system. Paul's books include the Wiley titles *iPad and iPad Pro 2022–2023 For Dummies, iPhone Portable Genius Sixth Edition, Excel All-in-One For Dummies, Fitbit For Dummies,* and *Teach Yourself VISUALLY Windows 11.* Paul invites everyone to drop by his personal website (https://paulmcfedries.com) and to follow him on Twitter (@paulmcf) and Facebook (www.facebook.com/PaulMcFedries/).

Dedication

For Karen and Chase

Author's Acknowledgments

The writer Dene October once observed that "A good editor is someone who cares a little less about the author's needs than the reader's." This is particularly true for a technical book because if you, dear reader, can't make sense of what's between these covers, this is a failed book no matter how well its author wrote it. But if this book is one that reads well, is accurate, and is helpful (and I happen to think it's all three), those are the result of Wiley's amazing editorial team caring more about your needs than mine. For this and so much more, I send out profuse thanks to Project Editor and Copy Editor Susan Pink and to Technical Editor Guy Hart-Davis. I'd also like to thank Associate Acquisitions Editor Kelsey Baird for asking me to write this book.

Publisher's Acknowledgments

Associate Acquisitions Editor: Kelsey Baird

Project and Copy Editor: Susan Pink

Technical Editor: Guy-Hart Davis

Production Editor: Mohammed Zafar Ali

Proofreader: Debbye Butler

Cover Image: © best pixels/Shutterstock; Screenshots courtesy of Paul McFedries

Leverage the power

Dummies is the global leader in the reference category and one of the most trusted and highly regarded brands in the world. No longer just focused on books, customers now have access to the dummies content they need in the format they want. Together we'll craft a solution that engages your customers, stands out from the competition, and helps you meet your goals.

Advertising & Sponsorships

Connect with an engaged audience on a powerful multimedia site, and position your message alongside expert how-to content. Dummies.com is a one-stop shop for free, online information and know-how curated by a team of experts.

- Targeted ads
- Video
- Email Marketing

- Microsites
- Sweepstakes sponsorship

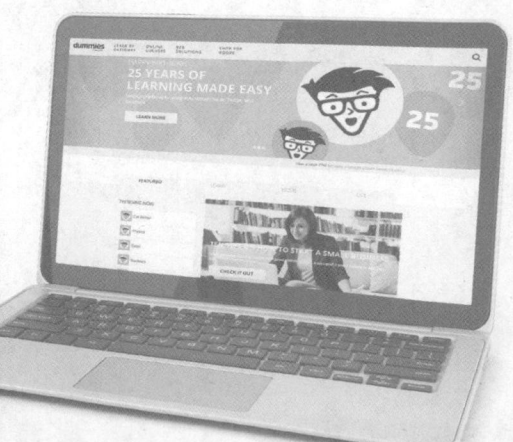

20 MILLION PAGE VIEWS EVERY SINGLE MONTH

15 MILLION UNIQUE VISITORS PER MONTH

43% OF ALL VISITORS ACCESS THE SITE VIA THEIR MOBILE DEVICES

700,000 NEWSLETTER SUBSCRIPTIONS TO THE INBOXES OF *300,000* UNIQUE INDIVIDUALS EVERY WEEK

# of dummies

Custom Publishing

Reach a global audience in any language by creating a solution that will differentiate you from competitors, amplify your message, and encourage customers to make a buying decision.

- Apps
- Books
- eBooks
- Video
- Audio
- Webinars

Brand Licensing & Content

Leverage the strength of the world's most popular reference brand to reach new audiences and channels of distribution.

For more information, visit dummies.com/biz

PERSONAL ENRICHMENT

Staying Sharp dummies

9781119187790
USA $26.00
CAN $31.99
UK £19.99

Facebook dummies
Carolyn Abram

9781119179030
USA $21.99
CAN $25.99
UK £16.99

Guitar dummies
Mark Phillips
Jon Chappell

9781119293354
USA $24.99
CAN $29.99
UK £17.99

Investing dummies
Eric Tyson, MBA

9781119293347
USA $22.99
CAN $27.99
UK £16.99

Beekeeping dummies
Howland Blackiston

9781119310068
USA $22.99
CAN $27.99
UK £16.99

Digital Photography dummies
Julie Adair King

9781119235606
USA $24.99
CAN $29.99
UK £17.99

Meditation dummies
Stephan Bodian

9781119251163
USA $24.99
CAN $29.99
UK £17.99

Pregnancy ALL-IN-ONE dummies
6 Books in one

9781119235491
USA $26.99
CAN $31.99
UK £19.99

Samsung Galaxy S7 dummies
Bill Hughes

9781119279952
USA $24.99
CAN $29.99
UK £17.99

iPhone dummies
Edward C. Baig
Bob "Dr. Mac" LeVitus

9781119283133
USA $24.99
CAN $29.99
UK £17.99

Crocheting dummies
Karen Manthey
Susan Brittain

9781119287117
USA $24.99
CAN $29.99
UK £16.99

Nutrition dummies
Carol Ann Rinzler

9781119130246
USA $22.99
CAN $27.99
UK £16.99

PROFESSIONAL DEVELOPMENT

Windows 10 dummies
Andy Rathbone

9781119311041
USA $24.99
CAN $29.99
UK £17.99

AutoCAD dummies
Bill Fane

9781119255796
USA $39.99
CAN $47.99
UK £27.99

Excel 2016 dummies
Greg Harvey, PhD

9781119293439
USA $26.99
CAN $31.99
UK £19.99

QuickBooks 2017 dummies

9781119281467
USA $26.99
CAN $31.99
UK £19.99

macOS Sierra dummies
Bob "Dr. Mac" LeVitus

9781119280651
USA $29.99
CAN $35.99
UK £21.99

LinkedIn dummies
Joel Elad, MBAs

9781119251132
USA $24.99
CAN $29.99
UK £17.99

Windows 10 ALL-IN-ONE dummies
10 Books in one
Woody Leonhard

9781119310563
USA $34.00
CAN $41.99
UK £24.99

SharePoint 2016 dummies
Rosemarie Withee
Ken Withee

9781119181705
USA $29.99
CAN $35.99
UK £21.99

Fundamental Analysis dummies
Matt Krantz

9781119263593
USA $26.99
CAN $31.99
UK £19.99

Networking dummies
Doug Lowe

9781119257769
USA $29.99
CAN $35.99
UK £21.99

Office 2016 dummies
Wallace Wang

9781119293477
USA $26.99
CAN $31.99
UK £19.99

Office 365 dummies
Rosemarie Withee
Ken Withee
Jennifer Reed

9781119265313
USA $24.99
CAN $29.99
UK £17.99

Salesforce.com dummies
Liz Kao
Jon Paz

9781119239314
USA $29.99
CAN $35.99
UK £21.99

Coding dummies
Nikhil Abraham

9781119293323
USA $29.99
CAN $35.99
UK £21.99

dummies.com

dummies
A Wiley Brand

Learning Made Easy

ACADEMIC

9781119293576
USA $19.99
CAN $23.99
UK £15.99

9781119293637
USA $19.99
CAN $23.99
UK £15.99

9781119293491
USA $19.99
CAN $23.99
UK £15.99

9781119293460
USA $19.99
CAN $23.99
UK £15.99

9781119293590
USA $19.99
CAN $23.99
UK £15.99

9781119215844
USA $26.99
CAN $31.99
UK £19.99

9781119293378
USA $22.99
CAN $27.99
UK £16.99

9781119293521
USA $19.99
CAN $23.99
UK £15.99

9781119239178
USA $18.99
CAN $22.99
UK £14.99

9781119263883
USA $26.99
CAN $31.99
UK £19.99

Available Everywhere Books Are Sold

dummies.com

Small books for big imaginations

9781119177173
USA $9.99
CAN $9.99
UK £8.99

9781119177272
USA $9.99
CAN $9.99
UK £8.99

9781119177241
USA $9.99
CAN $9.99
UK £8.99

9781119177210
USA $9.99
CAN $9.99
UK £8.99

9781119262657
USA $9.99
CAN $9.99
UK £6.99

9781119291336
USA $9.99
CAN $9.99
UK £6.99

9781119233527
USA $9.99
CAN $9.99
UK £6.99

9781119291220
USA $9.99
CAN $9.99
UK £6.99

9781119177302
USA $9.99
CAN $9.99
UK £8.99

Unleash Their Creativity

dummies.com